The 'Wall
=
Passion Not Patience

The 'Wall = Passion Not Patience

Barrie Stradling

Text © Barrie Stradling 2019
except where otherwise stated

Table of Contents

	Dedications	7
	Introduction	11
Chapter 1	More Memories From The Dens	12
Chapter 2	The Media – Millwall are Evil Perception	46
Chapter 3	The REAL Positivity of Millwall	87
Chapter 4	The Wailing 'Wall – Millwall Serenades And Other Pleasantries	139
Chapter 5	The Absolute Proof That No One Likes Us Chapter – The Referee And Assistants Section	321
Chapter 6	The Holloway Age – The Horror The Horror! Keep Taking The Tablets	349
Chapter 7	The Millwall Factor – Give A Lion A Bad Name	362
Chapter 8	Old Traditions Fade Away	426
Chapter 9	From Village Bobby To Robocop	433
Chapter 10	A Passion For Fashion To Bash In!	450
Chapter 11	Talk Your Way Out Of That!	455
Chapter 12	Eat Football, Sleep Football; Drink Too Much, Talk Bollocks!	460
Chapter 13	'He's Only A Poor Little Hammer' – Lions Not Irons	493
Chapter 14	'Me And Me Mates'	534
Chapter 15	The Many 'Joys' of Away Travel aka 'Been There Done That!'	548
Chapter 16	Mad Lions And Englishmen Stand Out In The Morning Sun	598
Chapter 17	'UEFA Cup We Had A Laugh!'	605
Chapter 18	'Mad Ted's Big Adventure' – Carlisle United Away Saturday 7th October 2006 2pm; League 1 Won 2-1	627

Dedications

To start my dedications, I would like to dedicate this book to a true Millwall Playing Legend – Barry Kitchener who sadly passed away on 30th March 2012. RIP Kitch.

To a real Millwall fan legend – The Lion Of London Bridge Roy 'F*** You I'm Millwall' Larner, an anti-Terrorist hero unarmed against three machete wielding Terrorists in Blue and Black Restaurant Borough Market near London Bridge, Saturday 3rd June 2017.

A true Millwall fan Legend who is no longer with us – Ian Garwood. RIP Tiny.

As I did in my 'I Was Born Under The Cold Blow Lane' book I'd also like to dedicate this book to all my home and away Millwall companions over my numerous Millwall years both past and present –

My East London Cousin Roy Munro, the Essex contingent of my Family – my Cousins, the Brothers Paul and Gavin Huish, their late Father Peter and Mother Joan and all their/my Millwall Family.

My lifelong Grammar School friends and their family and friends Colin 'Top Tips' Briden and his late Dad Bob Briden, Paul 'Night Moves' White, Paul 'Biker' Jackson, Brothers George and Peter Webb, Steve Kimberley, Peter Gibbins, Tony (Joe) Church and Peter Desmond.

Swedish Millwall fans Michael and Catarina Karlström and their sons Benjamin, Christoffer and Sebastian, Henrik 1 Kullberger aka Lundgren, Henrik 2 aka Agren, Mattias Rydberg and Daniel Österman.

Jim Stephenson, Bob Kensell and the boys, 'Striker', 'Win or lose have a booze' Jason, Dave Murray, Simon Watson. Book 'Em Dan-no and his Brother, Phil, Trevor and Fathers and Sons Eddie and Mick & Big John and Laupie.

People I know from Coach 1 – Tony Russell, Rob, Big Dave, Andy, old Dave, Peter Hudd, Mick Murphy, Martin, Nick, Adrian, Stephen, Tina/Chris, Liz, Alex, Kenny Denham and Pam Cooper.

To a Coach 1 legend and true Millwall fan – RIP Marmalade aka Richard (Mohammed) Vogel.

CBL and away friends' Father and son Sam and Dave Weller, Mother Kay, daughter Chelsea and son Charlie Wallace, a Millwall family. Tom, Barry, Chris and Jim, plus Father Alan Palmer and twins Gary and Neil Palmer.

CBL Block 9ers Dick and his Daughter Joanne Day and Home/Away regular Paul and son Liam, Cliff, Gary Hurley, Ian and Gordon Toal, 'The Mumper' author Mark Baxter and Angelo's Chippy and away regular Steve.

The Essex contingent of Andy Bell and his sons, his brother Mark Bell and friends Glyn Kerry, Laurie Carrigan, Jordan Carrigan, John Brown and South East London/Essex CBL couple now in Kent Trevor and Audrey Cox.

My East London contingent of Simon, wife Mary, Patrick 'Pat Nav/Tunnel Of Thought' Barrett, Lisa Barrett, Grandson Rudie, Dave Simms and wife Mary, Paul Simms and wife Sian Simms and daughter Violet, Nathan Simms and wife Katie and children Harry and Mia Simms; Clive Whates, wife Christine and their twins Lois and Aaron, Mad Ted Mayhew, Johnny Lynch, Brothers Steve and Micky Fisher and his sons, Peter and Dawn Ironside.

Harvey Millwall Brown of course, plus Dean and Victoria, with many thanks for your involvement in this book.

Barney Ronay of The Guardian for all his support against Lewisham Council's CPOs.

Last but certainly not least Grandad John.

My apologies to any of those that I may have forgotten to mention. Again, I'd also like to dedicate this to all Millwall fans everywhere.

My final dedication goes to a Millwall club legend Neil 'Bomber' Harris, a man who scored 138 goals a record for the club, overcame Testicular Cancer to return to playing again, took over the Management shambles left by those pair of c***s Lomas and Holloway, taking us to 2 League 1 Play Off Finals, winning one and gaining promotion to the Championship, taking us on two FA Cup runs to Quarter Finals, being in all honesty one of the clubs best Managers and a true Millwall Legend. He was forced out in my opinion by Fans Social media abuse and finally live abuse from the away section gathered for the Luton Town away game on 2nd October 2019 that we threw away late after leading, forcing him in my opinion to decide that it was in his best interest to leave his managerial position with Assistant Dave Livermore, I would like to leave my last Dedication to a 100% Lions Legend Neil Harris.

Introduction

To explain the title of the book, Millwall fans are passionate in supporting Millwall but not patient. As an example, players that come through our youth system are expected to be the real deal straight away never given time to develop, I give you Teddy Sheringham and Richard Sadlier. This policy seems always to have been in place so is part of our psyche unfortunately! For reference the season in which we won the Play-Off Final at Wembley v Bradford City was my 50th Anniversary season supporting Millwall! I have utilised Facebook and other Internet for the photos in this book, thought I should say this, also with many thanks a lot are used with the permission of the Millwall FC Press office, pictures aside I hope you enjoy the book.

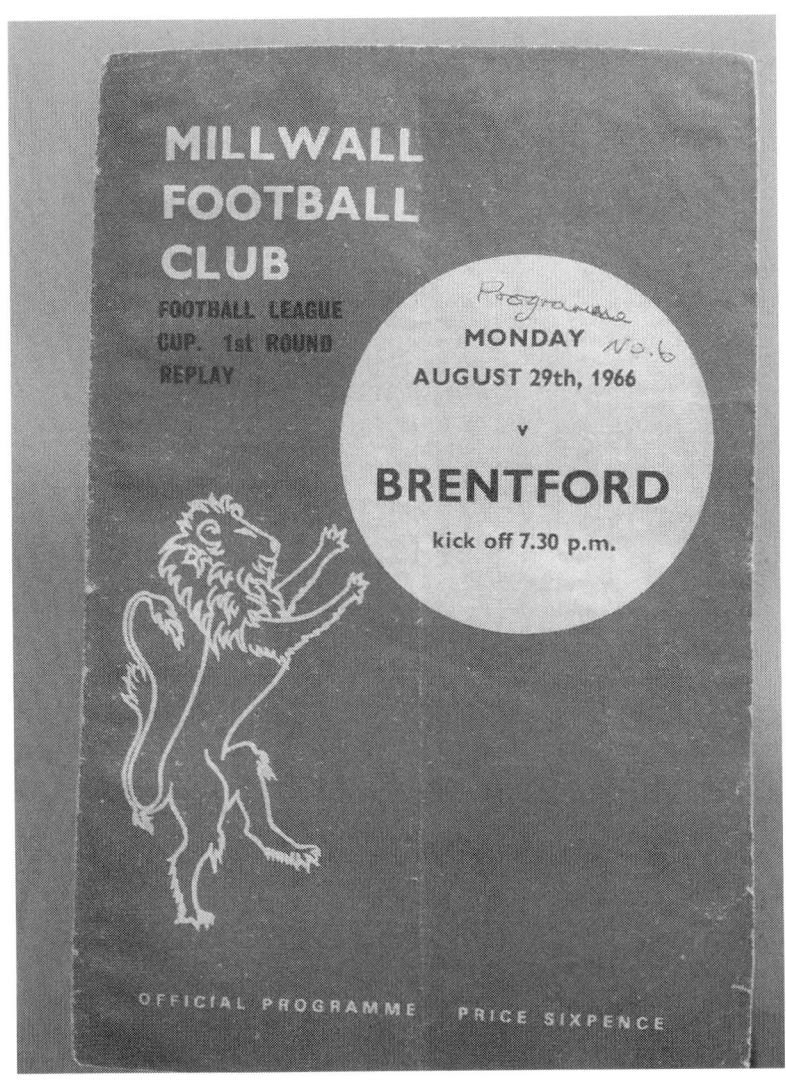

Above: Programme of the first game I ever went to at Millwall

CHAPTER 1
More Memories From The Dens

Continuing a rambling tradition from my other two English Millwall books here are some more memories of both Den(s) –

The Old Den –

To start a quote from Gary Lineker that was on the website wakeupmillwall.com, which in a way perfectly describes the true hostile nature of the Old Den –

„I remember running on to the pitch at The Den when I was a youngster with Leicester in the fifth round of the FA Cup. The place resembled a huge trap, and the venom that hit us from the Millwall fans was unbelievable. I remember thinking to myself, maybe it would be a good idea not to score at this place!" I remember this game at the Old Den in 1984/5, Lineker played for Leicester City up front with Alan Smith in a vile green kit and we won 2-0. I'm glad we frightened him and we beat them!! For interest for those who do not remember it was victory in this game that led us into the Luton Town away FA Cup Quarter Final riot night!

Nowadays it is very strange seeing the olden day footage of the Old Den on the historical videos/DVDs, post-war in black-and-white with 'Tasches and cloth caps aplenty, with people drinking from glass beer bottles in the ground, running onto the pitch to retrieve the ball, and running onto the pitch to celebrate a goal or merely to relocate themselves to seats in the stand, mind you apart from the glass beer bottles and a change in headwear fashions, not much changed during my Old Den lifetime.

There was the confusing time when they started using geographical names for the stands instead of CBL, Halfway Line, etc; this was at the time of the 'all-ticket' restrictions, leaving me for one thinking at the time – 'Which stand is the East Stand then?'

I never twigged what the 'E' numbers above my head in the CBL actually meant, I think at the time I thought that it meant Ecstasy Tablets were available, Doh!

I eventually got my bearings and realised what stand/terrace was what, I knew that geography O-Level I have would come in handy one day!

There was the time when we had a cuddly fluffy Lion mascot in the centre-circle in the 1970s.

There was a very big bloke who used to stand at the front of the CBL who would rant and rave all afternoon, over and above an Old Den occupant's obligatory abuse quotient.

He would assail our delicate young schoolboy ears with words we would not use ourselves; if you believe that I must show you this great time-share offer I have.

We always used to say of him, right or wrong – 'I bet he's henpecked at home and apart from ,Yes Dear, No Dear,' he doesn't give his wife any back chat', preferring instead to vent his marital spleen at Millwall for a few hours until he went back under the thumb at 5.00pm. Whether our diagnosis was true who knows, however, he certainly often seemed to be more wound up than anyone else around him, no mean feat in the old CBL!

There were the Sunday markets, Community Care and Crèche schemes, which were naturally largely ignored by the media.

During my Millwall Old Den lifetime, there were the management eras of –

Benny Fenton and his defensive policies when we seemed to take our foot off the gas whenever we were a couple of goals in front.

There was Gordon Jago and his attempts at Americanisation.

There was George Petchey and the 'Petchey Must Go!' Campaign, when petitions were passed around the terraces in an attempt to oust him.

There was the time when I did not know whether to laugh or cry during the Peter Anderson reign.

There was Barry Kitchener's dozen game caretaker reign.

There was our rebirth under George Graham.

There was the dream come true success under John Docherty and Frank McLintock and the sight of The Doc turning the dug out into a fog bank with his smoking.

There was the short reign of cardie man Bob Pearson.

There was the chase Bruce Rioch around the corridors 'Resign You Bugger!' stylee.

Not forgetting the Diamond System reign of Roy Keane's favourite Mick McCarthy.

For any manager Millwall were, and still are, a crowd that does not suffer fools gladly, as highlighted by the crowd reaction to any blatantly wrong or unpopular substitute decisions when the crowd would let the hapless manager become aware of their feelings in no uncertain terms.

When we played Liverpool in a Sunday TV game in 1989 and my mates Micky Fisher, Steve Fisher and I ran into Lou Macari and his sons on the Eastbound East London line return journey, we had a good chat with him, he seemed like a nice chap.

Finally on a personal note there were the mob handed Old Den post match pub crawls, invariably starting in The Albany and ending somewhere in the Old Kent Road, via the Five Bells, The Crown And Anchor, Cockneys etc and resulting in a stonking headache after practically every home match in the late 1980s, early 1990s.

As an aside in the 1980s Soul Boy era as an East Ender we always used to tour the pubs north of the Thames mostly in Bethnal Green, bars like Septembers, Queens and The Weavers, it was a land filled with mostly gorgeous scantily clad barmaids, half naked female bar top dancers, very lovely on the eye but a bit of a bugger to get served! Drunk or not our ears feasted on American Soul/dance music, early rap/hip hop and electro. My mates and I would also trawl south of the river to the Soul/Dance Music bars on the Bermondsey Side of Tower Bridge Uncles, Samsons, Gillys etc, ah happy days.

It proved to us that north and south of the Thames were similar Barwise and certainly in musical tastes anyway.

The New Den –

Some New Den memories in no particular order -

There were the penalty shoot-outs and there were the cinder track races against the away team's juniors, where it appeared that if we won either of them we would go on to lose the game for some odd reason. There were 'The Lion Roars' pre match challenges when ex Lion keeper Tony Warner regularly used to help out a toddler so that they could win a prize by hoisting them up and dropping the ball into the target at the behest of the home crowd.

There was the disabled boy who had a couple of kick-ins in front of the CBL and the kids who are only as big as the ball they're trying to kick, all of which are always carried out to the roars of the home crowd which must make the children's day. One of my usual home and away mates Nathan once won a mobile at this challenge, without Denzil's help I might add!

There was the setting up of the Neil Harris' 'Everyman Cancer Appeal' and his emotional return for a night match against Barnsley, when the whole crowd including the away fans applauded him onto the pitch. Millwall mates Nathan did a bungee jump, his second, to raise money for this charity and his brother Paul was involved in a half time 'The Lion Roars' style, goal scoring competition shoot out on Boxing Day 2002 against Gillingham, representing the CBL to raise money for the same charity.

There was the day that we helped a bewildered and deluded away fan by doing our Good Samaritan work in an attempt to get him into the ground undamaged. At this particular time, we were not driving to matches as we mostly do now but going by tube and for a period when the East London Line was previously closed for repair, they had a replacement bus service from either Whitechapel or Aldgate. For one match we went via Aldgate and saw an Ipswich fan sitting on the bus, seemingly oblivious to the possible pitfalls of wandering around aimlessly at the New Den wearing a vile maroon and dark green Ipswich away shirt, consequently, we decided to do our good deed for the day, so we took him in hand and escorted him personally to the North Stand. This led to our being the object of many suspicious stares en route. If you can help some idiot along the way, I always say.

On the first day of the original set of East London Line lengthy closures several years ago and subsequently required replacement buses, we were all battling at Whitechapel station to get onto a tube replacement single decker bus when my mate Simon Barrett asked the bus driver –

'Why the f***ing hell don't you have a double decker bus?'

The bus driver's reply was – 'A double decker bus would not go through the Rotherhithe Tunnel Sir!' Good point, Si you were shot down in flames or what!

On another occasion after we had lost at home, we were on another packed single decker ELT bus and someone kept continually ringing the bell. So much so that the driver threatened to stop the bus, until we, in no uncertain terms, told him that a bus full of Millwall fans whose team had just lost were not the best passengers to bugger about, we suggested that for his own well being perhaps he should just continue, which he did, good choice!

Simon also used start singing a circus theme tune as we lapsed into farce during the Jimmy Nicholl era, strangely apt considering the clown-like performance we were watching.

There was the game when Simon's son and daughter, Patrick

and Lisa and wife Mary were all on the pitch for Patrick's mascot day against Blackpool and Micky's son Michael was a ball boy at a home game and a mascot away at Preston North End a couple of years back.

There was the match that the fan dubbed Andy May's dad did his solo sit-down protest in the centre circle at the horror of it all at the time (see 'The Trouble with Millwall' cover picture).

There was the Project Life Lion event when they tried to raise money to protect the African Lions of the Serengeti where they had lovely fluffy Lion cubs around the ground. Speaking as a Leo myself, I am rather partial to Lions even though they would rip your throat out as soon as look at you when they got bigger.

There was the proposed ground share with Brighton blown out of the water, post their Goldstone ground exodus, due to Police concerns about Aggro, this was prior to The Sun's Seig Heil not Seagulls Millwall Racism chant slanderous and totally idiotic reporting Cock Up.

There was the day that we had to pass through a huge fire underneath the railway arches by the recycling plant when some bright spark had set fire to a large pile of tyres. On another day, there was a huge car yard fire away from the ground, both of which filled the New Den sky with thick black smoke. Amazingly, Millwall once again did not get the blame.

There was the time when there used to be a glut of paper planes sailing out of the CBL with cheers for the furthest and the confetti flurries when the team come out.

There were the free pint games.

There were the original Gents based Kitchener's posh food posters – 'Much Better Than Jellied Eels And A Glass Of Beer!' In my opinion a strange choice decision that mocked our 'common' roots us and 'Let 'em Come' !!!!

There was the story in the Nottingham Forest Programme on April 7th 2007 titled 'Swedish Fans Invasion' about me and some of my friends Henrik 1 and Michael and the rest of their Swedish

Millwall contingent, I was seriously injured by a Hit and Run car in Stepney Green and was Hospitalised in three East End Hospitals – The Royal London, Mile End hospital and Homerton hospital, where I was in a Glasgow Scale Grade 3 then Grade 4 Coma with Fractured Skull, Sub Arachnoid Haemoorage i.e. a Traumatic Brain Injury for approximately 6 weeks and in Hospital for 17 weeks, I was also given the Last Rites a couple of times whilst in the coma, so it was a bit worse than just having a bang on the head!

The Programme mentioned me being critical as I nearly died but that I had recovered enough to meet up with my Swedish friends for a drink in the West End and get back to The 'Wall's games.

It also mentioned that I was the author of two other English Published Millwall books 'Tuesday Night In Grimsby' and 'I Was Born Under The Cold Blow Lane'. I was both in the Programme and announced personally over the PA by Les, I must say that I got a great response when I first returned back to the New Den from the Millwall fans in the CBL who had seen me there numerous times before and also numerously at the Old Den and all around the country.

I really must add that I was very impressed to be so mentioned by the club that is for sure.

For information, I have done numerous Interviews, Articles and Questionnaires for the Millwall Swedish Fanzine and Websites. I wrote two away Match stories that came after the other English books were published, which the Swedish Millwall published on their Website or Fanzine, they were about me and my London Friends away travels. There was our Ferencvaros away story called 'UEFA Cup We Had A Laugh'

There was also a story I did about a trip that we had to Carlisle United away called 'Mad Ted's Big Adventure' – Carlisle United Away Saturday 7th October 2006'

For interest I have included them here with an added home section to the Ferencvaros Story, please see the very last two Chapters later on.

For reference when I was in Homerton Hospital where two of

my Millwall mates Simon Barrett and Dave Simms both worked at that time, they allowed me to go out with them and go to Millwall, which I did for a night match v Leyton Orient that we lose 5-2, Dave then drove me back to Homerton, after watching the game I was glad to go back to my hospital bed to be honest!

Highlighting how my brain works now, when we played Blackpool at home as they are a team whose fans are adorned in Orange, I think that the Orange jacketed Stewards are Blackpool fans who cannot find the away section so just plonk themselves anywhere in the stands or around the pitch, I said at the home game in August 2014, if all the Stewards in Orange went up to North Stand Upper Tier, it would be a big away following!

Wrong and bullshit obviously but I thought my assumption was funny, mind you I have had a bang on me nut!!!

On the marketing front –

There was Ogden's 'non events' performance, mind you how would you sell a club of Millwall's reputation and location? If a top advertising agency man like Peter Mead could not promote us positively who could?

There was the 'Bentt' boxIing match, no pun intended, promoted by his professing a life long Lions devotion on the pitch, yeah right.

We were home to 'Dream Team' shown on Sky TV, which often turned the outside of the New Den into the 'Dragon's Lair'. At one game we also had a strange green/purple Muppet creature and the customary new manager scarf aloft pose on the pitch, which was very confusing to me, mind you

I am easily confused.

They filmed a 'The Bill' episode at the New Den in March 2008 in season 2007/8 at our game against Leyton Orient. There have also been various television advertisements, filmed inside the New Den over the years, including Dennis Wise's Honey Monster Sugar Puffs, an ad for the Inland Revenue's 'Child Trust Fund' and a 'Nike' Streaker one among others and their Guy Ritchie Produced

NikeFootball.com Euro UEFA 2008 'Take It To The Next Level' TV Advertisement, Ian Wright, Harry Redknapp and Terry Veneables were together at the New Den advertising The Sun on TV Adverts pre the Premiership starting in mid August 2009. They also used the New Den club shop as a backdrop for BBC's Asian Radio Network advertisement in October 2002 and the outside of the ground was used for a Hyundai Getz advertisement in 2003 and very numerous Nissan Navara advertisements starting in 2007, which fill practically every ad break during 'Soccer AM' on Sky Sports, I thought I would mention this for all those who do not recognise the ground. There was also the bescarfed Millwall Peter De Savaray lookalike on the New Den pitch for the then new National Bingo game and the Kit Kat ad in February/March 2010 and Late Kick Off feature at same time. Paddy Power football coach trip that drives in to New Den in 2017. There are in fact numerous instances of The New Den featuring in TV ad campaigns, I won't try to list them all but this is true!!!

Moving away from The New Den to Wembley, still featuring Millwall Sky Bet Televised football bets in 2017 feature two versions of Steve Morison's goal v Bradford City in the Play Off Final 2017 one of him missing and one true one of him scoring in their TV advertising!

I have a couple of ideas of how to raise money commercially for Millwall not yet tried –

1) What about putting in swear boxes next to the seats as a fundraiser?

It would make a fortune; it would certainly bankrupt me if no one else!

In my defence I would say 'I can't keep putting my money in the c***ing swear box, It's not my fault continually f***ing well swearing, I have f***ing Tourettes you c***, honest! How could I have been going Millwall for 5 decades and not have f***ing Tourettes?'

2) The marketing policy is usually to try to play down any 'Mill-

wallness' in our crowd, which hasn't exactly worked has it? So why not go the opposite route.

Bite the bullet and instead of trying to make Millwall less hostile, why not go the opposite way and play up our supposed evil aspects by staging kindred like events – Bare-knuckle fighting, demolition derbies, cockfights, bear baiting, biker conventions, Satanic Covens, Nazi rallies and Ku Klux Klan meetings.

It is what everyone thinks we are like anyway so why not?

PS just joking.

Moving away from marketing ...

There are the modern Lion's Muppet family of Zampa and Roary and the shock of finding out that Zampa was a woman and was pregnant!

There was the brief return of John Docherty and Terry Hurlock.

Some Home Events Per Season In No Particular Order Of Importance Or Occurence –

Season 2002/3

There where what looked for the entire world like snipers positioned on the West stand roof in the North corner at the early games (?)

There was the putting up of stripy blue and white goal nets and the cinder track was replaced by a Millwall coloured tarmac making it like other grounds nationwide, which in later seasons became blue Astroturf, that many players deemed as dangerous or responsible for twisted ankle injuries that they received.

There was the attempt to attract more women in to the New Den for the Pompey game, with a pound admission, a bit sexist I would have thought, anyway what was to stop a great glut of cheapskate Lady Boys or transvestites turning up?

There was a pancake race in front of the East stand at half time on Pancake Day against Burnley.

We had Scandinavian TV at the ground, most noticeably for the Dennis Wise death threat game against Leicester City; hence, the resulting foreign pitch side adverts.

Wise and Wilkins brought in Goalkeeping coach Tony Burns whose pre match warm up policy seemed to be to try to break Warner, Marshall or Gueret's wrists when he booted the ball at them as they dived on a ball, good plan! He was ousted and then returned in 2007/8, then was replaced in 2012/3 by Kevin Pressman.

One humourous incident during the 2002/3 season was when we had a girl sitting a couple of rows in front of us in the CBL wearing a skimpy T-shirt and tracksuit outfit. This rode up to show a fair amount of bare flesh as she sat down and on the expanse of skin close to her bum, we saw that she had adopted the modern fashion for having a tattoo, in her case she had a Lions badge etched onto her lower back, naked female flesh and a Millwall badge – mmmm perfect. Rather like the tantalising glimpses of thongs that you see all too occasionally peeking above girls' jeans nowadays this was like a moth to a flame for all of us red blooded men. The hypnotic effect meant that it was almost impossible not to look at her nether regions. I can just imagine the conversation at the tattoo parlour –

'What do you want love and where do you want it?'

Her reply was no doubt – 'Millwall, my Arse!'

Season 2003/4

There was the appearance of the then larger than life Lions fan Andy 'The Viking' Fordham, the 2004 Lakeside BDO World Darts Champion, who paraded the winner's trophy on the pitch at half time against Sunderland on January 17th 2004. He is now massively slimmer although at the time it was said that he also apparently supported Glasgow Rangers, can you do that? Mind you he was so big at the time I was not going to tell him that he can't support 2 teams!

At the AFC Wimbledon at home in the 1st round FA Cup game on November 9th 2009, it was a mere couple of days after Millwall fan David Haye had won the WBA World Heavyeight Championship and he came onto the pitch at half time to be lauded by we Millwall fans briefly.

At the Nottingham Forest game on 1st November 2003 there was a whistle emanating from the East and/or West Stands throughout the match, this prompted an appeal for it to stop over the PA and in typical Millwall fashion everyone started whistling, again only at Millwall!

This whistling happened at the Derby County and Norwich City games as well, which was reported to the FA by the referees, the narks!

We played Derby County on the afternoon of England's Rugby Union World Cup triumph on Saturday November 22nd 2003 and the game consisted of both sets of fans singing the patriotic 'Ingerland, Ingerland, Ingerland' and 'Swing Low Sweet Chariot' throughout the match.

Season 2004/5

There was the sadly premature death of 1970s Lion favourite Keith Weller which prompted a photographic montage shown on the Jumbotron pre kick off against West Ham United on November 21st 2004, presumably it was done like this rather than having a potentially explosive minutes silence if the Hammers fans did not observe it properly.

There was the brilliant idea to play Iran in a pre-season friendly, which strangely got cancelled, something about security I believe, can't think what! On a lighter note there was the comic sight in the same West Ham United match of Dennis Wise gathering up the £7 worth of coins thrown at him from the upper tier of the away North stand before giving them to a young Millwall fan in the West Lower and then giving the coin throwers a 'thanks for the cash' thumbs up.

There was the shock of Adrian Serioux's enormous throw in from practically the half way line that set up a goal against Leicester City in August 2005. This was his home debut and brought gasps of shock from the crowd and subsequent throw ins were accompanied by the crowd's German Bundesliga style floppy raised wrist shaking.

There were the various schoolboy football teams dotted around the East Upper at the Stoke City home game in February 2005 who sang 'She fell over!' in high pitched voices everytime a Stoke player hit the deck.

There was the 'Everybody Out!' Scenario of Wisey, Theo and Muscat all leaving at or after the May 8th 2005 Burnley game. Bizarrely it was before this match that Clive, his daughter Lois and I were approached by what looked like very stylishly dresssed Italian Ultras on Oldfield Grove, they asked me where the New Den was and how long it would take to get there, they then asked where the 'Golden Lion' was and how far! Do you think they were here on a Hoolie holiday? In the end they plumped to head directly to the ground, me and Clive found it all very odd that they wanted to know where Millwall's Firm pub was.

If you thought 2004/5 dramatic I give you –

Season 2005/6!

Well what can you say about this little lot –

Players

In addition to the departure of Wise and Muscat, Ifill, Ward, Dichio and youngster Sweeney are all sold. Throughout the season numerous old pro loan players came in and went out with both Lee and then Tuttle adopting a revolving door policy.

Managers

Steve Claridge in – Steve Claridge out.

Colin Lee given Steve Claridge's job after Claridge tried to bring him in as his assistant.

David 'Tuttle Football' Tuttle, (sorry I meant Total Football), then coming in as Lee's assistant, before Lee was moved upstairs to the mystery job of Director of Football, whatever that means, before being booted out.

Tuttle becoming the stand in Manager, Wilkins returning to help out.

We naturally get relegated in 2005/6 after losing 11 home games and gaining more red cards than wins.

Tuttle inevitably leaves with McLeary coming in as caretaker number 2, with Tuttle's oppo Tony Burns.

Chairmen

Chairman Paphis out – Burnige in/Chairman Burnige out – Paphitis in.

Reg Burr passing away, Paphitis out again following the arrival of Peter de Savaray and his ridiculous tub thumping soap box speech before the Birmingham City Carling Cup game about his 5 year plan for Millwall to become a top 15 side and his development plans, 'kin good luck!

Then the end of season upheaval with Stewart Till and Heather Rabbatts coming in as Chairman and Deputy Chairman with De Savaray moving more towards Millwall Holdings.

De Savaray then leaving completely and Rabatts taking over the redevelopment project. Welcome to a real Football Farce. Moving away from the above mostly early Hokey Cokey farce there were also the games when PA Les played the stock rabble rousing type music like Prokofiev and Europe's 'The Final Countdown' shortly after PdeS arrival, not forgetting the Fireworks before league leaders Reading at home in December 2005 and a Shotokan Karate exhibition before the Brighton game on April Fools Day 2006.

Last but definitely least the Sheffield Wednesday disallowed 'goal' and the subsequent Wednesday winner with half the Millwall team off the pitch refereeing debacle.

During the season and the unprecedented turmoil we tried to prepare Simon's son Patrick for the inevitable relegation that you did not have to be Nostradamous to predict. Patrick had not experienced such emotional turmoil so we tried to mentally prepare him for what real football supporting is all about. Sadly Patrick's experience of Play-Off Semi Finals, a Wembley Final, a divisional Championship, an FA Cup Final and a UEFA Cup trip isn't the normal way of the Wall as any adult Millwall fan will know.

If Millwall 2005/6 was submitted as an idea for Dream Team it would have been laughed at as too far fetched, but sadly it was all true.

As seemingly not a season can go by without real or imagined Millwall hooligan controversy in May 2006 prior to the World Cup there were a series of well publicised Millwall specific Police dawn raids, going under the operational name of 'Operation Devine'. This followed alleged trouble in various home games – Wolves, Brighton and Crystal Palace and supposedly daming CCTV footage.

Not that I'm biased but please rearrange the following 'Reaction Police Top The Over An'.

I suppose we should be used to it, after all it is nothing unusual for Millwall to be made the scapegoat and media pariah immediately prior to any big occasion.

Season 2006/7

This season was to start in no less a bizarre fashion ...

We now had a big blue bus parked in the car park for a kick off.

Massive ousider and posh named arcade game Nigel (S)packman came in as manager via Ray Wilkins and the Chelsea old boys network.

Spackman's managerial tenure saw him trying to go for the world record squad size with nearly twenty players coming in permanently or on loan, it's quantity not quality that counts I say! He and Wilkins were shown the door after a quarter of the season with the team at the foot of the table all bar a team who had been deducted 10 points themselves and the underswell of crowd animosity beginning to grow.

To add to the ridicule possibilities in late August one of these signing was the 'Only Fools and Horses' surnamed Liam Trotter, who returned to us in 2009/10 and was captain in several games in Paul Robinson's injury absence in 2011/12 and later.

There was the 2006/7 post Nigel Spackman then outing and intro of Scotsman Willie Donachie! With a West Ham Chief Scout of Pat (Patsy) Holland in 2006/7 at his side!!!!!

There was the crowd swelling 'Let 'Em All Come Back' fan initiative, there was also several aesthetic changes to the New Den, the rusty old girders on the stands were painted blue, there was the 'Millwall heroes' mural on the side of the North Stand and on banners and the addition of Millwall player photographs to finally brighten up the drab grey concourses.

There was the September 2006 Brighton game when three American fillies were introduced on the pitch before the kick off, as part of a Fox TV reality TV show, from their vantage point at the front of the West Lower god knows what they made of it all!

This was also the game when a local youth's friends sort help at the New Den for their friend who was in a very bad way following recent brain surgery, a very good idea as they were able to get him urgent attention rather than wait for an Ambulance, naturally the Police treated the whole incident like a crime scene, Millwall until proven innocent again!

There was the 2006/7 Dockers G, with 'Shoeshine Boy' hitting the PA airwaves and we had a great crowd's hat shot on front of the programme!

Away from the Den there was the start of the London Underground posters that tried to attract floating fans to the New Den with the strapline – 'Real Talent, Real Football, Real Passion', it also stated that Millwall is only 7 minutes from London Bridge, which cynic that I always am made me think and 'a million light years away from the Premership!' These ads were not surprisingly ridiculed and lampooned in the media, BBC radio and Metro to name but two, strangely I don't remember Spurs or Chelsea's previous radio campaigns receiving the same mocking response.

There was the major shareholder with a 28.9% stake of the club, the Isle of Man's supposedly dodgy financial man Graham Ferguson Lacey getting slagged heavily on the 'House Of Fun' website in March 2007 and by Millwall's Board in April 2008 and again on the 'House Of Fun' following a Daily Telegraph article which indicated that Millwall's Board had blocked an EGM he had called, as he appeared to be trying to bugger the club's running up, because his proposals would have stopped the Board making any decisions, without putting every one that they had to make to all the shareholders. Why did he not just take up a position on the Board as he was apparently offered? I am a Shareholder but to me doing it this way would be like trying to run the club by a bloody large committee, that would make every decision take an eternity from experience of this sort of thing. To my mind speaking as someone who ran their own business what a sound plan that would not be in a way to run a business! His side seemed to totally revolve around the Regeneration of the area around the New Den rather than Millwall as a Football club, that is where he appeared to stand in his letter or at least that is what it seemed to imply to me anyway. I suppose to get him out in the open and making him face all his Millwall detractors the board eventually constituted his requested EGM in July 2008, when he would effectively have to face, in other words our undoubtedly hostile entire Shareholder Millwall family. He would certainly find out what or who he was up against in these circumstances, especially if it became apparent that in reality it was a purely personally selfish financial speculative position that he was in and particularly if it became apparent that he had no interest in what Millwall as a football team did. In reality we as a hardcore Millwall Football Club fanbase, Shareholders or not, are interested in us as a team not a business, unless we again went into Administration that is, especially because in the current era when clubs like Rotherham United, Bournemouth, Luton Town and Leeds United when it happened to them in 2007/8 and in Luton's case in 2008/9 again. All the clubs listed were deducted umpteen points for getting in a financially perilous position and were consequently put into a probable relegation situation.

Thank God this did not happen to us when we were actually in administration.

With Luton Town's 2008/9 30 point deduction, the authorities should just have relegated them to the Conference directly that is effectively what they had done, as Luton were in the position of needing 11 wins to get 3 points I think without doubt they were down already, if they survived from that position in my opinion Love or rather in my case Loathe them Luton should be put in the Champions League!

Season 2007/8

Pre 2007/8 there was the Friendly at home v African National side Sierra Leone which had the loudest Reggae style sound system plonked down in the Lower tier to the right of the empty North Stand and was used by a vocally rambling Sierra Leone DJ.

Never mind that we won a trophy for our 2-1 win or not and that we both sang our own National Anthems, and they had dancing Africans pre match or not, whatever, for me it was just too bloody loud!

In 2007/8 Stewart Till became Vice Chairman before moving on in 2008 and John G Berylson became Chairman in October 2007, after Donachie's sacking.

Also in 2007/8 'The Golden Lion' was now no more, I heard rightly or wrongly that the Old Bill were miffed about this as they normally knew it would be full of Millwall's Boys, now they would need information of where they were, shame! Police intelligence would now need to be real no longer a misnomer!

Unfortunately although we survived relegation in 2007/8 there was the sad death of a real Millwall character 'The Lion On The Roof' Steve Veakes. It was a real shame to lose him early in the season from a Heart Attack.

Post Season 2007/8 on May 24th 2008 my Millwall home and away mates Simon, his son Patrick, Brothers Paul and Nathan all played as Block 9 in the 5-a-side tournament on the New Den pitch, me, Dave Simms and an array of Friends, Girlfriends and Family all went to see them, they finished in 3rd/4th Place amidst the 24 teams as there was no 3rd Place Play Off. Their record was excellent 5 wins, 1 Draw and only one defeat in the Semi Final against the winners of the tournament.

Season 2008/9

In 2008/9 there was the weird incident of Zampa having a pre match rumble with a mascot type thing dressed as a man sized Cigarette, against Tranmere Rovers at home in January 2009. I know that it was a ploy to stop people smoking but it was very bizarre to watch I thought! Finally, there were 2 of the most bizarre things that I have ever seen at Millwall games home or away, mind you I have only supported the Lions for 5 decades so maybe I have not been going long enough! They were both in the Sky Sports Televised game in the crunch League 1 match on Easter Monday in April 2009 v Peterborough United.

When we clapped off the 3 Officials at Half Time and also continually sang 'Lino' after the Penalty shenanigans, without the usual concluding 'you're a C***!' part, I said to Nathan who I was sitting next to on the night in the CBL about the applause – 'Am I at a Millwall match? I only ask because I have never seen that before, mind you I have only been going for 42 years!'

Speaking of why they got the clap, as it were, none of us that were there in my contingent had ever seen a 3 times taken penalty either, for or against us.

We all said our getting 3 in a season is pushing the boat out for us let alone our taking one 3 times. We also said if it had been given against us it would certainly not have been so friendly and they would definitely not have been applauded off.

There was either the intentional piss take or cock up score on the Jumbotron scoreboard at the Stockport County game at the New Den on 27th March 2010, when Stockport's Swailes scored an own Goal, the score came up on the Jumbotron as Millwall 0 Stockport County 1, did that mean that when another of their players Huntington scored another own goal to make it 4-0 in the real world, that it was now 2-2? It never came up on the Jumbotron so I assume that we did actually win 5-0 not 3-2!

Finally in the same season there was the man who did an on-pitch bended knee marriage proposal to his chosen lady before the Norwich City game on 6th February 2010, which was greeted by male shock and awe and some chanting – 'You don't know what you're doing!' Who said that romance was dead? This was also sung to the Jumbotron operator after the above score debacle had appeared.

31

Season 2009/2010

This season saw the home start for two charitable Events –

The home game v Charlton Athletic on 13th March 2010 following the instigation on 19th December 2009 game at the Valley when both sides wore the adapted kits, in honour of murdered teenagers Millwall fan Jimmy Mizen and Charlton fan Rob Knox where the two families were together on the pitch and fans' money was donated to The Mizen Foundation, v Charlton Athletic home and away.

There was the Help for Heroes day, v Wycombe Wanderers at home on Saturday 21st November 2009, which had soldiers abseiling down from the roof of the West Stand to deliver the match ball among other things pre match and there were numerous able bodied soldiers and seriously injured personnel marching around the pitch side at half time.

Season 2010/2011

This season with the closure of the Silwood Path/Recycling Plant railway arches, meaning that to approach the CBL from Oldfield Grove aka Surrey Quays, we had to go via Silwood Street and then through the Bolina Road railway arches, leading us behind the North Stand away section with the away fan safety zone walkway above our heads. To do this we naturally had to walk through a Police state, you know the form enough Police to run a third world state fully equipped and with enough horses to have a Police Horse of the year show, naturally the Gee Gees where excited at being there and the road was filled with horseshit!

I thought if this Police state situation continued as I am sure that it would with the 18 month closure, as a marketing option, Millwall could introduce a rose growing section to the club shop where they could produce club insignia bedecked plastic buckets and shovels, so that you could shovel up the knee deep horse shit after the game, a positive boon for rose growing horse shit and it would clean the street, it would attract all would be rose growing gardeners of a Millwall persuasion and it would raise money for the club, seemed like a sound plan to me!

Season 2011/2012

In 2011/2012 the most poignant moment along with many others was the very very sad passing of Kitch, with the on-pitch religious and family/player service before our first win at home since Boxing Day when we beat Hull City on 7th April 2012, which was massively fitting given the circumstances.

The game after when we beat Leicester City at the New Den on 14th April 2012 to keep our Championship status with our third consecutive victory in a week, following our win at Pompey on Tuesday 10th April, there was an amazing half time moment when Extreme Endurance athlete Alex Panayotou completed her 188km run in on the pitch, which she had run to break her 24 hours record for Endurance, and to raise money for the local food for needy families The Trussell Trust (Foodbank) Charity, sod that I won't even run for a bus, that is endurance in my head!!!!

Season 2012/2013

The opening game in 2012/2013 v Blackpool on Saturday 18th August 2012, when the West Stand was officially renamed by Kitch's youngest daughter Nikki at the end of a charity cycle ride from Great Yarmouth when she and several fellow cyclists entered the New Den, as The Barry Kitchener Stand, a 100% deserved renaming, I am sure all Wall fans agree. In the same season there was the very funny incident in the lower part of this stand near the dugout when a bloke tried to catch the ball to throw it back and in doing so fell straight over the stair barrier, crashing into stewards against Bolton Wanderers on Saturday 6th October 2012.

I said it looks like a practice jump for something like the Cardiff City fan did from the upper North stand!

I know it was not a practice jump, but we all thought that it looked funny when he did it; it was like a stuntman jobby!

Season 2013/2014

In 2013/4 I was under 24-hour Psychiatric care as soon as Lomas' appointment was announced, so have not listed anything from 2013 sorry, but my medical team would not let me use anything sharp like a pen or pencil!!!!

I thought I was healing then I went to Southend United away in the FA Cup EEEEEEEEEEEEEEEEK!!!!

Further healing appeared in my mind when Ian Holloway arrived and I saw the messiah, sadly I must have been dreaming because we seemed to go strangely even more bizarre on the pitch! Then the Messiah did his job and we survived relegation, going from bottom up to sixth from bottom!

There was the Charlton home game on 15th March 2014 entitled 'Jimmy's Day' for the teenage demise of Wall Fan Jimmy Mizzen, this has become a customary event both home and at The Valley where it is always allied to the Charlton fan Ben Kinsella, both whom died as teenagers aged 16 through violence in 2008.

There was one funny thing at The New Den on 19th October 2013 when Harry Redknapp QPR manager and Joe Jordan his oppo both got hit by ball, the amiable Jock had his glasses broken and Botox mush laughingly was hit in the face by a ball thrown down from the Kitchener Stand, turned to moan at the fourth official and missed Easter's goal from the resulting throw in.

This was hilarious as it hit whinging Vermin as well as his Jock oppo nutcase Jordan, but the rest of season pre Lomas being booted out required my continually having to have electroshock treatment, I am only joshing, but not far off!

Season 2014/2015

If I thought Lomas was bad this was the season of 'I would rather be serving time in Holloway Prison' year than be involved with any of the on-pitch lunacy of this bumpkin, so let's focus on the unmentioned positives sorry less horrifying negatives –

Millwall are always perceived in the media as Racist or Homophobic or Hooligans, anyone that you meet once you mention your team, go straight into their preconceived vision of what we are, do other clubs get it? Strangely enough no.

With how bad we were to watch at home the Euroferries are skint pleasure that we did not have a working Jumbotron to watch replays of the Evil one Holloway's absolute shower of shit we had just watched.

For reference the jumbotron came back to life albeit smaller than its frame on 21st November 2015 v Colchester United, which we won 4-1.

Seasons 2015/2016 and 2016/2017

Well praise the lord Holloway was ousted albeit rich the swindling bumpkin bastard but in comes a real Wall man the legendary Neil Bomber Harris! I have listed various events during these seasons later on in the book.

There was the horrified reaction by all Millwall fans to the Regeneration plans around the New Den when Lewisham council announced in 2013/14 that they intended to flog the land including the Lions Community Centre and the car park area around the ground to Property Developers Renewal, causing a Millwall fan petition and several attempts to get the council's decision to sell to the only offer, which miraculously became the best offer they received overturned by Millwall FC with support from Bermondsey and Old Southwark MP Simon Hughes and a couple of Millwall fan petitions.

This reared its ugly head again in 2016/17 when Lewisham announced whether they were going to make the acquirement of the land a Compulsory Purchase Order after John Berylson had blocked the original proposal and amazingly Millwall's proposals and offer to work in conjunction with Renewal was rejected out of hand, now pardon me if I suggest that Lewisham Councils decisions are based on greed or a nice palm greasing from Renewal on Wednesday 7th September they announced by 6 votes to 1 with 1 abstention that CPOs were what they would grant, conveniently ignoring all the good work the Millwall Community Trust has done In the community that comes under their auspice or the fact that Millwall fans and players helped to Save Lewisham A & E, palm greased heftily by Renewal me thinks.

The CPO issuing was investigated by Lewisham's internal Committee after a vote orf 7 – 1 abstention 20th September because it was apparent that there was no firm facts that there was justification for issuing them, i.e, there was no thought regarding the social implication on the Bermondsey committee, be they business or residential.

Renewal a company that was offshore, strangely had a Mysterons policy for their board members, and in truth no record of capability to produce such a project, to be honest they appeared to be another EuroFerries make believe entity! The Lewisham Mayor Sir Steven Bullock was apparently a Millwall Community Trust Trustee, and the rumour mill had it aso on Renewal's board, though whether that was proved I do not know.

However, on the Millwall Community Trust Trustee front as the centre, the Millwall Café, some of the Den car park and The Memorial Garden, is that not a shit on your own doorstep Policy issuing CPOs against something you are effectively on the board of, or does an earner come his way with it being issued?

I know what I and all Millwall fans think, palm greasing aplenty, sod the fact that they were not planning to supply what by definition to the issuance of a CPO, like sufficient ample socially affordable housing, also I wondered what would happen to Kings Ferry wanting to park their coaches in the Den car park, if it was to become a work in progress building site, therefore being presumably another source of money thar Millwall FC would lose, from the CPOs actually going ahead.

This CPO issuance was actually stalled by Lewisham Council Scrutiny themselves when it became patently obvious that Renewal were a firm that the Former Mayor and other Councillors were on the board of, the company had no record of having the capability of being able to do such a project, they had offshore ownership a mysterious board, which no nepotism here contained the Lewisham Mayor before Bullock, David Sullivan, who until 2006 owned 26% of Renewal, and more worryingly for them a document was found that implied that they were up for selling their freeholding for a profit pronto, I cannot believe that there are such a thing as shifty underhand Developers! A meeting that was arranged for Wednesday 28th September 2016 to re vote on whether CPOs were actually viable and in fact to the benefit of the Lewisham Community, not just the pockets of Renewal and its links to Lewisham Councillors, was cancelled at the last minute when the document turned up, it being deemed serious and warranting an external examination so dodgy were its implications, with alleged links to an Estate Agent's who were to act on Renewal's behalf to flog the land as soon as CPOs had been enforced essentially.

The National media for once fell on our side with a couple of lead articles in The Guardian, one entitled 'Millwall Score An Early Goal As They Seek The Ultimate Home Win' and one on The Sun, it was also in The Standard and on BBC News relaying the truth about Lewisham's dodgy dealings.

So at this particular moment this was all up in the air with the media actually seeing that the situation was not only bad for Millwall FC but for Football clubs nationwide in general should such a practice as this become legal and cha ching for Property Developers time! Just a thought but with our reputation do you think the Police really think that turning areas around The New Den into a Building Site was a good idea? We are Policed like we are ISIS already, so you turn Millwall's ground into what amounts to an Ammunition dump and not think there will be a violent response to builders affectively breaking into our domain and will very well be treated like burglars shows how much consideration has gone into the local Labour council's decision, none apart from greed, self-interested and inherent nepotism between members of the Council and Renewal jumps off the page to me, but what do I know.

The Curtain Comes Down,

what I said in the above paragraph was obviously right as Lewisham Mayor Sir Steven Bullock, saw the light on 25th January 2017, with the media, Football Teams, Sports people, politicians, Local Businesses, Millwall supporter groups, with a lot of the outcry led by Barney Ronay of The Guardian, picking holes in the corrupt nature of the CPOs, Renewal, Funding issues, well pretty much everything the shifty sods instigated! Ordered the withdrawal of the process, the biter bit!!!

Millwall groups pursued the issue with call for an independent enquiry by Parliamentary sources, with another petition, this follows the deluge of Petitions including 13,000 signatures being delivered to London Mayor Sadiq Khan, the week prior to Lewisham Crumbling.

The horror came back when in a report commissioned by the Lewisham Council Retired Judge Lord Dyson cleared the Council of any wrongdoing in his Report about the CPO published in November 2017, so the battle is not over. The fight will continue against Lewisham Council CPO/Renewal.

In essence pick on the wrong club, pick on the wrong fans, be as corrupt as arseholes, have not got the bottle to fight and you get blown out of the water!!! Sadly not completely so, see the part in 2018/2019.

Dockers' Day at the Den

Above is a picture from 18th March 2017 game v Bury on Dockers Day, an annual event that marks Millwall's affiliation with Millwall Docks and Dockworkers from our formation in 1885, the above shot features players who featured in Millwall's Famous 59 Home Game Run, standing in front of the Blue Bus before Kick Off they were also introduced on to the pitch pre-match.

Finally in this season there was emotional day at the Den on Good Friday 14th April 2017 when we played Northampton Town, it was a day based around Jimmy Mizen's Charity, which was supported by home fans and the travellers from Northampton Town, which showed the enmity between both sets of fans, this was heightened when in the second half of a game that Millwall were winning 3-0 there was a major incident in the Dockers Stand in the blocks slightly nearer to the away North Stand than the CBL, messages echoed via PA Les about keeping access points clear and Millwall fans were encouraged to vacate certain blocks, which they did. From where we were in the CBL it was not apparent initially what had happened, but it transpired as Medical staff flooded the area that something serious had taken place, we later found out after the game thar Lions fan Antony Murphy had collapsed in the Dockers Upper and Medical staff were in the process of giving him CPR in situ on the Dockers stand hence the request for areas to be cleared. The CPR continued until after the game had finished and Lions fans did exactly as was requested of them over the PA via Les, the atmosphere in the crowd had dropped when it became apparent that this was a serious if not life threatening incident, our response to this situation was supported by the attending Northampton Town fans, who chanted Millwall and we applauded them for their support. Many thanks and much respect to Northampton fans for accepting what the real Millwall are and donating financially to the cause.

We thought that the few people who invaded the pitch from Kitcheners lower to encourage the referee Graham Salisbury to blow his whistle in the Extra Time period, accompanied by chants of 'Blow Your F***ing Whistle' by we in the CBL, would be the medias focal point, you know Millwall fans threaten Ref in pitch invasion bullshit, it was not like that in this instance but this media biased idea will become apparent when you see the next chapter highlighting the sort of bollocks we usually get.

At first glance it seemed that in this instance the Media realised this was serious and not unjustified well those few that mentioned did.

The Millwall Official Site relayed the information that Antony Murphy was able to breath and was taken from the Den still alive, which we were all glad to hear. The matches relevance was lessened dramatically as was the atmosphere at the time when compared to someones life or death scenario, he was thankfully taken to hospital to recover. It was later reported that he had had a Heart Attack, he had been operated on in the hospital and was put into an induced coma, to aid his recovery. They opened a fund to donate to the medical staff via Just Giving, which we Millwall fans did. Sadly Antony passed away on the eve of the Play-Off Final v Bradford

City, more info on this later in the book. In response to the respect shown by each set of fans Millwall and Northampton Town to each other, this was Tweeted by a Northampton Fan.

> ↻ Northampton Town Retweeted
>
> **PC 1025 Price**
> @NorpolFootball
>
> Nice touch as @MillwallFC fans clap 👏 the @ntfc supporters coaches as they leave. #respect @sixfieldstravel @ntfc_trust
>
> 14/04/2017, 17:16

This is just a small sample of the Millwall reality rather than the preconceived media Lions fans character assassination, the full complement of which comes slightly later in this book.

Oh yes and we beat Premier League Bournemouth, Watford and reigning Champions Leicester City at Den in FA Cup, and we won promotion via Play-Offs, so all in all quite and eventful season 2016/2017

Season 2017/2018

The New Den was put on the highest Terror alert at Reading home game on Tuesday 26th September 2017, with following Saturday 30th September 2017 game v Barnsley on high alert as well, this was because of a threat that Terrorist Police recognised when a Millwall Steward of ten years, converted to Islam and was sending information by Phone to Pakistan of the New Den, he also had Facetime links to the infamous Finsbury Park Mosque. The threat was not a firm one but full security precautions were taken in case anything happened. The employee was hospitalised on fears of his Mental Health, whether this had any link to Roy Larner's Borough Market reaction who knows!

The Return of Tim Cahill on Monday 30th January ex Lions Messiah the man who scored in FA Cup Semi at Old Trafford v Sunderland in homage the Ex Lion return at 38 prompted –

'We're on the pitch if Timmy Scores' and 'Timmy Cahill he's one of our own'

Season 2018/2019

At Remembrance Day v Ipswich Town on 27th October 2018 Johnny Garton, Millwall fan and British Welterweight Champion, brought his title belt out onto the pirch before match as did another Millwall Fan and boxing champion Ted Cheesman, British Super Welterweight Champion who displayed his belt before the home game v Bolton Wanderers on Saturday 24th November 2018.

Two Comedy Official related games at the New Den, Bolton Wanderers game on 24th November 2018 and the Blackburn Rovers game on 12th January 2019, when the officials had to be changed during first half of each match Bolton Wanderers was really comical when Ref went off then to become 4th official who had replaced him they then changed the Linesman for someone from crowd who was qualified but a Millwall Fan, something seemingly not taken on board not that it bothered me his allegiance, even when he celebrated Skalak's equaliser from sidelines, and in Blackburn Rovers game it was only one official the Ref taken off and replaced by 4th official, I had not seen having to replace a Ref during the game before then for it to happen again in same season, I should have had a bet on it, got bloody good odds! Maybe they were the now referred to weakness Snowflakes moments by Refs, i.e, in a the crowd are being beastly to me, I want to leave or they were injured moment I don't know, or care,

Returning to The CPOs in early 2019 new Lewisham Mayor Damien Egan was patently on Millwall's side wishing to keep Millwall FC as part of Lewisham's community, and after the change of Mayor, Millwall, Renewal and Lewisham Council seemed to be working in conjunction not against each other, so hopefully it is finally all over – hoorah!!! Until we heard that the Lewisham Council still has a conditional land sale agreement (CLSA) in place, so as they say it Ain't over till it's over!!

Fairy Tales Do Come True, because despite my doubts in this section, here comes the final truth from Millwall's official Website on 11 October 2019

Millwall Football Club warmly welcomes the announcement by Lewisham Council that it will terminate the conditional land sale agreement that exists between the Council and Renewal. This agreement was concluded in December 2013 and provided for the sale by Lewisham to Renewal of the freeholds of the land adjoining Millwall's stadium. The agreement in effect inhibited Millwall from proceeding with its plans for the development of the land it leases.

Millwall equally welcomes the announcement by Lewisham Council that the leases owned by the football club and its community scheme will be varied to allow Millwall to prepare development plans for the land around The Den.

The Council's statement is as follows: Following a period of intensive collaboration over the past eighteen months, Lewisham Council, Millwall Football Club and the development company, Renewal have agreed a new approach to enable their sites to go forward for housing and other development. The previous plan had included a potential compulsory purchase order to develop part of a site currently leased by Millwall Football Club. Following months of negotiation facilitated by the Mayor of Lewisham, Damien Egan, the previous Conditional Land Sale Agreement will now be terminated. Plans which involve building on leasehold land are now being revised. This paves the way for an increase in much needed social housing for Lewisham residents and retains the Millwall stadium.

CHAPTER 2
The Media – Millwall are Evil Perception

"WE ARE A CONVENIENT COAT-PEG UPON WHICH FOOTBALL HANGS ALL ITS EVILS" -REG BURR, FORMER MILLWALL CHAIRMAN.

To start above is the never a truer word said in jest statement by former Lions chairman Reg Burr

I hope the Northampton fan post near to the end of the last chapter has not led anyone who does not know to thinking that the media must have seen that and now think that all Millwall fans are sweetness and light!

I am not saying that we are all angels, far from it, and I am obviously focussed more on my Millwall allegiance than non Millwall fans would be, but this perception could not be farther from the truth because the Negative angle adopted across the board by the Media gets on your wick, or should I say our Millwall wicks, this led to the creative creation of The Liar – please see how we perceive the tabloid red top press in particular also a mock up of Daily Express –

I know we used to chant 'We Are Evil' at the Old Den, so perhaps the media heard that, wrote it down and that is that, forgetting that was a hoolie firm chant, not confirmation verbally that we are all Satanists!!!

Thought I would put the above as an idea as to why the Media are predominantly so anti Millwall.

In truth it is because it is a perception that the media are happy to perpetuate, in this chapter is one very small bit of proof of what they will publish and what they will not, you will say very small??? But I say very small, because if you went on an anti Millwall press cuttings exercise the amount that I found would be the size of 'Encyclopedia Britannica'!!!

To start below I thought that I would show some Anti Millwall stories, the first one was following a crime raid, second when we played at Highbury in the FA Cup and George Graham had become the Gunners manager and the gutter press came up with the accusation that Millwall fans who had been allocated the Clock End would steal the beloved Arsenal Clock, and when we visited Upton Park for first time in a while, certainly our previous trip there had been pre the erection of the Moore, Hurst, Peters Statue, on the first picture it is uncovered, following this is the Millwall are coming board it up picture version, as the media again implied that we would either de- face it, which was possible I suppose but ludicrously as they said with the Highbury clock they said that we would steal it, funnily enough we stole neither, I think even the Old Bill might notice if we brought in heavy lifting gear!

Whilst these were ridiculous several years before the above two claims, there was one even more scandalous, libellous, ludicrous media report (your choice) when it said Millwall were involved in a bank raid, with Millwall FC Old Den images accompanying a totally unrelated story about a bank raid in South London, I am a bit vague about the facts as I could find nothing on the internet that related to this story D Notice Internet as we Wall Conspiracy theorists would say, I am not lying, this really certainly did happen, I remember us all being disgusted with how it had been thrown together in the gutter media.

To highlight my Millwall are treated one way other teams are treated entirely differently perception, everyone else especially Premier League clubs are sweetness and light, one example –

On Sunday 22nd November 2015, Tottenham Hotspur played West Ham United at White Hart Lane, two hated rivals and one West Ham fan was stabbed in clashes outside the ground about an

49

hour before kick off, this was only fleetingly mention, in some on-line newspapers, and on TV, it was not on Radio news on Monday morning, it was not mentioned in The Sun or Daily Mirror, that I saw either!

Now excuse my Millwall perception but if this had involved us, it would have been a media blitz along the same line as the terrorist attack on Paris the week before!

Moving on to a television media example I just had to mention as it was a really original blame Millwall story, on one Jeremy Kyle show, I am not sure when it was aired on TV I only saw the clip on You Tube. In it there was one woman who had cheated on her man. So as I did not see full programme I don't know what their relationship was, but that aside the reason that she gave for her cheating on him was because he went to watch Millwall play and had not taken her!

Now I have heard Millwall blamed for most things but infidelity!!!!

Well if everyone had her attitude, that was and is most people at New Den or Old Den f***ed then!

If this reasoning became rife today we should open up a relationship and marriage counselling service in the Den Executive Lounge!!!

Paranoia And The Media

The usual newspaper headline for any Old Den game with even a hint of trouble was/is –

'Riot At Den!'/'Den Of Shame!'/'Animals!'

More specifically, Referee Norman Burtenshaw's apparent assault in 1967 at the Old Den in a 2-1 home defeat to Aston Villa when allegedly he was knocked unconscious by Wall fans this saw the headline

'Thugs Maul Ref!'

There was the prophecy of trouble – 'Rivers Of Blood' headlines for a midweek night match against Manchester United on 16th September 1974, which sadly for the press passed off peacefully when the Red Devils, then notorious fans, did not turn up.

Not forgetting the 1978 Ipswich Town FA Cup Quarter Final 'riot' 'Shut The Lion's Den!'/"Burn These Bastards!' Headlines. It did seem at this time that when tabloids reported on any Old Den incident anything constituted a riot from a small amount of coin throwing to a full scale Rodney King inspired LA job, any of which would be worthy of the same definition, as you will see nothing much changes.

Millwall, rather like England, do suffer from a sweeping generalisational attitude in the media, which demeans the plus points of Millwall fans, for example the loud vocal support that we generally give to our side, especially away, again like England. In Millwall's case, it also ignores the major advances the club and team have made since our imminent financial extinction a few years back.

However, the tabloid end of the market in the press has always meant sensationalism; it sells papers.

In the 1960s/70s, you would frequently have many headlines of a 'Hooligans on the Rampage!' Style in the press, especially in the Sunday papers, this was an era when Saturday WAS the day for Football, with only occasional midweek games, today as you know you can watch Football every day of the week – 'When Saturday Comes' yeah righto not nowadays chummy! For example I went to the Vetch Field twice once on a Friday and once on a Sunday, I have also been to the Liberty Stadium three times at the time of writing also twice on Friday and once on Sunday, never on a Saturday told you!!!

Once the season was over, the press would revert to the seaside bank holiday invasions by Teddy Boys, Mods, Rockers, Skinheads, Suede heads, Punks or whoever were the relevant menace to society at the time, they would then switch back to Football when the season started.

Something that was different in the early days of the Bovver Boy era was that no one particular side was the scapegoat. You therefore had reports of trouble from most clubs, complete with the customary Police photographs of weapons hauls, smashed up 'special' trains, on pitch battles and terrace rucks featuring bloodied victims, who had often been hit by bottles, nail studded golf balls or darts inside the grounds, there is nothing like a bit of claret to sell papers.

Apart from the focus on certain scapegoat clubs the main difference in the modern era is that everything is now in colour. As I implied earlier nowadays there seems to be less focus on trouble unless it involves us or Cardiff City, with most other incidents only being mentioned if they were on television or just too heavy to ignore, even then it's only a few days coverage not weeks/months like we have had numerous times.

It seems that we get more of the shitty end of the stick than anyone else does.

Is there one rule for Millwall and another for everyone else, or is it just me?

I'm not saying that Millwall do not often deserve the bad press that we get for some of our fans' actions, far from it, however reporting of Millwall related incidents can stretch a connection a bit to say the least and whilst largely justified post Luton and the Birmingham Play Off, it has often been a case of 'The Journalist Moves In Mysterious Ways' school of reporting, some examples to whet your appetite –

1) There was the fuss that was made in The Sun after the alleged Ian Wright coin-throwing incident at Highbury, with its prolonged 'Find the Bobble Hatted Thug' picture campaign; it should not have been hard it is hardly normal headgear is it?

Compare the response to the above to other high profile incidents of missile throwing that have occurred in recentish past seasons between Premiership sides, inside the ground and captured by TV and press cameras, for example –

Arsenal fans threw coins at Jamie Carragher against Liverpool at Highbury, which he threw back.

Burnley fans threw coins at Didier Drogba at Chelsea, which he also threw back.

Manchester City fans threw coins against Manchester United at Maine Road, specifically at David Beckham.

Everton fans threw bottles at Fulham players.

Chelsea and Spurs fans threw lighters and bottles etc at Stamford Bridge.

Spurs fans threw bottles at Sol Campbell against Arsenal.

Chelsea fans threw missiles at Thierry Henry in the FA Cup at Highbury and Stamford Bridge.

Portsmouth fans threw two bottles at officials during their 2003 game against Charlton.

To name but a few that, whilst reported, strangely this mostly did not result in such an extended witch-hunt, as the Ian Wright incident or our Pie throwing Assistant Referee incident against Birmingham.

2) There was the time when the Isle of Dogs, Millwall, admittedly our spiritual home, suddenly metamorphosed into Millwall F.C. SE16, presumably so that the BNP's win in the Isle of Dogs by-election could be connected with us. Apart from the name 'Millwall' as a connection, there is no link at all, still never let the facts get in the away of a good story. E14? – SE16?

An easy mistake to make, what are a river and a few miles in pursuit of a story?

3) In the past the Millwall fanzines have highlighted, the disparity between a quarter page article about Reading away on 'Spanner Night ' and a much smaller report on the same page about that year's Notting Hill Carnival, which appeared in the Evening Standard at the time.

I was at Elm Park on the night and standing close to the area where it happened, in reality it was a minor incident, obviously, it could have been a lot worse if the missile in question had actually hit the keeper but in truth it landed nowhere near him. Nevertheless this Reading missile-throwing incident was reported like the Kennedy assassination, whilst the usual carnival sideshows of rioting, drug dealing, muggings, rapes, stabbings and multiple arrests, were scarcely mentioned, put down to carnival high jinx or summarily dismissed as nothing very much!

4) There was the scurrilous tabloid article that famously linked Millwall (club badge and shots of the outside of the Old Den and all) with an armed robbery on our ground several years ago that I fleetingly mentioned before, this was naturally also given front-page status.

5) There were tabloid headlines, that went something like –
'For God sake don't let them get promoted' following supposed crowd trouble at our 1988 FA Cup-tie at Highbury. Problems caused solely by bad organisation, Arsenal's refusal to make the game all ticket and aided by the Police's liberal use of force I might add. It resulted in late comers being crammed into a corner stand; and having to push their way into a decent position whilst being manhandled by the fuzz, still never let the truth get in the way and all that.

6) Finally, there is the plethora of 'They're Coming!' shock-horror reports that are invariably to be found in regional papers countrywide prior to a visit by us.
Dire warnings not to travel to Millwall are also popular in local papers.

7) In addition to 'factual' sic reports in the media that we Millwall fans have also had to endure numerous 'humorous' comedy skits and cartoons at our club's expense over the years. For example

in the inflatables era of the late 1980s the Evening Standard had a 'witty' cartoon showing a Neanderthal/skinhead Millwall fan carrying a blow up Stanley Knife standing in a queue behind someone with a blow up banana waiting to go through an entrance marked 'Millwall F.C'.

8) In a similar vein because of our reputation, we are the first club that a comedy scriptwriter thinks of when they want a Football hooligan punch line, no pun intended. As a result, we have been used as a violent comic reference on Harry Enfield's Television Programme, 'Drop the Dead Donkey', 'Alexei Sayle's Stuff' to name but three of many, please see later section in this book re this.

Although 7 and 8 above are not a press story, this sort of thing still acts as a negative reinforcement in the public's mind of our bad image. I can only assume that comedy writers/cartoonists have never had the pleasure of a trip to the likes of Elland Road, Ninian Park, Maine Road, The Britannia Stadium, Ashton Gate, Molineux, St Andrews, Fratton Park, Bramall Lane, The Vetch Fields/Liberty Stadium or Turf Moor.

To name just a few that I have visited in recentish past, because unbelievably, a trip to any of the above can be 'interesting' to say the least.

I suppose as they have a perfectly good whipping boy for society's ills in Millwall why change it? Moreover, the public, who have not had the pleasure of any of the above, would not understand a joke about say 'Swansea Jack Army hooligans', so Millwall it is every time. The words cheap and shot spring to mind.

Returning to the press and media, the local paper scare stories that I mention above appear season after season and most of the others that I refer to are several years old now and were highlighted in the Millwall fanzines at the time and in 'The Trouble With Millwall' book a few years back.

I am glad to say however that this proud press, media, advertising and general bad reputation tradition is still alive and well, some examples from the previous years in no particular Alphabetical order –

A) The People ran a double-page article on 17th March 2002 about one of West Ham United's Top Boys Cass Pennant and his new book about West Ham's hooligans – the Inter City Firm – called 'Congratulations You've Just Met the I.C.F'.

In this article, it had excerpts from the book and a large picture of the author superimposed over a double-page spread photograph of the Luton FA Cup Quarter Final riot!

Cass Pennant was a main player in Bravo's 'I Predict A Riot', that I mention later where I also mention that the programme did feature the Luton riot and also the Birmingham riot as well, that aside the programme didn't start until 2005, despite the time difference he did say on this Programme that Millwall's Hooligan following were the only ones who had regular run in battles with the police, true I'd say.

A few questions getting back to The People article, why feature the Millwall Luton riot in relation to a West Ham book?

Mind you as I mentioned in the anti West Ham chapter later on, footage of our Luton riot also features heavily on West Ham's 'Hooligan' Documentary. Why? What does the actions of the ICF have to do with us?

Why did they not use specific ICF shots from West Ham's own hooligan documentary?

West Ham themselves have several Hoolie books available, Millwall don't really have any to be honest.

That doesn't stop West Ham United more or less getting away scot free when it comes to having an unblemished Hooligan reputation, why I've no idea. See the specific West Ham United section later on.

B) Prior to his arrival the mere possibility that Dennis' Cabbie/ Callum Lamper' Wise may come to Millwall prompted some tabloid newspapers to imply that we deserved each other and were kindred spirits as it were. The Sun did an article calling the move 'A Marriage Made In Hell' complete with comparative Wise and Millwall Rolls Of Shame to highlight the fact. There was as much, if not more, outcry surrounding Lee Bowyer's move to the Happy Hammers following his alleged involvement in a racist attack on an Asian and the fact that West Ham's ground is in a largely Asian area. This was headline news on TV and in the press for several days in January 2003; however, the media made no link between Bowyer and West Ham's chequered hooligan history, as they had done with Millwall and Dennis Wise, strange that!!

Naturally, it did not get any better for Wisey when he was promoted to our Manager thus allowing the 'They're Made For Each Other' comparisons and slurs to flare up again.

Strangely his later Managership of Hooligan club Leeds United was not mentioned from memory!

C) I believe it was the Daily Mail or Daily Express, same meat different gravy, which did a classic of image manipulation when they published a press photograph in colour taken from behind the normal Police presence in the corner of the North and West stands at the New Den.

This was for the Birmingham City League game in 2001/2 (Pie Night as its known.)

This photograph, allied to the incidents in the game, meant that the image was portrayed in a way that implied that the Police had been called in as a fluorescent yellow thin line keeping us evil pastry throwing Millwall hordes at bay. In truth, they were in the position that they always stood in, with most of those pictured standing there with their arms folded and watching the match.

Mind you with a floodlit New Den as a backdrop, it was a spectacular, if very misleading, shot to use.

The press did miss a couple of tricks here though –

1) With the events surrounding the Afghanistan war and anthrax alerts being well publicised at the time and following in the wake of BSE and foot-and-mouth I am surprised that they did not say of the pie attacker – 'Millwall Thug in Chemical Attack!'

2) Can you imagine the outcry if the assistant referee had been Jewish and somebody had thrown a pork pie at him? You could then have the headline – 'Millwall Racist Thugs in Anti-Semitic Attack!'

You can see it all now can't you. To my mind, the pie thrower was more likely a food critic than a hooligan!

At the same time as the Birmingham game pie incident there were very serious incidents at Cardiff City v Leeds United, Aston Villa v Manchester United and Chelsea v Spurs, games, which included pitch invasions, fence scaling, away fan baiting and glass bottle and coin throwing.

Incidents that were initially covered on TV and the press but which then disappeared, unlike the Millwall problems. All of these incidents combined, with our pie lobbing being by far the most trivial, saw the usual – 'Hang ,Em And Flog ,Em' Brigade coming out in force.

There were also suggestions to bring back the perimeter fencing; didn't these contribute to umpteen deaths at Hillsborough? Anyway, Cardiff City at the time of the Leeds game at Ninian Park had fences so that works doesn't it!

I cannot see anybody who has paid up to £40 or higher for a seat in the Premiership objecting to sitting behind a metal grille can you? I suppose we could go continental and adopt the Italian style glass partitions, but these don't stop trouble either; however, they are a positive boon for the window-cleaning industry. I am sure that they are a joy to watch a match through when it rains as well.

'Send in A Gunboat, Bring on the Water Cannons and Baton Rounds!' sorry the brigadier has woken up again

D) There was a Persil Non Bio poster a couple of years ago that featured a father sitting next to a baby in a pram with the slogan – 'Of Course He's Sensitive, He Cried When Millwall Lost'. Is there no escape?

E) In late 2002, the press made much of the fact that RMT union boss Bob Crow was a Millwall supporter.

This gave the media many opportunities to use the 'No One Likes Us' analogy whenever he threatened any industrial action on the tube with headlines like – 'No One Likes Him, But He Doesn't Care'. Mind you, he was quoted in the press and on TV interviews using this comparison himself, between his union, his Millwall allegiance and the fact that we were equally despised. I suppose you could say that he brought it upon himself.

F) The Daily Mirror had a front-page picture of Tony Blair at the same time as the rail problems in the latter part of 2002 with the banner headline – 'No One Likes Me? I Don't Care!'

G) Princess Anne, whose Birthday is the same day as mine bizarrely, was referred to as the Millwall Royal, because no one likes her and she didn't care! On a similar royal tack and just to show how my mind works – I watched The Queen's Christmas Speech in 2001 and she appeared to be wearing a Millwall colour blue outfit, I thought to myself 'Surely not? She can't possibly be a closet Lion can she?' Imagine it – Millwall by Royal appointment. Mind you we would have to change our badge and nickname to the Corgis, it would be rude not to. I thought to myself that there is only one way to be certain, if a butler comes in and brings her 'Jellied eels and a Light Ale' then we can be sure! 'No One Likes One, One Doesn't Care' Up The Lions Ma'am!

H) There was a press review in the Daily Mirror on 3rd December 2002 for a BBC TV programme about aggressive Bulldog ants; the review included the line – 'The Millwall Fans Of The Insect World Bulldog Ants Are So Hard They Even Turned On The BBC's Ant Cam'

I) Continuing the TV theme in 2003, an episode of 'Two Thousand Acres of Skye' referred to Millwall when talking about unruly animal behaviour. 'The Salon' Channel 4s camp documentary about a poncy hairdressers managed to include a comment from a hairdresser that a customers new haircut made them look hard enough to go to Millwall. Quentin Willson on 'Britain's Worst Celebrity Driver' managed to compare the incompetent celebrity driver's road rage as being akin to a Millwall fan's response to being caught in a revolving door.

J) Two stories that I highlighted at the beginning of this chapter –
When we played at Highbury in the FA Cup on January 9th 1988, the press was rife with rumours that we were going to steal the Clock End clock, all several tons of it, obviously we didn't.
On a similar tack, Millwall played at West Ham United on Sunday 28th September 2003, for the first time in over ten years. In the weeks preceding the game the local East End press speculated about the probable trouble, the huge police operation and, like the Clock End accusation, they said that we were going to steal Bobby Moore's head from the brass statue in Barking Road, again not exactly light, obviously we didn't do this either.

K) On Monday March 15th 2004 the possibility that goalie Andy Marshall, on loan from Ipswich Town at the time, could make the move permanent prompted The Sun to report the possible move as him switching the Tractor Boys for the Bovver Boys.

L) On May 14th 2004 'The Football Factory', a football hooligan film based on a fictional book about a Chelsea 'Headhunter', was released at the cinema. Naturally, there was a media furore surrounding its release so close to June's Euro 2004. Specifically from a Millwall perspective, despite the fact that it is based on a Chelsea hooligan's life, it does feature a battle at the end of the film with Millwall hooligans filmed near to the New Den; consequently the media chose to the focus almost entirely on the supposed Millwall aspect of the film. Its release in the week before the May 22nd FA Cup Final did not help obviously as it gave the media carte blanche to mention it and our Final appearance together in their bulletins or articles. Strangely, from what I saw anyway, they chose largely to ignore the fact that the film is about Chelsea hooligans and also featured clashes with Spurs and Liverpool fans in the film and decided to use the New Den as a backdrop for the TV reports instead.

M) In February 2004 when black Millwall teenager Moses Ashikodi allegedly threatened fellow black Lions player Mark McCammon with a knife in a training ground canteen bust up it was naturally spread all over the media. Whilst such a major incident is undoubtedly newsworthy, with it being a Millwall incident the News Of The World on Sunday 8th February managed to incorporate a dig at our hooligan reputation and Manager Dennis Wise's chequered history including the Callum Davidson incident in their article. With the implication being, that anything associated with Millwall is violent. All I can say is thank god that the knifeman had not been a white player or we would have been buried in a Millwall are racist deluge, see later on.

N) The Lion Roars carried a snippet from a Sunday tabloid in their issue 171 In November 2004 with a snippet from an article quoting scouse transvestite 'comedian' Lily Savage aka Paul O'Grady regarding the Gay charity Stonewall where he was quoted as saying of his Gay rights aspirations –

'I'm not interested in equality, I want superiority. I do not wish to be equal with some Millwall supporting, pitbull-breeding, wife-battering arsehole'. No one at Millwall wants to be on equal footing with Scouse gay Transvestites either I'd say. I haven't got a dog let alone breed them and I'm not married so he/she can't mean me!

O) 'Murder Team Investigation'

On July 11th July 2005 the above renamed CSI style ITV series returned to our screens.

During the first episode of its new run in a storyline about a computer oriented murder game called 'Fone Tag', a competitor was stabbed to death and top copper DI Trevor Hands said something like 'No one dies for a game' to which a colleague replied 'That's rich coming from a Millwall supporter!' Oh how we laughed!!!! Let me think Heysel, mmmm Hillsborough were they not both Liverpool related?

P) 'Shop the Yobs'

The Sun and also the BBC website on July 20th 2009 ran a full page with the above mentioned headline and a mug shot gallery of a game at Hull City in a 3rd round FA Cup game on 24th January 2009. This was because Crimestoppers in collusion with the Police and The Sun wanted to get the public's help in finding the supposed offenders, strangely Millwall were the first side ever to be featured on a Crimestoppers appeal, unusual for us, well no it bloody isn't!!! Given the time that these things drag on for and how the media circus kicks in you have to ask is it a conspiracy against us? Isn't paranoia wonderful?

In the articles pursuit of fairness there was no mention of how many of the 32 supposed yobs featured in the mug shots were Hull City fans, none as it transpired, they were all Millwall and the Old Bill were going to raid 24 of the identified, supposed Millwall hooligans, it was reported in the Hull Daily Mail press up there in early August 2009 as it had a link to the article on the website in the House Of Fun.

Therefore the assumption by the local plod and the media was that it was Millwall causing all the trouble in the ground! Wrong, they were obviously not there on the day and therefore conveniently ignored what the home fans did in the ground.

For those of you who were not there at the KC Stadium, to my Millwall mind, it was the KC without The Sunshine Band, as it was certainly not That's The Way I Like it, mostly because we lost and also as we always do, we got the customary Police State treatment and got blamed for everything.

At the game unusually for a Millwall away game there was a huge Old Bill operation, where we were strangely treated like terrorists pre match. The six of us, that went left Harlow at 9.30am, drove up there and arrived at about 1.20pm.

When we found the Ground, we asked the Old Bill where the away Car Park was; we spoke to the ones who were standing with umpteen other Old Bill bouncers outside a pub opposite the ground that had chalkboards outside the doors saying No Away Supporters.

We then parked up in the Ground's huge, but soaking bleeding wet and extremely muddy Car Park opposite. This was after the copper that we asked had said that there was a pub further on which was accessible to Millwall fans. So after we parked up we wandered across to it, and in fact it wasn't a pub, it was the huge New Walton Social Club, that had hundreds of Millwall inside and dozens of Lions drinking outside, with many dozens of Old Bill, Police Dogs, Horses vans, etc, etc surrounding the place.

When we went inside, we found that the bar was packed like a January sale in the West End; I decided to stay Teetotal and had nothing, fortuitous actually, as it took two of our number about 20 minutes to be served. As we stood there a bloke in a Hull City top got on a mike near the stage at one end and said that we Millwall supporters would be escorted to the ground, which was just across the road at 2.15pm. We all said sod that so we headed outside at about 2pm. The Cozzers lined up outside would not let us go to

63

the ground without our being mobbed together in their mass Escort, we argued with them about why this was necessary? As we were extremely close to the bloody ground from where we were, but they argued against our departure and therefore we were all held there until about 2.20pm.

When the Police cavalry and Riot Police were sufficiently in huge numbers, they marched us across the road and through the Car Park's mudbath.

When we arrived at the ground close to kick off, they had sold all the programmes so we could not buy any. I went to the loo and the others went inside but we lost each other, as I had no idea where they were and our mobiles were unlistenable inside the ground, so I sat on my own for the whole game.

The Hull City fans to the left of us, up the side of our section behind the goal, in a ground that was similar to Leicester's Walker Stadium, were mouthy buggers and the nearby Millwall and they exchanged pleasantries from the start.

Missiles started flying between the sections, mostly bottles and some broken seats from both sides, and the Stewards and Riot Police separated the two sections with clashes erupting on both sides.

The Police state operation was naturally mostly against Millwall's section as we are naughty boys.

All of you fellow Lions know how these bleeding operations are so biased, i.e. if they are not Millwall they can practically do nothing wrong. Fully clad Riot Police were stretched across our entire section at the front pretty much the whole game,

Because of the fracas in the first half, as had happened at Southampton a few years back in a relegation season, they shut the buffet at Half Time, so they could sell us nothing.

Near the latter part of the game, the missile, particularly the broken seat chucking, stepped up from both sides, loads of broken seats flew from our bit and there were more clashes between fans and Old Bill Riot Police again. At the close, they rode four mounted Police horses out and plonked them in front of our end near the left hand side where all the clashes had happened.

Millwall inevitably got all the blame, they continually said on the Radio news after the fracas that there had been 12 arrests, whether they were all Millwall or Hull City as well they did not say.

However it said in the reports that the Old Bill were happy with the success of their operation, good for them, I don't suppose it had occurred to them that if you treat people like shit, trouble is more likely not less likely to happen, but what do I know!

Q) On Monday 3rd January 2011 The Sun carried a report about our crushing the Palarse on New Years Day and Jason Puncheon' hat trick. Typically the headline to the report was 'Punch Up' and the first line was 'Millwall fans used to love a punch up now they prefer Puncheon' sod the victory!

I wonder do any other teams have this sort of linkage? They don't blimey!

I am amazed that when Uwe Fuchs scored at a victory at Crystal Palace in the 1990s that they did not say 'Fuchs Up' if they didn't, opportunity missed there I reckon.

R) The Night Of The Scousers –
The Carling Cup third round tie at the New Den against Liverpool on October 26th 2004 caused a major stir in the media. The thing that caused most of the media indignation was the West lower and East upper home stands singing 'Hillsborough' to the Scousers' continental 'Liverpool' tune.

In the outrage that followed it was alleged by the northerners and the tabloids that we also sang 'You should have all died at Hillsborough!' And 'There's only one Boris Johnson!' in the wake of the Iraq hostage Spectator rumpus earlier in the month. The Spectator is naturally an enormously popular read at the New Den.

According to the Daily Mirror we also chanted about the deaths of James Bulger, John Peel and Ken Bigley. Only The Beatles, Jimmy Tarbuck, Cilla Black, the Liver Birds and Ken Dodd's tax fiddling seems to have escaped our attentions. I personally heard nothing Hillsborough-related at all, I am not doing a Wenger but from where I was sitting in the CBL it was far too noisy to discern anything, although I am assured that the 'Hillsborough' chants did happen by friends who sat nearer to the Dockers stand perpetrators on the night.

We in the CBL certainly never sang any of the above abuse, we only sang the customary Scouse stereotype and social deprivation repertoire – 'Does the social know you're here?' And 'Sign on', etc.

The Scousers for their part on the night sang 'Shit on the Cockneys, shit on the Cockneys tonight!' and the bizarre variation 'Shit on the gypos!' not to mention other anti London chants.

According to tabloids they were also singing 'Budapest! And '4 nil to the Hungary' referring to the 4 Millwall fans stabbed at the Ferencvaros away game. Again, I didn't directly hear this but if true what is the difference between singing about accidental death and attempted murder?

Whilst I would agree that chants about the dead are out of order, the Scousers themselves have sung about Manchester United's Munich air crash in the past, which apparently isn't glorifying in death as they accused Millwall of, conveniently they never mention Heysel, hypocrisy anyone?

The Liverpool fans on the night ripped out 68 seats in the North Stand, hurling several down from the upper tier, they also tried to invade the pitch and were prevented from doing so by dozens of riot police and stewards. They injured one of their own wheelchair bound fans in the ensuing rumpus, it resulted in all of their disabled fans having to be moved along the cinder track behind the goal to safety. In response to the Liverpool fans' violent reactions we in the CBL sang – 'Scum, scum, scum!' And 'Disgrace to the Premier League!'

The Scousers hostile reaction was initially attributed in the media to their taking umbrage at the Hillsborough chants, however it really only seemed to escalate following a suicide mission by one

19 year old Scouser, James Harrison rather than occur as a result of any chants.

This Scouse nutter sat in the West upper and allegedly took offence at what Millwall fans around him were singing about the 1989 Hillsborough disaster, consequently he threw a punch at one Lions fan and shouted out 'Liverpool' which resulted in his receiving the inevitable hiding.

He pleaded guilty to affray and was referred to as the 'catalyst' to the Liverpool fans' violence at his court appearance, where 4 other Scousers were also on trial for violent disorder, which they pleaded not guilty to.

As the catalyst tag implies it was the Scouse kamikaze's actions rather than any direct Hillsborough abuse that triggered the Liverpool fans violent response.

As an aside I don't know if Stoke's announcer/DJ at the Britannia Stadium in the following Saturday's game was being ironic but he played 'Happiness' by Scouse comic Ken Dodd at the end of the home sides 1-0 win, sorry did that sound too paranoid!

On December 8th 2004 Millwall and Liverpool were both cited for the incidents on the night, including Millwall fans allegedly using racial abuse, more of which later.

The media for their part covered the FA charges by mentioning the crowd trouble, injured disabled fan and 68 broken seats but most of them conveniently didn't mention that it was the Scousers who caused the physical trouble.

Why do the media have a seeming double standard when it comes to us? Is it a simple oversight? Do they bear a grudge? Is it a conspiracy? My innate Anti Millwall paranoia tells me which ones it is!

On the evening of the FA charges there was a fictional BBC2 programme about a terrorist attack on a London bank called 'The Man Who Broke Britain', this featured civil unrest on the streets and to highlight it they showed helicopter camera footage of the Birmingham Play Off riot outside the Cliftonville Tavern on the Ilderton

Road. As I said before undoubtedly there's no other footage of any London non football related civil unrest/rioting available so Millwall it is!!!!

Continuing the Liverpool theme on October 29th 2004 BBC's 'Have I Got News For You' had MP Robin Cook as its host. Following a story about a Royal Navy sailor being given permission to continue being a Satanist whilst serving in the Navy. The panel asked Robin Cook if he was a Satanist, which he obviously denied.

Later in the show during the missing word round one of the tabloid posers involved Millwall fans alleged singing 'There's Only One Boris Johnson!' to Liverpool fans earlier in the week. Ian Hislop identified it as a Millwall chant and Cook was queried about his opinion of Boris Johnson and whether it tallied with ours in response

Robin Cook said something like – 'I've already been accused of being a Satanist tonight, I certainly don't want to be mistaken for being a Millwall fan!' Oh how we laughed! I for one would not want to be mistaken for a philandering Scottish ginger minger Labour MP either.

Naturally in June 2005 despite the police and numerous officials present on the Liverpool match night refuting the racist abuse claims against us Millwall were clattered with a £25,000 fine this was compounded by the warning that if Millwall were unsuccessful in their appeal the fine would rise to £32,500 with the prospect of a game having to be played behind closed doors, thereby upping the actual fine substantially, kangaroo court justice at its best, the seat and missile throwing Scousers, who were by now European Champions, got off practically Scot free, strange that.

Such was the outrage caused by the unfairness of the fine that several then MPs, including Millwall fan and local Lib Dem MP Simon Hughes and former Sports minister Kate Hoey, tabled a motion in Parliament against the 'Guilty when proven innocent' fine.

There was an online petition that had numerous clubs fans' support including support from Manchester United, Newcastle United, Spurs, Portsmouth and Chelsea.

In September 2005 the sentence, the racist chant accusations, fine and all additional punishments were dropped on appeal, so FA justice is not such an ass after all, although Millwall still had to foot the legal bill, so despite being not guilty the club were still financially punished, ain't life fair!

S) The return of Birmingham City to the New Den in November 2005 in the League Cup saw Fleet Street, Wapping and Canary Wharf's finest turning out in force for the expected violence, it was a night of mass policing and posturing, with the only 'violence' being Millwall in the East Upper ripping up the segregation netting and surging towards the Brummies the other side of the Jumbotron, tens of yards sorry Metric metres apart, that was about it apart from the police rushing around from the West Lower to the East Upper, some missile throwing from the Brummies and 5 arrests, again all Birmngham fans who were later released, it still prompted these headlines in the next days 'quality' press – 'It took several dozen police officers to separate the fans of these two clubs' The Guardian and 'Fans clash again' The Times.

Although I expected nothing else to be honest, Millwall's press office summed it up for me when they questioned how many other games have the number of arrests listed in the press match reports.

T) BBC News website said on 23 July 2010 despite the minor detail that he had only played 4 games for Millwall, the headline on a story about him shooting someone dead said –

'Former Millwall striker Gavin Grant guilty of murder'

The mere fact that he also played for Gillingham, Tooting & Mitcham, Grays Athletic, Stevenage Borough, Wycombe Wanderers and Bradford City seems irrelevant, strange that!!

U) As I mentioned a few pages earlier cable/Digital TV station Bravo had a programme which started in March 2005 called 'I Predict A Riot' presented by James Brown (not the Godfather of Soul version but a Leeds United fan who said he had never been to Millwall v Leeds United, basically because he implied that he was cacking himself coming to the New Den!) The programme was named after the Leeds band The Kaiser Chiefs' hit, the advertising trailers they used featured the Luton riot footage, thank god for that I thought it had been forgotten!

The Luton footage, together with the Birmingham Play-Off riot was actually very heavily featured in the programme, more so than the Heysel deaths, I know that it was in Belgium not a UK riot as the series was focussed on but it was far worse than Luton or Birmingham put together.

The programme also largely featured Millwall's 'Ginger' – Bob Payne

V) Factually Millwall related footage is not the only available football riot, very bloody true, however that detail aside it seems to be as the Luton Riot and the Birmingham riot together with our 'Panorama' programme, were also featured on another Bravo programme West Ham's Danny Dyer's 'The Real Football Factories' in May 2006

W) In addition there was an ITV 1 programme called 'Surveillance City" shown in August 2006, this programme focussed on the fact that CCTV cameras were everywhere today and part of the programme showed the 32 CCTV cameras that were in place at Selhurst Park, in this instance to spy on the plethora of top boys (sic) on show at that notorious hooligan game Crystal Palace v Southampton, stop laughing!

This was at a match in the 2005/6 season, as a closing piece they implied that CCTVs had stopped hooliganism and to highlight how bad it could get they showed footage of Millwall rioting after the Birmingham Play-Off Semi Final.

X) Back to the newspaper domain on 8th October 2014 The Daily Mirror focussed on a MSC vote about the choice of our away kit for 2015/6 when they published a story with the Headline 'Let's all make Millwall play in pink next season'. What a laugh that would be encourage non-Lions fans to vote for something that would wind us up, the ones I have listed from the Anti-Millwall media witch-hunt are only a snippet, I could fill an entire website with Anti Wall Media stories of a scurrilous nature, but I will just leave you with this nugget.

Y) A cheap shot that really annoyed me was when a lazy supposed journalist from The Sun on Wednesday 2nd November 2016 wrote in the football section under the banner View To A Dill Andrew Dillon 'Lion's Win' so I read it and 100% wished I hadn't because the smug faced arsehole wrote about Millwall v Lewisham CPOs.

His shock was why someone as clever as Dr Robert Winston took to Twitter to show his support for Millwall FC against Lewisham Council's scandalous CPO regeneration scheme, this journalist sic wondered why someone so intelligent would ally himself with us thick Millwall people, until genius Dillon who obviously possesses a brain the size of a planet discovered in his anti-Millwall shit for brains head what the link could be – it was because Winston had been involved with a BBC documentary 'Walking With Cavemen'.

Thank Christ you solved that you absolute genius I was getting worried that someone was planning an intellectual takeover of us!!! I should be used to seeing this anti-Millwall shit but this particular one annoyed me so much, especially as it was at the same time as FIFA Poppy ban and West Ham United's massively overpriced renovation and crowd trouble, this ground should be rebuilt from scratch not fit for use paid for by us Football Stadium was splashed across the real media, instead of focusing on a real problem in modern football let's take the piss out of Millwall!

Let me run these few minor Millwall FC and Millwall fan reality points by you Dillon –

Neil Harris Everyman Appeal re testicular cancer research fund/Prostate Cancer UK sponsorship/Help for Heroes/Headley Court Defence Medical Rehabilitation Centre/Saving Lewisham A & E from Closure/Jimmy Mizen Foundation and Toby Alabi Heart-4More Foundation.

As Jack Nicholson says in A Few Good Men – You cannot handle the truth!

If you are the actual View From A Dil, Journalist sic or a person who knows nothing about the real Millwall only what the media has drummed into your head, do not read the next bit in this chapter and especially do not read the next chapter where the above list plus more is gone into in more detail or your whole Anti Millwall head might explode and you then have to think for a living. Jolly good luck with that one.

I would just like to say Dill Aka Der brains if you would like to challenge myself or any of a number of Millwall fans to an intellectual battle bring it on you smug c*** sorry is that my being a Millwall Caveman?

If you think it is then I would like to say that I prefer to stay where I am in my supposed cave than join you on your The Sun's lazy journalistic alleged intellectual higher ground!

I wrote a letter that I emailed to The Sun Feedback about this Millwall slandering lazy supposed journalist in November 2016 stating a lot of what I put above without swear words, and do you think I received a response to it? Does the phrase did I bollocks answer this query?

Z) Fairly recently the final slur and the end this time honest New Statesman in 30th March 2017 issue the former Conservative Chairman and Lord Chris Patten said after Prime Minister Theresa May had started Brexit Article 50 that 'Theresa May is creating "Millwall" Britain – 'No One Likes Us We Don't Care'. Glad that Brexit whatever your thoughts are be they for or anti-Brexit I feel that it is great that Millwall are used as the literal scapegoat for it by a man, who don't forget gave Hong Kong back to the Chinese, does the phrase pot kettle and black mean anything to you, you freeloading Lord?

AA) Finally in The Let's Hate Millwall FC Section – Millwall 3 v Everton 2 FA Cup 4th Round New Den 26th January 2019, the media especially the gutter press and BBC had a field day.

Millwall's second equaliser came off Jake Coopers arm, whether deliberate or not was debatable, but no magical VAR, so goal granted despite Everton players badgering the officials like Billy O.

Murray Wallace then gets a winner in 94th minute continuing the line of 5 Premier League sides beaten in the FA Cup by the Lions at the New Den in recent history – Aston Villa/Bournemouth/Watford/Leicester City and Everton.

I was glad that Everton had a full strength side out so could not use the resting players excuse but upset that Jake's equaliser was controversial as it gave media a plot to build their anti-Millwall stories on instead of praising an excellent performance by the Lions against a side who had spent over £80 million in season on transfers, instead because goal was controversial potentially they focussed on the negative things on the day.

Back to the Everton FA Cup game let's have some reality – the Scousers come down to South East London mob handed and giving it the big un and one gets slashed with a knife, whilst I would never condone the use of a knife, the truth is this, if you come to a club like Millwall and threaten people willy nilly when you meet your opponents on the street at ground level and get punished for it, how can you complain?

Quite a simple solution don't put yourself on the frontline looking for trouble in the first place, rather than what this victim did find it and then launch a social media campaign about it, simplest way to avoid this was don't come to a working-class club like Millwall giving it the big I am as there would not have been a problem if you had done this would there?

Effectively the Scouser with initials JB, not James Bond in case you wondered from the County Road Cutters Everton firm, apparently came down with a couple of hundred strong firm and had boasted what he/they would do to Millwall, these posts on Facebook were soon deleted when the reality struck. They attack a small family pub, Whelan's, which although Millwall fans frequent it, is not a Millwall pub, it certainly is not The Golden Line or Bramcote, if they were so heroic they should have gone to The Blue Bermondsey where there are several Millwall fan pubs, see how clever you feel then!

Pictures/video of the face slashed Scouser with knife in hand during the ruck he was slashed in, lots of rumours he dropped knife and he was slashed with his own weapon, even more reason to have no sympathy for him whether he dropped blade or not, then goes in to self-promoting poor me media roadshow bullshit as he was nothing more than a Scouse warrior media whore plastering his face all over Facebook and social media, whilst professing he was afraid to look in the mirror not afraid to see your mug all over social media though, even going to The Sun Merseyside's most hated media, still if they give me money f*** the Hillsborough principle.

The media, focussed on outside ground trouble already mentioned and also on another juicy piece for them where around a dozen Wall fans in Dockers upper sang 'I'd Rather Be A Paki Than A Scouse!' for 14 seconds, foolishly filmed it on mobile and it goes viral on Facebook social media.

Thus, causing the FA/ EFL to threaten to close the Den, and after due consideration not to forget incorporating Millwall hating bias, they brought the punishment down to £10,000 pre 2019/ 2020 season, forget all the chants other fans have sung this is most heinous crime known to man!

Because it was Millwall fans, leading to Millwall replacing in ground CCTV, asking for Wall fans to report any offensive abuse they are within hearable distance of in a grassing action, whilst Racist/ Homophobic chants or verbal attacks should not be rife, why is there only one rule when it comes to this not Millwall okay to sing/ say anything if Millwall then you are instantly guilty!

Just my thought – does the Everton firm name County Road Cutters not sound like they are a knife carrying enterprise? Or is it just me!!! Even if not his knife pretty obvious he came for trouble and got more than he bargained for

The gutter press had Luton please see next section, Wembley trouble v Wigan Athletic which was Millwall v Millwall fans and dragged as much derogatory stuff up as they could.

Strangely and specifically about Millwall's opponents Everton, why was there no mention of the 7 Millwall fans stabbed at Goodison Park in FA Cup game on 3rd February 1973, when a Millwall coach load were directed into the home Gwladys Street End and the Scouse stabbings started?

Oh, sorry that was against Millwall so that is perfectly okay!!

I thought I would give you an alphabet sized list well 27 letter alphabet list, which if I was more awake, I am sure I could have expanded several fold!

Never Let The Truth Get In The Way Of A Good Story

Sadly, with Millwall/Luton riot footage being the most recognisable hooligan image and therefore an easy option, expect it to continue, for a good while yet! Despite its non inclusion in BBC March 2019 programme mentioned in the above section.

Here are a little couple of surprise images for you, what Luton Town was really like pre the Riot and actually what caused the riot. Not that I am paranoid but whenever the media show stock football riot they show Luton Town FA Cup 1985 Quarter Final riot, but they never show images like this do they, the reality of this night was Luton Town's greed in not making it all ticket and cramming people like sardines into an end far too small or the crap undermanned policing, in what as I am sure you can see could easily have been Hillsborough fan death carnage, still never let the truth get in the way of shabby journalism, so let's just show how nasty Millwall fans threw seats and ran at the police –

The media in general again before it is highlighted by a real anti-Millwall person in the next section.

On February 19th 2017 Millwall beat Premier League Champions Leicester City at New Den in FA Cup 5th round, prompting a jubilant pitch invasion, with Wall fans congregating in front of Leicester City fans in North Stand, the Leicester fans throw bottles and coins down, which Millwall throw back and in Media TV and

77

Press make it sound like we had just bombed Pearl Harbour, not reacted to us a third division side beating English Premier League Champions, Lincoln and Sutton United fans storm the pitch following their victories v lower league side, natural exuberance is explanation, we do same it is portrayed like a murder spree!

After the above Leicester City snippet and the aforementioned 1-8 and A-AA I lead you on now to a REAL Millwall hater and her media perception of the incident v Leicester City.

To highlight the media obsession with being Ani Millwall I give you our friend Karren Brady also in The Sun Monday, February 20th 2017 onwards and Labour MP for Streatham Chuka Umanna Wednesday 15th March 2017

Before I highlight her attitude, can I ask one question how is she in a National Paper allowed to write what is effectively a West Ham United Official Programme/Fanzine?

Anyway that aside here you go following Millwall's Victory v Premier League Champions Leicester City in the 5th round of the FA Cup 5th round a giant killing of England's Premier league Champion by a League 1 aka a 3rd Division side, so what does she write –

'YES, I know a few Hammers fans like a ruckus but they aren't in the same league as some of Millwall's who even made a mess of their team's FA Cup win.

Today, Leicester complain about those who celebrated by charging on to the field, confronting visiting fans, throwing coins and spitting at players.

Millwall's response is that Leicester said nothing on the day — as if that mattered — and to offer cut-price entrance to the next home match as a thank-you to fans.

I wonder if they will give back the coins, too.'

Hilarious last line eh!

Strangely she did not mention Leicester City fans throwing bottles on to the throng of gathered celebrating Millwall fans after the match, thereby starting what she saw as a civil war scale situation. Please let me point out that this is from the C*** who blamed Millwall for being bombarded by Birmingham City fans from the stand above us at St Andrews, where she had put them when we were in lower part of same stand, and we are naturally blamed by her for our audacity to have been where the missiles were falling, the self-interested Baroness, how the f*** does this happen?????

Now let me think I have sussed it – jobs for the boys or in her case girls, in her expertly written article very conveniently forgets West Ham United being given a council funded stadium, which their 'Appy 'Ammers fans have caused serious trouble in several times in the first season there 2016/17, I wonder how she reported this, because in this context is referred to as a few Hammers fans like a ruckus, what a complete C****!

Her esteemed article was festooned with pictures of Millwall fans, the Stewards and Police Horses, which I will not give the dignity of including here, we lifelong Wall fans should be used to this Wall assassination but from such a source makes it far less easy to bare. A person who has put herself in a self-interested position of power that amazingly gives her a regal audacity to write what she likes, by conveniently switching away from the reality of her own club's fans and focus on those beastly Millwall rotters!!!

You have seen how Millwall are treated by the media and Brady in particular now see how other teams are treated by the Media more recently.

If you can explain the disparity for the coverage or lack of it for the next few recent events, I would love to hear them, here we go!

The following things really happened on April fool's Day 2017 – Leeds United fans threw bottles on the pitch at Reading adding loads of time to game, and Palarse fans had several flares blazing at Stamford Bridge, Leeds not mentioned at all really in Sunday press.

A bit and only vaguely on Championship TV programme, and Palarse mentioned on Match of The Day a smidge and in Sunday Media a bit where it said Palace and Chelsea might face Punishment, had not heard what happened about this at time of writing.

On separate occasions Leicester City fans cause trouble in Sevilla on 22nd February 2017 and Atletico Madrid on 12th April 2017 clashing with fans and Spanish Police in the Champions League away legs, including racially abusing Spanish in Madrid with chants about Spain having no say on Gibraltar as that was ours, strangely whether in defence of UK Sovereignty or not that is not racist but we sing chants about DVDs to Spurs Korean player and it's portrayed in UK media as a diplomatic incident!!!

If it was Millwall it would be Headlines across every red top in particular with headlines like –

‚Millwall fans start Syrian Civil War!!!!' And 'Millwall DVD of Son Abuse Pushes North Korea To Use Nuclear Weapons!!!!' and 'Brexit all Millwall's Fault!'

I would just like to point out how f***ing big flares are, I mean the ones you have on boats not type of Noel Edmunds style Pavarotti size trousers, I know what they are like from personal experience having stood under one at Malmo v Hammarby, they are size of a f***ing great Dildo and it is like having a bucket of soot tipped on your head if underneath one when they are aflame as I unfortunately was when at the game in Sweden.

Consequently the Steward searches must be top notch at Stamford Bridge, because unless the flare was shoved down front of the Palace person with the flares underpants and Steward would not touch there as saw bulge and thought geezer was built like a Donkey, they are a bit bloody hard to miss!!!

I investigated what a slating Leeds and Palarse fans got for Saturday 1st April shenanigans from that mouthy no nothing c*** Baroness Karren Brady, in The Sun, I was looking forward to it so searched online on Sunday 2nd April and I was mortified that she had not mentioned it at all as at then, buggered if I would buy

The Sun on Monday or throughout week to check, so if I missed sorry! Am I B***ocks!!! I think I missed the Leicester City incidents as well!!! I really must try harder to find this stuff!!

On 22nd April 2017 Port Vale v Bolton Wanderers fans staged a pitch invasion with the standard for the 1970s on pitch ruck at Vale Park, I know that the League 1 unless Millwall are involved is not necessary to report but this failed to hit any with Brady or headlines elsewhere.

An incident that I mentioned earlier our beloved Baronet Brady managed to not mention that a Millwall fan collapsed at The Den on Good Friday 14th April 2017 v Northampton Town, and was given lengthy CPR on site, respect was shown by Millwall and Northampton Town fans, for the medical work that was going on at a very serious Cardiac Arrest situation, Millwall fans applauded the Northampton Town fans for their support and respect of a real life situation, they understood it was a real world situation and we applauded them for their support, which also included putting money in to the Trust that was set up for the medical staff, did the useless C**** Brady mention it or contribute? Of course not, she cannot waste her mega wealth on that and from a media perspective it was positive about Millwall and her computer has a cannot allow Millwall positives filter installed, hang on she could have overridden this, if she had mentioned it she would have focussed purely on the fact that several Millwall fans ran on the pitch to get the referee to stop the game early and that would have fulfilled her slag Millwall criteria! Missed that one Brady!

Brady was strangely reticent to mention West Ham United along with Newcastle United and Chelsea were involved in an apparently serious HMRC Tax Fraud investigation in late April 2017, could not find anything on her West Ham Fanzine the Sun Sports Diary, I investigated Miss Marples on the interwobble and, I found an article on a West Ham section of a London Football Clubs where she adopted the classic it wasn't me gov approach, re arrange the phrase F*** As Shifty and As. Not me mate must be those dodgy

French investigators. Is denial the best way for a Baroness/Baronet or whatever she bloody well allegedly warrants being? Suppose it must be.

On a similar tack I have to mention an article from the Evening Standard Wednesday 15th March 2017 which for reference was after the Spurs match Son DVD chants Police Investigation, Labour MP for Streatham Chuka Umanna whose father was a Crystal Palace director apparently the first black director at any top football club, Chuka worked in a box office at Selhurst Park in the article entitled 'How I banned racist fan at Palace, by MP Umunna' he goes on about an abusive incident at Crystal Palace when he effectively grassed a Port Vale fan who was arguing with him face to face and racially abused him and he barred his entry to the ground. In the same article he mentions West Ham fans on the phone being extraordinarily abusive. Having mentioned this, for balance he must by a clause in the contract mention Millwall fans 'not always being very nice', not that I am biased but what the hell have Millwall got to do with his being racially abused by a Port Vale fan in person or by West Ham on the phone?

I assume there is something in all the media manifesto that to be able to mention West Ham, you must also besmirch Millwall, ah a balanced Media eh!!! As it was not pro the 'Appy 'Ammers this could be Brady related or does that sound too paranoid?

To close the anti-Millwall media deluge I leave you with –

Play Off Final v Bradford City at Wembley 20th May 2017 The Truth v the Media

Pre this Final the media in some areas went in to it will be carnage mode at Millwall v Bradford City, especially bearing in mind the trouble at the games v Wigan Athletic in FA Cup Semi Final and 2016/2017 Play Off Final v Barnsley.

Not saying that there was none at all but from what any of my party on the day of the Bradford City game there was not, the truth of what happened strangely largely ignored in the media was that on 40 minutes Millwall fans clapped for a minute in memory of the sad passing of Antony Murphy the Millwall fan mentioned previously who had a heart attack at Northampton Town home game and sadly passed away at the age of 40 who as I mentioned passed away the day before the Play Off Final, the 40 minute mark was in conjunction with his death at a young age.

On 56 Minutes Bradford City fans clapped for a minute in homage to the 56 people who passed away in the Bradford Fire on Saturday, 11 May 1985 at Valley Parade. Millwall fans joined in this applause. Was this largely mentioned in media?

Strangely neither incident was, however as we won with a late Steve Morison goal, at the end Millwall fans invaded the pitch, I said to my mate's I was with in Club Wembley well there are tomorrow's headlines then!

There were only about a couple of hundred or so on the pitch, so bear in mind Millwall fans there numbered near 30,000 so what is that percentage?

We did not condone the invasion as it held up Millwall players' celebration, but here is what it was like.

There were very few stewards behind the goal where we were located, those that were there opened gates at the pitchside that allowed entry onto the pitch, the main group of stewards only showed up several minutes after this pitch invasion had happened, why had they not been sent out to get in position before the final whistle as they should have been, this was the first time any clubs fans had invaded Wembley, nothing to be proud of and we sang Off The Pitch/Off Off Off type chants and the PA announcer repeated that it was illegal to be on the pitch etc.

Now I am not condoning this invasion at all but if Millwall's average crowd is 9000 or so and 3 times that amount are at Wembley how hard core are these from a Millwall point of view?

None of we hard core thought what we must do is invade the

pitch and ruin our own club's celebration. Bradford fans had all pretty much gone and some Bradford players still in the pitch area were no doubt abused as losers, but the way their manger talked was like Millwall fans had threatened them, still talk that up and wash over your defeat eh McCall!

I think the media missed a big opportunity here, why not compare the pitch invasion with when the Scots won 2-1 at the old Wembley v England in 1977 and the Tartan Army went mad, invading the pitch like an invading army, with Millwall's link to Scottish jam workers, the Rampant Lion badge why did they not imply it was as bad as the last Scottish Wembley Pitch invasion, that Millwall fans swung on the crossbar etc, this didn't happen but what the hell has truth got to do with the media??? I just thought I would reinforce the sort of media tosh we get with my own flight of fancy!

Bomber and Steve Morison criticised the invasion, no doubt as they knew, as we did that the victory and clapping homages would be ignored, Millwall fan invasion – there are the media reports written then! Do not know what the situation is as I write but the FA were looking into the incident according to the media, I would like to say why was Stewarding so shit, i.e. why open gates onto the pitch as I mentioned, something I think worthy of mention is when Wembley had the audacity to charge £2.40 extra per ticket price not per transaction, making if my calculations are correct Wembley a profit £127,000 could they not have spent some of that on professional stewards or giving them proper training?

As you can see from the piece above the anti-Millwall ethos continues at full steam ahead, and I am certain I have only mentioned a tiny portion of cheap shot journalism that Wall have had to face, I am certainly not pushing myself to a frenzy hunting any more down!!!!

> Ryanair was "the Millwall of the skies" – no one likes us: we don't care. Now, it would seem, it is the Crystal Palace, complete with foul language prohibited family enclosure.
>
> Apple addiction is a genera[...]

I believe the above came from The Evening Standard in January 2018, referring to an old quote when Ryan Air had been referred to that way.

Forget about all this aforementioned mentioned Anti Millwall unreality watch out Media here comes some dreaded Millwall Reality!

Think of this part as an appetizer to the real Wall Reality deluge I would like to start by mentioning some positives re Millwall that are not in the media's frame of reference – we were the first team to play a live match on Sunday 20th January 1974 v Fulham.

Millwall were the first Football League club to open a crèche, which was in the primary school very near Cold Blow Lane, it employed two qualified crèche workers, loosely referred to by us as Millwall Minders, children were provided with a meal and played games in the school on match days at home at the Old Den, to allow parents to have their children looked after safely whilst they attend the matches and picked their children after the match, did this or the Sunday Community Markets get mentioned frequently by the media? Strangely not they also ran a Soccer School for kids and looked after older people in the area with one to one support.

If you can get a copy of it check out 'Millwall In The Community', a book that was produced in the mid-1980s under the auspice of Reg Burr, that lists a lot of the clubs communal work, it is referred to as 'The club that gave itself back to the people' by author Sunday Times writer Chris Lightbrown on the back cover. Do you want truth or media perception? If you want the latter avoid this booklet at all costs.

Millwall currently hold the record for the number of fans at the new Wembley Stadium by one club, taking 49,661 to the League One Play-Off Final in 2009 v Scunthorpe United.

Millwall also hold the one club's fans record at the old Wembley when we brought 47,349 fans against Wigan Athletic in the Auto Windscreen final in 1999.

The media might ignore this but this is the reason why Chairmen at Millwall think that we are capable of massive crowds, with the belief that these people are or will become regulars. Unfortunately NO they won't!

They are only right on one level – if we include the Woodwork aka Glory Hunting faction at a high profile game, the crowd is also swelled if we include our core non-English fans base, then yes, if it is regular club games then this is not our hard-core support as we 100% Real Wall know!

As I said in my other books, the opponents are irrelevant in my decision to go to see Millwall home or away, I don't care if we are playing Real Madrid or Rushden and Diamonds, I am going!

Now sit down, do some Mindfulness, and have a breather, before Reality hits you the reader and hopefully the media in the face, turn to the next Chapter if you can!!!!!!

CHAPTER 3
The REAL Positivity of Millwall

Let's move in to the total unknown by the media, the real world of recent or previous in house and South East London Millwall positives!!

Now excuse me if you feel I am being paranoid but Millwall do anything good and it gets pretty much ignored, I should be used to it, as they did not sodding mention the aforementioned Crèche and neither did they mention the Community Market much at the Old Den donkey's years ago or the work in the Millwall Community nowadays either, and they wonder why we are so paranoid, read the rest of this chapter.

Another personal thing that will never be mentioned in the media, if they were told about it, in March 2010 Peter Huish, a hardcore Lions fan, father of Paul and Gavin my cousins, all of whom I mentioned in The 'Wall dedications, sadly passed away. A friend of Paul's went to the same school as Neil Harris, he told Bomber about Peter's Millwall devotion and sad departure Neil got a Millwall shirt all the side signed it and Harris had it sent as a present for Peter's funeral, which as a good deed by Millwall would never ever be mentioned, as negativity is the only way the media looks at us!

From here onwards Ladies and Gentlemen I give you Real Millwall FC and Fans – Enjoy it is all real honest! –

In late November 2001 Neil Harris in conjunction with Millwall FC launched the Everyman Cancer Appeal, below is a clip from a BBC article – mind you they are not the gutter end of media!

Harris launches cancer appeal

Harris aims to raise awareness of testicular cancer

Millwall striker Neil Harris, who has fought testicular cancer this year, launches a campaign on Thursday to increase awareness into the disease.

The Neil Harris everyman Appeal, set up in conjunction with the club and the Institute of Cancer Research, will raise money for medical studies into the alarming increase in the problem over the last few years.

There was the Help For Heroes day, v Wycombe Wanderers at home on Saturday 21st November 2009, one of several, which had soldiers abseiling down from the roof of the West Stand to deliver the match ball among other things pre match and the numerous soldiers and seriously injured marching around the pitch side at half time, I found it enormously moving to salute our soldiers who had been in Iraq and or Afghanistan below is an article from The News Shopper Lewisham Tuesday 3 May 2011 with comments from Help For Heroes organizer

HELP for HEROES
Support for our Wounded

Millwall fans raise £10,000 for Help for Heroes

With money still coming in, the Lions say their fundraising for charity Help the Heroes on April 23 at The Den was a roaring success. Forces sweetheart Kelly Ann Sproul had led the crowd in singing Jerusalem before the game against Preston North End, and Land of Hope and Glory was sung at half time, while a number of serving troops took a lap of honour.

Organiser Karen Bain said: „Once again Millwall and its fans have done themselves proud. "Not only is their generosity incredible during a time of economic hardship for many, but the support they gave to the service personnel and to the event as a whole was very moving."

Millwall Share Allocation to Help for Heroes

In the mid-2010s us Millwall Shareholders who had less than 100,000 shares were given the option that they could either up their allocation to the requisite amount or donate the shares to Help for Heroes, which a lot of us did, I had 23,700 shares so I donated mine to them.

Below is a picture of John Berylson with Help for Heroes in 2013

Jimmy Mizen Foundation

The 19th December 2009 game at the Valley when both sides wore the above adapted kits, in honour of murdered teenagers Millwall fan Jimmy Mizen and Charlton fan Rob Knox where the two families were together on the pitch and fans money was donated to the Mizen Foundation, v Charlton Athletic home and away, and subsequent local encounters between the two sides, did that get widely mentioned in all the media? Err, not much no, strange that! If a half-eaten meat pie is lobbed at an incompetent tosser of Lino in a Birmingham City home game as it was it is like we had just invaded the Sudetenland or tried to poison the Lino with E coli!

Jimmy Mizen Foundation as a Millwall supporter murdered at a young age, has a regular day once a season to respect the family called Jimmy's Day which was on Good Friday 19th April 2019.

Millwall FC Become Allied With Prostate Cancer UK In A Sponsorship Deal

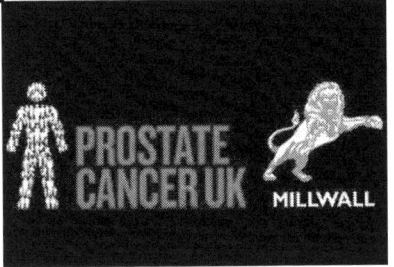

The piece below is taken from Prostate cancer in the media, which I took from the internet

Another strike for Men United as Millwall FC partnership triumphs at Third Sector Awards

There was joy for Prostate Cancer UK and Millwall FC last night (Thursday 18 September 2014) as we triumphed in the Best Corporate Partnership category at the Third Sector Awards. The victory, at The Grand Connaught Rooms in London, came after a hugely successful 2013/14 season in which we worked closely on and off the pitch with the Championship club.

Following on from this on October 18th 2014 Millwall FC presented a cheque pre-match v Wolves of £25,000 to the charity Prostate Cancer UK, see picture below –

Lions Take On The Iron In Designated Charity Fixture –

The visit of Scunthorpe United to The Den on Saturday 1st April 2017 was the club's focus match for Prostate Cancer UK in season 2016/17

Below Is A Press Article Millwall Fans Raising Money For Soldiers' Fund In 2015

Headley Court Defence Medical Rehabilitation Centre Section

For the home game v Brentford on Saturday 9th November 2014 i.e. the day before Remembrance Sunday, Millwall wore a Camouflage coloured kit that they had been allowed to do, to raise money for Headley Court, a rehabilitation centre for injured British Service Men, they donated £10 for every kit that they sold to the Centre, Sky Sports featured a video supplied by Millwall of this, so at least some acceptance I suppose, see all the pictures below for the reality –

Headley Court Staff Collections outside the New Den

Old Veterans inside the New Den Pre Match

95

Millwall FC plus Mascots in especially designed Camouflage Kit that were sold to fans to raise money for Headley Court

Millwall FC Lined Up Pre-Match with Seriously Wounded Soldiers From Headley Court for the Remembrance Silence

macron
HEADLEY
COURT

We Remember.
macron
HEADLEY
COURT

THE BARRY KITCHENER STAND

sky BET
macron
HEADLEY

Above Headley Court based Fundraising and more pictures of Millwall FC especially designed kits inc Subbuteo Set of Millwall in the kit

In closing the Headley Court Affiliation Tony Craig Lions club captain made a donation from proceeds of his Testimonial in late July 2016 v Brentford to Headley Court

British Legion Poppy Appeal
31st October 2015

Millwall supporters donated a superb £2,247.43 in just two hours when a bucket collection for the Poppy Appeal was held at The Den on Saturday prior to the home game with Bradford City.

Fundraiser in aid of veterans and wounded servicemen ...

A team made up of Millwall Legends took on decorated members of the PWRR

On 14th May 2017, a team made up of Millwall Legends will take on decorated members of the Princess of Wales' Royal Regiment (PWRR) in a special one-off charity event.

Under the watchful eye of Les Briley – who famously captained Millwall to the top-flight for the first time in the club's history in 1988 – the likes of Teddy Sheringham, Maik Taylor, Sean Sparham,

Jimmy Carter, Gary Alexander, Kevin Bremner, Mark Beard, Stuart Nethercott and David Livermore will face stiff competition from PWRR, managed by Brian Wood MC.

Sean McCarthy Millwall Fan and Poppy Seller outside His Stall In Cannon Street in the City Of London

Leading up to Remembrance Sunday Millwall fan Sean McCarthy has sold Poppies near to Cannon Street station for years, especially Millwall specific poppies in the last couple of years, for reference when he became more focussed on his Team in 2013 he raised £38,000 then in 2014 he raised over £60,202 and again in 2015 £65,637.35 so in three years £163,000+. I wondered how did that compare to other Fundraisers for the British Legion Poppy Appeal?

Never saw him mentioned in media, is that because he is a Millwall fan? Because if it is positive in a Millwall related way the national media can't be arsed to mention it!

If you think I am paranoid prove me wrong!!!! Moving along a bit, Sean was introduced to us at New Den v Bury on 28th November 2015 in the wake of his record in 2015, as he walked onto the pitch the announcer said that the amount that he has raised now over the years £350,000+

Pre 2016 Poppy sales, I went up to his stall in Cannon Street outside Boots and thought it strange that he was not there in late October when I went there, I later found out why he was disgustingly stopped selling Poppies after 2015 having done a 14-year stint and his stock confiscated by the authorities that legislate Poppy sales, this was because of some dodgy buggers pilfering from the sale of the Poppy's. This to me is on a par with FIFA's bullshit Poppy England v Scotland banning, had it not occurred to the powers that be that if Sean was dodgy, why on earth did he raise so much money over such a long period of time for their cause?

Now pardon me but tarring with the same brush as the scumbags who were actually corrupt and any Millwall Scapegoating springs to my Millwall mind!

I saw from Fan on The Board in 21st December 2016 Charlton home programme that he had raised £62,000 whether that was in 2016 it did not say I assumed so as it was a piece about him not being barred by Millwall which the joys of social media had applied in some places so I assume it was 2016.

Not seen anything about this achievement mentioned in national media either. Again, if I have missed it, I am sorry, I have the feeling I have very little to be sorry for!!!

Excuse me if what I have put above re his not being outside Boots in Cannon Street is incorrect but that is what I was told.

Now pardon me if I am presenting my Millwall paranoia but as quite a few of our fundraising exploits are regarding British armed forces charities and institution, I am surprised some no nothing lefty c*** in the media has not said we always do this because we are typical violent Millwall – i.e. warmongers!

Millwall Community Trust Ex Service Leaver Employment Support 2018

Millwall FC Armed Forces Reduced Ticket Price Offer 2019/2020

Sleeping Bags For Homeless Military Veterans Appeal

Lions supporter Ayse Smith at The Den continued her project of collecting sleeping bags for homeless veterans a Norwich City Community Day on Saturday 2nd March 2019. "I'm looking for people to donate sleeping bags for homeless veterans," she said.

The Millwall supporter urged fellow Millwall fans and the community to continue helping those less fortunate by supporting the UK Homes 4 Heroes charity.

Sky Bet Championship match against Rotherham United Saturday 2nd February 2019 club hosted its second annual 'Memorial Day'

Memorial Day honoured those Millwall supporters who we lost in 2018, with all names sent in appearing in the matchday programme and on the big screen prior to kick-off, where a minute's applause was observed.

103

Millwall Football Club hosted its first-ever 'Community Day' when Norwich City visited The Den Saturday 2nd March 2019 Highlighting what happened on the day (Copied from Millwall Official site)

The new initiative will see the club showcase the varied and far-reaching work of its Community Trust throughout an action-packed day in SE16. Participants on the Trust's Post-16 education course will be holding a bucket collection and giving away wristbands while the Lions Centre's 3G pitch will host two matches – one for Premier League Kicks attendees and another between Millwall's and Norwich's respective down's syndrome teams. Also taking place in the Lions Centre, in the Sports Hall between 12.30-2pm, will be Millwall's regular matchday family fun zone but there will be added activities to mark the special occasion, including a bouncy castle, badge making, dart football, pool football and inflatable Twister.

Elsewhere there will be an inflatable penalty shootout next to SE16 Bar, while Community Trust staff and Post-16 students will also be present to inform fans of different courses and programmes from a marquee next to the Blue Bus. Also next to the Blue Bus will be the Millwall Supporters' Club marquee, where supporters can leave donations to Southwark Foodbank as the club uses its first-ever Community Day to re-launch the partnership with its local centre.

Staff and volunteers from the 'Back the Bakerloo' campaign – which the club is actively supporting – will also have a presence by the Blue Bus and will be handing out information leaflets about what is undoubtedly an important project for the local community. Participants from the Trust's regional training centre (RTC) and down's syndrome team will adorn the cover of the matchday programme, which will also contain more than six pages of content covering the Trust's yearly activities.

Young Lions fans Harvey Brown and Ellice Barr – two names familiar to fellow Millwall supporters – have been invited as special mascots, while all ball girls for the game will be from the RTC U16s group. The Trust's down's syndrome team and all RTC age groups will take part in a half-time lap of honour while a special video, telling the story of the Trust's work, is played on the big screen.

Millwall duo Steve Morison and Aiden O'Brien have also donated match-worn boots which will be auctioned in the Sponsors' Lounge to raise money for the Trust after the game.

Sean Daly, the Trust's Football Development Manager, said: "We want to extend our heartfelt thanks to all who support the Trust, from players and club staff to fans, partners and the local community. As a self-financing charity, events like Community Day are so important in allowing us to continue our work in the local community, so please come and join in the celebrations."

You can find out more about all of the Trust's different programmes and initiatives on their website www.millwallcommunity.org.uk.

The Big Sleepover at The Den Donate to Crisis

Millwall Football Club is pleased to be hosting 'The Big Sleepover' at The Den in aid of Crisis.

From 6.30pm on Wednesday 29th May, families will be able to camp out on the pitch for the night, with all profits being donated to the homeless charity.

Returning To The Poppy Here Are Numerous Examples of Millwall Related Poppies –

106

107

Just to finish the Remembrance theme, below are the gates of the New Den on Saturday 4th November 2017 day of Burton Albion game the nearest to Remembrance Sunday the following week as it

108

was an International break w/c 10th – 11th November 2017. At this game Millwall fans raised £5165.20, a record-breaking amount at the New Den for the Royal British Legion.

General Millwall Team and Club Related Hospital Supporting Projects, Visits and the Save Lewisham Hospital Appeal

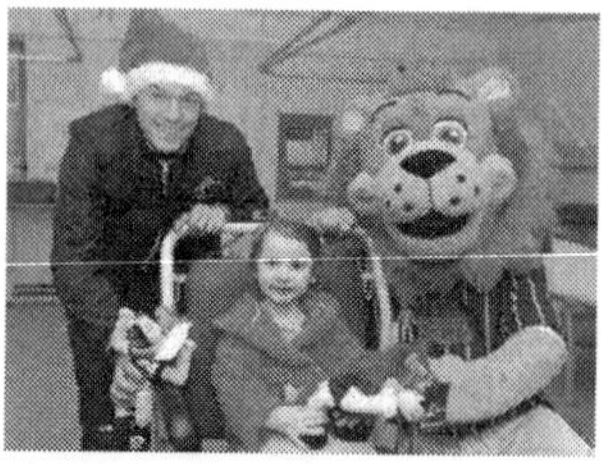

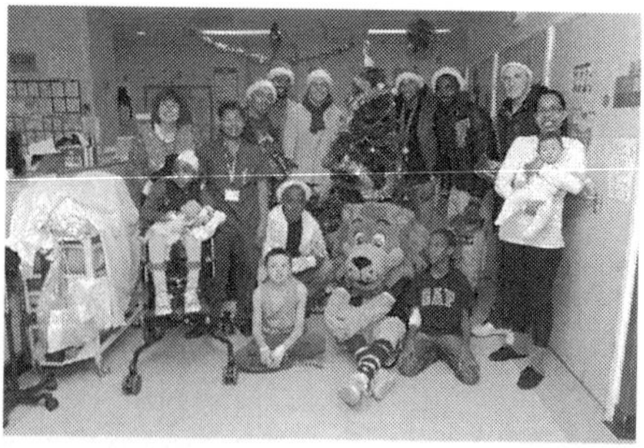

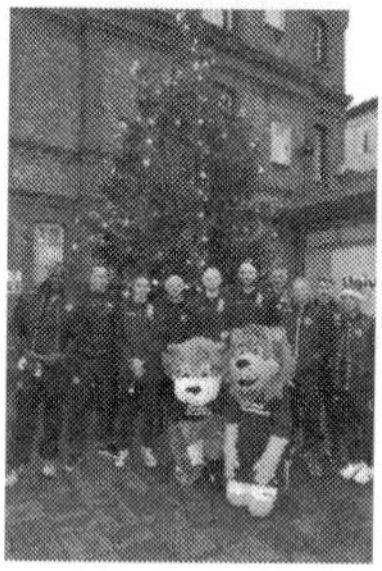

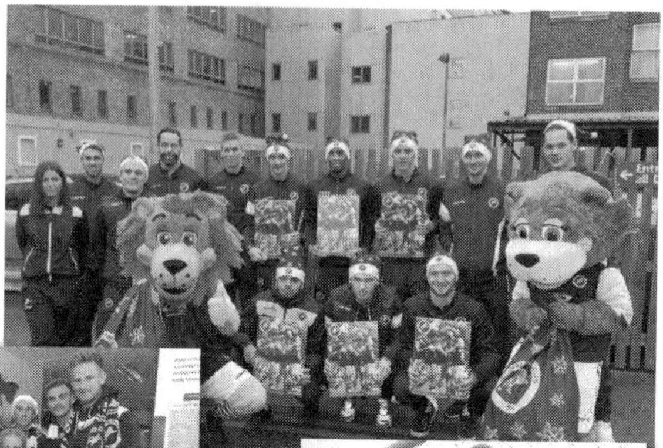

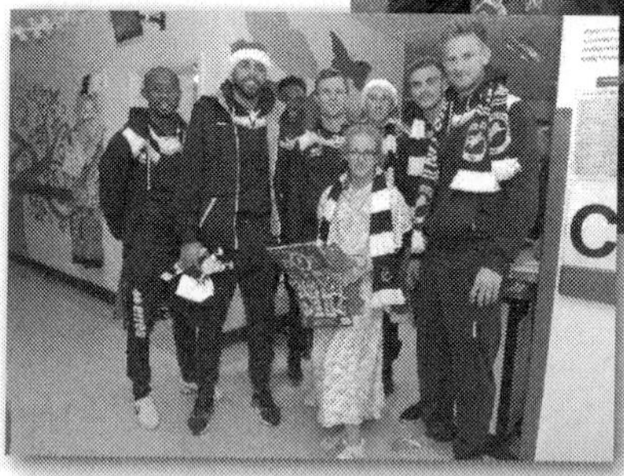

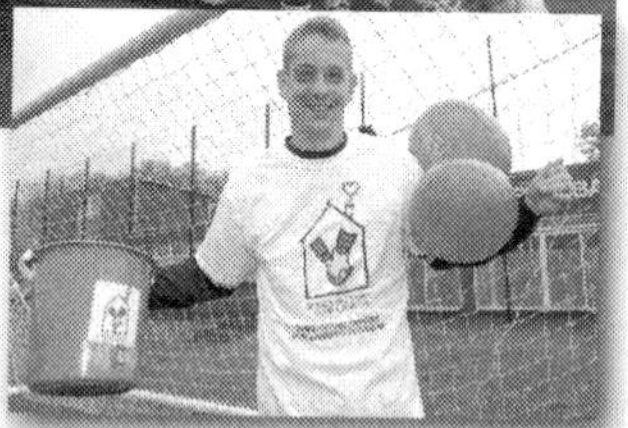

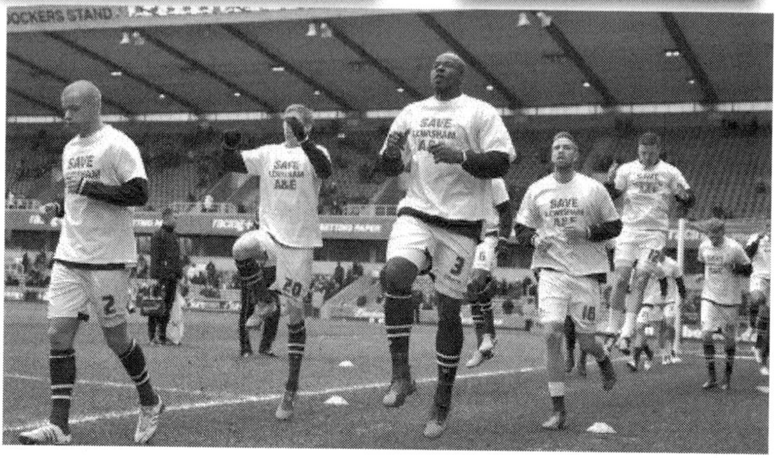
SAVE LEWISHAM A&E

Toby Alabi Heart4More Foundation

Tobi Alabi had an 11 year long stay as a Lions youth player before founding the Heart4More Foundation due to his suffering two serious cardiac incidents, ending his playing career early, which following his Millwall stay had also contained playing for Swedish Second division side Ljungskile SK.

Tobi had to retire at 19 when he suffered an on pitch collapse due to a Heart Condition, on retiring he founded Heart4More Foundation to raise awareness of Heart problems, especially to highlight this problem to the Football community, consequently after the 2014/5 season on 5th May 2015 there was a Fund Raising match at the Den between Millwall Legends XI v Heart4More Foundation XI.

The foundation's aims are to get professional footballers from the age of 14 upwards to be screened on a yearly basis to check for any heart conditions, this Foundation is backed by Millwall stalwart Danny Shittu and he was presented before the Birmingham City game on March 25th 2014, the pre match announcements were to turn out to be the nights highlights as we were beaten 3-2 by the Brummie Boks!

Neil Harris Donates Unique Prize

The copy below comes from Millwall Official Site In November 2015 –

Millwall have joined forces with some of the biggest names in world football to support an online charity auction in memory of Sir Bobby Robson. Bidding on the Sir Bobby's Online Auction runs until the evening of Sunday 29th November with more than 140 incredible money-can't-buy items donated in memory of the legendary former England manager from the world of sport, celebrity and lifestyle.

Among the star prizes, Millwall have donated the chance to be a ‚footballer' for the day, including joining in with the first team for a training session as well as sitting in on the technical analysis meeting between manager Neil Harris and his players.

The prize also includes starting the day with breakfast with Neil and his coaching staff at Calmont Road, lunch with the players and, generally, having the same access as the manager and players to all areas on a general working day.

Millwall First Football Club to support Sugar Smart Campaign announced October 2016

SUGAR SMART

Below was received from Bolton Wanderers Supporters Association after a match at The Reebok 18th November 2016, when Millwall fans had contributed individually to a collection that Bolton Wanderers fans were holding, the Millwall truth from Bolton Fans!!

> **The BWSA**
> 1 hr
>
> On Saturday when Bolton played at home to Millwall, there was a collection going on outside the ground for a young girl who is really ill and will need expensive treatment to get through it. A Millwall fan took the collection cartons into the Millwall end and made sure they contributed as well. Millwall fans always get bad press, this proves otherwise! Well done Millwall!
>
> #bwfc #millwall

THE OFFICIAL SUPPORTERS ASSOCIATION

Thank You! to the away fans from MILLWALL FOOTBALL CLUB on Saturday 20th November 2016

Proving that Millwall fans are fantastic such a nice gesture from Derby's Steward. Below is an Email from a Derby County Steward working when Millwall Fans Visited on Wednesday 20th February 2019

I would just to take this opportunity to say a big thankyou to your supporters who made the trip up to the Derby match last Wednesday. Although your club & fans sometimes get a lot of bad publicity, the fans behaviour on the night was exceptional.

I have just lost my wife and her funeral was arranged for the following day so I was not in a very good place anyway. I don't know how but some of your fans found out about this, and at the end of the match the kind thoughts and gestures shown to me by quite a few of your supporters especially the group who came up on the coach made me feel ten feet tall.

Might I add that in the 43 years I have worked for Derby County I have never been on the receiving end of so many kind thoughts from the away fans. So could please pass on a big thankyou to your fans for me and I hope to see them again next year.

Dave Manning (Away Stand Supervisor)

Lions Collect Prestigious League One Gong At The EFL Awards

Millwall Football Club picked up the Nickelodeon Family Club of the Year trophy at the annual EFL Awards in London on Sunday 9th April 2017.

The Lions collected the prestigious award for the first time in the club's history.

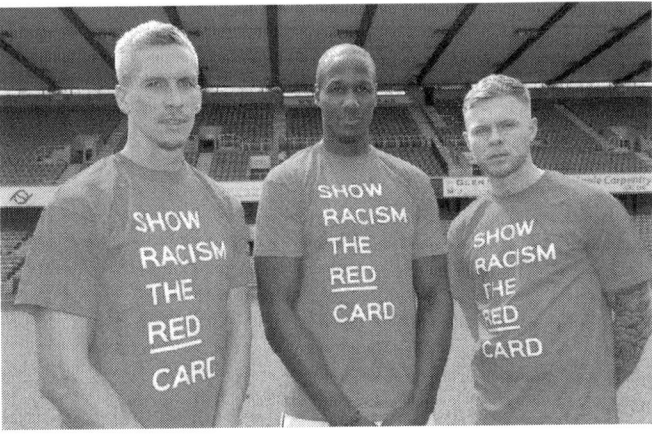

And again in September 2018 Millwall Awarded EFL Code Of Practice

Millwall awarded EFL Family Excellence status

Millwall are one of 63 EFL clubs to have achieved Family Excellence status in the 2018/19 campaign.

The record-breaking number, up from 56 Clubs in 2017/18, recognises continuous improvement and best practice in family engagement across the Leagues and supports clubs' efforts to attract and retain young fans of the future.

Following the 2016/2017 season Millwall Legends played this fundraising match for Military wounded soldiers and veterans

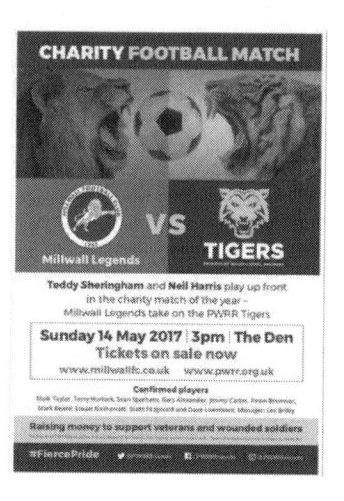

Millwall fans donate £2800 to the Bradley Lowery Foundation at Sunderland 18th November 2017

Miracles Do Happen – Hostile Football Rivalry Aside The Isla Caton Section

Millwall fans rally to West Ham cause

By Sean Whetstone   16 Feb 2018 at 19:54   7 comments

Millwall fans have raised over £4,500 for West Ham fan Isla Caton to demonstrate that football has no colours when it comes to cancer.

The above article is from January 2018 highlighting what Millwall fans are really like, charitable and considerate, not the antisocial demons we are always perceived to be!!!

Quote from Twitter –

Millwall fans are by far the most generous fans in the world! Isla Caton is our 3-year-old girl with the rare form of child cancer called Neuroblastoma, Mummy, Daddy, Family & Friends are trying to raise 200k for a vaccine to stop her cancer relapsing.

Millwall Fan Hits Fundraising Target After Running Big Half In West Ham Shirt

Millwall fan Jamie Pearce, 25, trebled his fundraising target for young cancer sufferer Isla Caton after running the Big Half in a West Ham shirt on Sunday 6th May 2018

Jamie Pearce, 25, bravely donned the Hammers' colours on Sunday as he ran 13.1 miles, passing through the streets of Southwark in the first ever Vitality Big Half.

The runner's initial aim had been to raise £500 for three-year-old Hammers fan Isla Caton who suffers from rare childhood cancer neuroblastoma and needs specialist treatment in America.

But a quick check of his sponsorship page after the race on Sunday revealed he had almost trebled his original target by so far raising £1,250.

To end this section some fantastic news, forget the rivalry an update on Isla –

In March 2019 now a Five-Year-Old cancer victim whose incredible battle brought one of football's fiercest rivalries to a standstill is now „completely free" of the disease, her parents have confirmed.

Brave young Hammers fan Isla Caton needed £400,000 to get treatment for neuroblastoma – and received donations from West Ham supporters and from rivals Millwall as well. Inspiring Isla Caton is now 'completely free of cancer'

119

Millwall Fans are also involved in Toby Nye a Leeds United family foundation

We were refunded £9.50 after £37 stitch up by Leeds United in 2018 options were either take a refund, donate to Lionesses/Millwall Community Foundation or to Isla or Toby or split between both Isla and Toby via FOTB.

> ♥ Millwall Fotb and 2 others liked
>
> **BermondseyBoy**
> @Bermondsey1885
>
> I see some Millwal fans are offering to give their refund from @LUFC to Toby Nye a 4 year old Leeds fan suffering from neuroblastoma and @islasfight You can't buy class. That's why I love @MillwallFC and I mean all of you.
>
> 10:06 pm · 22 Jan 18
>
> 42 Retweets 108 Likes
>
> **Kev** @millwallkev76 · 6h
> Replying to @Bermondsey1885 @LUFC and 2 others

England fans wreck ambulance after World Cup Quarter Final v Sweden win
7th July 2018 in Borough Market. Millwall fans raise £10,000 approx to help London Ambulance Service Replace/Repair

Emergency call

Millwall FC Supporters' Club raised almost £10,000 this week to repair the ambulance trashed near London Bridge after England beat Sweden in the World Cup quarter-final last Saturday.

You can join their lion-hearted gesture by donating at justgi­com/crowdfunding/millwall supportersclub.

Any extra funds raised go London Ambulance Service.

Millwall Supporter Conor Moorcroft Fundraising Plane Jump 2019

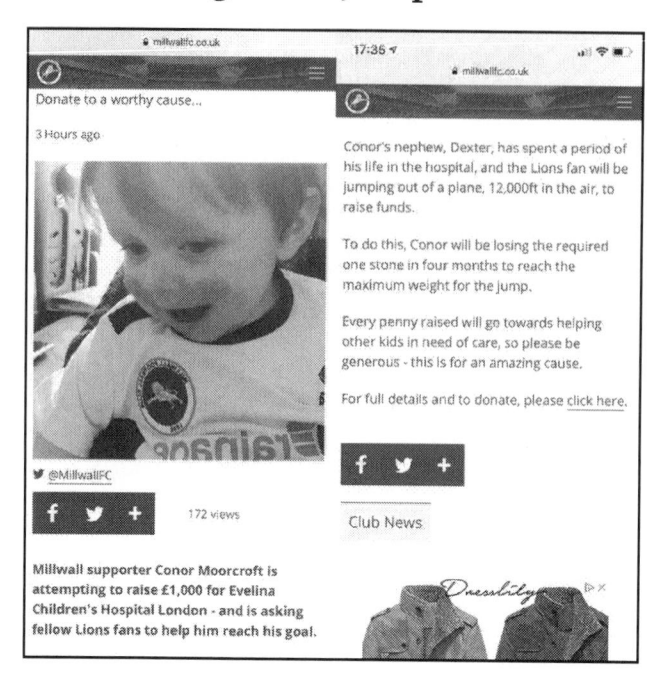

Members of Millwall's Academy were sat down on a Friday morning in May 2019 as National Epilepsy Awareness Week came into focus at The New Den

Millwall FC fan Ellice Barr from Deal enters The Den

Jed Wallace had expressed his excitement at the prospect of being led out onto the pitch at The Den by young Millwall supporter Ellice Barr, as The Lions took on Brighton & Hove Albion in the Emirates FA Cup Quarter-Final tie. Wallace met seven-year-old Ellice last season 2017/2018, with the Lions man becoming aware of the youngster and her family's support for the club – and notably her favourite player.

Ellice suffers with diplegia cerebral palsy, which has affected her mobility since birth. Her story has touched the hearts of Millwall fans and supporters of other clubs worldwide, with her family's early fundraising efforts raising money for surgery to increase her mobility.

Further fundraising, started by Millwall Supporters' Club, is underway to raise the required amount for an evenly laid garden for Ellice to be able to play with her brother and sister this summer, a campaign her idol Wallace – along with the club – is wholeheartedly supporting.

Ellice, along with 10-year-old fellow avid Lions fan Harvey Brown – both well-known and endeared to by the Millwall family – were also among our Community Day mascots in our home match with Norwich City, and Wallace is grateful for the platform as a footballer to be able to give back to the community.

"They are an inspiration to us all, of course. Football's a massive thing for all of us, and it has given me an opportunity to have an impact on people.

The mascot opportunity arose after Ellice's dad Joe tweeted Jed Wallace asking for support in his daughter's campaign to raise £65,000 for life changing surgery to help her to walk unaided. "The same as with Harvey – I know that Aiden [O'Brien] and a few of the lads have been really involved with helping him, and that's what this football club is all about – the community, a family and being there for Ellice, Harvey and hopefully more kids in the future."

Wallace finally went on to laud the tireless work of Millwall in the community and reiterated his delight at his opportunities to help those less fortunate. "It's brilliant what Millwall do for the community. For one reason or another, this club can get a negative spotlight on it, but credit has to go to a lot of the things that especially Nena and the club do in the community.

Were any of the large selection of aforementioned positive things featured widespread in the media?

Millwall Paranoia time again – does anything that is positive re Millwall ever get reported? Does it b****ocks! Surprisingly they would rather highlight on something that they think is humourous, like the Away kit ruse, how we chuckled not! Or say focus on any minor incident involving Millwall fans as though it were the start of a Nuclear War!

I could expand this reality against a manufactured Media perception for many, many columns, proving my case easily but I hope that what I have put at least gives you a brief insight in what Millwall fans have to put up with, something that I have had to endure in all my Millwall life, which started in 1966.

There is more media proof showing how they will always show Millwall fans as naughty Lions in a previous chapter, with the ethos let's just focus on a negative preconceived preconception not the positive truth to flog more papers!

If you can get a copy of it check out 'Millwall In The Community', a book that was produced in the mid-1980s under the auspice of Reg Burr, that lists a lot of the clubs communal work. It is referred to as 'The club that gave itself back to the people' by author Sunday Times writer Chris Lightbrown on the back cover. Do you want truth or media perception? If you want the latter avoid this booklet at all costs. The preconceived National media cannot ruin their template of Millwall FC practically being in league with the devil, so minor negative = major outrage, major positive = blissfully ignoring.

I hope that for all those non Millwall people who have only ever taken their perception of what Millwall fans and club are like from the Media's ultra-biased preconceived perception, I think that what has gone before in this chapter highlights perfectly what Millwall Fans and Club are really like.

However if you need any further proof of this ethos, please look on the next few pages of the closing section of this Chapter, the finishing section displays what Millwall fans and club are really like, f*** the media's prewritten perception!!!

Showing that Millwall are a family club, and by family I do not mean like Watford, Fulham, Ipswich Town or god forbid Palarse, I mean we look after our own, both the club and their fans so to finish The Harvey Brown Section on the next page.

The Harvey Brown Section

The aforementioned Harvey Brown, here is his story and picture library. I don't precisely know how much attention the national media outlets gave this, I know social media and local South East London media did and Millwall Football Club definitely did.

In 2015/16 season when Millwall supporters Victoria and Dean Brown launched their Petition to get Jeremy Hunt MP to make NHS England to fund Vimizim for Morquio Sufferers for their 6-year-old son Harvey, shown below. For those who do not know for an MP/office to acknowledge the petition it must be 10,000 signatures long, to hope that Parliament discuss it must be 100,000, no pressure on the people pressing to get something right done there then! They reached 10,000 in October 2016, with only a couple of months to hit the big 100k target, the pictures following show the players and Mascots including manager with Harvey at Millwall's Training ground and when he was chosen as a mascot for Millwall's home game v Rochdale on Saturday 26th September, when it was proved that good can prevail as his being mascot led to our first home league victory following a run of defeats, god must have done that!

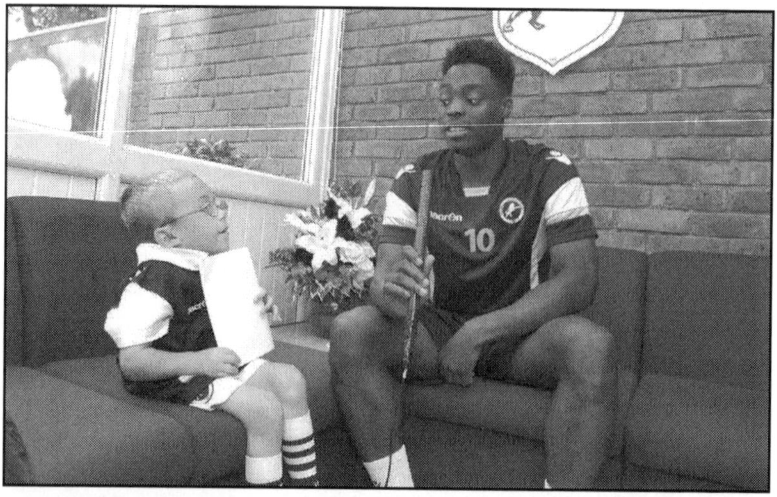
10

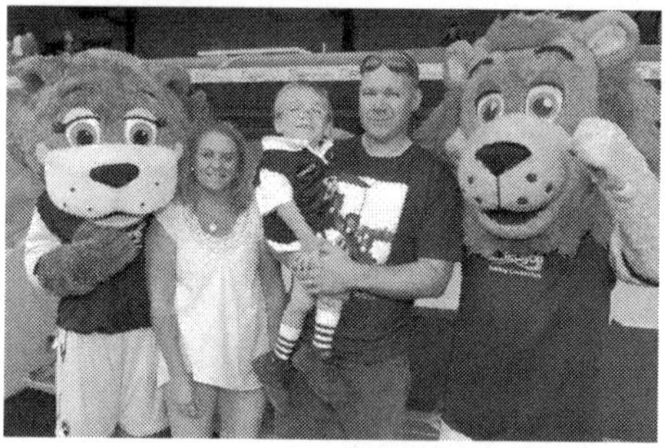

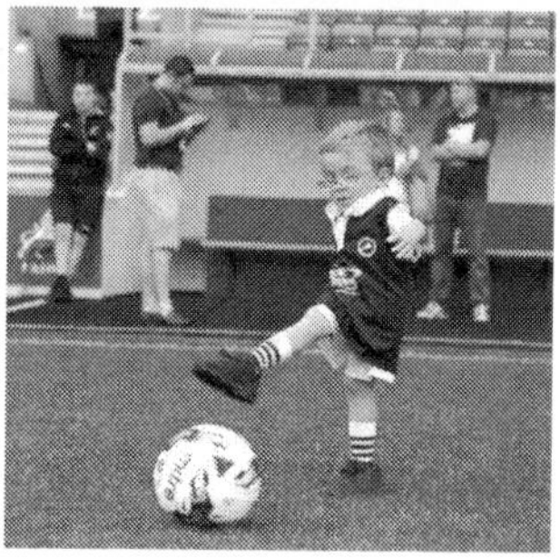

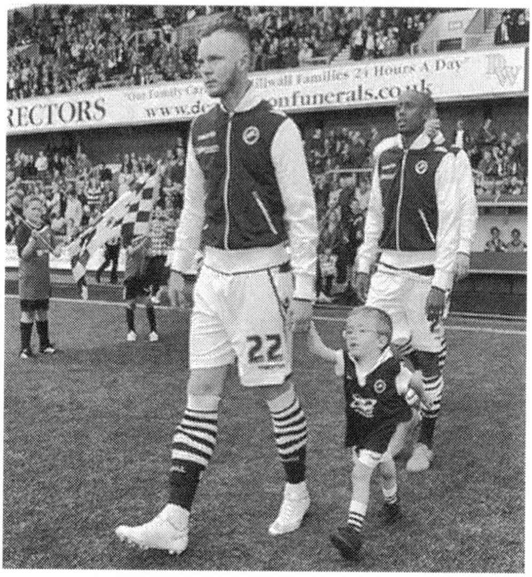
22

129

In late November 2015, the Brown's received the brilliant news that their attempt to get the NHS to fund the necessary medication had been successful, thanks to the enormous amount of work the family had done, by family I mean Victoria and Dean Brown family and backed by the Millwall family of fans and club. This was featured in local South London media and on ITV London, so had some acknowledgement!

Then the evil Millwall came out with this idea called Millwall Disabled Football – Join Our Team, then pre season 2016/2017. See the following images.

A highlight of the Harvey Brown section at the end of 2015/2016 Millwall FC did this –

Young fan set to lead the team out on Sunday League 1 Play-Off Final Sunday 29th May 2016

131

Some more photographs in the first Harvey being held aloft on his 9th Birthday by Lions Captain Steve Morison outside the New Den. In the second picture is Harvey in his Millwall wheeled wheelchair outside Great Ormond Street Hospital in November 2018.

I would like to close the Harvey Brown Section with a further highlight, a selection of pictures specific to one day when Harvey was selected as one of the mascots for Millwall's big home clash with Norwich City on Saturday 2nd March 2019 on the aforementioned 'Community Day' along with the Ellice Barr.

Harvey being held aloft by Steve Rendell who was doing the London Landmarks Half Marathon Fundraiser for the MPS Society the Society for Mucopolysaccharide Diseases on Sunday 24th March 2019, pictured with Harvey's dad Dean Brown, several Millwall Players and Bomber Harris, plus Johnny Garton Millwall fan and British Welterweight Champion on Saturday 24th November 2018 at The New Den.

Stephen Rendell at the completion of his fundraising run having raised at the time of writing £6,180 on Sunday 24th March 2019 and on its completion when fundraising page on Facebook closed this sum finished on £6665, over the target figure of £6,620 by 166 supporters of the fund.

Kevin Downey, a 60 year old Millwall fan, ran his 30th consecutive London Marathon also raising funds for the MPS Society, the Society for Mucopolysaccharide Diseases, with his final London Marathon on Sunday 28th April 2019, pictured above with Stephen Rendell and Harvey Brown in front of the Blue Millwall bus also photographed on the pitch.

Pictured with an away Millwall team signed by all the Millwall players etc. There was a raffle in front of the bus on Good Friday 19th April 2019 with this shirt as the prize and Kevin and Harvey pictured outside the Barry Kitchener Stand. At the time of writing Kevin had raised £3,895 for Harvey's Charity the MPS society.

Harvey being held up by ex-Lions skipper Danny Shittu inside the New Den on Sunday 26th May 2019 Wonderwall Cup Day.

Final thing in the Harvey Brown portion was his being awarded Young Citizen Of The Year Award in Southwark Civic Awards 2019

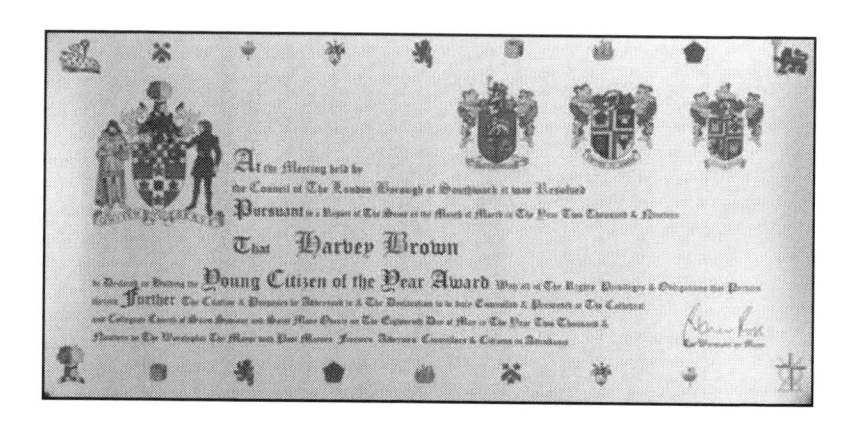

The Worshipful the Mayor
Councillor Catherine Rose

The Mayor's Office, Civic Suite
Third Floor North, 160 Tooley Street, London SE1 2QH
Office 020 7525 7303
E-mail: mayors.office@southwark.gov.uk

25 March 2019

Dear Harvey Brown,

It is my pleasure to inform you that you are to be honoured in the Southwark Civic Awards 2019 with the **Young Citizen of the Year Award 2109**. Each year these awards publicly recognise the exceptional contributions of various individuals and organisations to life in Southwark, and you may be justly proud of being included in their number.

Your award will be presented at a joint civic celebration at Southwark Cathedral on Saturday 18 May 2019, combining the Southwark Civic Awards and the formal election and installation of the new Mayor of Southwark.

The civic awards ceremony will commence at 11am and will be followed directly by our second ceremony (Annual Council and Mayor Making). This will be followed by a Civic Reception to which you and your guests are invited to attend. Honorands will need to assemble in the cathedral at 10:30am, with all

All attendees will need to be seated by **10:45 am**. You may bring four guests to the civic awards ceremony and you and they will be most welcome to join us for light refreshments afterwards in the Cathedral at around 1 pm.

You may bring as many guests as you wish to the civic awards ceremony in the cathedral, however due to a restriction on space and numbers attending, we can only allocate one guest place to each honorand for the civic reception.

We would be most grateful if you could complete the enclosed reply forms and return them to us in the pre-paid envelope provided as soon as possible.

We take this opportunity to congratulate you on your achievement and we very much hope you can join us on the day.

Yours sincerely,

Jacqueline Brazil

Jacqueline Brazil
Civic Officer and Private Secretary to the Mayoralty

Enc3

Closing Chapter 3: The REAL Positivity of Millwall a lot of the highlights of Millwall FC positives that have been mentioned in the chapter

CHAPTER 4
The Wailing 'Wall – Millwall Serenades And Other Pleasantries

To start a general note this song, chant and comment chapter is dedicated to all of those away fans who have ever sung at us 'You've only got one song!' Wrong!!!!

Free Speech My Arse – No Offence!

I feel it only fair to warn you that although I have tried to make it as PC as possible as I am anything but PC I have probably failed miserably, because Free Speech me like, someone's PC agenda of what is acceptable aka right or wrong me no like!!!!

Just like to point out something you may or may not have seen to establish how racist our Asian abuse of Son in the FA Cup Quarter Final at White Hart Lane listed elsewhere in this chapter was, they brought in a cultural expert, try to rearrange the following words into a phrase – Total for up post waste f***ing a money of a PC made. The answer in case you are struggling: Total waste of f***ing money for a PC made up post!!!

I heard that our offence v Son was racial stereotyping. As a Millwall fan I never feel that we are stereotypically treated, I could have that wrong I could mean that is all we ever are, the Millwall Tar With The Same Brush Society is how we are treated.

I would love to know which PC bod decides what can and cannot be said.

Free Speech oh yeah, vaguely remember that, I would just like to mention that if anti-ginger hair chants are constituted racist or wolf whistling blonde haired or metro sexualesque players is homophobic, Wall games will be like a bleeding library stadium! I have put Non-PC alerts, for those of a not from this planet persuasion also rather than delete all non PC chants from Millwall and opposition fans I thought that like Rappers CDs do I should include the following at the start of this chapter –

PARENTAL ADVISORY EXPLICIT CONTENT

Devotions To The 'Wall

To start a typical Millwall chant came when we won Promotion to Division 1 pre naming it the Premiership in the late 1980s, we'd won the Division 2 Championship now called the Championship and we sang – 'Now you're gonna believe us, now you're believe us, now you're gonna believe us, we've won the f***ing League!'

I thought I would list a few oldies, oddities and self-effacing Millwall chants.

To start several chants which seem to have disappeared of late, the first one I previously listed in one of my other books, but it was a real favourite at the Old Den –

'The Lions, the Lions, da, da, da, da, da, da, da, da, da, da roar! (war!)'

Usually accompanied at the Old Den by surging and 'On the pitch' type gestures, sung to the tune of the film 'The Vikings' horn line, an Old Den favourite, as was – 'Come on you Lions!'

This is yet another old chant that seems to have disappeared without trace, as has the more modern –

'We are, we are Millwall!' Sung to the tune of Queen's 'We Will Rock You'.

The reason for the next chants infrequent use in some of the last 10 years is self-evident –

'We're proud of you; we're proud of you, we're proud of you Millwall' and 'We're the pride of London town!'

To continue, some more golden oldies –

'We are the C B L, we are the C B L, we are the C B L, we are the C B L.'/

'We are the Millwall, we are the Millwall, we are the Millwall Cold Blow Lane!'/

'Millwall here, Millwall there, Millwall every f***ing where, na na na na, na na na, na na!' and

'Na na na na, na na na na, hey hey hey – Millwall!'

'We're here, we're there, we're every f***ing where Millwall, Millwall.'

Some chants that occasionally get an airing today –

'You are my Millwall, my only Millwall, you make me happy when skies are grey (and blue and white), you'll never know dear how much I love you until you take my Millwall away, etc – bush!'

'When I was just a little boy I asked my mother what will I be? Will I be Arsenal? Will I be Spurs? Here's What She Said To Me – Millwall, Millwall, Millwall, Millwall. Millwall. Millwall, Millwall, Millwall, Millwall, Millwall!'

The latter sung to the tune of the Beatles' 'Hey Jude.'

Not forgetting the more modern 'Millwall' chants to the tunes of 'Vindaloo' and 'The Great Escape' and the late 'Lion on the Roof' chant – 'Lovely jubbly Millwall!'

There was a song popular for a short time a few years back in CBL to the tune of Oasis 'Wonderwall' – 'And maybe you're going to be the one that saves me, because after all you're my Millwall, Millwall, Millwall.'

Some more general 'Wall chants now to start – 'EIO, EIO, EIO, EIO, etc.'

Recently stolen by Middlesbrough, Spurs and Luton!

There was a golden oldie chant next to raise the volume –

'Sing up Millwall, sing up Millwall, sing up Millwall, sing up!'

In 2005/6 some newly acquired alleged 'Wall took to singing an adapted chant, that to my mind is only really associated with northern teams from my experience –

'Millwall till I die, I'm Millwall till I die, I know I am, I'm sure I am, I'm Millwall till I die!'

Some general devotional chants –

'Stand up if you love Millwall.'/'Cold Blow Lane Barmy Army'/

'We are the famous, the famous Millwall.' And 'Millwall, Millwall, Millwall, Millwall.'

The last one sung to either – 'Amazing Grace, Here We Go, Que Sera, Sera or You'll Never Walk Alone.'

Then there is – 'Miiiiiiillwaaaaaall'

Our version of the Monks aka Gregorian chant that sends shivers up my spine when it echoes around the grounds, sad isn't it. It was this chant/song that the Old Den crowd, in particular, used to use as a springboard to bring other chants in at full volume, songs like – 'Give me an M... etc.' culminating with – 'Who's the best team in London? Or 'Who's the best team of all? Millwall, Millwall, Millwall.'

'We Love You Millwall We Do, Oh Millwall We Love You'/'Come on Millwall, come on!'/'Let ,em come.' And naturally 'No one likes us!'

The latter subsequently pinched by Gillingham, Burnley, MK Dons and bastardised by Glasgow Rangers, etc bloody cheek can't you © copyright this bloody stuff?

Finally as an aside I saw a banner on TV from Ajax v Arsenal in the Champions League in February 2003 that I thought we should adopt at Millwall to back up our 'No One Likes Us' posture it said – 'Hatem all' It probably means something warm and snugly in Dutch but in Pidgin English I thought it was a marvellous Millwall type sentiment!

Harry Boy Cripps

Here is an old un a proper charming Harry Cripps song –
'Harry, Harry Break Us A Leg, Break Us A Leg, Break Us A Leg, Harry, Harry Break Us A Leg, Just Above The Knee!'

Celebrate Good Times C'mon!

Chant from League 1 Play Off Final May 29th 2010 after 1-0 win, against Swinedon –
'Wemberlee, Wemberlee, we are the famous Millwall and we won at Wemberlee, Wemberlee!'
Blimey, we now win Play-Off games, number one time Yahoo get me Jackett! Number two time actually did this again v Bradford City in May 2017, this winning at Wembley is getting boring now obviously not really just thought I would say that it was!!!!

Pride Park Home Fans' Heat Treatment Abuse

In our last game of the relegation threatened 2012/13 season on 4th May 2013 our trip to Derby County at Pride Park is a classic lesson in highlighting it never being a good idea to wind up Millwall fans, especially ones who were on a relegation knife-edge.
The home fans in giving their perspective on why to our customary 'No One Likes Us We Don't Care!'
They sang – 'No One Likes You Cos You're Shit!' Thanks much appreciated!

Non-PC Alert –

In response to highlight the Derby mass murderer Michael Philpott we sang –

'He's One Of Your Own, He's One Of Your Own, Micky Philpott He's One Of Your Own!'/'You Set Your Kids Alight That's What You Do!' (In a skit on Leeds United Jimmy Saville abuse at the New Den and Danny Shittu's That's What We Do!' at Charlton both from the same season you can find both later in this chapter.

Regarding his horrific crime of killing 6 of his kids by burning them alive they/he got –

'You Burn Your Kids Alive!'/'Arsonists, Arsonists'!/'Murderers, Murderers!' and 'You Set Your Kids Alight!

In addition, a bloke behind me sang solitarily the abstract – 'You Sleep In Your Sisters Hearth!'

Finally, the abuse aimed at the mouthy home fans to our right attaching them to him by family links –

'Micky Philpott F***ed Your Mum!'

Ex Hammer Comes To New Den with Derby County

Frank Lampard Derby County Manager at the New Den 18th August 2018 the obligatory ex West Ham links chants – 'West Ham C*** West Ham C***!' and non Vermin 'Lampard Lampard You're A C***!'/'John Terry F***ed your Mum, he's Your Father!' and 'Frank Lampard John Terry's Your Dad!'

At 2-0 to Millwall the obligatory lose to Millwall sacking society chant 'You're Getting Sacked In The Morning!'

Reading About Wall Sarcasm v Reading at the New Den Tuesday 27th January 2015

In the second half with Reading kicking towards their own fans in the upper North Stand, there was a period when every time the ball was in our area and was touched by a Millwall player the Reading fans shouted 'Handball' in an attempt to get a Penalty.

To highlight their obsessive shouts we started shouting 'Handball!' every time one of their players touched the ball with any part of their body, and so to make it more humorous we sang – 'Handball, Handball, Handball!' which echoed around the New Den.

This time at Reading away Saturday 3rd February 2018 to Fat bird in home stand to our right giving it large no pun intended -

‚There's only one Vicky Pollard!'/'Whose the slapper in the White?'/'She Takes it up the Arse!'/'She's expecting Triplets'/'Have you ever seen your c**t?' ‚We can smell your c**t from here!'

To her bloke

‚She's so fat she pays you for sex!'/'Has she ever seen her c**t?'/'You silly bastard you're shagging a pig!' And ‚You silly bastard your birds a fat slag!'

Also a black Reading player Tiago Ilori I think I could be wrong had dyed blonde hair at the top of his head got usual 'He's Got Bird shit on his head' and the adaptation at 2 – 0 to Wall 'Bird Shit Bird Shit What's The Score?'

Fishy Grimsby

There were numerous Lions chants aimed at Grimsby Town in a New Den game in April 2002, some mentioned in 'I Was Born Under The Cold Blow Lane'.

Chants were all about the Fisherman fraternity with several fishy folk chants like – 'We can smell your fish from here!'/'You're not fishing anymore!'/'You're going home to your lighthouse!' Moreover, 'There's only one Captain Birdseye'

There was also the more offensive and bizarre – 'You sleep with your sister's fish!'/'Captain Birdseye sex offender!' And 'You're S… and you stink of fish!'

A 'Ladies we won! – Now you can Dance around your Handbags in white stiletto's' or a 'We had a happy Essex Night in the Weston Home's Community Stadium'

We played at Colchester United's new stadium on October 21st 2008, identikit Stadium or not it was infinitely better than Layer Road, which putting it technically was a S***hole! We won there to take us to the joint top of League One, 2nd only on Goal Difference, to highlight our assent and Spurs pre 'Arry Boys arrival at the time having only 2 points and looking like having an impending Relegation demise, combined with the home side's lowly League Position we sang the following…

From us to them– 'Tottenham Tottenham here we come!' and 'We're playing Tottenham next year!'

To highlight the home sides then lowly position and the fact they had not won at home at the time in their new stadium, we sang a variation on the above chant – 'You're playing Barnet next year!'

We also sang the customary Relegation explanation chant – 'That's why you're going down!'

From them to us –

Colchester United fans to the right hand side of the away section at the Weston Home's Community Stadium in October 2008 sang – 'We pay your Benefits!' Implying we were all unemployed.

I doubt that very much! But thanks anyway, they also sang this West Ham United implication –

'You're just a Bus stop in West Ham!' Wrong!

Mouthy Home Fans Get Riposte

Queen's Park Rangers and West Bromwich Albion in consecutive away matches 19th September 2018 at Loftus Road and 22nd September 2018 at The Hawthorns the mouthy home fans got this family assessment – 'Your Mum's A Slag – Your Dad's A Nonce – Your Gran's A Brass!'

'Essex Girls We Won Again! –You Can Dance In Celebration Around Your Handbags In A Mega Micro Mini On The Pier, In A Kiss Me Kick Hat, By The Outside Winkle Stall!'

By the way Ladies by winkle stall I do not mean a Dildo/Vibrator emporium, I mean a seafood stall!

At our Tuesday 3rd March 2009 away match at Southend United's Roots Hall, by the way again I do not mean it is the best place to get a Root aka sex, Essex Girls, just thought I'd explain it again, it is Sarfend's Stadium name.

Pre match two weird home Mascots were on the pitch, one called Elvis, with a buffed up black quiffy hairdo and the other Sammy, who was I assume supposed to be a Shrimp, allied to the Shrimpers nickname, however he wore a high whiteish hood/head whatever and looked like he came from an American Deep South, cross burning society, so we sang – 'Are You Ku Klux in disguise?'

We were discussing between us what time the half time on pitch cross burning and lynching started, luckily it didn't, sorry just us being daft!

The home fans to our right were accompanied by a bass drummer I think it was and to highlight this we sang – 'You can't sing without a drum!' and 'Your drum is too big for you!'

On a stereotypical assumption, right or totally wrong we also sang to the home fans –

'Are you West Ham in disguise?' and You're just a town ful of inbreds!'

The Referee performance was Hometown Harry Central. His name was East, which Southend is in England so that might have been a bit of a clue that he was not going to give us sod all unless it was in a nothing position! He didn't, so job done, well sort of as we won 1 – 0.

Because he was as bald as a coot with Alupecia, to give him our opinion of his outrageously biased display we sang –'The Referees a bald C***!'

In a approximate combined variation on the customary –
'The Referee's a W*****!' and 'Lino Lino You're a C***!'
We also sang – 'Are You Goody in disguise?'

As his lush barnet or total lack of it made him look like the then terminally ill bald headed Jade Goody who was featured heavily in the media at the time.

When we went 1 – 0 up, we sang to tell him that his overly biased performance had failed, so to highlight this we gave him – 'I – 0 and you're still a C***!

Multicultural fun at PNE's Deepdale on Saturday 23rd October 2017

There was a Sikh festooned in White t shirt, turban and Beard with a Blue Union Jack sitting in the Tom Finney Stand to the right hand of the away section in the Bill Shankley the, here his is outside on his bike

The chants he received at Deepdale 'There's Only One Father Christmas!' and the less polite 'You're Just A Shit Father Christmas!

Fattist Abuse

When we played Premier League? Watford at the Den in the The Emirates FA Cup 4th Round on Sunday 29th January 2017, one of their players the Slimfast Version of Akinfenwa black Watford forward Stefano Okaka, whinged about everything, which naturally as he is on a Kings Ransom a week he feels he is entitled to, to point out what we thought of him from CBL, Akinfenwa comparisons were shouted at him.

When he came on The Dockers sang 'You're Just A Fat Danny Shittu!!!' to first team regular who had been on benchTroy Denney. We won 1 – 0 so his and in fact ALL of their teams continual moaning worked didn't it!!!

Leyton Building Site Lullaby's

We played at Leyton Orient's Brisbane Road aka Matchroom Stadium, on Saturday 22nd November 2008, Stadium? I like a laugh, it looks in reality much more like a Building complex for private houses and flats. Why would you want to have a balcony inside a stadium (sic) that hung over the away section? That would sod up the tenants there listening to their TVs, DAB Radios, IPod's, MP3s, Stereos, talking to each other or using their Mobiles or Telephones, especially if us noisy buggers were there in vast numbers as per usual. To highlight the Stadium's scaffolding and Building complex nature we 2700 sitting in the old East Stand, which hasn't seen a bit of work on it since the 1950s from what I could see, sang – 'You got your stand from Ikea!'

This was to the Os in the stand with the scaffolding on it's roof behind the goal to our left.

When the attendance of 6951 was announced, we sang the slightly mathematically inaccurate –

'We've got more here than you!'

Anoraks Chuff Chuff alert New Den aka South Bermondsey station 12th March 2010 and Good Friday 2nd April 2015

To welcome the Anorak strewn prats to their customary defeat to us, we sang 'Trainspotters, Trainspotters, Trainspotters' to highlight their natural pastime, we also sang this joyfully when they started leaving early as our goals flew in left right and centre, so that they did not not to watch the slaughter but could go and add to their trainspotting numbers collection they left the ground in droves, yea Gods!

On Good Friday 3rd April 2015 in a game when Millwall beat Charlton after being a goal behind, Charlton Athletic see us as their arch rivals, when in all honesty they are totally irrelevant to us, lets look at the all time record between the two sides home and away, at the point when we reached 70 games between the 2 teams, the record at this point was Millwall Wins 34, Draws 25, Charlton Wins 11! There is the most recent version of this at the time of writing slightly later on.

The record between the two sides is ever so slightly heavily laden in our favour don't you think!

Millwall sing the customary 'You'll Never Beat Millwall 'or 'You Never Beat Millwall!' either version true as you can see from this 70 games statistic above.

To highlight this and shoot down all their South London dominance boasts they make, we in the CBL sang –

'F*** Off Charlton – South London Is Ours!l

Anoraks Chuff Chuff arrival again pre Christmas 2016, Wednesday 21st December 2106

Well surprisingly Millwall won this rearranged game that had originally been cancelled due to International call ups 3 – 1 naturally we sang the 'You (You'll) Never Beat Millwall' chant and 'F*** Off Charlton South London Is Ours!' in addition to these we sang 'You're F***ing S***, You're F***ing S***!'

When they sang a chant about removing their hated Belgian Chairman and 95% owner Roland Duchâtelet in response we sang the helpful 'You're Getting F***ed by the Belgian!'

We played them again on Saturday 14th January 2017 at the Valley, they sang something about us being on Jeremy Kyle I think, so we sang the Belgian and You'll Never beat Millwall chants, mentioned above in a game that ended 0 – 0.

On the Video screen to the side of us pre-match they showed a video that had a banner saying Historic Matches or words to that effect at top which highlighted the last time they beat us 2 – 0 in

1996, so over 20 years ago!!!!! To highlight this and update the previous mentioned 70 games statistic the record between Millwall and Charlton Athletic League games at the time of writing in 2019 is Played 74, Millwall 35 wins, Draws 27 and Charlton Athletic wins 12!!!! Nothing much changed eh!

Coventry City Away Saturday 4th February 2017 Ricoh Owners SISU Home Fan Protest and also the I would not do that if I was you ethos

At the Ricoh Arena in February 2017 in the wake of our victory against Lewisham Council's CPO, Coventry City fans outside handed out A show of support Flyers asking for our support, along with Blackpool/Charlton Athletic/Blackburn Rovers who in there and the other listed clubs cases were being destroyed by their board, unlike us who were being tortured by an outside Council,

Coventry City Fans along with many other club fans had supported us and asked for our support, I took a few leaflets for distribution to my mates inside and myself and another Millwall fan waiting for turnstiles to open warned the Coventry fan handing out the Flyers about one of their demonstration plans a pitch invasion where they said that would try to get us to support them, me and the other Wall fan said do NOT come into or at our section as we will kick off, which will be counterproductive for you.

I said best go the way Wall did v Lewisham peacefully, the Coventry City bloke I was speaking to said we have tried to do it the peaceful way for 10 years it has got us nowhere, so we want to step it up!

In the game in the first half with Millwall attacking the South Stand where we were gathered, Wall got a corner, at which point the Coventry City fans to our right bombarded the pitch with tennis balls, which had to be cleared before we could the take the corner, and when we took it we scored!!!

In support sic we sang – 'You're Getting F***ed By Your Owners!'

Without another goal Millwall Goal following the first one in the 1st half and the Tennis ball barrage seemingly ending we sang – 'Where's Your Tennis Gone?' and 'We Want More Tennis Balls!' To try and encourage another goal!

The same type of thing happened at Shrewsbury Town on Tuesday 4th April 2017, anniversary of Tim Cahill's FA Cup Semi Final at Old Trrafford. The home fans with a sodding drum to the right of us sang 'We Should Be Beating This Shower Of Shit!' meaning Millwall, strangely as had happened at the Ricoh as soon as they did this we scored, keep singing chaps!!!

For those who did not go up to Wales sorry Oop North West there was a weird banner at the back of the home stand to the right that said 'Breathe On The Salop' what the bloody hell that meant god knows, I know Salop was an alternative name for Shropshire but Breathe On Them?????

Do they have rank breath in Shropshire so is a defence mechanism?

The ethos of not singing a certain chant applies to us as well, like the first ever rendition of 'Bobby Moore Is No More' at Upton Park, we were leading 1- 0 from a Jamie Moralee goal right at the beginning, we start singing Bobby Moore and Amsters get two goals quick time, a bit like insulting players like Marlon King, or Tottenham's Son, do that they will invariably score, in their cases hat tricks each on one occasion.

A Light Grey Whistle And Fluted Geordie Manager At Huddersfield Town Play Off Semi Final First Leg, Saturday 15th May 2010

When Huddersfield Town Manager Lee Clark went garrity in his Technical Zone after a perceived dodgy decision, he was greeted by we away hoards with ' Sit Down You Geordie C***!' and 'You Shop At Matalan!' reflecting his roots and what we thought of his suit's quality, he got pretty much the same at the home 2nd Leg, although his suit was darker, not that we gave a f***!

When Birmingham City manager at St Andrews on 1st October 2013 he received 'Lee Clark, Lee Clark You're A C***!'

He must bore us now becase when he returned to the Den as manager of Bury on 18th March 2017 we could not even be bothered to abuse him!

The Minnow Shots Arrive At The New Den, Ah, The Joys Of The FA Cup

When we played our FA Cup 2nd round tie at home to Aldershot Town on November 29th 2008 there was a largeish turnout of away fans, in what for a lowly placed in the table League 2 side, was a big tie for them against a recentish FA Cup Finalist and at the time of the game a high flying League 1 side the Lions, there were some interesting chants.

With a smallish crowd only around 6000 and only the upper tiers being open, the Aldershot fans sang at us – 'Your ground's too big for you!'

When we sang our customary West Ham hating chants, which gets an airing whoever we are playing they sang – 'I'm Forever Blowing Bubbles' which can only have been to take the piss and to wind us up.

In our observant state of their quality during our 3 – 0 win we sang –

'Aldershit!' and 'You're shit and you know you are!'.

By way of explanation we were taking the piss and checking is their name AlderShots or AlderShits? It was an easy play on words mate.

From The National League North The Even More Minnow AFC Fylde Arrive At The New Den Ah The Deep Joy Of The FA Cup First Round!

With relegation to Division 3 or League 1 or whatever it is called this week, we now had the pleasure of playing teams that not only have we never played before but we have never heard of, in this case AFC Fylde a team who come from below the Regional section of the Conference. This was first time they had gone this far so we were their first ever game in the real FA Cup, respect to them for getting this far, we won the game v them 3 – 1 on 7th November 2015 at the New Den, one good thing with playing a real team their fans did not sing all the bollocks that Premier wannabe teams sing which drives me up the wall, who the f*** wants to think they are Palarse Utras!!!!! AFC Fylde old had one chant for the team 'Fylde Fylde' which led me to think well that is nice you have filed it so desk/office now tidy, sorry how my brain works, my apologies. Obviously they were not referring to their office duties, but I thought there were far more variations on a theme, based on their name 'A F, AFC, AFC Fylde'/'Fylde Fylde Fylde'/'We Are, We Are Fylde!'/'Give Me An F, etc' all 4 are real football chants not Premier League wannabe arsehole chants. AFC Fylde could make plenty of variations, I know that I do not go to Everton games every week but they have only had one chant when I have seen us play them 'Everton, Everton, Everton; as have Aston Villa with 'Villa Villa, Villa Villa!' Moving On.

Wall's Fred Onyedinma name sarcasm or poor spelling or bad hearing – whatever!

At Burton Albion away Saturday 24th February 2018 he received – 'Oh Fred Or Me Dinner'/'Oh Fred And Me Dinner!'

Numerous Travelling AFC Wimbledon minnows arrive at the New Den, continuing the joys of the FA Cup early rounds

We played mid table Conference side AFC Wimbledon at home in the FA Cup first round on Monday 9th November 2009 and we won 4 – 1 hoorah!

3339 followers of the enforced bedouin team who were encamped in the upper and lower tiers of the away North Stand sang, among other things at us –

'Your grounds too big for you!'

Ostensibly to take the piss and as the 20,000 capacity New Den was just under half full.

In response we sang –'Your grounds in Milton Keynes!'/'Milton Keynes, Milton Keynes Milton Keynes!' and 'MK Dons, MK Dons, MK Dons!' to highlight their forced abandonment of Wimbledon FC in the league for the enforced Milton Keynes/MK Dons formation and their subsequent reinvention as an at this point Amateur side.

Trip to NAM in FA Cup 3rd round January 7th 2012

Lovely day out in Essex just thought I would list some chants from us and them.

Chants from them –

They sang 'I'm Forever Blowing Bubbles' to wind us up, I suppose they were trying to show us that they were really Wet Spam Untied herberts, yeah righto schoolchildren!

To Liam Feeney – 'You're Just a fake Aaron Lennon!' i.e. the Spurs winger.

To imply that we were caravan dwellers, like Wet Spam always focus on as well they sang –

'Where's Your Caravan?' and 'Wheels on your house go round and round!'

Non-PC Alert –

Chants from us to them –
In reply to gypsy reference we sang –
'Oh East London is Like Bengal!'/'Where's your Taliban!' and 'Dale Farm, Dale Farm, Dale Farm!' These were in relation to the large Asian population in East End/Essex and the Police's 2011 massive eviction of gypsy's on an Essex site.

Gloryhunters

A few chants to the big game crowd swellers in the CBL and the rest of the ground that emerge during a cup run or promotion push, 'I'll have a seat by the skirting board please'. If you get my drift. Who needs them? Only the bank I suppose, whatever to serenade them we have sung – 'Where were you when we were shit?'/'Will we see you here next week?'/'Three games a season, only 3 games a season!'/'Glory, glory hunters!' And 'Glory hunters, you're just glory hunters!'

This is only In my opinion but only turning up for Bertie big Bollocks games is rather like only going in to a cinema to watch the end of a film, you will see the climax but not the whole plot.

'Very Very Non Glory Hunting, I Must Get Me Barnet Done!'

In total non Gloryhunter mode, me, Simon, Patrick, his mate Ricky, Dave, Paul and Nathan all went to Underhill on 1st September 2009, this was a week to the day after all the fun and games at West Ham United in the Carling Cup, to watch the 'Wall in a slightly, sorry much less hostile/violent Johnstone's Paint game against League 2 side Barnet, who we had never played before.

We joined hundreds of fellow Lions there to watch our side succumb marvellously to the mighty minnows 2 – 0. That aside it added to our grounds visited list, taking my total then to stadia that I had seen Millwall at 101*, including Ferencvaros in the UEFA Cup, Altrincham and Telford at their Amateur grounds in the FA Cup, Wembley stadium, the Millenium Stadiium.

PS *This away ground number is larger now if you use trips to an away team at several grounds, like Bristol Rovers at Eastville/Twerton Park and The Memorial Stadium and any clubs added after this 2009 date there is a list later in this book, the numbers at time of writing are League clubs 94, Amateur clubs 3, Overseas clubs 1, Wembley x 2, Millenium Stadium 1, however if you use grounds I have seen Millwall at a team who have moved the total is 126,

Moving away from ground gathering itself, just to explain what Underhill was like it was a real Conference level ground with bits and bods of seating sections and terracing all around the ground, some roofing on the side Terraced section etc, but naturally as we are Millwall, there was a large Old Bill presence for such a Mickey Mouse game, this being essential following the previous week's game at Upton Park/The Boleyn Ground or whatever they bloody called it!

We stood on a side terrace near the front, because if you stood near the back on it's 6 or 7 steps, you had a perfect view of the roofs pillars in your way, this way we didn't have them in our eyeline, still too bloody low down, but whatever!

There were a couple of very strange signs in front of us, for those who were there or had not seen them on the night, to our left there was a sign that said 'Watch Your Language' and just to our right one that said 'No Standing', marvellous! I assumed that it meant that you had to sit down on the terrace but not swear? If it meant that, we all naturally ignored it and to be honest you would be a bit F***ed if you had Tourettes or Piles! Telling a Millwall crowd to not swear will work a treat, Not!

I think that the other sign was meant to stop those in the seats standing up in them, good luck with that one as well!

Moving on to the chants. The home fans in the section to our left behind the segregation fencing and line of Old Bill bravely sang in response to their North London position – 'South London is full of S***!'

In response to the highly publicised violent events at West Ham United, which they were obviously not bloody at they sang 'You're not scary anymore!'/'You all ran from West Ham!'/'Where were you at Upton Park?' and to wind us up properly they continuously sang stuff like –

'West Ham, West Ham!'/'United!' and 'I'm Forever Blowing Bubbles!'

We naturally in response sang 'Who are ya!'/'You What?' etc and the following –

To highlight their lack of fans in the ground, we sang 'Shit ground No Fans!'/'Can You See The Barnet fans? We can't see a f***ing thing!'/'We've got more fans than you!' and 'There's more Old Bill than you!'

The last two were not strictly mathematically accurate we had 743 out of the 1623 attendance, but bloody close!

To highlight their 'You all Ran from West Ham!' And 'You're not scary anymore!' chants we sarcastically sang 'Barnet's lot are scary!'/'Barnet ran from Fisher! And the usual 'You'll run and you know you will' and a sarcastic variation of this 'We'll run and we know we will!'

Oop North v 'uddersfield Tahn 20th April 2013 at the then entitled John Smith's Stadium January 11th 2014

They had a drum accompaniment, which I could not bloody see, we sang to the bleeding racket –

'Millwall Don't Need A Drum!' plus 'Can you sing without your drum!' and more politically re miners strikes in a week when she was buried –'There's only one Maggie Thatcher!' and on a similar tack – 'There's only one Arthur Scargill!'

The drum accompanied I know what I like and I like what I say locals sang the bizarre chant –

'You're Just A Town Full Of Bastards!' What????

'Very very very very Real Wall non Glory Hunting, I must get me bumps felt!'

Three of us, me, Paul and Nathan went to Carlisle United on a Tuesday night 9th March 2010, only 7 hours up on the club coach and 6 hours back so a doddle, I was in bed by 4.15am, and we won so happy! That aside I should probably get my head read, as should the other two plus, Glyn Kerry, Mark Bell, and brothers Laurie and Jordan who had driven up from Essex themselves, the support at the game by us was excellent and there was one funny chant that we sang to the massed ranks sic in the 3,853 crowd, there was an adapted olden Millwall chant –'They're here, They're there, They're every f***ing where, empty seats, empty seats!

What's The Worst That Could Happen?

Ipswich Town away 21st April 2012, as we took a two goal lead a Tractor Bald Headed Top Boy in the comatose crowd noise home stand to our left, went mental and started clamouring across the meshing offering us all out.

Non-PC Alert –

Now I am not a betting man but I think the odds that he faced of 1298 to 1 where not in his favour, unless he had a tank, napalm, a thermo nuclear device or a bazooka!

Which we did not think he had so we greeted his insanity with –

'You Take It Up The Arse!' to which he bent over towards us pointing at his arse

'Wanker, Wanker, Wanker!'/'Sit Down And Behave Yourself!'/'2 Nil And You've Got No Hair!'/'Baldy Baldy What's The Score Baldy Whats The Score?' and 'Baldy Baldy You're A C***!'

As we took our winning score of a late 3 – 0 lead he was not very happy so got up and left to which we sang – 'Where's Our Baldy Gone?' and 'We Want Our Baldy Back!'

On 10th August 2013 the same bloke I assume appeared again this time in the upper tier.

This time in a green vest bizarrely he looked like a Bruce Willis Die Hard clone, when strangely we had Die Hard 4.0 on way up

He got some of the above not all as we were losing this time, a new one that he got was -

'Do What the Steward Says' when they sat behind him when he was standing an larging it,

He also got 'Does Your Boyfriend Know You're here?'

And 'Baldy's Got A Boyfriend La La La' and 'Your Boyfriend is your brother!' when a young bloke sat next to him.

Wet and wind Swept in West London, well Middlesex at a 'real' football ground – Brentford away 14th November 2009

This game was played at what can be considered a real football ground as it had terracing, as much as many people want terracing brought back at all levels, but going to an old style Football ground at this level really puts all seater grounds in to perspective.

For those who were not there the weather was horrendous, rain drenched and very windy.

Loads of us went to the game, in the seats in the tier above us were Simon, his son Patrick and his Grandson Rudie who was less than 4 at the time and it was his first ever away match to watch Millwall, I tried to explain to him that he now had many many many more years where he must endure the Millwall experience, whether he understood or believed me I do not know!

On the terrace below this stand at the Brook Road end were myself, Paul, Nathan, Dave, Swedish Millwall contingent Henrik Lundgren, Henrik Agren and Daniel Österman who in reality was a Scouse/AIK fan, who had come to his first ever Millwall away game as well as far as I know.

In the first half me, Nathan, Dave and Paul stood at the back, then me and Nathan joined up with our Swedish contingent who had located themselves at the front of the crowded terrace, on this terrace although technically undercover so not in the rain the roof leaked all over Nathan in particular at the back in the 1st half and then on me at the front all the 2nd half, I will freely admit that I am a large enough target but I had enough water dripping on to my nut to film a Timotei TV advert of me washing my hair, it was a very similar situation to the QPR League Cup game at Loftus Road when the pipes p***ed all over my head at a night match there in 1987, that I mentioned in 'Tuesday Night In Grimsby'.

The water feature aside we also moved as we could not see sod all, Paul and Dave stood on a raised step at the back of the terrace but as there was not enough room for all of us, me and Nathan were on the Terrace itself and could not see much, there was a plethora of obstacles, i.e. we had heads in our way, we were at best in line with the crossbar peering through the coloured goal net, there were posts in various places in our eyeline and we were not high enough even on the terrace back step to overcome the lack of height and see our own end let alone the other end, ah the joys of terraces

To the chants –

In the stand to our right there were dozens of young chavs who were continually gesturing at us, so that they could say 'I took the piss out of Millwall me' to show how hard they were to their mates at school on Monday I would imagine, well done yoof, how brave of you!

We sang to their gesturing and bravado the usual repertoire –

'Little Boys, Little Boys, Little Boys!'/'You'll run and you know you will!'/'Does your Mother know you are here?' and 'Sit down Shut up!' and 'Sit down and behave yourself!'

More originally we sang 'Where's your Mum?'

To close this part a misrecognised 'celebrity' spotting chant pre match there was a Brentford bloke with a beard and balding head, walking around the pitch side with a ladder over his shoulder, he was greeted with –

'There's only one Uncle Albert!' ala Only Fools and Horses, sea fairing old salt.

Where's Inspector Morse and Lewis Someone Has Nicked Their Stand!

Oxford United away at the Kassam Stadium, Saturday 29th October 2016, our second visit there following the Johnstone Paint Southern Area Final Second Leg, in the game mentioned above, it was a daytime early kick off 1pm due to aggro at aforementioned night game, so gave us a far better perspective of the stadium in daylight, which only has three stands, with the area to our right behind the goal an advertising hoarding with a car park behind it, what I thought was funny was that they even had their own jews hill with a small number of presumably Oxford fans standing on highest ground they could find gawping in to the ground!

Anyway that aside herewith some observational chants – 'You've Only Got Three Stands!' and 'Your Grounds Embarassing!'

'Get 'Orf My Pitch!'

There are the annual ritual of end-of-season pitch invasions that very often ruined any laps of honour by the team, these invasions often led at the Old Den to the players being surrounded, manhandled and sometimes stripped down, often ending up in only their jockstraps!

On such celebratory days at either Den when a pitch invasion has spoilt the party, the pitch invaders have been greeted with chants of – 'Off, off, off!'/'Off the pitch, off the pitch, off the pitch!' And 'You're just a bunch of wankers!' Not forgetting the difficult to misinterpret – 'C***s! C***s! C***s!'

Grandad We Love You!

Grandad John was my Millwall fan hero recommendation to Sky One's Programme makers Granada, almost an anagram of Grandad itself! For "Football's Hardest Away Days" when they asked me to be the lead man in it, I turned it down because my elderly Mum was in hospital at the time and recommended Grandad for it.

I was in it a bit having been interviewed outside a store in Gillingham, but as I say Grandad John was the star of it, in my small part in it I said that Grandad was our spiritual Leader, our Dalai Lama, mind you I am mad!

This was also shown partially on '8 out of 10 Cats' on Channel 4 in November 2008 pre umpteen repeats since..

This section features a few more dedications and chants.

His rare non-appearances at home have prompted the chants -

'Grandad's gone to Charlton!'/'Where's our grandad gone?' And 'Grandad's in Bulgaria!'

Pre our Uefa Cup match chants included –

'Grandad's got his passport out!' And 'Grandad's going on a European tour!' which he did!

Most sarcastically, Mark McGhee's departure in 2003/4 was heralded with–

'Grandad for manager!' At least I think it was sarcastic!'

At Stoke City away in October 2004, we sang –

'Grandad is a sex god, Grandad is a sex god, la la, la la, la la, la la!'

An extension, as it were, to the 'Grandad's on viagra!' chants.

You can always rely on Grandad piping up with the following when asked for a song, it's not exclusive to Millwall, Chelsea sing it as well for one however, it sums up Millwall's mentality a treat and along with songs like 'No one likes us' it complements our siege mentality and paranoia perfectly.

To finish this grandad section his equivalent of 'My Way', his theme song -

'F... 'em, f... 'em all, United, West Ham, Liverpool, 'cos we are the Millwall and we are the best, 'cos we are the Millwall so f... all the rest!'

Sung to the tune of an old World War Two Song 'The Long And The Short And The Tall.'

West Country Wizard Alert Bristol City away Sunday 2nd December 2018

To a baldy headed hippy Steward with a beard standing in front of us in the away section, he got

'Gandalf Gandalf give us a spell!'

'Gandalf Gandalf give us a song!'

'We love you Gandalf we do!'
And when he did not respond we also sang
'We love you Catweazle!'

Physio Ho Ho Ho

When Millwall played Port Vale on Valentines Night 14th February 2017, when there physio run on continually to aid their apparently mortally wounded players, the Dockers sang – 'You're Just A Shit Bobby Backache!'

A play on the surname of our own physio Bobby Bacic.

Very Non-PC alert –
Tottingham

At the Rhino testimonial match at the New Den in August 2001 the Spurs fans were serenaded with very non pc racist/anti Semitic/gay references for example – 'We've got a foreskin, we've got a foreskin, you ain't, you ain't!'/'Where's your foreskin gone?/'Hello, hello Jewish Jew boys, Jewish Jew Boys!' And 'Jewish, Jewish nancy boys, Jewish nancy boys!'

On the non-racial piss taking front, the Sol Campbell Arsenal affair could not go by without comment, his newfound Gunners connection led to –

'Where's your Campbell gone? Where's your Campbell gone?'/'Campbell, Campbell Champions League, Campbell Champions League.'/'Campbell is a Gooner, Campbell is a Gooner! La la la la – la la la la.' And 'There's only one Sol Campbell.'

Additionally we Millwall fans sang the following after the first game of 2007/8 on Saturday 11th August 2007 at Doncaster Rovers, returning from Doncaster station we were bundled by the Police on to a train that had both Sunderland fans and supposedly a Tottenham Hotspur 'Yid's' Firm on board returning from the Stadium of Light. Strangely, Spurs 'Firm' all got off the train early at Stevenage rather than get off it with the largish Millwall firm at Kings Cross, I cannot think why, perhaps the hiding they would get, following Millwall running the Doncaster Rovers fans inside the Keepmoat Stadium at the game and fighting the Police outside the ground.

On the train home, we Millwall sang the aforementioned – 'We've got a foreskin, we've got a foreskin, you ain't, you ain't!' and the religiously bizarre –'Allah ran From Jesus!'

Very Very Non-PC alert required apparently! – Still Tottingham FA Cup Quarter Final at White Hart Lane Sunday 12th March 2017

This game had a gamut of what Millwall are like and what we have to endure in the media/FA.

The game which we lost 6 – 0 unfortunately, had a range of sarcastic, abusive and comical chanting.

Ex-Lion Harry Kane, went down injured in first quarter of an hour and to signal that a top club and England goal scorer now, had said that his stay at Millwall whilst 18 made him what he is, to honour this we sang –

'Harry Kane He's One of Our Own!'

Delle Alli was doing the seemingly Premier League obligatory prima donna act of seeming like he was mortally wounded for any tackle and therefore pleading for every little thing to be given his way, to highlight what we thought of this Spurs and England player's antics we sang – 'Alli, Alli You're A C***!' and the European Championship specific chant 'You Let Your Country Down'

Herewith the chants that I mentioned at the start of the chapter that required a cultural expert being brought in to assess the level of racial stereotyping that the chants displayed.

167

Despite a Third Division Side reaching The Emirates FA Cup Quarter Final En route disposing of three Premier League sides including reigning Premier League Champions Leicester City all they were going on about in the Media in England be it TV or Newspapers after the match televised on BBC was the FA were investigating the racial abuse of South Korean Spurs Player Son Heung – Min because we sang our customary Asian Stereotype chant of 'DVD' and a new additional stereotypical derivative of 'He's Selling Three For A Fiver'

This alleged racial abuse must have mortified him as he only managed to score three goals, thank Christ we left out our chants about Korean dog eating restaurants otherwise he would have had to declare!!!

Strangely the fact that Spurs fans sang 'YIDS' and 'YID ARMY' all afternoon also they sang "No Noise From The Pikey Boys' at us, none of this was mentioned as racist, the YID reference ones despite there being a large Jewish Community up the road from White Hart Lane and a Jewish Carnival on that day in nearby Stamford Hill, also according to what I saw on a The Sun Twitter page Spurs sing re their South Korean player 'He'll Shoot, He'll Score, He'll Eat Your Labrador, Min Son, Min Son – Come On You Spurs'

Apparently this Asian Stereotype is not racist, presumably as they are a Premier League side who sang it, that is perfectly okay!!! Does the phrase one rule for them, one rule for us sound right?

Spurs fans seem to have nicked EIO a Millwall invented goal celebration, adapting it to YID I O, as their goal celebration, in their case to highlight their alleged Jewish routes, when I hear it on TV I always think that we could sue them from a copyright angle as a money raiser for Millwall! Worth a try!

Glad that Spurs did not YID I O each goal at this game they got six and would really have wound us up, perhaps they thought about my Copyright idea? Doubt it but just a thought.

Back to the FA Doddery Old Git Committee, does this mean that our being allegedly beastly to one player is more important to the dithery old bastards at the FA than clubs like Leyton Orient, Charlton Athletic and Coventry City being dragged in to the financial abyss by their owners in the two London Clubs case by European chairman and the midlands club by a Hedge Fund, glad that the FA have their priorities so right!!!!

To close sarcastically as it became obvious that Spurs were going to the Semi Final they sang their 'Spurs Are on Their Way to Wembley' and the customary clubs wide 'Que Sera Sera, Whatever Will Be Will Be We're Going to Wemberlee!' In sarcastic response to this we sang –

'Que Sera Sera, Whatever Will Be Will Be We're Going to Shrewsbury!'

The Laughing Policeman!

At Bournemouth on Saturday 29th November 2014 there was a black policeman, standing initially to the right-hand side of us, then he moved to the throng of Stewards and Old Bill stretched out in front of our side section, he had black gloves and dark glasses on, to make sure he knew that we had noticed him we sang –

'There's Only One Eddie Murphy!'/Eddie, Eddie Gis A Wave!' and when we made it 2 – 2 'Eddie, Eddie What's The Score?' he was smiling and laughing all the way through this that was in the latter part of the match, so Millwall are racist eh! What? He did not think so neither did the fellow Police and Stewards most of whom also laughed at these chants.

Millwall Engine Djimi Abdou!!!

I know Djimi had his own chant from the Leeds United Play Off Semi Final at Elland Road in May 2009 when he scored he got 'Djimi Abdou, etc. etc.!' but at Oldham Athletic on 25th February

2017 I heard the first rendition of the following 'We've Got Abdou, Jimmy Abdou, I Don't Think That You Understand, Super Neil's Man Who F***ing Hates West Ham, We've Got Djimi Abdou!

Non-PC alert –
Millwall Fan Is A Paedo Abuse From Reading's Mouthy Buggers At Madejski Saturday 26th October 2013

Giving it the biggun Reading fans to our right abused a bloke in our section, who my mates said appeared to be middle aged, wearing a green top and dark glasses, was the focus of their Paedo abuse presumably because he had the audacity to give them some verbal!

At one nil to them he got - 'Who's The Wanker in the Green?'/'See You On Jeremy Kyle!'/'Does She Take It Up The Arse?'/'She's Got A C*** Like A Bucket!'/'You're Shagging Your Sister'/'Paedo, Paedo what's The Score?/'You're Shagging Your Daughter!'/' You're Just A Sad Old C***!'/'Are You Saville In Disguise'/'Paedo' and 'Paedo, Paedo Give Us A Wave!' We sang to these mouthy bastards– 'Whose the Wanker In The Shorts?' and 'You Fat C***!

Very Non-PC Stereotypical Nationalities long section alert –
Soul Crew Serenades –

Herewith on a hooligan theme some exchanges with one of our perennial enemies Cardiff City -

From Them To Us –

On their various visits to the New Den the Soul Crew have sung -

'We're only here for the trouble!'/'You'll run like the rest of them!'/'Ran away!'/'You're not famous anymore!'/'Where's your famous Bushwhackers?'/'Bushwhackers, wank, wank, wank!' And

'You're too scared to come to Wales!'

The above relate to their alleged Hoolie victory in Cardiff a few years back, the last chant was particularly relevant for any sheep in the crowd I believe!

Finally they also sang the following charming Welsh style song at home against us the last time we played them 'Harold Shipman Is Our Friend He Kills English!'

From Us To Them –

In response we have sung numerous chants for example in the League Cup at home on 21st August 2001 the East Upper sang to the Bluebird Boys – 'Shit team no firm!'

There was also a rare rendition of an old classic to the Men of Harlech tune that went something like –

'Men of Swansea f*** their Mothers, Men of Newport f*** their Brothers, Men of Cardiff f*** each other – f*** off back to Wales!'

Alternatively –

Men of Swansea f*** their Brothers, Men of Cardiff f*** their Mothers, all the rest have f***ed each

other – f*** off back to Wales!'

Your choice!

In addition to these 'firm' chants we always sing about sheep abusing, dragon inserting, etc as listed in my other Millwall books, to the Welsh, we also sing further minor state and World Cup loss chants, for example.

Regarding the Welsh's supposed third world country persona we sang –'You're only here for asylum!' And not forgetting a chant referring to England's 2 – 0 World Cup Qualifier win over Wales we sang –'We're the famous England and we're going to Germany!' And '2 nil to the Engerland!'

Against them in March 2011 on the final day of the 2011 Six Nations Rugby, with England top of the table they got 'Engerland'/'God Save The Queen' and 'Swing Low Sweet Chariot'.

Not Cardiff City bit in addition our other Welsh enemies Swansea City sang to us – 'Where's Your Football Factory?' And 'Where

Were You In World War 2?' The first one's backdrop is en route to the CBL end outside of the ground including the Railway arches, what the second chant was about I have no idea, very strange.

Back to the Bluebirds at the new Cardiff City stadium 25th September 2010, we sang 'I'd rather be a Paki than a Taff!' Racist I know but in addition to 'You can stick your f***ing dragon up your arse!' and 'Ingerlund Ingerlund Ingerlund' it had to be said to the English hating Welsh.

Closing on Cardiff City at the games at New Den on 19th March 2011 there was one of the strangest incidents I have ever seen, when the Taffs took the initial lead against us in the game that ended 3 – 3.

One of their fans Ryan Oliver plummeted on to the lower tier from the upper tier, it was like a scene out of Casualty's Christmas Special, with umpteen medical staff treating him for umpteen minutes on the North Stand lower stairwell, see the story of what happened in the last part of this section.

At the game to help the patients recovery we sang –

'Suicide!'/''He (She/You) Fell Over!' and 'Let Him Die, Let Him Die, Let Him Die!' from CBL.

From West and Dockers Stand when we went 2 – 1 up '2 – 1 and you lost a fan!'/'2 -1 and your mate is dead – jump!' and 'Cardiff is a shithole you might as well jump!'/'Crippled and a long way home!' and 'He's going home in a London Ambulance!'

When they scored again to tie the score 2 – 2 we in CBL shouted 'Jump!'and as he obviously never jumped we sang 'You Only Jump When You're Winning!'

When we got a late equaliser to make it 3 – 3 we sang ' You're Not Jumping Anymore!'

The story of Cardiff City fan Ryan Oliver –

He called Millwall in the week after the incident, thanking the Millwall medical staff for saving his life, it transpired that he confirmed that it was nobody else's fault apart from his own, he had his foot on the tier wall, it slipped and he plunged to earth, he was really really lucky, as he landed on a seat which he split in half, this saved him from severe injury as it broke his fall, he was also very fortuitous that he did not land on two very young ball people, a boy and girl, who were sitting there on the empty lower tier totally not expecting a grown man to suddenly emerge from above, he actually only broke a couple of fingers, bruised his ribs and had whiplash, if he had landed on the concrete he would have been lucky to survive intact or in truth at all!

In this game Cardiff City fans smashed up the North Stand toilets and broke 86 seats, not mentioned much strangely, so must have been our fault somehow, probably Millwall poltergeists!!!

The following Season in our last home game pre Christmas on 10th December 2011, the Taffs return was greeted with – 'Jump Jump Jump!'/'You'll jump and you know you will!'/'You might as well jump!' and 'You'll jump in a minute!'.

I thought that we missed a trick though we should have requested Van Halen's 'Jump' from Les, also the bloke jumped well fell last time after they scored, did the song 'You'll jump in a minute!' imply they would score? Eek!!!! They did sing 'We Only Jump When We're Winning!' Told you it was bad singing that to them!!!!!

They also sang Band Aid's 'Do They Know it's Christmas' song adapted like this –

'Feed Millwall – Let Them Know It's Christmas Time' which we have sung before to Swansea City who are Fat Bastards according to Cardiff City

At the return game on 31st March 2012 in now their soulless identity kit Stadium they sang 'Is That All You Take Away!' to which we replied 'Go Home and F*** Some Sheep!'

To their 'We Are Cardiff City We Are Top of the League!' chant we sang –'You Are All Welsh C***s!'

Pre match and early in the game highlighting the Cardiff City fan falling out of the upper tier at The New Den, we sang –'You Might As Well Jump!' and 'You're Gonna Jump In A Minute !'

And as Cardiff fans left early in droves we sang – 'Is There a Fire Drill?' At the next match at the New Den Saturday 25th October

2014, we sang 'Suicide' a chant referring to the fall from the Upper Tier of the North Stand of Ryan Oliver in the 3 – 3 game, we also sung the customary to any country dwellers– 'Sheep, Sheep, Sheep Shaggers!'

Humorously in response to this the Cardiff City fans there sang – 'We Know What We Are – Sheep Shagging Bastards – We Know What We Are!'

I loved the honest sarcasm of this response, made all the more cheerful for me as we won 1 – 0 SHITTU stylee!

Very Very Non-PC very long Section alert – We All Hate Leeds And Leeds And Leeds, Leeds And Leeds And Leeds And Leeds, Leeds and Leeds And Leeds! We All F***ing Hate Leeds!
Our Pigeon Fancying, Mushy Pea Noshing, Cloth Cap Wearing, Whippet Worrying Yorkshire Chums Lengthy Section –

My first visit to Elland Road a trip on Sunday December 19th 2004 was naturally a volatile encounter.

For the record I travelled on a club coach that had as part of its entertainment a video featuring the BBC's 'Panorama', Channel 4's 'No One Likes Us' documentary, followed by news footage of the Luton riot, trouble at Manchester United, Bristol City and Southampton from the 1980s and the Derby Play – Off riot and the Chelsea FA Cup trouble from Stamford Bridge in the 1990s.It set us up nicely for our trip to West Yorkshire!

There were plenty of exchanges between the fans during the game, I thought I'd list a few for you.

For info our next trip to the following season to T'Yorkshire's Revie glory hole, when we bought food at the in-ground refreshment stalls we were not allowed to have any plastic cutlery to eat the food with, presumably in case we decided to attack the Yorkshre folk with the lethal plastic!, bizarre, moving on to chants from my first trip there.

From Them To Us –

'Come in a taxi, you must have come in a taxi!' And 'Taxi for Millwall!'

To our couple of thousand travelling fans, it would have to have been a bloody big Taxi!

When they took a lead late in the first half they also sang their 'big' club chant

'One nil in your Cup Final!'

From Us To Them –

In response to the above we replied with the honest – 'Three nil in our Cup Final!'

The Man Utd FA Cup Final defeat at the Millenium Stadium.

Additionally when ex Leeds Player Jody Morris equalised late in the game we sang –

'One-one in your Cup Final!'

Peter Ridsdale–

'There's only one Peter Ridsdale!' And 'Where's the money gone? Where's the money gone?'

Fallen giant abuse–

'Champions League (Championship)? You're having a laugh!'

Some observations to Leeds fans sitting near the away section, to start the customary –

'Who's the wanker in the hat?'

To a trappy home fan and his good lady we sang – 'Does she take it up the a…?'

In response men around him nodded vigourously. We also sang 'Your bird is an ugly c…!'

Yorkshire Ripper –

'Did The Ripper f*** your Mum?'/'Did The Ripper Rape your Mum?' and 'One Peter Sutcliffe, There's only one Peter Sutcliffe!'

At The Play Off Semi Final on May 14th 2009 2nd Leg at Elland

Road we sang – 'Karen Matthews Is Your Mum!'

Relating to the Mother who kidnapped her own daughter with an accomplice and was based in the Leeds area.

The following chants are old hat I know but we had not played them for years so it had to be done -

Istanbul murder flavoured abuse – 'Always look out for Turks carrying knives!'/'Where were you in Istanbul?'/'You're not famous anymore!' And ''Galatasaray!'

At the Play Off Semi Final away in May 2009 in addition to the above we sang –

'You Let Your Country Down!'

By their not doing the Turkish fans I assume?

In October 2008 they apparently complained about us singing the chants above at home, which we continually did, strange as they sing 'Munich' re the 1958 Munich Aircrash to Man Utd, they sang 'Aberfan' about the South Wales 1966 Primary School Children Coal mining disaster to Cardiff City, etc, etc. They also sang 'Ferencvaros' to us, where there were several Millwall stabbed there, so they have no excuse for being offended at all in my opinion,

On a similar tack to above there was great animosity shown in the media etc after the home game with Leeds United in the following season on 24th October 2009, when a Millwall section in the East Upper had a bloke dressed in a Galatasray shirt, what the press etc did not mention was the fact that Leeds United in the upper North stand waved a large Hungarian flag, the purpose of both things was the same to highlight the damage received by both sides fans, so why not mention both?

Highlighting another reason for their having no excuse for our being offensive to them, re the two Leeds's fans murdered in Istanbul in the Champion's League v Galatasaray.

Following the death of George Best, we played Leeds United at the New Den and their fans sang –

'We hate Man U and we hate Man U, we are the Man U haters!' Throughout the pre Match 'silence' prompting the referee to truncate the minutes silence early, we naturally called them scum, which those chanting were in my opinion.

We sang 'You're just a town full of bombers!' not strictly accurate but Bradford and Dewsbury are close enough I suppose.

In the game at the New Den on Saturday 9th April 2011, the next home game after the Cardiff City one mentioned before this section, in the Leeds United game that we won 3 – 2 there was some marvellous stuff on display in the crowd and vocally.

We also sang ' You might as well go home, you might as well go home, you might as well f*** off!' adapted to 'you might as well jump!' and another chant at them when they were behind 'Jump Jump Jump!' as listed for Cardiff visit in December 2011 above.

Leeds fans threw umpteen bottles and some seats I believe in to The Dockers Stand aka East Stand, apparently due to their waving Turkish cards and Galatasaray references to t'northerners, one bottle was thrown at Leeds' keeper, who insisted on giving it to the ref, which was nice of him, see the story of his day below. I dare say that every bottle thrown be it from us or our Oop North chums it will be or fault, no matter what! Oops my Millwall paranoia has bubbled to the surface again!

Top of the people in glass houses delusional chart is Captain Birdseye aka then Leeds United Chairman Ken Master Blaster Bates, after this game, when he launched his attack on us in an interview utilising his speciality maximum biased blinkered vision. He castigated Millwall fans for abuse regarding the Galatasaray murders of two Leeds United fans in Istanbul, when minature turkish flags were waved, throat slitting gestures were made and 'Istanbul' and 'Always Look Out For Turks Carrying Knives' fillled the air, there was also a St George's flag that said something like 'Leeds Is A Shithole You Might As Well Jump' relating back to the Cardiff City upper tier plunger the previous home game.

Whilst all of this did happen, the great bearded one conveniently forgot that Leeds United fans definitely threw bottles and other missiles in to The Dockers Stand to their left before the game, he also forgets the Ferencvaros stabbing chants and Hungarian flag from previous games against them at the New Den. Their apparent chants about the death at the police's hands of Millwall fan Ian Tomlinson at G20 at the flag flashing game on St Georges Day at Millwall,. Not forgetting their Munich 58 chants and grafitti v Man Utd regarding the Munich air crash, also the fact that George Best's Minutes silence was at a game v them at the New Den when their pigeon fancying, whippet worrying, cloth cap wearing contingent chanted anti Man Utd stuff all through it, forcing the Referee to have to abandon the Minutes silence, they sang 'Aberfan' about the South Wales 1966 Primary School Children Coal mining disaster to Cardiff City as I mentioned previously. Isn't blinkered stupidity a marvellous thing,

Returning to Master Bates, he also said he hoped they did not play us again, 'why is that Ken because you very very very rarely ever beat us, especiallly aI the New Den?'

Moving on to the T'Leeds next visit to New Den on Saturday 24th March 2012, the one among them who had learnt how to write had produced a large hand daubed coloured ink banner that they briefly unfurled that said something like 'Millwall have only got one song – Wankers' referring to plethora of Galatasaray abuse that they get I think, doubt it referred to 'No One Likes Us' because if it did 'Marching On Together' anyone?

When they also sang during the game 'Where were you at Elland Road?' to the West Lower contingent in particular I think, in response we in the CBL sang –'You Let Your Friends Down!' and the previously mentioned 'Where Were You In Istanbul?' and at another visit in September 2013 Millwall sang 'You Left Your Mates To Die!'

One thing I would like to mention to our whippet molesting chums in response to their enquiry, when we travel to their domain, games are often played in midweek, we have to buy vouchers to meet the Yorkshire police at Woolley Edge services on Junction 38 on the M1 before we get given our tickets in return for the voucher, consequently people are f***ing fed up with the palaver, so the northern plods masterplan must be working as it has been in place for umpteen visits to their northern paradise

However when they come to London there are no such restrictions, like their having to meet the London filth at South Mimms services on M25 or some such masterstroke, in fact the only restrictions are when the Police deny us access to parts around our own ground, like the Millwall Café or Club Shop by closing down Bolina and Zampa Roads, meaning we have to go all around the houses to park and get in to our own ground.

Sorry I forgot Leeds are a big Premiership Champions League level club so deserve the best service, where as we are nobodies in Police eyes, yeah righto are they and do they b***ocks!

This Old Bill Voucher system was still in operation for the clash at Leeds United on 22nd March 2014, Wall fans at Barnsley on 22nd February 2014 sang this appreciation of the Yorkshire plods prowess –

'West Yorkshire Coppers You Ain't Got A Clue!'

True enough but their brilliant plan has stopped us travelling as numerously as we would have, so job done for those scumbags!

Another trip to T'Leeds the Circus/Funfair Valentine's Day at Elland Road game on Saturday 14th February 2015

'Hello lass it's Valentine's Day, fancy a go on Dodgems at Elland Road?'

I don't remember anyone asking their lady this on Millwall coach, but it obviously had to be prerequisite oop north, we met the Security Dingles at Wooley Edge on the M1, to swap our vouchers, for our beloved match tickets, we were then held on the coach for an unnecessary 20 minutes or so, presumably so that we could sit on our coach and fully taking the pleasures of the jewel of the north T'Leeds, T'United.

We were escorted in by plod motorcyclists, to find that since my last visit for the Play Off Semi Final that they had moved the away section to the opposite side of the land of milk and honey or is that delusional living in imaginary past Whippet Worrying fan base! I think it is the second, moving on, it is always an adventure following the Wall, and today was a real surprise, the plod drove us to our away section through a funfair, if you don't believe me, a little further below is a photo that I took out of the upper tier window refreshment bar where as you will see, from the Kings Ferry Double Decker coach, was where we had been plonked.

As we were getting off someone on our coach said – 'Don't forget to take all your stuff with you, don't leave anything on here, this place must be full of pikeys, so as soon as we go in, they will ransack the coach!'

Enjoying the reality of our parking space on my way to away end I was almost arrested for greeting the locals with a customary Milllwall greeting – 'Nice To See You Are Here You Northern C***S, Happy New Year!'

An elderly Northern Police Officer then came running towards me, grabbed me, told me to stop trying to pull away, and he said 'A Bit Old For Effing and Jeffing arent you, if I hear you swear again, I will arrest you!'

I was about to say 'Righto you northern c***! Do NOT follow me in to the ground, as I have to f***ig swear watching the Wall!' But thankfully my brain went in to shut the F*** up mode, and I was able to get in to the ground, having gotten to the bar. Herewith a lovely picture I took on my mobile from the window there to prove that I am not making this funfair scenario up -

Moving on to the fun and games inside Elland Road, we only had a couple of hundred fans there, aside from some Wall being stuck in the M1 and M40 serious road accidents, this aside it was largely due to the long running palaver for Millwall fans only of the Voucher system, which for those who do not know, is a massive restriction, for example if you flew to Leeds/Bradford Airport or went on a train to Leeds, to say spend sometime in a hotel up there, you would still have to go to Wooley Edge Services, to swop your voucher for a ticket, because the northern Plod, think we are that much of a threat that you cannot simply pick up your away tickets at Elland Road! I am sure that then employed Andy Ambler had checked this out, but doesn't this sodding infringement impinge our human rights! On to the abuse, sorry pleasantries ....

Them To Us –

'F***ing Embarrassing!'/'Must Have Come In A Taxi!' and 'Is That All You Take Away ?'

Us To Them –

'Stick Your F***ing Vouchers Up You're A***!'

A chant pointing out why we were so thin on the ground, because of the Police enforced Voucher for ticket performance,.

Not that they would hear me, but I did shout at the Leeds Fans abusing us, 'Have you ever heard of the Police restrictions you northern B***ards!' I also mentioned the fact that they would absolutely love all the shit we have to go through the northern c***s!!

Us To Them –

'He's One of your own, he's one of your own – Jimmy Saville he's one of your own!'/'Jimmy Saville F***ed Your Mum He's Your

Father!' and 'Jimmy Saville He's probably your dad!'

Them To Us –

In response to this Saville abuse they sang 'Frank Maloney He Might Be Your Dad!' and 'Kellie Maloney he's one of your own!' In relation to ex Boxing Promoter Frank Maloney a male Millwall fan who now wanted to be a lady!

I would like to point out how delusional these whippet fiddlers are they were singing – 'We Are the Champions, The Champions of Europe!' really when was that then?

They also sang 'There's Only One Billy Bremner!' that is as maybe, but he died in 1997!

Finally, then ex Lion Steve Morrison played for them and they sang 'Steve Morrison, Steve Morrison, Steve Morrison' in response to their homage we sang to the same tune 'He's F***ing Shit, He's F***ing Shit!'

Ah this section is getting quite long but herewith some more We All F***ing Hate Leeds! our Pigeon Fancying, Mushy Pea Noshing, Cloth Cap Wearing, Whippet Worrying chums

Continuing The Leeds Section Herewith The Cloth Cap Whippet Worriers Paedo File Collection

Yorkshire Paedo Jimmy Saville Leeds United front, at the New Den on Sunday 18th November 2012, we sang – 'Jimmy Saviile is your Dad!'/'Jimmy Saville F***ed your Mum!'/'He's Under Your Bed!' and finally a full ground Milllwall crowd chant to the gathered Yorkshire folk –

'He's one of your own, he's one of your own – Jimmy Saville – He's one of your own!'

Which shut them up big time, apparently it said on HOF that In response T'Leeds sang –

'He Shags Who He Wants, He Shags Who He Wants, He's Jimmy Saville He Shags Who He Wants!'

Not now he don't he is dead. F*** me praising a paedo because we had the audacity to be abusive about him, talk about Yorkshire shit, don't know about Yorkshire grit.

I did not imagine this I actually saw a video of them singing it filmed at Elland Road, now if that does not prove that they have the morals of a Serial Child Molestor, I don't know what does and our anti Saville chants are abusive? Really I would rather be abusive to the sick C*** than think his being a celebrity from your area means he can do what the F*** he wants to anyone of any age, if that is your perception I think you should seek psychiatric help now!

When they played again at the New Den on 28th September 2013 in a game Millwall won 2-0 there was a huge additional collection of Paedo chants – they got the 'He's One Of Your Own!' from the whole ground again, plus the other ones previously listed but there were loads of new ones at this game they got -

'You're Just a Town Full of Nonces!'/'You're Just a Club Full of Nonces!'/'Your Support Loves F***ing Kids!'/' You Sleep With Your Neighbours Kids!'/'You're Going Home on a School Bus!'/'You're Going Home with Rolf Harris!' another celebrity who was an accused child abuser, at the time, pre-sentencing.

At 2 – 0 to Millwall they got 'Two Nil and a Bag of Sweets!' And 'Can You Hear The Paedos Sing? No, No!'

In closing in this game after a miss the Leeds United player got – 'You're Shit and a Paedophile!'

Continuing the theme at the Yorkshire folk's next trip to the New Den on 9th August 2014,which coincidentally was also a 2 – 0 Lions victory, throughout game, they got some of the above and some new ones –

'You're A Paedo – That's What You Do!' in a Danny Shittu chant skit,

'Saville's been in Your Home!' and continually 'Saville F***Ed You're Mum – He's Your Dad!'

More broadly to T'Leeds folk – 'You're Shit and Northern C***S!'

In response to the latter Leeds sang to us – 'You're Just a Town Full of Bastards!'

A bit harsh Northerners, we were deeply mortified!

The most recent and best away game ever -

183

Elland Road Leeds United 20th January 2018 Millwall's 4000th League Match we won!!!

A real game of 2 halves we are 2 – 0 up, have a goal disallowed as well and they have a man sent off in first half, start of second half they get 3 goals, we then get 2 late goals and win 4 -3!!

A lot of Millwall abuse to the Marching on Together Scarf twirling Northerners all around us.

Our connecting Jimmy Saville with Leeds fans led too –

'No Noise from the Paedophiles!'/'Who's The Paedo in the Blue?'/'Can You Hear The Paedos Sing? No No!'/'you're Just a Town Full of Nonces!'/'Wave Your Scarf If You're A Nonce!'/'Paedo, Paedo What's The Score?'

One Real original in response to their We All Love Leeds chant we adapted it to 'You All Touch Kids – You All Touch Kids!'

Then with us winning away for what could be our first away win in 2017/2018 season –

'How Shit Must You Be we're Winning Away!' and 'We Scored Two Goals You Must be Shit' We gave them 3 – 2 and you f***ed it up at 3 -3 but were going mental after 4th so did not get t that one.

Non-PC alert –
Paedo Abuse Moves South To The Cottage Saturday 16th August 2014

The week after the Leeds United victory at The Old Den listed above we played at Fulham for the first time since April 1999, where we had around 5000 or so Real Wall, and the support was fantastic having finished the true reflection on what Millwall support is, on to the Paedo Chant, in connection to Fulham's former chairman Al Fayed's connection with the King Of Pop who had a statue erected outside the Cottage, he was our paedo target for today, we sang 'Michael Jackson F***ed Your Mum, F***ed Your Mum, F***ed Your Mum, Michael Jackson F***ed Your Mum, He's Your Father!' and

'Michael Jackson He's One Of Your Own!

At the home return v Fulham at the New Den on Saturday 21st February 2015 we sang a more bizarre variation on the King of Pop chant – 'Michael Jackson F***ed Your Son, F***ed Your Son, F***ed Your Son, Michael Jackson F***ed Your Son, He's Your Uncle!'

Following Ian Holloway's caustic comments about his perception of disgraceful abuse of T 'Yorkshire folk the week before, we sang – 'We Are Millwall We Sing What We Want, We Sing What We Want!'

As a play on our Jimmy Saville Paedo Leeds abuse, at a time when middle aged/old Millwall fan Boxing Promoter Frank Maloney announced that he was going to have gender reassignment and changed his name to Kellie, we sang the sarcastic –'Frank Maloney He's One of Our Own!'

Paedo abuse seems to have become our Bet Noir; I said to some Wall as we walked through Bishops Park back to Putney Bridge Tube, 'We are going to run out of Paedos to abuse. I would be amazed if we could find enough famous Nonces to link with every club that we played!'

To be honest whoever started the link the paedo to our opponents chants would need a lot of internet research, and they would get banged up as one of them as they would assume the researcher was looking for fellow Nonces, best vary our abuse I think, we seem quite capable of that, but just thought I would mention my concerns!

This is not at Fulham or Paedo just a celebrity who always announces who he supports one, when we played Bolton Wanderers at the New Den on Friday 19th December 2014 we sang – 'Peter Kay F***ed Your Mum – He's Your Father!

Non-PC alert –
Paedophilia Abuse Goes Back To Its Yorkshire Hotbed Up – Rotherham Place Where 1400 Children Were Abused Sexually over a 16 Year Period and Largely Ignored by Police and Authorities, at the quaintly named New York Stadium –

On Saturday 28th February 2015, we visited the home of the worst Child Sex Scandal aka Rotherham, at the new stadium of Rotherham United New York Stadium, as 1400 were the estimated figure to have been sexual groomed by Muslims over 16 years I thought that The Jimmy Saville Memorial Stadium was more apt!

Still moving on it was a 6 pointer Relegation game there were 1309 of us there.

As it was our first trip to Rotherham since the paedophile scandal erupted, naturally apart from our loud vocal support of the Wall, we abused the home fans to the left and right of us, to highlight the repertoire, to start some standards –'Sex Case Sex Case Hang Him Hang Him Hang Him!'/'He's One of Your Own – Jimmy Saville He's One of Your Own!'/'You Sleep With Your Sisters Kids!'/'Jimmy Saville F***Ed Your Mum He's Your Father!' And 'Paedos, Paedos, Paedos!'

The new stuff specific to the Child Sex abuse scandal –

'You Let Your Children Down!'/'You Let Your Daughters Down!'/'You're Just a Town Full of Nonces!'/'Town Full Of Paedophiles!'/'You're Just a Town Full of Paedos!' and the best one 'You Knew, And You Did F*** All!'

The hard Yorkshire men prats to the left and right of us seemed to be pleased that we were insulting their town and them; in fact I am sure I heard 'There's only one Jimmy Saville!'

I think that they were abusing someone in our end who they had also accused by singing 'Are You Saville In Disguise!' either way, we took their lippyness badly, and surged through the netting on either side of our stand, strangely their heroism faded rapidly when they realised that Wall were serious and on their toes they went, only for some of their heroism to return when the South Yorkshire Police waded in truncheons flying, realising that the old bill were doing their job for them

At Rotherham United for next away visit there on Sunday 26th August 2018 they got the additional -'Paedophiles Paedophiles Paedophiles!'/'You Only Sing When Your Grooming!' and 'Who's the Paedo With The Drum?'

Individually Rotherham United fan Barry Chuckles of The Chuckle Brothers who passed away in 2018 got – 'Barry Chuckles Sex Offender!' And 'Barry Chuckles He's One Of Your Own!' in a Jimmy Saville Leeds United stylee

Not Rotherham but their posher brothers from up the road at Dean Henderson Sheffield United's loanee from Man U goalkeeper in match v Millwall at Brammall Lane on 13th April 2019, received a deluge of abuse for an alleged porn type pictures he sent to a 14 year old girl, guilty or otherwise he got – 'F....ing Paedo!'/'Paedophile, Paedophile!'/'Paedo'/'Nonce!' and the old favourite 'Sex Case Sex Case Hang Him Hang Him Hang Him!

I love to go a Wandering a Treat them mean to keep them keen day at Molineux Saturday 12.15am 2nd May 2015

Back to earlier games v Wolverhampton Wanderers before I start I'd just like to say that the Wolves chant

'We Are Wolves' always sounds like 'Millwall, Millwall, Millwall' to me and I get confused, mind you for me it is easily done.

In the final game of the 2014/5 season and the first official Neil Harris game at Kenny Jackett's Wolverhampton Wanderers in the week following our relegation to League 1, first the chants.

Them To Us –

Early on in the game as former Lion Kenny Jackett was Wolves manager they sang the original 'Kenny Jackett is a Wolf, is a Wolf, Is a Wolf f*** off Millwall!' and the highly unoriginal 'You're Going Down, You're Going Down, You're Going Millwall's Going Down!'

Us To Them –

That we warmly applauded and EIOd, we also sang the sarcastic, won't insult us chant 'Going Down, Going Down Going Down!'/'We are Going Down Say We are going down!' and 'Que Sera, Sera Whatever will be will be we're going to Shrewsbury!'

As it became apparent from other scores that Wolves would not be in the Play Offs we sang -

'You are staying down, say you are staying down!'

The chants continued as they went in to a 3 – 1 lead they sang 'We only need three more!' due to Goal Difference as they went in to this lead.

In response following our getting a second we sarcastically sang 'You only need 4 more!'

Wolves won 4 – 2 but due to other results did not reach the Play Offs.

So with the chants over I will move on to the OTT police exercise that this game was –

Dave, Paul, Nathan Simms and I drove to Wolverhampton and arrived a bit early, so were amongst the first ones there when we approached the Stewards outside the away block in the Steve Bull stand lower tier, the stewards asked us to show them Season Tickets or MSC cards to prove who we were, OTT or what, if anyone knew Millwall's ticketing policy they would have known that we had tickets that we had needed proof i.e. Teamcard or MSC card to purchase with in the first place, so what was the genius behind this plan?

As we were going in Dave Simms, Paul and Nathan's Dad as our elder statesman, asked the Stewards if the needing club-based proof was for everyone? The steward answered no only for you and Leeds!

We said really? Now there is surprising!

When got in to the ground following the full body search, and approaching the Refreshment we found that they had blocked up all the Alcohol points!

Also the Policing was over manned on a grand scale, I have seen trouble at Molineux several times, and I assume that as we could conceivable have had a game where Wall had to win to survive relegation hence an invading Wall army, the Police had instigated a full Robocop/Running Man policing strategy whilst this was still a possibility, sadly not so, as we had been relegated on the Tuesday before this final game of the season, one question – is Police policy chiseled in stone and therefore like the Ten Commandments can never be changed?

Before the end of the game we were effectively kettled by Police and Stewards inside the ground right the way along the Steve Bull Stand that we occupied and it was announced to Millwall's fans that there would be restrictions around the ground at the end of the game, no shit! Although we were not kept in when we got outside we found gates to stairwells to the right of us leading towards Wolves main stand and the Molineux Subway were shut off and manned by stewards, and exits to the left of us towards the Wolves Stan Cullis stand had a huge wall in place, I mean Berlin Wall scaled replica as did the road to our left hand side and behind us so we could go nowhere, consequently we were forced to march up a steep street hill in front of us, to get on to a road that we could get on to try to find Paul's car, which was parked behind the Billy Wright stand on the opposite side of the ground.

I did point out to the kindly West Midlands plod that if you treat people like shit you are liable to create not stop trouble, strangely I had no response to this from the boys in blue! For their successful wasting Midlands populaces money escapade.

Moving back to events seasons before this game –

In April 2002, at the New Den the away fans were invited to a post-match 'discussion' outside.'Hooligans' TV star Lenny and his

'Subway Army'/'Yim Yam Army' chums were asked the following – 'Will we see you in the street?'

From them to us –

I thought I'd list just a few exchanges from our ignominious exit from the FA Cup 3rd round at Molineux a few years back and the Championship game at the New Den in January 2005 -

'FA (UEFA) Cup? You're having a laugh!'/'You've Never Won F.. All!'/'We hate Cockneys and we hate Cockneys, we are the Cockney haters!' And 'F… off back to London!'

From us to them –

'Premiership? You're having a laugh! And 'Hungary we had a laugh!'

Wolves then manager Glenn Hoddle was targeted –

'Glenn Hoddle?You're having a laugh!'/'You've got that c… Hoddle!'/'Glenn Hoddle sex offender!'/'Hoddle is a weirdo!' And 'Hoddle, Hoddle give us a hymn!'

This was followed by a bizarre CBL rendition of 'All things bright and beautiful'.

Hair Today Gone Tomorrow

Fleetwood Town away Easter Monday 17th April 2017, there were several Wall chaps adorned with what looked like a range of Jason Price Black Curly Perm wigs, at half time a young groundsman with a fork poked about in front of our terraced end in the goal mouth. He had black curly perm haired like Kevin Keegan in his prime, so in honour from our Wall bewigged choir he received – 'Wiggy Wiggy Wiggy!' and 'You've Got A Wig On, Your One Of Our Own!'

Then having considered again they sang –

'Give Us Our Wig Back You're Not One Of Us!'

Bradford City!!

In a Muslim Terrorist/Yorkshire vein MFC sang at early Afghanistan War time – 'You Ran From The Taliban!'.

Politically re Muslim radicals we have never sung 'Let's Go Fundamental!' instead of 'Let's Go F***ing Mental!' Just a thought!

Moving away from Islam when then League 1 Bradford City played at the New Den on 3rd January 2015 in the 3rd of the FA Cup they took a 2 – 1 lead and started going in to the greatest Team the world have ever seen bollocks, with typical Lions gallows humour we sang in the Docklands Upper – 'You're Nothing Special We Lose Every Week!'

This was the end of a week when we had just plummeted to third from bottom of the Championship and were seemingly in couldn't hit a cows arse with a banjo form!

There's Been A Burnley!

When we visited Turf Moor 25th February 2012, for what was our second consecutive win with 3 goals scored there, to remind the locals that they were Northern and not Southern like us we sang –

'Der Der Da Der Northern Monkeys!' and 'Sit down you Northern C***s!'

Call For A Priest I Need The Last Rites! The Mortally Wounded Players Who Writhe In Agony Syndrome

I know that this is prevalent in modern British football, especially since the foreigner influx, that said Kenny Dalgleish and Franny Lee!!!!! This was in a game at the New Den on Saturday 12th April 2014 v Watford, managed by Italian Giuseppe Sannino, when Ikechi Anya, laid on the floor writhing in agony in front on the CBL on two occasions we naturally gave him –

'Let Him Die, Let Him Die, Let Him Die!' and 'W***er, W***er, W***er!' and the original 'There's Nothing Wrong With You, There's Nothing Wrong With You!'

Whether Anya was mortally wounded like he appeared to be or his ears were burning I don't know because in the first half he was substituted, and he walked off, perhaps he was a Zombie?

Or had to either shoot off to Guys ICU or to The Old Vic Theatre for his afternoon acting class!!

I would just like it noted that I was given The Last Rites twice when I was in a Coma following my Brain Injury, as I was sparko I don't remember if I writhed about as the Professionals do, or don't you have to if what you have is real?

We've Got A F***ing Big Ostrich!

Continuing the Watford players seeming ethos of I am mortally wounded in the game mentioned above when another Watford player lie in a heap face down in the six yard box in front of the CBL after a collision from a cross with his own goal keeper Almunia and our Austrian Giant Stefan Maierhofer it was not a foul but the player whose name escapes me, because I was bored stiff with the Watford writhing mentality to be bothered to look it up in the programme, we sang –

'Don't F*** With The Austrian! Don't F*** With The Austrian! Don't F*** With The Austrian!'

Continuing our Stefan theme in the next game at Middlesbrough on 19th April 2014 our 6ft 7in Austrian turned goal machine and it launched a few specific chants to highlight his two goals, one the title of this section, well that is what it sounded like initially around me but was –'We've Got A F***ing Big Austrian!'

He also got – 'Feed The Hof And He Will Score!' as I am sure you know a revised version of Man City's Shaun Goater 'Feed The Goat' chant' Sadly this was not true!

At the next game v Doncaster Rovers on Monday 21st April 2014 Maierhofer got 'Hof, Hof, Hof!'

'Infamous FA Cup trip to KC Stadium – That's The Way I Like It!' Is it Bollocks!

The home fans sang 'We Are Hull' which sounded very much like –'Millwall, Millwall, Millwall' to me, like it did regarding the Wolves chant, I got very confused, it is easily done as I am quite mad!

Apart from the alleged Millwall 'Riot' inside the ground or whatever it was wrongly called, there were a lot of chants going between the London and Northern fans.

From Us To Them –

At the end of the match to the home fans who had been giving it large all game behind their Riot Police and Steward Lines, we sang the customary 'You'll Run and you know you will!'/'We Can See You Sneaking Out! And a new version chant – 'Let's See How Brave You Are!' i.e a derivative of the olden day chant 'We'll See You All Outside!' Which we didn't, not a soul!

It was pretty much nearly all Credit Crunch/Recession era social abuse, particularly as it was played the day after the UK actually being in recession had been confirmed in the media, for we old Lions the abuse dated back to the 1980s trips to merseyside, there was money note waving, i.e. a renewal of Harry Enfield's Loadsamoney and there were social depravation chants regarding the supposed North South divide, we sang –'You're Skint and you know you are!'/'Loads and Loads of Money!'/'We pay your Benefits!'/'We've got loads of money!'/'Does The social know you're here?' and the golden oldie chant usually aimed at the Scousers, where new words are used over Liverpool's 'You'll Never Walk Alone' theme tune – 'Sign On, Sign On, with a pen in your hand and you'll never get a job, you'll never get a job!'

From Them To Us –

'You're Going Home To Your Shithole!'

London is a Shithole is it,? In what Tykes' Der Brain is this considered correct?

During our drive through Hull it looked like we had stumbled on Dagenham from my observation of it and that is hardly Xanadu is it! – 'You're only here to see the Tigers'/'You're only here for Hull'

Wrong, I myself thought as Millwall were playing there I might get up in the middle of the night to venture umpteen bloody miles north so I did, not to specifically watch your bloody team trust me!

'You're not English Anymore!' What? at least I think that is what they sang, difficult for a Cockney like me to decipher a chant in their unintelligible local dialect!

Regarding our 2 – 0 defeat to the home Premier League side they sang the very old chant

'1 nil in your Cup Final'/'2 nil in you Cup Final' and 'You're not very good, etc Shit!'

Wrong to first and 2nd chant and to the 3rd chant neither were you!!

This was a new chant that I had not heard before a derivation from the losing score followed by it's a long way home chant – 'All this way for nothing!'

Finally a specific big cat Tigers v Lions comparison chant – 'You got mauled by the Tigers!'

Non – PC Alert
Sarfend United Essex Girl stereotype

At Roots Hall on Friday 21st August 2009, there was a green bedecked home fan in the stand to our right who seemed to be giving it the big one, in response he got the customary – 'Who's the wanker in the green?'

He also got the Essex Girl stereotypical 'Your Mum is an Essex slag!'

Sarfend Away Again The Local Lads Stereotype Time Now Plus A Bit For The Ladies – Monday 28th December 2015, Wall Won 4-0!!!

Today it seemed like there had been some intensive chant writing over Christmas, and a perfect collection to show that Millwall fans are the worst people you should give it large to, unless you're a masochist!

To prove that Downton Abbey isn't big at Millwall to mouthy git in stand to our right with a lady was greeted with and then asked – 'You Midget C*** You Midget C**t!' and 'Have You Ever Seen Your Dick?'

Then regarding his companion he got 'Does She Take It up the Arse?'

To which he implied that she did, so when another Essex Boy emerged the first one got 'You're Getting Dumped in the Morning!'

The lady herself got 'We Can Smell Your C**t From Here!' and implying she was a cheap prossie –

'She's only £2 An Hour!' Then when she disappeared her first lover man got -'She's Getting Rumped in the Toilet!' and when she emerged again she got 'You're A Dirty C***, You're A Dirty C***!'

The man in green who had implied she was easy also grassed us up to Stewards and Police, he got – 'Who's The Fat C*** in the Green?'/'Grass, Grass, Grass!'/'You Dirty Grass, You Dirty Grass!' and

'Fat C*** Fat C*** You're A Grass, Fat C*** You're A Grass!'

When he vanished he got 'Where's The Grass in the Green!'

Another fat git in a leather coat and a red beard like an extra from Deliverance or ZZ Top, was also greeted with 'Where's The Fat C*** Gone, Where's The Fat C*** Gone?' after he appeared to give it the biggun climbing over wall towards us in first half at which point he got 'He's Got A False Beard!' only to disappear in second half. When he also got 'Where's The Fat C*** Gone Where's The Fat C*** Gone?'

In general the mouthy chav divs next to us on our right got 'Have You Finished Your Homework?' And 'You're Only Here Cos It's Half Term!' And 'Have You Ever Had A Beer?'

The dodgy looking elder top boys and stewards guarding them got –

You're Just a Stand Full of Nonces!'/'You Only Come For The Children!'/'Paedo, Paedo, Paedo!' And

'Your Only £4 an Hour!'

The home fans essential annoying drummer got 'He's got a Silver Stick!' Implying he was well equipped in the drumstick department, then when asked to serenade us he got 'Drummer, Drummer Give Us a Song, Drummer Give Us a Song!'

When he didn't, he got 'You Only Sing When Your Drumming!' And ''Drummer, Drummer You're A C***!'

To finish the only way is Essex section, home goalie Bentley, made a complete hash of a Shaun Cummings cross letting it sail past him and land in the bottom corner of the net, to point this out to him he got 'Two Nil And It's All Your Fault!'

Wonga aka The Show Me The Money Millwall Travelling Financial Advice Service on Boxing Day 2010 and 10th April 2012 Fratton Park

On Boxing Day 2010 at Fratton Park the perennial Play Up Pompey Pompey chimes was greeted with 'F*** of Pompey – Pompey F*** off!' but this day there was an original financial situation chant – 'Bankrupt Pompey – Pompey Bankrupt!'

Next trip to Fratton Park was a 6 point relegation clash that we won 1 – 0 at on Tuesday 10th April 2012 when Pompey had been docked 10 points for their non Tax paying, financial shenanigans and entering Administration not to say possible closure were languishing second bottom of Championship they received a vast array of chants –

Financially F***ed Section –

'Dut Dut Dut Dut Dut Bankrupt Pompey!'

'Skint Skint Skint!'

'You're Skint And You're Going Down!'

'Bankrupt Pompey, Pompey Bankrupt!'

'You're Skint And You Know You Are!'

'Bankrupt Pompey, Pompey Bankrupt – You're Skint!'

'You're Skint, You're Skint, You're Skint You're F***Ing Skint!'

'You're F***Ing Skint And You're F***Ing Skint!'

'You're Not Getting Wages!'

'We Pay Your Benefits!'

'You're Skint And You Know You Are!'

'You Are Very, You Are Very, You Are Very Poor!'

Who has the money? section -

'Where's Your Money Gone?'

'Harry Redknapp's Got Your Money!'

'Grandad's Got Your Money!

And finally to Fat Pompey bloke giving it the biggun to us to our left –

'Fatty Where's The Money?' and 'Fatty's Ate Your Money'

Tax evasion advice section -

'Pay Up Pompey – Pompey Pay Up!' and 'We Want Our Taxes Back!'

Millwall financial help and piss take section –

'Shall We Lend A Score To You?'

'Loadsa And Loadsa Money!'

'We've Got Loadsa Money You Ain't!'

'Whe've Got A Tenner You Ain't!'

'Singing I've Got A Tenner, Singing I've Got A Tenner – Haven't You?'

'We'll Never Play You Again!'

Waving Pompey goodbye section–

'Bye Bye Pompey – Pompey bye bye!' – 'F*** off Pompey Pompey F*** off!'

'Bye Bye Pompey – No More Pompey – Pompey No More!' 'We'll never play you again!'

More fan based than financial section–

To Pompey's Drum, trumpet and bell ensemble in the game we sang –

'Millwall don't need a drum!' and 'You can't sing without your drum!'

To mad John Portsmouth Football Club Westwood the multi colored bloke replete with bell who is always on telly when Pompey are shown who was not there early on when we sang. –

'Where's the wanker with the bell?'

I said at Pompey, what the bloody hell would you feel like if your season ticket was very close to the bell ringer, drummer or trumpeter? By the way I always wonder why the trumpeter isn't now as good as Miles Davis he should be he seems to practice all season and has done for donkey's years!

What about a marketing idea for the skint South Coast side what about club badged ear plugs or ear muffs?

To protect you from the bleeding racket at Pompey games!

Just a thought, I am at the other end and feel that I have tinnitus every time I have been to Fratton, so God knows what your lugholes must be like if you have to endure this every home game and probably every away game if the home club stewards foolishly allow the musicians sic in with their instruments that is!

You Better, You Better You Bet! Michael Chopra playing for Ipswich Town at the New Den October 29th 2011

The day after admitting his gambling addiction following Rehab in The Sun newspaper he paid a visit to Millwall, the perfect venue, so in sympathy he was greeted with –

'You're not betting anymore!'/'You F***Ing Spunked all your money!

At The start of the match, then as we dashed in to an early two nil lead '2 – 0 and you F***ed your bet!' and in conclusion '4-1 And You Lost Your Bet!' as we ran out 4-1 winners near the end.

I had missed the story myself and only sussed out what the chants meant when we started singing about gambling at the start, I had to ask Paul Simms what the chants meant, he explained and I said to him that explains an Email that I got yesterday that I did not understand then.

I knew we would warmly greet him after all we are a family club unfortunately we can be in the mould of the Manson Family!

He must also have loved playing against us a team with RACING+ a betting newspaper festooned across our shirts and all over one stand the day after his epiphany!

On a similar tip, DJ Campbell aka Dudley Junior was brought in on loan to Millwall from his club Blackburn Rovers, in the transfer window January 2014.

This was following his match fixing NCA arrest in December 2013, so in his first full game for the Lions against Reading at the New Den the CBL sang – 'DJ, DJ What's The Score, DJ What's The Score!'

People like a bet at Millwall and the innocent until proven guilty is not a consideration, if a pisstaking opportunity arises!

Walk Like An Egyptian!

On Saturday 6th April 2019 we played West Bromwich Albion at the New Den, Egyptian international Ahmed Hegazi, scored an own goal for our second in a 2 – 0, then got sent off, an as he walked like an Egyptian off the pitch he was helped off by the chant – 'You're A Just A Shit Mo Saleh!' Liverpool's Egyptian goal machine.

I've Got A Nice Scarf I Have – Look!

At Chesterfield on August 27th 2016, the Ched Evans abuse game as you will see a bit later, there was a bald cuddly bloke in the stand to our left who kept holding his Chesterfield Blue and Red halfed scarf over his head, his consistent performance also included a wander down to the bottom of his stand where he fell arse over tip!

I thought why does it say United on it also why do people have split colour scarves usually with another team they have played or are playing on it, i.e.a lower League team playing someone like Chelsea/Man City/Arsenal/Man Utd or Liverpool etc? As they had scarves like this and also a drum I think they are in need of psychiatric help in Chesterfield, the scarf aside the need for a drum unless you are Brazilian should be certifiable I think!

Moving back specifically to our scarfing idiot at Chesterfield in a game we won 3 – 1, he got –

'Who's The W***er With The Scarf?'/'Who's The Paedo With The Scarf?'/'Fat C*** Fat C*** What's the Score?' and 'Are You Evans In Disguise?' I sussed out who Chesterfield United. the name on the scarf. were, they are a modern US Soccer (sorry!) team based in Virginia, so I assume that he was showing us that Chesterfield had a a UK and US branch?

I may be wrong, but no one would know what he was trying to display, until they Googled it as I did for the book the day after, you made your arms tired for no reason mate!

Hull City Away On Tuesday 6th March 2018 For 2-1 Win

A night match in Yorkshire with bloody annoying young northerners banging on metal fence at back of stand next to us, so where do Police and Stewards look? At us!!!

Them to us

'Going Home To Your Shithole!'

What London???

To which we sang 'London's a Shithole I want to go home!'

We sang 'Jeremy Kyle He's Coming For You!' and 'We Saw Your Sister On Jeremy Kyle!'

So they sang re a girl in our section

'You're Birds On Jeremy Kyle!'/We Saw Your Girl On Jeremy Kyle!'/She's Going To Cry In A Minute and 'She's Got Chlamydia!'

We sang 'We Pay Your Benefits!

To which they sang 'You Pay Our Benefits!' recognition eh!

Us to them

To imply they were poor not Hull City not scoring – 'Have You Ever Seen A Score?'

Implying they were schoolboys 'Where's Your Pencil Case'

Oop The North End

The Section title is as a Northern Actress might answer the Bishop's 'Where would you like it?'

In truth it refers to Millwall's visit to Preston North End in January 2006 that had some good sarcastic exchanges.

There was a black Preston fan in the mouthy home section next to us sporting an Afro of monumental proportions to whom we sang – 'There's only one Macy Gray!' and 'Macy Gray sex offender!'

From a culinarily perspective the technically and probably a tad awkward, culinary placement we suggested –

'You can stick your F...ing hot pot up your arse, sideways!'

The youth and kids in the drum beating home section next to us in the Shankly Stand sang about us -

'W*nkers, W*nkers' and 'You're shit and as soft as f...!'

In response we sang to them – 'You'll run to your mum and dad! And 'Does your teacher know you're here?'

In response they sang the bizarre – 'Does your postman know you're here?' something to do with delivering our Giro's I think (?)

In response to their 'You're shit and you talk funny!' chant I listed in another book, we sang –

'Aye Oop! Aye Oop! Aye Oop! Aye Oop! Aye Oop!'

Millwall icon 'Tank' standing near the back of our section was getting plenty of fatist abuse from the mouthy young Preston fans for example – 'Who ate all the pies?'/'Get your tits out for the lads!' And

'Have you ever seen your dick?'

'Tank' replied to this by doing 'mine's a whopper!' gestures with his hands.

We collectively responded to their abuse by questioning their virginity -'Have you ever used your dick?'

Near the end at 2 nil up the home fans started to leave to which we sang –

'2 nil and you're f...ing off!'

We sang – 'Who's the slapper in the pink?' To a young girl in the home section, in her defence they sang 'Sit down shurrup!' which we mocked so they replied with the same chant in a mock Cockney accent.

Non-PC alert –
'Everton, Everton, Everton!'

In the 2 games against Everton in the FA Cup in January 2006 there was a plethora of pleasantries exchanged, we naturally sang the golden oldie chants– 'You Scouse c...s!'/'I'd rather be a Paki than a Scouse!'/'Sign on!'/'You knicked my stereo!'/'Only happy on Giro day! And 'One job between ya!'

Some newer chants on a similar stereotypical tip –

'You live in a tracksuit!'/'Town full of scaggies, you're just a town full of scaggies!'/'Your mum is a prostitute!'/'Where's my wallet gone? Where's my wallet gone?'/'Woke up this morning and my hubcaps were gone!' And 'Where's me hub caps gone? Where's me hubcaps gone?'

We naturally also sang – 'Rooney, Rooney!' And 'There's only on Wayne Rooney!'

We sang – 'Premiership? You're having a laugh!'

They sang – 'Championship? You're having a laugh!'

The Scousers for their part also sang – 'You're shit and your mam's a slag!'

As Abusing Players Is Somehow Wrong a Very Non-PC for reference nearly every opposing player is called A C*** so to avoid C word central alert I took those chants that said xxxxx you're a C*** chants out but left person specific versions in! -

You're So Hurtful 2

Continuing a theme from 'I Was Born Under The Cold Blow Lane' some personal abuse against Player's at the time many of whom now have moved on or retired –

Players ...

Notts Forest's David Johnson, handballed a goal into our net in front of the CBL in 2002/3, which he later admitted, which was nice of him, at the time he got the harsh but true 'Johnson you're a cheating C...!'

When both played v us for Ipswich Town at the New Den on 29th October 2011–

Lee Bowyer an Ex Wet Spam Untied player was greeted with 'Bottle Job, Bottle Job, Bottle Job!' as he made the most of an alleged injury and went off the pitch early doors.

Jimmy Bullard got 'Bullard you're An Ugly C**t!' a great player on the day Man Of The Match on their side by a country mile, massive defeat for the bumpkins or not, but it had to be said unfortunately, right or wrong on the ugly tip!

Portsmouth's Tim Sherwood got the following, which as a spectator I thought he thoroughly deserved – 'Sherwood you're a dirty c...!' And 'F... off Sherwood! F... off Sherwood!'

QPR's Stefan Bailey came out to warm down after our game at Loftus Road in February 2006 and was greeted by the observant, although not offensive – 'There's only one Dizzee Rascal!'

Arsenal era Jermaine Pennant was playing for Watford at the New Den in January 2003, the fact that he appeared to be on perpetual loan at the time meant that we had to point it out to him –

'You'll never play for Arsenal!'

Blackburn Rovers David Dunn a slightly portly and aging player got the usual abusive –

'You Fat C*nt!' and the original 'David Dunn Days Are Done!'

Birmingham City's then player Emile Heskey at the New Den in the Carling Cup on November 29th 2005 and then Crystal Palace's Andy Johnson in the following game at Selhurst Park on December 3rd December 2005 both received – 'You'll never play for England!'

At the New Den on February 5th 2005 QPR's peroxide player Andrew Davies was greeted with the pre paedo revelations perennial – 'There's only one Jimmy Saville!'

A real popular figure of Millwall fun was Ade Akinbyi on April 12th 2003, Stoke City played at the New Den with the Palace loan player in their ranks he received the following observation – 'He's shit and he knows he is!'

At the away return at the Britannia Stadium in October 2004 he got – 'You're worse than Mark McCammon!' And 'Akinbyi sex offender!'

Carrot topped Crystal Palace player Ben Watson an alleged Millwall fan, played at the New Den in August 2003 he got – 'Who's the C… with ginger hair?' And 'We hate gingers and we hate gingers, etc, we are the ginger haters!' Not forgetting the hard to misinterpret – 'Ginger C*** ginger C*** ginger C***!'

Naturally he scored against us.

Continuing the ginger theme Ipswich Town's Jack Colback made a couple of glaring errors when we played at Portman Road on October 30th 2010, we sang to the redhead– 'Ginger C***, Ginger C***, Ginger C***!' and 'Strawberry Blonde? You're having a laugh!'

Further continuing the ginger theme at Fratton Park Portsmouth on Boxing Day 2010, Pompey red headed forward Dave Kitson got 'Kitson you're a ginger C***!'

At Watford on Boxing Day 2013 in the first half when kicking towards our away section, Troy Deeney received –'She Said No Deeney, She Said No!'

God knows what that was about, as he is not even remotely like Marlon King!

Also when Danny Shittu approached Fernando Foresteiri before Danny's early dismissal, seemed to bottle it and fumbled possession of the ball out behind the goal rather than face him, he got the mock chant based on Danny's surname – 'He Made You Shit Yourself!'

Derby County's long haired defender Shaun Barker at New Den February 11th 2012, did something that we did not like in front of us in the CBL, so we sang the he looks like the Messiah, sacriligeous chant –

'Jesus Jesus You're a C***!' I'm sure the archbishop of Canterbury must love that one, not!

Rotherham United's blonde haired Brazillian Junior was play acting and trying to get our players booked at the New Den on 2nd January 2005 and was greeted with –

'Junior, Junior, Junior you're a C…! Junior you're a C…!'

Sunderland's Jason McAteer playing at the New Den in January

2004 got the following chant -

'He's fat, he's queer, his name is McAteer!'

Gary McAllister the ageing follicly challenged then Coventry City player/manager at the New Den on

May 4th 2003 was lauded with- 'Old Man, old man, old man!' And 'F... off old man, f... off old man, f... off old man, f... off!'

Then Brighton starlet Leon Knight missed a penalty against us at the New Den on 11th December 2004 and was greeted with – 'Leon, wank, wank, wank!'

For some reason Norwich's former Lion Darren Huckerby continually seemed to try to get Millwall player's sent off, particularly Kevin Muscat, his perceived dive in gaining the penalty at Carrow Road in 2005 prompted a chorus of 'He's gonna dive in a minute!' to echo around the New Den at the return game in November 2005.

On a similar tack Brighton's Gary Hart hit the deck in the wake of a Chelsea diving scandal, we sang – 'Are you Drogba in disguise?'

At Rotherham United 28th February 2015 the paedophile sex scandal area Rotherham's almost peroxide blonde and headbanded Ben Pringle got – 'Are You Saville In Disguise?'

Crystal Palace's Republic Of Ireland International Clinton Morrison also got the diving chant at the New Den in February 2006, more so he got this observational chant – 'No way you're Irish, there's just no way you're Irish!'

When Phil Neville played for Everton against us in the FA Cup especially at Goodison Park in the replay, we sang the Luke Chadwick patented – 'Neville you're an ugly c...!'

Darren Beckford the blatant Elbower of Forde in the televised League game in 2008/9, was greeted in Play Off Semi Final 2nd Leg with deluge of C word abuse home and away and at Elland Road the aforementioned for Stefan Bailey – 'There's only one Dizzee Rascal!'

Martin Keown playing for Leicester City at the New Den in August 2004 got –

'Keown you're an ugly C...!'/'You've got a face like a

monkey!/'There's only one Quasimodo!'/'Keown is a monkey, la la, la la, la la la, la la, la!'

When Millwall went 2 – 0 up we sang – 'Monkey, monkey what's the score?'

Swansea City's then Forward Lee Trundle received – 'You Fat Bastard – You Ate All the Leeks!'

Stockport County's Craig Davies, he was not singer Craig David for anyone not there, but his name was very close! He wore black gloves to match his sides all Black kit in November 2008 at the New Den, to highlight his winter warmer dress sense he got – 'Who's the Wanker in the gloves!'

Why he wore gloves when it wasn't cold, apart from his being a Northern Jessie, God knows!

Not Millwall or abusive, but great if you are a West Indian Cricketer however in a football sense funny I thought at Crewe Alexander in November 2004, Crewe's fans sang 'Trinidad, Trinidad's number one!' to their keeper Clayton Ince.

Middlesbrough's Scottish player Chris Boyd at our first visit to the Riverside on 20th November 2010 was serenaded with – 'Chris Boyd you're a Scottish C***! Chris Boyd you're a Scottish C***!'

At Blackpool on bonfire day 2011 Jonjo Shelvey ex Charlton Athletic and on loan to Pool from Liverpool, was greeted by –'Shelvey You're A Charlton C***!' And 'Shelvey You're An Ugly C***!'

For info for non Wall we like to encourage people, with our fashion eye for beauty!

Against Doncaster Rovers at home on Dockers Day Saturday 5th February 2011 new signing Darren Purse had an altercation with Donny's Billy Sharp, where they stood in mid pitch in the second half head to head, the newly renamed Dockers Stand Formerly East Stand sang – 'Pursey, Pursey knock him out, Pursey knock him out!' From a sensible point of view, he did not do as the Dockers and us in the CBL requested and therefore did not give the short arsed ref a chance to straight red him!

Not insulting more sarcastic, Nicky Maynard for Bristol City at New Den on 20th November 2011, before he scored his two goals in our 2 – 1 defeat. He was greeted by a bloke behind me with – 'You're just a packet of sweets!' I.e., Maynard's the sweet company, shame that he was not just a packet of sweets then he might not have scored two against us in this Sky Sports live game.

On a similar tack, Leicester City's Souleymane Bamba got the bizarre pisstake -

'Bamba you're a bowl of rice!' and 'Bowl of rice Bowl Of rice, Bowl of rice!' Not as daft as it sounds because Bamba is in fact an Israeli Cholesterol free snack made from peanut butter-flavored puffed corn, whoever started the chants at the back of CBL must have been a food buff!

Ex 'Appy 'Ammer Nigel Reo – Coker played for T'Bolton Wanderers against us in FA Cup in February 2012, and his former club allegiance was greeted with the customary chant for players with Wet Spam links –

'West Ham C***! West Ham C***! West Ham C***!'

At Watford on 1st November 2014 dreadlock Black Watford Defender Juan Carlos Paredes in the second half when they kicked towards us, we sang – 'E Bola, E Bola, E Bola!' Because he was black, we assumed that he must be West African, so liable to have Ebola, ignoring the minor fact that he was from Equador!

Cardiff City's Man City loaned Welsh mega whinge bag, Craig Bellamy, at the game at New Den on 19th March 2011. He moaned at everything all game and was like the love child of Cristiano Ronaldo and Dimitar Berbatov; you know the world's biggest miserable delusional git, always looking on the Shite side of life! He was greeted warmly with the adapted standard abuse especially for him 'Bellamy you're a F***ing C**!' and when giving it large re anything that he did not like to Millwall players in front of CBL we extolled several Millwall players to lamp him – 'Trotter/Fordey/Pursey knock him out, knock him out!'

Closing this section on a Taff tip on 18th September 2012, we played Cardiff City, well I think it was Cardiff City as they were in red not blue, moving on! Scot Kevin McNaughton a grey/white haired player received the comparative chant – 'One Philip Schofield, There's Only One Philip Schofield!

Sky Sports Expert, Presenter Watford 1st November 2014

To the left of the away section at Vicarage Road there was a Sky Sports team, with a presenter holding a microphone the one and only John Solako to welcome him we sang – 'You're Just A Shit Chris Kamara!'

Multiple Criminals Very Non-PC alert – Crime Triplets Serenades –

When Dangerous Driving Murderer convicted/jailed Felon former West Bromwich Albion forward and at the time an Oldham Athletic forward Lee Hughes played against us at the New Den on 15th December 2007 naturally he was very deservedly abused. I believe that this was totally justified, speaking personally because as I mentioned earlier I was run over by a Hit and Run Driver and put in a Grade 3 Glasgow Coma, the death end of this scale, for approximately 6 weeks. I was very nearly killed, so naturally I think that Hughes should still be in Jail not on a Professional Football club's books receiving pocketful's of dosh from his massive Oldham Salary.

The game itself was a Football Fan's Fantasy or in our case a Millwall Fan's Nightmare.

The match had five goals, a dodgy Penalty awarded against us, a Player from each side sent off, practically everyone on the Pitch on both sides booked; totally bloody awful officialdom from all 3

Officials and an added 7 Minutes of Injury Time at the end. Hughes naturally scored a Hat Trick including converting the highly dubious Penalty awarded by the completely useless Referee and he mocked us with his goal celebrations Dance.

One of our scorers in the 3 – 2 defeat Jay Simpson was sent off by the completely incompetent Referee Kevin 'Not Fit For Sunday League'/'3 – 2 to the Referee' Friend, for his goal celebration towards home fans in the West Lower.

The chants that Murderer Hughes received were as follows – 'Scum, Scum, Scum!'/'You're Scum and you know you are!'/'Lee Hughes is a murderer!'/'Murderer, Murderer, Murderer!' and 'Bang Him up, Bang Him up, Bang Him up!'

Naturally he gave the Bald Headed Dangerous Driving Murdering bastard Hughes no punishment whatsoever for his mocking celebrations towards us. Of course, it was very galling to us all particularly his one for the First Goal tap – in which he did in front of us at the corner flag in the First Half at the Cold Blow Lane end of the ground. Friend whose performance made Uriah Rennie look like Pierluigi Collina, ran off the pitch totally Millwall Friendless at the end like Linford Christie with a rocket up his arse because he was so very rapid and largely because he was so scared of us I presume. During the game, a slight fan ran on to the Pitch from the East Stand to try and justifiably whack Hughes when he scored his Hat Trick. Sadly, he was not successful in hitting him or the massively incompetent Referee as he was bundled off the Pitch by Stewards before he carried out the attack on the Murdering Bastard or the Friendless One.

According to an entry on the House of Fun in October 2008 prior to his moving to Sven's Notts County, whilst at Oldham Athletic their fans apparently sang – 'Lee Hughes wherever you may be, you were drunk and disorderly, you killed a man and you did your time, and now your Oldham's number 9!'

Why they sang that about him, the Slap headed C*** god alone knows.

As far as I am concerned whether he was a great goal scorer for them or not, they could f***ing well have the murdering C***, F*** him and F*** them as well!

Ched Evans convicted of raping a 19-year-old girl and jailed for 5 years in 2012, had his case retried in October 2014 his conviction was quashed and was released having done half his sentence in October 2014, now shit sticks in Millwall mentality, so guilty or not guilty his appearance for Chesterfield United against us on 27th August 2016 at their new ground Proact stadium, which we won 3 -1. In our customary style we bombarded Evans with abuse justified or not, rude not to – 'He's Got the Touch of a Rapist'/'Paedo!'/'Paedophile!'/'Ched Evans Is A Rapist!'/'Ched Evans Sex Offender!'/'Sex Case Sex Case Hang Him Hang Him Hang Him!'/'She Said No Ched (and Evans) She Said No!'/'Rapist!'/'Evans Sleeps with Children!'/'Evans Evans You're A C***!'/'Are You Marlon In Disguise?' And at 3 – 0 to us 'Rapist Rapist What's The Score?'

I did say to a bloke standing behind me who was going in to Ched Evans abuse meltdown, I would be careful mate, look at what happens every time we bombard Marlon King with abuse, he always scores! Speaking of whom -

Non-PC Marlon King Specific alert – Serenading Marlon The King Of Crime

Closing this section Mr Versatility on the offence front be it motor crime or sex or any other option to be truthful!

The persistent KING of Crime, –

Marlon King Incidents and legal cases -

While on loan to Hull City, King was alleged to have head butted teammate Dean Windass in a casino in Scarborough. Hull City stated that the matter had been dealt with internally, and both players remained with the club Windass later described the incident as a "storm in a teacup".

King has convictions for 14 offences, dating from 1997.

He received fines, driving bans, community service sentences, a rehabilitation order and orders to pay compensation on convictions including: theft from a person and from a car, criminal damage, and attempting to obtain property by deception; fraudulent use of vehicle licence document, driving without insurance, speeding, drink driving; a wounding incident while playing amateur football, and two cases involving assault of young women rejecting his advances in the Soho area of London.

Two cases have led to imprisonment. In May 2002 he received an eighteen-month prison sentence for receiving stolen goods, in relation to a BMW convertible that he was found driving. He was found not guilty of a charge of assaulting a police officer in a related case. His solicitor commented that "His reputation will be tarnished forever, whatever success he achieves, he'll always be referred to in a Tyson-esque way as someone who has had a criminal past and that is a considerable penalty.

Gillingham continued to pay his salary while he was in jail, and supported in his appeal, which resulted in the sentence being reduced to nine months, and he was released on licence after five months, returning to the Gillingham team within two days of his release.

In December 2008, again in the Soho area, King was arrested on suspicion of punching a 20 year-old female university student in the face, causing a broken nose and split lip for which she was treated in hospital. He was later convicted of sexual assault and assault occasioning actual bodily harm, and sentenced to 18 months in prison and placed on the sex offender register for seven years. Wigan Athletic immediately initiated the cancellation of his contract. King's agent, Tony Finnigan, said he was confident that his client would find a club on his release, which was on 29 July 2010 and accused the Professional Footballers' Association (PFA) of failing to offer support.

Gordon Taylor, the incumbent chief executive of the PFA, said that the PFA did not represent players when they have broken the law and been convicted on non-Footballing matters. It would support members with anger management or other issues if approached but no approach had been made by King. After his release, he made an appeal against the conviction which was unsuccessful.© Wikipedia

Continuing the King of crimes lengthy and versatile crime career he was again arrested time his time in connection with a hit-and-run incident, which left a man with a head injury, been there done that myself!

King, then 33, was arrested by City of London Police officers and was released on police bail until mid-September 2013 pending further inquiries that Detectives from Westminster were pursuing.

He was held on suspicion of failing to stop at the scene of a road traffic collision following the crash in central London in the early hours of a Saturday morning the last weekend in July 2013.

Police and ambulance crews were called to Bishops Bridge Road in Paddington, following reports that a car had hit a pedestrian and not stopped.

A man in his late 40s was taken to a central London hospital, although his injuries were not believed to be life-threatening.

As I myself was involved in a very similar incident where I was run over by a Hit And Run driver on a red light as a pedestrian, in my case receiving a severe Traumatic Brain Injury and spent 6 weeks in a coma, my hatred of The Wonderful Marlon Just Got Deeper When I Heard The Above, His Chants Homage Prior To This -

Marlon King – In previous games he has had –

Formerly a Gillingham player King, then at Notts Forest at the time a convicted felon for motor offences got the following at the New Den on 3rd October 2004 – 'Pikey!'/'Marlon you're a thieving c…!'

More humourously, he came on in the second half with a white bandage around his head and got –

'There's only one pint of Guinness!'

On March 25th 2006 Marlon King now at Watford received the following chant to highlight on his alleged BMW thieving– 'Where's your Beamer gone? Where's your Beamer gone?'

He also received the following Prison 'man love' oriented chants – 'You got raped in prison!' And 'Marlon Marlon pass the soap, Marlon pass the soap!'

His serenade rhapsody got its full reign when he was at Coventry City's where we played at the Ricoh Arena on Saturday 16th April 2011, and he scored both goals against us in our 2 – 1 defeat, this was irrelevant really it was more to do with the plethora of criminal activities he has allegedly been involved and imprisoned for, Car dealing shenanigans, assaulting a Police Officer, sexual assault and across the board he got in general –

'Marlon Marlon You're A C***!' '

Referring to his time in prison –

'Marlon Takes It Up The Arse!

Referring to the sexual and physical assault on a 20 year old female in a Soho nightclub, for which he served 9 months of his 18 months sentence, he got 3 old sexual offender favourites -

'Marlon King Sex Offender!'/'Sex Case Sex Case Hang Him Hang Him Hang Him!' and 'You Sleep With Your Sisters Kids!'

Specifically re his Sex crime he got –

'You Beat Your Women Up!'/'He'e Got The Touch Of A Rapist!'/'Rapist Rapist Rapist!'/'Does Your Victim Know You're Here?'

And a real quality original 'Marlon's A Rapist, He Don't Need Consent!'

One question – what genius at the FA decided to allocate the 2011 Women's FA Final at Coventry City i.e. the home of a convicted sex offender? Just a thought.

When we returned to the Ricoh Arena on 17th April 2012, and as you will see below he was no longer with Coventry City, we sang – 'Where's Your Rapist Gone?'

He moved on to Birmingham City for 2011/12 but had been injured so did not make his debut until he came on as a sub, v Millwall right in front of us in the 2nd half at St Andrews, he must love playing us, he got pretty much all the previous chants plus some new ones –

'Marlon You're a dirty C***!' and the classic 'She Said No Marlon She said no, She Said No Marlon She said no, She Said No Marlon She said no, Oh Marlon She said no!'

In the home game of the same season on 14th January 2012 he did play in the whole game and obviously scored in a game where we were down to 9 men due to ref and lost 6-0, he got pretty much all the above plus –

'You Had Sex With Your Cellmate!'/'Marlon, Marlon you've got AIDS!' and less sexually he got 'Marlon, Marlon Show Us Your Tag!'

When he next played at the New Den on Tuesday 23rd October 2012, he got a bleeding hat trick, after we had taken a 3 – 0 lead in less than 20 minutes only to draw 3-3!

As he had moved on to Sheffield United from Birmingham Cty and obviously did not play against us the home bods at St Andrews on 1st October 2013 got the same questioning chant listed above. – 'Where's Your Rapist Gone?'

Some more chants at the lovely Marlon -

At 3 – 0 –'Rapist Rapist what's the score?'

In the wake of the Jimmy Saville child sex abuse scandal, he got 'You're Just a Black Jimmy Saville!'

Moving away from Marlon but to a Saville oddity the gathered Crystal Palace massive at the New Den in our last home game of 2012/3 on Tuesday 30th April 2013 sang to Alan Dunne when he had the audacity to confront their ex player Wilfried Zaha in front of them continued the Saville theme with – 'Oh Jimmy Saville, He's F***ed Alan Dunne!' How the f*** those Ultra wankers worked that classic out I have no idea, for info it was not lately if he had because A) Dunne is too old for that Paedo and B) Paedo Now Then Now

Then Now Then is dead!

Back specifically to the King of Crime In one game he pulled the rear of the shirt/shorts of Millwall's Mark Beevers in front of the Barry Kitchener stand near the CBL and got the adapted 'He Said No Marlon He said no, He Said No Marlon He said no, He Said No Marlon He said no, Oh Marlon He said no!'

I said I think he must have thought his name was Beaver I will have some of that!

Whilst at Birmingham City and he was scoring his customary glut of goals v Millwall as he always seemed to do the Brummies sang his name, so in response we sang – 'You Idolised a Rapist!'

King always scored against us five goals in consecutive seasons at the New Den for the Brummies,

just a thought someone had previously suggested on an away coach trip, when King is playing against us we should shut up and not abuse him as he always bloody scored no matter what club he was playing for. Perhaps we should have sung his praises! Nah sod that ...

Marlon has now retired, well from Football anyway, when he was released from Sheffield United in December 2014, however his criminal mind is still thriving, adding to his umpteen criminal convictions as listed previously herewith info that I saw in the news on 15th May 2014 re his latest shenanigans -

King was arrested and bailed in April 2013 after a car crash which left one man seriously injured, and in July of the same year, he was again arrested in connection with a hit-and-run incident which had left a second man injured in London

In the April 2013 incident Marlon was eating an ice cream at the wheel when he caused a three-car pile-up on his 33rd birthday April 2013.

In May 2014 for he was jailed for 18 months dangerous driving after a crash, which left a motorist having to be cut out of his car and airlifted to hospital, he also handed King a three-year driving ban. The QC who sentenced him said: "I do not regard your case as merely impulsive or silly behaviour. It was aggressive. It was arrogant."

King had pleaded guilty to a charge of dangerous driving at Nottingham Crown Court in March 2014.which was nice of him, having usually adopting a policy of it wasn't me gov!

The offence that he was sentenced for was that he had been eating ice cream that he had bought at McDonald moments before the concertina crash. This was whilst driving his Porsche and because of his lack of attention to his driving he caused a three car pile-up on the A46 at kick off time coincidentally 3pm, on his 33rd birthday April 26th 2013.

Marvellous Marlon had been seen weaving in and out of traffic before he undertook a VW Polo whom who he perceived as travelling too slowly in the outer lane.

King slammed on his brakes in frustration, forcing the driver he undertook to perform an emergency stop in his black VW Polo. As the driver in the VW Polo stopped a silver Vauxhall Astra who had pulled out behind him, collided with the stationary VW Polo. The "concertina effect" forced the Polo into the back of King's Porsche.

The driver of the VW Polo had to be cut out of his car and airlifted to hospital after the collision at Winthorpe, near Newark. He spent three weeks in hospital and required surgery for a fractured and dislocated forearm. The Vauxhall Astra driver was also taken to hospital for cuts and bruises.

King had done Lee Hughes's Hit and Run routine and drove off after the crash that he had called however he was called back as other motorists thought that the driver who had to be cut out of his car had died.

Just a thought why not bang Lee Hughes and Marlon King together they could then form a team and it would be like a professional Mean Machine Football team!

Adding to the dynamic crime ridden duo is a real criminal, makes Marlon look like a beginner Nile Ranger, if you wonder what the hell I am talking about look on Wikipedia under his page and click on Controversies it is too bloody big to copy to here, versatile in being a Rude Boy is his profession!

He played for Blackpool at the New Den on August 30th 2014, and was barracked mercilessly as he warmed up, when he came on as a substitute in the second half the abusive fun began –

'Rapist C***! Rapist C***!'/'Rapist, Rapist, Rapist!'/'She Said No, Nile She Said No!'/'Nile, Nile you're A C***!'/'Sex Case, Sex Case Hang Him, Hang Him, Hang Him! And 'Ranger, Ranger you're A C***!'

Naturally, he scored, as I intimated whenever we abuse those who deserve to be abused they always score against us, we should just shut up, tactically better that way, even though it goes 100% against a Millwall Fans nature, but we should consider it!

I give you a final one former Lion Darius Henderson playing against us for Scunthorpe United on Saturday 22nd August 2015. As a former Lion who had had the nerve to leave us, we naturally felt the need to be abusive to him when Scunthorpe United kicked towards us in the first half. in his case relating to his incident with his wife and prostitute and his ABH charge he got – 'She said no Hendo, she said no, she said no Hendo she said no, she said no Hendo, she said no oh Hendo she said no!'

Wrong on two levels one a Prostitute will not say no that is against her job description! And two don't abuse goal scorers!!! In his case he was substituted and did not score, it had led to three mates and me I was there with Martin, Jordan and Laurie to implore the chanters to shut up! It is not always fatal but not in this instance, I would not use this as a test case and look at whom we aim to abuse!

Tactical Plan Possession Obsession – Let's Bore Them In To Submission Coventry City at New Den 1st November 2011

Coventry City seemed to think that they were playing in a European away tie, so the tactical ethos was pass pass pass, ideally sideways and backwards, that seemed to be their plan, they must have been possessed by Ray Wilkins I reckon, with the most exciting cry being keeper on!

As they tried to bore us to death in the first half the Dockers Stand sang the following to show their pleasure – 'Boring C***s! Boring C***s!'

Non-PC Manager alert PS not the manager of PC World a Football Club Manager – Let's Abuse Everyone, Be Rude Not To!

The Managers...

Derby County's then manager John Gregory got the following at the New Den on Saturday

26th October 2002 a game we won 3 – 0 -

'We want Gregory out, say we want Gregory out!' And 'And now you're gonna believe us you're gonna get the sack!'

At the return match at Pride Park in April 2003 Gregory was on suspension and the home fans chanted for the instatement of stand in George Burley, as we twice took the lead in a 2 – 1 win

we sang – 'We want Burley out, say we want Burley out!' And 'Gregory, Gregory, Gregory!'

Kevin Keegan got 'Keegan runs from pressure!' and the adapted Hoolie classic –"Hit him on the head, hit him on the head, hit him on the head with a baseball bat, Keegan, Keegan!' In reference to his baseball bat assault of several years before, when I assume his bubble perm must have cushioned the blows.

Similarily we also sang 'We want Hoddle out!' to the then very very newly appointed Glenn Hoddle for our victory at Wolves in December 2004.

In March 2003 then Walsall Manager Colin Lee, did not exactly go a bundle on Mark McGhee so in McGhee's defence he got the following adaptation of the classic Old Den Dalglish chant, this time to the tune of 'London Bridge Is Falling Down' – 'Colin Lee can't sit down, can't sit down, can't sit down, Colin Lee can't sit down, he's got piles!'

In March 2004 at Sheffield United's Brammal Lane, we gave our first rendition of –

'Stan Ternent is a liar, is a liar!' In response to Stan Ternent then Burnley manager's Mo Camara monkey noise allegations

An Ex Hammer and then Crystal Palace's beautiful (sic) Manager Ian Dowie received the following facist abuse 'Dowie you're an ugly c…!' He also naturally received this at the Ricoh Arena when he was then the Coventry City Manager and we played there in the FA Cup in January 2008.

Another Ex Hammer Harry Redknapp at home against Southampton when he Managed them on October 22nd 2005, got some very innovative observational chants, about his appearance –

'Harry needs a face lift!'/'Harry needs botox!'/'Collagen, Collagen, Collagen!'

Not forgetting the classic – 'Face like a foreskin, you've got a face like a foreskin!'

He also got these type of chants when he was at The New Den as QPR manager on 19th October 2013, when laughingly he was hit in the face by a ball as I said earlier on.

Away at QPR's Loftus Road on Saturday 26th April 2014 dear Harry Boy got above mentioned Foreskin chant naturally plus a couple more the perennial – 'Harry Redknapp Sex Offender!' no evidence but that does not stop it being sung and the original – 'Harry Redknapp He's Having A Stroke, He's Having A Stroke!' due to his ruddy faced glow.

Finally in October 2006 Bournemouth's then new manager Kevin Bond visited the Den, following in the wake of the Panorama corruption expose, consequently he got –

'Bung in a minute, he'll take a bung in a minute!'

On 15th January 2001, Paul Jewell made his managerial debut for Ipswich Town after a two year absence from the managerial hot seat at the New Den, a game that we won 2 – 1, during the game as he loitered in the Technical zone he was serenaded with – 'Sit Down You Scouse C***!'

Whenever he stood or complained in the technical area. As we were heading to our 2 – 1 win in his first game in charge he got the usual defeat chant – 'You're Getting Sacked in the Morning!' and this more personalised sacking chant 'He's Short, He's Fat, He's Gonna Get The Sack, Paul Jewell, Paul Jewell!'

He got this again when we beat them 4 – 1 on 29th October 2011

On 13th August 2011 Ex England manager Steve McClaren came to the New Den with his then side Nottingham Forest, pre match Zampa paraded around the pitch holding up a brolly, taking the Michael out of his famous/infamous England dreadful display when McClaren was featured standing with his brolly unfurled in the rain, to laud him we sang 'You let your country down!' and humoursly 'Where's your brolly gone? Where's your brolly gone?' in a game that we won 2 – 0, yahoo

Steve Bruce at the New Den when we played Hull City on Saturday 2nd February 2013, as he ranted and raved in technical zone we sang – 'You Fat C***!'

'You Are Really Getting Sacked In The Morning – You Can't Beat Millwall!!!!!! You're Fired!'

Owen Coyle was sacked the day after Millwall beat them 2 – 0 on Saturday 6th October 2012, we seem to get everyone sacked if they lose to us, it seems to be a cannot beat them you're fired. To highlight the ethos of their inability to beat the Lions and off they go as I said we saw off Owen Coyle, we have also seen off – George Burley, John Barnes, Steve McLaren, Sven Göran Erickson, and Steve Coppell twice

Sammy Hyppia stepped down 10 days after we beat them at Amex Friday 12th December 2014, I suppose that counts.

As this seems to be a Millwall thing we sang –'You're Getting Sacked in the Morning!' to Lee Clark manager of Birmingham City as we took a 3 – 0 lead early on in the game on Tuesday 23rd October 2012, sadly we blew this sacking opportunity when we let in 3 goals and drew 3 – 3.

Still it will happen again to some poor sod, because Dougie Freedman was released from Crystal Palace to replace the sacked Owen Coyle after we had drawn with Crystal Palace the Saturday before the Birmingham City game at Selhurst Park on Saturday 20th October 2012.

I could be wrong but Palace had relinquished a 2 – 0 lead to us, so the board may well have thought sod that bye bye then!

Continuing the 'Millwall won I am leaving' scenario a few days after we beat Luton Town away in the FA Cup in February 2013, by mutual Consent whatever that means!!!! Luton Town manager Paul Buckle left.

Blackburn Rovers Michael Appleton was sacked the game after we knocked them out of the FA Cup by beating them in Quarter Final at Ewood Park Wednesday 13th March 2013, he was not sacked straight after our win there but after their not beating hated local rivals Burnley in the game on the Saturday after our Wednesday match, not exactly after losing to us but close enough!

Psycho Stuart Pearce then Notts Forest Manager was sacked the day after we won 1 – 0 at the City Ground on Saturday 31st January 2015, and was replaced by a previous Wall victim Dougie Freedman, this just gets better!

Mark Cooper Swindon Town manager was sacked after Wall beat his team 2 – 0 at the New Den on Saturday 17th October 2015

Finally

After our defeating, them in FA Cup Premier League Champions Leicester City sacked their manager Claudio Ranieri in February 2017 following another defeat several days later by Sevilla in Champions League following defeat by us in FA Cup 5th round, their second defeat in a week.

Sorry the finally was misplaced because Claudio Ranieri was not the last lose to Millwall manager to be given the sack, because on Saturday 26th October 2019 Millwall beat Stoke City and within a week then manager Nathan Jones was sacked, if you are reading this book a while after it was issued do not be surprised if there have been more!

To my mind this highlights football's hypocrisy, Ranieri spoke very honestly after our beating them unlike Watford Manager Walter Mazzarri and Agent Orange Southend United's Phil Brown, who came out with every excuse and blame Millwall theory under the sun why their teams were beaten at the New Den in the same season 2017/18.

Claudio Ranieri on the other hand on TV after the defeat said that in these types of matches he needed Warriors/Gladiators and Millwall had that, whilst his team did not, he said especially after going down to ten men when we battled harder. Ranieri affectively did not get warriors, he got wimps too frightened to take a throw in in front of a real crowd, not the Happy Clappy Premier League type of fake support,

Ranieri was too honest for his own good here is opinion pre-match from conversation me and Clive had in Millwall Café with two Leicester City women, when I asked why had Leicester City gone from Premier League Champions to languishing in the relegation zone in real danger of relegation to Championship, bearing in mind this was before we knocked them out. They said the Board had given each player a flash new car for winning a League that the odds of winning was 5000 – 1, they also practically trebled the players wages, thereby giving them all a Bertie Big B**llocks cannot be arsed mentality, not a fighting mentality.

To my mind, they are to blame for the sides demise the Board and Players not someone as honest as Ranieri.

Non-PC alert –
Stewards ...

At West Ham United away in April 2005 as we were being held in the ground we were naturally surrounded by stewards and police unfortunately for him on steward became our main target, chubby steward number 195 received –'195 sex offender!'/'195 is a homosexual!' And '195 ugly c...!'

A skinny, dark haired, bespectacled steward then walked along the length of the away stand swishing a plastic bag and got the obligatory 'There's only one Harry Potter!' which I mentioned previously in 'I Was Born Under The Cold Blow Lane' both stewards entered into the spirit of it all and the gathered police all had a good laugh, well as long as we entertain someone!

At Brighton in December 2005 two stewards walking in front of we away fans were serenaded with these 'gay' questions–'Are you going for a shag?', 'Does she wear a strap on?' And

'Which one takes it up the arse?'

At Watford in March 2006 stewards attempting to get Millwall fans to sit down were greeted with – 'Get a proper job!' And '£3 an hour, you're earning £3 an hour!'

At Leyton Orient's Brisbane Road Building site on Saturday 26th September 2009, there was a black dreadlock thatched Steward with black shades on standing in front of us, we serenaded him with – 'He's got a pineapple on his head!'/'There's only 1 Stevie Wonder!' and 'Stevie, Stevie give us a wave!' which the miserable sod didn't! I only realised at the next home game that he was a

Milllwall Wise Security steward when I saw him outside the New Den, small world eh!

At Brentford's Griffin Park on November 14th 2009 at the front of the terrace standing pitchside behind the goal there were two Asian Stewards facing towards us, at half time they were greeted with 'Immigration knows you're here!'

At Sheffield United's Brammal Lane in February 2011 three girl stewards walked along the front of our behind the goal stand and were greeted with the customary– 'Get your tits out for the lads!' and less complimentary if that is the phrase to a fat member of the female steward contingent –

'Arse like a rhino, she's got an arse like a rhino!'

A Brizzle City Steward Who Are Ya? A black steward was in the line-up in front of us at Ashton Gate as we were held in the ground after the game in August 2010, to relieve our boredom and cheer ourselves up we sang the sarcastic– 'One Kolo Toure, There's only one Kolo Toure!' Which he laughed at bless him.

Finally at Scunthorpe United on April 25th 2011, they had positioned a young female steward to the right of the goal in front of us, this poor sod got –'She takes it up the arse!'/'Get your tits out for the lads!'/'We can smell your C*** from here!' and '400 of us one of you!' implying I think that she was in for a treat, a four hundred man seeing to, like a porn star Shagathon!

The girl took it well, amazingly, but the head steward who like the CBL steward's top boy looks a smidge, well very like Harry Potter! Replaced her she was moved back into the Steward collective. He got 'There's only One Harry Potter!'/'Harry, Harry give us a song!' and 'We want the young girl back!'

London –

As a Londoner and a cockney to boot, which some have tried I can tell you, I would like to include a golden oldie London song, which in my opinion, we should be obligated to sing whenever we play Northern teams especially 'Oop North'.

There is nothing strange about the song but the added lyrics are a bit odd – 'Maybe it's because i'm a Londoner, that I love London so, maybe it's because i'm a Londoner, that I think of her wherever I go, I get a funny feeling inside of me (spunk!) Just walking up and down, maybe it's because i'm a Londoner, that I love London town (get off me sister!)'

I have no idea who added the 'Spunk' and 'Sister' portions, but I am glad to say that I have never felt a funny feeling inside of me, I am not Gay so particularly not someone elses spunk! And I do not have a sister so it was not me. It is not quite 'New York New York' but we like it.

Country Boys –

Naturally, every 'yokel' side get 'You only sing when you're farming!'

More specifically a few years back we gave Ipswich fans a damn good bleating at Portman Road –

'Bah, bah, bah, bah! etc' To the tune of 'Love and Marriage' popular on TV adverts at the time, which I think they enjoyed.

Generally we have also sung country comparisons, for example we sing –

'You only sing on your tractor!' and 'You're going home to your tractors!'

Yeovil Town's first ever visit to the New Den in August 2006 had a couple of variations on the rustic theme, Yeovil sang 'You've only got one song!' to 'No one likes us' to which we replied –

'You've only got one farm!' And the surreal 'Does your tractor know you're here?'

A couple of questioning statements –

'You must have come on a tractor!'

Answer 'No I usually come in the hayloft with the farmer's daughter!'

'Is your tractor parked outside?'

Answer 'No but my top of the line 4 x 4 Land Rover is!'

Norwich City fans at Carrow Road in October 2005 naturally got the usual 'I can't read…' and rustic chants, they also got 'You only sing when you're ploughing!'/'Town full of in breds, you're just a town full of in breds!'/'In breds in breds what's the score?' and 'There's only one Jerry Springer!'

Another in bred reference I assume?

Norwich City fans at Carrow Road New Year's Day 2018

'You've Got More Toes than Us!' and 'Six Thumbs No Fans!'

On 29th October 2011 Ipswich Town fans left in their droves as they crashed to defeat, they were greeted with – 'We Can See You Sneaking Out!'/'Cheerio, Cheerio, Cheerio!' and 'F**K Off, You Might As Well F*ck Off!' in addition to the 'Town Full Of Inbreds and 'I Can Drive A Tractor 'deluge they also got 'You're Going Home to Your Sister!'

We London Lion Divas Pestering the Welsh aka Sheep Worriers Chester in the Deva Stadium –

For the FA Cup 1st Round trip to Chester City on November 8th 2008, at their newish Deva Stadium (sic)! Stadium? As I said re Leyton Orient's one, Stadium? I like a laugh!!!! It was a slightly vamped up Amateur ground in my opinion, it was my 103rd away ground watching the 'Wall at this time and a first trip for me to Chester City, just thought that I would mention it.

It is a ground that is apparently partially in Wales and just to inform any Taffs who have not visited there yet, we saw enough sheep as we drove through the rural countryside roads en route, to fulfill a Welshman's ultimate pre/post match entertainment and

Welly boot filling Sexual fantasies. Although it was a small crowd 1932, it had a piss poor atmosphere and they had a drummer in the terraced end behind the opposite goal, which is a real sign of how shit the home support will be, having to have a drummer or band playing to back any chants in my opinion, except at Leicester with Drummer Lee Jobber as you will see later on, we 389 there sang some interesting chants –

Due to Chester City's blue and white kit, Millwall played in our third kit the Stewards/Blackpool brightly coloured Orange one, so we sang – 'Kenny Jackett's Tango Army!'

Implying that our side looked like thin versions of the fat orange Tango advertisement man.

The home stands to our left and right had bizarre names emblazoned on the front of them.

The left hand west stand was called 'The Liversage Stand' this got – 'You're sitting in a sausage stand!'

The right hand East stand was called 'The Vaughan Stand' this got –

'You're sitting in the Johnny Stand!'

To imply that it was something to do with Johnny Vaughan or was something to do with condoms I think!

We also sang 'Are You Johnny or Frank?' to imply that it was named after either entertainers Johnny Vaughan or Frankie Vaughan.

The terraced stand I mentioned above was called the Harry McNally Stand this got no abuse because we couldn't think of anything funny or abusive to sing about it I don't think..

Regarding their new partial Welsh position we continually sang 'Sheep Sheep Sheep Shaggers', bleated Sheep noises at them and we sang 'You Welsh C***s!'/'Can you hear the Taffy's sing?' and 'You're not English Anymore!'

We also sang 'England, England, England!' to highlight that we were English and they weren't! They sang this too, but we just refused to believe them!

They sang 'You're just a bus stop in West Ham!' and 'You're just a small town in West Ham!'

In response we sang 'You're just a small town in Wales!' and most humourously

'When you was just a little boy, you asked your Mother what should I be? Should I be English? Should I be Welsh, here's what she said to you, just F*** a sheep my son, Just F*** a sheep my son, just F*** a sheep my son, F*** a sheep, a sheep!'

We also sang 'Shall we F*** a sheep for you?' in reply to their 'Shall we sing a song for you?'

In the land of Captain Pugwash's Seaman Stains at Staines 'Massive' Town Saturday 28th November 2009

This FA Cup 2nd round trip was a real trip back to the world of non league football, for a kick off they did not sell meat pies, what! The loos were portaloos that were behind our side terrace and some tactical construction genius had put wooden boards in front of some of them so that you could not open several of the doors, so we had a lovely ablutions trip to piss up the trees, whilst ankle deep amidst the piss strewn leaves and mud, it was lovely, strangely they did not have anyone there offering hand towels, washing delicacies or scent, like they do in West End clubs/bars, why not!

At the game in the land of Ali Gs, Staines Massive, which is a real slip up in the Trades Description Act department, massive what? There was an Ali G impersonator handing out pitchside literature pre match and they had a player nicknamed Ali C, because his name was Ali Chaaban, who was sentenced for a drug offence, when he pleaded guilty at West London Magistrates' Court to possessing a class C controlled drug with intent to supply 845g of cannabis, and was jailed for 8 months in 2007.

He obviously became the main target of our abuse and naturally scored a late highly dubious equalizer from a penalty given by one of the most dodgy bent refs that I have ever seen, which is certainly a tough group to top, the Ref (sic) Anthony Taylor was an amalgamation of the 'reffing biased talents' of D'Urso/Rennie/Friend and Tanner combined, please imagine that to envisage what he was like to give you a flavour of his display for those who were not there.

Enough reffing rants on to what Ali C, got – 'You're supposed to be inside!'/'Ali C's a dealer!'/'Dealer, Dealer!' and 'How much for a line?'

The home Chav fans opposite us in the stand (sic) who sang 'It's just like watching Brazil!' due to their kit colours were greeted with 'It's just like watching AC Milan!' from us for our red and black striped away kit, they also were greeted by we gathered Lions for their 'we're hard!' stance with 'Back to school on Monday!'

Non-PC alert –
Caravan Dwellers v London Townies –

Continuing the exchanges between us and our Kentish chums Gillingham, some chants from the 12th February 2005 game at Priestfield Stadium.

From Them To Us -

To start the anti Millwall and Fulham adapted Man U chant –

'Build a bonfire, build a bonfire put the Millwall on the top, put the Fulham in the middle and then burn the f***ing lot!'

In homage to our late late Play Off defeat at the New Den against Birmingham City they sang –

'Stern John in the last minute!'

There was of course the customary Townie/Gypsy abuse and response -

'We can't read, we can't write, we wear gold and Nikes, we all come from Gillingham and we're all f***ing pikeys!'/'You live in a cardboard box!' And 'We've all got a garden!'

From Us To Them –

On a caravan/gypsy/carnie tip we sang '5 kids, 4 dads, 3 dogs, 2 cats!'/'We've got running water!'/'Wheel's on your house go round and round, round and round, round and round, wheel's on your house go round and round all day long! And 'Fairground time – Saturday night!'

Finally in this section a chant that West Ham United had previously sung to us earlier in the season, it was sung to the tune of The Addams Family –

'Your sister is your Mother, your Father is your Brother, you all f… one another – the pikey family!'

We sang a chant about an old Millwall favourite Not!!! The sadly Gills departed Andy Hessenthaler–

'Where's your German gone?'

The customary mouthy home fans next to us included one individual who stood for the whole game right next to the segregation meshing between the two sets of fans. As a fashion statement he was wearing a blue and yellow woolen hat, a la Benny from 'Crossroads' and a home shirt, which unfortunately had a later to be a Millwall player's name 'Spiller' plastered across the back. Here's a selection of just some of the abuse he received, all of which he stoically did his best to look like the barbs were water off a duck's back, staring straight ahead with his arms folded.

The Lions fans standing near to him mockingly sang 'Let's all do the Spiller!'

And crossed their arms with a scowl on their face to copy his continual demeanour.

On the sartorial tip we sang – 'He's got a shit hat on his head!' And the bizarre 'He's got a Malteser on his head!' Finally on the paedophile front we sang – 'Spiller's bird is only 4!' And 'Watch out Spiller's about!' I'm sure he'll choose his wardrobe more carefully each time that we visit, especially as Spiller later moved to us!

At the New Den in August 2006 for the League Cup game the Gillingham fans showed their colours by unveiling a St George's flag with 'Pikey Army' emblazoned across it, I think it was more a case of if you can't beat the abuse, join the abuse.

At the Priestfield Stadium game on October 13th 2007 the above mentioned flag was on display at the back of the home section next to us with their young 'Boys' located next to us.

To show their youth and Chav behaviour Millwall's fans sang – 'You've all got nappy rash!' and 'You only sing when you're thieving!'

Not specifically to the mentioned games but a couple of old favourites that get a frequent airing –

"You Can't Read, You Can't Write, You Wear Gold And Nikes, You Are All From Gillingham And You Are F****** Pikeys." And "You Can Shove Your Lucky Heather Up Your A***."

Non-PC alert –
Death –

We have sung about the demise of Bobby Moore, Dodi Fayed and Matthew Harding in the past, which I have listed in my other two English Millwall books, continuing the tradition at Telford United in the FA Cup in 2003/4. On a pitch like a very sandy beach and in the wake of the then Morecambe Chinese cockle picker's tragedy – 'There's a load of F...ing Chinkies on your Pitch!'

Non-PC alert –
Sex Rears Its Ugly Head, Again –

To start a few opposition chants –
Former Millwall player Jody Morris also ex Chelsea, Leeds, etc star was involved in a sexual assault case that was subsequently dropped, prior joining us in 2004/5. Innocent or not he was lambasted by Plymouth Argyle fans at Home Park in August 2004 who

chanted – 'Rapist! Rapist!' Each time he was involved in a challenge. On a similar theme Cardiff fans at the New Den in October 2004 sang –

'Jody Morris is a rapist, is a rapist!' As did Leeds fans in March and August 2005.

Graham Stack on loan from Arsenal and only two days away from a rape trial surprising played against West Ham United at the New Den on Sunday 21st November 2004 consequently the 'Appy 'Ammers sang 'Sex Case' and 'For rape, your going down for rape!'

Moving on to Millwall –

The sadly departed Paul Ifill and Matt Lawrence (aka Shaggy) were shown in the Sunday Sport a couple of years ago cavorting with 'Sport Stunnas' with a headline of –

'Millwall stars get stuck into Sunday Sport babes'.

Paul Ifill in particular was pictured sucking on a pert mam this was reprinted in our fanzines so for the next home game he got – 'Ifill got her tits out, la, la, la, etc.' The Sport from experience is the only paper that nobody admits to buying, because anyone I have found reading it invariably claims to have found it on the bus, train, tube, bench, pavement or wherever, yeah of course you have!!!

Fulham fans on 20th April 2018 at the Den sang 'Ryan Sessegnon He's One Of Our Own' not sexual but I response we sang -'Michael Jackson He's One Of Your Own' in a paedophile inference hence sexual reference

When Keith Gillespie played for Leicester City at the New Den on August 14th 2004 as one of those accused in the La Manga sex scandal he got – 'Keith Gillespie sex offender!'

Collectively Leicester's team got –

'Leicester City sex offenders!' And 'You're just a town full of rapists!'

Notts Forest played at the New Den on October 3rd 2004 and their fans were serenaded with –

'Robin Hood sex offender!' In 2008 at the City Ground many sang a variation on this by singing –

'Brian Clough sex offender!' Which many Lions fans objected to as he was in reality the greatest Manager that should have been allowed to Manage England's National Side and the only away manager to get a standing ovation from tunnel to dug out at the Old Den..

Delia Smith at Norwich City's Carrow Road in October 2005 got some new abuse, see 'I Was Born Under The Cold Blow Lane' for our previous repertoire. The new/adapted chants were –

To start the non sexual celebrity chef reference–

'One Gordon Ramsey,There's only one Gordon Ramsey!'

Then the Sexual references –

'Oh, Delia, wowo, Oh, Delia wowo she's only 5 foot one, she takes it up the bum!' and 'Delia, Delia you're a slut, Delia you're a slut!'

At the New Den game a few week's later we added this Delia culinary talents appreciation chant –

Oh, Delia, wowo, Oh, Delia wowo, she's only 5 foot two, she makes a lovely stew!'

I dare say that she does but as none of us have ever eaten one I would imagine, it was just a she's a great cook guess on our part, that and the fact that 5 foot two rhymes with lovely stew, at least it was very poetically correct!

At Ipswich Town in March 2006 we sang – 'Paedo!' to their horse Muppet thing and their bumpkin fans, God knows why!

On a similar tack at Watford's Vicarage Road land of the Elton John abuse as listed in previous books and in the wake of the Jimmy Saville scandal on Tuesday 7th November 2012 we sang to both a chav standing in the stand next to us and to Watford's Troy Deeney – ' Jimmy Saville touched your Mum, touched your Mum, touched your Mum, Jimmy Saville touched your Mum, he's your Father!'

On a sexual tip former Watford's enemy Luton Town's one time Manager David Pleat with his kerb crawling was included with – ' David Pleat F***ed your Dad!'

Closing the section on a Watford front in a play on the we forgot that you were here chant, Milllwall to the quiet Watford fans next to us we sang – 'We forgot that you were queer!'

Finally sexual cuckoldry ex England player at Reading on Saturday 26th October 2013 got – 'Terry F**ked Your Mrs!' and 'There's Only One John Terry!'

Aston Villa fans at Villa Park with John Terry now playing on 9th December 2017 at Villa Park got – 'John Terry He's Shagging/F***ing Your Mum' in response we got 'John Terry He's Shagged More Than You!'

Not Terry but there was also a strange chant from us to one of them 'You're Just A fat Danny Dyer!' and in reply they sang 'Danny Dyer He's F***ed More Than You!'

Finally, some chant queries –

Can the Young Boys of Berne fans really go? – (Clap, clap, clap, clap, etc.) 'Young Boys!'

Like a paedophiles glee club, a Jiimy Saville/Rolf Harris/Jonathan King/Gary Glitter rally or a Baden Powell 'Scouting for Boys' Appreciation Society. Surely, they cannot sing at all can they?

Not so much the chant, but an odd club name in a similar paedophile vein to some of the other sections in this chapter, great for the Scout who is scouting for Young Boys, eek!

Be like Nancy fans singing 'Hello Hello We Are The Nancy Boys!' Makes you think doesn't it.

Rangers In Our Midst At The New Den March 2011

We gave QPR the league leaders in the Championship a very warm Old Den style welcome for our

2 – 0 victory on Tuesday 8th March 2011.

Here we go with a selection –

To delusional Cyber Warriors Rangers fans – 'What's it like to run at home?' following incidents at the away game at Loftus Road and around Sherperds Bush.

To their beloved then manager Neil Warnock, star of a video about a trip to the New Den with Sheffield United, when Paddy Kenny had a cosy fire side chat with Kevin Muscat in the Tunnel.

Moving on to his QPR tenure whilst standing in his technical area –

'Sit down you Northern C***!'/'Sit down Pinnochio!' and 'Big Nose, You've got a f***ing big nose!'

Moving to Paddy Kenny and adding to the repertoire listed in the goalkeeper section later, whilst standing in front of us in the CBL – the Peschisolido song 'You're s*** and your wife's a slag!'and 'There's only one Kevin Muscat!' as listed above.

QPR's Moroccan maverick Adel Taarabt for his arabic background got –

'Your Mum is a terrorist!'/'Terrorist, Terrorist, Terrorist!' and 'Shoe Shoe Shoe Bomber!'

To highlight our victory we sang – 'Who The F*** are QPR?'

T'Barnsley Away January 21st 2012

We played Barnsley at their whippet worriers Oakwell outpost on 21st January 2012, at the end of what had been a very strange week –

On the Saturday before 14th January 2012 we lost at home 0 – 6 at home to Birmingham City, due to having to play them and all the officials, hence being forced to play with 9 men due to 2 dubious reds.

We then played Dagenham And Redbridge at home in an FA Cup 3rd Round Replay on Tuesday 17th January 2012 and win 5 – 0.

We then travel Oop Norf to South Yorkshire to finish the week and win 3 – 1 with a second consecutive hat trick by Darius Henderson, in homage to the victory we sang –'We've Got Our Millwall Back!'

Additionally to any woeful yahoo by Barnsley we sang the bizarre adaption of 'What The F***ing Hell Was That?' by singing – 'What The Shitting hell was that?'

Whether this final chant has any grammatical connection to the English language I am not prepared to say!

T' Barnsley Oakwell again this time on Saturday 17th March 2018 St Patrick's Day and a 2 – 0 win for the Lions 6th consecutive away win, equaling Kenny Jackett's previous record from League 1

Chants re 29th May 2016 Wembley Play Off Final Trouble

'Where Were You At Wembley?'/'You'll Run Again!'/'You Shit Yourselves!'/'Did You Run At Wembley?

Something that I always find funny at Northern Grounds are Hoardings around pitch especially at Barnsley that say Bapps For Bolts, I always think it should say Bolt For Baps! i.e. Hurry To The Boobies!!!

'Just Say Ah!'

There is the bog-standard injured player euthanasia suggestion of – 'Let Him Die, Let Him Die, Let Him Die!'

Specifically to show our compassion any injured Northern player's get – 'Let the northern b...... die!'

Finally and even more specifically, any prone Gillingham player gets – 'Let the f...ing gypo die!'

Star Spotting

Real

Lennox Lewis was in an executive box behind us on Highbury's Clock End and we serenaded him with –

'Bruno, Bruno!' This did not work as he beat him and forced him into perpetual Panto.

Imaginary

Next, not so much celebrity spotting as mass-murderer spotting – Many years ago, any game that we played in Yorkshire would prompt us to sing –

'There's only one Jack the Ripper!'

Due to the then reign of terror of the Yorkshire Ripper and to remind them of the real London original.

Relegation Stations

This is not only a Millwall trait but at the time of any relegation pushes to take the sting out of any detractor's barbs the best idea is to insult yourselves so –

'Que sera, sera, whatever will be will be, we're going to Barnsley, que sera, sera!'

Which I first heard us sing at Derby County, when we were relegated from the old first Division.

More recently we have sung – 'We're going down; we're going down, Millwall's going down!'/

'We're so shit it's unbelievable!'/'Where shit and we're going down!'/

'We're shit and we know we are!' And 'Going down, going down, going down!'

Moving away from self abuse to relegation haunted team abuse when we played a second from bottom Nottingham Forest at the City Ground on Gary Megson's managerial debut on 15th January 2005 we sang the following – 'Brian Clough? You're having a laugh!'/'Gary Megson? You're having a laugh!'/'We'll never play you again!' and 'You're shit and you're going down!'

As Millwall languished at the foot of The Championsip in August 2005 at the early stage of what looked like a relegation battle in the soap opera that was the 2005/6 season during a 5 – 0 defeat at Reading, with gallows humour we sang – 'We are bottom of the League, say we are bottom of the League!' We also sang 'The football League is upside down!'

At a 4-0 defeat at home to Sheffield United in October 2005 and with Millwall languishing at the foot of the table we sang –'Now you're gonna believe us we're gonna win the league!' This was reprised again after our first home win against Norwich City in November 2005.

At Coventry City's Ricoh Arena on December 10th 2005 we were losing 1 – 0 and the home fans sang the regulation relegation chant 'Going down, going down, going down!' to which we replied with the sarcastic 'So are we, so are we, so are we!'

Against Brighton we sang 'That's why you're going down!'

To every Seagulls wayward shot or pass, not to allege their fans are going down obviously!

Derby fans at Pride Park in April 2006 sang the sadly accurate – 'You're going back to the Football League again!'

Against the Pikeys/Clothes Peg floggers/Lucky Heather flogging Fortune Tellers – sorry Gillingham, I didn't want to be anti Gypo racist, oh I do don't I sorry! At the New Den on April 10th 2010 when we won 4 – 0 to go second whilst the Kent folk were heading in to the danger zone we sang '3 nil and you're going down!' then '4 nil and you're going down! Not forgetting the sexual intimation – 'Going down on your sister -You're going down on your sister!

Sarcastic Fantastic

I suppose you could say that the whole chant chapter is sarcastic, but anyway -

To start obviously not a Millwall original and something that I've mentioned before in my other Millwall books but I will never forget the fantastically ironic rendition at our first visit to Anfield in

November 1988 – 'Who the f***ing hell are you?'

In the past in response to Sheffield United fans anti Wednesday chants we have often sung the following oddity 'We hate Tuesday and we hate Tuesday, we are the Tuesday haters!'

When we lost a 3 nil lead at home to Crewe at the New Den on 9th April 2005, the home crowd naturally booed the team until we got out of jail with a late penalty to make it 4 – 3 at which point the CBL sang – '5-4, we're going to lose 5-4!'

Continuing the theme at Reading during a 5 – 0 defeat in August 2005 we sang the following …

At 3-0 we sang – 'Were gonna win 4-3!'

At 4-0 we sang – '4-nil and you're wife's a slag!'

Additionally as the goals rained in we sang to the quiet home fans we sang –

'3/4/5 nil and you still don't sing!'

At Luton Town on Bank Holiday Monday 2005 we scored only our 3rd goal of the season so we sang –

'We scored a goal, you must be shit!'

On the team inspiring front who can forget –

'Will we ever score a goal?'/'Will we ever win a game?' And 'Shit, shit, shit!'

The latter chant in 2007/8 followed a bad showing by the Lions, especially at home, that should encourage them! No it bloody wouldn't!!!!

At an unusually quiet Britannia Stadium Stoke City in February 2006 we sang –

'We only sing when we're losing!'

Some more popular sarcastic Millwall observational chants –

'(...) nil and a long way home!'/'You might as well go home, etc. you might as well f... off!' And 'You're not very good, you're not very good, you're not very, you're not very; you're not very good – shit!'

There was the time after we sold Steven Reid when every free kick that we won near to goal was greeted with sarcastic chants of

'Reidy!' forlornly hoping for one of his pre departure specials.

Similarily for any shot shy performances post Neil Harris' initial departure we would sarcastically break into 'Super, super Neil, super, super Neil, super, super Neil, super Neil Harris!'

Coventry City's eventual fall from the top flight and visit to the New Den in November 2001 saw them suffering from delusions of grandeur. As their ginger magician Manager Gordon Strachan had taken them down, only then to depart, we felt it only fair to remind the away fans so we sang -

'There's only one Gordon Strachan!' And 'Where's your Gordon gone?'

During the game, we lost our 1-0 lead to go 2-1 down, and their delusions kicked in, so they sang of their 'We Won't Be Here Very Long' superiority – 'Who are ya?/Now you're gonna believe us we're gonna win the league!/'You'll never play us again! And 'Going up, going up, going up!'

You get the picture. Sadly for them these songs were sung far too soon I'm afraid.

Millwall clawed their way back and eventually ran out 3-2 winners, which prompted the whole of the home crowd to stand as one and chant/point at the away fans – 'You're Going To Win F... all!'

Sweet when that happens isn't it? This put them in their place that is for sure.

At QPR in November 2004, we sang this old favourite –

'QPR, QPR, QPR – QPR Ha, ha, ha, ha, ha, ha, ha!'

For the New Den return in February 2005 we sang 'The Hokey Cokey' as QPR did their team huddle in mid pitch.

Against our beaten 2003/4 FA Cup Semi Final opponents Sunderland at home on bonfire night 2004 we sang the sarcastic – 'If you all went to Cardiff clap your hands!' And 'We all went on a European tour!'

Referring to the old away game police policy of locking us in the ground for hours we used to sing – 'We're not going home, we're not going home, we're not going, we're not going, we're not go-

241

ing home!' At Brighton & Hove Albion in December 2005 the home fans sang the old chestnut –

'Is that all you take away?' In response we sang – 'Is that all you allocate?'

More humour than sarcasm to close the Withdean chants–

We also sang 'Let's all do the relay, let's all do the relay, la, la, la, la, la, la!'

As we stood behind the goal with a running track between us and the distant goal.

Some self-abusing sarcasm -- the opening home league game of 2002/3, a humiliating 6-0 defeat against Rotherham United, prompted pleas for mercy, when it began to rain heavily and we capitulated, we sang – 'Call it off, call it off, call it off!'

There were also requests to show the cricket test match being played that day on the video screen instead of this embarrassing debacle with chants of – 'Put the cricket on the box!'

Also v Rotherham United this time in Yorkshire on Saturday 28th February 2015 we took the lead 1 – 0 and we sang – 'How Shit Must You Be We're Winning Away!' didn't last we lost 2 – 1!

More bizarre than sarcastic at Scunthorpe United on Easter Monday April 2011 we sang to one of their players 'There's only one Justin Bieber!' God alone knows who this was aimed at and where it came from!!

At Ipswich Town in March 2006 as a snow storm blew around Portman Road we sang –

'Lets' all build a snowman, la la la, la la la!'

At Crewe Alexandra on 16th September 2006 that old crowd favourite, the dog running about on the pitch prompted our following chant to the comatose home fans –

'Get your Mother off the pitch!'

Brizzle City Away first game of the season back in Championship on Saturday 7th August 2010, pre match they were greeted with – 'You sleep with your sisters kids!'

The game ended 3 – 0 to us and we sang to the Bumpkins, sorry

Local Yokels, sorry is that a bit regionally stereotypical? 'In Breds In Breds what's the score?' and 'Championship? You're having a laugh!' which they had sung to us pre match. As our goals rattled in and near the end to a lot of home fans who had not left many of their compatriots had done as we rolled the home side over, we questioned there staying by singing the sarcastic –' What are you still doing here?'

At Reading's Madejski Stadium for the opening game of the following season on August 6th 2011, in tribute to Reading forward Shane Long the much sought after player, rumoured to be playing his last Reading game as the Transfer window edged towards it's closure in a few weeks,, their fans sang 'There's only one Shane Long!' in response and slipping back in to sarcastic reality we sang – 'Shane Long – he won't be here for long, he won't be here for long, he won't be here for long!'

Finally Barnet at the New Den on 11th August 2015 in the Capital One Cup the magnificently named Michael Gash came on as substitute and the Barnet fans all sang the classic – 'We Love Gash!' no sexual connotation there at all obviously!!!!

Grounds For Improvement –

They say that no one is more self-righteous than a reformed person is, so our newish ground prompted us to give it the big one at away matches at clubs with an old style ground particularly -

'Shit ground, no fans!' And 'Shitty ground, shitty ground, shitty ground!'

We have very often sarcastically sung the first chant if we are locked in by the police in an otherwise empty stadium and at super swish new grounds like the Madejski and Ricoh Arena.

Specifically relating to a hail lashed afternoon on the away section of the open to the elements Brian Moore temporary stand at Gillingham's Priestfield Stadium in February 2005 we sang –

'Shit ground no roof!' On a similar tack as rain teemed down on us on the open Meccano kit away stand at The Withdean in December 2005 we combined a crap ground chant with a gay chant–'Shit ground – Queer fans!'

At Goodison Park for the FA Cup 3rd round Replay in January 2006, we sat in the upper tier of an old style side stand, complete with restrictive view pillars consequently we sang – 'The ground is worse than QPR!'

'Quiet Here Isn't It?' aka 'Are You Off?' –

Leicester Ciity fans on Tuesday 28th December at the New Den sang 'Can You Hear The Millwall Sing? No No I Can't Hear A F**Ing Thing!' and 'It's So Quiet At The Den!' isn't delusional deafness a wonderful thing! Sorry, 2 – 0 to us wasn't it?

Moving on to the real Librarians -quiet fans i.e. Watford, Northampton Town, Sheffield United, Leyton Orient, Colchester United, Ipswich Town, Crystal Palace, etc etc, especially at their place get – 'Will you ever sing a song?' And 'Do you ever sing at home?'

At sombre and solemn Pride Park Derby County on Monday 3rd January 2011 we sang the above plus 'More noise in a library!'

Northampton Town's largely silent presumably Hungover from New Year's Eve fans on 1st January 2008 at Sixfields sang 'We Only Sing When We're Winning!' when they burst into song after they had taken a 1- 0 lead prior to shutting up for practically the rest of the match that they led until we equalised before the very near end.

The Millwall innovated 'You're Support Is F**ing S***!'

Was what we could definitely have replied to them but we couldn't be arsed to when we scored a very late equaliser.

When then table topping Ipswich Town came to the New Den on Boxing Day 2004 their fans sang –

'We are top of the league!' As we took an unassailable 3 – 1 lead we sang –

'Top of the league? You're having a laugh!' And 'Top of the league – you still don't sing!'

At Crystal Palace in December 2005 we sang to the slumbering suburbanites –

'It's nice to know you're f…ing here!'

At Colchester United on Bank Holiday Monday at Easter the crowd was 7393 with over 3000 of us, so to highlight this we sang – 'We're supposed to be away!'

On a bizarre quiet home fans front against a very unusually quiet Stoke City fans in February 2006 we sang – '2 – 1 and you still don't sing' and 'You quiet Northern bastards!'

What about at Reading's Madejski on 22nd February 2011 to their bloody drum accompaniment we sang –

'Make some noise without your drum!' too bloody right, an annoying bleeding racket and positive signs of non passionate support.if you need a bloody drum in my opinion!

Southampton in a FA Cup 4th Round Replay Tuesday 7th February 2012 in a quarter full only St Mary's they sang our enemy's chant 'I'm Forever Blowing Bubbles', in reply we sang their enemy Portsmouth's 'Play Up Pompey' that aside re quiet home support we sang – 'Where's Your F***ing Home Support?'

QPR fans at The New Den 19th October 2013 sang to us – 'No Noise from the Pikey Boys!' in reference to the caravans parked along the Ilderton Road between South Bermondsey station and Zampa Road.

The final chant is an ever-popular Millwall chant that I have mentioned before it is sung to fans that try to get out early, in some cases they are streaming out in droves hence – 'We Can See You Sneaking Out!'

Why leave early, you wouldn't leave a film before the end unless it was rubbish would you?

Oh! I see! In some cases, it is just the 'Boys' trying to leave early to get into position for the post-match festivities.

At Sixfields in 2008 Norhampton Town fans sang that we were all Pikeys but original and wrong, The home fans to our right sang the offensive, to us anyway – 'You Make West Ham Look Posh!'

I know their intention was to wind us up by comparing our supposed lack of sartorial elegance to West Ham United fans our very very hated local Rivals, but speaking as an East Ender, the Farmer's fans team might be named the Cobblers but that was what they sung as they must have never been to the Newham part of the East End! A Saville Row fashion style area it ain't.

I Want A Ground With an Atmosphere, Goodbye To That Nowadays

I hate going to grounds like Portman Road Ipswich Town or Vicarage Road Watford especially as the atmosphere is totally non existent, which as a Millwall fan used to the Den annoys me massively and makes me wonder how on earth do the home players play in this ground, where is the encouragement?

I know what to expect at these grounds but what really upsets me at modern football is the loss of grounds with proper Denlike home atmosphere's, grounds like Ninian Park Cardiff City.

Having been replaced by a new all seater stadium's and lost the fan mentality completely, seemingly, the hostility of Ninian has been replaced by happy clappy taffs – eek!

I hated it and feel sorry for real Cardiff City fans having to endure what it has become, Cardiff City Stadium is now about as hostile as Reading, Ipswich, Brighton or Watford or perish the thought Palace!

I think that the Soul Crew must have retired!

The same has happened at Middlesbough, their old ground Ayresome Park used to be a proper football ground like Ninian Park. and The Old Den

However as Cardiff City Stadium is, Middlesbrough's Riverside is, it is a nice stadium, but a seen that, been there done that, modern copycat, it is another PR creation, i.e. ground must.have a drummer and people waving flags, type of b***ocks.

Their old ground had a proper atmosphere, as an old Wall fan something that I am used to and think how it should be.

On Saturday 19th April 2014, we were in a side section on the corner in line with the corner flag, and behind the goal next to us, they had a drummer, which is the mark of something that is definitely wrong in my opinion, apart from Leicester's Lee Jobber who you will see a section about later in this chapter.

There was also someone waving a big flag, god knows how that reflects a good atmosphere or inspires the home team! To him/her we sang – 'Whose The W***er With The Flag?'

Strangely after we sang this they stopped waving for a while, only to restart a while later, perhaps they are on a time and motion contract and have to do for X amount of time per game!

To highlight what it was like we sang numerous chants –

Stick Your Drum Up Your Arsehole!'/'Millwall Don't Need A Drum!'/'Is This A Library?'

We also sang –'Sit Down In Your Family Stand!'/'Sit Down And Behave Yourself!'

Specifically aimed at an elderly bloke in this Family section to our right – 'Sit Down Grandad!'

This was not our Grandad but a bloke sitting near the halfway line, who was standing and lambasting Boro, nothing wrong with that, but we thought we should take the piss out of him so we did!

You might have gathered that I hate lack of atmosphere grounds and really hate the loss of grounds that used to have proper atmospheres.

In the Identi Kit Stadium modern era it is probably some sort of Health and Safety ethos, cannot sing too loud as you will end up with a sore throat! Do not show any real passion you will need therapy!

Where Am I? Who is performing tonight?

Not chant related but modern happy clappy identikit stadia –

Speaking along the same lines as I said above about Middlesbrough and Cardiff City I give you Coventry City's Ricoh aka Event Arena! On Saturday 16th April 2016, we travelled to Coventry and found inside that the Refreshment staff all had Millwall T Shirts on and there was a bloody great Millwall flag behind the counter.

I know they were trying to appease our hostile nature, but this tactic goes straight over our heads, we were given 1800 tickets approx. and had tried to get more, which were turned down enabling the West Midlands Police to adopt their heavy handed tactics, now excuse me for interfering with Police and Coventry City intelligence, but if they had given us more tickets that would have made Millwall people who could not get tickets happier, also the Bar in the ground was shut, nothing unusual there!

However, I think the following highlights that giving Millwall the requested additional tickets would have made far more financial sense my reasoning Ricoh holds 32,500 approx.

The end of the ground directly opposite us was empty save for a few people in wheelchairs and a huge Flag with Jimmy Hill's black and white photo on.

Not that I can know more than the professionals! But as a team usually like to kick towards the home end in the second half, in this instance as Wall were the only occupants at one end and the other end was pretty much completely empty, so the kick towards the home end fans was impossible at the Ricoh.

The crowd was announced as 11,000 or so, so they had over 20.000 empty seats, therefore would it not have made more sense financially to sell us more tickets. After all as I have highlighted above there were plenty of empty seats, for example next to our section itself it was like a vast wasteland cover partially in netting, and stewards/Police.

Respecting Your Own Players –

The Old Den and to a lesser degree the New Den crowd breeds a Millwall type of player. 'Kick, Bollock and Bite' as I called them in my other book.

A Millwall crowd's mentality was and still is, give a hundred or one hundred and ten percent and the players will have no problem, swan about and be afraid, be very afraid.

I suppose it probably happens at every ground but over the years especially at the Old Den, it seemed that different sections of the ground disliked different home players, with a player barracked and hated in one section being replaced by a different hate-figure in another part of the ground, I know not why

Before I start could you imagine if the great ex player Uwe 'The Duvet' Fuchs had been joined at Millwall by his German international compatriot of the time Kuntz? Thus summing up nicely what the rest of the Football world think we are anyway, the dream pairing.

In the early days of the New Den, we had Tony Witter who was very popular despite his tendency for last minute lapses; he used to get – 'Walking in a Witter wonderland!'

Millwall Youth product given the Captiancy in 2014/5 on the Good Ship Holloway In one game as a local boy Sid Nelson gets – 'Sid Nelson He's One of our own!'

Humourously loanee Andros Townsend at Scunthorpe United Easter Monday 25th April 2011, got

'There's only one Andros Townsend!' and the adapted ' There's only two Andy Townsends!' allying Andros wth ex top pro now ITV Sport pundit Andy Townsend, clever eh!

On September 27th 2005 at the New Den then QPR's defender Danny Shittu received the classic – 'You're Shittu and you know you are!' He signed for us in 2010/11 and received 'Shittu, Shittu!' each time that he touched the ball, he also received an adapted version of the above Witter chant 'Walking in a Shittu Wonderland!'

this was sung by us on a Friday 10th December 2010 at Swansea City, it was chilly night but little did we know that we were about to enter Ice Station Zebra Narnia Wonderland a week or so after!

Hero to villain time when he returned with his chosen team QPR at the New Den in March 2011 he was greeted with ' Shittu Shittu, You're a C***!' and due to his money oriented decision to join high flying Rangers rather than us – 'There's only one greedy b***tard!' and when we took a first goal lead he got –'Shittu Shittu, what's the score?' his dismissal that lead to a Penalty that extended our lead to the final score of 2 – 0 was greeted by us warmly.

How opinions change, in his second spell hen he became Millwall captain in 2012/3 he receives 'Shittu!' everytime he wins a tackle or more so when he wins a header hich he does practically everytime!

After he had scored the winner in the FA Cup Quarter Final at Blackburn Rovers on Wednesday 13th March 2013, when asked how we had won he said 'That's What We Do!' this echoed around Charlton Athletic's Valley on the Saturday 16th March the next game, when we sang 'Danny Shittu That's What We Do, That's What We Do, Danny Shittu, That's What We Do!' this also prompted a T Shirt to be brought out, that said the same with a caricature of his face on the front on sale for the Semi Final

On the first Home game of the 2015/16 season Fred Onyedinma against Barnet in the Capital One Cup received his first full name chant – 'Oh Fred Onyedinma!' mind you one bloke at the back of the CBL kept singing his own version when this was sung – 'Freddie Shagged My Sister!' true or not who knows but he seemed to be enjoying himself!

I am not sure if this chant was sarcastic or not.

Modern day ex Millwall player David Livermore now Neil Harris's second in command came in for some very undeserved sarcastic abuse, although he did also have a personalised chant sung to Liverpool's continental style tune – 'Livermore, Livermore'

There were also the very unfair and less complimentary versions including – 'Livermore Very Poor!'/'He's Shit, He's Poor, He's David Livermore!'/'Livermore Out The Door!' And 'Livermore He Can't Score!'

After a particularly left-footed performance, this was also adapted to –

'No Right Foot, No Right Foot!'

On 12th April 2003 when he scored a screamer with his right foot against Stoke City, it prompted his one footed goal celebration dance where he held his lethal right foot. This resulted in the following chant – 'Where's your left foot gone?'

He also scored a cracker against Forest in October 2004 at home and got –

Livermore, you're having a laugh!' The poor sod just couldn't win!

When it was mooted that Livermore wanted away in August 2005, possibly to newly promoted

Premiership side Sunderland in the home game versus Stoke he got –

'Premiership? You're having a laugh!'

Bearing in mind that the above were sung when he was one of us, god knows what he would get if he ever returned to the New Den with clubs like Lee Hughes era Oldham Athletic.

Ex Lions Full Back Robbie Ryan was not exactly a goal machine there I have said it!

This is why away forwards who missed would sometimes get – 'You're worse than Robbie Ryan!'

Robbie himself used to be greeted with – 'Will you ever score a goal?'

We sang this for any of Robbie's hapless nosebleed efforts, until he scored his first ever goal after almost two hundred appearances against Gillingham on Boxing Day 2002.

A goal that won me £12 in a first goal scorer sweepstake that we run amongst ourselves at each home game, at the time cheers. This goal was greeted with chants of – 'I was there when Ryan scored!'

Having scored the first goal, he naturally scored a spectacular effort in the very next home game against Watford.

He was well on the way to becoming Steve Lovell. This second goal prompted a deluge of sarcasm.

Firstly, an observation, a bloke sitting behind me shouted out – 'You're just like a London bus Robbie!'

There was also a glut of chants in addition to the Roberto Carlos classic mentioned elsewhere -

'Robbie, Robbie give us a wave, Robbie give us a wave!'/'I was there when Robbie scored!'/

'We love you Robbie, oh yes we do, etc, oh Robbie we love you!'/'Walking in a Robbie wonderland!' And 'Robbie! Robbie! Robbie!'

The last was just like The Jerry Springer Show.

He got the West Ham Paolo Di Canio comparison of –

'They've got Di Canio; we've got our Robbie-O!'

He got the Neil Harris comparisons of – 'Are you Harris in disguise?' And

'Super, super Rob, super, super Rob, super, super Rob, super Robbie Ryan!'

Also whenever he was in the opposition's half he was request to – 'Shoot!'

Ex Wall Loanee Martin Waghorn at Ipswich Town in 2017/18 was abused particularly at the Easter Monday 2nd April 2018 fixture at Portman Road, he got 'Martin Waghorn You're A W***er, You're A W***er!'/'Waghorn Waghorn You're A C***!'/'You Fat C***!'/'Martin Waghorn Your Bellies Offside!' and 'You're S**t And You Know You Are!' naturally he scored twice as he had done at the game at the New Den on 15th August 2018, I think we should not insult people who are likely to score i.e Waghorn, remember Lee Hughes and Marlon King?

Less than popular or prolific striker Kevin Braniff returned to Millwall from a loan spell at Canvey to play against Rotherham

United in January 2005 and was greeted with – 'Kevin Braniff? You're having a laugh!'

He was also greeted with 'Take him off, take him off!'

After a hapless yahoo at Brighton in December 2005, he also got the even more sarcastic –

'Super, super Kev, super, super Kev, super, super Kev, super Kevin Braniff!'

At QPR in February 2006 Berry Powel was substituted when the away following thought Braniff should have been, consequently after the substitution we sang –

'10 men we've only got 10 men!'

Similarily against Brighton at home in April 2006 when Braniff came on for Ben May we sang –

'10 men, we'd rather have 10 men!' So would their fans allegedly!

Finally re Braniff there was this bizarre chant sung in response to a hapless Hull forward 's wayward effort on goal in front of the CBL in the following game at the New Den on Valentines Night –

'You're just a small town in Braniff!'

Ex Lion Jody Morris was lambasted by us for his lack of high in his early appearances –

'Stand up Morris – stand up!'

On the positive front Ex Lion Alex Rae sat among us Millwall fans at West Bromwich Albion in a black baseball cap. With his Wolves connection The Hawthorns is probably not the best place for him nowadays, which is presumably, why he sat with us, he was greeted warmly by us with chants of – 'Stingray, Stingray!'

When Ex Lion Paul Ifill scored a great goal against Brighton at home in December 2004 and got the following comparative chant – 'Thierry Henry? You're having a laugh!'

Ex Lion Willie Gueret Swansea City era got – 'Willie, Willie You're A C***!' And the Welsh variation 'You're Shit And Your Wife's A Sheep!'

Play Off Final v Swindon Town goalscorer Lions Captain Paul Robinson had an adapted version of The Graduate theme season ago 'Here's to you Paul Robinson, Millwall love you more than you can know!' and also got 'Robbo Robbo!'

Lion Keeper in 2008 – 2009 etc David Forde following his Penalty save v Oldham Athletic at home on Tuesday 18th August 2009, at Southend United away on the following Friday, we sang –

'Forde is taking Steroids!' and 'Forde is on Viagra!' why we sang either and especially the usually aimed at Grandad latter chant I do not know! In the latter part of his Lions career post departure he got 'Ireland's Ireland's Number One!' for his Republic Of Ireland goalkeeping position.

Additionally former Lion star Josh Simpson has been lauded with a few tentative renditions of the theme tune from 'The Simpsons'.

On a similar tack 2010 Lions loan striker Shaun Batt got his own chant – 'Der Der Der Der Der Der Der, etc – Batt man!' to the theme of the original Kapow/Shazam 60s Batman theme tune when he scored at home against Gillingham in April 2010!

Jason Puncheon then loanee who got a hat trick v Palarse on New Years Day 2011 at Den got his chant to tune of KC & The Sunshine Band 'Give It Up' – 'Nah, Nah, Nah Nah Nah Na Jason Puncheon, Puncheon, Jason Puncheon!'

2015 Loan recruit Diego Fabbrini got the Man City adapted chant of 'Diego Oh Oh Oh, Diego Oh Oh Oh, He Came From Italy To Play In Bermondsey!' Not abusive more complimentary.

Tony Craig at the Play Off Semi Final at home v Huddersfield Town in May 2010 got – 'He's Hard, He's Blue, He's Millwall Through and Through – Tony Craig, Tony Craig!'

This was years before his leaving for Brentford and return at which point it was more like the why is Craig playing society!!!

Blonde haired then Liverpool loanee Zak Whitbread was greeted by this comparative chant at his debut against Leeds United in November 2005 – 'One Boris Becker, there's only one Boris Becker!'

When now ex Lions Marvin's Williams and Elliott both scored whilst at Millwall in the home game against Derby County in January 2006, the usual 'There's only one …!' chant was adapted to

'There's only 2 Marvin's!'

Not really sarcastic just funny I thought at the Coventry City home game in August 9th 2005 new Portuguese signing Carlos Fanguerio was greeted with the Strictly Dancing bizarre connection – 'There's only one Fandango!'

In the same Coventry City game now ex Lion Adrian Serioux was sent off and was greeted by –

'Chim, chiminey, chim, chiminey, chim-chim-cheroo, we f…ing hate Adrian Serioux!'

Similarly ex Lion Big Bob Peeters received the above chant and a rousing sarcastic rendition of –

'There's only one Bob Peeters!' And 'Super, super Bob, super Bob Peeters'

When he emerged against Burnley in the final game of 2004/5 in May 2005 at the New Den.

He took it in a 'my public love me' sort of way, I'm not sure it was meant that way Bob!

At the 2005/6 season pre season friendly v Gillingham when Big Bob was warming up in front of the West Stand one wag near me shouted out – 'Sit Down Bob You're Frightening The Kids!'

In 2014/5 Booby Peeters was now Charlton's Manager, so to greet him at the Valley game on Saturday 22nd November 2014 he got – 'Bobby Peeters He Looks Like A Nonce, He Looks Like A Nonce, Bob Peeters He Looks Like A Nonce!' he also got 'Bobby Peeters Sex Offender!'

Sod any accusations, proof or evidence lets just accuse him!

In response to this the Charlton Massive sang 'Bobby Peeters Is Our Mate, Is Our Mate, Is Our Mate Bobby Peeters Is Our Mate He Hates Millwall!'

To inspire our own team at home Alan Dunne in 2008/9 got the following from one bloke at the back of the CBL's whinging contingent– 'Alan Dunne, Dunne, Dunne – He's a C***, C***, C***!'

That must have really inspired him, I don't think!

Dany N'Guessan, the man who walked off like a spoilt schoolchild at the Kitch memorial game, came back to the New Den on Tuesday 27th October 2015 with Doncaster Rovers, for whom he was on the bench, when he came on as he substitute he was greeted by an original less than hail fellow well met chant of – 'Dany N'Guessan You're A Sh*t C**t!'

My favourite humorous one came at the home game against Derby County on 22nd September 2004 Millwall's then young prospect Barry Cogan was serenaded with – 'There's only one Terry Wogan!'

Being Selective With Who You Chose To Confront

Happy New Year to Bumpkin Massive at Portman Road on 1st January 2019, when An Ipswich fan decided to confront the 900 Millwall fans to their right, from the Sir Alf Ramsey Stand, he had a lady besides them, who walked up the stairs to the exit during the match and as she made her way she received the following, or he did 'She's Getting F***ed In The Toilet!' and 'She's Getting F***ed By Her Brother!'

When she returned to the brave one confronting us, with an elderly person presumably his Mother he got – 'Your Sons Embarrassed!' and 'Ugly C***, Ugly C***!'

This is a classic example of why you should not get obviously noticeably cocky when confronting Millwall fans, we are not the best opponent to pick believe me!

Respecting Your Chairman

During a 5-0 rout at Reading In August 2005 the pre season madness that preceded this crazy campaign saw Theo Paphitis and the board becoming the focus of the abuse as chants like – 'Sack the board!'/'Support Millwall – F… the board!'/'Theo, Theo what's the score?'/'Where's the money gone?'

And not forgetting the sarcastic, I think – 'Grandad for Chairmen!'

Echoed around the Madejski.

Continuing the theme during a 0 – 4 home defeat to then Championship leaders Sheffield United on October 18th 2005, which saw us sink to the bottom of the table, the CBL sang – '4 nil to Theo!'

Some also sang the less than complimentary Millwall copyrighted chant – 'Theo, Theo you're a c…!'

As we languished at the bottom of the Championhip following a humiliating 3 – 1 home defeat at the hands of fellow strugglers Crewe Alexandra on November 5th 2005, the Theo abuse continued inside the ground and post match in the car park, a selection of the additional abuse –'F… off Theo, F… off Theo, F… off Theo – F… off!'/'We want Theo out, say we want Theo out!'/'Theo out!'/'Thief, Thief, Thief!'/'F… off back to Cyprus!' And 'Run a kebab shop, you couldn't run a kebab shop!'

By this time, pre Peter De Savary's arrival, Theo had faced a torrent of abuse, the Autowindscreen Final, the Divisional Champions win, Play Off Semi Finals and FA Cup Final and UEFA Cup were a dim distant memory and the long honeymoon was well and truly over!

At Derby County an additional less than complimentary chant was aimed at then Dragons' Den not Lion's Den Paphitis – 'Thieving bubble c…! Thieving bubble c…!'

Again highlighting his Greek roots and sung to the tune of 'Chirpy, Chirpy Cheep Cheep'

With Millwall still languishing in the relegation zone against Luton in February 2006 during the match the chants turned against DeSavaray with – 'F… off DeSavaray!'/'Where's our Millwall gone?/'We want our Millwall back' and 'You've killed our football club!'

Marvin Williams late late winner saved him a post match verbal deluge. In contrast to the above Chairmen deluge's at the end of our success in the Play Off Semi Final on May 14th 2009 2nd Leg at Elland Road we sang, to then and at the time of writing still our Chairman the American John Berylson when he came on to the pitch with all the squad, management staff etc, and came over to us, were he was greeted with- 'There's only 1 John Berylson!' and 'USA, USA, USA!'

The Ex Files – From Hero To Villain

Former Millwall GOD Teddy Sheringham was guilty of committing the cardinal sin when he joined our hated enemy West Ham United in 2004/5, made worse by his supposed professed childhood support of them consequently the following insulting anti Teddy chant sprang up in August 2004 –

'Oh Teddy Teddy, he went to West Ham and now he's a c...!'

Continuing the Teddy abuse, his absence in the home game against West Ham United in November 2004 saw us trying to pick him out in the crowd, we spotted a lone figure on the West Stand roof and sang – 'Is that Teddy on the roof?' And we sang 'Teddy Teddy what's the score?'

As we eased to our now customary home win against them. There was also a banner on the East Stand that read 'Turncoat Teddy Judas'.

At the return game at Upton Park in April 2005 Teddy played and got his abuse personally, he got the above plus 'Judas!' and the less polite 'Teddy Teddy you're a c...!'

With reference to the particular anti West Ham United/Teddy chant when Neil Harris equalled Teddy's goal scoring record with his goal at Walsall on 13th December 2008, we naturally sang 'Super, Super Neil, Super Super Neil, Super Super Neil, Super Neil Harris!'

Some Millwall there also sang '1 More and you've beat the

Scum!' I think this Teddy animosity is purely because of this alleged 'Appy 'Ammers affiliation, if he went anywhere else, apart from Crystal Palace of course, he would still have been deified at Millwall in my opinion.

James Henry when he returned to the New Den for the first time as a Wolves player on 18th October 2014, the former favourably received Winger, now in a Gold Kit got – 'There's Only One Greedy Bastard!' and the now customary to treacherously perceived he left us – 'Henry Henry You're A C***!'

Tony 'Denzil' Warner's alleged wage demands and contract refusals which saw him miss the FA Cup Final and subsequent UEFA Cup adventure meant that he was greeted with a barrage of abuse when he returned to the New Den in October 2004 with his new club the hated enemies Cardiff City, including several plays on former very masculine positive chants for example – 'Denzil's got a small cock!'

The antithesis of the old Millwall era favourite – 'Denzil's got a big one'

To continue – 'Denzil (Warner), Denzil (Warner) you're a c...!'/'There's only one greedy bastard!'/'Tony Warner sex offender!'/'You Scouse c...!'/'We hate Denzil and we hate Denzil, etc we are the Denzil haters!'/'You're just a Millwall reject!' And 'Judas!'

When Millwall scored in front of the CBL he got – 'Where the f... was Denzil?'/'Denzil, Denzil what's the score?' And 'Dodgy keeper!'

He also got some of the abuse when he played against us for his then side Hull City at the KC Stadium in the FA Cup in January 2009, he is now back as one of Wall fans favourites as he often appears in the away end with us at games, and is encouraged to lead the singing, like he was at Roots Hall in recent visits for example.

Ex Lion Darren Byfiled came on as a late Sub for Oldham Athletic on 18th August 2009 against us at the New Den, he got 'He's got a malteser as a head!' the customary 'Byfield, Byfield You're a C***!'

and 'You're Shit and your Wife's a slag!' A chant usually reserved for Paul Peschisolido whenever he played against us in the past.

Lucas Neill was roundly booed when he played for Blackburn Rovers at the New Den in the FA Cup a few years back. He got the Judas treatment for having the audacity to leave us and every time he touched the ball he got 'Lucas Neill is a wanker, is a wanker!'

God knows what he would have gotten if he played for our bitter enemies West Ham United against us!

Zak Whitbread the player who apparently wanted to play for a big club, moved to Norwich City in 2009/2010 and was a sub against us at the New Den on 6th February 2010 he was given a very warm welcome whenever he warmed up and then came on as a sub late ib the game, if this counts –'There's only one greedy bastard!' and the sarcastic 'You're supposed to be at Wolves!' a rumour of the big club pre his move.

To take the piss out of his blonde albinio bonce he got 'He's got birdshit on his head' and the complimentary 'Whitbread Whitbread you're a C***!'. And questioningly when we went 2 – 1 ahead he got 'Whitbread Whitbread what''s the score?'

Marc Bircham's first game against us came at QPR in November 2004, where the lion tattooed one, now sporting a blue and white Mohican, was greeted less than cheerily by the several thousand traveling Lions, a sample of the chants – 'Bircham, Bircham show us your arm!'/'Bircham, Bircham you're a c…!'/'Bircham takes it up the a…!' And 'Marc Bircham sex offender!'

The best though was an adapted evangelical rendition of 'He's Got The Whole World In His Hands' that we continued practically all night –'He's got a Lion on his arm, he's got a Lion on his arm, he's got a Lion on his arm, he's got a Lion on his arm. He's got a bird shit on his head! He's got a bird shit on his head! He's got a bird shit on his head! He's got a bird shit on his head!

With the additional optional lines of 'He's got a dildo up his a…!' And 'He's got Ian Holloway up his A…!' Even so he applauded us at the end of the match.

This was before Bircham returned to Millwall as Hollowhead's assistant during the keep taking the tablets thieving bumpkin era in the recent past.

Not that he was ever a Lions hero but ex Lion Lewis Grabban then at Bournemouth played his first against us for them on Saturday 5th October 2013, whilst we were winning 2 – 0 having taken the lead in the first 10 minutes, Grabban got 'Grabban Grabban You're A C***!' and 'Grabban Grabban What's The Score?' thankfully we did not ask him this when he scored Bournemouth's 4th from the spot in what was to end in a 5 – 2 defeat!

For some reason he never played at the vital return at the Den Relegation survival fight late season, probably just as well, I don't think he would have liked our reaction to him much. He was still with them and actually played at the New Den when we knocked then Premier Leagure Bournemouth out of the FA Cup in the 3rd Round on Saturday 7th Januray 2017, he was serenaded mostly with the 'Grabban Grabban You're A C***!' Chant.

The Millwall failure in 2018 was now at Notts Forest, and we played at the City Ground on Wednesday 3rd October 2018 when he was featured in the programme with an Islamic style beard, to great this new look he got the standard 'Grabban Grabban You're A C***!' Chant.and the new selection –

'Grabban You're An ISIS C****!'/'ISIS C*** ISIS C****!'/'Lewis Grabban He's Shagging A Goat!'/'Lewis Grabban You're Going Down For A Stabbing You're A Terrorist!' and 'Lewis Grabban He F***s All Your Goats!'

Not that Mr Moonwalk was ever anything like a hero at the 'Wall, but when Bas Savage played against us for his new side Tranmere Rovers at the New Den in January 2009, he had blue hair, why I do not know, it may have been a blue rinse that went tits up, what do I know?

A bloke behind me in the CBL said 'His head looks like a chalked up Snooker cue!' strangely true.

To highlight this we sang a portion of the Bircham chant from above, 'He's got bird shit on his head!' It was obvious that he had to be abused for having blue hair but it was a strange chant, I thought I could not think of any bird that crapped blue stuff myself, but I am not an ornithologist so what do I know!

We also sang, when we went 1 – 0 up 'Savage Savage what's the score?' and ruder but necessary when he appeared to try to get any Millwall player booked with his card waving hand motions -

'Savage, Savage, You're a C***!'

We played at Blackpool on 10th January 2015, and ex Lions loanee Jamie O'Hara got a range of sexual abuse, aimed at his split with ex model Danielle Lloyd and his alleged string of affairs pre split, he received 'Jamie O'Hara He F***S Who He Wants!' then aimed at his ex wife ' Jamie O'Hara Your Wife Is A Slag!'/'She Takes It Up The Arse!' and 'She Sucks Who She Wants!' and 'You Married A Slag!' this last one he put the thumbs up to us in recognition

When he was a Millwall player Peter Sweeney had 'The Sweeney' theme tune dedicated to him however when he left to join Stoke City and we played them at home in August 2005 and even though he was injured and didn't play he still received – 'Sweeney, Sweeney you're a C...!'

Sweeney did play in the return at Stoke in February 2006 and was greeted with the above and –

'You Scotch c...!'/'Sweeney is a rent boy, Sweeney is a rent boy, la la la la, la la la la!' And

'Peter Sweeney sex offender!'

On 10th September 2005 ex Lion Daniele Dichio returned to the New Den with his then new club Preston North End and was 'greeted' unkindly having been deemed to have left us in the lurch in our time of need, he received the adapted Teddy chant –'Oh! Danny, Danny he went to Preston and now he's a c...!'

And the more general – 'Danny, Danny you're a C...!'/'F... off Dan Dichio, F.. off Dan Dichio!' to the tune of 'La Donna e Mobile' for all you opera buffs out there. Dichio also received the insultingly sarcastic –

'You're worse than Bobby Peeters/Kevin Braniff!'

On 18th October 2005 Paul Ifill returned to the New Den with his new side Sheffield United this followed much London press speculation about the likely response from the home crowd, in truth apart from some low key booing the most sarcastic thing he received was – 'I I Iffy, Iffy I, singing I I Iffy, Iffy I singing, I I Iffy, I I Iffy, I I Iffy Iffy I – Ifil!' But sarcastically sung in praise of Spurs loanee Phil Ifil, his near namesake and utilising Paul Ifill's own chant.

In the next game on Saturday 22nd October 2005 Dennis Wise returned to the New Den for the first time playing for his new club Southampton he got a mixed reception, on the positive front he got the old favourite 'Oh Wisey... he's only 5ft 4 he'll break your f...ing jaw!' and the sarcastic chant aimed at the Saints fans 'Wisey loves Millwall!'

He was applauded off the pitch by most of the crowd at the end, however in contrast he also got 'Oh Wisey wowo, oh Wisey wowo, he's only 5ft 4 his wife's a f...ing whore!' And 'Wisey, Wisey you're a c...!'

Like Wise Tim Cahill got a largely positive response when he returned to the New Den with new club Everton in the FA Cup in January 2006, although we did sing – 'Cahill, Cahill, what's the score?' as we took the lead, the game ended in a draw, in the replay at Goodison Cahill got more mild abuse – 'What a waste of money!' Naturally he scored the goal that knocked us out, so the Everton fans sang the chant back at us to take the piss.

Ex Lion, Mark McCammon playing for Brighton & Hove Albion on New Year's Eve 2005 received –

'McCammon, Wank, Wank, Wank!'

Sam Parkin a part time Millwall loanee who only played a small amount of games for us received 'Parkin, Parkin you're a C***!' When he played against us for Leyton Orient in November 2008 at their Building complex site.

A less blonde than he used to be Darren Ward returned to the New Den with loathed rivals Crystal Palace in February 2006, he received a less than complimentary reception – 'Darren Ward, is a wanker, is a wanker!'/'Wardy Wardy you're a C...!'/'Darren Ward sex offender!' And 'Judas!'

When he rejoined us in 2009/2010 Ward was not abused but serenaded with the old chant

'There's Only One Peckham Beckham!'

When ex Lion Marvin Elliot played against us for Bristol City at Ashton Gate in August 2010 he was greeted with ' Marvin Marvin you're a C***!' At home in April 2011 he got the above but he also got 'There's only one greedy bastard!' ah how feelings change!

Ex Lion Ben May when he came on as a substitute for Scunthorpe United at their place in October 2008, was greeted with – 'Ben May you're a thieving C***!' and 'Where's your Toilet Seat, where's your Toilet Seat?'

After his apparent robbery of a Toilet Seat etc whilst at Millwall.

In 2012/3 whilst still at the club Liam Trotter was deemed to be lazy so from CBL he gets – 'He Runs When He Wants, He Runs When He Wants – Liam Trotter He Runs When He Wants!'

At the start of the Ian Holloway era, Liam Trotter refused to sign a new Millwall contract and went on loan to Bolton Wanderers with a transfer at the end of the season, who were one of our opponents at home in a relegation dogfight on February 15th 2014, he could not play against us due to being on loan, but the CBL chanted a less polite or humorous version of the above chant – 'Liam Trotter He's One Lazy C***!'

In a three for one former Lion deal, when Bolton Wanderers played at the New Den on Friday 19th December 2014, in the starting line up was ex Lion Liam Feeney he got the Millwall Copyrighted – 'Feeney Feeney You're A C***!', on the bench but coming on a substitutes were ex Lions Liam Trotter – he got the usual – 'Trotter Trotter You're A C***!' and 'Liam Trotter He Runs When He Wants!' a chant that he used to get when he was playing for us as you will see from above. Behind us in the CBL a couple of blokes chanted 'You're Not Fit To Have The Name!' this a play on Trotters

Independent Trading 'Only Fools And Horses', not loud but original I thought. When ex Lion Youth Player who said that he wanted to play for a big club 'Conor Wilkinson came on he got – 'W***er!' and 'C***!' we decided not to mention his name, so that must be more insulting I suppose.

Darius Henderson whilst playing against us for Nottingham Forest at the City Ground on 5th April 2014, former hero got – 'Hendo Hendo You're A C***!' he also received 'She Said No Hendo!' chant at Scunthorpe United when playing for them as listed earlier

Finally George Saville the 2017/18 Millwall player sold for big bucks to Middlesbrough apparently for him to get a better quality footballing side and get promoted played against us at the Riverside on 19th January 2019 was thanked sarcastically when near us for letting us make some money by selling him then got 'Saville Saville You're A C***!'/'You're Only Here For The Money!' and after a less than inspiring display he received "What A Waste Of Money!' and when Wall players came over to applaud we travelling Lions fans, so did he and was told in no uncertain terms to F**k Off Saville!

Gallows Humour etc From I Suppose A Friar Tuck Is Out Of The Question Land On Saturday 5th April 2014 and just a Little Bit From Middlesbrough Saturday 19th April 2014

To start at the game non Gallows Humour Stuart Pearce soon to be appointed Forest Manager received – 'Stuart Pearce Is A W***er, Is A W***er!'

The Trapdoor Chuckles Cometh –

As we were in the dreaded dropzone on the trip up to Nottingham a comment from Tina Collins on Coach 1, this was in response to Kenny, who said that he could see Millwall winning at Forest, she replied –

'I Think That You Have Got More Chance Of Seeing The Pope Have A W*** On A Sunday Than That Happening!'

Funny I thought and happily she was wrong as we won 2 – 1!

Our Gallows Humour chants at The City Ground pre taking the lead we sang – 'Going Down Like A Malaysian Plane!' With reference to the missing plane mystery, flight MH370 and about our expected demise – 'We're Gonna Win League One!' and 'Que Sera, Sera Whatever Will Be Will Be We're Going To Crawley!'

As we took the lead 1-0 and then 2-0 –

'You Must Be S*** We Scored A Goal!'/'Staying Up Staying Up Staying Up!' and 'How S*** Must You Be We're Winning Away!'

At Middlesbrough on Saturday 19th April 2014 another game we won 2 – 1 we sang – 'We Scored Two Goals You Must Be S***!'

Middlesborough Fans Accused Of Being Skinflints And Fashion Victims

In the match on 21st December 2013 it was a £5 entrance fee game presumably in an effort to raise the crowd the way we played even that was exhorbitant! At Boro fans we sang 'You're Only Here For A £5!' implying that if it was full price they would not have come to the game.

In response to their 'London's A Shithole I Want To Go Home!' we sang –

'You're Just A Town Full Of Tracksuits!'

Tractor Boys Stereotypical Tar With The Same Brush Accusation

At the New Den for Ian Holloway's first home game the Tractor Boys, on 18th January 2014 obviously they received the perennial bumpkin insult'I Can't Read I Can't Ride, etc! Chant.

But today to say that they were all related to The Suffolk Strangler we sang –

'You Murder Prostitutes!'

A Load Of Mouthy Won't See Their Arse For Dust Outside Madejski Or New Den Reading Fans Saturday 26th October 2013

To we gathered Wall next to them, the heroes sang to us

'Go Back To Your Shithole!'/'You Are Embarrassing'/'Millwall Are Shit!' and ''F*** Off Millwall You've Always Been Shit!' and 'You Support A Load of Shit!'

They sang this after we sang 'Your Support Is F**king Shit! to them.

Finally, the original, well to me anyway, 'Same Old Millwall Always Cheating!' following a Millwall foul.

Evening All!

Home-and-away it would be remiss of us not give the Police their traditional greetings of –

'The Laurel And Hardy Tune''/'Kill the Bill! '/'We hate old Bill!' Not forgetting 'Harry Roberts'

I have listed these elsewhere but as an aside, I noticed in the Millwall history book that a Harry Roberts played for us in the 1930s!

The Police also occasionally get – 'He's got a silver tit on his head!'

Following yet another Police incursion onto the CBL, the Police were requested to –

'Old Bill, Old Bill give us a song. Old Bill give us a song'

Which they didn't so – 'Can you hear the Old Bill sing? No, no, can you hear the Old Bill sing?

No, no, can you hear the Old Bill sing? I can't hear a f...ing thing, ah!'

At the time of yet another New Den upper tier invasion there was a less than polite request from the CBL for the Police to vacate our stand – 'F... off Old Bill; F... off Old Bill, F... off Old Bill, F... off!'

Millwall and Neil Harris Shirted Ian Tomlinson's death at the hands of the truncheon welding Old Bill Riot Police at the G20 rumpus in early April 2009, had us singing 'Harry Roberts' at the west Country police force strung out in front of us at Yeovil Town on Good Friday, we also sang to them 'Murderers!'

This theme was continued at our next away match again in the West Country this time to the Riot Police in front of us and also all around us at Bristol Rovers on April 18th 2009, we expanded the repertoire, in addition to singing the above, we also sang –'Justice For The Millwall One!'

The above 'Murderers!' was used and we also sang the following to tell the Hampshire Old Bill what we thought that they were doing at Southampton in the first game of the season 2009/10 on 8th August 2009, as they did the usual surrounding and filming us routine, we sang – 'We're just a bunch of Cattle!'

Implying that the local plod thought that they were shepherding their cattle on a farm, wrong!!!

After A Fashion

Assistant Referee Jarnail Singh ran the line in a very fetching micro turban against Cardiff City at the New Den in August 2001, strangely he never got 'We Only Sing(h) when you're flagging!'

The main fashion victims though have been players –

Paul Birch was the funniest at the Old Den, although if memory serves Chelsea's Teddy Maybank received this type of abuse some years before Birch and Efetebore Sodje at the New Den as listed in my other books.

Another fashion victim was Watford player Anthony McNamee who said in an interview about his funniest moment in Football, that he said was at Millwall, where he played sporting a massive Afro hairdo and each time he was on the ball the home crowd nearby sang Jackson 5 songs to him

Non-PC alert –
Cussin' The Custodians

Unfortunately, a goalkeeper is stuck directly in front of us for 45 minutes, hence the usual need for them to wear industrial ear protectors or to get a bit of distance between themselves and the home stand behind the goal.

The usual practice is/was for them to wander off outside of their goal area, this was particularly prevalent at the old place.

Some Old Den highlights –

When Liverpool's Bruce Grobbelaar looked up at the CBL with a 'What Are These People On?' expression on his face as the abuse rained down on him.

David Speedie did his short arse in goal impression for Coventry City in the old First Division, he came out in the second half in front of CBL; turned around looked up into the crowd and waved at us, his appearance was greeted with hoots of derision and laughter.

Peter Shilton got – 'Shilton f...s his Mother!' God knows where that one came from?

As an aside at the Old Den, we always used to acknowledge any goalkeeper who stayed put in his area, joined in with us or took the abuse in good heart. Paul Cooper of Ipswich springs to mind for one,

Moving to the New Den and away -

Straddling the line between 'After A Fashion' and 'Cussin' The Custodians' in September 2005

Preston's glamour boy keeper Carlo Nash complete with sun tan and blonde highlights in his hair was greeted by the CBL with the inevitable barrage of 'Cooes' and wolf whistles, he also got the catalogue of usual chants – 'Carlo takes it up the arse!'/'Does your mother know your queer!' And 'Has your boyfriend got gonorrhea?'

At 1 – 0 to Millwall at Carrow Road in October 2005 Norwich's much lauded England prospect now a QPR keeper Robert Green got – 'Greeno, Greeno what's the score' and more specifically 'You're worse than David James' And 'You'll never play for England!'

After the latter he took off his cap and gestured with his fingers towards us the number of games that he had played already played for his country, unfortunately he did play again and f***ed up big time in the 2010 World Cup v USA whilst horror of horrors he was at that time the Vermins keeper!

Still at QPR he got 'You Let Your Country Down!' Referring to this and 'West Ham C***!' Reerring to his former employer at The New Den on 19th October 2013.

In the game at Carrow Road mentioned above then Millwall Keeper Andy Marshall was being continually barracked by the home fans because he left Norwich for arch rivals Ipswich, also mocking Green's England prospects we sang 'Marshall for England!' Marshall got his own back on the home fans by saving Darren Huckerby's late penalty in front of the main baying home section, sweet!

Burnley goalie Brian Jensen, aka the Beast as they called him, was a 'big boned' keeper, to highlight his cuddly nature he was greeted by the CBL in the second half of our League game at the New Den on February 28th 2004 with 'Who ate all the pies?' In response, he did a mime of munching a pie, which prompted a smattering of applause and resulted in him getting less abuse than he would ordinarily have got.

Brighton's goalkeeper Andy Pettersen was not able to escape the gay references due to his side's gay capital status he got an adapted 'Fat tosser!' chant when we sang the charming –'Ah! you s..t stabber!'

David Seaman was the target of a post Holland 1994 World Cup fiasco tirade of -

'Where were you when Koeman scored? Or Nayim or Ronaldinho or Sakiri or Zola, or... '

Goalkeepers a few years back also received to the chant of 'Are you Seaman in disguise?' For any errors he made. Seaman's predecessor at Arsenal John Lukic was haunted in the press by rumours of Seaman's imminent arrival, so in the Division 1 game when we played them at Highbury he got –'Seaman, Seaman, Seaman!' A real Hello Sailor if I have heard it.

I cannot remember his name but a Charlton goalkeeper in the 1990s sporting a Beatles style Mop Top hairdo playing in one of our customary wins at the New Den got – 'She loves you yeah! Yeah! Yeah!'

I am sure he did not understand why we sang it at all, I couldn't!

Walsall's keeper James Walker at home in September 2002 got this bizarre obscure effort –

'Are you Bosnich in disguise?' Eh?

In December 4th 2004 Sheffield United played at the New Den and cuddly keeper Paddy Kenny got a bloody chin after foolishly getting involved in a bust up with Kevin Muscat in the tunnel at half time. As a result both he and Muzzy were sent off during the interval. In the second half outfield replacement Phil Jageilka came on as stand in keeper and took up his position in front of the CBL where he was greeted with – 'Where's your fat C... gone?'

In the following season's game at the New Den in October 2005 Kenny was greeted by the CBL with – 'Kenny, Kenny how's your chin?'/'There's only one Kevin Muscat' And 'Muzzy, Muzzy he'll kick the f...ing shit out of you!'

At QPR under Warnock again for our clash at Loftus Road 28th September 2010 Mr Kenny was greeted again by us, we ourselves were wondering what some of the following chants were about but I looked on Wikipedia and I found out why he was getting the abuse that he was.

In November 2006, whilst at Sheffield United their then Manager Warnock told him to lay low, but instead Kenny went for a night out in Halifax and he was involved in a drunken brawl outside a curry house with a former friend, who admitted to having an affair with his wife.

Kenny ended up having his eyebrow bitten off and required 12 stitches.

When in front of us in the 2nd half, he got no Muscat abuse but because of his past and his previous cuddliness he got – 'You Fat C***!' And 'Paddy, Paddy You're A Druggy, You're A Druggy '

And due to the above mentioned marital bliss, he specifically got – You're Shit and you're wife's a slag!'/'Paddy, Paddy where's the wife?'/'Does she take it up the Arse?' And 'There's Only One Mrs. Kenny, One Mrs. Kenny!'

Estonian spiky haired blonde then Southampton's keeper Antii Niemi playing at the New Den on 22nd October 2005 was serenaded with 'There's only one Annie Lennox!'

Reading's bald American goalie Marcus Hahnemann at home in August 2004 implying that he looked like a member of 'Right Said Fred' to highlight this assumption he got – 'I'm too sexy for my goal!'

Ian Walker playing for Leicester City at the New Den in August 2004 got –

'You'll never play for England!' And the Millwall copyrighted 'You're shit and your wife's a slag!'

Pre Lions stay Southampton's Welsh goalkeeper Paul Jones playing in a pre season friendly at the New Den

in August 2003 was serenaded with Welsh stereotypical comments; he was the target for numerous sheep references and requests for mint sauce. Each time he took a goal kick, he also got a chorus of bleating and the adapted Fat Tosser chant – 'Ah! You sheepshagger!' Which he seemed to enjoy.

Sheffield Wednesday keeper David Lucas managed to injure himself and twice collapsed in an undignified heap in the CBL goalmouth prior to being carried off on a stretcher during the infamous Steve Tanner game at the New Den on February 4th 2006, to aid his recovery we helpfully sang – 'Again, you'll never walk again!' And as he continued to be treated in the goalmouth to aid his recovery we sang – 'Get the fat c... off the pitch!'

At the first home game of 2005/6 against Coventry City on 9th August 2005 City's keeper was ex 'appy 'ammer and in the modern era under Lomas Millwall second keeper Stephen Bywater who had been sent off in our historic 4 – 1 coshing of our hated foe. When he positioned himself in front of the CBL in the second half he got 'West Ham reject!'/'We hate West Ham, etc'/'Chim chiminee, etc!'/'We beat the scum 4 – 1!'

More specifically he got – 'You're not wanted anymore!' He also got the following sarcastic West Ham goalie collection – 'There's only one Roy Carroll/Shaka Hislop/Jimmy Walker!'

One bloke behind me even added Phil Parkes to this list! What about Bobby Ferguson from the 1970s, He must have been a latent 'Appy 'Ammer to know any of the buggers in my opinion, I looked Ferguson up on Google to highlight my point, I am certainly not 'kin West Ham!

Returning to the Ex West Ham United goalkeeper he played against us for Derby County in the FA Cup game in January 2010, was greeted when he was in goal in front of the CBL in the 2nd half of the match with 'West Ham Reject'/' Bywater, is a wanker, is a wanker ! ' and specifically '4 -1 and we took the piss!'

Continuing the Derby County in Championship at Pride Park on Monday 3rd Januuary 2011 now Derby keeper Bywater when in front of us got ' We beat the scum 4 – 1!' and 'West Ham C***, West Ham C***!' Bywaters then played for Cardiff City against us on 19th March 2011 at the New Den and got the same last chant, he must love playing against us, or come to that for us, as he signed for us in June 2013,

At Chester City in the FA Cup 1st round in November 2008 their Goalie John Dandy whilst in front of us in the 1st Half to highlight his customary warm weather Goalkeeping clobber got – 'You shop at Matalan!'/'You shop at TK Maxx!'/'He's got his Mother's tights on his legs!' and 'He's got his Daddy's thong up his arse!'

One similar chant of note from a rainy windswept night on an open terrace at the far far lesser of the 2 St James's Parks at Exeter City on Tuesday 24th November 2009, for some bizarre reason their keeper Andy Marriott got serenaded with 'Your Mum shops at Lidls!' God knows why, this was taken up!!

In the 1990s when Kasey Keller was our goalkeeper prior to going through his dotage at Fulham in the mid 2000s, he would often get the American national anthem sung to him or 'Where's your caravan?' due to his now sadly departed flowing gypsy style locks, this was particularly popular by Leicester City fans.

Perpetual whilst at Millwall stand-in goalkeeper Willy Gueret, a Frenchman, often got the French national anthem when he played. On a personal note if anyone caught me singing the French national anthem they have my permission to give me a good slap!

Continuing the French theme when we played Cambridge United at the New Den on 28th October 2000 they had ex Sunderland and Scunthorpe goalie Lionel Perez in goal, wearing a short sleeve shirt and looking like a cross between shamed German goalkeeper Harald Schumacher and Harpo Marx.

He sported a long curly blonde (?) perm (?) hairdo. A fatal combination of Paul Birch portions to us. Consequently, he got a barrage of 'Cooes!' and wolf-whistles; however, unlike Birch who seemed to shrink from all the attention, dear Lionel seemed to take umbrage, it is unlike a Frenchman to get in a strop! Foolishly, he then tried to get Tim Cahill sent off in front of the CBL, which did not go down too well. What this meant was that the anti French/Hairdo abuse stepped up a pace and he began to posture in front of us like an old time circus strongman. He also gestured towards the CBL upper tier, which was the main source of the abuse, once again, his gestures to the upper tier resulted in the old stand up and give him a damn good 'wankering' routine and an escalation of the abuse, so he got all manner of insults including –

'You French c...!' And 'Lionel takes it up the a...!'

He also got the less abusive – 'Lionel, Lionel what's the score?' 3-1 as it turned out.

After a while, he must have twigged that trying to get a Millwall player sent off in front of a home stand, combined with a confrontational approach probably wasn't the best policy.

He then began to adopt the usual pattern of wandering outside of his box as per the Old Den, so much so that he left his towel in the goal at the end of the match and shot off the pitch, a wise move.

A chant from the away stand in August 2005 Ipswich Town's normally mute following sang the following to Millwall's ex Tractor Boy and Norwich City keeper Andy Marshall following a kick out cock up 'Give it to Marshall!'

T'Bolton's ginger haired keeper Adam Bogdan was in front of us in the CBL in the second half at the New Den in the FA Cup in February 2012.

He suspiciously wore a pink shirt and socks and I wondered whether he tried to use this as a distraction to his hair colour? If he did it did not work, he got –

'Ginger C***, Ginger C***, Ginger C***!'

Continuing the ginger thread because he was red haired as was the ex-Lions manager Steve Lomas at the game at The New Den on 15th February 2014 in the wake of the Lomas departure he received – 'Are you Lomas in disguise?'

David James, ah bless him, he must love playing against us. He made his debut in League football on 25th August 1990 for Watford, at Vicarage Road against us and we beat them 2 – 1.

The fact that he also played for West Ham United and Pompey, i.e. 2 enemies and had appeared in England's disastrous showing in the World Cup. He then made his debut post the 2010 World Cup disaster for Bristol City against us. To highlight the comic options he played with a huge afro, I have thick hair but his Barnet looked like he had stuck his fingers in the plug socket on first day of the season on 7th August 2010, where we also coshed them 3 – 0. In this case, to greet his appearance in the Brizzle team in front of our away following in the first half we sang –'You Let Your Country Down!'/'Wanker, Wanker, Wanker!'/'David James Sex Offender!'/'Sex Case Sex Case Hang Him Hang Him Hang

Him!'/'James, James what's the score?'

We also sang 'England England's Number one!' because the Yokels had sung this to him pre kick off, and we sang it as we racked up our 3 goals.

To highlight the International team goalies difference we sang to our keeper David Forde –

'Ireland Ireland's Number 1!' As he kept a clean sheet!

Tomasz Kuszczak Brighton and Hove Albion's goalkeeper v Millwall at the New Den on Saturday 22nd September 2012, was deemed to be the cheating reason why Chris Taylor got sent off was greeted with the obligatory – 'Cheat, Cheat, Cheat!' and the nationality specific 'Polish C***! Polish C***!'

Highlighting, That You Should Never Ever Offer A Challenge To A Millwall Crowd, The Leeds United Then Kasper Schmeichel Section –

In the Evening Standard in the week leading up to a Leeds United game at New Den in April 2011 Peter Schmeichel's son Kasper did an interview re his entering the New Den's hostile atmosphere, the article had a headline -'Kasper Schmeichel will not be shocked with Millwall trip'

In the article Schmeichel said: "The atmosphere we see at Elland Road compares to anywhere. It means that the atmosphere at other stadiums isn't going to shock you or intimidate you."

Wrong, this is the New or Old Den mate, a smidge more hostile, well massively more hostile than Elland Road 'Marching On Together bullshit and any other ground.

He was greeted in the 2nd half in front of the CBL with many repetitions –

'You're S**t and you're Dad's a C***!' he also continually got 'Wanker' and at 2 – 0 and then at 3 – 1 to us he got 'Schmeichel,

Schmeichel what's the score, Schmeichel what's the score?' and was confronted by the whole of the CBL standing to abuse the deluded prick.

His body language did not indicate that he was happy at all, I am not medically trained in anyway but thought that I would point this out!

Having moved to Leicester City he enjoyed the delights of The New Den again in a game that would secure our Championship existence again in April but this time 14th in 2012, having presumably won the toss we were made to kick towards the CBL in the first half so Kasper got our unfriendly Kasper the ghost treatment earlier this time, as he ran towards us, he blew kisses mockingly and looked smug but was still greeted with most of CBL upper where I was, getting the full c***! Treatment pre KO, having positioned himself he got the above mentioned chants plus – 'Kasper, Kasper you're a C***, Kasper you're a C***!'

This as you may have gathered already is a traditional Millwall greeting, which ex Leeds United then Leicester City player Jermaine Beckford was greeted with any time he came within earshot.

Schmeichel also got – 'Schmeichel, Schmeichel you're a grass!'

This was early on in half and probably following his reporting a coin or a plastic bottle being lobbed near or at him during Leeds United game.

He also got – 'Did he name you as a joke?' and 'Is your sister named Snow White?'

Referring to his dad Peter Schmeichel's naming choice.

He seemed pleased to get the first half over with even though his team were losing 1 – 0 and stand in front of Leicester's fans for 2nd half, who loved him more, well it could not have been less!

Shame we went 2 – 0 at that end though must have upset him again, another defeat Kasper 2 – 1 this time and making Millwall safe!!!!

For his next trip with Leicester City to the New Den on Saturday 15th December 2012 he was warmly greeted by a lot of the above mentioned chants plus one new one –

'You're just a Shit Peter Schmeichel!' In a who's the Daddy, the Daddy or son skit!

On the Schmeichel front one thing that I would advise people not to do, that is to give us a challenge, i.e. if they say that they won't intimidate me, we naturally really put in a great effort to make sure that we intimidate him as much as possible, we like a challenge! And abusive consistency being the Millwall way he will be greeted the same whenever he has the pleasure of playing against us again, be it away or especially at home and for whoever the team they play for is.

There is Posh – Not!!!!

When we beat Peterborough United at home on Easter Monday 2009, a game also shown live on Sky, each time that their manager Darren Ferguson's mug came up on the Jumbotron we sang –

'You're S*** and your Dad's a C***!'

This was to pay homage to the Footballing Darren and Alex Ferguson family, to add some nationalism to the

Homage we also sang – 'You Scotch C***!'

The Haggis noshing Fergie Family must love a real Millwall Home night, well I suppose they wouldn't sorry, well no I'm not sorry at all F*** 'em both!

Agent Orange aka David Dickinson, oh sorry Phil Brown PNE Manager at New Den St Georges Day 23rd April 2011

This was another game shown live on Sky Sport at Easter again this time v relegation threatened Preston North End, a great 4 – 0, Lions victory, to highlight this we sang to the relatively small gathering of PNE fans – 'Going Down, Going Down, Going Down!' and 'That's why you're going down!' as they missed chances and we took them.

There was one great new original chant that we sang at 4 – 0 –

'F***ed on the telly, you're getting F***ed on the telly!'

Moving on to the trade's description act misnamed Phil Brown!

A man who was greeted every time his orange coloured mush appeared on the Jumbotron with –

'You've got a face like an orange!'/'Sit down you orange C***!'/'F*** off you orange C***!'/'Who's been tangoed, who's been tangoed over there?' and 'You've been tangoed!'

When it rained as he stood by the technical zone, we sang –

'Smudge your mascara, you're gonna smudge your mascara!'

As he walked on the pitch to join the two physios to help an injured Preston player from the field we implied that this was a promote yourself moment– 'You just want to get on the telly!'

As we racked up our four goals, we sang –

'Spray Tan and a long way home' and Fake tan and you F***ed it up!'

We also sang 'You're getting sacked in the morning!' this was then adapted to –

'You're getting sprayed in the morning!'

Making Your Opposition Team/Fan's Feel At Home And Away

In addition to what has gone before some general chants to start, sung to the away fans in their North Stand comfort zone – 'Sit down shut up!'/'Who's the wanker with the flag?' And 'Who's the wanker in the white?' Your club flag/shirt colour choice, sung to the extrovert types in their ranks.

We played perennial underachievers Wolverhampton Wanderers at home after they had let a points lead slip to let in their bitter rivals West Brom in 2001/2 in homage we sang - 'The Wolves are going nowhere!' And 'You f...ed it up, you f...ed it up, Wolves have f...ed it up!'

We sang a similar type of chant v Wolves at the New Den on 18th October 2014, when we were 3 – 0 down only to draw the game 3 – 3, to highlight this we sang the hardy perennial – '3 Nil and you f***ed it up!'

When we played Premier League side Bolton Wanderers in the FA Cup at home in the FA Cup 5th Round on 18th February 2012, T'Bolton fans had a flare or something in the away end, so smoke was blowing across the upper tier, from where we were it could have been a fire for all we knew, in support we sang – 'Let 'Em Burn, Let 'Em Burn, Let 'Em Burn!' and 'Terrorist, Terrorist, Terrorist!'

At Colchester United on 21st October 2008, to highlight our very good form and near top of table League One position and Spurs rock bottom of the Premiership and at the time on only 2 points position, we sang – 'We're Playing Tottenham next Year!' We beat Colchester United 2 – 1 on the night, they had not yet won at their new Weston Homes Community Stadium at that point and consequently they were languishing in the lower reaches of the League, to highlight the we're up the top and you're down the bottom plight, we sang to them – 'You're Playing Barnet Next Year!'

Sheffield United played at the New Den on 4th December 2004 in dayglo orange kits, that clashed with the stewards and was ideal should the floodlights fail, to highlight their garish kit, we sang –

'You look like a traffic cone!' And 'You only sing for the stewards!'

In addition to the gay insinuations Brighton's fans in the past have been informed that –

'You look like a Tesco's bag!' To highlight their stripy blue and white shirts with red trim.

At Reading in the August 2005 game I mentioned above we sang serenaded the mouthy home fans with among other things –

'You're just a small town in Oxford!' And "Town full of wankers, you're just a town full of wankers!'

Wimbledon FC's visit to the New Den in February 2002 prompted -

'You're just a bunch of squatters!' And 'Shit team no home!'

Not forgetting – 'You can stick your f...ing Wombles up your a... – sideways!'

Particularly Uncle Bulgaria! We lot are all Tweenies fans in the CBL private joke sorry Clive!

Finally moving away from The New Den to Luton Town's trappy fans at Kenilworth Road in August 2005 we added to our non pc Asian area chants repertoire when we sang –

'Small town in Delhi, you're just a small town in Delhi!' And 'Luton smells of curry, Luton smells of curry, la, la, la, la!' More specifically to an extrovert/gobby ginger minger home fan in the side stand at the same game we sang –'There's only one Chris Evans!'

Luton Town in FA CUP 5th Round at Kenilworth Road 16th February 2013

When Millwall kept the ball in our stand Luton Town's mouthy fans shouted 'Gypo!'

Then 'Where's your Caravan?'

To which I started – 'Where's Your Taliban?'

Re massively Asian nature of Luton

Luton Fans sang

'You're Just a Small Town in West Ham!'

We replied

'You're Just a Small Town in Bengal!'

Knocked 'Em In The Old Kent Road!

A selection of chants from the Bovver Boy era through to the present day –

To start a few golden oldies from the Old Den was sung to

a slushy tune from the 70s 'Seasons In The Sun' by Terry Jacks, George Jacks relation? The first went something like –

'We had joy we had fun, we had Chelsea on the run, but the fun didn't last 'cos the bastards ran too fast!'

Chelsea old Headhunters era fans used to sing – 'We All Agree That Harry The Dog Is A Poodle'

I seem to recall that we also sang a chant that went something like -

'Hi, Ho, it's off to Wolves we go, with a knife and a brick and a shooting stick'

If memory serves this was sung in the 1970s when Millwall were due to play at Molineux in the FA Cup, although memory being what it is the shooting stick part may be wrong, what the bloody hell would you do with a shooting stick?

If memory serves, there was an old Bovver boy chant sung to the tune of Nancy Sinatra's 'These boots are made for walking' that went something like – 'These boots are made for kicking and that's just what they'll do, one of these days these boots are gonna kick the shit/f*** out of you!

There was another old 'You'll never make the station!' era one when we used to sing –

'The **** sing we don't know why, 'cos after the game they're gonna die!'

Some more Millwall golden Hoolie chants, ancient and modern – 'Will you turn up (Will we see you) at The Den?'/'Where were you at The Den?'/'We are the hardest in London!'/'Millwall Millwall run, Millwall Millwall run, Millwall Millwall run, Millwall run from no one!'/'Come and have a go at the Millwall agg(a)ro!'/'You'll get the same as Luton!'/'You'll run and you know you will!'/'The .... Sing we don't know why – Cos after the game they're gonna die!'/'The Lions, The Lions Da Da Da Da Da Da War (Roar)!' And 'Hello, hello Millwall aggro, Millwall aggro!'

More up to date variation of the above at Loftus Road QPR in September 2010 the home boys (sic) to the right of us got – 'You'll

Run Like You Always Do!'

A couple of more modernish firm chants – 'Bush, Bush Bushwhackers!' And 'Bush, Bush, Bush!'

No specific chants yet from the more recentish Firm addition Millwall Youth.

Some general Hoolie chants that Millwall have obviously sung over the years...

'You're gonna get your f..ing heads kicked in!'/'Oh! Hoolie, hoolie, hoolie, hoolie, hoolie, hoolie Hooligan!'/'Ag, Agr, Agro, Aggro!'/'''You're just a bunch of wankers!'//'What's it like to run away?'/'We'll see you all outside!'/'Will you stand and fight outside?'/'Let's go f...ing mental, let's go f...ing mental, la la la la – la la la la.'/'Walk on, walk on and you'll never walk again, you'll never walk again!'/'Come and join us, come and join us, come and join us over here.'/'On the pitch, on the pitch, on the pitch.'/'Millwall's gonna get ya!'/'Come on, come on, come on, etc.'/'Ooo! Bat round the head! I say ooo! Bat round the head!'/'You'll get a boot wrapped round your head!'/

'Hit him on the head, hit him on the head, hit him on the head with a baseball bat, on the head, on the head!'

A lovely collection I'm sure you will agree. The last chant was probably derived from The Ramones 'Beat on the Brat.' It is an example of bloody Americanisation, what is wrong with a good old English cricket bat or croquet mallet coshing?

There was also a replying chant to the opposing fans 'We're hard!' chants in the 60s/70s the storytelling TV reference – 'Jackanory, Jackanory!' Implying that they were making all there Hoolie victory chants up.

Some more specific chants from us and the opposition now -

From us to Bristol City anytime –

'Their name is Bristol City and they like to run, they do run, run, run, they do run, run!'

From us to Portsmouth at home, 13th December 2001. A real charmer sung to them about a Waterloo pub battle before the game initially and the inevitable post-match clashes –

'Going home in a body bag!'

To end this section a few from various opponents –

In reply there was a hooligan bravado chant from Stoke City's fans at The New Den in February 2004 when they sang -'You're shit and you're scared of us!'

On a similar front a chant sung by Brighton fans at the New Den in Setember 2006 and Doncaster Rovers in August 2007 prior to the Yorkshire folks mass running away to disprove their chant, both teams sang the following chant to highlight our supposed modern lack of hooligan threat –

'You're not scary anymore!'

On a similar tack Derby County fans at the New Den on Saturday 23rd October 2010 sang 'You've Got No Football Hooligans!' a brave accusation when you are behind police/steward lines and with bloody great gaps between them and Millwall fans.

Southampton fans previously sang the above and 'Does your teacher know you are here?' and 'Where's your boys gone?' to the East Upper and our modern perceived lack of threat nowadays, where did it all go wrong? Who wants the Den to be friendly? As an Old Den veteran I bloody don't!

Non-PC alert –
Birmingham City – 'We Want To Be Together!' –

St Andrews Serenades

When we played there 1st October 2013, the mouthy Brummie boys to our right, and I mean boys in an age sense, got the plethora of back to school type chants, but here is a selection of other chants they received –

'Jeremy Kyle In The Morning!'/'You're Shit And You Talk Funny!'/'I Can Smell Your Fear From Here!' and 'Shittu F***Ed

Your Mum!' On a racial tip they got – 'Birmingham Birmingham Taliban!'/'You Ran From The Taliban!'/'You've Got The Mosque In The Morning!'/'Happy Ramadan!'

Racist I know sorry! All the Brummie young herberts seemed to be white from what I could see, but I suppose it is open season on abuse!

Continuing the hooligan theme some earlier exchanges with perennial enemies the Brummies.

At the return of Birmingham City to the New Den in the Carling Cup on 29th November 2005, naturally there was a heightened expectation of trouble it being the Brummies first game against us since the Play Off riot. It was a night of massed stewarding and Policing and a few witty exchanges between the East Upper and the away fans in the North Upper.

From Them To Us –

They sang the cheeky – 'You've got more stewards than fans!'

And the hooligan boast – 'Zulu's gonna get ya!'

In a previous game in the League game in 2001 the Brummies sang the insult of all insults to the East Upper – 'You're all Palace over there!' At least I think that is what they said with their Brummie accent it's like trying to decipher a pissed Ozzy Osbourne statement.

When we played the then Premier League side in the FA Cup 3rd Round at the New Den in January 2011 their fans sic sang this classic –

'We want to go home, we want to go home, London is a shithole, we want to go home!'

What! You want to go home, goodbye you best f*** off back to a real shithole i.e. Birmingham then, my Gods deluded, stupid or Premier League brainwashed morons or what!

From Us To Them -

Millwall Boys sang the following to the Zulu Warriors as they emerged in the ground and began to hurl abuse– 'You're white and you know you are!'

One question – If they are Zulus why the bloody hell wasn't Michael Caine fighting them from the Millwall section in a red uniform with a white Pith Helmet on? Just a thought!!!

I heard a rumour on an away trip to Birmingham City on 1st October 2013, on the club coach when we had a film on that had him in it Now You See Me, that when he was 19 he as a Bermondsey Boy came to the Old Den to support the Wall, got hit by a brick aka missile, said this is too rough for me and decided to go support Chelsea instead, wise move not as this was when Chelsea had a proper firm!

As an aside on this coach we had another DVD, that was White House Down, i.e. not exactly legal at the time, which when the driver put it on, on the small overhead screens was replete with Chinese subtitles! Brilliant it was unwatchable and driver was told unceremoniously to take this f***ing thing off! Which he did, real pub or on the street Chinese DVD job 100%

The Voice of the MK Dons Mysterons

When we played the created entity that is MK Dons at the New Den in 2008/2009, their fans sang our chant – 'No One Likes Us!!!''Kin cheek can't we © this bloody stuff as I have said before!

As my mate Simon said when they continually sang it –

'I don't know about nobody liking you, no one knows who the F*** you are!'

At the away game against the MK Dons on St Patrick's Night in 2009, we gathered 1800+ Millwall sang –

'AFC Wimbledon, AFC Wimbledon!' and 'You've got no history!'

To ally to their emergence from the ether of the alleged remnants of the former Wimbledon club.

A Joyful Winning Night in the middle of Nowhere aka a Joyful Winning night In The West Of England's Tractor District

4 of us, me, Laurie, Paul and Nathan went to a Tuesday night match at Herford United on 27th January 2009, it was the first ever visit there for any of us. It was a strange place in the middle of God knows where, with an Amateur type ground, that had strange terracing in our end of the ground, we had half the end, divided by metal fences and a roof over the small stepped section at the back, however from where the roof/terrace steps started to the surrounding pitchside wall, there was a flat tarmacked area. As it was a night match there were only 258 of us there in this and the seats section to our left, what happens if they have a huge away turnout on the terrace itself, I have no idea, if they all stood on the flat ground area, they would have to put them in to height order, i.e smallest at the front gravitating to tallest at the back to watch the match! Bizarre.

Some chants from us -

To the Millwall people standing at the very front out in the open in the pissing down of rain, we sang –

'Wet Lot, Wet Lot give us a song!'

They did and also replied with 'Dry Lot Dry Lot give us a song!' so we did as well.

As the rain poured down heavier, we sang 'Wet Lot Wet Lot Come Up Here!!' I.e under the roof, some did!

There was a young home boy at the front leaning on the pitchside wall behind the goal in the home part next to us, he was white and clothewise well chavved up, so when we took the lead we sang – 'Rude Boy, Rude Boy What's the score?'/'Rude Boy Rude Boy You're a C***!' and 'Rude Boy Where Do You Keep you're gun?'

The Hereford United goalie Craig Samson in the 2nd Half was in front of us, he unfortunately for him had vivid ginger hair and got the customary 'We Hate Gingers!' Chant.

We also sang – 'Strawberry Blonde? You're Having A laugh!'

He was also compared to Soaps Gingers relating to Eastenders Bradley Branning he got – 'There's Only one Bradley!'/"Bradley, Bradley Give us a wave!',and after he made a ricket and we scored he got 'Bradley, Bradley You F***Ed it up!'

Relating to Coronation Street's Chesney Battersby – Brown he got –

'There's only one Chesney!' At 1 – 0 he got 'Chesney Chesney What's the score? And sporadically during the whole 2nd half he got 'Chesney Chesney Give us a wave!' Which he didn't, bloody celebrity!

I Love To Go A Wandering… err no I F***ing don't! Wycombe Wanderers 20th February 2010, where we lost again!!!!

Adams Park is a bok ground for us, I have seen us lose there 3 times, draw once and win once, today was another Millwall playing worse against the lesser sides routine, I thought that I would list down some of the chants that occurred there. Here we go –

There was a blonde female press photographer on the pitchside in front of us who a bloke next to me kept singing this to – 'Can You Take A Picture Of My Cock!' whether she could we thankfully never found out!

Their ginger forward Matt Harrold on the day after the live Eastenders Archie Mitchell murderer live episode and Bradley Branning's death to highlight this ginger link he got the following in the first half in front of us –

'Are You Bradley In Disguise?' and 'You're Dead and Your Dad's A C***!'

To conclude the specifics there was also this chant from near me at the back of the stand – 'Shit Ground No Beer!' Therefore proving that Wycombe Wanderers' home is more Adams Park than Adnams Park, for all you CAMRA folk out there!

Mascot Diagnosis

At Scunthorpe United pre kick off on 17th December 2016, Scunthorpe United's Mascot Bunny was at our end and to show him what we think about these creatures our Christmas greetings were –

'You're Just A Nonce In A Costume!'

'Ah Ha Nahrich! The Mystical Land Of Delia Smith/Stephen Fry/Bernard Matthews And Alan Partridge Arrive At The New Den For The Holloway Era Away Teams Customary Three Points Saturday 7th March 2015

In a stereotypical abusive fashion re inbreeding we sang – 'Does's Your Sister Know You're Here?' And more modern 'You've Got More Toes Than Us!' abuse or not did us no use, we lost 4 – 1.

'Halloween Eve 2010 in The Land Of The Non Vocal Yokels!'

As you may have gathered if you have read any of my Millwall books, I hate grounds where the atmosphere (sic) is like the noise abatement society i.e. Ipswich Town, who are allied to the likes of Watford, Palace, Charlton etc, this was as bad if not worse than any I have been to,

To highlight this we sang – '1 nil up and you still don't sing!! 'then '2 nil up and you still don't sing! And more originally ' 2 nil and you've all f***ed off!' which we sang to the leaving droves to our left behind the goal.

A couple of original chants relating to the Suffolk Strangler Ipswich Prostitute murderer that we sang –

'Where've your prossies gone?' and a variation ' Where've your brasses gone?'

At The New Den return game on a less horror movie more religious day Easter Monday 2013, we sang –

'Inbred C***s! Inbred C***s!'

To the yokels there singing something like 'You're just a small West Ham!' could be wrong it was something comparing us to Wet Spam Untied, could not hear it properly, unfortunately I could hear their following inaccurate chant though – 'Millwall is a shithole I want to go home!' sorry to upset you better say bye bye then!

'Just Because You Are from the West Country Does Not Mean That You Are West Ham You Yokel Prats!'

Continuing the Bumpkin theme we won another game in Gloucester at Cheltenham Town also on a Tuesday night, in February 2009, here are some Yokel Vocal serenades from the locals. There was a small section of home team crooners in the miniscule home crowd in tractor country to the right of we away fans behind the goal, they sang several West Ham Utd related chants, to us including their continually singing 'I'm Forever Blowing Bubbles', to wind us up, our winning 3 – 1 at the match there on Tuesday 24th February 2009 didn't help them! To have a go at us they also sang – 'You can stick Green Street up your arse!''and 'You're just a small club in London!'

Additionally they sang 'You're not scary anymore!' i.e. a revised version that I had never heard before, it was a variation of the of the oft sung modern chant 'You're not famous anymore!' wrong!!!

Once again in the West Country Yeovil Town fans on Good Friday 2009 also sang 'I'm Forever Blowing Bubbles', they also sang – 'F*** off back to West Ham!' Both wrong but sung to wind us up,

I think our losing 2-0 there was enough torture, ya smock wearing, straw chewing, Cider/Scrumpy guzzling bumpkins! losing there was bad enough for me let alone hearing your Claret and Blue rhapsody!

Finishing my 2008/9 season ramble of the West Country and continuing the 'Appy 'Ammers routine, in addition to the above at the next away game at Bristol Rovers on Saturday 18th April the home fans not only sang – 'I'm Forever Blowing Bubbles', they also sang 'United' and 'You Always Run From West Ham!', strange their singing the first one and incorrect their singing the second one.

To additionally wind us up at the end of the game, after our 4 – 2 defeat the PA blasted out Palarse's 'Glad All Over', well that worked I was not Glad in anyway after watching how we had performed and continually hearing the scum rhapsody without hearing bloody Palarse's theme tune!

Luckily the Old Bill let us go straight out after the game and did not retain us until we had gotten the full wind up from The Dave Clark 5 tune.

Non-PC alert –
Taunting The Titfer!

Derby County on January 3rd 2011 at Pride Park to the boys to our left a couple of newish sartrorial sexist titfer chants – 'Whose the pooftah (prat) in the hat?' and 'You won your hat in a raffle!'

Mouthy Opposition At The New Den And Beyond.

Continuing the Mouthy fans theme in addition to the previously mentioned Mouthy opposing fans chants here are some more ripostes that away fans sang to us at the New Den –

Brighton & Hove Albion in September 2002 to our depleted East upper contingent sang -

'There's only five of you singing!'

In December 2004 they sang – 'Worst support we've ever heard!'

In response to the 'gay' chant bombardment at The Withdean

in December 2005, they sang a couple of social stereotype chants – 'What's it like to wear a tag?' Moreover, 'You wear fake Burberry!'

They also sang 'Have you ever wondered why?' in response to our 'No One Likes Us!' Chant

Southampton fans in the League Cup second round on 19th September 2006 sang –

'Where's your Millwall gone? Quite!'

Reading fans sang the first of many renditions of – 'UEFA Cup? You're having a laugh!'

At the April 24th 2004 game at the New Den, this was whilst we were in our pre FA Cup Final wind down phase. In a similar vein at Reading's Madejski on 5th April 2005 the home fans sang –

'You were shit in Europe, you were shit in Europe, la, la la, la la la la!'

At least we were in the UEFA Cup in Europe!

On January 3rd 2005 Rotherham United fans sang to an injured and prone Dennis Wise –

'Shit on the floor!' They also serenaded the stretcher bearers when they came on to carry Wisey off with ambulance noises – ' Nee, naw, nee naw!'

Watford's fans, sang the following at the New Den on December 28th 2005 –

'We've got more fans than you!' That is as maybe but the Watford fans that we saw all looked like they were from a rural rambling club rather than football fans.

Hereford United's travelling fans at the New Den on October 28th 2008 sang a variation on the 'You're not famous anymore!' Apparently we've lost our Hooligan reputation chant, they sang an aforementioned chant–

'You're not scary anymore!' I doubt that very much, as well as the fact that we won it and was also very near Halloween!

Leyton Orient fans to highlight their supposed superior East Endness sang the massively inaccurate –

'We hate West Ham more than you!' At the New Den on March

15th 2008, my God is that inaccurate, never heard the 'Bobby Moore Is No More' or 'Chim Chiminee Chim Chiminee Chim, Chim Cheroo We Hate Those Bastards In Claret And Blue' chants then O's? You have certainly never been to a Lions v Irons game either!!!

In Millwall fan stereotypical pisstake mode Crystal Palace's supposedly Posh Suburbanite fans were very unusually mouthy at the New Den in February 2006 they sang this suburban superiority chant –

'We pay your benefits!' Thanks Suburbanites ta!

At the New Den pre-season friendly in July 2006 they sang – 'We've got more fans than you!'

They also sang the sarcastic hooligan chant – 'Let's all run from Millwall!'

Presumably implying that they would not I assume, my arse they would not as the 'Royle Family' Dad might say!

In Neil Harris's Testimonial 1st July 2010 the Hearts contingent, pretty much sang continually apart from when we took the lead, 99.999% of their chanting was totally unintelligible to our English ears apart from, one that they sang to us – 'You've Got More Blacks than Arsenal!' implying that we have more black players than Arsenal do. We do have many black players, so what! A player's colour means nothing, in the real world of Millwall; it is more to do with give us 100% and if they do, based on their effort and achievement players are either good or bad, whether they are orange, green, black, white or purple it makes no difference! People will think that this cannot be true as we are always a team whose fans are perceived by all and sundry who know F*** all about nothing as all racists, wrong!!

Non-PC alert –
The Championship Era Party's Over – Southampton's St Mary's Easter Bank Holiday Monday 17th April 2006

There was a glut of chants from this particular relegation game at St Mary's, although they could have gone in to other sections, I thought I would lump them together.

Saints rivals Pompey –

'Pompey's staying up, they're staying up, they're staying Pompey's staying up!'/' There's only one Harry Redknapp!' In addition, 'Play up Pompey!'

Messiah or Gypsy -

To Romany looking Southampton substitute Kami Kosowski warming up in front of us.

The Southampton fans sang 'Jesus, Jesus give us a song!'

We sang 'Your Mum reads tarot cards!' along with the usual caravan and Pikey references

Paedophile and Rent Boy Gay Sex -

To an effeminate looking home fan in the section next to us in a hooped green top we sang–

'Does your Daddy touch your arse?' Moreover, 'Rent Boy, Rent Boy How's Your Arse?'

We also sang the customary – 'Rupert Lowe Sex offender!' all non PC sorry!

Little Britain Social comment –

To Chav style girls in the home section we sang –

'There's only 1 Vicky Pollard' before spotting another and singing 'There's only 2 Vicky Pollards'

To A Fancy Dressed Steward -

As we were held in the ground we sang the following to a bespectacled black steward in the massed ranks of Police and stewards surrounding us at the end of the game -

'One Edgar Davids, There's only one Edgar Davids!' In addition,

'Edgar, Edgar give us a song!'

He took his glasses off so we sang – 'Where's your goggles gone? Where's your goggles gone?'

To the orange jacket stewards in front of us we sang – 'RAC, RAC, RAC!'

To Us and About Us and Ours -

Gallows humour - As the away section stood all afternoon the Saintly fans sang to us – 'Sit down – you're going down!'

Southampton also continually sang – "Going down, going down, going down!' Sarcastically so did we.

We also sang – 'Bristol, Bristol here we come!'/'Millwall's going down, we're going down, we're going, Millwall's going down!' And 'We are going down – say we are going down!'

More Sarcasm –

'Where've our players gone, where've our players gone?'

Moreover, the sarcastic, I think! 'We want Bob Peeters back!'

When now an ex-Lion Ben May hit the bar with a late header, we sang the sarcastic –

'You must be shit, we hit the bar!'

At Portman Road Ipswich Town on 2nd April 2018 we were in a season where we had scored 4 goals in the first minute of a game, so as the game was about to start we sang – 'We're Gonna Score In A Minute!' we did score in the first half but sadly not that early today.

Non-PC alert –
Our Championship era has started again – the Long-Awaited Return to the Land Of The Delusional Suburbanite Nigel's and their return visit to us –

Our trip to Selhurst Park on October 15th 2010 was hilarious, as usual, Norwood Junction was like Police State, and all the pubs were shut or Home fan only, although they did sell beer inside the ground strangely, money money money! Springs to mind. We got to Norwood Junction quite early and strolled past a pub The Albion, which was policed by several Old bill and the heroic home Ultras gestured at us through the window.

This was very daring of them, as they were safely behind police lines and a very strange choice of pub for the delusional homeboys. Why would you plot up in a pub with a name of your hated rivals? In their case Brighton and Hove Albion, it was like Millwall replacing the Golden Lion/The Bramcote etc with a pub called The Hammers, weird!

In the game, which we won 1 – 0 in our first visit there since the Holmsdale Ultra revolution, hilarious, they were greeted with the usual Eric Cantona naturally, and we accompanied their drum ridden we are Italian style Ultra bollocks, by continually singing – 'You Take It up the Arse!' to their tedious continual drone.

Additionally, we adapted 'Who The F*** Are Palace?' to also fit this monotonous dirge and we also did a limp wrested arm raised continual dance to accompany what the home pr**s were doing, our anal chant and limp wrested waving seemed to shut them up, good!! I thought that this was all very funny; mind you, I am a bit biased.

To my mind any teams fans like Palace who need a drum are a joke, continuing this vibe, but to real fans not delusional Ultras, the Italian firms are dangerous and passionate, Palarse are just laughable.

The return game at Millwall on New Year's Day 2011, was marvellous, they only sold just 2000 tickets in North Stand upper tier and I was quite, well deliriously happy that we made Palarse look like the mugs that they are.

They are a very big embarrassment, as all Millwall reading this know, for example bringing some Coaches from Surrey aka Croydon to South East London yea gods.

The lengthy journey price was about as much as I paid to go to Derby County on Monday 3rd January 2011, When we went to their shithole we went on East London Overground Line, doddle, or is this too dangerous for them to attempt as they might run in to Charlton's Notorious Anorak Train spotter Firm on the way! I wondered whether the 1.30pm kick off was made that time yesterday so that they got home early enough for their mums to read them a bedtime story and tuck them in bed early?

In their deluded heads probably good to get home early so that they could go online immediately and boast about how they took over Bermondsey, Ultras my arse, Suburbanite Cyber Warrior tossers!

On the same tack for information QPR fans could also get coaches from West London to Bermondsey in March 2011, at the bargain sum of £24, kin hell the following Saturday 12th March 2011 after this game on Tuesday 8th March 2011 I paid £25 for a coach trip to Burnley! It had to be a bit more expensive as it is more than 200 extra miles!

Moving on to the game and day, we dominated a game that we won 3-0 against a piss poor relegation level side, loved it.

Pre-match Les played Alice and the whole ground gave the Suburbanites 'Palace, Palace Who the F*** are Palace?' At full volume, something that we did before in a previous game at New Den until Jordan complained to Theo and it was banned at his request, as he has now gone off to his Avatar but Orange coloured man wonderland, back it came – hoorah!

They had an ultras flag at back of North Stand and foolishly sang their drone, which was responded to by our sell-out crowd this time singing – 'You take it up the Arse!' obviously it had not occurred to them that this would definitely happen.

As the upper tier of the away stand suddenly appeared to be emptying out, we sang 'F*** off you might as well F*** off!' and 'Where's your Ultras gone? Where's your Ultras gone?'

As we had done to him at Derby when he stood in after Gregory, there we abused George Burley as I mentioned earlier. At this game the then Palarse manager during this match as he stood in testical sorry technical zone – 'Sit down you Scottish C***!' and at 3 – 0, 'Sacked in the morning you're getting sacked in the morning!', wrong it didn't take that long, he was booted out on the night of the game, bye bye!

Our return to the Land Of The Police Escorted To Their Own Ground Nigel's. Saturday 26th November 2011, naturally the trip, was the usual police state bollocks day of being f***ed about, i.e. a proper Millwall away day. For example, the allocation was only a bit more than half of what Wet Spam Untied had been allocated, we had 2600 they had 4900, brilliant strategy by plod, losing Palarse mucho thousands in lost revenue, well done!

There was apparently trouble when the academy mob were there so they then blame us, that sounds about right, in second half from our section and at the Ultras there were a couple of bottles thrown, which was bloody stupid and led to it being focussed on Football League show on BBC.

Whilst I would, 100% say that all the bottle and coin lobbers were doing was affecting our club financially no doubt and giving the filth a reason to show why we need such restrictions.

One thing that I thought was stupid was for Palace to sell beer in bottles inside the ground in the first place, wouldn't plastic containers be less dangerous?

Moving on to the chants –

I would love to know who else would do this; I would say no one but us.

When The Crystal Girls, their scantily clad pom pom dancing bints ran on pre match, we greeted them from the Arthur Waite shithole stand with – 'You take it up the Arse!' the above-mentioned chant solely sung at the Holmsdale Ultra knobs section the season before. I thought one part of their dance did not help, when they bent over towards us! I am not a choreographer just thought we could say, see told ya as they did it towards us.

Moving on to the Nigel Ultras we sang 'Stick your drum up your arsehole!' to one of their entrance on to the pitch tunes we also sang 'Millwall don't need a drum!'

They Will Need Their Wellies in the Hillsides – Swansea City Friday 10th December 2010

We had a lovely trip to Swansea City on a Friday, one thing I wondered as an Englishman as our coach sailed past hundreds of what the locals probably deem very shaggable sheep, the flocks occupants had different colour paint brands on their back, was that to highlight who the sheep belonged to? Alternatively, was it a colour coding that indicated what sexual act the Woolly Bah Sex Machines would be prepared to do? I knew what it really meant, but I might have been wrong!

From a sheep shagging perspective I thought that we should adapt Palace's 'You Take It up the Arse' chant mentioned several times above to 'Sheep Take it Up The Arse, Sheep Take It Up The Arse!'

On the way there I text some mates who were not able to go to suggest this idea.

I also said that if we did sing this adapted chant, then if anyone suddenly shot off, we could imply that they not only could we see them sneaking out, but we knew that they were heading home to anally pleasure their livestock!

I had a very bad sore throat on the night so could not Grandad this chant myself, so it never was taken up unfortunately, so we could not open up another Welsh-abusing angle!

Moving on to what was sung by us on the night of our 1 – 1 draw at the Liberty Stadium, or should that be taking Liberty's Stadium? I have put a brief explanation of where I think the chants came from –

Nationality assumptions – 'You wish you were English!' and 'Where've All the Sheep Gone?'

In reaction to what Cardiff City's Soul Crew always say about Swansea's Jack Army i.e. Fat Bastards, we sang Band Aid's 'Do They Know It's Christmas' song adapted like this –

'Feed the Welsh Let Them Know It's Christmas Time'

Continuing the fattest theme, we also sang 'Is the Camera Big Enough?' to the riot police surrounding and filming us all match, we were implying that the cuddly Jack Army should be filmed not us, in widescreen probably better!

Finally to the screeds of riot police coming up the stairwell all around us for no apparent reason

'You Got Done By Students!' This was the day after Students rioting and bashing whom they considered the Old Bill fascists at a University Student Fees Demo.

Can You Handle It Can You Handle It? Cos You Ain't Had Nothing Like It! Respecting Your Own Manager Reprise

Millwall fans have a habit of hounding managers out of their job or acknowledging former employees, just a few examples –

My first recollection was the 'Petchey must go' chant and signature campaign when petitions were handed around the Old Den terraces in an effort to try to oust our manager George Petchey in the late 1970s early 1980s.

Bruce Rioch was another manager forced out, in his case he was chased around the corridors at the Old Den in the 1990s by irate fans at a reserve match following a 6 – 1 hiding at Portsmouth; strangely, he thought that it was time to leave, 'Rioch out!' was the cry.

Also in the 1990s when Mick McCarthy was our manager I once saw him standing outside of Charing Cross station in a green and orange outfit that made him look like a particularly Irish colour-blind test, just thought that I would mention it. To my ears, his shouts to the players on the pitch from the dug out always used to sound like the foghorn of a boat in distress, very apt in some cases. The crowd turned against McCarthy when the Republic of Ireland management rumours began to emerge and he was told in no uncertain terms to – 'F… off Mick McCarthy!'

His return to the New Den as Sunderland's Manager on 17th January 2004 and again on November 5th 2004 resulted in him getting a substantial amount of abuse, including -'Mick McCarthy is a wanker, is a wanker!'/'Sit down Pinocchio!' And 'Sit down big nose, sit down big nose, sit down big nose, sit down!'/'Big nose, big nose, what's the score?'

Not forgetting the 2002 World Cup chant – 'Keano, there's only one Keano!'

The horror that was Jimmy Nicholl's reign left us all mute in a state of shock so no chants I am afraid.

From what I can recall Billy Bonds did not have any specific abuse either apart from the obligatory Anti Hammers chants, I think 'Appy 'Ammer or not that we respected his playing career attributes.

Mark McGhee's return to the New Den with his new team Brighton in December 2004 and in every subsequent game he got the following abuse – 'He's Scotch, he's bent, his a… is up for rent! Mark McGhee, Mark McGhee'/'Cheer up Mark McGhee (sad) fat Scottish bastard and a shit football team!' And 'Mark McGhee sex offender!'

Under Dennis Wise prior to our eventually beating Ipswich Town at home on Boxing Day 2004 our perceived Wilkinesque (or Alan Dorneyesque for our older readers) sideways/backwards tactics led to the CBL singing – 'Sideways, we only pass sideways!'

Colin Lee manager in our Hokey Cokey management season in 2005/6 was greeted with – 'Will we ever score a goal?' And '4 – 4 – 2!' for his one man up front policy in August 2005.

Lee's mid season replacement David Tuttle was the focus of varied abuse as we continued to struggle in February 2006, for example – 'You're taking Millwall down!'/'F… off Tuttle!'/'Tuttle is a wanker!' and 'You don't know what you're doing!' These followed some seemingly strange substitutions in the game against Luton Town at the New Den, which we actually won!

Similarily when Tuttle had a habit of only bringing on Marvin Williams in the second half, we sang –

'Where was he at 3 o'clock?'

Nigel Spackman's less than impressive start at Millwall led to – 'F… of Spackman!' and Spackman, Spackman you're a c…!' that didn't take long did it?

In 2006/7 Willie Donnachie prior to being sacked in October 2007 got 'You Don't Know What You Are Doing!' for what we decided were bad tactical decisions and after substitutions at Southend United, he also got chants for Byfield, Williams, Elliott, Hubertz and Hackett not forgetting anyone else that had gone or not been squad selected.

Kenny Jackett largely always had positive chants –

'One Kenny Jackett, there's only one Kenny Jackett' being the usual and 'We love you Kenny We Do!' a new one at our victory at T'Burnley in February 2012.

Unusual for Millwall fans who perceive anyone leaving like a horrendous divorce, when Kenny Jackett returned with Wolverhampton Wanderers on Saturday 18th October 2014, he was warmly applauded and also from the back of the CBL he received what some Lions fans perceived as slanderous – 'There's Only One Kenny Jackett!' we came back from 3 – 0 down to draw the match 3 – 3 so I do not know if he would have got slaughtered for beating his former team, back to his departure when KJ left at the end of 2012/3 a Wet Spam Untied Ex Captain came on board, let the real respect your own manager really start here –

'Our second 'Appy 'Ammer Manager Steve Lomas in 2013/14, pre his Boxing Day 2013 Bye Bye

Following in the wake of Billy Bonds umpteen years previously Steve Lomas former West Ham United Captain became our manager in 2013/14, although we lost our first League game, which was the first game of the season at the New Den on Saturday 3rd August 2013, he did not receive Lomas Out! Well not yet anyway.

From the opposition the piss taking began when we played AFC Wimbledon at New Den Tuesday after the 6th August 2013 in the Capital One Cup First Round, lippy AFC Wimbledon fans sang these wind them up chants to encourage us to slag off our manager - 'Stevie Lomas – he comes from West Ham' and 'He's West Ham till he dies, he's West Ham till he dies, he knows he is, he's sure he is, he's West Ham till he dies!'

The Ginger One's Torrent of Abuse Begins with Millwall going the first 6 league games without a win and at our third consecutive home defeat v Derby County on Saturday 14th September 2013. the torrents of abuse began in earnest, especially as it was a 5-1 defeat, he got a deluge of 'Shit, Shit, Shit' at half time and full time

More specifically for his West Ham association and Ginger hair as Derby's goals totted up he got –

'F*** Off Lomas!'/'Sit Down You Ginger C***!'

At 5 – 1 he got 'You're Getting Sacked In The Morning!' and 'Lomas, Lomas You're A C***!'

Like Wimbledon had Derby County fans sang 'There's Only One Stevie Lomas!' to take the piss as if we needed any piss taking!

Even the CBL sang some chants implying that he we had excused him when we went on a three game winning run in September 2013, this at the Leeds United victory, the third in a row.

The lets lambaste Lomas torrent really began at the two games in a week absolute horror parade, three wins on the trot followed by a 4 – 0 defeat at Birmingham City on Tuesday 1st October then on the following Saturday 5th October 2013 with a real debacle at Bournemouth a 5 – 2 defeat that included Millwall being 2 – 0 up in first 10 minutes!

Following Millwall is never ever dull, you need psychiatric help but it is never dull, always a Goalfest under Lomas, but usually in our bloody net!

Following Bournemouth scoring their fifth from their second penalty near the end of the game heard chants of

'Lomas Out Lomas Out!' came to the fore in addition to the aforementioned 'Lomas, Lomas You're A C***!'

In the wake of 'We Hate Those Bastards In Claret and Blue!' aimed I think at Stephen Henderson Bournemouth's keeper on loan from Wet Spam and Jack Collinson ex 'Appy ' Ammer were also serenaded with 'West Ham C***s! West Ham C***s!' both of which were early in the game when we were coasting, was also sort of indirectly aimed at ex Vermin captain then Wall manager Lomas.

At home v QPR at The New Den 19th October 2013 QPR fans sang –

'Stevie Lomas He's Taking You Down!'

At an unfortunately Live Sky Sports match v Middlesbrough at The New Den on 21st December 2013, where Millwall were abysmal and lost 2 – 0 to a team one place below us in the relegation area in the Championship, Lomas was serenaded with 'Shit, Shit, Shit!' and 'We Are Going Down, Say We are Going Down!' in general about the team's atrocious performance.

Specifically aimed at Lomas himself he got a mass serenade of some previously mentioned chants plus plenty more –'Lomas Out!'/'We Want Lomas Out!'/'West Ham C***! West Ham C***!'/'Ginger C***! Ginger C***!'/'Chim Chimineee, Chim, Chim Cherooo, We Hate Those Bastards in Claret And Blue!'/'F*** Off Lomas!' and 'You're getting Sacked in the Morning!'

This was inside and additionally outside the ground with a fairly large demonstration outside The Barry Kitchener Stand, the above chants echoed as did the general 'We Want Our Millwall Back!' and in reference to anti Lomas chants 'Are You Watching Berylson?' asking was he seeing the massed Millwall fans demonstration outside in the car park.

In the next match which was to be his last at Watford on Boxing Day 2013, he was warmly greeted by us at our 4 – 0 defeat, he received all the above specific anti Lomas chants and whilst standing in the technical zone as Watford goals rattled in all afternoon he got –

'Sit Down You Ginger C***!'/'You Don't Know What You're Doing!' And 'Four Nil To The West Ham C***!' and We're Shit And We're Going Down!'

As Watford not only scored four goals but made a mockery of Lomas's tactical nous he got the aforementioned and also the prophetic 'Bye Bye Lomas!'

He got the aforementioned 'You're Getting Sacked In The Morning!' he did not last till the morning as it turned out, getting sacked straight after the match.

'Super Super Neil, Super Super Neil Super Neil Harris!' Also echoed around during the game, a psychic chant as it turned out because, two former Lions on the staff at The New Den Bomber and Scott Fitzgerald were put in temporary charge for the next game the following Sunday at Doncaster Rovers.

Not specifically about Wet Spam Untied's undoubted planting of Lomas as an avenger for our Avram Grant banner airplane abuse at Wigan in our midst, we also sang the aforementioned 'We Want Our Millwall Back!' which we all naturally do,, however in my and most of my Millwall mates minds this means with spirit, with bottle and with passion whilst playing for the club we love.

Something that those of us at Watford objected to were some in our section cheering Watford's dominant possession each time they passed to each other, and booed whenever a Millwall player got the ball, The wrestler Big Daddy 'Easy Easy Easy' chant echoed as did 'It's Only Four You Must Be Shit!' and 'We Want Five, We Want Five!'

I know the above three chants were sarcastic at the shower of shit that was overseen by the tactical genius that was Steve Lomas that we had paid to admire, but this type of mentality, I.e, taking the piss out of the Wall, never has been and never should be the Millwall way in my opinion, as I expressed above true Millwall or HOF favourite Real Wall is not taking the piss out of your own team, but supporting them, especially if they are giving their all for The Wall, even if in this instance they were far from giving their all, slag Lomas the instigator and organiser of this monstrosity off big time by all means, but do not sarcastically take the piss out of your own team, whether thoroughly deserved or not.

At Doncaster Rovers on 29th December we drew 0-0 because Millwall had returned with commitment and passion under Bomber Harris and Scott Fitzgerald's caretakership, we sang -

'We Got Steve Lomas Out!'/'We've Got Our Millwall Back!' and naturally 'Super Super Neil, Super Super Neil Super Neil Harris!' echoed again.

As we had got rid of our main abuse target the tactical mastermind that was Steve Lomas we decided to pick on other people, so up at Donny we picked on a ballboy who had made a bit of a balls of getting the ball back in front of us –'Ball Boy, Ball Boy You're a C***!' And more specifically towards Millwall Chief Operating Officer and Finance Director Andy Ambler –

'Andy Ambler Is A W***er, Is A W***er!'/'We Want Ambler Out, Say we Want Ambler Out!

And the Millwall abusive favourite 'Ambler, Ambler you're A C***! Ambler you're A C***!'

The Only Way Out Is Orange Southend United Away FA Cup

At the next away game after Doncaster Rovers following a 3 – 1 home defeat v Leicester City, which was not a bad performance came the horror show at Southend United's Roots Hall on 4th January 2014. With Bomber and Fitzgerald in charge this performance looked like Wall's team were still possessed by the tactical ghost of Lomas! In the land of Orange skinned ladies, as a homage I think, plus the fact that Southend wear the same dark blue colour as us, we wore all orange.

Pre and during the match as a Steward kept wandering in front of us who had Ginger hair got –

'Are You Lomas In Disguise? As the Ginger Lino at this and Leicester games also got,

At this game the shrimpers steward Because he had a beard I think also got –'Paedo Paedo!'

The shrimpers physio was cuddly, well a fat git in shorts and he got – 'You Fat C***!'

Which he acknowledged by pointing at fat blokes in our section chanting the abuse and laughing, I am not svelte but I was fine as I was sitting. standing in the penultimate row!

We started if that is the word and as we were one nil down the floodlights went out, the home fans held their mobiles and I Pads in the air in a way to get some light on to the pitch, did not work but there was our wishing for the ref to abandon the game, sadly he did not but re started and then sent Jermaine Easter off.

During the blackout we sang –

'You're Supposed To Pay The Bill!'/'Shit Ground And You've Got No Lights!'/'Shall We Lend You Twenty Quid?' and 'Call It Off, Call It Off, Call It Off

We also sang ' Southend Is A Shthole I Want To Go Home!' Unusual for Wall to sing this sort of chant but in this instance I don't think this was anything to do with Winkle Stall and Kiss me quick hat land, more to do with Millwall's utterly inept performance.

To highlight our crap performance against a team two divisions below us from annoying home fans with the bleeding annoying drummer we got – 'Championship You're Having A Laugh!'/'We'll Be Playing You Next Year!' and 'Da Da Da Der F***Ing Useless,

F***Ing Useless!' At 1-0

Back to the horror show that was the match from a Millwall prospective we were shit with 11 and certainly did not improve with one less, our appalling performance meant the return of – 'We Want Our Millwall Back!' as the 4 – 1 defeat goals rattled in, in the pissing down rain.

A true story to end to highlight how bad it was

My Cousin Paul called me Sunday after the match, while I was watching West Ham United being massacred at Notts Forest on Sky Sport.

He called to tell me that after being at that shower of shit at Sarfend the day before, he went around to Kelly his Fiancés house for dinner in Leigh on Sea; he was having Dinner when his hands turned blue! Naturally they were worried and Kelly rushed him up to A & E in Southend area, where he was told that it was not a Heart problem as they were worried that it might be, they said that it was a circulation thing caused by stress,

When told, this Kelly said to the Nurse it is football related, she said Southend United won today didn't they. They both said yes we know, but he is Millwall!

Paul's Fiancé had said to him when he first arrived at her place after the Sarfend debacle that she had never seen him so wound up after a Wall loss!

Paul said that he was okay on the Sunday, especially when I told him that Wet Spam Untied just got massacred that cheered him up no end, I said that aside sue Millwall, for having to visit A&E due to their shit performance related stress!!!

Moving back to Southend United they played at the New Den on Saturday 19th September 2015 in a League One game, with a physio who made Fatty Arbuckle look like he had anorexia, if he has a brother their singing he ain't heavy he's my brother, would really be pushing it, to cheer him up, he got 'You Fat C***! You Fat C***!'

Very Non-PC alert –
The For Fox Sake Section

To Start Foxes Rhapsody Chants 2008 -

Before I close of the chant chapter I thought that I would highlight all the humorous/insulting chants that we sang at the Walker Stadium, on September 13th 2008. This was pre-our return to the Championship but it was a real Millwall day, it had fantastic vocal backing from us all afternoon, a great performance from the team and we won 1 – 0, Yahoo! It was a great day. For those not there, I have included some of my explanations of when the chants happened and my assumption of why.

We were in a corner section of the stadium, 1103 of us. In the Alliance & Leicester home stand to our left, there was a hugely fat bloke Lee Jobber aka Jobber The drummer, he was certainly a Big Jobber, I am not exactly slim myself, well I am fat if I am honest but he was about twice the size of me and made Bad Manners Buster Bloodvessel look anorexic!

He sat behind a huge Bass Drum with a stand arrangement that held it up at the back of the home stand, he was shirtless/topless and foolishly, as he was so obese, he was attired only in shorts that must have been the size of a Circus tent. Speaking myself as a fashion guru it is not a good look for someone so grossly cuddly. To his credit, he continually banged out a loud Bass Drum rhythm all afternoon to inspire the home fans in front of him, this was In case the home fans could not sing without a drum rhythm I suppose. We have had the appalling racket of a newish era home band next to us or too bloody near to us at several away grounds, positioned as close as possible to annoy us I think to be honest. Preston North End in the away Shankly Stand being the worst in my opinion, with their bloody noisy band very near to the away section. However, Leicester's Drummer gets wicked style was a spectacle that I have never seen anywhere else. He looked like a massively cuddly Geordie often does when they take their shirt off and stand there topless, in the Geordie's case whether it is Freezing/snowing or not! In this case, we serenaded or abused him if you prefer all afternoon.

'Oh fatty, wowo, oh fatty wowo, he's banging on his drum and takes it up the bum!'

Implying that not only was he hugely obese but was also the Gayest in the Leicester village.

He also got – 'Is your Wife as fat as you?' whether his supposed betrothed was Male or Female, we did not specifically ask.

As we did not know his marital or living status we implied that he was a Mothers Boy as he got –

'You Live With Your Mum!' presumably implying that he still lived with her, whether he was thirty year old looking or not as she fed him his presumably vast daily calorie intake requirement.

'You're not fit to play that drum!'/'You're not fit to wear the shirt! Moreover 'Die in a minute, you're gonna die in a minute!'

These were sung when he stopped and slumped down over his percussion, seemingly shagged out after a lengthy and continual banging of the Bass Drum with his beaters practically all afternoon.

'Have you ever seen your dick?' If he has, it would be via a mirror on a stick I reckon, as I said before in one of my other Millwall books about an Assistant Referee at Crewe Alexandra. This was not an original chant today I know it was not invented just for this man, as it was also sung at Crewe Alexandra to a linesman, in fact in addition to this it is an oft-sung fat boy chant, which we started at Upton Park..

This was penned by us from the South Bank when it was an away terrace to the 'Appy 'Ammers mega cuddly photographer umpteen years ago, in one of our top-flight seasons from memory.

'Fat C*** what's the score?'

We sang this when we took the lead, and we sang – 'Fat C*** Fat C*** give us a song!'

As well, he did not sing to us as he preferred to bang his big drum, instead it seemed.

'You Fat C***!'

We continually sang this whenever he played the perpetual vocal backing rhythm, to Johnny Cash's Burning Ring Of Fire tune I think it was, if it was I am sure his ring does have that sort of anal curvature and temperature with all the curry that he must eat based on his cuddly magnitude!

'Oh fatty wowo, oh fatty wowo, you've got to lose some weight, you look a F****** state!'

We sang the next to show our expert fashion and Dietary sense, yeah right!

'Oh fatty wowo, oh fatty wowo, you've got a massive gut and look like Jaba the Hut!'

We sang both of the above to our 'Oh Wisey!' tune, the latter comparing his large demeanour to Star Wars huge fat creature.

Taking out his Big Bass Drum –

Moving specifically away from Mr Jobber In a variation of 'Bellies gonna get ya!' which also got a sporadic airing to the drummer man, we sang 'Fatty's gonna get ya!' This was after he had departed and was aimed at a bloke and a young boy who took the big bass drum and beaters away down the stairs towards the pitch after the game

'We love you fatty we do, we love you fatty we do, we love you fatty we do, oh fatty we love you!'

We sang this as at the end of our victory he danced around the drum as we sang abusive chants at him, he then walked down the stairs applauding us, and to be honest after his display we did admire his temerity.

He was in fact very complimentary of our support and chants and Millwall fans in general in an interview that Southwark News did in late September 2008, he was a top man in truth

He responded well to our attention, in fact applauding us as he left at the end and said in the interview that our recognition brought a tear to his eyes. He realises what real support is, as I said it was a proper Millwall day fan support and team wise, good luck to him.

To the general home fans we sang -

'Oh Wisey wowo, Oh Wisey wowo, he's only 5ft 4, and he broke your f***ing jaw!'

I am sure that you know it was a revised revival of the old Millwall chant about Wisey's Leicester's Callum Davidson incident that got us banned at the time from the Walker Stadium.

To highlight our perception of Leicester's massive Asian population, we sang -

'Shoe, Shoe, Shoe Bomber!'

This was re the Asian shoe bomber who was arrested on an Airplane a few years back.

'Town full of Muslims, you're just a town full of Muslims!'

This was specifically aimed at Leicester's home fans in the city's very large Asian population

'Off to pray, off too pray, off to pray!'

This was a chant regarding a Muslim's regular daily prayer hours, as the home fans left early and we accused them of sneaking out to pray at the Mosque.

To various home fans on their way out, we sang -

'Yiddo, Yiddo!'

We sang this to one of them who was gesturing to us from behind the goal to the right of us, it was implying that he was Spurs I assume, God knows why

'There's only one Gary Glitter!'

This was sung to the same or a different bloke near him on the right, none of who looked like the paedo nonce to me, so God knows why he was abused with that.

'Who's the C*** in the suit?'

This sartorial question was to a bloke in the Drummers section to our left, sitting down in a suit near the front.

As we never found out why he was so snazzily attired he also got 'Does she take it up the arse?' this was questioning the sexual exploits of the woman he was sitting with, he didn't let us know this either!

Steward –

Finally to a Zak Whitbread hair coloured steward standing in front of us near the front after the game we sang – 'One Boris Johnson, there's only one Boris Johnson!' and 'Boris, Boris give us a song!' and when he wouldn't he got – 'Boris, Boris – you're a C***!' To show our Political sense and to imply that he looked like not like our Zak but London's second loopy Mayor.

Still Leicester City but this time Sven At The New Den – Leicester City Home which we Won 2 – 0 on Tuesday 28th December 2010

The next game following Pompey away saw Sven-Göran Eriksson's first club management trip to New Den a

2 – 0 defeat saw him greeted with –

Shouts about f***ing off back to IKEA/'You Let Our Country Down!' and 'Sit down You Swedish C***!' Whenever he was standing in the technical area.

As we were heading to our 2 – 0 win he got 'You're Getting Sacked in the Morning!' from the back of the CBL.

I said to one of my Millwall mates Clive, who I was sitting next to at the game –

'Are they singing 'You're Getting Sucked in the Morning?' '

He said 'I think they're singing 'You're Getting F***ed In The Morning!''

With Sven's alleged rep with the Ladeez anything was possible I suppose!!!

Foxes Rhapsody 2 Return Game Journey To The Land Of Sven Leicester City Away Lost 4 – 2 Saturday 22nd January 2011

I will be truthful we could not understand much of what they sang but herewith a selection of what we sang, which I definitely understood and their chants that I sort of understood!

Sexual dig at Sven

In this game Mr Eriksson was serenaded with sexual misconception abuse –

'Sven is a Paedophile, Sven is a Paedophile!'

Banging On The Big Bass Drum

Back to our away section next to Lee Jobber, he did not get the full repertoire that he had endured in our first encounter with him in 2008 as I listed previously. Today he arrived at his drum from pitchside at the back of the stand to our left in a bomber jacket shorts and trainers, close to the kick off, he then prepared his drum and disrobed to display his naked tattooed body in its full beauty.

At this game he only got – 'Fat boy fat boy give us a song!' adapted from the previous version of 'Fat C*** fat c*** give us a song!'.

We also sang a not sung last time song of 'Have you ever pulled a bird?'

To further highlight our perception of Leicester's massive Asian population and their perception of London both sets of fans sang.

Us to them -

'Leicester, Leicester Taliban, Leicester Taliban!' we sang 'Ingerlund, Ingerlund, Ingerlund' to highlight our place of birth and homeland perception and 'Pakistan, Pakistan, Pakistan!'

To highlight the local populace background.

Them to us -

'We all hate Cockneys! In response, we sang 'We all hate Pakis!'

Stereotypical non-racial perceptions -

Them to us –

We pay your benefits. We pay your benefits!'/'Have you ever met your dad?' and 'Going home to your tower blocks!'

Us to them –

'We want to go home we want to go home, Leicester is a shit hole we want to go home!'

Them to us –

Delusional chant by them –

'We're just too good for you!'

A few points to note in our defence, we beat them 2 – 0 at the New Den in December 2010, In this game, we missed a Penalty in the first few minutes of game, their 3rd goal came from a totally delusional dodgy referee awarded free kick, and we had a man sent off! Straight after we came back to 3 – 2. I admire your bias but what you said was delusional in the extreme!

They also sang – 'Your song is all bullshit or (You are all Bullshit' you ran from West Ham!'

What? I would not even run for a bus, and it is always sensible to believe the media perception of the battle of Upton Park Carling Cup game, sod the truth best just believe what we want!

Their perception that we were not as numerous or vocally passionate or as persistent as usual –

'Can you hear the Millwall sing, no no, can you hear the Millwall sing I can't hear a f***ing thing!' and ''worst support we've ever seen!' They also sang a chant I had never heard before

'You're so quiet we'll sing a song ourselves!'

As some left early as we were down to ten men and losing 4 – 2 –

'Time to go, time to go, time to go, time to go, time to go – F*** off!

Premier League Champions Foxes Come To Lions Den and Wish They Hadn't on 18th February 2017 in FA Cup 5th Round

We beat the reigning Premier League Champions Leicester City at home with 10 men, against their 11 men inc Jamie Vardy and Referee Craig Pawson, so 10 beat 12!!

Some complimentary chants to a team languishing in the drop zone of the Premier League the season after being champions, welcome to the Den!

'Champions Of England? You're Having A Laugh!' and

'Going Down Down Down, Going Down Down Down, So F*** Off Jamie Vardy You've Had You're F***ing Party, Going Down Down Down, Going Down Down Down!'

Re Premier League victor in 2016/17 and the follow on Champions League -

'Champions League You're Having A Laugh!'

'Are You Going To Seville!' Their next opponents but in the Champions League in week after there defeat at Den.

To finish this chapter with some non-Leicester City chants, another return to the Championship 2017/18 and 2018/19.

Back With the Championship Big Boys Again Nottingham Forest Away Friday 4th August 2017

Ah a Friday night first game of the season due to being buggered about by Nott's Forest a T20 Match at Trent Bridge on Saturday, etc. etc.

The chants from a game we dominated massively missed god knows how many chances, do not score apart from cheating ref disallowing Moros goal they score we lose.

The mouthy Forest youth next to us behind Police and steward lines and netting sang about Forest being champions of Europe which we'd never be probably true but in response we sang –

'Champions Of Europe? You Weren't Even Born!'

As the City Ground crowd was 28.000 plus they sang to us –

'What's It Like To See A Crowd?'

We replied -

'We Took Wembley!' and 'We Are Millwall – Wembley Is Ours!'

Notts Forest Away again Wednesday 3rd October 2018

In the following season we were at Nottingham Forests City Ground were losing 1 – 0 in a game we had dominated as we had in our last visit the first game of 2017/18 where we lost 1 – 0, in this game trailing again the floodlights went out, to recognise this we sang – 'Brian Clough He's Turned Off The Lights!'/'Let's All Have A Whip Round La La La, La La La!'/'Pay Your Bills, Pay Your Bills. Pay Your Bills!'/'We Want Our Money Back!' and 'Call It Off Call It Off'

The lights came back on after ten to fifteen minutes and Forest then scored again! Thankfully Wall staged a brilliant late comeback and we drew 2 – 2 also having one disallowed in the process!

Bristol City at Ashton Gate Saturday 19th August 2017

To Bristol fans who seemed more Happy Clappy than ever before with drum and flags they got the adapted – 'Stick Your Flags up Your Arsehole!'

The Londoners regional estimate – 'If It Wasn't for the River You'd Be Welsh' and 'You Sleep with Your Sisters Sheep!'

Tom Elliott apart from 'We Want Elliott! At Ashton Gate he also got 'He's Big he's black he'll rape your centre back Elliott Elliott!'

Reading about Reading at The New Den Tuesday 26th September 2017

This display by Reading the team not a book! Was the most depressing performance we had seen for a long while, they played in Orange Shirts, Black Shorts and Orange socks so got –

'You're Just a Team full of stewards!'

To be honest I think their manager Dutchman Jaap Stam must have thought that they were Holland in their total football era. In this instance they seemed to be possessed by Ray Sideways Wilkins, as it was possession with no forward momentum all night, to highlight this with sang to Mr Stam –

'Jaap Stam You're a boring C***! Jaap Stam You're a Boring C***!'

Warnock's Welsh Wales at the New Cardiff City Library Stadium Saturday 28th October 2017

For those too young to have been there Ninian Park was like the Old Den, hostile and passionate, the new Cardiff City Stadium is like somewhere possessed by Watford/Ipswich or Palarse Ultras!

28th October 2017 our chant selection –

Re Wales going out of World Cup Qualifiers whilst England didn't 'There'll Be No Sheepshaggers In Moscow!'/'Clap Your Hands If You're Going To Russia!'/'Will We See You In Moscow?'/'Are Your Scotland In Disguise?'/'There'll Be No Welsh Flag In Moscow! – To a Welsh Flag waver and 'No Gareth Bale In Moscow!'

Normal ethnic stuff now – 'Same Old Welsh Shagging A Sheep!'/'You Shag Sheep My Lord You Shag Sheep!'/'What's It Like To Shag A Sheep?'/'Same Old Welsh C***S Shagging A Sheep!'

Mr Warnock abuse – 'Warnock Is A Paedo!'

To mouthy Liam Gallagher impersonator home fan in a red coat to our right – 'Red Coat, Red Coat You're A C***!'

And as there were two white plastic inflatable sheep bouncing around in the away section, one of which went sideways near home fans and seemed lost, we sang 'We Want Our Sheep Back!' a very nice steward went and got it and returned it to us, he was greeted with 'EIO, EIO, EIO!

An Interesting Trip To Stoke City's Britannia Stadium Saturday 22nd December 2018 Plenty Of Material For Abuse

I arrived on Coach earlier than some of my mates who had driven up, I walked in to block on ticket unquestioned by stewards there but in customary Millwall stylee I walked to somewhere better located than my seat up near the corner flag so went right behind goal, I sat down when some old jobsworth steward came and said can I see your ticket sir, I said what for no one asked for it when I walked in, and you are wasting your fucking time mate, because unless you personally put people in correct seat no one gives a monkeys, so good luck with 1400 plus Millwall here today, he said we have had more than that here, I said that is as maybe but fuck your luck controlling Millwall's sit where you want mentality, as it was early I walked to where I was technically supposed to be, it was a shit seat so I walked back near centre but away from jobsworth's entrance, when my friends Dave, Paul, Nathan, Kay and Charlie turned up we sat right on jobsworths domain and he kept trying to give it the big one with loads of Millwall arriving just before KO, strangely failing miserably and being slagged off big time, I was going to go and personally tell the twat, told you mate! But could not be arsed.

Something that struck me was the body search outside pre turnstile when they touch you down, but in my coat apart from keys and wallet etc, I had mobile and two bloody great phone Charger Batteries, I said what they were but the Steward never asked to see them, not that I would have been pleased if he did but what is the point of a search that proves nothing? Also Stoke fans whose home ground used to be passionate and vocal, was now like a happy clappy ground soulless, the Premier League occupation must have killed the real Stoke City mentality, it has happened to many clubs that have been there see what I mention above with Cardiff City's new ground and Soulless Soul Crew crowd nowadays, Stoke fans had a drum, I rest my case!!!!

One thing that the Stoke fans did have to the left of us was they unfurled a flag that was of a burning image and had the words The Tropics on it, highlighting a Stoke Petrol Bombing of this venue near South Bermondsey later to become The Golden Lion.

The players abuse now to the chants

Ex England number one goalkeeper Jack Butland got 'You Let Your Country Down!' and the original 'England England's Number 6, England's Number 6!' implying how far down the England's chosen keeper list!

The real abuse starts here with Irish Republican James McClean facing us, with his pro IRA, anti-British Army anti-poppy wearing mentality, when he refused to wear any shirt that contained the Remembrance Poppy on, something that happened to start in 2012, this was greeted with the following –

'James McClean You're A W***er!'/'F*** James McClean!'/'F*** The IRA,F*** The IRA!'/'Terrorist Terrorist Terrorist!'/'McClean You're A Terrorist!'/'You Support The IRA'/'James McClean Sex Offender!' and 'McClean You're A F***ing C***!'

This was accompanied also by God Save The Queen and 'Ingerlund Ingerlund Ingerlund!'

CHAPTER 5
The Absolute Proof That No One Likes Us Chapter – The Referee And Assistants Section

Moving on to referees specific they must test all reffing officials that come to Millwall games to make sure they have the anti Millwall gene in place themselves! – enjoy this undoubtedly very non PC Officials chapter, Non PC or not I am not editing the truth sorry! By the way I did not continue this up to 2018/2019 season as would have filled whole book on its own.

Mr Inconsistency Aka You Don't Know What You're Doing!

To start here is some evidence from season 2011/12 of why refs and linos are so despised at the New Den in particular, please see who wins prize Lord Inconsistency at the end -

Leeds United at the New Den March 20th 2012 game and Sheffield Wednesday also at the New Den on 28th January 2014 and Brentford away 14th October 2017 were ruined by Lee Probert an alleged Premier League Ref, f*** knows how, love to know who

321

picks these totally incompetent dodgy anti-Millwall c****!!! It is a conspiracy I tell Ya.

If it is meant by Refs to prove a Millwall crowd won't intimidate them because they are very important, then it works because of all the points go out the window, we don't get them back due to being f***ed over by their pisspoor decisions.

As all Lions fans know we are proliferated by away biased dodgy cheating useless bent c****! At The New Den or Home Biased bent c***s away.

Without going into it too deeply there were 4 x 100% penalties turned down that I can think of without really trying Nott's Forest away 1, Peterborough United away 1, in the Leeds United game the c*** of a ref turned down 2 blatant penalty decisions, after the second one the whippet worriers go up other end and score, he then gives us a penalty. With the top official allegedly blowing up just before Kane scores when Keogh was brought down, Henderson misses the penalty or keeper saves it, same thing!

Sod advantage, surely the goal is advantage for the foul.

To prove my anti-Millwall conspiracy theory, apart from the Penalties we had two Millwall players sent off at New Den caused by that cheating Giraffe beanpole dodgy cheating c*** Visic of Birmingham City. Apparently, he had been doing it regularly all season, strangely, officials had not taken this in to consideration, in this game, his theatrics put us down to nine men, so we get beat 6-0.

Away at Vermin's drum West Ham United's second goal was the most blatant foul on a keeper that you will ever see whether Forde should have caught and not punched it or not, foul was waved away and their goal caused by the Forde foul allowed them to win 2 -1.

At home Reading winning 2 -1 by their being allowed a goal when one of their players was so offside that he was lonely in our half and would not go near ball as he would become active, so instead he lets another player run wide cross it and he runs in and scores, is his scoring not active then? It was bad defending I admit, schoolboy errors, i.e. they did not play to the whistle, or in this case the lino shoving his flag up for offside, but stopped on the assumption that he knew what he was doing, wrong!!!!!

I know that it is not 100% all down to officials as keeper David Forde cost us goals and we did not convert our chances often enough especially at home.

However, in the games that I mentioned whilst we won away at Peterborough United, due to piss poor

incompetent cheating reffing decisions, here are the outcomes of several games –

we lost away at Notts Forest and West Ham United and at home v Leeds United, Birmingham City and Reading, so that is 15 points gone west as we only got 3 points out of a possible 18 points, putting us in position that we were, they must be f***ing delirious at the FA!!

Sorry did not include the game before Leeds United in March 2012 Southampton getting two consecutive Pens in injury time leading to another defeat at home, so in reality 18 points gone west, with our only gaining 3 out of 21 points!!! We would be just outside or inside the Play Off zone pretty much, I wonder why we have been in the relegation zone a lot of the time?

Referees are not exactly popular and are objects of ridicule in my opinion this abuse and unpopularity is due to several factors -

A)   Anti Millwall bias.
B)   Having a chip on their shoulder.
C)   Incompetence (a catchall phrase that covers a multitude of their sins).
D)   Physical imperfection.
E)   All of the above.

My personal opinion is that referee's performances would be improved if physically torturing them was used by us, so in my Millwall conspiracy theory mode I would like to use the following pre match questioning approach – 'Are you on orders to try to stop Millwall winning or getting promoted? When he does not reply –

'He's told us nothing Igor attach the genital electrodes!'

That should sort out our long held Millwall fan conspiracy theory and would improve the official's performances instantly!

Nowadays the Millwall programme usually does not print where the officials come from, which they used to in the old days. At that time you could play a geographical guessing game to try to deduce just how close the officials lived to your opponents and whether they had in fact come to the game on the away teams coach. Today you can no longer ascertain if their performance is down to regional bias or just good old incompetence. In 2004/5 the programme did carry an interview with the refs called 'Oi Ref', in which practically every ref said that they like refereeing at Millwall because the crowd's hostile response helps to focus their mind! What on earth would they be like if we weren't abusing them!!!

To explain what we visualise as their reffing performance, it is if an opposition player commits an offence, wave play on if a Millwall shirted player commits the same offence, a shrill parp will emerge and the Millwall player will invariable get a strict talking to at the least or more likely booked, where as the opposing player was not deemed to have committed an offence at all, isn't paranoia marvellous!

The Millwall We Always Get Shit Refs! Pick Us A Wanker Selection For Worst Wall Referee!

You have quite a few to choose from, enjoy your choosing!

Paul Danson.
Ginger Barnet who was the flame headed Referee against Cardiff City at home in August 2001 was serenaded for his pro Taff decisions with – 'The referee's a Welshman!'

R.D. Fernandiz.

The Referee against Swindon Town at home in November 2001, appeared to have an anti townie bias, so he was serenaded with – 'The referee's a farmer!'

PJ Joslin

Received – 'You're Racist To The English!'

In a similar vein – John Brandwood and Graham Laws the referees against Gillingham at home in 2001/2 and 2004/5 respectively got the gypsy alternative for their pro Gillingham decisions –

The referee's a gypo!' And 'The referee's a pikey!'

Billiericay 'Dodgy' Dicky – Andy D'Urso an ex Premiership Referee (God knows how!) had a biased hometown stinker in our opinion whilst refereeing Gillingham v Millwall at Pikeyville in October 2007, to highlight his Gillingham flavoured bias he was also lauded with the above chants. Additionally when he refereed us at the New Den on 15th March 2008, if that was what he did! When we played Leyton Orient he switched his bias 100% to the away team, i.e for the East London side, he highlighted this by sending off Mark Laird with a straight Red Card and he also turned down 3 blatantly obvious Penalties for us and therefore he was serenaded manfully by us with the adapted Lino chant ' D'Urso, D'Urso You're a C***!' He was serenaded with this again when he referred (sic) our game on 18th August 2009 v Oldham Athletic, it was particularly popular to tell him what we though of his ineptitude when he gave Oldham Athletic a highly dubious Penalty ! Which his Steve Tanner/Kevin 'Not Fit For Sunday League' Friend style blatantly incompetent/biased anti Millwall performances whenever he referees us thoroughly deserved in my opinion. Continuing the 'Blimey it s Andy;" theme we had the pleasure of his reffing talent (sic) again this time at Colchester United on Easter Bank Holiday Monday on 5th April 2010. It was a very important top of the table game, for the record one query that I had – as the Billericay based D'Urso is a member of the Barking & Dagenham Referees Society, how is a ref from Essex, a ref in any of our games v Essex or East London opponents? Pre match in his and his trusty partially sighted Anti Lions Linos warm up we gave him a hearty greeting as mentioned, as they trotted past us we sang –' D'Urso, D'Urso You're a C***' D'Urso, D'Urso You're a C***!'

He had a blinder again he only turned down 3 blatant penalties in front of us in the first half among umpteen other things he f***ed up! To focus on the level of his incompetent, blatantly biased performance we sang a more specific chant– 'D'Urso, D'Urso You're a cheating C***!'

This may sound paranoid but I reckon that he is a Wet Spam Untied fan, he must be that would certainly explain and aid his incompetent bias, I say this because apart from his Billericay base, near where we were parked in the Car Park around the ground, there was a car with a West Ham United Badge Car sticker in the backwindow, I reckon it must have been his, or does that sound a bit bonkers?

I don't care to be honest he is a cheating useless, one way, anti Millwall c*** whether he is Wet Spam Or not!!!!

Paul Simms who was next to me at the game said that I broke the World Record for calling one person a C*** in a football match, hoorah, shame that The Guinness Book Of World Records Peeps weren't there, that must be a record that they would include, er perhaps not!!

I said to Paul 'Glad that I broke the record but really glad that they didn't have swear boxes at Colchester United, or I would have had to apply for bankruptcy!'

When they made Kevin Lisbie, ex Anorak and their goalscorer the Man Of The Match pre his coming to us, I said 'If it is only Colchester United players they include in these type of things, why not give it to D'Urso, he has been their most influential article and effective player!'

Concluding the joy of a D'Urso game section, when we played at St Mary's Southampton on 20th August 2011, he was our Reffing nightmare, and true to form he managed to miss the most blatant penalty in all christendom from close range just before half time when we were trailing 1 – 0, the final score of the match, to highlight his perceived anti Millwall bias we sang the original – 'What Chance have we got with this C*** in charge!'

How true that is even today!!!

Kevin Friend

The aforementioned Millwall hating Reffing disaster at the Lee Hughes debacle at the New Den, was installed again as the horror show at Portman Road, to highlight the terror it was humorously on the day before Halloween in 2010, in the game he admirably managed to confirm his anti Millwall bias, incompetence and downright cheating by turning down two blatant penalties in the 1st half for us, whilst instantly awarding a highly dubious Penalty to Ipswich Town in the 2nd Half. To highlight our pleasure with his display, we sang the general Reffing 'We always get s*** refs!'/'The Referees a w***er!' and more specifically 'Kevin Friend is a C***, is a C***!'

We had this reffing expert again in FA Cup v Bolton Wanderers at home in February 2012, as he magically is deemed as a top flight, i.e. Premier League quality ref, what! How! In whose bloody referee assessors opinion?

We had him yet again in a vital clash at QPR when we were in relegation trouble, so a game we just could not lose, the second from last game of the season on Saturday 26th April 2014, if his installation does not confirm that it is an Anti Millwall conspiracy I do not know what does, with my Millwall paranoia I thought that Harry Redknapp and the FA conspired with a plan to pick the most objectionable ref possible to Wall fans, probably leafing through their thick Anti Millwall cohorts library files and picking No Friend of ours Kevin, in this game early on Lee Martin was carried off on a stretcher after an horrendous tackle! By QPR midfielder Tommy

Carroll when he stamped on his leg and cut it, badly enough for him to have to be carried off, naturally the reffing inefficient Friend deemed this not even a foul, let alone a yellow card minimum, he then gives a dubious penalty for a alleged handball by Simeon Jackson, that A was not deliberate and B was not actually possibly in the area, f*** the rules get on with it stylee, he gave a 77th minute Penalty, which they scored from, sadly his job was not done as Scott Malone scored in injury time and we drew, sorry about that Kevin my Friend, I would Unlike this C*** 100% if anyone was fool enough to make him a friend of mine on Facebook!!!

We had Friend again v Middlesborough at The New Den Saturday 4th August 2018 opening season game, when he played on until Middlesborough equalised sod the real time allowance shown, once they scored their equaliser at nearly 100 minutes the whistle went to his lips happy to end a game we led 2 – 0 only to throw away 2 points.

As I mentioned re D'Urso at Colchester, at this match I nearly broke this calling the ref a C*** world record, I think I will blame it on peer pressure this time as I was certainly surrounded by plenty of equally minded Wall at the QPR and Middlesborough games!

Brendon Malone

I like a laugh and got one when Berndon Malone referee at Watford's Vicarage Road on Tuesday 27th September 2011, was near the centre circle and a clearance managed to hit him on the head and he went arse over tip, which prompted – 'EIO, EIO, EIO!' a Millwall goal celebration.

The leaguewide customary –'You don't know what you're doing!'

Moreover the Millwall original – 'He fell on his arse – the refs a wanker!'

Strangely after this compliment he seemed to never give us a decision for the rest of the game, that will teach us!

Dean Whitehead.

Following the D'Urso reffing! performance at home to Oldham Athletic on 18th August 2009, in the next game away at Southend United on 21st August 2009, we had Dean Whitehead who again continued the inevitable incompetent performances of Referees and Linos that we have, to point this out we sang –

'Are You D'Urso in Disguise?'

He did not let us know, but I do not think he was, that aside it was very close!

Uriah Rennie.

Much loved along with Rob Stiles, Gurnham Singh, Steve Tanner and Andy Hall, etc, etc. and many others too numerous to mention. Uriah was a real New Den favourite it was always a treat when he Referees us, he was welcomed away as well. This antipathy has nothing to do with his colour, just his ineptitude. What I would like to know is if Rennie was deemed unfit for the Premiership how could he possibly be good enough for any other professional Football League or Cup competition?

They all have the same rules don't they? As we pay our money as well, we are entitled to a good referee, if such a thing exists. Apparently, Uriah had an Agent to handle his PR image he must be bloody busy! Rennie was a perennial Millwall, and every other Football fan, 'favourite' I mentioned a raft of chants in 'I Was Born Under The Cold Blow Lane' some slightly more recent abuse came at Stoke City away in October 2004 when we sang – 'Rennie, Rennie you're a c…! Rennie you're a c…!'

More humourously at the New Den against Luton Town in February 2006 and against Nottingham Forest in January 2008 when he was the Referee we sang the above and 'You've got a Malteser as a head!'

Continuing the Rennie theme – any error that black referees Trevor Parkes and Joe Ross made was greeted with 'Are you Rennie in disguise?' I would sue for slander or libel! Millwall's modernish penchant for booing, mocking and abusing the officials in their warm-up does not help us gain there affinity and neither did the following the aforementioned Trevor Parkes was the Referee against Bury at home in 2000/1 very foolishly looked up into the CBL upper tier to see what all the 'Encouraging' remarks coming his way were, only to be met by practically the whole of the upper tier rising as one to give him a damn good wanking hand signals display.

Geoff Eltringham gave what I would consider the worse most ill judged penalty decisions against Brighton And Hove Albion, that lost us the game 1 – 0, to thank his reffing wisdom. We in the CBL in front of which the penalty(sic) happened we sang – 'Cheating C***! Cheating C***!'

I know I am ever so slightly Millwall biased but Eltringham displayed the perfect example of Little Man aka Napoleon Complex in proving we could not intimidate him!

Steve Baines was the referee (sic) against Ipswich Town at home on 24th August 2002 was at the time apparently the only ex pro footballer currently a ref. Putting the 'ex pros should be referees' school of thought in to context he was a strong contender for the worst ref ever, a very fiercely contested section when Millwall are involved in any game. For his part he managed to disallow two goals and miss three Millwall penalties of the most blatant nature. He did not have any specific chants aimed at him because we were all too traumatised by his inept display to think of anything original so all we could manage was – 'Cheat!Cheat! Cheat' And 'The referees a wanker!'

It is supposed to make you go blind isn't it? So that would explain a lot.

He did get the customary masturbatory hand signal display though. He had a northerner's tasche although where he came from I do not know, he could quite possibly just have been a Village People fan or perhaps he was in disguise to save him from any retribution. As Ipswich had two 'Bents' in their squad, I wondered why he didn't just swap shirts with one of them at the end and be done with it!

Thereby giving a true reflection of his performance i.e. Bent not in a sexual sense but ineptitude, It is a conspiracy I tell you!

Paul Armstrong.

The white referee against Sheffield Wednesday at home in 2002/3, who booked Millwall's then 15-year-old Black striker Moses Ashikodi after he kicked the ball away got – 'The referee's a racist!' It was more like child abuse than racism I would say.

Paul Taylor.

The referee at home in September 2004 against Watford was awful so got –

'You're a joke, you're a joke, you're a joke!' As well as less complimentary abuse.

Matt Messias/Clive Penton.

Messias was the referee for Brighton's visit to the New Den in December 2004 and he seemingly decided in the second half to give the away side every decision including a late penalty.

Similarly Penton was the referee at Watford on New Years Day 2005 and in this instance he managed to be an especially blatant hometowner, he sent off Danny Dichio and Watford subsequently scored. In recognition in each Refs case we sang – '12 Men! You've Only Got 12 Men!'

Exhibiting a very open display of bias referee Mike Thorpe and his trusty assistant Referee's appeared in bright canary coloured yellow shirts when we played Norwich City at home on 6th December 2003 ostensibly because the away side were wearing their

331

away dark green kits, well that was the excuse but at least we knew where we stood!

More humourously was a Dermot Morgan aka Father Ted lookalike whose name escapes me appeared to be the referee against Port Vale at home in season 2000/1, this was a bit of a worry, as the actor who played him was dead by then!

G Cain, the referee at the Sunderland home game on Saturday 17th January 2004 was the best comedy referee ever, choosing to ignore any foul or misdemeanour by either side, he was the classic example of what I like to call a 'F.... the rules, let's get on with it!' type of referee.

Keith Hill.

Moving away from Millwall chants Hill refereed Millwall v Reading in August 2004 and denied The Royals 3 penalties so the away fans sang – 'Stand up if the ref's a twat!'

When he refereed our home match against Brighton on April Fool's Day 2006 we sang –

'The referee's a pooftah!'

At the infamous Hull City FA Cup 3rd round the Referee (sic) was a completely homer and gave them every decision. For those who do not know the match Ref was Stuart Attwell the referee that gave the extremely extremely bizarre goal in the Watford v Reading earlier in the same season.

Apart from being biased against us all game was completely F***ing useless.

For example ex Lion Denzil who was their goalkeeper, against us there, in the first half was right in front of us and he made a balls up when he picked up a back pass in the area about 15 yards out just after they had scored their first goal. The ref, if that was what he was supposed to be! Gave us a free kick inside the area which was nice of him, but he never counted the distance that the wall was back and allowed them to line up outside the 6 yard box, which was nowhere near as far back as they should have been, we took the kick and blasted it wide.

Continuing this theme Mike Jones was another Referee (sic) that administered sorry F***ed up our clash at Charlton Athletic on 19th December 2009.

It was a great game 4 – 4 to aid this goal glut he gave Charlton Athletic 2 highly debatable Penalties, pretty much straight after each other, sent off Djimi Abdou for the second and was a completely biased incompetent twat, it will come as no surprise that this moron was the same referee that gave the Sunderland Beach Ball goal v the Scousers,

I think that the FA draw these idiots out of a hat to Ref us up, see Watford/Reading mystery goal ref Stuart Attwell above that we had at Hull City in the FA Cup, it is all an anti Millwall conspiracy I tell you!

Jonathan Moss

To all Millwall fans who were not there it may surprise you but the Referee at Scunthorpe United on Easter Monday 2011 was a complete C***, geographically he came from South Yorkshire just up the road from Sunny Scunny! And his name in programme was Jon Moss.

Mmmm, the only Jon Moss that I know was the gay drummer in Culture Club, the lover of Boy George, I think the drummer version knew more about football than this dodgy as f*** C***, but we won so f*** him! He was serenaded with the descriptive – 'Cheating C***, Cheating C***!'

He was the Referee again! Who had come in as a replacement for the one named in the programme in our home match v Birmingham City, my God, again as at Sunny Scunny we would have been far better to have had Culture Club's Drummer in charge again to be honest. In this game this genius sent off Shane Lowry and then Allan Dunne, in a game that saw us lose 6 – 0 with 9 men and about half the defence in the dugout/dressing room at the New Den on 14th January 2012, It was a fabulous display of really remarkably dodgy reffing, generally we sang – 'We Always Get Shit Refs!'/'You Don't Know What You Are Doing!' and 'The Referee's A W***er!'

More specifically in Brummies game he got -

'Referee, Referee you're a C***!' and 'Are You D'Urso in disguise?

Wish he had been in charge that shows you the level of unbiased quality on display; we usually win if D'Urso is in charge.

In this game the Linesman as we call him as opposed to the Referees Assistant stupid title that they have, disallowed a Millwall goal at 3 – 0 his name escapes me, he got – 'There's Only One Lino'

What I think the Football authorities do is employ some YTA Yoofs and get them to watch umpteen hours of footage of live football to be able to pick out the most incompetent biased officials to stop Millwall, sorry does that sound paranoid? I know it does, but it is a bloody coincidence that we just randomly get such high level reffing incompetence for decades isn't it!

Special mention must go to the 'referee' of the Sheffield Wednesday relegation struggle at the New Den on February 4th 2006, a day that will live in Millwall refereeing infamy. Ladies and Gentlemen I give you the aforementioned – Steve Tanner, a man who among other things managed to turn a Millwall goal celebration, players in a huddle, crowd EIOing and 'Let 'Em Come' blaring out, into a Sheffield Wednesday attack and goal, with just a wave of his ambiguous hand, a finger pointing to the centre circle for a Millwall goal suddenly morphing into a secret free kick for Wednesday. Innovative thinking if nothing else.

No original chants for the grate man i'm afraid as we were all in a ref induced state of shock, I just had to mention it. We had the very dubious pleasure of this incompetent useless C*** at Leyton Orient on 26th September 2009 and to highlight what we though of him we serenaded him with – 'Tanner, Tanner you're a C***!'

By the way he wasn't one of those, they are very useful!! He was just a f***ing nightmare as per usual!

On 16th January 2010 against Southampton in a League 1 game at the New Den, referee (sic) Andy Woolmer, gave Millwall a free kick about 20 or so yards from the Saints goal in the 2nd half in front of our stand, he positioned the ball for the free kick then did the usual counting out the distance of the wall walking routine, however to add to the fun Southampton seemed to not want to move back any more, so to get the required distance he picked up the ball and moved that back to gain the extra distance between the free kick and the wall!!!

Leaving Southampton thinking, to use his first name 'Blimey that is 'Andy!' Innovative thinking and something not even I have seen in 4 decades of watching live and televised Football, brilliant and all that for achieving the required distance between ball and wall, but not exactly the letter of the law is it? Perhaps I am wrong and it will become the norm, eek!!!

Back to Andy Woolmer when we played Oldham Athletic on 30th April 2016 in our last home game pre Play Offs in 2015/16 we had Mr. Woolmer again, and this time I thought he must have been a Millwall Fan ringer as he gave us most of the decisions, NOT Oldham, I kept asking my mates there with me if Millwall were really the ones in dark blue as something seems to be going wrong here we have got a ref who is refereeing the game not exhibiting the Football League remit of being anti-Millwall, but it was real!!

In reference to the above he did a similar thing though, he looked at where the Oldham wall was standing in front of their goal and then sprayed a line in front of them, now I am not an official but isn't the rule, measure the distance for free kick wall first then ask facing team to move back there, then spray line? Not let them stand anywhere find them and spray line there? Not that it mattered. I can honestly say in truth he is the first Referee that I have not included the word C*** about match reports to non-attending Millwall mates, Millwall mates thought my texting Tourette's was cured.

As you probably think I am, I freely admit that I am very Millwall biased but in recent seasons we Lions have had to endure the like of Rob Styles, Andy D'Urso and Uriah Rennie! Not to name umpteen other reffing tossers, so I rest my case; biased wankers or absolute shit, are not strong enough phrases to describe incompetent wankers like these 3 and the numerous others that we have had to put up with.

To highlight what we have to endure, another example of the high level of tosspots that we have to endure, for our FA Cup 3rd round tie in January 2009 at Premier League Hull City's KC Stadium we had Stuart Atwell, the official that gave the extremely extremely bizarre supposed goal in the Watford v Reading game, shown nationwide on TV etc. at the time earlier in the same season, his refereeing in our game very successfully highlighted his wide range of total f***ing incompetence perfectly!

As did Mike Jones the Sunderland v Liverpool Beach ball referee (sic) that we had at Charlton Athletic in December 2009, it is all a conspiracy against Millwall I tell you, terribly sorry my innate paranoia as arisen again! To try to prove my, it is an anti-Millwall Reffing conspiracy theory, another couple to add to the 'Respect them? For what!!!!' list.

Nigel Miller
Was the ref who gave us a real masterclass in ineptitude, incompetence, cheating, bias and uselessness at the Den v Portsmouth on Boxing Day 2011, we won though so he f***ed that up!

Other than 'Cheat' and 'We Always Get Shit Refs' there were no chants specific to him unusual for us but I think that it was because we had all lapsed in to a disbelief inspired coma.

I tried hard though as I broke the The Guinness World Record that I mentioned under D'Urso for calling the Ref a C*** the most times in 90 minutes, he was that bad that I did it with ease!

Trevor Kettle

The Referee if that is the word for what the useless c*** is, at home v Barnsley on 22nd December 2012 he gave Adam Smith a straight red for a tackle that was not even a foul, let alone a yellow and certainly not a straight red. His decision made me boil with steam coming out of my ears even more so when I saw his name!

I would like to finish the Effing Reffing section with a drumroll and introduce The Lord Of Inconsistency, with the special award for worst Referee I have ever seen in charge of a Millwall game and that is NOT a short list of suspects – I give you Robert Madley, who we had the pleasure of at Watford on 1st November 2014 and Darren Deadman see a bit later.

They were in my opinion without doubt 2 refs whose comparative inefficiency made Uriah Rennie or Andy D'Urso or Steve Tanner or Kevin Friend or Mike Jones or Stuart Atwell, just some of a long list of reffing incompetents we have had the pleasure of at Wall games as you will have gathered in reading this section of the chapter, Madley's performance also Deadman's made any of the other listed suspects look like Colina!

Madley got the customary – 'We Always Get Shit Refs!'/'You Don't Know What You're Doing!'/'Cheating C***! Cheating C***!' and 'Cheat Cheat Cheat!'

We lost 3 – 1 thanks to his missing fouls on Millwall players, ignoring a blatant penalty on Ricardo Fuller and giving Watford a free kick slap bang in the D of the area, which even the Watford forward Troy Deeney who ran straight in to Alan Dunne said was not a foul at all, and naturally they scored from it to take a 2 – 1 lead.

He carried on his performance in the second half when there was a foul on a Millwall player in midfield which he totally ignored, waved play on and then Watford scored their third in the latter stage of this run of play.

He managed to book Millwall players for fouls or complaining about his incompetent decisions, only to ignore any similar incidence by a Watford player. I do not like Millwall losing but if we do lose if it is a fair, even sided official to a better performing side then I can accept it however when you are cheated for 90 minutes by a 100% useless c*** then I need psychiatric care.

To highlight that we gathered Wall all thought the same we sang '3 – 1 to the referee!' and when the PA announcer announced the nominated Watford Man Of The Match, we sang 'Ref, Ref, Ref, Ref!'

I have nominated my worst Wall ref ever, cue drum roll it is the above mentioned – Robert Madley, and well anyone the EFL sends us to be honest!

To appease Madley the competition for top tosser became a situation for hot debate only 4 days later on the Tuesday 4th November 2004 in the game at home v Blackburn Rovers.

Apart from Kevin No F...ing Friend of Millwall's poxy performance in first home game of 2018/2019 v Middlesboro and his extra time adding of I will play till they equalise the 2 Millwall goals, which Boro obviously did, another top contender for most incompetent one eyed away team biased referee was John Brooks he was referee v QPR at home on 6th April 2019, well I know my Millwall paranoia is rife but he gave us nothing, whilst they dived about like Tom Daley at the Olympics, full I am premier League style, he gave their I am mortally wounded dives as fouls. yet he miraculously missed a blatant last defender attack on Lee Gregory on the way to a one on one v QPR keeper, just outside the box he waved play on as thought nothing had happened, he professed all of the balanced view of a nine bob note, he got 'We Always Get Shit Refs!'Yo don't know what you are doing!/'You're not fit referee!'/'Cheating C...!' Cheating C...!'

For reference we had had the pleasure of his undoubted reffing skills before –

I give you Darren Deadman, Aka Deadman Cheating! A useless bent cheating incompetent hometown Wanker who we had the highly dubious pleasure of at Sheffield United on 12th February 2011 must be added to the reffing Millwall hating list as he managed to give United a penalty that was unique, in that it had not accounted for in any rules in the game – ever. I think that his real name is hyphened with his first surname Brain missing, is name is Darren Brain – Deadman!

Moving on to his performance three year or so after the Sheffield United game, in the game following Madley's performance at Watford, the inimitable Darren Deadman showed how versatile he was he can not only be a Homer but an Awayer as well, there's talented for you! He did not give a foul as such for Danny Shittu being booted in the face, apparently trying to kick someone's head off is okay and does not warrant a yellow card.

He like the Watford maestro ignored a blatant penalty again on Ricardo Fuller, as I said at Watford,

it is either a Penalty or a yellow card for diving, to do neither is just piss poor refereeing.

Far be it from me to imply that there is a Millwall specific Referee's Rule Book that it is against the laws of the game to give Millwall a penalty, seemingly there is also a proviso that certainly players must not be awarded a penalty,, I give you Ricardo Fuller! Either there is an FA edict or the refs are biased, your choice!

Back to Deadman he ignored any foul on a Millwall player, but seemed to really appreciate the Blackburn Rovers dying swan efforts, i.e. roll as many times, as you can, make the noise of a Cow Calving in order to make sure that you attract the Refs attention.

This Rovers tactic worked a treat, to highlight his bias he then sent off Millwall full back Andrew Wilkinson for a straight red, which even Rovers manager said was not a straight red, he however waved play on when a Rovers player did exactly the same thing, after this Rovers extended their 1 – 0 lead to a 2 – 0. He also sent Ian Holloway and Marc Bircham off for their complaining about his ineptness.

This brilliant plan to make Millwall lose in consecutive games, blew up in his face, as it raised the crowd to Old Den like levels and it inspired the team, to get 2 goals back to draw a game with only ten men! Deadman had received the customary deluge –

'You Don't Know What You're Doing!'/'We Always Get Shit Refs!' and '2 nil to the Referee!'

In the game v Rovers, he received the particular to him –'The Referee Is A Cheating C***!'

Moving On With General Reffing Incompetence Chants –

Some general referee chants, to start the old time Old Den one of –

'How's your Father? How's your Father? How's your Father referee? You ain't got one, you're a

b......, you're a b...... referee!' and in April 2010 v Brentford ' We Only Get Shit Refs!'

Nowadays as common as 'No One Likes Us' At Millwall games be they home or away.

There has been a chant sung to several anti Millwall officials, if they have tried their hardest to stop us and we are still winning!, bad luck! To highlight this we have sung to the official –

'1 nil (or whatever the score is) and you're still a c***!'

Nowadays our preferred general chant which I have listed before is – 'The Referee's A Wanker!' Or 'Who's The Wanker In The Black?' Green, purple, yellow or whatever other colour that the Referee have tried wearing over the seasons to stop the chants rhyming.

They have got to have a hobby I suppose and a version of self palm manipulation is there's!

The Not Even Good Enough To Be The Referee So On The Assistant Ref Front Some Incidents And Observations –

At Wycombe Wanderers Game on 20th February 2010, forget about what Andy Gray and Richard Keys said about her on Sky Sports in 2011, to the same female Assistant Referee then named Sian Massey in this game a year before she was greeted, if that is the right phrase, by us with – 'Get Your Tit's Out For The Lads'/'We Can Smell Your C*** From Here!! and 'Lino, Lino You're A Slag!'

With her name now Sian Massey – Ellis, presumably her married name she Assisted again at Scunthorpe United on 17th December 2017 and got the smell chant above, but also a biological correct one as well –

'Lino Lino's Got A C***! Lion's Got A C***!'

For us to know this was impressive, as she ran the line at the opposite end of the ground from the away end!

The assistant referee aka lino against Portsmouth on 'sex offender' night in December 2001 made Millwall keeper Tony Warner move his blue towel which was hanging on the side netting, presumably because he may mistake it for a Millwall shirt, it is this quality of eyesight that fills you with optimism about his likely performance doesn't it?

With regard to the pie lobbing It's nice to see that the New Den's Upper East Stand aka The Dockers Stand in the modern era had carried on a proud Old Den tradition of pelting the linesman with food, etc naturally nowadays the 'Assistant Referees' have a vast selection of food available to be thrown at them due to advances in catering. There was a Linesman (sic) against Reading in 2000/1 who wore a baseball cap whilst running the line on a sunny New Den day, was it to shield his eyes from the sun or was he psychic and had had visions of an imminent meat pie attack?

To conclude this section some modern general Linesman/Assistant Referees chants, different name same incompetence, they invariably get – 'Who's the wanker with the flag?' And 'The linesman is a wanker, la, la, la, etc.'

Not forgetting the 2004/5 additions –

'Lino, lino you're a c...!' And 'There's only one David Blunkett!'

At home to Ipswich Town on 18th January 2014, the linesman whose name escapes me because I was in a state of shock, who was in front of the Dockers Stand, reversed the Referees decision of giving a corner to Ipswich Tiown in front of the North Stand to one of giving us a goal kick, so to highlight our admiration for such an usual decision we sang – 'We Love You Lino We Do, We Love You Lino We Do, We Love You Lino We Do, Oh Lino We Love You!'

Specifically Assistant Referee I. J. Woodward at the Ipswich game on Boxing Day 2004 threw a wobbler pre Half time. Allegedly he was injured, however my opinion was his ears were on fire as he was being treated to the above type of chants and was a broken man! His replacement G.L.Ward came on and was greeted sarcastically with 'pro' chants of 'Lino, Lino!' When he waved his flag in our favour. To make sure that he didn't think we would be so positive for the whole of the second half we in the CBL sang – 'C... in a minute, you'll be a c... in a minute!'

Whilst I freely admit that I am not exactly sylph like but at our FA Cup 3rd game at home v Derby County on 2nd January 2010, we had a massively portly, seemingly bloated and very biased, partially sighted Assistant Lino Stephen Artis, one of his appalling decisions was greeted with –

'You Fat C***! You Fat C***!'

I would like to end this section with a question – What I would like to know is why linos very often look at Referees to give decisions when they are infinitely closer to the incident? One of nature's great mysteries.

The Anti-Millwall Referee's Grading System –

As you may have gathered from my references in this chapter there appears to be quite a few awful anti-Millwall officials, consequently after the Blackburn Rovers game mentioned above, I devised the Referees Assessment Glossary below.

I thought we should instigate a referee assessment panel of our own, so that we could send it to the referee's assessor, we could have a you show me yours – we will show you our referee's assessment!

I thought from a Millwall fans point of view there could be a most biased anti-Millwall ref table, as a season long project in 2014/5, be a close vote between Madley and Deadman, but having the grading system in place would be more exciting than the Champions League not that I give a toss about that.

Back to Referees, I devised this Referee C***edness Grading System, with 5 levels, 1 being the least biased 5 being the most biased –

1. A Bit Of An Anti-Millwall Biased C***
2. Quite A Bit Of An Anti-Millwall Biased Cheating C***
3. Bent As A Nine Bob Note Anti Millwall C***
4. Top Notch Anti Millwall C***
5. So Biased We All Want To Kill The Anti-Millwall C***

With a proviso saying if you ever send him to referee us again, we will kidnap his entire family and not release them until after we have received our own referee assessment!

The Assessment would also have another Grading System that highlighted how self-important the ref was when refereeing a game, this is again on a level, system 1 least self-obsessed – 5 most self-obsessed.

1. A Bit Of A Big Head
2. As Self Obsessed As F***
3. Ego The Size Of A Small Planet
4. The Game Is All About Me – Me – Me

5. I Am Suffering From Small Man Completely Self Important Overblown Ego Syndrome

These options would be followed by a box that you ticked to select your option.

I had thought that you could include a please put your comments below box, but from a Millwall fan perspective as it would only contain a variation of The Ref and two Linos were all useless, cheating C***s, I decided against this. I did think that it was a good idea to make a deal to get the Official Referee's Assessment and have a monthly competition though.

In this competition, you present them with an unnamed Official Referee's Assessment, with two sections -

1. You had to guess which referee they were talking about,
2. You had to see if you could guess which comedy scriptwriter had written this comic masterpiece, with a note saying for reference, please do not put Danny Baker as this will be wrong!

I also had a thought that you could hand out x amount of ballot papers at home games containing all the option boxes that you could tick, these could then be collected outside the three home stands at the New Den after the match, with the results assessed collectively to get a consensus;

For away matches you could hand out the same ballot papers on Coach 1 that were completed on the way home to London and collected by the Coach Stewards, for another more focussed assessment to get a consensus.

You may think I am biased, well I am. Isn't every club fan?

Nevertheless, to highlight the level of referees that we always get, when asked who the referee is today.

I give them one of the three options –

A) It is a C***

B) It is the posher double barrelled – A Absolute – C***

C) It is the ref who retained his wife's name – A Two Bob C***!

When the enormous hullabaloo erupted over Racing, Cricket and Football match fixing and betting syndicates, etc., the Cricket authorities were thinking of introducing lie detectors into their Umpire equation to weed out the dodgy dealers, an idea that they got from Singapore's Football League, who brought them into their League in 2000. I think that they should at least make them compulsory for Referees in all English Football.

Given the consistent bloody awful Refereeing that I have seen from Referee's against my side Millwall at away or at home, forget Respecting them in my opinion a better option would be that the officials had to endure a pre-match Dressing Room Guantanamo Bay style torture, this to my mind would bring about a vast improvement in their anti-Lions fans 'They won't intimidate me!' attitude that they all seem to arrive with at the New Den, continuing the policy that they always used to have at the Old Den!

Hence the Millwall chant 'No One Likes Us We Don't Care!' the bloody Refs and Assistant Refs do not like us that is for sure!

I'll be honest it would please us massively I reckon if they showed the Official's 'SAW' style torture on the Club's New Den Jumbotron Video Screen that is for sure.

If this was impractical I'd settle for the old bright light in the eyes, Chinese water torture; red-hot needles down the fingernails or the simple beat the truth out of them with a rubber cosh, there would be volunteers queuing around the block for performing any of these routines, this would apply to all clubs fans, but especially with us due to the cheating W***ers that we Millwall have to continually put up with!

Alternatively, they could attach a simple electric shock device to a 'sensitive' area on the ref and set it off each time that it was apparent that he was about to give a highly dubious penalty for the opposition, which he would undoubtedly turn down if it was for Millwall. As I said earlier you probably think that as I am hardcore Millwall, I am obviously insane, well I am a bit, sorry, well I am certainly not sorry, just thought I would say that I was!

Being slightly less violently minded, I would settle for the Referee's having to have pre match lie detector tests to ascertain whether they would truthfully endeavour to be as biased as possible against Millwall and if it was proved, replace them with someone who wasn't, if one actually really exists in the Millwall world.

One thing that galls us all watching Millwall at League 1 or Championship level is –

if a Referee has had a bad performance in a Premier League match and consequently been booted out of the Top Flight they can then demote them to our levels, where they can prove conclusively how crap they really are! Why?

To our minds if they cannot Referee at the top level they should not Referee at any level, be it professionally or in Pub Team match in a park, because correct me if I am wrong, but it is the same rules whatever level it is at isn't it? 'You're Not Fit For Sunday League!' a very apt chant that I think in reality every team outside the Premier League has to put up with post these demotions.

Some very apt chants that we have sung after watching high level incompetence, in our mind cheating biased Refs/Refs assistants, we sang at a home game on 2nd April 2010 v Brentford, when a goal that was slightly offside, well only about ten yards! Amusingly I read a Teletext report on TV when I got home that said that the forward, an ex-Lion player Carl Cort, received the ball to score when he was in a lot of space, well that is true, but it was only because he was bloody yards offside!!!

To highlight this we sang our customary Linesman chant, very apt in this instance as he was one of the worst Referees Assistants or cheating b***tards if you prefer we have ever had and that is saying something given the competition for dodgy Linesman/Assistant Referees that we have to put up with.

This one was consistently awful, and seems to have lost the ability to raise his flag or see sod all, to thank him for his fantastic display we sang – 'Lino, Lino You're a C***!'

To the referee in particular we sang 'We Only Have Shit Refs!'/'We Always Get Shit Refs!' this was a very apt modern day chant for what we in my Millwall paranoia have to always put up with, this always gets them on our side, oops wrong it does the complete opposite!!!

To prove it is not just me the referee's assessor said that it was definitely offside, marvellous!

But the goal will not be deducted from the score or the points that we lost for it being allowed, with us after the goal getting a 1 – 1 draw rather than the win will never come back, so how is it beneficial having assessors who can see what shit they are? Beats me!!!

The above honest assessment aside I assume in general that all the match assessments at whatever level they have performed at professionally are carried out by people from within their fellow Football referees contingent, be they current or retired. Therefore, to my mind they themselves are not liable to be overly dispassionate, in case it reflects badly on their own careers as Referees and what training/courses their Refereeing association has put these apparently qualified Referees through successfully.

I had an idea – in conjunction with the official body's match performance review why not have them also assessed by a small team of random home and away fans for games, whereby they have to fill in a supplied questionnaire of the Referee's performance, if allied to their official assessment and you did it with both sets of fans you are liable to get a much more balanced assessment, I say question both sides fans in case the officials have been home or away team biased.

To show you how consistently useless they are, there are the nonspecific Millwall modern crowd chants –

'You Don't Know What You Are Doing!' And 'You're Not Fit To Referee!'

These highlights their inefficiency perfectly from both teams perspective, because I have very often heard both sets of fans sing these chants in the same game to the Referee, from my experience this is usually the most accurate and pertinent vocal assessment highlighting how their regular level of incompetence should be viewed. So my idea would never be allowed to happen at Millwall anyway, seemingly having their fellow Referees assess them is somehow okay, alternatively does this level of reviewers also reflect their peers incompetence in performing the assessment? Just a consideration!

Why do referees not have their names on their shirts like the players? Perhaps their criminal performances qualify them for anonymity under the witness protection programme. I suppose the ref having their double-barreled name with 'Incompetent Wanker' or 'Cheating Bastard' emblazoned across their shoulders would hinder this as well? Who can tell!

CHAPTER 6
The Holloway Age – The Horror The Horror! Keep Taking The Tablets

This chapter is undoubtedly Non PC, but I am f***ed if I am changing anything an 100% am never apologising to this thieving from Millwall useless c***!

For those of you who did not have the pleasure of witnessing this c***s Millwall Managerial reign especially games like Bradford City away on a midweek in FA Cup a visualisation for you, the zombie film Sean Of The Dead was filmed in Millwall fan pub near the old Den The Albany, if you can envisage we fans being the ones inside the pub watching hordes of zombies trying to get us, that was what watching Wall was like under him, players past their Best Before/Use By Dates, crocks and last season pension topper upper Zombies that he brought in!!!

Holloway Arrives Hoorah!!! – How Wrong My Joy Was, More Aptly My Thoughts Become I Would Rather Be In Holloway Prison!!

After the Southend United horror show there was the appointment of Ian Holloway as manager, up at Huddersfield Town on 11th January 2014, Holloway's first game, he came running up the line towards we gathered Lions fans in the Away end pre match, clapped us and bowed down to us, it was patently obvious to me and my mates there Dave, Paul and Nathan that he understands Millwall fans, give 100% we will back them win, lose or draw, for example as highlighted when we applauded Millwall off the pitch at The New Den after Birmingham City beat the 9 man Lions team 6 – 0 we applauded them roundly at the end of the match, as they had battled manfully, however swan about like Bouaza and N'Guesson did in a couple of games and we will batter you verbally.

Holloway got far better chants than Lomas, with 'Holloway Holloway!' echoing as he did his greeting towards us and 'Ollie, Ollie, Ollie, Oi. Oi Oi!' To highlight what we thought of the teams performance, even though we lost 1 – 0 to a late late Huddersfield goal, we stood and applauded the Lions at the end of the match. A bit different to Watford under Lomas and Southend United when Lions players coming towards us at the end were told to F*** off!

At Ian Holloway's first game at the New Den on 18th January 2014 against Big Mick's Ipswich Town it really felt like we had our Millwall back, the team played with spirit, passion and the crowd roared like the Millwall I have known for 50 plus years, it felt like we had comeback from a horror show, which we had with the incompetent Lomas reign, or should that be rain!

At this game watching the passion of a manager who feels like we do really made us feel like the real Wall had returned, he loves us and we love him.

We sang 'Ollie, Ollie, Ollie. Ollie – Ollie, Ollie!' to Ole Rhapsody.

There was another chant at Burnley on 8th February 2014 – 'Ian F***Ing Holloway!'

I personally honestly cannot really remember a manager being so well liked and respected especially being taken on board by us so quickly, my god proves what a load of bollocks first impressions being lasting impressions is! Holloways madness shoots that analogy straight out of the water.

My god my messiah has arrived ethos seems to have been sadly misguided as we sunk without trace!

After two defeats one at Leeds United on 22nd March 2014 and the following Tuesday 25th March 2014, we played a must win cannot lose game at home v Birmingham City and we lost, we then played another must win game v Blackburn Rovers on Saturday 29th March 2014 we take the lead, via a penalty they get a man sent off for a foul, they then equalise, we take the lead again by another penalty in 88th minute, and they equalise again and we draw 2 – 2.

Holloway got – 'You Don't Know What You're Doing!' re his tactical strangeness, then the honest 'That's Why We're Going Down!' as the second equaliser went in, well on the positive side I would soon be able to collect a few new grounds in League 1!

We turned the corner in late March and April after two draws and three away wins, when at Middlesbrough on 19th April 2014 we sang – 'Ian Holloway, Ian Holloway!'

I had been right Holloway the Millwall Messiah had arrived because with our last 8 games resulted in 8 unbeaten games till the end of the season, 4 wins and 4 draws, and we stayed up I rather liked that– MIIIIIIIIIIIIILLWAAAAAAALL!!!!!

Before 2014/5 season in Holloway's first full season along with Paul, Dave and Nathan Simms I was at the Fans Forum 7th August 2014 at the New Den. At this Forum Hoolyway said something that we all suspected, that the players that Lomas used were overpaid don't want to be here wastrels, Holly said what he had discovered was that these useless cannot be arsed tossers had used Wall fans Appy Ammers hatred as an excuse to not try, they could blame our hatred of Wet Spam Untied and Lomas's link with why they were performing so crap and disinterested not the fact that they couldn't be arsed, this included ex Lion Steve Morison who basically did not want to be at Millwall, apart from the high wages that we were paying them obviously, higher than we had paid Lions players previously, Holly said he was disgusted when he arrived at this attitude and cleared the crap out pre season, I like that as well, in our opinion it should be people who want to play for Wall stay, players at Wall for a last hoorah jolly, cannot be bothered to try can all F*** off!

Holloway = The Man at C&A

I would just like to start with this question about the adored Holloway's sartorial splendour –

Mr Holloway was always very smartly dressed, with a seemingly endless wardrobe of natty attire.

I wondered as his Football staff are all absolutely kin useless tossers, does he have a Fashion Stylist/a Valet/a Dresser/a Butler or a Batman? Alternatively, does his Mum or Wife dress him before he comes in to ruin our day, be it home or away! I think rather than get in a fancy advisor, a Football advisor should have been brought in, you could look like Compo if Wall played like Wall should, but dressing like you were meeting The Queen, didn't wash with us!

Holloway's A Messiah Mmmm Let's Think? Was He B***ocks It Was More Like Holloway A Mad Shower/It's A Holloway Mess Here!

He Was Not The Messiah. He Was A Paid Up, Rich Failure And A Very Naughty Boy To Steal From Python Or The Wall Based Truth An Absolute Useless C***!

In 2015, we started well then plummeted like a Russian submarine or Malaysian Plane your choice; an especially good week we were defeated at bottom club Blackpool on Saturday 10th January 2015 herewith a summary of the days entertainment –

None of my mates fancied it so I went on my own on Coach 1, at 7.30am, a short while in to the journey, someone sitting at the back who was asleep vomited like Regan in The Exorcist, the second driver and Tina cleared it up, tried to wake him up unsuccessfully then still asleep he was sick again! So another clear up required, air freshener etc.

We then went on to Blackpool where it was as windy as a bloody hurricane, which we found out, when as we arrived so did Millwall Team coach, the sharp minded local Old Bill decided that we should not park in the Car Park anywhere near the team.

Consequently, we were driven away escorted by motorbike plod on to a main road, so we then had to walk back to the ground. Brilliant planning as some people on the Coach had mobility problems, not that the Old Bill cared about this!

When we arrived back at the ground, I decided to go in to Blackpool's Club Shop to get out of the bloody wind; I then felt brave enough to head to the away stand, where a Steward with a Sniffer Dog met me. He wandered up and down the few-gathered Wall and he asked if those standing there had any drugs, I said why do you want some? He said no that is what the Sniffer Dog was for.

Only one problem was that the dog's real focus was a large plastic Wheelie bin that people used to piss in or at, and doggy focussed on pretty much only this, thereby I am sure missing and Charlie, which I saw people sniffing in the bog.

With the weather a tad windy, I discovered something that I had missed previously that at the back of Blackpool's away section is not a solid entity but an open grid, I have been there before but as it had not been so bloody windy had not noticed, well that is my excuse anyway!

I had missed the Refreshment stand on the way in and was going in to I am up North and not able to get a meat and potato pie meltdown mode, until I realised that it was actually there and now open so had my obligatory northern delight.

The weather was shit bloody freezing and windy and to add to our entertainment the pitch looked like someone had ploughed it, Millwall were absolute cack it was what I would call a wage thief central performance so to the chants – Blackpool fans collectively chanted their own Chairman abuse –

'We Want Oyston Out, Say We Want Oyston Out!' I said to a bloke behind me that I would like to get Kelly Brooks tits out but it is not going to happen unfortunately!

In the second half Ricardo Fuller missed what looked like an easy chance to us, he got some stick, so stuck his two fingers up to us, which just escalated the abuse to the customary – 'Fuller, Fuller You're A C***, Fuller You're A C***!'

He got this as well as he was substituted and seemed to go in to Caribbean abuse mode, it is always a good idea to irritate people who had travel hundreds of miles from early in the morning, whilst you are paid, and we had to pay!

Blackpool fans received 'You Can Stick Your F***ing Tower Up Your Arse!' and 'Your Pitch Is F***ing Shit!'

Along the same line as Oyston Out, we sang 'We Want Ollie Out, Say We Want Ollie Out!' in a game that we lost 1 – 0 to a team below us in the Championship.

On the walk back to the coach we were greeted with a refreshing heavy fall of hailstones lovely, we then boarded and drove off, as we stopped in a very small Services in the Midlands unfortunately it had three coaches of QPR on their way back from Burnley in it.

Not that they are any threat it was just that this was only a short stop, 15 minutes, and the Q in WH Smith was over a hundred, so we all predominantly left empty handed.

When I got back to the Den I waited for a bus, then a cab came along so I got that, naturally.

As I sat down the Cab Driver asked if I had been out for a beer, I said I wish I had I have just come back from Blackpool watching Millwall lose. He said I better not tell you who I support then, I said West Ham mate, he said yes, I then tried to go in the local Tesco's only to find it was after 11pm so shut, all this ended the day perfectly!

We then move on to the real Hammer House Of Horrors that was the FA Cup 3rd Round Replay at Bradford City on Wednesday 14th January 2015, four of us travelled up, myself, Dave, Paul and Nathan Simms on Coach 1 again this time a double Decker that left at 12.30pm.

We arrived at Bradford having passed snowbound fields in the Midlands on the motorway, after a couple of beers the second of which had a proper Northern six inch head on, poured out of a bottle by a Northern moron, moving on!

The pitch was again rough, with pitchside snow piles that had been taken off the pitch, with pitch coverings also piled up with the snow on our side of the pitch.

My Wall friends I give you what I would vote the worst Millwall performance that I have ever seen, including Watford and Southend United away in the previous season.

Please feel free to vote for your own away disaster but this is mine –

Beevers got sent off in the first six minutes so we were down to ten men, but that aside the Lions soulless, gutless, spineless and useless performance that led to a 4 – 0 defeat, which if you look on the bright side, stopped us getting annihilated at Chelski in the 4th Round !

The night was only memorable for the diversity of the gathered Millwall fans abuse –

'Ollie, Ollie, Ollie – Out, Out, Out!'/'There's Only One Kenny Jackett!'/'We Want Ollie Out Say We Want Ollie Out!'/'Bye, Bye Ollie, etc F*** Off Ollie F*** Off!'/'You're Getting Sacked In The Morning, Sacked In The Morning!'/'Ollie, Ollie You're A C***!'/'There's Only One Steve Lomas!'/'We're Going Down, We're Going Down!'/'Stevie Lomas He's Better Than You!'/'We Want Our Lomas Back!'/'We Blame The Pitch, Say We Blame The Pitch!' and 'We want Our Millwall Back!'

As our first shot on target was on 86 minutes at 4-0 we sang – 'Can We Have A Shot On Goal!' and 'You're Not Fit To Wear The Shirt!'

Then when we did have the late shot, we sang –

'Let's Pretend We Scored A Goal'/'EIO 'and 'Let's Go F***Ing Mental!'

I know that it was not a League game but they were from a division below us, so we sang – 'Championship You're Having A Laugh!'/'We're Coming Back Next Year, We're Coming Back Next Year, Were Coming Back Were Coming Back Next Year!'/'We're Going Down, We're Going Down, We're Going – We Are Going Down!'/'You're Nothing Special We Lose Every Week!'/'It's Only Four Nil How Shit Must You Be!'/'We're All Going On A League One Tour!'/'We're F***Ing Shit, We're F***Ing Shit!'/'We're Shit And We're Sick Of It!' and at 4 – 0 we sang '5 – 0 And We're On The Pitch!' We also sang – 'We Want Our Money Back!' and 'We Paid For This You're Having A Laugh!' We did get our tickets refunded so it was almost like the 4 – 0 rout had not happened, unfortunately it had!

Thanks JB For The Blessed Relief!

On Tuesday 10th March 2015, it was announced that Ian Holloway, had been sacked HOORAH!!!!

Following the traditional sign of death this came a short while after he had received the accursed full Backing of The Chairman.

I can honestly say that he was without doubt the worst Millwall manager that I have ever had the highly dubious privilige of watching in the flesh at my umpteen hundred home and away games,

Please bear in mind that I have been going Millwall since 1966, and therefore had the privilege of enduring the careers of –

Peter Anderson, George Must Go Petition Petchey, Jimmy Nicholl, Kevin Spackman, Willie Donachie, Steve Lomas and David Tuttle.

I would just like to say bye bye Mr Holloway You Tactically Inept, Talk The Talk But Can't Walk The Walk, Sheep Shagging, Tractor Driving, Cider Guzzling, Wage Thieving, Yokel Bumpkin C***!

I had a thought about what we could do with the useless bastard to get recompense, I thought we should try to get him banged up, banged up NOT banged, in his namesake Holloway Prison.

I thought he should be done under the Trade Descriptions Act, because he referred to himself as a Professional Football Manager, he proved that very wrong, as he had about as much tactical Football nous as a 3 year old has about F1 racing with a large Scalectrix kit.

Or what about the Jobs Description Act, because his CV, was fraudulently filled out that he had experience as a Professional Football Manager, when it really should have said was he had bags of experience as a Coco The Clown Tribute Act, with the side option of Worzel Gummige, aided by his sidekick Marc Bircham as Aunt Sally, because he acted like a c*** so was perfect for the female role, he also had the alternative option of Kellie Maloney if Birch was unavailable of course.

Okay if the above did not work what about imprisoning him under the Mental Health Act, I can honestly say that most of us mistook passion for lunacy, I am not medically trained but would suggest that people who are as far away from their marbles as Holloway was, should not be allowed out unguarded in to the real world.

I am sure that we could get an enormous amount of medical confirmation if we all went to a Mental Health clinic assessment that he had scrambled our brains to such an extent that we all thought that we were Napoleon as well! I would just like to point out that my birthday is the same date as Napoleon, but I have never had any problems at Waterloo myself, apart from trains not bloody running different gravy that!

As I am sure it is against Health and Safety too punish someone so Mentally Ill, so I would just like to say – May You F***Ing Rot In Hell, or Hull Your Choice – Holloway You Incompetent Self Deluded Bertie Big B****cks Bigging Yourself Up Absolute C***!!!

For info I heard that Bumpkin Snake Oil Salesman Holloway refused to walk until he was paid off the full amount which I heard was £1.3 million, kin hell this sort of agreement makes even a print union agreement at their peak look reasonable! Not that I don't think that they must do due diligence but who the f***ing hell is this abject crook a Football Expert on Sky Sports, and in 2018 on Quest, talk about money for abject failure, i.e. failure from a disaster of his own making! If this C*** is a Football Pundit aka Expert I would like to say that on that basis I must be the Archbishop of Canturbury!!!!

Bomber Command!

Neil Bomber Harris temporarily replaced the Holloway disaster zone and we seemed to have a team that looked like Millwall back, not the shambolic shower of shit under Holloway.

However sarcastically when we went 2 – 0 up at high flying Brentford on 21st March 2015, he got plenty of 'Super, Super Neil, Super Super Neil, Super Neil Harris!' but sarcastically we away fans sang 'You're Getting Sacked In The Summer!' this was a sarcastic version of 'You're Getting Sacked In The Morning!' and in Bomber's case it was because he was only theoretically there in the short term, until a permanent Manager took his place, that was unless he decided to stay or was deemed good enough to.

Harris became permanent manager in early May 2015 the week that we were relegated, that aside HOORAH!

He was alongside David Livermore.

Prior to the season start myself Simon, Paul, Dave and Nathan went to a Fans Forum at Harry's Bar, I asked Neil a question, along the lines of you know exactly what we are, players give 100% we will back them passionately, give a half hearted performance and we will be right on their backs, have you told the young and new players, I asked this because in season 2015/16 18 players were ousted and Bomber began his rebuilding, for example Tony Craig hardcore Wall man came back and became Captain and Steve Morison returned for his third and hopefully most successful stint. Bomber replied yes we have always stressed that myself and Tony Craig especially as well as old stalwarts like Morison had also always told the more inexperience what to expect.

Hopefully our first league game of the 2015/6 season away to Shrewsbury Town on 8th August 2015, where we played well, the backing was proper Wall 1500+ of us and we won 2 – 1, would highlight what the players can expect from us.

Morison scored one of our goals in the Shrewsbury Town win, and he scored his 50th Millwall goal at home in the second game of the season v Barnet in round one of the Capital One Cup aka The League Cup on 11th August 2015, onwards and upwards mind you he also missed a penalty!!!

2016/2017 lays Hollowhead to rest, we beat Bournemouth, Watford and Leiester City the reigning Premier League Champions In three FA Cup games, and at the end of the season we win the League 1 Play Off Final on 20th May 2017 at Wembley v Bradford City,

Millwall were definitely back, from the non entity that Holloway and Lomax had turned us in to, also our Promotion to the Championship meant that we would play QPR in 2017/2018 so we would see Holloway in the flesh twice, that will be nice for him!!!!

Can you plan sick leave? As I was sure he would suddenly develop something on dates of both of those games, it won't be a conscience as the scumbag is well past that, strangely he was actually at the Loftus Road and New Den games, albeit like a pantomime villain! Also Lewisham's CPO disgrace was shot down Holloway and CPO gone, not a bad season then eh!

Then in 2017/8 we get into a Championship Play OIfs position after a 17 game unbeaten run, with a string of away wins record previously held in League 1 by Kenny Jackett only to lose v Fulham at Home and Middlebrough away in last 3 games, but beat Aston Villa in final game and only just miss out for the Play Offs, not bad for a team favourite for relegation pre season eh!! 'Super, Super Neil, Super Super Neil, Super Neil Harris!'

Our Millwall are back all Hail Super Neil !!!!

Hollowhead Serenade At Loftus Road Tuesday 12th September 2017

We had the pleasure of the tactical genius thieving bumpkin in the flesh well from a distance when we played his then present team QPR at Loftus Road, unsurprisingly he was greeted warmly!!! We were amazed he had the bare faced front to be there, but he was about 50 yards away from us.

Holloway, Holloway You're A C***.

Shit C*** Shit C***

He Can't Read He Can't Write But He Can Drive A Tractor He Is Ian Holloway And He's A F**King Wanker

He's Gonna Cry In His Dugout

Paedo From Bristol, Your Just A Paedo From Bristol

Ian Holloway You C***

Harris, Harris Knock Him Out

Sex Case Sex Case Hang Him Hang Him Hang Him

Will We See You At The Den?

Ole, Ole, Ole, Ole You C***! You C***

Holloway, Holloway Give Us A Wave

You Bald C*** You Bald C***

He's Gonna Cry In A Minute

Your Just A Bald Jimmy Saville

He's Gonna Hide In The Dugout

In the return at the New Den Friday 29th December 2017 at Millwall we win 1-0 and in homage pantomime villain Hollowhead got –

Thought we would really go to town big time on Bumpkin bonce but all the above and 'He's Gonna Cry in the Dugout!' dressed looking like Peaky Blinders wardrobe had a clear out.

Following the information that said Neil Bomber Harris had

taken control, in section mentioning Bomber Command earlier. Bomber himself resigned after the Luton Town away game on Wednesday 2nd October 2019, Neil resigned along with David Livermore, leaving us hunting for a manager, Adam Barrett One of his coaching staff stood in for his departure, overseeing the defeat of Leeds United at home. the disastrous defeat at Brentford away and the score draw v Cardiff City, again at home.

Then in week commencing 21st October 2019, Millwall appointed the very experience Gary Rowett, former Burton Albion, Birmingham City, Derby County and Stoke City manager, his first game in charge was at home versus his last employer Stoke City manager at the New Den on Saturday 26th October 2019, the game held as Remembrance Day and his first game a win, a good appointment.

We all said whoever joins Millwall must be able to wholeheartedly understand passionate aka hostile Millwall at home, Gary appears to understand us, if he doesn't he must learn otherwise he is in for bit of a nasty surprise abuse.

CHAPTER 7
The Millwall Factor – Give A Lion A Bad Name

A Certain Reputation
In response to the assumption that we were not scary or famous anymore, wrong, as Millwall are football's equivalent of a traffic warden – i.e, no one likes them either but they don't care, and given that you cannot actually teach an old Lion new tricks and specifically hating Millwall and castigating us in the media is on a par with hating Manchester United as a national pastime, it's no wonder that our bad name and reputation perpetuate is it?

It was helped by the very, very well reported and long drawn-out Birmingham Play-Off riot coverage or the Liverpool 'Hillsborough' chants that happened many years ago now that is for sure.

The mythology of Millwall as a trouble club is a long-standing one with crowd problems dating back some almost a century, with the first real trouble as far as I know on October 16th 1920 when we played Newport County at home. This was a supposedly violent clash resulting in County's goalkeeper being pelted with missiles, taking umbrage at it and getting a right-hander for his trouble, sounds similar to Paul Roberts Brentford K.O doesn't it? As a result the Old Den was closed down from the 22nd November 1920 until December 4th 1920; obviously Millwall life has a way of repeating itself.

Our crowd reputation was enhanced, if that is the right word for it, by the infamous 1977 'Panorama' hooligan programme, more of which later. It has been kept in the public eye ever since by the numerous high profile real incidents and the way that we are portrayed in the media and TV's obsession for showing the Luton riot at the drop of a hat whenever there was any Football related trouble. With the high technology CCTV/video of today it has also allowed the most recent Football hooligan undercover/covert documentaries to be compiled, in all their gory detail, more of these later as well.

Seemingly we are to blame for everything apparently, for example there were 2 highly publicised incidents in 2007/8 – one of the Groundstaff/stewards at Chelsea v Manchester United was Sam Bethell (Millwall's Chris Bethell's son) who is also a Millwall fan who was blamed for the trouble in The Sun on 28th April 2008 when it all kicked off after the game between Manchester United players warming down and Chelsea's Groundstaff, the newspaper obviously had to say that he was a Millwall fan and blame Sam Bethell for attacking Man United's Patrice Evra, because typically it had to be Millwall's fault.

Similarly when Glasgow Rangers fans rioted in a square in Manchester when the TV screens installed for the hundred's of thousands of Rangers fans there who could not get tickets for the UEFA Cup Final v Zenit at the City of Manchester stadium in May 2008. Strangely according to the Scottish Daily Record, despite all of those arrested listed being Scottish – Millwall and Bolton casuals, what the bloody hell is a casual in the modern era? We and the fairly local trotters were blamed for it all kicking off, when running battles started with the Police because one of the TV's packed up and the Rangers fans could not watch the match on one of the screens, some other reports said that it was Stoke City fans involved as well. It seems that it is essential or at least much easier to blame us in every incident because we are Football's Hooligan pariahs, much better than blaming the mega rich Chelsea and at the time they were financially viable Glasgow Rangers for the trouble.

As I said in 'I Was Born Under The Cold Blow Lane' one 'Old

Time Musical' philosopher once wrote – 'It's the rich what gets the pleasure, it's the poor what gets the blame, Ain't it all a bleeding' shame!'

Being a young fan of a team with such a perceived violent fan reputation gave me a perverse pride because it gave me an ill conceived air of menacing threat, violence and notoriety, This was acquired merely because I was Millwall, however as I get older and hopefully wiser this same hard man reputation becomes a largely undeserved millstone around my neck.

The violent perception of our fans must also ultimately act as a definite negative when it comes to any business or commercial activities.

Promoting a club of Millwall's reputation in a positive way is not easy that is for certain, especially with a pre conceived media assisted image that makes a trip to South East London look about as appealing as spending a fortnight in Afghanistan or Iraq, when shit sticks it sticks!

Equally, I am sure that many away fans think twice about coming to the New Den, particularly after the documentaries and the Birmingham City Play-Off riot. I am certain that we get fewer away fans than other less volatile clubs do; you only have to look at the normally less than full North Stand with its oceans of empty seats. Even before the recent bad publicity sides like Crystal Palace and Charlton, i.e. local sides, have stayed at home in droves rather than risk it, even trouble clubs like Birmingham and Cardiff have not turned up in any numbers, unlike Millwall who more often than not take more to a dodgy away game not less.

The threat of attack at Millwall for away fans is a real one, but generally not for every club, however, if you're a fan of a recognised 'Firm' team then you will invariably be in for a warm, if unfriendly, South East London welcome. Any away fan about to embark on their first trip to Millwall would not be consoled by ground Hopper Guides that's for sure, their apprehensions would not be allayed from reading that it isn't advisable to drink anywhere near the ground that is likely to contain any Millwall fans, including London Bridge and Waterloo stations. In truth there are not too many, if any, pubs that I can think of in the locality that I would call away fan friendly, that was when there were pubs, as apart from pubs in The Blue, the Wetherspoons, Whelans at Surrey Docks (Quays) all Millwall pubs nearest to the New Den and The China Hall, The Bramcote, The Barnaby and The Golden Lion are now no more.

There is one positive result of this 'Don't drink In South East London' policy and that is that any away fans who like a Light Ale would have to quench their thirst in the ground itself, thereby putting some money into the club's pockets, so that's something I suppose.

One game that highlighted the effect of our image was when Leigh RMI were drawn against us in the FA Cup first round at their ground in 2000/1. I was in 'The Barnaby' near the ground when the draw was made live on TV after a home game. As this particular tie was drawn out the most prevalent question in the Millwall filled pub was 'Who? Where's Leigh?' Notwithstanding this Leigh, in their opinion, were forced to switch the game to a Sunday noon kick-off and move it to Millwall.

Their reasons for having to do this was Millwall's fans notoriety and Police intelligence, very very often an oxymoron, that the whole of Greater Manchester and Lancashire's hooligan community were going to join forces to fight the Army of Darkness on it's way from South East London.

I don't know if this was true, I know we have had trouble in the past at Wigan, Manchester United, Preston North End, Burnley and of course Manchester City in the recent years, but I seriously doubt that Leigh RMI were a major target.

The less than complimentary comments about Millwall's travelling fans missed some vital points –
A) Those most likely to go would be the normal away following, which is generally vocal but non-violent and the new ground gatherers.

B) No one even knew where Leigh was, the only Leigh that most of us knew was 'On Sea' and near Southend. I doubt Millwall's usual coach drivers would know that Leigh RMI was up near Wigan/Oldham and we would have ended up having a paddle in the 'Kiss me quick' resort in Essex!

C) Why would a huge Millwall 'Firm' be expected to travel 200 plus miles to a semi-pro side that no one had even heard of? Apart from away grounds visited gathering obviously

D) With the supposed code of the 'Firm's' being to only fight like-minded individuals or those clubs that can enhance a reputation, why would they want to fight an amateur club with no enhancement value at all? I know that we have had trouble in the past at non-league clubs like Slough but as far as I can recall that was against Chelsea fans and anyway it was fairly local.

Perhaps I am making false assumptions and a trip Leigh would really have been like a Civil War but I seriously doubt it. Kudos/reputation is the real point that was overlooked here. My usual travelling contingent and I have often commented that you only find the 'Boys' in any numbers at the real trouble games, you will not see them at games on Wednesday night up at the likes of Crewe Alexander and there is the rub.

A blanket away fan ban or switching a game only really punishes the normal hardcore week in – week out fans of both sides, i.e. the largely passionate but innocent fans.

With Millwall being the second-biggest side that Leigh RMI could have played, with local rivals Wigan being the plum draw, the result was that a potential money-spinner went out of the window when it was switched to London.

The game at the New Den attracted a small crowd with only about 100 Leigh RMI fans in attendance.

On the plus side they did have a fat goalie who we took the piss out and the Leigh RMI fans chanted the universally popular – 'Stand up if you hate Wigan!'

This went down very well with both sides and we naturally joined in. given Wigan's favoured nemesis status at the time.

The Leigh RMI manager Steve Waywell said –

'The Hooligans Have Won, No Doubt About That!' I would say if anything that the hype had won.

To finish this section on reputation a strange overheard conversation -

I was on a train en route to see England v Scotland at Wembley in the Euro 2000 Play-Offs with Millwall mate and fellow England member Dave Murray. In our carriage, we had Burnley 'Boys' the 'Suicide Squad' jumping about and chanting 'Su, su, suicide!' We stood next to them on the crowded tube and heard them having a very strange conversation. These Burnley fans were discussing who the top Firm were, naturally, Millwall came up as a contender and one of the Burnley fans said something like – 'When We Went To Millwall They Bullied Us!' This struck me as a very peculiar expression to use for a Football Firm, what did he expect a cheery greeting? Very odd.

Sweep It Under The Carpet

If you did not know any better with the media sweep it under the carpet mentality in place you could be forgiven for thinking that apart from Millwall and Cardiff everything in the garden was rosy, with Football violence largely a thing of the past, especially in the Premier League.

Anybody who travels away with Millwall regularly knows that there are numerous likely trouble spots, where violence always happens i.e. the Police Category C top priority Hoolie games -

Stoke City, Bristol City, Leeds United Wolves, Swansea City, Cardiff City, Sheffield United, Burnley, Birmingham City and Portsmouth, etc. To name just some recentish trouble spots outside London.

I'm sure that there must be regular trouble at these clubs; I cannot believe that violence only occurs just because we are playing them.

Due to our lowly status in recent seasons, whilst I can vouch for the trouble that I have seen in the lower Leagues, I have to rely on the media and Football authorities to tell me what is happening in the Premiership. Because very little trouble is reported, if I knew no better, I could assume that all was well. There is seemingly a concerted effort in the media to try to portray the Premiership as a sort of – 'We Have No Trouble Here' place, to paraphrase 'The League of Gentlemen's Edward, absolute tosh obviously. The top-flight non-trouble assumption was blown out of the water initially by the Channel 4 documentary 'Football's Fight Club' whilst it was more a history of hooliganism than a current documentary, it provided evidence of the widespread nature of the Hooligan problem. There were interviews with 'Top Boys' from Chelsea, West Ham United, Glasgow Rangers, Liverpool, Aberdeen, Man Utd and Southend United (?) With details of past and present misdeeds.

Naturally, It had to feature Millwall with one fan interviewed and footage shown of the political implications that followed our FA Cup Riot at Luton.

This was followed by BBC2s far more in depth and up to date 'Hooligans' documentaries on which they mentioned around fifty large-scale violent incidents that had happened in England in 2001/2, most involving Premiership sides. Millwall were obviously still main players in many of the events mentioned and we had the privilege of 'Starring' in the first of the Hooligan trilogy entitled –

'Hooligans – No One Likes Us" bit of a clue there!

The second programme in this series was a far more damning expose of Cardiff City with the third one being about Italian and Argentinean hooliganism.

I must admit I sat down to watch our episode with a certain amount of trepidation and whilst we did not exactly come up smelling of roses neither did Cardiff in their programme.

It seems they were vying with us for the most hated fans in the country, well the Welsh contender anyway!

Incidents like Nottingham Forest's trip to the New Den, a Battle of Waterloo against Portsmouth, trouble outside the ground at various games, running battles with the Police near South Bermondsey station and various other less than savoury events closer to the ground, It is very difficult to defend our fans actions when it is shown in all its raw glory like this.

I assume that the Birmingham footage must have come too late to be included extensively, thanks for small mercies. The documentary emphasised that the club had not agreed to be involved in the programme, which they put across in such a manner as to give the impression that Millwall Football Club did not care about what happened. Contrary to the truth and more a case of many times bitten many times shy I would imagine, however by having no right of reply it did the club no favours. That said, I could certainly understand the reticence on the clubs part to get involved.

One good thing that did come out of the 'Hooligan' series overall though was that it highlighted that other clubs had problems as well, with video footage and interviews shown featuring England, Nottingham Forest, Manchester United, Sheffield United, Chelsea, Stoke City, Oldham Athletic, Bristol City, Wolves and Cardiff City to name but a few. Whilst many wrongs do not make a right, it is at least refreshing that the programmes highlighted that it is not solely a Millwall problem.

We were also naturally featured in the Bravo programmes The Real Football Factory about the firms in London edition, presented by the West Ham United supporting actor Danny Dyer.

Wall are also featured in a 2012 Documentary by Sheffield United fan Sean Bean 'Hooligan'.

I suppose that it was impossible not to mention Millwall in this sort of programme especially with the glut of undercover footage available.

Wall are the go to guys to use an Americanism when it comes to this sort of malarky it seems.

There was a remarkable BBC1 programme called 'Riot Cops' shown in May 2003 that highlighted the work of Cardiff riot police, it showed trouble between Manchester United, Liverpool and Cardiff fans over the weekend of the 2002/3 League Cup Final at the time the Worthington Cup. Remarkable because in all of its 30 minutes or so it neglected to mention Millwall once! Naturally, I dashed off a letter of complaint to the BBC immediately after watching it, informing them that they had somehow inadvertently broadcast a hooligan programme and had not mentioned Millwall! Heads will roll for this oversight I am sure. Ps just joshing.

If you had not watched any of the above programmes or did not live in the real Football-going world, you would probably be left with the misconception that the much-vaunted Premiership in particular is trouble-free. You also only have to visit a Sport bookshop or a general bookshop's Sports section to see a vast array of available Hoolie literature including Premiership sides, they cannot all be total fiction. Lets be honest it is a problem at all levels from International Football downwards, which has been with us for decades.

From the personal accounts by people I know who support West Ham United, Manchester United and Spurs about recent incidents that they have witnessed I would say that trouble today is still rife.

One Rule For Them, A Different Rule If It's Us –

You might say that I am biased and paranoid, but here is my view of the Middlesbrough game at the New Den Saturday 19th February 2011 and it's media response, Due to Lino ineptitude in my opinion, coins, plastic bottles and lighters I think were thrown at the non offside flagger, he then got the Ref Sergison over to report the bombardment, only for Stewards and finally Plod to get involved, leading to a pitch invader attempting to confront the officials, not making it and being dragged off by stewards pitchside and the bombardment to escalate.

Following some dodgy antics by Boro's keeper Jason Steele a plastic beer bottle was lobbed from the CBL Lower after this the ref decided to suggest taking the teams off, prompting the tunnel cover to be pulled out, only for the managers of both teams to tell Ref that this was not a good idea. prompting Kenny Jackett to get the ref to ask Boro's keeper what he thought, the keeper picked up the bottle and pretended to drink it and the game was sensibly allowed to continue. This was reported in the press on a parallel to North Korea's alleged nuclear tests, with Millwall having to announce that they were helping Old Bill to find culprits via CCTV and would ban them for life, as announced by John Breylson and then Fan On The Board Peter Garston combined. Even this was slagged off in the media, as was Kenny Jackett's partial defence of why it had happened when he said that he did not condone it but it was due to Millwall's inate passionate crowd, which overspilt following the plethora of terrible officialdom we have to endure.

The events of a game with 5 goals unfortunately 3 of which were Boro's resulted in longer than usual highlights on the BBC Football League Show, which focussed on the missile attack! I am not denying that it happened and I do not condone the missile chucking individuals who bear no financial responsibility for their actions, with the club suffering the consequences of their misdemeanours..

We were not punished by the FA amazingly given our history although they said that we will be monitored for any other missile events that occur in 2010/11, although any incidents occurring again meant Middlesborough incidents being reinvestigated within any further enquiries,.

When a plastic bottle was thrown at a surly Watford player at Vicarage Road straight after this Boro game, I said to my Millwall mates on the day, that the incident would be added to our crime list, implying that we always lob missiles and we would be slaughtered behind closed doors, big fine etc etc,

After this Watford incident we all had to cross our fingers big time, this was before the FA's decision had been announced, luckily due to an honest Referee's report realistically reporting that he did not handle the situation well. fortunately the FA were lenient, something that was more than we expected, as we all slid in to worst case scenario mode, given how we are usually treated, however the actions taken, helped by the Refs report I would say, with Millwall's attitude in trying to combat these sorts of incidents and arrests/listed punishment for the people who caused the trouble if captured was taken in to consideration.

All the 'Wall fans that I spoke to or heard discussing the situation want the Den to be hostile loud and passionate as it scares the opposition teams and fans, hence the 50 odd game home unbeaten run from Old Den in the 1960s. There really is no need to throw missiles, however much it is deemed that the officials should be bombarded. Let's be honest the missile throwers will not pay any fine imposed by FA on Millwal FC and if the FA decided that behind closed doors games were necessary, they would not recoup the money to Millwall FC, for the lost revenue.

This seems to have been totally disregarded when they decided to throw things pitchwards.

The FA decision was especially good as the Railway upgrade from March 2011 for 18 months coincided with Leeds United, Cardiff City, Swansea City and Bristol City all due to play before the season ends at the New Den It had made the way into the ground from the North for us CBL people a tad precarious, with Silwood footpath up to Surrey Canal Road past recycling plant being closed, leading our having to walk through a plethora of horseshit deposited by the Police Horse Of The Year show that we have to endure, along with meat wagons, Plod aplenty etc etc. in Bolina Road passing the away section and the Railway walkway.

I came up with a marketing idea due to the plethora of Horseshit we have to wade through following the Railway works and Silwood footpath closure, why not have club badged buckets, spades and plants for sale in the club shop? It would raise some money for Millwall and enable people to clean up all the knee deep horseshit that the Police State generates with it's anally hyperactive police horses! Bloody good for helping plants grow Horseshit apparently, when I was a kid shovels and buckets were the norm to gather as much as you could of the equine fertiliser for your garden!

Moving on to the unfairness the next day West Bromwich Albion played Wolves, their bitter rivals, WBA's late goal resulted in a lit flare being thrown in to Wolves fans section and one Wolves fan getting a damaged bloodied head wound, I watched MOTD 2 that night and unlike the 'we're all doomed Millwall are involved' mentality, this was not highlighted at all, therefore I can only assume that a flaming flare is less dangerous than a plastic bottle!!! What do I know? Well having been at a game in Sweden at Malmoe v Hammarby and having a flare the size of a small baseball bat lit above my head I can tell you it is not fun!!!!

Gaby Roslin and Lawro seemed more interested in referring to the game as a passionate Derby, yeah righto, if that is the case Wet Spam Untied v us is a passionate local derby so that must mean that anything that happens in our games is obviously okay! I know that the onus is financial and that the Premier League is as pure as the driven snow, whilst Millwall are different, we are perceived like a pandemic of Hooliganism. All complete bollocks, trouble happens at umpteen Premier League games a season but is largely ignored, whilst if Milllwall are concerned it is reported with dire consequences like the outbreak of World War 3!

Moving back to our own division what happened to Palarse after their Ultra tossers bombarded QPR's Paddy Kenny with plastic bottles aplenty at Loftus Road, following a Penalty and sending off against them.

They are not us, so naturally were deemed as saints whether it was filmed and shown on BBC The Football League Show on

March 12th 2011 or not, selective decisions certainly come in to play here, lazy journalism!!

Finishing on FA Cup Semi Final v Wigan 13th April 2013, now let's say the bleeding obvious, the game should never have been a 5.15pm Kick Off with all the pubs open, thereby allowing everyone who was that way inclined to get plastered!

It did kick off in the ground for a fairly long time no denying that, it was Millwall fighting Millwall, until the Old Bill waded in at which point Millwall reacted to those steaming in from the Plod, a Millwall response to violent or aggression aimed at us.

The Media went in to Millwall have reintroduced the bad old days of Football Hooliganism single handedly!

On a week that Maggie Thatcher was being buried, I thought Luton Town FA Cup Quarter Final from 1985 would be plastered all over the media big time, but I did not see it unless I had blacked out ! However the newspaper media went mad, conveniently ignoring that Newcastle United kicked off big time in the streets of the Toon with the Toon Plod, with one genius deciding to punch a horse! Brilliant idea a You Tube instant hit!

The fact that there were three times more arrests and far more violent scenes after the Toon lost 3 – 0 to Mackem enemy Sunderland at home especially with the Police, instead they seemingly implied that we caused it all, seemingly because we played on Saturday the day before the North East enemies clashed on the Sunday!!!

Not that I am paranoid, much! But it is certainly convenient for lazy journalists to simply pick on Millwall as a matter of principle, stopped them blaming North Korea from wanting to start a Nuclear war with South Korea and America, amazingly Millwall fist fighting inside Wembley was more of a disaster!

On the Tuesday 16th April 2013 v Watford at the New Den the usually vocally comatose Watford fans sang – 'You Only Fight One Another!'

In response the CBL sang – 'You Only F*** One Another!'

In the same vein as their chant above they sang another chant that went something like –

'There's Only One Fight Club – Millwall!'

They also chanted 'Fight Fight Fight!' as used to be always chanted in School playgrounds when anyone argued.

Ah the joys of being high profile in the media, eh! We won 1 – 0 so they can sing what they want in my opinion, we beat them!

Very Non-PC Alert –
Proof That It Is Not Paranoia!

To explain that it is not Millwall based paranoia hopefully you have realized this anyway after Chapter 2 earlier, we do get this sort of bollocks please see the next Millwall are like ISIS/Taliban/Ku Klux Klan, etc. etc., guaranteed to kick off at the drop of a hat assumption.

To continue on the above ethos, please see this from Brighton and Hove Albion v Millwall 12th December 2014 A sixth-form college triggered anger by offering sociology students a trip to watch a match with the "notorious" Millwall Football Club to learn about working-class habits, masculinity, homophobia and racism.

Varndean College in Brighton were accused of perpetuating out-of-date stereotypes after arranging tickets to a match featuring the London club. The trip for students of AS-level sociology, was proposed as an opportunity to "observe and even talk to football fans from Brighton and the notorious Millwall".

At the game we sang the Paedophilic not homophobic 'Jimmy Saville F***Ed Your Mum – He's Your Father!'

Naturally there was Homophobic chants, instigated by the home fans, bending over and showing us their behinds, or waving limply at us, on a homophobic bent we foolishly then respond with – 'You Take It Up The Arse!'/'We Can See You Holding Hands!' In addition, 'Does Your Boyfriend Know You're Here!'

We sang to flag wavers 'Stick The Flags Up Your Arse!' is that

Homophobic, more fashionistic I would say.

Darren Bent played for Brighton and Hove Albion, so if we were racist homophobes this would have been perfect, the only chants he got were – 'You're Fat, You're Bent, Your Arse Is Up For Rent!' not strictly homophobic, more because he was on loan to Brighton and he was not very good.

There was a Gay link as well I suppose but, nothing racist, unless our singing 'Danny Shittu That's What We Do!' the then Shittu chant, was deemed racist!

The Brighton fans to the left our section were giving it the big un to us, and looked like Students on a Demo, Millwall fans pulled up the meshing between us and them and surged towards them, far be it from me to imply that these were the students from the Sociologists trying to prove something but prove me wrong!

We also sang the chant that had 'East London Is Like Bengal!' in it largely because it is aimed at West Ham fans and the game was on Sky Sports.

The article mentioned previously that featured the Flyer/Poster see below, was in The Times Education

Published at 12:01AM, December 11 2014 by Greg Hurst Education Editor

Unfortunately, if provoked Millwall always rise to the bait so we are obviously a reliable target.

Great being a Social Outcast isn't it, we should charge people for using us as a Scapegoat, see below as well -

'Millwall Are A Comedian's Scapegoat For Their Football Hooliganism Material'

Millwall are Comedy's scapegoats – how could I possibly say that???

In addition to the 'factual' sic reports in the media that we Mill-

> **AS Sociology Students**
> **Join us for a night at the AMEX**
>
> **MILLWALL**
>
> You will see...
> - Football (obviously)
> - Gender Performance – The *New Lad* and *Hyper Masculinity*, Hegemonic Masculinity and women challenging gender norms
> - Working Class culture and Habitus
> - Issues around Sexuality, Race and Ethnicity
>
> You can...
> - Enjoy the game – cheer, sing and chant on your local team!
> - BE A SOCIOLOGIST! Observe and even talk to football fans from Brighton and the notorious Millwall FC
> - Buy a delicious Pie
> - Warm yourself up with a cup of tea or a nice warm beefy Bovril
>
> **What will it cost?**
> Just £20.25 or £18.25 with a NUS card, including train and/or bus fare!
> **When is it?**
> Friday 12th December: 6:30pm-10pm
> **Speak to your teacher for a trip letter**
>
> **I WAS A MILLWALL HOOLIGAN!**

wall fans always have to endure, there have also been numerous 'humorous' comedy skits and cartoons at our club's expense over the years.

For example in the inflatables era of the late 1980s, which was never ever popular with we Millwall at the Old Den or away, never mind this reality, the Evening Standard had a 'witty' cartoon showing a Neanderthal/skinhead Millwall fan carrying a blow up

377

Stanley Knife standing in a queue behind someone with a blow up banana waiting to go through an entrance marked 'Millwall F.C'.

In a similar vein because of our reputation, we are the first club that a comedy scriptwriter thinks of when they want a Football hooligan punch line, no pun intended. As a result, we have been used as a violent comic reference on Harry Enfield's Television Programme, 'Drop the Dead Donkey', 'Alexei Sayle's Stuff' and 'Black Books' in one episode about Bill Bailey's first day at the shop to name but four of many.

To add to this shortlist in September 2008 on Challenge TV I watched Bullseye with Jim Bowen.

I am not sure from what era it came from but I believe it was fairly ancient as it looked like it was from one of the original series. There was a question on there about which Ancient Briton tribe Boadicea ruled. They said The Iceni and Jim said something like "Or Millwall fans as we call them nowadays!"

Oh how I laughed! Did I b***ocks! He apologized to we Millwall fans saying that we were to not take it seriously as he did not mean it to. Too late he had already enhanced our Public Enemy Number 1 reputation on public television! Great smashing super, ta!!!!

I can only assume that comedy writers/cartoonists have never had the pleasure of a trip to the likes of Elland Road, Ninian Park, Maine Road, The Britannia Stadium, Ashton Gate, Molineux, St Andrews, Fratton Park, Bramall Lane, Upton Park, The Vetch Fields/Liberty Stadium or Turf Moor.

To name just a few that I have visited over the years, because unbelievably, a trip to any of the above can be 'Interesting' to say the least. I suppose as they have a perfectly good whipping boy for society's ills in Millwall why change it? Moreover, the public, who have not had the pleasure of any of the above, would not understand a joke about say 'Swansea hooligans', so Millwall it is every time.

On Dave there was a showing in October 2008 of a 'Have I Got News For You' from November 2007, with Michael Aspel as Presenter. They showed a piece about the damage that Howard Carter's lot did to King Tut's Mummified Body when they found his tomb, an American Comedian on Ian Hislpop's team Reginald D Hunter, said after Aspel announced the breakages to the body something like, 'Sounds like he met Millwall Fans!'

Later in the Programme, Michael Aspel spoke about the possibility of the Olympic Stadium being taken over by a local Football side after the Olympic's in Stratford, the mentioned side were Leyton Orient, he said something like 'With the 55,000 seats being taken out when Millwall are there'.

Oh how I laughed, no I bloody didn't did I.

Leading on to the Racist scapegoat association assumption section next we were also mentioned by an Iranian Comedian Omid Djalili basically he said that he was a Racism Counsellor at Millwall FC sarcastically, how I laughed, NOT!!! Strangely we had also suddenly become Racist Public Enemy number 1 again this was on 'Jack Dee Live at the Apollo' in 2008.

Andy Parsons from Mock The Week in 2010 I think when talking about then Prime Minister Gordon Brown's attitude before the up coming Election to how the public perceived him, said something like – 'He is like Millwall 'No One Likes him but he doesn't care!'

I was not upset by that as it was a valid observation in my opinion.

Previously on 'Mock The Week' in July 2009, Russell Howard used Millwall as a joke buffer, when they were talking about Wimbledon Tennis being synonymous with Strawberry's, and he said

'Good Game – Guava?' relating to Millwall's fruit of choice, what a laugh we had, er no we didn't.

Are we the only football team that has ever had any hooligan trouble associated with it?

Apparently yes seemingly, although it has been a widespread problem at numerous clubs for decades, isn't it great being a comedic scapegoat!? Well not it bloody isn't!!!!

Comedic creation Paul Kaye aka Dennis Pennis in Crime Drama/

Comedy Lilyhammer 2 in sections refered to as Millwall Brick and Millwall Brick Part 1 in 2014 demonstrated how to make and how to use a Millwall Brick, another handy weapon to use against us! Oh yes and by us!

Finishing away from the hooligan ethos but back to 'Have I Got News For You' with Victoria Coren Mitchell as the presenter of the show shown first on the BBC on Friday 24th October 2014 the show ended with the customary closing shot this time with the Queen sitting alone on blue seats, looking slightly befuddled, the comment over this was something like ' After Millwall lose again The Queen looks bewildered' probably not verbatim.

But in my considered non biased opinion it shows that Millwall are the comics scapegoat, how can I say that we are the only club with blue seats, hence comedy scriptwriter choosing Millwall for the punchline, oh hang on so do Chelsea, Blackburn Rovers, Everton, Leicester City, Birmingham City, QPR, Ipswich Town, Sheffield Wednesday, Brighton and Hove Albion and Wigan Athletic, have blue seats and that is only in top two divisions, do you still think that I am paranoid.

The Millwall FC And All Their Fans Are Racists! Media Induced Perception Section –

To show that the media have perpetuated a racist ethos for Millwall, in February 2012, I was speaking to a black lady where I volunteer when she asked what I was doing at the weekend I told her that I was going to Millwall to see us v T'Bolton Wanderers in FA Cup 5th Round.

She said that she had never been to a live football match, so her perception only came from how the media have always portrayed Millwall fans, when I told her what I was doing she said to me -

'Do Millwall have any black players?

Talk about tarred with a media brush, perhaps tarred is not a good phrase as you would end up looking like one of Black and White Minstrals that aside once brushed never forgotten or forgiven

I said -

'Of course we do, we have several black players, many of whom are Millwall fan favourites one black player has been our Captain in several recent games'.'

Any Lion will know that this was Liam Trotter when Paul Robinson was injured, although I did not mention who it was as she would not know who he was at all.

She said 'I thought Millwall was a racist club?'

I said –

'To be honest we hate everybody whatever creed, colour or persuasion, it is much easier that way, so everybody who are not Millwall are open to abuse in our book!'

I explained to her where the racist theory came from, i.e. the situation in the 60s/70s when the National Front/League of St George etc used football grounds as a recruiting ground and turned up en masse with literature to distribute aplenty trying to boost their membership, it being seen by them as an ideal place, with there being so many white youths there, this was at umpteen clubs, certainly not only Millwall.

Continuing the Millwall Are A Racist club ethos -

Ian Wright in The Sun Tuesday 23rd October 2012 said about Marvin Sordell accusation that Football Authorities would sweep it under the carpet and fine us lightly if we were guilty we should be fined heavily, and he supposedly supports Millwall also he was not at the game!

In a column on October 23rd in The Independent Yasmin Aibhai – Brown wrote an article about Racism that said 'Millwall Fans and others too still behave like animals when they watch black players' again not actually having been at the Bolton game or I would imagine at any Millwall game in wake of the John Terry Racist cases and Kick Them Out Rio Ferdinand and Jason Roberts etc. T shirt boycott and also paying homage to the Sordell Twitter allegations.

The following excerpt which I edited slightly comes from News At Den -

Yasmin Aibhai-Brown, The Independent columnist made an unconditional apology.

Aibhai-Brown's comments provoked outrage from Lions supporters and prompted 15 complaints to the Press Complaints Commission, who vowed to investigate, I am sure that happened!!!

Millwall also released a statement following the publication of the article last Monday, condemning her "sensationalist and ill-informed opinion." But Aibhai-Brown admitted she was wrong, following in the footsteps of the newspaper's deputy managing editor, Will Gore, who offered his own apology soon after the outcry occurred against The Independent. She said: "I do want to unconditionally apologize to Millwall fans for writing that they "behave like animals" when black players come on.

"I should have said "some fans" and not tarred all the supporters carelessly. Many are committed anti-racists and I upset them. I was wrong."

However, Aibhai-Brown claimed she had received racially abusive emails in response to her article and said her apology "did not extend" to those individuals,

On reflection from me as a Millwall fan perspective the apology is one step forward one step backwards.

Non PC Alert –

Bolton Wanderers Reebok Stadium 12th January 2013 Visiting Marvin Sordell At His Then Home

We visited the Reebok Stadium for the first time ever where we came across Marvin Sordell who accused Millwall fans of Racidt abuse, see the Racist accusation section later on. The chants from the day, ps, I said on way to game, I know that he will get abused big time but I hope none of it is racist, otherwise this is playing directly in to his and the medias hands, there was none thankfully.

Marvin Sordell was a sub again but he still got – 'Marvin Sordell He Looks Like A Fish!'/'Nemo Nemo Nemo!' accompanied by numerous thrown and waved Nemo blow up fish! And at one nil to us 'Nemo Nemo What's The Score?'/'Sordell You're A Lying C***!'/'Sordell You're An Ugly C***!'/'Liar Liar Liar!'/'We Can See Your Eyes From Here!'/'Sordell Sordell Can You Swim?' and 'Sordell Sordell You're A C***!'

In defence of our Sodell tirade Bolton fans to our right sang – 'Marvin Sordell He Tweets When He Wants!'/'Sordell He F***ing Hates Millwalll!' and 'You Racist Bastards You Know What You Are!'

In The Mirror on Monday 14th January 2013 it referred to how poor Marvin had been treated by vile Millwall fans as 'Sordhell!' There is unbiased media bollocks for you! Is abusing fish racist?

There were other chants, when Benik Afobe came on we thought it was Marvin Sordell and started stepping up the deluge, until PA announced it was him, so we sang ' You Look Like Sordell, You Look Like Sordell!'

Two other Bolton Players ex Millwall player Kevin Davies got – 'You Look Like A C***!' and David Ngog following a miss got – 'You're Just A Shit Emile Heskey!'

Changing tack to regional abuse non Sordell the home fans sang the bizarre – 'London's A Shithole You Should Have Stayed Home!'

Continuing the racist theme Crystal Palace at Selhurst Park on Saturday 20th October 2012 had a Banner with a Monkey dressed in a Millwall shirt with other supposedly humourous tosh, one question – why is a large Palarse Monkey image banner in a Millwall shirt not referred to as racist in the media?

When you think about the reality of the black players at Millwall in recent times in addition to Liam Trotter's and Danny Shittu captaincies.

We had Tamika Mkandawire as Millwall Supporters Club player of the season in 2010/11 and another real fan favourite Djimi Abdou, who to highlight how racist we apparently are is a black Muslim!!! Was the 2011/2 MSC player of the season and also again in 2014/5, another real fans favourite Danny Shittu was Millwall Supporters Club player of the season in 2012/3, Milwall racist bastards three black players on the trot fans favourites!

Going back decades there was the adoration of players like Tony Witter, John Fashanu, (Chicken) George Lawrence, Trevor Lee and Phil Walker.

Naturally there are a lot that were not liked but that relates to all players be they white, black or purple if they do not give 100% for the Wall they are hated! It gets worse; Sky Sports News did a real assassination -

Sky Sports News Special Report Racism In Football' Monday 11th February 2013

Basically, the let's slaughter Millwall show!

They showed a video of Millwall fans in lower Block 28 Kitchener's Stand singing 'No One Likes Us' straight off the bat to imply that we could be as abusive as we liked to anybody and we did not care!

They focussed on Marvin Sordell's alleged racist accusation, where a 13 year old boy was charged, implying that we teach them young at Millwall.

They also focussed on Marlon King abuse when he scored a hat trick for Birmingham City at New Den after we were 3 – 0 we are not allowed to abuse someone who scored a hat trick for Birmingham City at New Den against us, all King's abuse is about his criminal sexual shenanigans, if they bothered to listen it was not racist, a bit like the Seig Heil by Millwall not Seagull accusation, sung by Brighton fans, don't let the truth get in the way of a scandalous attack. They focussed on, Millwall v Leeds United Jimmy Saville abuse how is that racist and was against Leeds fans not player, they also focussed on Galatasaray 'Always Look Out For Turks Carrying Knives', chants how is that Racist also that was aimed at Leeds fans who also sang about Millwall fans stabbed in Budapest at previous games, never mentioned funnily enough!!

They focussed on Leeds player El-Hadji Diouf who allegedly reported it to ref, reported what? He said himself that he heard no racist abuse he was complaining about a ball boy at a throw in.

Clever editing when Diouf is shown signaling in the Kitchener Stand direction, signaling what was not apparent, it was only presupposed racist abuse, based on what evidence? Never let the reality of what he was alleging apparently indicating get in the way of what you as Millwall assassins are trying to portray eh!

This came in the wake of the New Den Marvin Sordell allegation and punishment of a 13 year old Wall fan it was reported that Millwall "considered a potential courses of action" after The Daily Mail reported that Leeds United's El-Hadji Diouf had been racially abused at The Den on Sunday 18th November 2012, after the usual Twitter allegations that Diouf himself denied hearing Monkey chants that Twitter deluge claimed, the media went to town with this, although The Daily Mail was the one that majored on him being racially abused in an okay let's jump on the Millwall fans are all racists bandwagon.

In the Sky Sports News Special Report Diouf refused to be interviewed but they said that Diouf gave his Leeds shirt to a disabled Leeds fans after the games to show how lovely he really is in the barrage of alleged racism that he was enduring, that he subsequently denied.

They claimed we abused Millwall captain Shittu in Leeds United home game, what no mention of the plethora of Millwall's black players or Diouf being a Craig Bellamy style moaning c***!

No cannot do that it would not be biased enough if they went that tack.

Shittu himself bemoaned minority racism at his club but did point out in a club statement in response to the Sky programme being shown how much work Millwall had done to eradicate any Racist or he said Homophobic player abuse, not sure about the latter but former definitely.

They said at Millwall in undercover investigation against Leeds United they heard 56 instances of racist abuse from 5 people aimed at El – Hadji Diouf, might not be cricket but not exactly the Nuremburg Nazi rally as the media perceived was it? Or am I Millwall biased? I am, terribly sorry – NOT! In fact the non-abused Danny Shittu actually gave El – Hadji Diouf a lift home after the game and asked him whether he heard any racist abuse and he said that had not heard anything.

They went to see Leeds United at Birmingham City where there was no racism at all naturally cos the Brummies unlike Millwall are lovely.

Brilliant idea to only film in certain blocks around different grounds at certain games and hear nothing racist anywhere apart from at Millwall so must be100% right is it my Arse!!!!

Sky Sports News took the Millwall footage to Sepp Blatter who having seen it demanded action like relegation of teams who had any racism, great to get that from someone as up standing and as noble as him!

They also took it to Parliament to show black Tottenham MP David Lammy, who was appalled naturally.

They also showed Millwall v Charlton Athletic subs Danny Haynes and Emmanuel Frimpong took to Twitter claiming they were the victims of "disgusting" racial abuse at the match against Millwall at the New Den on Saturday 1st December 2012 They also heroically took to Twitter claiming they were the victims of "disgusting" racial abuse at the match against Millwall

Mr Haynes's tweet read: "The MILLWALL fans 2day was disgusting. The racial abuse I received was embarrassing. Not impressed at all!" Naturally literacy was not high on Haynes agenda!

In the Special Report, sic Haynes and Frimpong both alleged Lions supporters had racially abused them during the goalless game at The Den. Then the players concerned made it clear that they did not wish to make a formal complaint to police, and in the absence of any corroborative evidence of racism, we consider this matter closed. Another cowards way out Twitter, don't have any evidence so bottle it, Millwall naturally won't get any apology at all for the racist allegation, they showed coin throwing from a Millwall fan and trouble outside v Charlton, what has that got to do with alleged racism? They did not feature Charlton fans larging it behind Police and Stewards and throwing things inside the New Den after the game! They also covered Leicester City at home and they said there was nothing – kin hell dropped a Bollock there!

They said Marvin Sordell had received Death threats from Millwall fans, however not one person arrested for racial abuse at all, implying Police and Stewarding shit.

They said that the Sky Sports News Special Report programme came about via Marvin Sordell's accusations, where Sordell claimed that he was called a slave and received more abuse from Millwall fans at Reebok, he was the only one who wanted to talk on camera they mentioned death threats on social websites and blood strewn images, at the Reebok it was our fault for abusing him for his slandering us at Reebok, nothing racist have a look at the real I was there Reebok fish and liar chants.

Strange that Benik Afobe who played v Millwall at the Reebok and was one of the Bolton Wanderers player allegedly racially abused in the Sordell accusation at the New Den game, joined Millwall on loan until the end of the season several weeks after our alleged onslaught on Sordell at the Reebok, funny that if we are so racist he would want to come here innit!

Black Lawyers v Millwall is now the next step! Millwall are apparently the only club or people in England who are racist, bollocks and total bollocks or what, selective editing.

It Is Millwall So Must Be Racist – General Comments Or Chants Perceived As Non PC Racist Abuse –

Please see below for a real perspective of Millwall FC –

Lions honoured for Anti-Racism work Millwall FC 2011/12 Show Racism The Red Card campaign, why pick that as according to media we are practically like the Ku Klux Klan sports division, sorry the truth --

From 2003 Millwall Anti Racist programme spread.

Following the Everton FA Cup game on 26th January 2019 where a section of around a dozen Lions fans in The Dockers upper Blocks 17/18/19 nearish to the away North Stand, bear in mind this was in a crowd of umpteen thousand Millwall fans, the dozen or so filmed themselves singing 'I'd Rather Be A Paki Than A Scouse' then foolishly placed said film on social media and it went viral.

Following the social media outburst it prompted the FA to consider fit in their eyes punishment, please see later and in the end with our getting off leniently effectively with them fining us £10,000, also effectively enforcing Millwall to install a state of the heart CCTV system and mikes see a bit later.

It also prompted the instigation of a campaign meant to get home fans to report any racist. Homophobic abuse near them and report it is called –

'Hear Hate? Don't Hesitate Report Racism Protect Your Club' Anti-Racism Millwall For All Campaign run by Millwall FC in conjunction with the Millwall Community Trust following Everton FA Cup racist allegations.

Whilst this might be considered a worthy cause it has been seen by many if not all hardcore Wall fans as a grassers/nark's charter! Which is not the Millwall Working Class ethos at all.

Following the social media outburst it made Millwall FC react, there was the video with the players and Neil Harris on shown on the big screen at the Rotherham United match on 2nd February 2019. Mentioning alleged Racist chant, the Scousers sang Pikey and Gypo chants at Millwall is that not racist to Gypsy Romany community? Also there was a place called Indo Pak Social Club in Stepney set up by Asians so Paki obviously just like saying Brit, Scot etc, what constitutes racism and who decides.

Microphones were put up in Dockers stand roof, at the game after re Rotherham Utd, the Paki chant was not aimed at South Asian community but at Scousers, what is the racism evaluation level? And set by who in PC World

Why was there a need to shut Dockers Block upper portions in Blocks 17/18/19 at this and following games, i.e. the area where filmed racist abuse came from, far be it from me to say but there seems a different rule to Millwall than anyone else, hence CEO Steve Kavanagh's decision re mike and part stands closure, before EFL jump on us.

Why no call to shut Chelsea sections down following their December 2018 racist abuse of Man City's Raheem Sterling at Stamford Bridge or West Ham United fans abuse of Liverpool's Mohammed Saleh at The New London aka Olympic Stadium, only a short while after Millwall v Everton.

Whilst not condoning the chants/comments all of this abuse was aimed not at people who were Jewish, Gypsies or Asians but rather it was aimed at a stereotypical perception of the areas where the opposing clubs comes from or the perceived make up of their fans. There have obviously been stereotypical jibes aimed at us Londoners/English by other club's fans nationwide. Like it or not it is all part of a Football crowd's make up, insults are a means of winding up the opposing fans or players. In reality like most clubs a

Millwall crowd's mentality is to mock the opposition, with whatever ammunition comes to hand and as Football is predominantly a white working-class male game, for the time being anyway, the crowd is not going to be too PC is it? If intense political correctness does ever get a real grip, you will have a very quiet crowd that is for sure.

Is it ever okay to use abusive chants against anyone? Is there such a thing as acceptable abuse?

For example can you have a go at opposing fans, players, managers or officials for any of the following – Size, sexual proclivities, hair colour, religion, nationality, regional identity etc, etc?

If so, what makes these insults any less offensive than Jewish, Black or Asian abuse?

Whilst I do not condone racism, it seems that when abuse is aimed at a non-indigenous ethnic British minority it takes on a taboo aspect, I have never heard anyone in the media complaining about fans abusing people for their weight, hair colour or for abusing other British nationalities.

Why should there be such a distinction?

In A follow up to Everton racism shock and awe I received a letter with my Brighton and Hove Albion FA Cup Quarter Final match ticket the after runner of the Everton win, saying that Brighton fans should get no homophobic abuse as they are want to do! PC World order coming to the forefront in my opinion.

Firstly, to highlight the stupidity of Social media, the BBC especially focus on minor racist chanting I'd Rather Be A Paki Than A Scouse by only a small group in the Dockers Stand near away fans, foolishly this filmed on mobile phone camera and whacked on social media, giving anti-racist Campaigners Kick It Out to get on their bandwagon about how disgusting it was. There was even talk that they should shut Den after these racist chants what for about 10 people! OTT or what, we in the CBL heard none of this but by Kick It Outs level of punishment you would have thought all 14,000 plus Millwall fans present were singing it, isn't perspective bollocks, it is Millwall all KKK so must be stopped!

No talk about White Hart Lane being shut for Spurs Yid Army chants or Spurs being banned from Wembley or Leeds United chants re Munich or their pro Jimmy Saville chants shutting Elland Road. Why not? Oh, sorry they are not Millwall so must be innocent!

Championship side Millwall beat Premier League side Everton so what do they focus on trouble before game near Surrey Quays, Whelan's and Southwark Park again filmed and put on Social Media, therefore open season for lazy journalists or broadcasters.

Millwall humour following Everton Asian Scouse Social Media Outrage. Caused lions fans to chant to Brighton and Hove Albion fans at FA Cup Quarter Final Sunday 17th March following Homophobic letter warning 'We Know Where You Take It, But We Are Not Allowed To Say!"

Extending my ethos of let's drag Millwall through the mud as long and as much as we can on Monday 4th March 2019 there was a BBC 1 programme called Inside Out London which was not only about Millwall but Homeless Eastern Europeans sleeping rough in London and Children in one London family waiting for heart replacements, but the Millwall part of this triumvirate was entitled – Can Millwall Ever Shake Off Its Notorious Reputation?

The show segments presenter was Sean Fletcher, our section featured chunks of BBC's 1977 Panorama, a programme that has effectively made Millwall FC and fans a media scapegoat for over 4 decades, our section of the programme included football violence, switching from Harry the Dog to video footage of the Everton trouble outside the Sillwood Estate/Whelan's. Incredibly probably due to an internal error at the Beeb the Luton Riot footage did not get yet another airing!

BBC Radio 2s Richie Anderson was the main man interviewer, not saying there was a racist agenda here but he himself is a black man as was Sean Fletcher, Anderson interviewed a couple of black men Quince Garcia and his uncle Norman Garcia in Arments Pie and Mash shop in Westmoreland Road South London.

Norman was an old school member of F Troop, whilst 1980s convert Quince was the younger man, the snippets from Panorama featured an interview with National Front Leader Martin Webster, who said he saw a market in white football hooligans and recruiting Millwall fans would be good, white hooligans eh Norman or Tiny were not white!

They also focussed on the small group social media footage of the anti Scouse/Asian chant, switching between the two items NF in 1970s and Racist chanting by a very small group in 2019 as though they were the same thing, really???

Apparently whilst Norman carried on his F Troop activities, Anderson said the racism was so bad that Quince's Dad who came over to England on Windrush with Norman stopped going.

White Millwall fans interviewed around the New Den elaborated on how much work had been done by both the club and Millwall Community Scheme this was given only vague attention, Anderson mentioned the club winning the Family Club Award but shot this down by speaking about this announcement receiving mocking on Social Media essentially disparaging the enormous amount of work that Millwall FC, the MSC and Millwall Community Projects do, he also stated that Millwall FC were contacted about programme but refused to talk inferring they obviously had something to hide!

It highlighted that ex F Trooper Norman has turned himself around by seemingly now being involved with the church, implying if he could change his ways so could the club's fans something that both the Garcia's implied.

I would love to know what does that actually mean? Does it mean the true reality of Millwall FC fans passionate mentality must be replaced by Happy Clappy, fake fans like Crystal Palace Ultra tossers – EEEEEK!!!

Not a Millwall incident but a wonderful example of the hypocrisy that applies to abuse.

There was alleged racial abuse at the Everton v Norwich City 3rd round FA Cup match in January 2004. widely reported in the media at the time. It was claimed that the visiting Norwich fans racially abused Everton's black player Joseph Yobo by chanting 'You Black Bastard!' Something that, they vigorously denied. The Norwich fans said that they were actually abusing then Everton star Wayne Rooney with chants of 'You Fat Bastard!' This was apparently perfectly okay then, why should there be a distinction?

As I said I freely admit that in the distant past there was racist abuse which I've listed in 'Tuesday Night In Grimsby' and chants I mentioned earlier however since these incidents I cannot recall any real abuse, this shows the advances that the club's anti racist stance has made over the recent years, you may very very very occasionally hear the odd monkey noise and there are some racist comments, it is only from odd individuals in the crowd and it is nowhere near as bad as a couple of decades ago that is for sure, nowadays in truth Millwall are no better or worse than any other club in the Premiership or League for racism. Which makes it even more galling when we are accused by the media in particular of being ranting racists. Contrary to the recent allegations from the 2003/4, 2004/5 home games against Burnley, Liverpool and Brighton in particular that you will find later in this chapter, Millwall is not a hotbed of facism.

The truth is that Black players who are abused nowadays are invariably those from the opposition who have done something to rile the Millwall crowd, rather than just because they are black and they are booed not racially abused, you will see various incidences later on.

One example of this was Notts Forest's David Johnson who was quoted in the headline in The Daily Mail on Tuesday 8th October 2002 saying 'Racism? Thierry Henry is lucky he doesn't have to put up with Millwall' David Johnson implied that he was racially abused, according to him, after he had scored in front of the CBL. What Johnson failed to mention was that in his case, he was targeted because he had scored a blatant handball goal in front of the home stand, which the officials missed, but we did not, and not because he was black. He later admitted that he had handballed it, unfortunately too late for it to effect the result.

Chants can also be conveniently misconstrued for example when black player Etienne Verveer (E.T) played for us his 'E.T!' chant at the time sounded like monkey noises to anyone who did not know any better.

The same thing applied to Aboubaka Fofana whose name was shortened to 'Abou!' for chanting purposes for obvious reasons and consequently it sounded as if we are booing him each time he got the ball. When the home fans at Reading and Bradford City continually booed Abou in 2003/4, I bet he thought 'Blimey I'm popular today they're all calling my name!'

Slightly more recently 2006 loanee Bruce Dyer received 'Bruce, Bruce, Bruce!'

Which could easily be mis interpreted as monkey noises if you chose to hear it that way.

Millwall fans, whilst held up as racist pariahs, have ourselves been the target of abuse numerous times, in recent seasons, as have our players, just a few post decade examples –

At Swansea City in February 2001, the home fans racially abused all of our coloured players, we English and The Queen at the Vetch Field.

Cardiff City did similar anti London/English/monarchy abuse in December 2003 at Ninian Park.

At Bradford City in April 2003, goalkeeper Tony Warner was being racially abused by the home fans, consequently he confronted them in the second half.

Finally, at home to Burnley in February 2004, their fans racially abused Paul Ifill.

Whilst many wrongs do not make a right in the recentish past Oldham Athletic, Hull City, Leeds United, Manchester City, Everton, Sunderland, Blackburn Rovers, Notts Forest, Arsenal, Port Vale, QPR, Stoke City and West Ham United's fans have all been cited for racist abuse.

However, for some reason these club's misdemeanours do not get such large scale, drawn out and lurid coverage as similar alleged Millwall incidents, which brings me nicely on to -

The perception that Millwall's fans are all rabid racists, really stems from real racist abuse and facist recruiting at games at the Old Den predominantly in the 1970s, this was not only happening at Millwall I might add, it was a national problem at the time.

The racist supposition reared its head again several years later when Ian Wright made racist accusations about us on Arsenal's clubcall on the eve of an FA Cup game at the New Den in the mid 1990s. This despite Wright allegedly being a Lions fan, he says so in his autobiography and to confirm this when he was a pundit on the FA Cup Semi Final between Manchester United and Arsenal on Saturday 3rd April 2004 he said – 'Come on you 'Wall' when they mentioned the next day's Millwall v Sunderland game at half time. Gary Lineker admonished him for his bias and Wright said – 'I love the 'Wall I always have!'

Returning to the racist assumption, years after the Wright insinuation a defamatory article appeared about a midweek visit to the New Den on December 4th 2001 by the then non-cream of Manchester – Manchester City.

There was an away fan ban imposed for this game by both chairmen in an attempt to stop the inevitable violence, following crowd trouble between the two sides the previous time that we had met. To show the quality of unbiased journalism that we usually have to put up with, the match was notable for the scandalous reporting of the evening's proceedings perpetrated by a London based Man City supporting 'Hack' who we somehow managed to let into our 'Members Only' Junior Enclosure in the Lower East Stand. The reporter naturally came with his preconceived 'They're All Racists' ideas and as such managed to write a fantastically inaccurate account of the night's proceedings for publication in The Observer Sport section on the following Sunday, carrying the headline

'A Truly Nasty Night Out In The Family Enclosure'

I suggest that the writer should have spent some time in their own club's Family Enclosure at Maine Road before they complained about anybody else's, if my experience of sitting next to it was anything to go on.

I also presume that whoever wrote the article must wander around Moss Side in their rose-tinted spectacles, it being such a shining example of a harmonious non-violent multicultural society.

The Man(c) who should not have been in our Junior Enclosure in the first place, exuded all the accuracy of a blinkered head in the sand account of events by the fragrant Karren Brady. To highlight the precision of the masterpiece -

The reporter failed to notice that we had any black players in our squad.

Only Warner, Reid, Gueret and Ifill, I agree they were not easy to spot.

The reporter managed to quote chants and abuse that neither myself or anyone I was with heard which isn't to say that it did not happen of course, but seemingly he did not hear what we actually did sing to Shuan Goater, Shaun Wright – Phillips either, for example -

Shaun Goater got 'Goater you're an ugly c...!' And 'Have you ever pulled a bird?'

Shaun Wright-Phillips in homage to his dad Ian Wright got – "Ian wank, wank, wank!' And 'You're shit and your Dad's a c...!'

The reporter also managed to infer that calling a Man City player a 'Northern Monkey' was racist, presumably he has never seen Lenny McLean dealing with the two Scouse burglars in the film 'Lock, Stock and 2 Smoking Barrels' ? I can only assume that the article, written by a deaf, dumb, daft and colour-blind undercover Manc, was published without checking for accuracy.

Naturally anyone who read it and who did not know any better would probably take it as gospel.

Call me naïve but I expect better from the 'quality' press.

Something that I found comical on the night was when City scored and practically the whole ground stood up scouting for any rogue Mancs, who were silly enough to be in our midst and celebrating the goal. Save for City's team, the director's and officials, one foolhardy soul in an executive box and the undercover 'reporter' (sic), they did not show up. Not humourous really I suppose but it just struck me as funny that so many people spontaneously stood with the same Manc hunting idea in mind. It was probably just as well that it was a home fan only game based on this reaction!

The reciprocal ban on us travelling to the return game in Manchester prompted the most controversy at the time, because it was deemed by many to be an infringement of their civil liberties -'I Should Be Able To Sample The Delights Of Moss Side If I Want!' Was the cry.

I suppose that the ban was sensible, although It did mean missing an away match, which

I do not like doing if I can help it. Manchester City v Millwall was no more volatile than the Cardiff City v Leeds United FA Cup tie of the same season so why was there no ban there?

Sorry, my persecution complex kicked in there again for a minute!

Presumably, to try to stop ticketless fans travelling the away Manchester City game was beamed back to our Jumbotron. I could not be arsed to go, therein lies madness to me, shouting and singing at what amounts to a television, I can do that indoors and rather worryingly, I occasionally have, whilst trying to avoid the neighbours phoning the authorities to get me sectioned.

Instead, I chose to flick backwards and forwards on Ceefax and Teletext when they both existed all night, as LIVESCORE Mobile phone Apps etc did not exist at the time.

When Millwall beat Burnley to reach the FA Cup Quarter Final on Valentine's Day 2004 the next day's News Of The World managed grudgingly to accept our victory whilst mainly choosing to focus on the alleged negative aspects of the day, implying again that we were all racists.

This was because Burnley's black defender Mohammed Camara was booed each time that he touched the ball, the reporter conveniently ignored the fact that he was being specifically targeted for getting involved in a fracas with Tim Cahill following an elbow on Matt Lawrence by another clarets player. Camara had not received any attention prior to this; however, following the incident he was picked out for personal attention, as other such miscreants are at every ground nationwide. I personally heard plenty of booing but no racist abuse, which is not to say that there was none at all. To prove that the reporter had some sort of ulterior agenda the article then went on to mention the relatively low crowd under the sub heading 'Empty' implying that it was because of our crowd's mentality that no one wanted to come to the New Den.

The reporter again ignored the contributory factors. For example he did not take into account the fact that due to the late playing of the 4th round Telford game we had little time to sell tickets to either home or away fans or that Millwall had refused to let the away fans pay on the day, hence their relatively low turn out. Strangely, Fulham's small crowd against West Ham and Sunderland's half-empty Stadium of Light against Birmingham City in the same round did not warrant a similar mention in the reports about the games in the same paper.

On Monday 16th February, The Sun reporting the same Burnley game saw it as its civic duty to mention our last FA Cup Quarter Final appearance in 1985 at Luton, where it said that 31 Police were hurt. One question –If Liverpool do not get Hysel mentioned in every report about any of their European trips and Manchester United do not get constant references to the death of a Crystal Palace fan each time they reach an FA Cup Semi Final – why do we warrant such reporting? Reporting on the same game and representing the 'quality' press, we have the home of Burnley fan Alistair Campbell – The Times aka 'The Thunderer' whose columnist Keith Pike wrote an even more scathing attack on us under the heading 'Fanning Fires Of Bigotry'.

He said of the crowd at the Burnley Cup game – 'The New Den, Like The Old Den, Remains

Unparalleled, A Uniquely Poisonous, Malevolent, Ugly Depressing Venue For A Sporting Contest. Ranters To The Left Of You, Racists To The Right'.

He also went on to include other less than favourable comments about our possible appearance at the Millennium Stadium sullying English Football internationally via the worldwide television coverage of the event. Although the writer admitted that various other crowds, were in his opinion, unpleasant to be in the company of, he held us up as the main culprits, nothing unusual there then. Perhaps he was just unhappy with the pressroom hospitality.

The saga of our supposed racist crowd continued when Burnley visited the New Den soon after the Cup tie, this time for a League match on Saturday 28th February.

Following the racist accusations Mohammed Camara was booed each time that he touched the ball.

However, this time Burnley's then manager Stan Ternent felt that he had to vent his spleen in a Lancashire radio interview after the game, saying that Camara was the target of disgraceful monkey noises and scandalous racist abuse, which was reported on Ceefax/Teletext on the night of the game. His outburst was also reported in the News Of The World on Sunday 29th February.

However, for a change, the reporter was on our side stating that whilst he heard plenty of booing from his position in the press area at the back of the West Stand he had heard no racial abuse.

Neither had any of our extended group sitting in the CBL and the East Stand or anyone else that I spoke to who had sat nearer to the dug out itself. Sadly, LWT's Soccer Sunday chose to focus on the alleged racist angle rather than the game, thereby overshadowing Millwall's 2 – 0 win and our ascent to 5th place in the League. To add flames to the fire The Sun on Monday 1st March had a double page spread in its Football section under the provocative title of 'Race War', where Stan Ternent said that the yobs who abused Camara should be locked up. He had also now suddenly decided that he knew that Millwall was a BNP stronghold, there goes that 'Isle of Dogs' by-election again! He said that, as Burnley was itself a real BNP hot bed, he knew what one sounded like, no sweeping generalisation there then.

The Sun article on Monday 1st March was again unusually positive, as it also did not corroborate Ternent's monkey chants claim. It also gave Theo Paphitis the space to reiterate the true facts that it was booing not racist chanting. Theo also stated in the media and on Millwall's website that he had had instigated plain clothes spotters in the ground and requested that the Police and stewards look out for racist abuse because of the Cup accusations. He later said that, the only racist abuse accusations at the game apparently came from Burnley fans who had complained to stewards about the Camara booing and their own fans who were calling Paul Ifill a 'Paki' Consequently there was a mass Police and steward invasion of the away stand during the League game and they led a Burnley fan away, presumably the racist abuser, I believe one Millwall fan was also apprehended. Ternent in response claimed that Paphitis was 'burying his head in the sand' by claiming that the abuse had not happened. As an aside I can only assume that Stan Ternent did not read the League game's match programme as it contained an advert for an 'MSC Race Night', which I am sure he would have interpreted as a Ku Klux Klan rally. Quite what he made of his side's local rivals Preston North End calling their programme 'Whites World' I do not know.

Returning to former Labour spin-doctor and Clarets' fan Alistair Campbell.

He was at both the FA Cup and League games; he was in fact

flashed up on the Jumbotron after the Cup match leaving the ground, following in the wake of his stable mate Keith Pike's article, Campbell himself wrote a less than complimentary article about how racist we are after the League game. The article in The Times was entitled 'Racism: No One Likes It And We Do Care'.

On Tuesday 2nd March The Sun had another half page article continuing the hypothesis that we were all racist. It mentioned the above Campbell article and for some bizarre reason it also sought comments from two totally unconnected black players Derby County's Michael Johnson and Wimbledon's Jermaine Darlington about the racist abuse that they had received both the Old and New Dens. In addition to the above articles as it was Millwall and therefore considered good copy Ternent's racist allegations were naturally in all the tabloid press for days, for example I personally read articles in The Daily Star, Metro and The Daily Mirror on Tuesday 2nd March on my way to an away match at Sheffield United. Nothing like dragging the 'incident' out for as long as possible and making a story from a non-story. Irrespective of the protracted tabloid interest the Police did not investigate the allegations, as there had been no official complaint.

I only mention it in passing but on the same Saturday as the Millwall v Burnley league game there were dozens of arrests when Hull City fans rioted in a Lincoln hotel during their local Derby at Lincoln City.

In addition, Bristol City fans rioted upon returning from their defeat at Sheffield Wednesday with Riot Police having to use batons and CS gas to disperse drunken fans. Two incidents that warranted a miniscule mention at the foot of page six in The Sun on the Monday following the games.

I also personally heard several first hand stories from several different East End sources of serious trouble at West Ham United v Cardiff City at Upton Park on the same day, which did not even find its way into the media at all from what I saw, funny that!!!

As I mentioned in December 2004 the FA charged Millwall and Liverpool over the incidents in the October 2004 Carling Cup game against Liverpool. Whilst Liverpool were cited with not controlling their fans violent actions, Millwall were charged with throwing missiles and more scandalously with our fans racially abusing Djimi Traore.

The racism accusation came like a bolt out of the blue this was the first mention of any such abuse and came some 6 weeks after the game. At the time racism was back in the headlines as a scourge in society following the Spain/England incidents in Madrid and Dwight Yorke's abuse at Blackburn Rovers in particular. Strangely the FA did not ask for Ewood Park to be closed or fine Blackburn Rovers themselves, they were content for the purportrators, captured red handed and faced on Sky Sports live coverage, to be charged so why charge Millwall with racism? Especially when as far as I heard there wasn't any. Nonetheless Millwall were to become the first team ever to be charged with the offence by the FA. We often sit in the stand and hear a black player being booed and jokingly say 'That will be deemed as racist abuse in the papers', many a true word said in jest as they say.

If abusing northerners is racist then guilty as charged your honour, but the FA charge of racism against a Liverpool black player was absolute tosh. Traore was actually being booed for a foul on a Millwall player, as per the Burnley Mohammed Camara incident not being racially abused.

On 22nd January 2005 Wolverhampton Wanderers played at the New Den and ex-Hammer Paul Ince was giving his usual petulant referee baiting performance for the Wolves, obviously he was greeted with anti West Ham United abuse for his unhappy Hammer affiliation and more specifically he got – 'Paul Ince is a wanker! And 'Paul Ince you're a mouthy c…!' Not racist just truthful!

In the same game Wolves' South Korean international Ki – Hyeon Seol was greeted with a stereotypical chant that referred to the modern phenomenon of South East Asians trawling London pubs selling bootleg DVDs –'DVD, DVD, DVD!' In a press interview with Paul Barry of the Birmingham Evening Mail on Monday 24th Ince implied that we had seriously racially abused the South Korean throughout the game, he implied that it was as bad as anything he had heard in the racist days of yore, strangely I saw no complaints from Seol himself. I spoke to my mates after these accusations appeared and we all agreed that all we had heard aimed at the Korean was the chant relating to Asian pub salesman and some 'Sweet and sour' type of chants odd yes but not really racist I wouldn't think.

As I said we abused Ince himself, see above, however from the CBL at least this was not racial either. In my opinion non racist Ince abuse is thoroughly deserved, if he wants to continually moan and wave his arms around like a petulant five year old all afternoon then he deserves all he gets..

Following the article Millwall investigated the CCTV and audio footage of the match and found no evidence of abuse, other than 'DVD' so they asked Ince to be more specific about the nature and location of the supposedly disgusting abuse that Seol was receiving so that they could investigate and ban any offenders. According to Ince in the Evening Mail interview the abuse had been so bad that he couldn't repeat it, As is the norm in many abuse accusation cases Ince produced no evidence. For their part Wolves made no official complaint. You might have noticed DVD returned again in the chant section re Tottenham's Son Heung-minearlier on

Saving the very worst till last The Sun carried an extremely scurrilous article, chockful of innacurracies on Tuesday 14th December 2004 -

The article entitled 'Moronic Minority Put Football Back In The Dock – Monkey Chants And Seig Heils ... A Family Day Out At The Footie In Modern Britain' by Raymond Enisuoh, who was the sports editor of the leading British newspaper for the black community New Nation

The piece followed his supposedly harrowing visit to the New

Den for the game against Brighton on December 11th 2004. Highlighting this 'serious' article about racism in English Football The Sun also carried a comment in 'The Sun Says' editorial section pointing readers towards the item.

The article was so inaccurate that it is difficult to know where to start but here goes –

Enisuoh said that he was warned not to go through a certain estate to get to the ground, implying that it was somehow a 'no go area' for black people. The truth is that both the old and new parts of the Silwood estate, the estate I assume he means, is multi cultural, there are also a couple of industrial units at the Surrey Quays end of the estate manned by black staff, not forgetting that Southwark itself has a large black population. He said that inside the ground when he sat in the CBL Lower no one would sit next to him because he was black. I would say that if people didn't sit near him it was because their were plenty of empty seats so people spread out. More likely than a black thing any exclusion zone around him was because people did not want to sit close to the photographer he was with.

For the record I had an empty seat next to me but did not naturally assume that it was some sort of personal slur that no one had sat there

I think must have been a different match to the one my mates and I were at, we fans were accused of everything from monkey chants, booing black players, including our own, the aforementioned missile throwing, racist chanting, complete with Nazi 'Seig Heil' salutes, although he did say that this was thankfully far away i.e. not from the CBL. We were also accused of unfurling a racist banner. The piece all but implied that we had all donned white KKK hoods and set light to crosses on the pitch at half time!

He said that Millwall fans threw missiles at black stewards, my London mates and I sat high up in the CBL so we did not see any missile throwing, however my cousin Paul who sat in the front row of the CBL Upper said that the missile throwing he was referring to could have been kids playing at the front of the lower tier who disposed of plastic bottles, a paper plane and a tennis ball by tossing them on to the pitch side netting, not by purposely throwing them at any passing black steward(s).

However I later heard, from Johnny Lynch, a Millwall stalwart, who was sitting in the West Stand, that the incident he was referring to did happen but in the away end. A black steward was scrabbling to release a ball caught in the meshing at the front of the north stand, as Brighton were chasing the game a Brighton fan in an attempt to speed the process lobbed a bottle down at the steward from the upper tier, this was pointed out to the police and apparently the offender was tracked by CCTV and ejected. The article mocked Millwall's Anti Racism banners along the north Lower implying that the club were advertising one thing whilst we fans did the opposite, it also belittled the real efforts that the club have put in at improving our tarnished image in recent years.

He inferred that most of the alleged racist problems emanated from the CBL Upper above where he sat, these accusations were completely and utterly untrue. For the record we did abuse Brighton's black player Leon Knight, see the earlier chant chapter, this abuse was not racial it was merely the time honoured tradition of abusing the opposition's star player, it was certainly not because he was black.

We did boo the substitution of our own black player Barry Hayles because we disagreed with the decision to take him off but we cheered his black replacement Paul Ifill, both when he came on and when he scored, we may have booed or shown our irritation if any black player made a ricket, but we did exactly the same if it were a white player who had done something wrong. If you choose to be selective with your hearing it is easy to ignore this fact and say that it was only a black player thing.

Additionally we abused ex Millwall manager Mark McGhee with anti Scots abuse and the Brighton fans were lambasted for their supposed 'gayness', which was accompanied by limp wristed waving towards the away end from the East Upper.

Millwall asked for proof from The Sun but Enisuoh was unable to back up any of his claims with any evidence at all, even though he had a photographer with him who could have photographed the mythical racist banner that we allegedly unfurled and the supposed Nazi saluting.

Millwall also asked why if it was so bad did he not report the supposed missile throwing or racist chanting to either the Police or stewards at the time? Again no response.

Brighton fans who were actually at the game very kindly leapt to our defence, despite our gay accusations. Their web message board 'North Stand Chat' was full of messages supporting Millwall and refuting every word that the 'journalist' wrote. They pointed out that their black goalkeeper Michel Kuipers had made no mention of the appalling racism that was apparently going on all around him and they suggested that the Albion chant 'Seagulls' emanating from the Away stand at the opposite end of the ground, must have conveniently been misinterpreted as 'Seig Heil!' and attributed to Millwall fans to suit the writers preconceived 'They're all racist' point.

Quite what the Nazi saluting was I don't know, perhaps it was the then called East Upper's limp wristed waving? More likely it was the Brighton fans doing a finger point towards the Millwall fans to their left or towards the pitch to accompany their 'Seagulls' chants.

I don't know how many games that Enisuoh actually goes to but he does seems very naïve with regards to Football fan culture, it is also rather worrying that he could not distinguish between home and away fans. Deeming it a media witch – hunt/stitch-up by The Sun Brighton fans wrote to Millwall's official website to confirm the truth, one writer highlighted on the site said that Brighton fans would write to The Sun, The Press Complaints Commission and the FA to put our case and relay the true events at the game. To my mind their opinion would carry far more weight than Millwall fans

407

complaining, because this would invariably have just been seen as our making excuses for our racist fans.

I have a few questions -

Why did The Sun commission him to go to Millwall in the first place?

Why not send him to the most high profile racial incident at the time hotspot prior to this – Blackburn Rovers? Their fans really did abuse Dwight Yorke as captured by Sky Sport.

If I was cynical I would say that Wapping is much closer to the New Den, Blackburn are not as easy a target as Millwall and anyway it is up north.

How come he could not distinguish between home and away sections? Did he not do any pre visit homework? Or would that have put an unbiased slant on his preconceived racist ideas?

Why did The Sun only print part of Millwall's response in the article?

Conveniently ignoring the parts where Millwall had asked for proof that was not forthcoming.

That said to their credit The Sun did print a small selection of the deluge of irate letters that they got from Millwall fans on the Dear Sun letters page a couple of days after the article.

In our defence several newspapers (The Standard/The People/ Daily Mail/The Daily Mirror/The Observer, etc) all lambasted The Sun article, point scoring on the papers part probably but it was at least good to have their backing.

BBC London's Tom Watt summed it up perfectly by stating that the article was a perfect example of not letting the truth get in the way of a good story.

This disgraceful article was journalism at its most biased and negatively creative. It was dangerous and scandalous, moreover it was completely at odds with the anti racism cause that the author purports to support.

One danger of this sort of piece is that if you were not at the game and had read his article you would have thought that it was all true, it is Millwall after all.

If accepted as fact it would encourage not discourage racism in my opinion, quite what purpose is served by writing such a flagrantly inaccurate piece I really do not know. As an aside the 'Seagulls!' chant was occassionally sung sarcastically by us, most noticeably to another previous racist accuser David Johnson at Forest in January 2005. Amazingly on February 5th 2005 Enisuoh had a decent sized article published in The Sun with the headline 'I Got It Wrong About Millwall'. This article admitted that his racist assumptions and accusations were in fact totally untrue and a matter of misidentification of events. Better than nothing I suppose.

There was the fairly modern accusation made by the Nathan Ellington the lying Twit on Twitter after their St George's Day massacre at the New Den in 2011 – 'Racists! Preston striker Ellington claims he was abused by fans at Millwall'

The above was a headline in an article by The Daily Mail's Matt Barlow, when he lifted the accusation directly from Preston North End's Nathan Ellington's Twitter about his allegedly being abused pre match, Ellington said that he was bombarded with Monkey noises and was called a thief because he was black and only he received this, purely geographically this must have been from the Dockers Stand aka East Stand or the West Stand as we heard nothing of the sort in the game warm up from our position in the CBL upper, I say this as the Preston warm up was in front of North Stand.

In my opinion The Daily Mail article was sensationalist, lazy journalism, by a man who I assume did not hear it himself as this was not mentioned, I cannot confirm it but I doubt he was actually at the match, it was on Sky Sport who themselves denied hearing anything either, strange as they had umpteen mikes there for the Live match.

I heard 'You Stole My Stereo!' echoing from CBL, but this is sung at every northern team to be honest by practically all Southern teams, particularly at the Scousers, not racist more Stereotypical Regionalization.

Several points –

If Ellington was so mortified by the alleged racial abuse, why not report it to match officials, police, stewards at the time, so that action could be taken instantaneously not fill up his Twitter afterwards, was it his excuse for Preston North End being slaughtered and the reason that he did not score? i.e. he was under duress by us nasty alleged Racists!

Had it also not occurred to him that he could mention it to the plethora of black players at Millwall FC in the present or recently Craig Eastmond, recommended by Jay Simpson who himself had been on loan previously via Arsenal, Mahlon Romeo, Liam Trotter, Hameur Bouazza, Carlos Edwards, Shaun Batt, Tamika Mkandawire, Paris Cowan Hall, Shaun Cummings, Jordan Archer, Kevin Lisbie, Nadjim Abdou, Andros Townsend, Kiernan Hughes – Mason etc. etc. not forgetting loaned players Nathan Tyson, Theo Robinson and Benik Afobe, etc etc etc if we are so racist why on earth would this amount of players want to play at Millwall? Just a thought. Sorry do not show him the list of 115 black Millwall Players past and present, or he might think it is a conspiracy!!!

It was reported in This Is London, London Evening Standard on Wednesday 27th April 2011 that 'Nathan Ellington could take action after alleged Millwall abuse' he alleged that Millwall fans are a disgrace to the human race and was consequently asked by the FA to formally report his accusation, in I think from a put up or shut up mate perspective. More importantly I just wondered what action the prick thinks he should take? Perhaps the best action would be getting treatment for his persecution complex would be the best place to start!

This Millwall fans are racist ethos returned in a game v Bolton Wanderers on Saturday 6th October 2012.

For reference in the Bolton game black player Danny Shittu was Millwall captain, black players Liam Trotter and Djimi Abdou were in the starting line-up whilst Shaun Batt came on as a sub.

Not forgetting the long awaited return from a lengthy injury of Tamika Mkandawire, which was warmly applauded when it was announced that he was on the bench, which also had black player Thierry Racon on.

Danny Shittu was applauding the fans big time at the end of the game because he had put in a Man of the Match performance defensively and the name and chant of 'Shittu' had deservedly echoed around the ground most of the afternoon

Not to forget other black club players either not in the squad for this match or injured Dany N'Guessan, Liam Trotter and Karleigh Osborne.

Re-emphasising a point that I mentioned earlier are all these Millwall's black players and others that I have either mentioned or not specifically included all oblivious to the supposed inherent nature of Millwall fans, so want to play for Millwall?

In the game where Bolton Wanderers players played their Premier League Prima Donna player ethos of diving, cheating, rolling about as if they had been shot and moaning at everything because they were somehow entitled to special treatment what!

With, in my opinion the worst player being ex Liverpool black player David Ngog, seemingly getting away with anything that he wanted, from the very start.

However, Marvin Sordell who claimed, on his Twitter aka TWATter that Millwall fans racially abused him whilst warming up, Ngog was not mentioned in a list of players that he also said had received racist abuse. In this apparent tirade of Millwall fans racist abuse that he said that he and Bolton players received, he included himself, Lee Chung – Yung, Darren Pratley and Benik Afobe.

Whilst I am obviously Millwall biased I freely admit that Lee Chung – Yung did get the full 'DVD' treatment when he came on, for explanation of what this means see a bit earlier on in this section. In relationship to the reality of the circumstances within the game if anyone was going to be abused David Ngog should have been the one in my opinion, I am not implying that he should have been racially abused because he is black, but we should have focussed specifically on his bloody antics and told him big time!

Whilst I am not saying that some people or as it turns out one young boy had not abused the T'Bolton players, sorry one Bolton player Sordell.

I heard nothing from the CBL upper, because the only high level of what you could classify as Den racist abuse was prevalent manger when Owen Coyle, who we added to our lose to Millwall get sacked list, rushed on to moan about something so got –'You Scotch C***!'

In addition, in the second half in front of CBL Bolton's Hungarian keeper Adam Bogdan kept getting Ginger abuse as he had Ginger hair, or is hair colour abuse not racist? As I wondered earlier on.

The main target in response to all his Prima Donna cheating antics was their goal scorer white player Chris Eagles, to show our appreciation of his antics he continually got –

'Eagles, Eagles you're A C***!'

Specifically when we scored our second to win 2 – 1 he got –

'Eagles Eagles what's The Score!'

The best and most humourous was when he missed a penalty at 1-1 and shortly after hilariously hit himself in the face with the ball in front of the Barry Kitchener Stand he received the full ground joining in the singing of – 'Wanker, Wanker, Wanker!'

It seems to me that in the wake of the racist allegations against Liverpool's Luis Suarez and the long drawn out Chelsea John Terry racist scenario, where Ashley Cole also tweeted following the FA Terry decision that he was rebuked by the FA for.

Twitter is seen as the seemingly best modern way to put your thoughts or opinion global as soon as possible. It had also been the method used by the previously mentioned Nathan Ellington.

Moving on to T'Bolton to my mind it is Sordell's excuse along with his colleagues as the return of the hostile Old Den atmosphere frightened them and they used the alleged racist nature of Millwall fans as the reason for their getting beat!

Naturally, it gives the FA another chance to scrutinise the number one public enemy Millwall, I cannot think where 'No One Likes Us' came from!

Steve Claridge on the Football League Show on Saturday night, said that Millwall is not a racist club, which he reiterated several times also adding how much work the club had done on eradicating any element of racist abuse. He said Racism is not the norm and if there was any racist abuse it is a very small minority, a sentiment that was also broadly echoed by black player Danny Shittu who was playing his second spell at Millwall.

People who want to believe the Millwall are racist ethos, unlike those who make assumptions based on the media, Claridge knows Millwall as he was actually at the club himself for several years so understands the reality of Millwall, not the preconceived racist ethos that the media seem to have.

This preconception gives black players who have had a nightmare or been ineffective against us the option of latching straight on to the Racist angle on f***ing Twitter this without their having reported any abuse to the match Officials, the Old Bill or match Stewards during the game when the alleged abuse happened. Let us be honest if they were that offended by the alleged abuse they should report it straight away not Tweet away from the ground in isolation, which is the cowards' isolation bullshit way out.

Sordell's accusation was effectively blown out of the water in early November 2012 when a 13-year-old boy was apparently found to have been racially abusive to Sordell.

No one else, as had been suggested, had been found to have abused him racially the Den was not like a Ku Klux Klan meeting or the Nuremburg Rally as was implied by the media after Sordell's Tweet/Twat or whatever it is called.

The FA and Bolton Wanderers accepted that Millwall's having offered to put him through one of the clubs education programmes, Millwall for All (formerly known as the Millwall Anti-Racism Trust) was closure of the racism issue, the boy also apparently wrote a letter to Marvin Sordell offering his apology, which was accepted.

What about Sordell writing to Millwall fans to apologise for his unfounded racist abuse shit storm! His Dear John never writes tactic led to him getting slagged off at the New Den on Saturday 21st November 2015 when he played against us for his new club Colchester United, he was warmly greeted not with any racist abuse but as he had been at Reebok Stadium with ugly and fish chants from the CBL, towards where his team were kicking towards in the first half, we must have upset him as he was substituted at half time, sorry to see him go, er no I wasn't.

No bloody way did that happen and neither will the media ever adopt a fair unbiased perspective whenever they deal with anything Millwall fan related, that would mean that their preconceptions would have to be rewritten, so too much hard work for the bone idol journalists!

White's v Blacks: How Football Changed a Nation

There was a Testimonial match on 16th May 1979 for Len Cantello of WBA played at the Hawthorns between a team made up solely of White players versus a team made up solely of black players.

It was undoubtedly a time when Racist abuse towards Black footballers was rife there is certainly no way you could deny that and this documentary with Adrian Chiles highlighted how bad it was for black players like Cyrille Regis, Brendon Batson and Laurie Cunningham, and when asked where it was bad Regis said Millwall and Chelsea, and Batson mentioned a deluge of bananas from

West Ham United, however this may surprise you the footage they used was all largely from The Panorama Millwall Documentary, Harry the Dog fighting on the terraces but also linked with National Front footage and highlighting Racist Literature on sale outside the Old Den, now whilst recruitment in the far right groups obviously happened at Millwall it also happened at football clubs with white working class backgrounds nationwide, so the Beeb decided to be lazy and just use Millwall, as everyone knows what they are like, or not like if you know the real world as we Wall fans do.

The Documentary focused on the small amount of Black Professionals playing at the time, and conveniently forgot to mention Trevor Lee 1975-1978 and Phil Walker 1975 – 1979 at Millwall, or the fact that one of Millwall's Top Boys was Tiny aka Ian Garwood all of whom Tiny, Trevor and Phil were all black and well-loved at Millwall, strange they missed that out eh!!!

To Prove That Millwall Are Not The Ku Klux Klan Here's The Evidence Section –

I would just like to conclude this section with a list, I have mentioned most of these players elsewhere in this section in particular but I thought I would include a list of all the Black Millwall players I could recall playing for Millwall sorry if I have left anyone out, -

1. Nadjim Abdou
2. Benik Afobe
3. Patrick Agyemang
4. Adebayo Akinfenwa
5. Tobi Alabi
6. Calvin Andrew
7. Steve Anthrobus
8. Jordan Archer
9. Chris Armstrong

10. Carl Asaba
11. Moses Ashikodi
12. Phil Babb
13. Zoumana Bakayogo
14. Shaun Batt
15. Jason Beckford
16. Omar Beckles
17. Marcus Bignot
18. Hameur Bouazza
19. Bobby Bowry
20. Matthew Briggs
21. Mark Bright
22. Byron Bubb
23. Darren Byfield
24. DJ Campbell
25. Noah Chesmain
26. Leon Constantine
27. Paris Cowan-Hall
28. Shaun Cummings
29. Jesse Debrah
30. Shaun Derry
31. Dion Dublin
32. Bruce Dyer
33. Lloyd Dyer
34. Jermaine Easter
35. Craig Eastmond
36. Carlos Edwards
37. Preston Edwards
38. Marvin Elliott
39. Tom Elliott
40. John Fashanu
41. Aboubacar Fofana
42. Liam Feeney
43. Ryan Fredericks

44. Ricardo Fuller
45. Ali Fuseini
46. Michael Gilkes
47. Dale Gordon
48. Lewis Grabban
49. Gavin Grant
50. Kim Grant
51. Andy Gray
52. Willy Guéret
53. Magaye Gueye
54. Jethro Hansen.
55. Barry Hayles
56. Danny Haynes
57. Justin Hoyte
58. Kiernan Hughes-Mason
59. Paul Ifill
60. Phil Ifil
61. Sammy Igoe
62. Andy Impey
63. Simeon Jackson
64. Glen Johnson
65. Juan Maldonado Jaimez
66. Trésor Kandol
67. George Lawrence
68. Trevor Lee
69. Kevin Lisbie
70. Samy Mawene
71. Christian Mbulu
72. Mark McCammon
73. Izale McLeod
74. James Meredith
75. Tamika Mkandawire
76. Karl Moore
77. Stefan Moore

78. Guy Moussi
79. Dany N'Guessan
80. Gifton Noel-Williams
81. Jonathan Obika
82. Leke Odunsi
83. Fred Onyedinma
84. Karleigh Osborne
85. Vincent Péricard
86. Jason Price
87. Jason Puncheon
88. Mark Quigley
89. Therry Racon
90. Steven Reid
91. Wesley Reid
92. Theo Robinson
93. Trevor Robinson
94. Mahlon Romeo
95. Robbie Ryan
96. Bas Savage
97. Danny Senda
98. Adrian Serioux
99. Daniel Severino
100. Richard Shaw
101. Danny Shittu
102. Josh Siafa
103. Jay Simpson
104. Jordan Stewart
105. Andros Townsend
106. Liam Trotter
107. Nathan Tyson
108. Etienne Verveer
109. Phil Walker
110. Danny Wallace
111. Tony Warner

112. Curtis Weston
113. Marvin Williams
114. Tony Witter
115. Keaton Wood
116. Jermaine Wright
117. Chris Zebroski

Sorry do not show the list of black Millwall first team Players past and present to Nathan Ellington one of our accusers listed previously, or he might think it is a conspiracy!!!

Probably say what only 117 black players excluding Youth and Young players, that is only enough for 10 all black teams, Millwall you racist bastards!!!! In opposition to this conjecture this list only includes players in first team or squad not U23 players who had not yet moved up, this list was to conclusion on 2018/2019 season.

Maybe now I have blown the black player ethos out of the window they could focus on there are NO Asian players, of a Indian/Pakistani/Bangladeshi persuasion, nice try who does!!!

Just Because You're Paranoid Doesn't Mean That They're Not Out To Get You!

Moving away from racism topping up our most loathed status and completing the unholy trinity of Millwall and Dennis Wise, we added Kevin Muscat to our squad. We do get some small crumbs of complimentary tabloid reporting, however even these are invariably offset in the same article by sarcastic references to us fans, our No One Likes Us persona, our Hooligan reputation and not forgetting Muscat and Wise's previous misdeeds or other real or imagined misdemeanours.

Having Wisey as manager, Muscat as captain, Jody Morris and Graham Stack's sexual assault accusations, the Ashikodi/McCammon incident and Stan Ternent's racist accusations naturally gave the less charitable element of the press an excellent opportunity to slag us off, which they naturally did. Highlighting the normal media requirement only to accentuate the negative on 23rd February 2002 there was a charity match between Millwall and Middlesbrough fans to raise money for Colin Cooper and his family at the tragic loss of his son Finlay. This was a match that raised more than £2,000; a positive act that was largely ignored by the press at the time.

In addition to my true Millwall chapter earlier on to also show how good we really can be there was another game played between both sets of fans for the Finlay Cooper Fund cause at the New Den on Friday 16th May 2008. this was ignored as well from what I saw or didn't see,

Amazingly, the press missed an opportunity to castigate us, for example -

They did not notice the 'Legia Warsaw Hools' graffiti that was accompanied by a Nazi swastika, which used to be found near the railway arches in Bolina Road but has subsequently been painted over.

Surely this must have been proof positive that Millwall were in league with the International Fascist Alliance (Football Division),

In a similar vein there was the weird incident at home in late 2008 when a bloke with a Millwall hat on, stood at the Entrance/Exit at the front of the upstairs part of the upper CBL during the game and unfurled a Legia Warsaw scarf over his head and held it aloft as his mate took pictures of him, he was pelted with tea/coffee and abused by all and sundry and he then came up the stairs towards the liquid missile thrower and looked like he wanted a row, before the Jobsworth on duty chucked the two Poles out of the CBL,it was a bizarre situation, why he thought doing any of what he did was a good idea, God alone knows!

As I mentioned previously from Rangers UEFA Cup Final Riot and the Chelsea v Man Untited Premiership rumpus in 2007/8 just because Millwall fans are not actually involved is naturally no reason not to blame or mention us. For example on TV reports repeated on the 'Hooligans' documentary Sam Hammam was shown comparing the atmosphere that Leeds could expect at Ninian Park as like the Old Den but 10 times worse! Really?

I do not think Wimbledon's visits to the Old Den were any indicator of the true hostile nature of our old ground or the waves of hatred aimed at the opposition that the Old Den could muster, due to opponent lethargy on our part. That said Ninian was very hostile and the Cardiff City v Leeds United FA Cup game, to anybody with half a Football brain, was a cast iron certainty trouble game; in fact, I almost videoed the match, because I knew it would go off whatever happened. Nonetheless, the aggro was somehow reported in the media as though it was a surprise, not to anyone who has actually been to a game at Cardiff City or involving Leeds United it was not. For some reason after the Cardiff/Leeds trouble 'Harry the Dog' and the Luton Riot was, trotted out. I can only assume that they did not have enough footage from Ninian from the live Sky game to put on television, so again had to resort to the stock Millwall footage.

My main reason for mentioning this game however was because the events provoked other guests to Ninian to pop their heads above the ramparts and complain about the sort of welcome their club's fans had received in the hillsides; rampaging Soul Crew, rabid hostile crowds, English hating, missile throwing Welshman, you know the sort of thing.

The complainant that I found particularly amusing was Bristol City's Chief Executive, who appeared on the Hooliedoc and in the press; he said that missiles had been thrown at his team and fans. I can only assume that he has never had the pleasure of a trip to his own ground as an away fan. The phrases 'Let he who is without sin cast the first stone' (or seat!) and 'Pot calling the kettle black' spring to mind.

To continue the Cardiff theme and how Millwall somehow have to be included in any Football hooligan reporting The Sun ran a story on the 16th February 2002 under the heading –

'Hooligan Blow For Bluebirds'. A lovely image of a pretty little bird worn by a Welsh meathead springs to mind, which spoils it for me as a keen twitcher myself, just kidding, to continue -

This report was based on a table of NCIS figures aimed at excluding 1000 known hooligans from travelling to the World Cup 2002. it featured a league of shame top-ten list of people excluded from watching Football at grounds in England, Wales or abroad. Inevitably, the Welshman topped this list with 99 exclusions followed by Stoke City, Leeds United, Derby County, Manchester City, Bristol City, Coventry City, Wigan Athletic, Manchester United and Birmingham City. Funny how this list had clubs from the non-trouble Premiership isn't it? I am sure we were probably very high on any priority list prior to the 2002 World Cup banning orders, irrespective of our low placing on this list.

Anyway, to my main point, despite the fact that Millwall were equal 10th with Birmingham City and Hull City with only 17 exclusions, it somehow managed to warrant half the article being about us.

Our only claim to fame being that we were London's top worse side, if you see what I mean.

Mind you this was prior to our visit to Portsmouth, Wolves visit to the New Den and the Birmingham games so I am sure that we must have climbed the national chart with a bullet by the end of 2001/2.

Naturally, the Evening Standard printed a London only version of The Sun table, under the heading 'The Roll Of Dishonour' this enabled them to show Millwall sitting proudly at the top.

Millwall stated that the NCIS figures were too low and did not reflect the anti hooligan work they were doing, as borne out by more complete figures for all the Divisions shown in the press for seasons 2000/1 and 2001/2 in August 2002. The NCIS figures indicated that our arrest figures were around or well above the hundred mark for the two seasons respectively.

Millwall had 104 Banning Orders in October 2006 even though Spurs had 162 and Chelsea's had130 extra Banning Orders they only mentioned us on Teletext, charming!

The arrests tables also had a breakdown of what the arrests were for with most of the Millwall related arrests being for violent conduct or public disorder, with none for racist abuse, strange for such a supposed hot bed of racism, as had previously been implied by David Johnson in the press and John Barnes on TV in October 2002 and in a fan poll on racism published a month later.

The spectre of Football racism had come to the fore once more because at the time there had been an outbreak of racist incidents in the Champions League and at an England away game.

Unsurprisingly the fact that Millwall had only 18 arrests (14 for Football related incidents) home and away in 2002/3, down from 119 in the previous season, was not trumpeted in the media as our high figures had been previously. In fact, Millwall fruitlessly complained to ITN after they reported the new NCIS figures on August 18th 2003 by showing old Stoke Hooligan footage and implying that it was us.

Millwall were also the only side mentioned in the TV report, despite the 80% reduction in our arrests.

To further highlight the getting 'roped in' theme the figures issued in October 2004 showed Portsmouth top of the 2003/4 league for arrests with 146, largely due to the local Derby against Southampton, they also topped the banning orders for the Premiership, followed closely by Leeds United on 109 arrests and Manchester United on 108 arrests. Championship side Cardiff City again topped the total banning orders chart with 107 arrests and 160 exclusions.

This prompted their fans to chant 'We Are Top Of The League!' as part of their Hoolie boasting repertoire at the New Den on October 23rd 2004. My main reason for mentioning it though was the BBC News report that I saw managed to show footage from outside the New Den with 'Welcome To Millwall' prominently highlighted behind police cavalry, even though the report was about the aforementioned teams and English fans actions at Euro 2004 and Millwall were not in the top ten and not even mentioned on the report.

A similar thing occurred in November 2005 when there was another list of banning orders published and despite Cardiff and Leeds filling the top spot, naturally the report on BBC News was done against the backdrop of the New Den, I know the reported items I have used above are a few years old, I had just picked out what was around when I started to write this particular section, I am sure when you have read the above comparative information it will answer my query – paranoid who me!

Sun Awning Man Civilising The Natives

To complete this ramble around my mistrustful mind and to close this section on my media mistrust,

I recall in the late 1980s/early 1990s an interview with the then Old Den security adviser John Stalker, a former top plod who later plied his wares as a security grill, garage door and sun awnings sales representative on TV ads and numerous other media based outlets.

This interview, supposedly filmed live outside the Old Den, was about the security improvements and the anti-racist/local community initiatives that were improving the home fan behaviour at the Old Den. The interview shown on London TV was allegedly filmed whilst a game was in progress.

As John extolled the virtues of the new arrangements and initiatives, the background had a Millwall crowd singing the likes of – 'The Banana Boat Song'/'I'd rather be a P… than a Scouse!'/'Who the f…ing hell are you?' And 'You'll never make the station!' etc.

You get the idea? All this was beautifully segued together to fit the interview length perfectly and thereby blow dear John's 'I'm Civilising The Natives You Know!' claims clean out the water.

The chants fitted the length of the piece to perfection was this –

A) Just a happy coincidence? Or

B) Down to hours of crowd rehearsals beforehand? Or

C) Was it not really live at the Old Den on a match day? Or

D) Was it cobbled together as a 'Once Again Up Your Cold Blow Lane' Parental Advisory mega mix?

Anyone who says C or D gets a gold star. I am not paranoid am I? Am I?

John Stalker – strange name, it sounds like someone in America who follows you about in a Male toilet.

CHAPTER 8
Old Traditions Fade Away

When I was about six years old my Mum and Dad took me to Margate; this was in the era of seaside Bank Holiday Mods and Rockers battles. On this particular day in the early sixties, we were walking along the seafront, turned a corner and found ourselves in the path of hundreds of Mods fleeing from the pursuing Police and running in our direction. In an effort to get out of the way, we became pinned against a wall, where we remained until the rampaging Mods had passed.

We later went on to the beach where we discovered that the opposing factions were now engaged in wide scale fighting, for reference see the film 'Quadrophenia'.

A few years later, I was at Great Yarmouth with my parents during the skinhead era.

We were again walking along the seafront when we walked into several dozen skins in Norwich City scarves; they were heading in our direction so naturally we moved out of their way.

As the skinheads were the feared tribe at the time they effectively had the run of the seafront and took over the promenade unopposed, they then proceed to attack anyone on a motorbike, mostly the Rocker and Greaser types. I recall that they threw several motorbikes over the beachfront wall.

I only mention these incidents because they both gave me grounding for the type of incident I would encounter during my succeeding lifetime following Millwall home and away.

This chapter is not solely about Millwall but it does relate to the Hooligan traditions, the ground restrictions that we all had to endure and the fashions that the Firms have dressed in which I have seen over the years, although not exclusively about Millwall, the three sections definitely applied to us.

In the good old days, there were several general behavioural traditions that seemed to have largely faded away over succeeding years for example -

The Terrace Traditions Of –

Overhead synchronised clapping and hoisting scarves aloft mimicking The Kop's 'You'll Never Walk Alone'. This doesn't look quite the same in an all-seater ground.

Bouncing up and down, on the terrace steps to 'Knees up Mother Brown', etc in a fashion like pogoing at a Sex Pistols gig.

Bombarding the goals with toilet rolls, this often left the goalmouths looking like an Andrex puppy's ultimate fantasy. If you did not have a bog roll you could always use a bus ticket roll, as long as you remembered to take it out of the ticket machine first! I thought it funny when Loo Rolls were thrown from the away section by our fans at Leyton Orient in 2007/8, sadly they didn't cover the goal only lay on the pitch in front of us, shame!

In the terrace era even at the Old Den there was the frequent sight of acrobatic crush barrier balancers, who thought that they were Olga Korbet, only to find that they were not when they feel off! Not so much at the Den but elsewhere were the even more daft fans who thought that it was a good idea to climb up on to the terrace stand roofs, only to find that they were now standing on a rusty, shoddy corrugated iron erection that could not hold their weight. Consequently, they would often plummet to earth, leaving them with two broken legs and two months in plaster/traction for their trouble, well done!

The Boot Boy Era Traditions Of –

There were the Firm's greeting cards, which were handed out to the prostate victim who had just had the dubious privilege of encountering someone's 'Boys' at a service station, train station, tube station or outside the ground. I'm sure these cards, which usually said something like 'Congratulations You've Just met...' must have aided the victim's recovery no end knowing whose boot that they'd just had the pleasure of tasting and feeling. This is no longer a practice as far as I know. There was the away match custom of being asked 'Got The Time Mate?' To ascertain your regional identity pre attempted lamping, I suppose this is unnecessary nowadays as all the would-be assailant needs to do is wait for the victims' mobile phone to chirp up with an often incriminating Club specific ring tone and bingo!

There was the Police policy of confiscating the boot laces from your 12 hole Dr Martens in the skinhead era, as they also used to do for the East End Southend Bank Holiday invasions. In pre segregated grounds 'End' taking was a great Aggro era tradition, it wasn't unusual to stand at an away match and watch a Millwall Boys covert operation take place in the home end. This was carried out by fans without colours who would infiltrate the opposition sections. What then happened was that the home end would burst into a flurry of boots and fists as the invaders announced their identity; the crowd would then open up around the trouble in a schoolyard 'Fight, Fight, Fight!' Fashion. The usual outcome of these skirmishes was that the Police would wade in to extract the invaders and then either march them to the Police meat wagons waiting outside or back to their own fan section via the cinder track, usually to the plaudits of the waiting fans, more of which later. I saw Millwall do this at many away grounds but very very very very rarely if ever saw anyone foolish enough to attempt it at the Old Den. There was also the 60s/70s sight of mass pitch invasions, more of which later. The film 'I.D.' highlights these Bovver Boy era customs perfectly.

More Bloody Fences!

The combination of the practices that I mentioned in the Old Den chapter allied to the type of Bovver boy traditions I have mentioned above, meant that the powers-that-be eventually decreed that perimeter and segregation fencing were required at grounds nationwide, at which point watching Football became a fairly unpleasant experience. Perimeter/Segregation fences were naturally an attempt to keep rabid hordes like ourselves out or in, whichever you prefer.

Whilst this fencing was obviously boom-time for fence erectors, it meant that we fans were now effectively in cages. It became an era when live Football watching was a real restricted view, often-claustrophobic experience at best, particularly on a small terrace on a crowded day.

Something that came about as a result of the segregation policy was to mark your arrival by draping flags on the fences, this applied at home but more particularly at away matches, where it was obligatory to drape the pitch-side fences with country and club flags at the ground as soon as we arrived. Another problem was that some grounds also had anti-vandal climb proof paint on the fences, like Southend for example, this sticky stuff was impossible to get out your clothes even if you had just brushed against it accidentally.

Whilst I moaned in my other books about the draconian and sinister perimeter fencing at the Old Den to highlight just how bad they could have been …

In 1985 the Chelsea Directorial Leader Ken Bates said that the fences at Chelsea were an insufficient deterrent after a pitch invasion and on-pitch trouble at Stamford Bridge.

He was interviewed on television where he gave his proposals to put up electrified fences around Chelsea's pitch, good to his word he actually did this, luckily or otherwise the fences were never turned on and had to be dismantled.

Whilst his plans probably seemed just the ticket to the 'They should gas them like badgers!' brigade, sadly he was stopped in his tracks when it was pointed out that his ideas contravened the Geneva convention on human rights, especially the extra items he proposed like the Piranha filled moat, machine-gun towers, jack-booted crowd control stewards armed with Bullwhips and electric cattle prods and the pack of rabid jackals that he proposed using to keep order outside the ground.

It is a shame to see such sensible ideas stymied isn't it.?

Just in case you are wondering, I have made most of this up except for the part about the electrified fences, which was true!

As an aside, in October 2001, Leeds United fans accused Ken Bates of mooning at them at Elland Road, at a particularly volatile Leeds/Chelsea games, which he strenuously denied. This was reported in an article in The Daily Express. They should have had an arse identity parade to see who the culprit was! Perhaps they should have persued it when he was their Chairman?

The original fences mainly came about because the 1970s were awash with pitch invasions and on pitch bundles. Millwall at home had a Tony Martin dealing with a burglar type of mentality, so anybody who went pitch-side to confront us would find half the home crowd joining them, which was not to be recommended, so these types of away fan invasions did not happen at Millwall.

However it was commonplace to see fighting on TV, normally for some reason from the Baseball Ground at Derby County! These incidents were shown on the new-fangled colour TV's at the time and the rucks were a remarkable sight to behold, especially if viewed today.

Do not forget that the 70s was an era that taste forgot and whilst the violence was not funny

I suppose, the dress sense and hairdos certainly were. Imagine if you can Trench (coat) warfare with hundreds of opposing Gordon Grimley's fighting it out. These 'flair' ups would often resemble an outbreak of hostilities at a Bay City Rollers convention. Picture if you will a bloody great Western saloon style brawl breaking out on the pitch with the combatants dressed in the fashions of the day for example – Bloody great bell-bottomed jeans, trench coats, loon pants, 'Wigan Casino' high waisted snug fit trousers, ideal for the fuller figure, not!

Tartan scarves and tartan inlays on your flared jeans, 'Rubettes' style caps, chequered V-neck sweaters, 'Starsky and Hutch' style tie up jumpers, cheesecloth grandad shirts, huge collared shirts, multiple hooped lurid coloured Tank tops, 'Budgie' jackets, kaftans and bib and braces dungarees like a kids TV presenter.

Accessorised by the obligatory silk scarf tied around the wrist or in the belt loop; or a woollen scarf tied around your neck and the obligatory hairdo like a heavy-metal band.

Unfortunately unless you wore Dr Martens the popular footwear of the day was not ideal 'Good hiding' attire, footwear like – Stack heeled shoes, cowboy boots and in some instances clogs.

My God what a sight it all was! Unmistakeably violent whilst at the same time hilarious if viewed today, when the true horrendous nature of just how naff this particular eras clothes were.

At the time nobody seemed to notice. I suppose if the 'casual' ethos had existed at the time the 'I have got to out dress my opponent' would have led to the combatants looking like Jason King, ask your dad. For a slightly more modern example, see Austin Powers, ghastly!

I suppose all Football crowds do is to follow the prevalent dress trends of the day, hence the above fashion disasters, thank God though that the more extreme 80s fashions did not find their way into Football attire, imagine a tear up between hundreds of New Romantics or Adam Ant look alikes!

To finish this chapter a friend encountering Millwall at a pub in Waterloo –

Dr Jekyll And Mr Millwall

A long time mate of mine Lee Glasby, who supports Arsenal but follows rugby more as a rule, told me of an incident at a pub in Waterloo.

He and his rugby mates were on their way back from a Saturday match at Twickenham and they decided to have an alcohol top up in the appropriately named 'Hole in the Wall' pub near Waterloo station. For a laugh they decided to re-route the traffic by piling up some boxes and cones in the road near to the pub. They then went into the pub to watch the ensuing traffic chaos and got talking to a bloke who had seen what they had been doing who thought that it was hilarious.

They bought each other drinks and had a good laugh. During the chat, he told them that he was a Millwall fan. Lee said that he was a nice bloke and they were getting on like a house on fire.

Suddenly some Wolves fans came into the pub at which point the Millwall bloke transformed from his amiable Dr Jekyll and Mr Hyde took over. He reached into the back of his coat and pulled out a large machete type weapon, which he waved around his head towards the Wolves fans, whilst informing them that he was Millwall, very sensibly the boys from the Black Country got on their toes sharpish and ran out through the pub door.

With his mission accomplished, Dr Jekyll returned and he replaced the blade into the back of his coat. He then picked up his drink and carried on speaking to Lee and his mates as if nothing had happened. Lee said that he had never seen such a transformation before and he played rugby! Consequently, he naturally thinks that when Millwall is upon us we are all like this.

CHAPTER 9
From Village Bobby To Robocop

You cannot have a Millwall book without mentioning the police continually somehow, we are inextricably linked. They have obviously raised their ugly head in my other Millwall books and here they are again!

As anyone of my vintage knows years ago, policing at Football matches seemed to be far more disorganised. It was certainly very different from today's technology mad world with its Riot Police, CCTV, Video camera crews, mobile Video vans, Robocop's, Hoolie vans, mass cavalry and helicopters, Pepper Spraying well at least that is what it is like at Millwall matches.

In the early days their shambolic unreadiness for what was gathering apace around them in a Football sense, meant that initially the bovver boys had carte blanche to run amok at will.

Police escorts were scarce, if they existed at all, in the late 60s/70s, making a trip to or from many tube or railway stations a real 'watch your backs' treat.

It was also always a pleasure to come out of an away ground in the era of Police inertia to find a large home fan contingent waiting to give you a cheery farewell, if you catch my drift.

West Ham and Chelsea were good spots for this practice in London, as was Millwall's Old Den for away fans obviously.

The real difference today from the birth of hooligans in the 1960s is that whilst violence still goes on, as we at Millwall know only too well, the Police state has stepped up alarmingly with large presences, surveillance, covert or otherwise and Police intelligence.

The grounds have obviously also, in the main, become all-seater during the modern era and therefore

I presume more Policeable. Whilst there is far less trouble inside the grounds themselves, it has merely been switched to the surrounding areas.

As my years of watching Millwall home and away have passed the policing and surveillance techniques have come on a bundle, this has been combined with an erosion of my civil liberties as an ordinary/non-hooligan Football supporter. Following Millwall all over the country for many years has meant that I have seen the Police numbers and equipment escalate and multiply first-hand. Practically all of Millwall's away matches are like visiting a Police convention and it seems that constabulary nationwide are very keen to show us their new toys.

For those of you who do not know what following the 'Wall is like from a policing perspective I thought that I would try to compile a list of the changes that I have seen or had to endure following the 'Wall -

1. I have been body searched and had any bags or pockets rifled through by Police and or stewards on a very regular basis.

2. I have had to endure dry, i.e. alcohol-free, trains (and coaches) very very regularly. I assume on Police insistence, with any train leaving London and heading vaguely in the direction where we are playing having this restriction imposed. Naturally, this policy has meant that on numerous return trips from nightmare away matches when a Light Ale would have been very much appreciated it has been denied to us.

3. I have had to pass through metal detectors like the type you would pass through at an airport having to first empty out my pockets on to a side table. This was at particularly volatile games – West Ham United away for example. This could have been tricky if done in my youth as I had a pin and plate in my leg following an

operation on a dislocated hip, which would have been a bit difficult to explain.

4. On the way to grounds I have been held in numerous train station Police escorts surrounded by riot Police, Police vans, barking Police Alsatians and cavalry, I have then been marched all around the houses to avoid the home fans and then been marched all over the shop back to the station again after the game. We are then invariably held for an eternity until the homebound train arrives, we also usually have Police patrolling up and down the trains as well.

5. I have been held in the ground for anything up to an hour or even longer at many an away match in the past, whilst the Police were clearing the streets, whether this was for our safety or the home fans, I could not tell you.

6. I have been filmed up close and personal hundreds of times both at home and away, via CCTV, Police hand-held video cameras, Digital stills cameras, the modern Police mobile video vans and not forgetting the Police eye in the sky helicopters.

7. I have been confronted by a huge Police/riot Police turnout at practically everywhere that I have been with the Lions, including any railway station platform where we could conceivably get off.

8. I have seen the Sixties/Seventies bobby on the beat evolve in to today's Robocop. Many of whom very often do not appear to be wearing any identification numbers. In addition, at the Southampton FA Cup game at the New Den in February 2003, some of the Police also had the bottom halves of their faces covered with black scarves.

9. I have seen and been on the receiving end of many Police cavalry charges, when they have attempted to re-enact the Charge of the Light Brigade, there's nothing like having a bloody great horse champing at the bit and frothing at the mouth hurtling in your direction to get the old heart pumping I can tell you!

10. I have routinely had to suffer Police coach searches, without a search warrant in sight.

Presumably, they are looking for booze or asylum-seekers or

whatever is supposedly hidden in the coach's hold.

11. I have had to suffer matches being moved about Willy – Nilly, with days and times being dictated by the Police, presumably in an effort to prevent us from travelling. Consequently, I have had to get up in the middle of the night to go to games played at noon up North because of the above.

12. I have had to suffer away travel bans, when I have personally done nothing to warrant it.

13. I have had to prove that we have actually come in a car and 'No thanks we didn't want to go back to the station four miles away.' Still doesn't sometimes work as we have had to march within the Train escort and then have to be let back in the direction where our car was bloody parked, honest!

14. I have physically been pushed or hit with a truncheon by the Police when I was innocent.

15. Finally, I have had to give up photographs and prove my identity in recent years in order to complete the mug shot gallery at Millwall, compiled at the Police's behest, in order to be able to get a season ticket or membership.

16. We had Police Horses join us away at Bristol Rovers' Eastville on the terraces, and at Chelsea and Leyton Orient in the Tube Station.

These are just some of the restrictions that I have had to put up with.

I say 'I have' I really mean, 'We have', as we Lions have all had to suffer the above.

The Police's actions home and away are now so commonplace for a Millwall fan that you almost don't notice how much crap that we regularly have to put up with any more, so insidious has it all become.

I would also say that there is a certain amount of truth in the theory that if you treat people like criminals, as the Police normally do us, then you will invariably get criminal behaviour back, whereas if you treat people with respect you will usually get respect back.

To lighten the mood an amusing item well something that amused me when we played Bristol City in a night match at the New Den in October 2000. With the East upper in a volatile mood, the riot Police moved in and Police cavalry came around behind the goal heading towards this section.

Mad Ted was getting excited at the prospect of trouble and he was pointing out the Police's action to me rather than watch the match, consequently, I to was drawn to watching the cavalry moving around the cinder track. We discussed how they were going to get the horses into the upper tier.

Some possibilities -

1) Were they going to take a good run up and bound with one mighty leap like Champion the Wonder Horse on steroids, into the upper tier?

2) Were the horse and rider going to be hoisted up by the Police tug-of-war team by a rope and dropped into the upper tier?

3) Would they use a Police helicopter to pick the horse and rider up on a harness like air-sea rescue and drop them into the upper tier?

4) Would they simply walk up the stairs?

Presumably unable to decide on which was the best course of action they turned around and headed back behind the goal. Shame, having an impromptu Police horse of the year show would make good half time entertainment. Well it amused me anyway.

For comedy value I will also like to add Police in Scunthorpe who have silver tits on their helmets, I mean Police Helmet not undercarriage!!!

I have an idea for the Police, which they have yet to try -

On the hooligan documentaries, it said that large-scale violence was curbed when combatants started going to Acid house parties and raves and were consequently too 'Loved up' to run amok or organise any offs. Here's an idea why not only play Acid house music at games, hand out spliffs, etc at the turnstiles and give everyone a whistle, on second thoughts perhaps not the last one.

This would make the crowd too chilled out to cause trouble, I am sure they must already do this at some club's grounds given the clubs with atmospheres that seem like they have been sponsored by the Noise Abatement Society.

Mr Away Plod Traditions

For me, rather like the first swallow's appearance highlighting the arrival of summer, hearing my first Police siren and spotting my first Police helicopter at an away ground heralds the new season's arrival, only when I hear and see these signs do I really start getting into the spirit of it all.

As I said due to our reputation, and the home town Police's perception of us, games are moved all over the shop, seemingly adopting a f*** your luck getting train tickets cheaply via APEX, where very often the game that was on X is now on Y, so all your train fare money allied to any outlay made on lodgings for an up north trip goes totally sideways! Additionally it also appears that the Police dictate the early coach departure times, so that our coaches can meet up with a Police escort at a designated spot and at a designated time.

If you are on the first coach of a convoy, it can mean a long wait; because the Police hold the first coach that arrives at the rendezvous point until all the other coaches arrive, as they want to take all of them in together. Not all away trips have escorts but for the games that do the Police clamour on board to give us a pep talk about our behaviour, etc. As the Police officer goes – 'No Bad Language, No Racial Abuse, No Running On The Pitch, Blah! Blah! Blah!' Everyone on board is thinking – 'Yeah, Yeah, Yeah! Just Take Us To The Bloody Ground Mate!' They also very often search our coaches looking for any dodgy items, on many occasions whilst we are at the match, I know this is true because they have told us that they would be doing it, which was nice of them, a bit like a burglar making an appointment, however, it is just a bit of an infringement wouldn't you say? Even though most of the 'Boys' invariably go by train or under their own steam, I bet that it still doesn't stop the Police having a preconceived idea of what sort of people they're likely to encounter on our club coaches. I am sure that they must board every Millwall coach thinking that they are about to encounter a bunch of desperate cutthroats, however what they will invariably find is that the 'normal' hardcore coach community consists of young kids, girls, middle-aged men and women, old men and women, some less than combative males and several blokes who look like they maybe a handful, more specifically there is a disabled bloke called Kenny Denham who travels everywhere and who is in a wheelchair. In other words, the coach community is a cross section of the general population; this must be a real shock to them the first time that they board a Millwall coach.

The Police at away matches very often use German shepherds to keep us in check, especially for train escorts, for some reason there are always strange people, at full moon time or otherwise, who decide that it is a good idea to bark at these already agitated and possibly rabid creatures to wind them up even more. It is just another part of the customary 'We've arrived' invasion posture that Millwall adopt at away matches.

As an aside at away games there are often Police on duty at the match, or in the escort, who support our opponent's rivals and who wish us good luck in stuffing them.

Finally a marketing idea for the Police -

With the amount of video footage that they take of all of us at an away match or home match, why don't they raise funds for their Policeman's balls, etc by selling personalised copies of each person's away trip? Like a football version of Ed TV or The Truman Show, if they got their fingers out they could sell these videos to us as we left the ground after the match. More than enough to finance Big Away Police Operations.

'Evening Wall!'

The Old Bill idea in 2011 seemed to be lets all get Riot geared up and kettle Millwall, is this because we had the audacity to complain about Millwall fan Ian Tomlinson being killed by the Police unlawfully, so they must show us how tough they are.

You may think that I have Millwall paranoia, but at home v Cardiff City in 2010/11 they blocked off Bolina and Zampa Road to Millwall fans, only allowing Cardiff coaches down there, they would not allow us to drive on the same road until the Cardiff Ciy coaches had passed, only being able to get in to our own ground via Surrey Canal Road or Stockholm Road. What other clubs have these restrictions imposed on them at home??

Away in 2011/12 at Southampton we parked in a car park behind the home stand, so we get kettled by fully equipped for battle Old Bill, and are not allowed to go back this way despite being told to go home, I pointed out to the wooden top that if you let us go back to our car the four of us that drove there would, so what do they do force us to go in completely the opposite direction with Police Dogs and their truncheons wielding, the eldest one of us was allowed to go back to our car, but we had to walk the streets of Southampton trying to relocate the bloody thing, which we luckily did as Dave who they let go this way did not have his mobile on him so we three who were forced the other way had no means of contacting him, what fun.

Birmingham City away 2011/12 inside the ground we had a line of police behind the mesh next to us, facing us, behind them some 50 metres or so away Birmingham youth gave us verbal, so we replied, who do the Police warn for this ? Us, we did point out we were only responding to the abuse we were getting and they should talk to them, did they? Did they bollocks!

Outside they had a line of meat wagons along the road and we exchanged pleasentaries with the hundreds of Birmingham walking behind the vans, the riot Police then start kettling us, with riot shields, truncheons and Shields, they maced one kid, and were pushing people willy nilly, we naturally reacted thus giving them an excuse to be so heavy handed in their opinion, again we parked in a car park a short walk away, which the geniuses would not let us back in to, Paul and Dave got in me and Nathan the remaining two were held behind Police lines, I did point out that we were f***ing parked there, and despite pushing us back after a few minutes they opened the Car Park gate and let us in, not exactly Storming Norman or Napoleon is it, had it not occurred to them that if you are heavy handed and treat people like shit forcibly they will respond, which must be what they wanted in the first place, that is the joy of having a reputation of Public Enemy Number One, like Millwall have!

Found this in Birmingham Mail -

Police arrest 12 fans during Birmingham City's match against Millwall at St Andrew's. A dozen arrests were made yesterday as Birmingham City beat Millwall at St Andrew's.

But West Midlands Police said the game passed largely without incident.

A police spokesman revealed that six Millwall and six home supporters were arrested for public disorder and alcohol-related offences before, during and after the match at St Andrew's, which Birmingham City won 3-0.

And he said that two police officers were treated for slight injuries at the ground.

A total of 17,901 home and 1,064 away fans attended the game.

The police helicopter was heard overhead before and after the 90 minutes. Match commander Chief Inspector Ian Marsh said:

"There was an effective policing operation put into place before, during and after the match.

"That meant that officers were able to deal quickly with any of the minor offences that took place.

"The small number of offences were caused by a very small number of fans from either side.

"The majority of fans who attended did so with good intentions and were there to enjoy the match."

There had been concern that the game might attract trouble because Millwall fans have a history of hooliganism.

What I thought funny in the above was the police implying that what they had done was an 'Effective Policing Operation' – Really!!!! Talk about load of f*cking old b*llocks, or do f*cking what?

Also ' Millwall's history of hooliganism' – Not denying that, but apparently in the twat who wrote it's mind Birmingham City don't have a hooligan reputation, okay ever heard of Apex or the Zulu Army, you f*cking prick, perhaps you should read Caroline Gall's 2006 book 'Zulus: Black, White and Blue: the Story of the Zulu Warriors Football Firm'.

The c**t who wrote this one eyed loving delusional nasty Cockneys not Brummies darling's, bullshit must be related to Karren Brady with the b*llocks that she spouted re large crowd trouble at a game at St Andrews in the early 2000s.

Obviously with his head up his Arse attitude it is all our fault and f*** all to do with Birmingham City or the Old Bill being heavy handed with a let's treat people like shit attitude.

I have had to put up with this sort of shit for much more than decades and it makes me f*cking sick!

Our passionate nature and our reputation will never change as we do have the occasional spectacular tear up, see the following chapter.

What It Is Like To Be Millwall Especially Away, You Wouldn't Bloody Believe It

The truth of attending Millwall games for those that do not know would be a yeah righto of course it is like that response.

I had a Brain Injury and Headway East London a Brain Injury Charity where I volunteer with fellow Brain Injured people, go on various trips. Ally one of the former staff there who organised some trips and was at Millwall when I had a party in 2011, suggested that it would be a good idea to go to a game at Millwall with the Members as there are dozens of football fans there.

I said no problem I can easily get you tickets but I will warn you that attending games at the New Den for the uninitiated will be a bit of a culture shock so need to be carefully chosen.

I said I will give you a list of home games and tell you which ones to go to and which ones to avoid, for example games like West Ham United/Cardiff City/Leeds United etc, because there will be closed streets around the ground to protect away fans from us, there will be Police everywhere, you will see the full range dogs, horses Hoolie vans, Riot Police, helicopters etc.

Anyone who has not seen this before would think what the hell is happening here!

I went to a Police Open Day at Bow Police Station, essentially to talk about a project for Brain Injured people like myself called The Justice Project, a card carrying scheme to highlight that your actions may be caused by your Brain Injury, this was established by Headway a Brain Injury Charity where as I said I volunteer, I spoke to a PC in the entrance way of the Police Station who said what a good idea this ID was, I said what is to see inside?

He said Riot Gear, Police Batons, Police Dogs, Police Horse Cavalry, Hoolie Van etc, etc, I said I will give that a miss mate I am Millwall and have probably seen more of that up close and personal than you will ever see!!

As an example of the sense of horror what to us is normal is perceived by non-Millwall fans, on a Saturday in 2013, a non-football mate of mine the late Bob Heffer and I were watching a boat race that started in the Isle Of Dogs. We tried to get to the Tower of London area to see the race from that part of the river, unfortunately there was an EDL march through Whitechapel and the City, so they diverted buses all over the place in East London.

After a right palaver we made our way via Limehouse DLR to

443

Tower Gateway DLR when we arrived there, we found that most if not all pubs were shut, and all the roads were strewn with Riot Police blocking anyone going down any of them.

Bob said what the bloody hell is this, I said this? It means nothing to me mate, we get this every bloody away game, piece of piss to me.

The most OTT Police/Steward State I have seen in UK, which has some stiff competition as you will know from other events that I have mentioned in my books, was at QPR on Saturday 26th April 2014.

We arrived at White City Tube at around 1.00pm or so, we walked along the usual road past the QPR main stand, when we got there we found the road blocked by Barriers and manned by dozens of Stewards. Whilst looking at this monstrosity, we said to some QPR fans 'does everyone get this palaver?', they said 'no only you!' What a privilege eh?

This was confirmed by a new volunteer at Headway East London on the Monday after the game, as she worked in the Executive Boxes there on the day and she said that QPR had laid on special security for Millwall, great to be special isn't it?

For me it all got better, there were seven of us, the others showed the foreign stewards their tickets, that mentioned that they were Millwall and all got through, my one was looked at alarmingly by an Asian steward I said I am Millwall mate, he said you have to go around the other way, I said what ? The away end is up there you C***! He said no you have to go the other way around the ground.

I said well F*** you then but set off to walk around the ground, which I did with a Millwall veteran who had received the same response.

We walked down the road towards Shepherds Bush, where we encountered umpteen blocked roads, I said to three Coppers, what the f***ing hell is this b****ocks? One of them asked is there a problem, I said being treated like a C*** is the problem mate!

He said nothing and we headed off further down the main road, we eventually found the Away end a short while afterwards, during this route march one of my mates Simon who I was with in our group at the barrier, called me and said 'where are you mate?' I told him the bloody nonsense I had gone through and said I will see you on the away stand,

After about a twenty-minute yomp the Millwall veteran and I arrived at the correct street.

To get to the away stand we then had to go through one line of ticket checking stewards at the first barrier, only to then encounter another steward and Police strewn barrier outside the Visitors entrance, we had the tickets checked yet again, and then had to be scanned by a steward with a metal detector.

I said to a copper what next an Anal Probe? He said no we only do them on Mondays a female Steward said I will do it, I said Goodo lets go over there. She declined my suggestion and I went into the shit heap that is Loftus Road.

We only had the upper tier, which in my opinion was another rouse to stop us getting at ref Kevin Incompetent Cheating C*** Friend or the hero Rangers warriors.

To continue this we were getting it I am hard from the twats in the stand to our left, one bloke continually Wanker signing us.

This particular arsewipe annoyed me massively I was not alone in this but in my instance it prompted me to keep offering the C*** an invitation to come and join us or meet us outside.

We had decided to actually sit in the correct seats at this game, a very un-Millwall like trait, as you must have realised if you have read any of my Millwall books. Our plan was that we would have a Butchers at our Gold top priced seats, what you mean we might actually be able to see the goal below us tickets! If okay we would stay there, they were the best of a bad bunch so we stayed, in the seats three rows behind the netting that had been strewn across the first three rows to stop us dropping anything on the Rangers sitting below us. The home boys sic, were abused all the game and to them to our left we sang -

'You'll Run Down The Stairs!' which they did quick sharp let's get the hell out of here style before the end of the game.

After the final whistle the home yoof came on to the pitch and started heroically coming towards us abusing us, we greeted this with – 'Who The F***ing Hell Are You?' plus the customary 'You'll Run And You Know You Will!'

The heroes who knew that we could not get near them as we were in the Upper Tier, and surrounded by Plod, were then pushed back down to the end opposite us and not doubt disappeared home into the we attacked the Millwall fans fantasy cyber warrior mist.

Outside we had Police everywhere who we questioned and suggested what they should be bloody doing; for example we asked who had paid for this OTT Police state? Moreover, said why don't you go and arrest real criminals like Rapists, Terrorists, Nonces etc.

On the way, we sang' DVD and some what could be construed as racist abuse, that I will not include to Asians looking out of their windows at the massed Millwall contingent going past on the street, when got near to Shepherds Bush Tube we passed one side street, where their top boys LOL were giving it large behind police lines Palarse style. I decided that I should discuss with them up close why they were all mouth in the ground and cannot see your arse for dust outside the ground in the street.

Saying along the lines of we are in your manor chaps, come and big it up now, you f***ing melts!

The end of the Loftus Road story we move up North, the Midlands and Kent now -

With mass Old Bill in front of us at Bury on St George's Day 2016, we were told there was a major Police Operation in place and below is after Bury fans pre match had surged towards our section behind the goal from the stand on the side to the left in the picture below. A few things, if Bury surged at us why were we surrounded not Bury fans. If you think Bury????? Apparently, they have a hooligan reputation, or so a TV Hooligan programme said when they confronted Oldham and Rochdale.

Now I think I ought to point out that attacking Millwall is like an Amateur Boxer deciding that he will fight The Undisputed World Heavyweight Champion for his title, give it the big one behind fences and Police lines and claim a victory as Millwall largely could not get to them – thereby enhancing their supposed top boys reputation!

Back to Policing, we were held in the ground behinds a multiplication of what you see below for yonks, to protect us or some Police Intelligence Sic, when we were eventually let outside they formed Police lines in front of our own coaches.

I did say to a copper, if you let us back to the coaches, we would go home and be out of your f***ing town quicker. Does the phrase felt like I was talking to the wall, a brick wall not a Millwall mean anything?

Their ingenious plan was we had to loop around the Police lines that they would not move and then back towards coaches, a brilliant plan. I did also say to a copper do you think winding us up is a safer policy? Strangely my enquiry received no talking to response again.

Below is not Bury but Millwall's customary away Police greeting escort outside an away ground.

Another Police wheeze is to reduce our allocation, their thinking being that Millwall will be less numerous, wrong! Two classic examples of this in 2015/2016 Coventry City Ricoh Arena Saturday 16th April 2016.

Bear in mind that the ground holds 32,500, and the average Coventry City crowd that season was well below half of this.

So give Millwall 1800 tickets including the second request increase, now excuse me if I am wrong but as our end with our allocation was only a third full, the opposite end was completely empty apart from some disabled fans, and the rest of the ground was far from full, with the crowd being something over 11, 000.

So either Coventry City have got so much money they don't need the many thousands of pounds they would have got or the Police were scared of having what they considered too many Wall there.

A worse one than this came for our Final game of the season when at the time both sides were battling for a Play Off slot.

I know that they are not London based but in reality a local derby game v Gillingham away on Sunday 8th May 2016.

The brilliant police plan in this event was to only give us half an end maximum allocation, and no doubt half the end would be covered in meshing as well so less than the full allocation, our allocation turned out to be 1100 or so.

Consequently, I and many other people who are regular hardcore Millwall away fans could not get a ticket, in my case this was for the first time ever.

I know that this was also due to away regulars with a proven number of away trips per season record not taking precedence but in reality, Kent Police had caused all this.

I assume that Kent Police do know this but a lot of Millwall fans live in Kent, so what was to stop them either getting tickets in Gillingham sections having established a booking history during the season with Gillingham knowing the crap they would pull.

Alternatively, Millwall just turn up in numbers anyway with or without tickets as this is a local derby with the only other games anywhere near Millwall being Colchester United and Southend United in Essex, no London Derby at all.

Excuse me for thinking that if it all kicked off, with Millwall fans who had turned up unticketed or ticketed via their Gillingham ticket history plotted up in the home sections having got their tickets that way then the Plod had nowhere to put the unticketed Wall fans.

I suppose then they could say Millwall caused all trouble and no blame would be associated with the REAL guilty party Kent Police at all.

It was this game that forced me to write to Millwall along with other away regulars who had not got tickets, that a priority points system of Away travel should be put in place for hardcore away travellers taking precedent in any allocation, I am not saying it was solely down to me but this policy was brought in on a Home and Away basis, I myself as a normal 20 away games Millwall fan, took up an Away Season Ticket as well, so I am guaranteed a ticket no matter how piss poor the allocation as the Away Season Tickets come out of the Allocation first before any tickets are sold, more about this in a much latter chapter.

I Watched the Gillingham 2016 game with fellow Millwall mates Dave, Paul and Nathan Simms on a beamback in the Executive Lounge at the New Den, not exactly like being there, fine for a beer but hardly the same.

CHAPTER 10
A Passion For Fashion
To Bash In!

This chapter was my mad marketing ethos for the high street clothes shops and the Old Bill in these financially straightened times to make money.

When I first started to go to Football in the 1960s, pre the bovver boy era, it was a far more innocent era. It was a time when the rosette and scarf sellers outside the grounds, would extol everyone to 'Wear the colours'. It was not unusual to see fans all mixed together in their uniform of woollen scarves, bobble hats and with club rosettes pinned to their coats, rather like the happy clappy image that the TV advertising executives try to portray as the norm today I suppose.

This 'Wear the colours' dress code became none too sensible as the years passed and the A.G.G.R.O. era arrived when anonymity become preferable.

In addition to the ghastly bobble and ski hats, Deerstalkers or what looked like Bulgarian army hats that I mentioned in 'I Was Born Under The Cold Blow Lane' headwear of varying hues and designs have also appeared over the years some more examples Bronx woolly hats, Tartan caps, Pork pie hats and vile blue and white sectioned 1970s Rubettes style caps.

More recently we have have a fashionable sea of Burberry or American baseball caps, yet another example of Bloody Americanisation, what is the matter with good old English headgear?

Why not a natty cloth cap that could be waved above your head or thrown in the air at goal times as they used to do in black-and-white land? Why no Beanie hats? Why no Henley style boaters? Why no City gent style bowler hats? It worked for Alex in 'A Clockwork Orange' and in my opinion; it would be an ideal hat to wear as 'Firm' apparel. Failing that why not a Top hat? That would stop hooliganism in its tracks; can you imagine the opposing team's 'Boys' turning up in Top hats looking like Lord Snooty and his pals, having the gall to kick it off? It would be like 'Flashman the Boot Boy years'.

As with the hat, the scarf underwent fashion changes over the years as well, with various types taking centre stage. The scarves in the 1960s were usually of a woollen alternate bar of colour variety with end tassels, which used to look like your maiden aunt had knitted them.

In the 1970s, we had the tartan scarf and the silk/satin scarf, with silk-screened club affinity and again the obligatory tassels; the latter club identity types of scarves were to become an ideal trophy during the Bovver Boy era. Not forgetting the modern era's machine knitted elaborate club messaged affairs.

Following the original Hoolie era we had the casual era, prompted initially, from a Southern perspective anyway, to take the piss out of Northerners, who we assumed were all 'tasched up and wearing out of date clobber, true or otherwise it led to the wearing of Lacoste and Pringle, etc.

I know today that the prevailing fashion is club shirt and merchandise but the casual hooligan era is still alive and kicking, judging by the uniform of the 'Boys' that I have seen at home and away and portrayed on the hooligan documentaries in 2002.

The ethos still appears to be to flash the cash and out dress the opposing 'Firm'.

Initially the casual outfit was meant to throw the Police off the scent, as nobody had any identifying team colours on, apart possibly from a discreet club badge. Whilst this worked years ago today it is an identifying uniform in itself. Nowadays it would be easier to hide in plain sight by dressing in club shirts like everyone else; this would certainly confuse the Old Bill.

This was echoed by a Police spokesman on the Cardiff hooligan's documentary who said that signs outside pubs and bars that you can often find in London's West End, that say 'No Football colours allowed', have been replaced in Cardiff by signs that say that people wearing certain fashion brands would not be allowed in. Brands like Burberry, Rockport, Henri Lloyd, Lacoste, Aquascutum, Stone Island, etc, thus leaving the bar staff and bouncers having to be fashion gurus to spot the troublemakers. As the 1970s clothes era bore out, it really does not matter what attire you are wearing to give somebody a good hiding. Someone in a drip-dry Bri nylon anorak from Millets is potentially as dangerous as anyone decked out in Bond Street's finest in my opinion.

After all the likes of Harold Shipman and Fred West were not exactly fashion leaders were they?

If what was said on the 2002 hooligan documentaries was anything to go on, the idea was and still is, to out casual your opponents, if you get it wrong you could potentially end up looking like Alan Partridge or The Man At C&A. On these programmes it had quotes saying that the 'Boys' would buy new expensive clothes for a big trouble game, in much the same way that a woman might buy a new outfit for a wedding, sort of 'I can't go to Cardiff I have got nothing to wear!' How about getting a suit of armour!

There was one Chelsea fan who said that he would consider not going to a big away game if his best clothes were not available! Bizarre.

I say again that clothes mean nothing, a man in a Tank-top could be equally as dangerous. as a man dressed in John Galliano's hooligan range, probably more dangerous, after all if he is brave enough to go out dressed in a Tank-top he must be absolutely fearless.

Bearing this clothes maketh the 'Boy' ethos in mind, I am surprised that with Football's pre eminence at the moment and the seeming never left us reality of football related trouble, that a fashion group have not opened up a chain of clothes shops nationwide catering specifically for Football hooligans, they could call it 'Top Boys'. They would make a fortune, as it seems that the more that the hooligans spend on a particular item of clothing the better.

With the way that my mind works this led me to visualise a pre-season catwalk show of casual collections on 'GMTV/This Morning' and the like, something like –

'Mad Trev is sporting an Alexander McQueen original from his 'I've Done A Bit Do You Want Some?' range.

Sorry Wall not grassing but some ideas for the Police –

1) Why not do dawn raids to confiscate Hoolies clothes?

If clothes are so important to the hooligan fraternity, if the Police impounded any known Boys clothes, surely it would stop them travelling.

2) Why not put CCTV's into the top end casual clothes shops?

The Police could then nab the 'Boys' as they tried on their clobber in the changing room cubicle.

I would have thought that it would be much easier to arrest someone with the their strides around their ankles than having to publish their mug shots in the press or on the internet and then having to wade into the home stands to try to extract the offenders with the modern equivalent of the snatch squads of days gone by. If the offender did get out of the shop before they got nabbed, the Police could then always publish the CCTV strip show photos of the hooligan down to his love hearted boxers or dodgy Y-fronts that should flush them out pronto!.

3) Why not set up a 'Sting' by installing clothes shops in all the trouble club's grounds?

These could be stocked with the most desirable 'Firm' attire they could then arrest anybody trying to buy the uniform. Obviously, I am taking the piss, but why does it matter what you are wearing if all you are going to do is spill beer all over yourself, have a punch up, throw a few missiles, roll about on the floor or get involved in a blood-spattered ruck? I would have thought it would be more sensible to wear your worst and cheapest replaceable clothes. I know that the idea is to dazzle the opposition with your sartorial elegance in order to gain the element surprise, in a 'My God I cannot attack him he is wearing a £500 Designer shirt!' sort of way. It all seems like a very odd idea to me.

For Reference a version of this Chapter has also appeared in a Joint Football book called The German Ground Guide that I co-wrote with Herman Thomsen published by Amazon as an eBook in December 2016.

CHAPTER 11
Talk Your Way Out Of That!

It must be in every Millwall chairman's job description that they be a spin-doctor or a PR specialist of Alistair Campbell or Max Clifford before he was banged up proportions in order to defend the clubs fans, which they will almost certainly have to do during their tenure, usually more than once.

In my years of following the Lions chairmen Micky Purser, Alan Thorne, Reg Burr, Peter Mead, Theo Paphitis, have all had to use their media savvy diplomatic skills to defend our fans real and fictitious actions from the slings and arrows of the media, the same applied to 2008/9 and still current chairman John Berylson after all the alleged Millwall hooligans tear up at Hull City in the FA Cup and Play Off Trouble v Barnsley and Bradford City and FA Cup Semi Final v Wigan Athletic.

Many of our fans are no angels and we do have a problem of that there is no dispute, whether we are any worse than other similarly inclined club's fans I doubt.

That said we do seem to have a 'spectacular' every few years to top up our reputation, with most of the incidents lovingly captured on film or stills camera and spread around the world and the media ad nauseam – There was the FA Cup riot at Luton Town away obviously, in addition, there has been largescale trouble against Manchester City, Cardiff City, Swansea City, Rochdale and Birmingham City a few times, both home and away and Hull City away. These are just a few of the modern era events that spring to mind.

Because of the above type of incidents it can often mean that anyone offending against us are given the benefit of the doubt and deemed innocent, as happened in the 1990s when Birmingham City fans caused trouble at St Andrew's.

Consequently, a Millwall chairman must choose his defensive stance.

The options chosen so far by Millwall's hierarchy have been to either –

A) Disassociate the club from the trouble element.

B) Deny anything actually happens.

C) Back the alleged wrong doers to the hilt.

D) Threaten to bring in sanctions and ban all and sundry to appease our accusers.

E) Threaten to pull the plug on the club and walk away if the trouble continued

Alternatively, they have utilised a combination of all of the above, depending on the truth of the events and not the media speculations and gossip.

None have yet adopted the Sam Hammam eccentric 'If you can't beat them take them on a beano or employ them' stance. Can you imagine if Theo Paphitis had acted the way that Hammam did? Ye gods! If he had done the same, bad publicity would not be the word for the coverage he would have gotten.

Some other club's chairmen have adopted various different approaches over the years when their fans have caused or been involved in trouble, some examples –

'They're Not Our Real Fans'– When pressed for an explanation beleaguered chairmen simply panic and this is the first thing that comes out of their mouths just prior to putting their foot back in.

This is best countered by, 'Really how do you know?

I assume that unlike Sam Hammam Cardiff City, most chairmen probably do not know their club's 'Firm' by name, like he did with the Soul Crew.

'Convenient Blindness' – Or if you prefer the full Arsene Wenger is another policy that can be used, simply deny seeing anything. This is plausible because the executive bar is not the best place to view the real world outside.

'Take The Moral High Ground' – Another alternative is to take up a holier than thou stance and shift the blame on to the pariah club's fans. For reference see Karren Brady's strategy of 'Not my little Brummie Angels, it's those nasty Millwall ruffians again', following the mid 1990s St Andrew's game and again following trouble at Upton Park in midweek League Cup game more recently.

Talk Gibberish' – A final alternative is just to lose the plot completely and when questioned just talk nonsense, which is what Coventry's chairman did after his fans had caused trouble at Maine Road in an FA Cup tie in January 2001. He said that the troublemakers, said to number 200, must have been a rogue coach! Presumably, a 200-seater coach, a Double/Double Decker and hundreds of feet long? Sod trying to park that!

The General chairman's pat response to any trouble of ignorance/blindness or stupidity, smacks to me of 'Hand-washing' and 'Arse covering', although the other way round would be more hygienic.

There have been continual anti-hooligan campaigns by my club, often met with all the success of King Canute trying to stop the tide, additionally there have been attempts to try to tame us by softening Millwall's image and aesthetically changing certain things. For example there was the recent pointless exercise of replacing the nasty cartoon rampant Lion with two cuddly old style ones.

In the 1970s then manager Gordon Jago suggested changing the name of the club to something of an American nature, like South London Tabbies or Southwark Fluffy Cats or some such nonsense, no New Cross Rowdies then? Thankfully, this did not happen. Call us what you like people's mentality will persist; aggro is a Millwall tradition and a way of life to some, which I am sure they will wish to continue. I think in truth it is impossible for a club to eradicate an element hell-bent on mayhem, let's face it if the Police with all their resources cannot control it how can a club?

Because of the troubles in the last couple of decades, everyone had to suffer ticket and travel restrictions, with photographs and proof of address needed to get season ticket smart cards and memberships.

In 2002/3 all the home games were designated as all ticket and required a membership in order to buy tickets, a policy that was rescinded in 2003/4, when only four 'trouble' games were all ticket.

All away matches are still designated as all ticket, theoretically with no pay on the day facility available and you need to be a MSC Member or Teamcard aka Season Ticket Holder to get tickets, simply really a way of identifying people if any trouble occurs.

Whilst I thought that some of the restrictions were a sledgehammer to crack a nut, there was a beauty in having an away/home game 'Members Only' ticket policy for us and that is, in theory, Millwall have control over who they sell tickets to.

They should therefore have a record of all those at a game, with their mug shots on the club's database, aliases and dodgy addresses aside.

For an away trip, if the home club adhere to the 'all-ticket' for Millwall fans request and trouble breaks out then Millwall can justifiably say –

'We did all we could to prevent troublemakers travelling, we made it all-ticket.

Any troublemakers who are identified will face life bans and have memberships revoked.'

A masterstroke with only one drawback from a PR point that I can think of and that is that the chairman cannot now trot out the old trouble chestnut of – 'The hooligans are not our real fans.'

As they obviously are, because you sold them the tickets.

Alternatively, if the home side disobey Millwall's request to make it all-ticket for we away fans and trouble breaks out, our chairman can then justifiably say – 'We asked for it to be all-ticket.'

As an aside I heard that both of my other English Millwall Books 'Tuesday Night In Grimsby (Diary Of A Masochist)' and 'I Was Born Under The Cold Blow Lane' were in the prison lending library at Bellmarsh Prison.

These two books were brought out together in 2007 in one book in German published in Germany but renamed 'Millwall For Life' Actually 'Millwall For Life – Lebenslang Millwall'.

Lebenslang means Lifelong in German, for info.

CHAPTER 12
Eat Football, Sleep Football; Drink Too Much, Talk Bollocks!

To lighten the mood after the chapters on Millwall's alleged less savoury side, I thought I'd do a chapter on the sillier things that I have experienced first-hand or that my weird mind has conjured up -

Warming Your Cockles

When I went to Football as a young teenager, my dad would often give me a bottle of barley wine to warm my cockles prior to leaving the house especially on cold days to prepare my body for the rigours of an afternoon on the Old Den terraces, purely medicinal you understand

Having endured the match it was sensible to ward off the effects of a three-hour marrow freezing by trying to defrost myself by having a large portion of my mum's home-made stew and dumplings, followed by a thawing out process in front of a roaring fire or a bubbling central heating.

Once my blood had returned to a normal temperature, it was advisable to hibernate for the rest of the night in the warm whilst watching all the best (?) That 70s Saturday-night TV had to offer.

Nowadays with global warming and years of intrepid travelling I am more hardy, Oliver, Fool or both you take your pick, I no longer need a barley wine to bolster my resolve and I do not need a stew or a raging fire to warm me up afterwards. The succeeding year's winter visits 'Oop North' has toughened my Southern softie nature, so I can now face a night match at the likes of Oldham in February without a vest, no bother, frostbite means nothing to me!

Billy No Mates

Many years ago at the Old Den when I used to go with schoolmates, we would often stand at the front of the CBL, next to the players tunnel, one of our number Peter Gibbins used to go with his uncle John who would often act as our guardian, he still goes regularly home and away today.

At this time, the late sixties early seventies, I recall a bloke who used to stand near to us with a radio permanently stuck to his ear for the whole game. You know the sort, they seemingly take no notice of the game in front of them due to their radio enthusiasm, and they then suddenly announce the most obscure of scores to anyone within earshot apropos of nothing, score updates like -'East Fife are losing 2-1!' To humour him we would thank him and edge away, saying that we had been waiting for that score, ta. Piss taking aside a radio was a positive boon for any 'Billy No Mates' in the old days because at half time a radio was like a flame attracting a moth. People would huddle around him to catch the latest scores. This was in an era when they still used to put the scores on alphabetical scoreboards around the pitch or they had someone marching around the cinder track, with the scores on a placard rather than read them out. Once halftime was over everyone would then drift away only to invariably re-enact the Pied Piper scenario after the match. 'Follow the Trannie', as it were, was the watchword and we would all get in step with the radio man as he walked away from the ground, trying to catch the relevant scores, any stragglers who couldn't keep up would then ask the radio man's disciples what the score of such-and-such a game was. I suppose the modern technological advances like, in ear devices, headphones, club electronic scoreboards, and being able to get scores flashed up on your mobile phone have curtailed the radio messiahs, combined with the fact that clubs nowadays announce the results over the PA at half time and after the game. You can still see this creature in rare isolation today, but in years gone by if you had a radio you had many friends, albeit briefly.

'Programmes!'

In a nostalgia mode –
My now sadly deceased Mum's Sister Aunt Lily gave me some old Millwall programmes that she had found when clearing out the cupboard after her husband Dave had died, he was a Millwall supporting uncle.

This collection of programmes, although not all Millwall, contained many Millwall programmes dating back to the 1920s with the most recent from the 1950s, including a bootleg programme and a kosher match ticket for the Football League South Cup Final played at Wembley Stadium on April 7th 1945. There was a stack of them in various conditions, mostly pretty grim. Sadly, due to being skint at the particular time I sold them with my Aunt's permission and I split the money with her. My main reason for mentioning them was the weird and wonderful advertisements that they used to have in them for the likes of Mann's Brown Ale, Watneys Porter, Mackeson Stout, all of which were about 1d a gallon, through to Will's Whiffs, Rough Shag tobacco and the best powdered egg and Spam shops in the district. These type of ads rubbed shoulders with other advertisements for the finest cloth caps and waving hankies and all manner of 'snake oil' sales pitches for the latest elixir of life and miracle cure alls, my own personal favourite was along the lines of – 'Buy De Witt's Salts To Excite Your Bile.' Why on earth would I want to do that? I have only just got it off to sleep! What a peculiar world it all was.

Face In The Crowd?

In the 1970s, the old programmes used to have a competition where they printed a photo of the crowd with an individual ringed, in an 'Is This You?' style.

The possible outcome of this competition was many fold -
1) The person ringed could be happy as Larry because they had just won a prize.
2) The person ringed should have been at work and his granny's funeral excuse was now blown wide open.
3) The person ringed had told his wife/husband that he/she had to work, only to now have this excuse blown out the water, as his/her deception was now there for all to see in black and white with match and date.
4) The person ringed was a wanted criminal or wanted by the CSA and bang went there anonymity.

No wonder they stopped this programme feature, too risky.

A Suitable Case For Treatment

Football helps to keep me sane(ish), I think all the primal screaming is good for the soul; it acts like a Stress relieving pressure valve to keep me mentally healthy. I like to think of each match as two 45-minute psychiatric sessions of Primal Screaming, as you can lift the worries from your shoulders and release your aggression by shouting things like – 'You Useless C*** Ref!' For 90 minutes with only a 15 minute, 10 minutes in the old days, piss and pie break midway through. It also helps your psychiatric treatment to see the match officials and realise that there really are people far worse off than you will ever be. 'Thank you doctor see you same time next week.'

In the early days of my Football watching life, in black and white land, if a player was carried off on a stretcher, he had either broken his leg or done something equally as nasty.

With a Football crowd's customary sympathetic attitude these olden day pitch exits were often accompanied by the crowd intoning the Death March.

Nowadays, any excuse for a lay down followed by a St John Ambulance stretcher ride, or a golf buggy jaunt if you are at Reading, seems the norm. Players now writhe around in agony only to rise like Lazarus and charge about for the rest of the game like Desert Orchid on speed, when they looked on the verge of the last rites minutes before.

We have all seen players at both Dens' giving it the old 'I'm not long for this world!'

'Best call his next of kin and a Priest' routine, only for them to spring to their feet once the free kick had been awarded their way, then often having the bloody cheek to take the free-kick themselves!

Moments earlier, the only cure appeared to be an amputation now they were running about like a hyperactive three-year-old who had just eaten a 2lb bag of sugar.

Actors they maybe but what I'd like to know is what genius decided that an injured player should have to hobble to the by-line and then wait for the referee's permission to let him back on?

There have been a couple of times when a Millwall crowds medical diagnostic skills have been off a tad and a player who was being told, none too politely, that he was making a meal of it and could be left to die if required, was really injured and not just giving it the old dying swan routine.

For example, Nigel Winterburn was playing for Arsenal at the Old Den and was laid out on the pitch with the crowd's helpful cries of 'Get up you cheating #! #!!' ringing in his ears, when he had in fact swallowed his tongue and was going a fetching shade of purple, it was at this game that I believe he was being pelted by coins from the home crowd as well, not really his day was it?

At Reading in 2000/1 a home player was lying prostrate on the pitch being serenaded with 'sympathetic' comments from we away fans who deemed him a 'Take two tablets and see me in the morning' case. In reality, he had been lying there not because he wanted a golf buggy ride but because he had a punctured lung!

The main on pitch cure in days gone by was a mystery item that for some reason was never featured on 'Arthur C Clarke's Mysterious World' aka 'Now that's what I call bunkum'.

This item was the magic sponge, never mind about Big Foot, the Bermuda Triangle, Ghost sightings, the riddle of the Sphinx or UFO abductions, etc, this item was the mystery item, a real eighth wonder of the world and modern day miracle, if it did actually bloody work that is. If it did to my mind if this piece of equipment had been adopted into the NHS, waiting lists and recovery times would have been drastically cut overnight.

I have seen its supposed awesome power myself many, many times. A player lying prostrate on the pitch even in the old days and really injured, right through to the modernish era of the writhing about in mortal anguish type of 'injured' players, merely had to have the magic sponge applied to their gonads and their life threatening injury was now more completely cured than a visit to an American evangelist's miracle mission.

Unfortunately, the sponge's powers did not stop all the abuse from stinging the player's ears from the crowd.

It was a cheap cure to – Simply take one average sized bath sponge, fill a bucket with ice or ice cold water, get the local Shaman or Witchdoctor to 'bless it' and Bob's your uncle.

Applying this sponge to the patient's nether regions as cold as possible, turned any supposedly critically wounded player into someone as sprightly as Linford Christie after he had been jump-started on his lunchbox. Sadly more likely to be replaced by an ozone unfriendly spray today.

Any Colour As Long As It Is Blue

The campaign to bring back the white kit for the very successful Division 2 championship season in 2000/1 must have been instigated by those whose early Millwall days coincided with the 1970s near promotion to the top-flight period.

What you consider to be the club's colours depends on what you first saw them wearing, which in my case would make a Millwall kit royal blue-and-white striped shirts, blue shorts and blue socks, or stockings as they bizarrely used to call them in the good old days, with white tops,. That was what the Lions first wore at my debut game all those years ago in the mid-1960s.

Similar to one of the kits put up for consideration prior to the 2003/4 season in fact.

Over the years, I have seen Millwall wearing various combinations of blue kits, with white collars, white sleeves, white pinstripes, white bands and sections and we have even had pale grey panels?

So for me royal blue is the colour, although an all-white kit does often seem to have a talismanic quality.

With regards to the away kit, to my mind it should always be red and black or yellow and black or at a pinch, all white. It should never be green and white halves like a Blackburn shirt made by the colour-blind or the other ghastly all green efforts of recent years and where the grey/silver, grey or tangerine kits that we have recently had came from I don't know.

The excuse for the original green kit can only have been that Mick McCarthy was our manager and related to his Irish connection. What was the excuse for the recent grey/silver, grey or tangerine efforts?

I think that the 2001/2 green shirt must be a collector's item in the club merchandise stakes, I only ever saw one coach away regular wearing it all season, and I probably only saw about a handful of other sightings home or away. If the club shop had moved quickly they could have sown an Irish badge on put Reid or McCarthy on the back and set up a stall in Kilburn or Cricklewood to flog the excess stock to the Irish fans pre World Cup, they would have gone down a bomb, no pun intended.

As we seemed to have two green away kits in 2003/4 a striped one and a plain green one, it appears that green was now our away colour, how did that happen? Whatever happened to tradition?

We sometimes wore a Brazil style away kit in 2007/8 but usually played awfully. it might be like watching Brazil but our lack of quality drove me Brazil nuts!

Finally in 2008 and in later years we have had a third or second kit that was as mentioned tangerine or bright orange and made us look like Tango Man, stewards or Blackpool or whatever.

Speaking as a tight wad, why the bloody hell do teams need three kits? Just a thought!

Where Have All Our Players Gone?

Not that I am bitter you understand but I thought I would list the Millwall players sold to fund the building of The New Den.

There was the car-boot sale/bargain basement clear out of our star players in order to fund the construction and running of the new ground, whatever the excuse was at the time.

Despite protestations to the contrary by Millwall's board, I can only see one reason for offloading your best players and that is to build a ground or service a debt, take your pick.

Anyway, the following Premiership quality/International players have been sold in the last few decades... Kasey Keller, Steven Reid, Keith Branagan, Aiden Davison, Tim Cahill, Kenny Cunningham, Phil Babb, Ben Thatcher, Andy Roberts, Colin Cooper, Lucas Neill, Neil Ruddock, Mark Kennedy, Alex Rae, Jimmy Carter, Chris Armstrong, Paul Ifill, Darren Ward, James Henry, George Saville, Tony Cascarino and Teddy Sheringham.

Mark Crossley, Andros Townsend, Jay Simpson, Chris Wood,

Harry Kane, Glen Johnson and Darren Huckerby were not signed whilst on loan, presumably due to lack of funds. All of the above have, do or will play at the highest level, and whilst it is, only conjecture would have proved a more than competent Premiership side, I may be wrong, but I can dream can't I?

The Family Game

I know times have changed Football wise and usually for the better, but however far along the executive and gentry path Football goes it should never forget that it is in essence a game for working-class males, it's not a family game in the strictest sense, well not at Millwall it isn't, and never has been, it is very family oriented, though I give you the previous Harvey Brown section, I mean not happy clappy land family orientated like Crystal Palace fans!!!!

It should equally never go totally along the route towards the Football experience becoming an executive box piss up sport either. For me it has to be a spectator sport for the committed fan, many of whom at Millwall probably should have been! Likewise it should never become a wholly family game as this would mean losing its working-class pressure valve aspect, and it should never only become an excuse for a spot of lunch, bottle of Chianti/Prosecco 'Oh! Look there's a soccer match!' Affair either.

Who wants Football to become a solely moneymaking enterprise bereft of a soul? Not me.

Wall fans are a family who will always stick together and help each other but as you know, Millwall is most definitely not on any list of the 'lovely family club' variety.

To my mind the modern concept of Football, being a happy family game is a myth along the lines of Big Foot, except that Big Foot probably exists. Sons and fathers yes, occasionally daughters and wives, but hardly ever father, mother, the kids, granny, grandad, the grandkid's and spinster aunt Maud.

Obviously many girls/women do go, but these tend to be of a girlfriend or friend variety.

Wives will sometimes go with husbands but that its the exception not the rule. In fact any of my mates who have taken their wives to games at either version of the Den, have returned home to any ear-bashing afterwards for exposing their wives delicate ears to the world of obscenity, hostility and rabid partisanship that Football is, well the Den's are anyway.

In the main Football spectating is still overwhelmingly a white working-class male dominated sport, outside of the Premiership anyway and whilst there is an increasingly large turnout of girls and women at both home and away games for Millwall, they are still a small minority.

Football has thankfully not become a 'Family that doesn't swear in company stays together, happy clappy smiley people' game – yet. I personally believe that this is just an advertising executive's fantasy.

Oh I Do Like To Be Beside The Seaside Blackpool Away On Whizz Bang Oooh Aaah Day 2011

A bit of information re my Bonfire Day at the seaside, land of Kiss Me Kick Hats, Sticks of Blackpool Rock and Donkey Rides, I arrived very early on Coach One and was in fact the first one in the ground in the away section, whoopee, no prize for it just thought that I would let you know!

The story of the day – the updated Bloomfield Road that I encountered on November 5th 2011 compared to my only ever visit there in the 1990s was the most bizarre ground I have ever tried to get in to, very much a case of where the f***ing hell are the entrances?

You needed a Sat Nav tracking device or a sniffer dog to find where the f*** you were, it was like Indiana Jones competing on the Krypton Factor all my yomping around the outside of the swish ground did was wasted some of the time incurred as I had arrived very early. When I did find the away section, at about 1.30pm they had not opened it as the man with the black box required to open it had not yet arrived a steward said, when he said it -

I said 'Did you say black box? What is he going to crash his plane into the entrance to the turnstiles to gain access! Once inside although there are posts holding up the side stand that we were given, the ground was infinitely nicer than the delapidated wreck that it was when I went there originally.

A bit of info for those who like a beer I would like to point out that they did not then have a drink licence, the steward said that they had applied but had not been given one, so if you want a beer I would suggest that you go to the Golden Mile and find a pub, just to let you know!!! If this still applied nearly a decade later.

I went there again on my own on Tuesday 20th October a few years back by train via Preston and stayed in Blackpool FC hotel, I asked if there was a restaurant in hotel and told yes, I wandered in there 6pm, only to find that the Restaurant was effectively a bloody great Executive Box as it overlooked the inside of the stadium, I was told that it was a Blackpool Hospitality deal, with restaurant for people on this Blackpool FC Hospitality package which I was not, so McDdonalds opposite it was, I asked if after the match the restaurant bar was open to one and all and it was, so had a beer after game, the next morning at 9am the Emergency Alarm went off and kept going till we evacuated the building, we were then let back in, and I found out that the Fire/smoke alarm kicked in to action because the Toaster had started it at the Breakfast which I was allowed in to, I went back to Euston via Preston and on board someone came over ill and we had to stop at Stafford for them to get medical attention, game was a draw, Blackpool is full of Rock and Candy Floss etc, but it was interesting on other angles I suppose.

The Millwall We Don't Need An Usherette Principle Some Guide Points To The Away Travel Newbys

If you've read my other books you'll know these type of people are one of my pet hates.

Away Travel Newbys are the type of creatures who only emerge for a successful season or for a local Derby, thus swelling the usual away following. These people consist of those who do not usually travel to 'proper' away matches and those wishing to watch a winning side, aka Glory hunters, don't get me started!!! They get a brief taste of the away experience before disappearing back to the comfort of Saturday afternoon shopping with the wife or spending their match afternoon listening to the radio or watching on TV/Teletext., where for any defeat they can have a bloody good whinge, boot the dog up the arse and take to the drink straight after any defeat at a game.

The hard-core Wall away travellers does not have that luxury, we often find ourselves facing a 4 – 5 hour homebound coach trip, which with complications due to road works, traffic jams, coach defects, etc. can often be a lot longer. Where is the spirit of adventure in only going to home games?

By way of explanation to non Millwall away travellers, Tickets are merely a means of getting through turnstiles and in to the ground be it the old fashioned human or barcode zapping way.

The block and seat number might as well be written in Martian as no one takes any notice of what it says, as an example or two in 2015/6 season at Colchester United the steward said do you know where your seat is sir I said yes it is one of the blue ones behind this goal! I said I think I should explain to you mate Millwall fans never sit in their allocated seats, so you are wasting your time! He said I have to ask sir it is part of my job, I said to be honest mate that is why I thought I should tell you, unless you had usherettes who took you directly to your seat by means of a torch as they used to do many moons ago in cinemas, they are wasting their time totally, I estimate that in the hundreds of away matches I have been to I have sat in the correct seat less than 10 times, the games I sat in allocated seat being old Wembley Auto Windscreen Final, Play Off Finals and the FA Cup Semi Finals at new Wembley and Old Trafford, and the FA Cup Final at the Millenium Stadium, other than that I cannot really think of any hunt for your real seat games, apart from one game at Nottingham Forest and Reading.

I seriously cannot think why it had not occurred to Football Teams expecting Millwall that Unreserved seating was 100% the way they should go, otherwise Stewards are overmanned massively and wasting their time on a grandscale!!!

At Fleetwood Without A Mac Tuesday 24th November 2015

To explain the real joys of a proper away trip in midweek oop north, as Fleetwood Town is only up the road from Blackpool, I thought I would continue the joys of away travel midweek.

We left the New Den at around noon, on the legendary Coach 1, I think I mean legendary!

The clock at the front of coach was 1 hour and 40 minutes fast! Which might not sound too distracting but it is, trust me, the driver turned clock off in fact, which was better, following the customary traffic block up on Motorway due to bollard exhibition, I think you know what I mean, with one stop at about half way we arrived outside Fleetwood Town FC after 7 hours on the road.

We walked in to ground, I bought the customary as I am oop north meat and potato pie, the five of us that went, me, Dave, Nathan and Paul Simms, together with his father in law Les who comes from near Blackburn and goes to quite a few up north games with us, went to buy a programme, to find it was an odd shape sort of like a programme cut in half, and it was only £1!! I did question the lady who sold it to me and she assured me that it actually really was only a quid.

The ground bizarrely called Highbury had a small capacity on around 5500, and consisted of two covered terraced ends, which we chose instead of seating because of the demise of terrace areas, which Paul a CBL regular and one of our other companions who travelled with us chose instead.

It was an odd looking ground, both ends consisting of two opposing covered terraces of about a dozen steps, Wall away fans in seats were to our right in a stand that had a curved roof not unlike Huddersfield Town, had seats on the lower tier, with people in the upper tier sitting in front of what looked like executive boxes, accompanied by a bizarre PA that from where we were standing sounded like one of Norman Collier's cast offs!

On the left hand side there was a social club for half the pitch, and a stand covering the other end near the home end, that for some strange architectural reason was built in front of an old half stand, which you could see behind it!

There was a large video screen, which I will mention a bit later on.

In the terrace at the opposite home end they had the customary bloody annoying drummer, which was greeted as it had to be with customary anti drum abuse.

The home fans in the game sang chants against George Saville, in first half when we were attacking their end, due to his name not his proclivities he got 'Saville is a paedo!' and 'Paedo Paedo!'

After a 7 hour journey up, we played awfully and lost 2 – 1 our first defeat following a run of 9 games unbeaten. At the end of the game, they played Fleetwood Mac's 'Dreams' and here comes the videotron there was a huge sign that had appeared on the screen that said Away Fans with a bloody great arrow beneath it highlighting the exit, in case you were too thick to remember how you had come in to the ground!

I did wonder what on earth the flag festooned in home end that said something like there is only one way in one way out meant, that explains that.

We boarded the coach parked outside the away terrace, and it was pissing down, strangely above my head there was a leak and to add to my fun it dripped on me from above for a good part of our return journey, I reported it to one of the drivers who said it is probably the air vent sorry!

We got back to New Den at around 3am, I then got a lift home and went beddy byes after 3.30am, a new ground but a bloody arduous trip, shit performance and I got soaked, this was a proper away masochists trip!!!!

Burton Albion Night Match Away Tuesday 1st December 2015

Minor compared to Fleetwood trip I suppose, debatable if masochistic enough but, had London travel grief to top off another defeat away, I was lucky enough to have a friend Paul from the CBL going on Coach 1, so I got a lift home as he was heading east after we dismounted at Den, the three Simms went but drove from Barnet and as we could not guarantee getting back there in time for me to get last tube back to Bank at midnight, I decided on Coach, and as CBL Paul could give me a lift home I thought all good, that was until we arrived back at Den at around 1am, drove to Rotherhithe Tunnel only to find southbound shut and northbound, I.e. the way east backed up, we though sod that lets go Tower Bridge, we arrived there to find that it was completely blocked off! So we drove down Tooley Street and thankfully found London Bridge open, I was back indoors by about 1.40am, all adds to the away travel fun, to continue real masochism, Burton's aftermath was nothing compared to Oldham –

I Told Em Oldham! 12th December 2015

To continue back to real away masochism 2!!!! The Fleetwood drip was still prevalent, but luckily this time it was above the seat behind me, blind luck in my case that I had not sat there again, I went on my own on Coach 1 at 8am, Paul Simms drove up there with a couple of CBL friends and was close behind the coach.

We arrived at the roundabout outside Boundary Park in the pissing down rain, in fact it had been raining all the time we were outside London, it was so overcast that you were not able to read the newspaper in the natural light of the coach as the ground came in to sight at 1.30pm, someone sitting behind me announced that his phone had just flashed up that the referee was about to do a pitch inspection, we waited a few minutes and as we arrived at Oldham Athletic that resembled a wet Building Site we heard it was off with the ball only bouncing on certain parts of the pitch, whoopee we were allowed off the coach and to use the toilets inside the ground, I went across the car park that was awash via a circuitous route, as I headed back to the coach I asked to buy the customary northern meat and potato pie, the steward said it was shutting, I said brilliant, what are you going to do with them then? Could do with one after over 5 hours on the coach, the steward saw sense and gave me a free pie, I then headed for the coach and foolishly decided to cross the muddy and wet sandbank type arrangement, not wise at all as my foot sunk into the quicksand pathway and my trainer was sucked off my left foot, my right knee hit the tarmac, and my pie flew out of my hand and hit the deck, Kenny the wheelchair user on Coach 1s carer headed towards me from the ground, helped get to my feet and whilst being helped himself to not overbalance he pulled my missing trainer from the quicksand, and I boarded the coach with my left leg completely covered in mud!!!

Not that I am a refereeing official, but as it had been pissing down for days would it not have been sensible to have done the pitch inspection before we left London or a short while after we had, so we did not have the pleasure of an 11 hour wasted coach trip! Sod sensible, f**k the travelling fans I will do it when I want.

Do You Think We Will Have To Bury Him ? Steward Going Down at Bury on Saturday 26th November 2016

Something that was funny to see was, in pre kick off when Kevin Pressman was warming up Millwall's goalkeepers with some shots, he cracked one ball that missed the post but hit a Bury Steward on the head and knocked him to the floor, we all thought it hilarious as he hit the floor in a heap, not sure he did as he moved away from the position at the front of the away stand right behind the goal, once he recovered enough he sloped away!

Charlie Charlie Charlie Chants

At Brammall Lane Saturday 14th April 2018 there was a load of Charlied up blokes behind who sang –

'We're Gonna Sniff In A Minute!'/'We're Only Here To Sniff!'/'We're Only Here For Cocaine!' and

'We've Used All Our Charlie!' There's honesty for you!!!!

They continued this to the pitch continuing the Kevin Pressman tip whilst he was doing his customary shoot in to the keepers pre match they sang – 'You Fat C***!' and 'You're Gonna Eat In A Minute!'

In addition to the two goalkeepers

To Millwall's Jordan Archer they sang –

'Archer Archer Archer' and 'Scotland Scotland's Number 3' Sort of respectful as he is an international but to show that also a piss take.

To Sheffield United keeper Jamal Blackman they sang –

'Jamal Blackman He Loves KFC!'and 'Hes Only Here For The Chicken!'

God knows where that info came from, unless of course they actually saw him in Kentucky Fried Chicken!

Strange Signs at Rochdale Tuesday 21st March 2017

At a night match at Rochdale not that the time of day matters but near the Refreshments area concourse on the wall outside the Ladies Toilets there was a sign on the wall that said something like Meet and Greet Spot.

What outside a toilet? That sounds more like some Hampstead Heath Cottaging spot!!!

Think Of The Money Mabel!

Something that occurred to me was that as Blackpool in 2011 were sponsored by Wonga. Com, what would have happened if they had played Brighton and Hove Albion in the nine years that they were sponsored by Skint, would the effeminate elite have gone Jerry Maguire on them 'Show Me The Money' stylee on seasiders! Just wondered

When I was growing up in the Sixties and Seventies there was no such thing as overt club sponsorship or any blatant use of advertising, like pitch side hoardings or merchandising, unlike today's if it moves whack a sponsors name on it. In fact, in this era it was very difficult to get an item like a replica club shirt anywhere but the club shop that was if they even stocked them. If you were lucky, you could buy a shirt and sow the club badge on yourself or get your mum to do it for you, if you could find a badge anywhere that was.

At Millwall during my boyhood I cannot recall actually being able to buy a club kit at all, however that could have been a tactic on my cousin Roys' part, presumably on my dad's orders, to not let me see such things, perhaps there was a vast Aladdin's cave of Millwall goodies on sale that I did not see?

Somehow I doubt it. I do vaguely recall at the Old Den in the old days that you could get items like metal badges, rosettes, mugs, plates and scarves, etc, it was all very low key. Unlike today's type of club shop, where there has been a huge amount of sensible Millwall items for sale and some not so sensible, for example – In addition to the club kit and clothing you could buy images of the New Den in the form of a mouse mat, a jigsaw puzzle and a card model. There are also various golf items and stranger still, you could buy an often-apt Millwall coloured and badged lifebelt!

Whilst I have not seen a Millwall version of the plastic grounds that you often see in the Sunday's you could get a crystal glass depiction of the New Den for about £130, a snip.

Very artistic and all that but what is the point? It was a shame though that you could not buy Old Den plastic replicas, in all its pomp, looking like a roofer's nightmare with the legend –

'The Den, Millwall v Ipswich Town FA Cup Quarter – Final Riot, 11th March 1978'

For an added bit of kudos, you could also have had little bloodied people and Police on the pitch for added authenticity.

One thing that you used to see years ago at the Old Den, were people, who had presumably been on holiday in the States, wearing Detroit Lions merchandise. you still see this in isolation today,

Things seem to change in the late 1980s when several unofficial T-shirts appeared like 'Millwall Enough Said' and the Terry Hurlock 'Jaws' one. From this period onwards it seemed that our marketing stepped up a gear. One item that you could buy at the time was a black Millwall bomber jacket with a large leaping yellow Lion on the back, an ideal aid to staying incognito, especially where I come from in the East End.

Some recentish modern items that were also a positive boon in the anonymity stakes -

Club credit cards with Millwall's name plastered all over them.

I have enough gyp with my unintelligible signature and snide quips about being an undesirable for following Millwall as it is, without adding flames to the fire by combining the two and whipping out my credit card with Lion's logos all over it. I am sure that would not have been very 'That will do nicely'.

A very useful tool when surreptitiously paying for food or drinks in a pub at an away ground, the same applies to mobile phones that have a Millwall phone cover with a club logo or a personalised ring tone like 'No One Likes Us/Let 'Em Come', which would have obviously gone off at the least opportune time, cover blown immediately. I have absolutely no problem showing my Millwall affinity but sometimes discretion is the key.

I found an old copy of 'Four Two Four' magazine which had an advertisement for (Howard?) Wilkinson Sword Protector safety Football razors, these were available for all the then Premiership sides and the Old Firm in Scotland, with a club logo printed on the handle, which was also in the club colours.

Sadly Millwall were not available, I know we were not in the Premiership so that was why, but you could imagine the witty skits we'd have had to put up with in the press –

Millwall + Razor = A media field day! Oh how we would have laughed.

Obviously money is the key in any marketing or sponsorship deal, but some of the ideas were odd, none more so than Millwall's association with cable station 'Live TV' in 1997/8.

As part of the deal we had 'Live TV – The Weather In Norwegian' plastered across the club shirts, which left any wearer looking a bit of a div.

This particular connection linked us with a very weird cable TV channel, for those of you who did not know it had as its main assets the following – Bare-breasted girls on 'Topless Darts'.

A bloke dressed in a rabbit suit called 'The News Bunny' who ponced about in a Football club Muppet fashion behind the newsreader.

There was an attractive girl called Tiffany who progressively did a 'But Miss Jones you're gorgeous!' strip, down to her bra whilst she ran through the day's financial news called 'Tiffany's Big City Tips'.

There was a glut of soft-core porn programmes and cheap and cheerful parapsychology type shows.

Its sports presenters were ex page 3 girls Gail McKenna, Kirsten Imrie and Louise Brady who would show off so much cleavage it was impossible to concentrate on anything else if you were a red-blooded male, it was far more Daily Sport than real sport.

Occasionally they had a weather forecasting midget called Rusty who used to present 'Britain's Bounciest Weather'. He used to bounce up and down on a trampoline whilst giving out the weather forecast. He had to use a long stick in an effort to point to anywhere on the map in the North or in Scotland, quality entertainment was not the word for it.

The shirt title 'The Weather in Norwegian' was the main weather bulletin and was presented by Anne Marie Foss, a gorgeous Scandinavian blonde who would invariably wear a very skimpy two-piece bikini swimsuit type of affair. During the sponsorship she would on occasion appear on the channel dressed in Millwall's home kit, which she also did at the New Den accompanied by Kirsten Imrie in the away kit, she was also shown in the club programme. Sod the sight of David Mellor in Chelsea kit! But seeing women and Millwall so beautifully merged together used to send me into a Leslie Philips cravat wearing, tasche twiddling frenzy I can tell you!

To return to the point about Live TV, aside from the very necessary financial benefits at the time I was not too sure of the reputation benefits of this bizarre combination.

If you had seen this channel on cable TV you will know of what I speak, sadly it's now defunct.

Like every other club, the players also have sponsors for their kits, home and away, so what happens if they were of a Phil Barber/Bobby Bowry popularity and do not have a sponsor?

Would they have to buy their own kit?

Would they have to bring something in from home?

Would they have to make the club supply them with something by bringing a note from their mum saying 'Bobby's kit is in the wash', like we used to do at school to escape games?

Failing all else – Would they have been contractually obliged to turn out in a club badged jockstrap to play?

Finally a question – Millwall in the past few seasons have had sponsored corners, goals and injury time. How long before sponsored gobbing, ref abusing or fouls?

Gooner But Not Forgotten

I know that we have also not played Arsenal for several years, thank god from a football perspective! However, I thought that we missed a golden record request opportunity the last time that we played them at the New Den.

What we should have done was to bombard DJ Les with requests to highlight the Arsenal players many addictions at the time, imagine it.

For the druggies we could have had 'Cocaine' by Eric Clapton, 'White Lines' by Grandmaster Flash and the Furious Five, 'Ebeneezer Goode' by Shamen, Afroman's 'Because I Got High' or 'I've Got 5 On It' by The Luniz.

For the dipsos we could have had – 'Little Ole Wine Drinker Me' by Dean Martin, 'Red Red Wine'

by UB40 or 'Milk And Alcohol' by Dr Feelgood.

For the gamblers we could have had 'You Better, You Bet' by The Who, the tune from Channel 4's racing or late-night poker.

Not forgetting of course the coup de grace – 'Cigareets And A

Whiskey And Wild Wild Women'

Which would have covered most of their numerous and very well documented addictions nicely, at the time Arsenal certainly gave new meaning to the term in possession!

That's Entertainment?

I have been to many matches over the years both home and away when pre-match and half time entertainment (sic) has been provided some examples –

I have seen numerous balloon bags ejaculated into the sky at big games.

I have seen doggy Football. Not dogging football, just to explain that!

I have seen and heard the modern phenomenon of crowd band accompaniment.

I have seen kids five-a-sides, penalty shoot-outs and target competitions.

I have seen Police dog handling displays.

I have heard Russell Watson's operatic belting and a local singer Stephen Bayliss crooning pre match both at Preston North End.

I have seen and unfortunately heard The Beverley Sisters singing 'I Love to Go Wandering', accompanied by a band of Guardsmen on the pitch at Wolves! The horror, the horror!

I have seen and heard the Guards band performing Cockney favourite in the away stand at Wrexham.

I have seen a vast menagerie of acid flashbacks in the guise of club Muppets nationwide.

I have seen the North Korean 1966 World Cup conquerors of Italy at Hillsborough.

I have seen and heard Highbury's North Bank singing mural.

I have seen the 'Hello Sailor' man at Portsmouth and the 'Posh' man at Peterborough.

I have seen acrobats at Wycombe.

I saw Les Dennis on the pitch at Birmingham City in 2011, when he was commendably promoting a charity that was great but with his Scouse accent and no subtitles I have no idea what he was talking about.

I have seen numerous American style cheerleaders.

I have seen and heard the rise of the crowd rabble-rousing and on-pitch DJs.

I have heard the modern requirement to play goal music.

At MK Dons in August 2016 they had to try to kick the ball in to the back of a car boot to win the car in a subsequent competition, shit to watch and a dismal failure for all involved.

I have seen a half time Halloween costumed Pumpkin ball Penalty kick in against a witch in goal at Ipswich Town the day before Halloween 2010.

At The New Den in 2014/5 there was the introduction of the bizarre seemilnly bubble wrap mega ball a Zorb apparently box to box race, for Juniors, initially Millwall Juniors v Millwall Juniors then it expanded to both teams Juniors, still a strange sight to watch but more logical I suppose.

I have heard the modern style of ridiculously OTT intros for the team's, with the intro just slightly out of kilter with the likely delights that we were about to be presented with.

Finally, I have seen numerous weird and wonderful half time prize competitions over the years.

The strangest ones being a kick the ball into a car boot pre-match competition at Northampton from a few years ago, a similar game called 'On me shed son' a half time game at Crystal Palace in December 2005 where a Palace fan had to try to chip a ball into a roofless shed and singularly failing dismally.

There was a reinactment of Ipswich Town's 1978 FA Cup winning goal in March 2004 at Portman Road and the opportunity to have a Domino Pizza delivered to your seat if you won a competition at Watford's Vicarage Road on New Years Day 2005.

On Saturday 16th October 2010 at Crystal Palace again, they had an Eagle flying to it's keeper on the pitch, marvelous, I suggested that they should have a pre match duel between an Eagle and a Lion, strangely I doubt if they would think this was very sensible!

There is the recent one I have seen at several northern clubs away the fan of each club half time spin around ten times around a post then once you complete 10 turns try to kick ball in to the net, which surprisingly they normally fail to do with the ground no doubt spinning around like a top in their head post turning effort whether they have had a beer or not.

On Saturday 17th November 2007 at Bristol Rovers there was a half time Crossbar Challenge for home fans from the Centre Circle that was so bad it was absolutely laughable, who said Variety was dead? Outside Bristol Rovers after the game there was a fan of the home side, themselves nicknamed the Pirates, who had a small Child with him and to entertain him presumably he himself was dressed like a Long John Silver, style Pirate, he was also waving a large Skull and Crossbones Flag, he looked absolutely ridiculous but as we had lost 2 – 1 with their first goal in the last 15 Minutes being a dodgy Penalty and their second goal coming for them in injury time, Paul Simms, Nathan Simms and I who went didn't have the heart to laugh at him or take the piss out of him as we should have done.

At Bournemouth on March 29th 2008 they brought out 3 Cement mixers and lined them up in the Penalty area in front of the Home Stand at Half Time and people attempted to get balls in to them which they failed dismally to do. As I said above who said variety was dead? If this was anything to go on, from an entertainment point of view it must definitely be a bit dicky!

At Leyton Orient in November 2008, there was a small kids v home dragon Muppet half time Penalty shoot out, where the girl on the mike running it said that one small kid had a lovely costume on, when what he actually wore was a football kit! Proving that some women know sod all about football!!!

At Ipswich Town on 10th August 2013 the half time entertainment was a race between a Millwall fan and an Ipswich Town fan, who raced against each other inside a clear plastic Zorb ball! Bizarre and I am not just saying that because Millwall fan lost.

Continuing the supposed Entertainment theme, some home memories -

In years gone by at the Old Den, I have seen various parachute displays, some of which involved delivering the match ball from the sky. These jumps were usually performed by the likes of the Red Devils or the Parachute Regiment or someone equally proficient, they always landed on a target the size of a 50 pence piece from thousands of feet up with a 100% accuracy, where's the fun in that?

What they should have done was to get in a very amateur parachuting club to perform the task with their most incompetent members doing the jumps, thereby giving the crowd far more entertainment; it would have been much more fun. The crowd could watch the incompetent part-time skydivers glide gracefully down only to miss the ground completely and land in the school nearby, on The Old Kent Road or New Cross Road or on Jews Hill. The Old Den also gave them the option of plummeting from the sky and straight onto the laps of the commentators on the rickety gantry above the Halfway Line.

I reckon that If they did land on the pitch they would probably have left the ball on the plane anyway if they were supposed to deliver it. Sadly they would not be able to fly back up to the plane to get it, unless they were Superman, highly unlikely obviously!

At the New Den we have had various entertainments, just a few examples -

We had Bell and Spurling performing a 'Live' rendition of the' Sven Song' a couple of years back.

We had the horrendous sight some years ago of a Ginger era Spice Girls cover act, and the bizarre male wearing female Suspenders and lingerie circling the pitch in 2007/8, ye gods what a fright it all was to. For a Sky Friday-night match against Brentford in our Division 2 aka now League 1 championship winning season we had a pre-match treat in the guise of a girl group, whose name escapes me, who mimed and jigged about on a podium to their latest 'hit'. Their choreography looked like I'd worked it out for them on a fag packet before the match; mind you if I had done it would have been more Christina 'Dirrty' Aguilera like.

To get us on their side they wore Millwall scarves tied around their waists in a Michael Bentt style display of club affinity. The girls naturally had to endure the backdrop of -'Get your tits out for the lads!' And 'You're miming!'

Strangely, with the wonders of television when I watched the video of this match when I got home, none of this barracking soundtrack was on the broadcast.

In 2014/2015 season at The New Den they introduced a Half Time race, in bloody great Rolling aforementioned Zorb Balls, that people, well Juniors get inside and their job is to race this Ball rolling from the inside style from box to box, this either features two sets of youngsters one from Millwall one from our opponents, and initially had two Zampa Zorb Balls, so that it was a race between two people at the same time, however to our great chagrin one of the balls burst, so they could only now use one, this was in October 2014, Chris Bethell who was doing the commentary re how the competitors were going in a excited style like Murray Walker on a bender, said pre the event on this day v Wolves 'We've Only Got One Ball!' too many youngsters there to burst in to 'Hitler He's Only Got One Ball The Other Is In the Albert Hall' singing, shame been more entertaining than this strange game!

When we sat down at Scunthorpe United on Saturday 22nd August 2015, Martin who I know from Coach 1 sat next to me, we looked at the pitch which was the most abstractly mown pitches I have ever seen, there was absolutely no concernable pattern to it, I said this is like an Art Council Project! I then saw that there was an advertising hoarding above the left hand side home stand for Scunthorpelawnmowers.co.uk now if this was done by then I would sack their marketing department pronto!

Not that this was a game merely a comment, but there was a bizarre half time game that I briefly mentioned previously when home fan only this for variety consisted of a Scunny fan and a Lion fan, having to spin around quickly with eyes closed then after x spins they were to try a shot on goal first one winning, this may be a bit strange to hear but most of post spinning toppers stumbled all over the shop in their attempt to shoot! To add to the Scunthorpe comedy value they played Benny Hill's theme tune whilst contestants spun around a pole/post!

Entertainment value of good DJing when at the end of Scunthorpe United v Millwall game he played Bob Marley's 'Iron Lion Zion' good choice as Scunny are called the Iron and Wall Lion, clever what.

A couple of crowd entertainments that as far as I know, have yet to be tried –

Police dog displays but using pit bulls or a pack of wild hyenas to track the unfortunate 'burglar'.

On-pitch 'Firms' fighting, like a hooligan's championship? At least the Police would then know where they were. If Football carries along its gentrification route I am sure it's just a matter of time before the match day festivities consist of hampers in the back of hatchbacks in the car-park followed by the likes of hare coursing, show jumping or grouse-shooting as pre-match of half time entertainment.

Mind you we would have no problem getting a member of the Royal family to come to the New Den then, I reckon that Prince Philip's diplomatic skills would be a massive bonus in defending our frequent problems as well, let's get him on board! We also have foxes at the New Den who try to get inside the club to ferret through the bins, they act as rat catchers if cannot find any other food, now as money is the name of the game why not have fox hunting in the car park or on the pitch at half time with the posh types in red on horses, on a horse with dogs, but to make it fair or more blood thirsty if you like accompany the fox(s) with a couple of Lions see how the trophy hunters get on then when the dogs see the real opponents.

South East London Mysticism

Shortly after our poor start at the New Den, the club decided to call in eastern Feng Shui advisers to tell them why. Bearing in mind that it might have been more logical to get them in before the ground was built, if they believed in this philosophy, they naturally found faults.

It was discovered that the ground was situated on a negative vibe line in a bad karma zone or the then named Connex South Central and still designated South East London as they are more usually called.

The whole ground should be rotated through 90 degrees so that the South/CBL stand now faced East, the seats should face away from the pitch and be replaced with lime-green deckchairs, this new direction for the seats would have been a bloody good idea during Jimmy Nicholl's reign!

The natives should be offered shiatsu massages and colonic irrigation in order to purge and cleanse them of negative thoughts, etc. The toilet seats should be nailed down and be made of a mahogany only found in a specific sustainable Brazilian rain forest, the toilet paper should immediately be replaced by the old School paper from the Sixties – 'Izal', the rough wood pulp variety that made a man of you, if being a man meant having a sore arse? This paper had – 'Now wash your hands – Property of the LCC' stamped on it.

A more beneficial suggestion might have been 'Now pick the splinters out of your own arse or go to A&E at the Hospital'

The club name should be changed Gordon Jago Stylee to the South East London Cuddlies, the team's colours should be changed to a nice pastel shade, and joss-sticks should be freely burnt, although I think they already do this in the East stand. Finally soothing Tibetan style monks chanting music should replace 'House of Fun' and 'London Calling'.

Mumbo and jumbo? I think not. Again, just in case you wondered I made this up, not the fact that Feng Shui advisers were called in just the proposals, but I bet the real recommendations that they gave were not any more sensible.

Revenge Is Sweet

The infamous Ipswich Riot prompted then Ipswich manager the now departed Bobby Robson to say something in the press like – 'Turn the flame throwers on them and burn these Bastards!' Ah the voice of reason!

As the years went by I assumed that he'd forgotten and forgiven us, especially when he brought his then team Sporting Lisbon to open the New Den in 1993.

However, I was wrong, little did I realise that behind the benign and amiable exterior he was just waiting for his opportunity to gain his revenge, something that he achieved by recommending two Russian International's Sergei Yuran and Vasilli Kulkov to Mick McCarthy.

At the time I remember thinking – 'My God I have actually heard of them!'

In fact, I'd seen them on television in the Champions' League playing for Benfica for God's sake!

After the initial euphoria had died down and they had played a few games it became apparent that we had acquired a pair of lazy, money-grabbing, massively waged wastrels, Yuran in particular had drinking habits a bit too close to Boris Yeltsin's for a professional footballer.

It became obvious that never mind the major coup headlines of

– 'Millwall Sign a Perestroikas'

What it should have said was – 'Millwall Sign a Pair of Wankers'.

I can just picture Bobby sitting back and thinking – 'Ah! Revenge is sweet.'

They say that revenge is a dish best served cold, how true, cheers Bobby!

It was due in no small part to the massive wages of these two that Millwall slid into the financial abyss at which point the buggers left.

What Kulkov did following his departure I do not know or care, but I last saw Yuran playing like Pele's more talented brother in the Champions' League in 2000/1.

In February 2002 Sergei Yuran graciously admitted that he was a total waste of space in an

Evening Standard article under the heading – 'Yuran: Yes I Am Top Of The Flops'

This was not too much consolation, but thanks anyway.

My Millwall Favourites

In 'I Was Born Under The Cold Blow Lane' I listed the likes of Cripps, Kitchener, Hurlock and Rhino as heroes, continuing a theme to start a few modern volatile players.

David Livermore and Kevin Muscat and not exactly heroes as such but what I would call old-fashioned Millwall style players, as was Pat van den Hauwe, the latter not exactly a Millwall legend, however, his first action in a Millwall shirt was to elbow a Charlton player in the face at The Valley, which is good enough in my book, Bravo! We cannot forget John 'Fash The Bash' Fashanu either or the more modern era, Andy Frampton and Shane Lowry 100 % Lions.

Some less volatile heroes came in the guise of Derek Possee and the sadly departed and deceased Keith Weller, Tony Towner, Alex Rae, Andy May and Gordon 'Merlin' Hill, whose motto seemed to be – 'Never a tap in when a 25 yarder will do'. For you old 'uns out there who remember Merlin our winger not the really really really old people who were around when King Arthur's magician was about, did you know that there is a Train Station in Enfield North London called Gordon Hill. Blimey he has is own station!!!

Not forgetting long staying Wall players Alan Dunne and Paul Robinson

Pre his West Ham move and claims of devotion Teddy Sheringham was obviously a Lions legend, and a real Millwall goal machine. For the record Teddy used to go out with my Cousin Roy's daughter Amanda during his Millwall days, how is that for name-dropping?

Teddy was loyal to the Lions and as a consequence was greeted with open arms when our paths cross, until he became an alleged lifelong Hammer that was!

Unlike Tony '30 pieces of Silver' Cascarino, well bugger me he wasn't Irish after all who'd have thought? So Crayford wasn't a satellite of Eire then?

A more recent hero obviously has to include Neil Harris, in his first stay a real goal machine in the Teddy mould and a brave man to comeback after his Cancer problems.

Deviating slightly it was always sad to see the likes of Teddy and Harris leave, however unfortunately a club of our size can never perpetually keep its goal scorers for very long, because if they are any good they are sold to the circling pack of clubs with their wallets out. It was strange though that both Sheringham and Harris both left us for Forest albeit Harris joined a different version of Forest to the Clough era side that Teddy joined.

As a consequence of this flog 'em policy there are no Millwall players who have scored many hundreds of goal for the club, similarly we are not renowned for paying too much for players, no several million pound players at Millwall, yet!

Returning to the point my favourite goalkeeper was Bryan King, although Pat Cuff was far funnier between the sticks.

491

I personally like to see wingers playing and another of my favourite players from the Old Den era was Jimmy Carter someone who supplied the crosses and ammunition for Teddy and Cascarino to get their goals, along with 'Chicken' George Lawrence and Kevin O'Callaghan.

He of the banana diet, a player who was like shit off a shovel (a technical Footballing term)

Friend of mine Steve Fisher and I went for a drink in the late 1980s, to a pub called 'The Charleston' in Stratford, as we stood at the bar, we spotted the Peanut Man, went over to him, and said -

'You're Jimmy Carter aren't you?' He persistently denied it until we convinced him that he was and that we were Millwall and not rogue West Ham United about to give him a kicking. Once he accepted who he was, we had quite a long chat and we spouted as much nonsense as we could, as was Steve and my wont. I bet initially he was glad that we were not Hammers but probably more happy when we buggered off and left him alone.

He must have thought that if he went deep enough in to unhappy Hammers country no one would recognise him sadly he was mistaken.

To finish I'd like to pay respect to the players who came to Millwall in the twilight of their careers and didn't just show up to top-up to their pension, have a bit of a run-around and then bugger off, home players like – John Jackson, Nigel Spink, Dave Mitchell, Dennis Wise, Kerry Dixon, Paul Moody and last but definitely not least a Millwall legend and very short lived manager Steve Claridge.

All of whom in my opinion gave a hundred percent in each game in a true professional manner and exactly how it should be.

CHAPTER 13
'He's Only A Poor Little Hammer' – Lions Not Irons

Very Very Non – PC Alert -

As you undoubtedly know we and our non chums the Happy Hammers have a long history of local rivalry, violence and piss taking. The two very very bitter rival's fans have a violent history that transcends football with dockers from two shipyards either side of the Thames frequently having tear ups in the early part of the 20th century. Millwall's docks were The Millwall London and Surrey Docks and West Ham's were The Royal Docks, The problems became more profound when Millwall's dockers continued to work whilst West Ham's dockers downed tools in 1926, sparking bitter rivalries from thenceforth, only put aside for serious outside of football medical situations, as you will have seen in Isla Caton section several chapters previously.

Although as an East Ender the assumption is that I must support West Ham United,.

Millwall FC, come from the Isle Of Dogs Milllwall which is a lot nearer to Whitechapel 3.8 miles, also the Den New Cross Gate version is actually nearer to where I was born as is the South Bermondsey version see below.

I know there is a River in between but Whitechapel to New Cross Gate is 4.8 miles, whilst Whitechapel to Upton Park is 5.8 miles, If we move in to Modern era South Bermondsey stadium is nearer 3.1miles from Whitechapel whilst Olympic Stadium in 3.5 miles, so there, I have never ever felt any affinity with the 'Appy 'Ammers, f*** em!!!!

The modern reflection of this rivalry and hatred is highlighted in anti-West Ham T-shirts/car stickers and naturally there are numerous 'We hate...' type chants sung by both clubs fans.

Before I start on these chants it always confuses me when we play West Ham and they sing – 'Come on you Irons!' because it always sounds like they are singing 'Come on you Lions!'. Mind you to explain this, confusion comes easily to me, pre or post Brain Injury!

From Them To Us -

Here are their chants about us -

West Ham fans used to sing an American military style 'sound off' Cricket Fans Barmy Army type chant that went on for about a fortnight– 'Everywhere we go people want to know who the hell we are, we are the West Ham, oh, oh, oh, oh! West Ham United and you are invited to Upton Park to have a row – Millwall, we hate Millwall, and we hate Millwall. we are the Millwall haters!'

Just in case you wondered, by 'Row' I mean an argument or ruck, not a romantic punt up the Thames.

Whilst I heard the above in the flesh, there were several golden oldie chants that I have never actually heard them sing, in truth I found all their chants on a football chant website 'footballchants.org', the first was apparently sung to the tune of the American Battle of Independence song 'The Battle of New Orleans' and referred to 1970s/80s Old Den battles and alleged 'ammers victories, it was called 'We Steamed Millwall!' –

'With his Treatment balaclava and his Millwall brick in hand, blue and white scarf around his neck – that nasty Millwall fan, we steamed Millwall but the Millwall kept a coming, there wasn't quite as many as there was a while ago, we steamed once more and they started a running, down New Cross Road to the Old Kent Road, they ran through the bushes and they ran through the hedges where a rabbit wouldn't go, we steamed once more and they kept a running down New Cross Road to the Old Kent Road!'

Secondly there was the following choice olden day ditty sung to a children's song tune –

'A West Ham train came a rollin' down the tracks – whoooo! Whoooo!

A Millwall fan got thrown on to the tracks – whoooo! Whoooo!

He nicked a scarf and got cut in half – hip hip hip hooray, hip hip hip hooray, hip hip hip hooray!'

They sang this and they say we're scum!!!

There was also this lot, many of which I had heard us or other team's sing a variation of, the Gillingham Pikeys sarcastically for example also sang the first one, well they must know what a Pikey is! --

I Can't read, I can't write, I wear golden Nike's, I live in a caravan and I'm a Millwall Pikey

Your Mother is your Sister, Your Uncle is your Father, Your Cousin is your Brother, You're a Millwall family

Or - 'Your Father is your Brother, Your Sister is your Mother, they all Fu*k each other a Millwall family.'

'I'd rather f**k a bucket with a big hole in it, than be a Millwall fan for just one minute.

With Hatchets and Hammers, Stanley knives and spanners, we'll teach those scum how to fight (how to fight!)'

'They come from Senegal they'll never win f… all, yes its Millwall, yes its Millwall!'

West Ham will find though that Senegal Fields their reference is in South East London and not Africa!

'One man went to war (War), went to war with Millwall, (Stamp feet shout Scum),

One man and his baseball bat went to war with Millwall (Scum)'

Lastly from the same website I found this olden day bravado song sung the to the 'Dad's Army' tune –

'Who do you think you are kidding Mr Millwall, if you think that West Ham will run?

495

We are the boys who will take your Cold Blow Lane, we are the boys who will throw you under trains, so who do you think you are kidding Mr Millwall if you think West Ham will run!'

Moving away from the website they used to sing a chant to Don't Dilly Dally (My Old Man)' –

'My old man said be a Millwall fan, I said f… off, bollocks, you're a c…!,(You're a c…!)

I'd rather f… a bucket with a big hole in it than be a Millwall fan for just a minute,

with 'atchets and 'ammers, Stanley knives and spanners,

we'll teach those Millwall scum how to fight (how to fight!)'

Finally in an East End pub I heard a West Ham chant to the tune of Pink Floyd's 'The Wall' that went –

'All in all they're just a load of c…s like Millwall!'

From Us To Them -

From our side there have been numerous chants.

To start a golden oldie –

'What do you do with a drunken West Ham? What do you do with a drunken West Ham?

What do you do with a drunken West Ham early in the morning? Stab, stab, stab the bastard!

Stab, stab, stab the bastard! Stab, stab, stab the bastard! Early In The Morning'

'All together now – we all follow the Millwall, over land and sea (and West Ham!)

We all follow the Millwall on to victory!'

'You look in the dustbin for something to eat, you find a dead cat and you think it's a treat, in your West Ham slums.'

To continue the Green Street Millwall featured chant –

'He's only a poor little hammer (hammer!) His face is all tattered and torn, he made me feel sick so I hit him with a brick and now he don't sing anymore!'

Not forgetting an Old Den chestnut Millwall version of the above West Ham chant to the tune of 'Don't Dilly Dally (My Old Man)' that went something like – 'My old man said be a West Ham fan, I said f.... off bollocks, you're a c...! (you're a c...!)'

We took Their end in half a minute, we took the North Bank with West Ham in it,

we hammered The Hammers with carving knives and spanners,

we showed those West Ham bastards how to fight,

oh you'll never take The Den with the Millwall in it, South London's my way home!'

If memory serves there were alternative versions that went -

'My old man said be a West Ham fan, I said f.... off bollocks, you're a c...! (you're a c...!)'

We took The Shed in half a minute, we took the North Bank with West Ham in it,

we hammered The Hammers with carving knives and spanners, cos that's the way that Millwall go to war, if you want to be a runner then you better be a Gunner just ask my old man!' because they're all runners when they hear The Lions roar!'

'My old man said be a West Ham fan, I said f... off, bollocks, you're a c...!

We'll take East London and all that's in it, We'll take The Boleyn (North Bank) with West Ham in it, With ratchets and hammers (We'll hammer the Hammers), With Carving knives and spanners, We'll teach those West Ham bastards how to fight,

Cos you'll never take The Den with the (Bushwhackers) Millwall in it, cos we're the pride of South London!'

There was a general old chant sung to the tune of Chuck Berry's 70s hit 'My Ding-A-Ling' that went something like –

'When I was just a little boy, my father bought me my favourite toy, a West Ham fan on a piece of string and told me to kick his f...ing head in, f...ing head in, f...ing head in, he told me to kick his f...ing head in!'

There was also an old plea to play the enemy, which due to their usual higher League position was our best chance for mayhem – 'We want West Ham in the Cup!'

This wish for a proper Cup game, not the Simod Cup game was achieved in 2009/2010 see later on!

I thought it was ironic though that their final Premier League game of 2002/3 a relegation season was at Birmingham City, which would have been us if we had gone up in their place via Play Offs, which would have been very interesting to say the least!!!!!!

More specifically on the player abuse front –

From Them -

West Ham sang a version of 'Oh Wisey!' the previously mentioned – 'Oh Wisey wowo, oh Wisey wowo, he's only 5ft 4, his wife's a f...ing whore!'

From Us –

For our part Bobby Moore used to get the very abusive 'Robin Hood' variation listed in 'Tuesday Night In Grimsby' He has also had 'Bobby Moore Is no more!' sung to the Liverpool/Livermore tune.

We sang to the former Happy Hammer and ever popular Czechoslovakian looney Tomas Repka 'Repka, Repka You're A C...!'

In addition to absent friend Christian Dailly we sang – 'There's Only One Christian Dailly!'

Ex West Ham United goalkeeper Stephen Bywater played against us for Derby County in the FA Cup game in January 2010, he was the keeeper in our 4 – 1 demolition of Wet Spam Untied at the last game against them at the New Den, he was greeted when he was in goal in front of the CBL in the 2nd half of the match with – 'West Ham Reject'/' Bywater, is a wanker, is a wanker ! ' and specifically '4 -1 and we took the piss!'

Pre Premiership demotion we used to sing of the Hammers favourite maverick Paolo Di Canio –

'Paolo Di Canio, he's going downio!'

Or as seemed more likely at the time – 'Paolo Di Canio, he's going to Lazio!'

Then he went to the Anoraks, instead. Rome or Charlton? No contest!

He came to his senses when he did move to Lazio the following season.

Prior to the 'Ammers relegation at the end of 2002/3 there was talk on a Millwall website of organising a plane to fly over Upton Park at their last home game, if it was confirmed that they were coming to join us in Division One, trailing a banner saying ... 'Welcome To Division One'

No need to take the piss – not bloody much!

After Roeder was ousted West Ham's then new Manager Alan Pardew had the following chant sung in the CBL in his honour months before we played the Hammers at home in 2003/4 –

'Chim, chiminey, chim, chiminey, chim-chim-cheroo, we f...ing hate that wanker Pardew!'

As an aside on the morning of Millwall's visit to Upton Park in 2003 Frank McAvennie had sensibly arranged to do a book signing of his ambiguously titled Autobiography 'Scoring – An Experts Guide' at Newham Books in Barking Road, near to the ground. This was organised by an old schoolmate of mine John who works there. West Ham's security advisers had pointed out to him that he could have picked a better day for it but it went ahead anyway and I wished him good luck. John later told me that there were no problems apart from the mulleted love machine turning up late.

Some exchanges from November 21st 2004 New Den game.

West Ham chants – 'Sheep, sheep sheepshaggers!' And 'Where's your caravan?'

Not forgetting –'Your Sister is your Mother, your Father is your Brother, you all f... one another – the Millwall Family!' A Chant I mentioned earlier and also in the Gillingham chant section.

The only vaguely logical explanation for these is that there are a few caravans along Ilderton Road near South Bermondsey and Millwall have an ex pat South London Kent supporting community, a bit tenuous I thought.

Millwall chants in reply –

'Where's your curry house?'/'You're just a shit town in Bengal!'

499

And 'Are you Walford in disguise?'

We sang 'West Ham are going nowhere!'

West Ham replied with 'You've never won f… all!'

We sang 'We beat the scum 4 – 1!'

West Ham sang of their own manager Alan Pardew –

'You don't know what you're doing!' And 'Are you Roeder in disguise!'

They started singing 'We want Pardew out!' when he substituted their best player Luke Chadwick for the less than popular Bobby Zamora, to assist them we joined them in this chant.

We helpfully also sang 'We want Pardew in!' And 'There's only one Alan Pardew!'

Not forgetting the old 'There's only one Glenn Roeder!'

In homage to the man who originally took West Ham down from the Premiership, well done!

At the Upton Park game in April 2005 where West Ham failed to beat us yet again making it 6 games unbeaten for the Lions we sang – 'History, history you're the famous West Ham and your f… ing history, history, history!' And 'Millwall – you'll never beat Millwall!'

From a stereotype standpoint -

West Ham shouted at us – 'Pikeys!'

We replied with the equally non pc – 'Pakis!' sorry PC World!!!!

From a reciprocal graffiti perspective on the recycling footpath approach to the CBL at the New Den it said – 'ICF = MUGS'.

From West Ham's perspective, I saw graffiti on a wall in the East End between West Ham and Plaistow stations on the District Line that said – 'Irons kill Lions'.

There were also dire West Ham Hoolie threats written on the gent's toilet walls in the CBL!

It must have required a real undercover operation to write this.

Someone who worked at the renovation of Upton Park told me at The Den before the Leeds United game 9th August 2014 that in the lift shafts of the Bobby Moore stand as a lot of the workers were

Wall fans, they put Millwall garfitti all the way inside the Lift Shaft and incorporated Millwall memorabilia inside the construction, knowing full well that Wet Spam could not remove it unless they renovated the whole lift shaft! Hope it is true because I loved the thought that they did this, shame they have know knocked this all down, Millwall should have bought it and opened a Millwall Museum.

With the modern phenomenon of having your ashes scattered on a club pitch, I thought that rather than have mine scattered on the New Den pitch I would have them spread on whatever ground Vermin, sorry Wet Spam Untied played at, I thought it would be a good idea as that should sod their pitch up, a bit like sprinkling holy water on to a vampire.

An aside when I worked for an advertising agency we had Newham Health Authority as one of the customers and they decided to use Trevor Brooking in a recruitment campaign. As the company hardcore Football fan I was dispatched to West Ham's programme printers to get a picture of Trev, so I had to brave looking through dozens of photos of one of the enemy, every one of which made him look like he had wind, it was not a pleasant experience!

There was a great opportunity missed in the 1980s when West Ham used 'Pony' as their shirt supplier because at the time, their president was a man called R.H.Pratt. What a shame that he didn't do a Robert Maxwell and have his own name on the shirt front like a sponsor, how it would have gladdened all our hearts at the Old Den when facing West Ham as they ran out in 'Pony' shirts with 'Pratt's' emblazoned across the front, what fun it would have been.

Wrong Place Wrong Time

A couple of examples of the type of mobile phone problems, both West Ham related -

Firstly, my cousin Paul Huish has been a lifelong Millwall home regular and away traveller and for a laugh his then girlfriend Alison, supported the Hammers, she very kindly had a West Ham logo put on to his mobile phone, which he was unable to shift. When he showed it to me at West Bromwich Albion away in 2001/2, I said – 'Look on the bright side she could have put ' I'm forever blowing bubbles' on it as well, which you would have had a bloody job explaining if it went off in a stand full of Lions!'

He naturally bought a new mobile that he put a Millwall badge on, obviously he did not let his then girlfriend get her hands on this one.

Secondly, I got talking to a bloke in the Birmingham City Play – Off queue who told me of a close friend of his who had taken some clients on a business trip to an executive box at Upton Park, he was standing at the bar when his mobile phone decided to chirp in with 'Let 'Em Come', which as you can imagine wasn't exactly greeted with open arms.

Two Millwall coaches pulled into a service station in the Midlands for one away match,

As we walked inside, we saw that there was a bloke in a West Ham shirt.

When we entered the building, his face changed from rosy coloured to deathly white and from blissfully happy as a sand boy to – 'Oh! My God!' He immediately bent down and picked up a small child who he then carried about with him until we left, whether he was a Paedo on a mission, it was really his child or he was just using it as a human shield I do not know, but it saved his bacon nonetheless.

After the Birmingham Play-Off queue marathon, I had to go blood doning.

Anyone who doesn't know the process, prior to actually giving blood is that you have to have a pinprick test on your finger to see if your iron level is okay, I sat down for this test and the nurse kept on continually rubbing my fingers, she said – 'You've got ink all over them!'

I told her that it was printing ink as I had been queuing for Football tickets and had been reading newspapers to pass the time while I stood in the queue, she said -'Who do you support?'

When I told her Millwall, she went silent for a few moments until she admitted that she supported West Ham, Oops! Pain time I thought. A blood doning nurse, rather like a dentist, is not someone that you want to get on the wrong side of as they also have the ability to inflict quite a lot pain, luckily for me she took mercy on me and my veins.

West Ham United played Tottenham Hotspur at Upton Park in a Sunday FA Cup match in 2001, a game which they lost, I had arranged to meet some mates at a pub in East Ham on the night of this game. Upon arrival, I found that it was full to the gunwales with unhappy Hammers; it was not an ideal place to show off my rampant Millwall Lion gold chain that I had foolishly chosen to wear over a T-shirt.

As I stood amongst a sea of claret-and-blue, it prompted numerous less than friendly glances at the shining Millwall symbol in their midst, if pushed, literally or metaphorically, I could have said that it was just a representation of my star sign Leo, which it also sort of is, although somehow I doubt this would have washed, luckily the Hammers were keener on drowning their sorrows than bashing me because I was a tad outnumbered.

When myself and Swedish Millwall mate Henrik Lundgren went into the Hamilton Hall at Liverpool Street station for post Play Off Final consolation Light Ales after coming back from Wembley.

There were loads of Millwall drinking outside and also Glasgow Rangers fans with them who were celebrating because they had won the Scottish SPL that afternoon. We went inside and as we stood at the bar, one bloke walked in with a West Ham United shirt on, he only wanted to play on the fruit machine as it turned out, but F*** me had he chosen the wrong shirt to wear in a pub replete with depressed Lions following our defeat by the other Claret and Blue, who put the C*** in Scunthorpe United!

Fanzone

It was a pity that Sky had not chosen to put any of our recentish matches against West Ham on live, because then we could have featured on the 'Fanzone' section where two opposing fans do the match commentary, if they showed Millwall v West Ham United they could have renamed it 'War-Zone'!

As an aside Fanzone is not something that I could represent Millwall at as they do not appear to have a bleep button and my usual language when watching the Lions would mean I could only do matches after the watershed.

Generally, I think that Sky has missed a trick with the way it was done though – I know the rival commentators are partisan and did get worked up but to bring it more in line with the modern obsession with 'fly-on-the-wall' type programmes, they should have let the two fans do the commentary from the bar whilst steadily getting lashed on Stella.

I am sure you would then get a far more realistic, entertaining and not to say abusive commentary, as it gradually degenerated into an argumentative mess. They could then have done a half time summary from each of the opposing fans at the urinal, as they leant on the loo wall and belched. At the end of the match Richard Keys could have announce a post-match round up from the two fans only to cut back to the bar as the two protagonists were now involved in a Wild West style bar room brawl.

Now that would be entertainment, a trick missed, Live TV would have done it!

Do not dismiss this idea if Jerry Springer can have a show about a man so in love with a horse that he married it and brought it on the show to profess his love, then anything is possible, I refuse to mention the Jeremy Kyle show!

From Panorama To The Real Football Factories – No One Likes Us And The Happy Hammers Connection

The infamous BBC Panorama documentary was screened in November 1977 and very kindly introduced Millwall into the British nation's consciousness as a byword for Football hooliganism.

I saw it fully for the first time in years on the coach to Leeds United in December 2004 I had forgotten that for some reason the reporter said that Spurs not West Ham were our bitter rivals, news to me.

Panorama is probably one of the main reasons why we are still the pariah that we are today; mind you, our much publicised high-profile aggro since then has certainly not helped.

Strangely, a West Ham documentary entitled 'Hooligan' made in 1985 did not have the same detrimental effect on the Happy Hammers fans reputation for some reason especially strange when you consider ex ICF top boy Cass Pennant has written or co written several Hooligan books including -'Congratulations You Have Just Met The ICF' and 'Good Afternoon The Name's Bill Gardner' specifically about West Ham hooligans exploits the latter co written with fellow ICF main man Bill Gardner about his Football hooligan life.

He also wrote/co-wrote a book called 'Want Some Aggro? The True Story Of West Ham's First Guv'nors' about West Ham's pre ICF firm'The Mile End'.

In the late 1960s, early1970s when Boot Boys and Firms first came to prevalence we had a tradition at our Grammar school in the East End, where we would profess to be good friends with the 'Top Boys' or leaders of the local 'Firms' in our case West Ham United and Millwall.

The Millwall names that were bandied about by us were Ginger and Tiny, for those who don't know the latter was a tall black man who like Little John wasn't Little he certainly wasn't Tiny.

The West Ham fans among us would claim to know Bugsy, another black man, or other members of the aforementioned Mile End Mob. Two black blokes must have stood out like the proverbial dog's Eli Wallach's at the time during any trouble, for interest this is my version of Cockney Rhyming Slang!

If you consider it Ginger's Carrot coloured hair wasn't exactly good camouflage either was it?

These claimed affinities, totally fictitious or otherwise, were our own urban myth and would give the people claiming the affinity an air of reflected menace, striking fear into any listener gullible enough to believe their, 'Yeah! The Top Boy's My Mate,' claims.

* The above was adapted for a Southwark News article that I did.

Both 'Panorama' and 'Hooligan' perpetuated the boot boy mythology and if anything bolstered its popularity in fact. Strangely the West Ham Hooligan documentary largely also featured footage of Milllwall's Luton Riot, strange that!

What the initial purposes of the documentaries were who knows but I would imagine all they did was to act as a recruiting campaign for the more impressionable and massage the egos of those involved, swelling their numbers and putting the two teams in the frame to be shot at metaphorically by other clubs 'Boys', who now had the chance to make a name for themselves by taking on the TV stars.

Whilst they did give an insight into the Bovver Boy lifestyle, all they really achieved was to enhance or create the reputation of two of London's most notorious sets of fans, bringing the names of their 'Firms' into the public domain.

For Millwall it was Treatment, The Halfway Liners and F-Troop.

Just in case you are too young to remember F -Troop was a TV comedy western series featuring an incompetent cavalry troop. Panorama also introduced the aforementioned 'Harry the Dog' and his kamikaze solo attacks in to enemy territory to the world.

For West Ham United it introduced the Inter City Firm aka I.C.F.

Highlighting their antics nationwide, it showed that they got their name by travelling on Inter City trains using Persil discount vouchers, which were available as a marketing ploy at the time.

The original Millwall hatchet job and West Hams' later effort both followed similar paths highlighting the away travel and invasion culture of the day. They both showed a day in the life of a 'Firm', a bit like a working-class version of posh people's blood sport – A train or coach trip, a card school, a piss-up, a bloody good punch up and a bit of a rampage around your chosen destination, before heading back home for your tea. The perfect way to spend a Saturday apparently.

Whether it has anything to do with the 70s/80s Millwall and West Ham documentaries or whether it is the real hostility between the two clubs fans or the East End heritage of both sides that did it I do not know, but Millwall and West Ham rivalry does appear to have a fascination for playwrights, TV and film companies, who put the two London clubs fans together as rivals for example -

'The Firm.'

A 1988 TV play with Gary Oldman as a thinly-veiled West Ham ICF top boy called Bex who was in a power struggle with his South London rival and leader of the Buccaneers called Yeti, i.e. Millwall and the Bushwhackers, subsequently relaunched in 2009 on the big screen when this time Millwall and West Ham United are actually specifically mentioned as the two main warring factions.

'I.D.'

Another poorly disguised Millwall/West Ham film, this time more from a Millwall perspective. For Shadwell Town, The Dogs and The Kennel please read Millwall, The Lions and The Old Den.

Its highlight is an FA Cup game between Shadwell Town and their bitter local rivals Wapping, i.e. West Ham.

'Bob Mills.'

Prior to his 'In Bed with Me Dinner' and those bloody London congestion charge ads,

I recall a very strange comic TV punch up, allegedly between the I.C.F and the Bushwhackers.

What it was all about and why God knows.

'In Sickness and In Health'.

Featuring rank Hammer Alf Garnett, in the TV spin-off from 'Till Death Us Do Part', who used to have next-door neighbours that were Millwall supporters and who used to sing Millwall songs through the walls to wind him up.

In West Ham's own right, as everyone undoubtedly knows, there was a hooligan film initially called 'Yank' about Elijah 'Lord of the Rings' Wood as an American moving to England and getting involved in The Green Street Elite, an imaginary version of the ICF, released in September 2005, its release title was either 'Hooligans'/'Green Street Hooligans' or 'Green Street' depending on which country you were in.

West Ham had apparently been duped into allowing themselves to be used for such a project and allegedly it was only called 'Yank' to fool them into allowing shots inside Upton Park. Frodo is featured in the film at Upton Park against Birmingham City and away from the camera he actually attended the Milwall v West Ham United 4 – 1 game at the New Den in March 2004, that must have been a real baptism of fire for him. Having seen the film and having the DVD for those who have not seen it it is like a tourist's guide to London and Cockney rhyming slang, for the American Market presumably. There were also too many bloody renditions of 'I'm Forever Blowing Bubbles' for my liking.'On the inaccuracy front Millwall is signposted as being in Tower Hamlets, which our initial formation home the Isle of Dogs one conveniently is of course and the chants from Millwall are very lame, not a 'No one likes us' or a

'Chim Chimnee' in sight, although the West Ham present top boy, played by Charlie Hunnam, has a London accent. That is so bad that it would make Dick Van Dyke blush with embarassment! Of the anti West Ham chants as I mentioned only 'He's only a poor little Hammer' gets a prominent and very violent rendition near the film's end.

I can't think why they didn't use our 'Bobby Moore is no more!' or our more smutty Robin Hood version can you?

The 'Green Street' GSE violence in the Tunnels v Birmingham Zulu's was actually filmed on Bolina Road i.e. a street that leads towards Millwall's ground, That aside the largest ruck in the film between West Ham and Millwall is actually shot with a Docklands backdrop.

The Lion Roars said that Millwall FC had turned the film company down even so, as we were in Football Factory, we are yet again the evil ones lurking like a bogeyman in the shadows as the sworn enemy who West Ham play in a cup tie, the film is permeated with violent clashes between the rival firms at length and it is by far the most violent of the 3 solely 'Hoolie' films I've mentioned.

There is another version of this Green Street GSE aka ICF tosh called 'Green Street 2 – Stand Your Ground' which I watched on Sky in February 2010 and looked just like a remake of Mean Machine Vinnie Jones version and Scum but also with an interned Football Hooliganism Milllwall/West Ham United additive, complete bullshit, best to avoid at all costs!! I actually regrettably watched Green Street 3 – Never Back Down on London Live TV in December 2018, this was even worse – avoid!

As I mentioned about their 'Hooligans' Documentary strangely, West Ham are not chastised for their Hooligan reputation, as Millwall would be, for example, the aforementioned Happy Hammer Danny Dyer is not castigated despite his Bravo Hooligan Documentaries The Real Football Factory and The Real Football Factory International and also continuously mentioning Millwall v West Ham.

Highlighting the Media largely ignoring any link between the West Ham ICF and their Football violence the 2007 film 'Rise Of The Foot Soldier' is a film based on the life of Carlton Leach, an ICF General, who became a Bouncer and then one of the most highly respected Gangsters in the London and Essex area of the country.

The film also shows the incident where three associated men to him were killed with shotguns infamously in Rettenden Forest in Essex.

I will admit that in the Media, he was mentioned as a feared ICF Football Hooligan General.

The film according to House of Fun allegedly featured West Ham beating the Millwall Bushwhackers so to see if this was true I went to see it at the Cinema to find out if it did which It doesn't, it does feature a violent clash on the Underground when Millwall Treatment era, dressed in blue surgical masks, attack West Ham on their way to Arsenal on a tube train.

Millwall are heavily armed with Knives and Axes and certainly do not lose.

In fact, in an interview with another renowned ICF Football Hooligan and Author/Publisher the aforementioned Cass Pennant, regarding Leach's book 'Muscle'.

Pennant asks him who the hardest Firm West Ham faced was. Leach says that it was undoubtedly Millwall, especially the incidents at the infamous Millwall v West Ham United Harry Cripps Testimonial at the Old Den, where he says that armed Millwall ambushed West Ham in the Old Kent Road.

There was a Favourite 2006/7 Millwall chant formerly aimed at Crystal Palace –

'Millwall Up And West Ham Down, Doodah, Doodah, Millwall Up And West Ham Down Doodah, Doodah Day!' Sadly (I say, mind you I am slightly biased) their dodgy looking dealings with 2 Argentinean Players at the 'Ammers caused them problems, especially the Carlos Tevez farce.

Much more worrying for a Lion it resulted in them staying in the

Premiership somehow, from what looked like an obvious Relegation position when we sang the above chant.

Because of their foreign Players shenanigans, they got a £5 Million fine.

Consequently, I would say that West Ham definitely gets particularly favourable decisions from the authorities, following such a lowish fine and no point's deduction based on the above.

The jammy buggers didn't go down or get forceably points deduction relegated, I reckon it was a bloody fiddle!!!!

Additionally on the factual front, we have featured on the various hooligan documentaries although really only Channel 4's 'Football's Fight Club', mentioned Millwall and West Ham together and it showed the footage of West Ham's 'Boys' taken by British Transport Police when they attacked 'The Crown and Anchor' and the 'Canterbury Arms' prior to a game at the Old Den in 1989.

As I briefly mentioned, in May 2006 West Ham fan and 'Football Factory' actor Danny Dyer presented a Bravo documentary series about football hooliganism called 'The Real Football Factories' the first programme focused on London rivalries, Chelsea's Headhunters and their rivalry with Spurs Yid Army and more specifically for us, Millwall and West Ham United, the programme incorporated footage of both Millwall's 'Panorama' and West Ham's 'Hooligan' documentaries.

Naturally it also had footage of our Luton Town and Birmingham City riots.

In our own non West Ham related right, we have featured in various other things, for example –

On the factual front there was the aformentioned historical programme shown on Channel 4 called 'No One Likes Us' a decade or so ago and 'Hooligans – No One Likes Us' documentary.

On the fictional front, our hooligans were obviously highlighted in 'Arriverderci Millwall', an England hooligan play/TV drama and featured in the aforementioned films 'The Football Factory', 'Green Street' and 'Rise Of The Foot Soldier'

Moving away from hooliganism we were also featured in the films 'Nil by Mouth' and 'Goodbye Charlie Bright'. Happy Hammer actor Ray Winstone had to wear a Millwall shirt in 'Nil by Mouth' and said that he had to wear a West Ham shirt beneath it, as he could not bear it to touch his skin.

As a hardcore Millwall fan I know how he feels, I have a job getting on a bus in the East End if it says 'Upton Park' on the front! Another problem is my going into a Pie and Mash shop, a London delicacy that I love with a passion, that have West Ham flags or Posters up.

Like the ones that I have been in in the recent past at Roman Road, Bow, East Ham and Shadwell, with Robins at East Ham being the worst for its overt West Ham memorabilia, Mind you it is very near to West Ham United Upton Park era itself so it is not too unusual that it is bedecked in 'Appy 'Ammers stuff I suppose

On TV there was of course Lottery Larry's favourite 'Only Fools And Horses' that often had Millwall references on it. Mind you I found out on the Internet that Buster Merryfield i.e Uncle Albert allegedly actually played for us once, that explains why it was always on the Video on the coaches if true.

One of the characters on an Alison Stedman, Jim Broadbent LWT programme from a decade plus ago, whose name escapes, me was a Millwall fan and was often shown on the terraces at the Old Den and one of the fire fighters on 'London's Burning' was a Millwall fan.

F.A Albin & Son's the family of Funeral Directors based near Rotherhithe Tunnel, featured on the 2003 ITV reality show 'Don't Drop The Coffin' were Millwall supporters who were shown at a game at the New Den.

'We want West Ham in the Cup!' – 'You do? There you are!' The Carling Cup second Round game at Upton Park, Tuesday 26th August 2009

Closing this Lions not Irons chapter, after beating Bournemouth in the Carling Cup 1st round and then drawing the unhappy 'Ammers in the second round draw. Our first real cup encounter since the 1930s which was in the FA Cup, not counting the Simod Cup game there, the Police naturally went in to f*** that aka s*** themselves mode because of this hated enemy away clash on 25th August 2009.

Whether this is all true or not I do not know, but a Millwall Steward we spoke to said that we originally were allocated 6000 tickets, West Ham then decided to halve this to 3,000 in the lower tier only

I know that West Ham United moved all the Wet Spam Season Ticket holders in this end to other home parts of the ground. Then the Plod halved it again to 1500.

What fun, it is very unusual for Millwall to get ballsed about, err no it is not!

Even though the actual Allocation had not been confirmed yet, Millwall assumed that it would be 3000, and said that we Season Tickets Holders could get tickets online or by phone Friday, then in person Saturday.

To make matters worse the company who did the Ticket Sales f***** it up, as we heard that they started selling them to Members on the phone or online Wednesday and Thursday,

In my opinion, they should not do this, as only Season Ticket holders were eligible first and according to Millwall site not until Friday with Members not eligible until Tuesday this week.

After all the ballsing about and the allocation being brought down, with us Season Ticket holders able to get tickets online and on phone, we sold 900, and we only had 600 left, this was after Millwall heard from the Plod.

As I said above Millwall were working on the assumption that we would get 3000, consequently after Old Bill's extremely wise – my arse decision, they stopped the phone and Online option at midday approx. Friday and only did it on a Personal Basis Saturday prior to our home game v Carlisle United.

One of my Millwall mates Paul Simms did not want to wait until Saturday and had gotten his, his brother Nathan and his Dad Dave's tickets on the phone Friday first thing.

The rest of us didn't fancy getting ours that way and when they halved our allocation again as I am our Ticketmaster, although it was my Birthday Saturday 15th August I got up at 5am and walked through Rotherhithe Tunnel, what else would you do on your Birfday?

I got over the Den at 6.15am and there was about 30 people in front of me, the Stewards went along the queue to the ticket office behind the CBL, asking people how many tickets everyone was getting and taking a tally, it was at about 140 where I was so I knew that I would be okay, so hoorah!

In celebration of me Birfday, I got the requisite five additional Wet Spam Untied away tickets that I needed with the Teamcards that I had from the boys. Just as well, that I did get there early as we sold out our Allocation of 1500 by mid-morning.

Re this main enemy 'Appy F***ing 'Ammers game, the Old Bill F***ed up big time.

As we had all one end and due to the reductions and our not being allowed in the upper tier, to give us less height to throw things I assume, there were only 2300 of us in it after the second wave of 800 tickets, consequently there were hundreds of Millwall over there without tickets.

Therefore, the Plod would have to try to find our lot in Upton Park and around the outside of the ground, during the outside battle, which we ourselves saw none of it as we were inside the ground.

The Police had to call in Reinforcements during the night's warfare to try to control it all. Why had they not realised that if it was going to be a war zone as they apparently thought that it would be, there should have been too many, not too few occifers there in the first place?

I do not suppose that it had occurred to them that if we had a standful of tickets they could keep track of us and know where we were! You know the form that we generally get anyway treat us as if we are terrorists surround us with Riot Police, Alsatians, Meat Wagons, Police Cavalry, etc and keep us in the ground for hours after the game, this did not really happen too much either, see later on.

I myself thought why not have a checkpoint to ascertain if people had match tickets and prove which team they supported outside the station in Green Street? As they often used to have outside the Cold Blow Lane at the Old Den at these sorts of games. Seems like a good idea to me, because that way if people did not have tickets then they could divert them away from the proposed battlefield, it would also stop Millwall fans who had gotten tickets in Wet Spam bits, as they could then move them in to the empty upper tier of the away stand, what do I know!

As we were given, the Sir Trevor Brooking end aka the North Bank as was and were initially allocated 3000, which the Police in their infinite wisdom halved to 1500, Millwall complained, and Wet Spam agreed with us that it was a stupid idea; the English National Fans Forum and Simon Hughes the MP for Bermondsey complained directly to the Old Bill and said that doing it this way would cause more problems not less. As an act of partial appeasement the Old Bill gave us 800 more tickets, so we had 2300, that aside it was still well below the allocation that we should have had.

The Old Bill after the complaint about the first massive ticket reduction naturally denied everything and blamed Tom Dick and Harry, strangely they did not see sense and give us the other 700 tickets to reach the promised 3000 at least. Police and Intelligence are certainly not words that you can put together in a sentence! I said at the time that the way that they planned it (sic) would require more plod not less. For a kick off delaying the announcement about the Allocation decisions obviously meant that, many Lions fans got tickets from Wet Spam mates.

If they had not f***ed about so much this would not have happened to any great degree, I suppose their thinking was as there would be a mass off this way they could then blame Millwall for it, as per usual!

On the day of the game John one of my mates, a Gooner, who works in a book shop right near the ground in Barking Road, phoned me mid afternoon to say that Wet Spam Untied mob were all firmed up and on the piss in The Boleyn where they were tooled up and singing songs about going to war with Millwall, he said that the pub itself had hired extra security, he also said that he had also heard previous rumours that it was all going to kick off big time in Green Street, how true that was.

When I told my Millwall mates about this call we all said why have they allowed pubs to be open all day? We usually have to put up with Alcohol free zones aplenty, the nearest open away fan pub is usually in the next county if it is played well outside London!

Another mate of mine Dave who used to live right near Upton Park, said that as it is such a large Muslim Ghetto that the alcohol business in the pubs has tailed off alarmingly therefore on such a big boozers game they would open up all day and pretend that it was New Year's Eve profit wise, rather than have one man, his pint and his dog sitting in the saloon bar, whether there would be widespread trouble or not!

On the night 3 of my mates Paul, Nathan and Dave drove there and the other 5 of us, me, Clive, Simon, Pat and his mate Ricky got the Tube to Upton Park from Whitechapel and walked to the ground, through the usual Police State, there were also hundreds of Unhappy Ammers Herbert's everywhere in Green Street, we walked to our away end and did not see any of the trouble outside.

Pre kick off they shut the Upton Park Tube station and Millwall got off at East Ham or Plaistow and it all went pear shaped for the poor non-Football sods on the trains or the Millwall who had to walk unescorted through the Wet Spam heartland, where it naturally kicked off several times, what a surprise, the Police apparently said to Millwall fans who asked them what the best way to go was, that they could not escort them and they could not guarantee their safety! Marvellous!

A couple of my Millwall mates the brothers Laurie and Jordan, were told to get off the train at Plaistow, they asked the Old Bill and were told the above so they trudged along with people walking that way, in what turned out to be amid a throng of Hamsters, when they got to Green Street, they managed to be let through the Police cordons there by telling them that they were Millwall, they then headed through the residential back street where it was unpoliced and the West Ham Herbert's spotted them having left the West Ham throng and were heading towards the Away section, sussed that they were Millwall, and sang at them 'Scum' in response and Jordan was hit in the back by a bottle that they threw at him!

Steve one of my mates who supports Spurs travelled back from Dagenham Heathway where he had been at another friend of ours Keith's house at about 6 – 6.30pm, they stopped the train he was on at East Ham I think and announced that they could not move on as there was trouble at Upton Park and they had to stop, he said that a train load of Millwall arrived as they were running trains on to Barking or somewhere, so they pulled the Communication Cord and their tube stopped on the other Platform, they got off the train and ran across to the Westbound side and the Driver in response had to shut all the train doors, which they tried to batter their way in too unsuccessfully, Steve caught in this rumpus said that it was terrifying, the Driver of the Tube said due to this Ag that as an Emergency Procedure he had to drive off so he did!

Unsurprisingly it kicked off big time outside, and inside there was Wet Spam trouble with Stewards and Old Bill, and three mass pitch invasions, and it was featured in the media, as if Hooliganism had suddenly reappeared out of the 70s/80s mist.

As we were inside the ground we did not see any of the outside trouble but we heard about all the Aggro going on in Green Street during the game from my Cousin Paul, who is a Millwall member and couldn't get an away ticket, he lives in Essex and he didn't trust himself with Wet Spam mates who said go with us we will protect you and I also heard from my Millwall Swedish mate Henrik who was also not there but watching it online or via the news on TV or listening on Radio, I got news via their mobiles, etc. while the game was on.

We saw the Wet Spam Aggro with Stewards and Plod inside the ground to our right and their 3 Pitch Invasions from all around the ground, all the TV and Press went in to 'it is the return of the Football Hooligan Warfare' overdrive, it was mentioned everywhere! This stupid assumption is only because all the Aggro that happens unless it features Millwall is not bloody reported! Hull City in the FA Cup in 2008/9 media overkill, I rest my case!

As you undoubtedly know It is always like tribal warfare between Millwall and Wet Spam Untied, but the Police caused a hell of a lot of their own problems, their halving Millwall's allocation from what Wet Spam had originally given us, caused Millwall to either turn up with no tickets, get tickets from West Ham mates in their section, get them online or simply turn up for the inevitable mass ruck!

It had obviously not occurred to the Police that if they had ALL Millwall in one section they could pen us in and they would know where everyone was, too easy that!!!

I myself naturally know which away games are going to be dodgy and which aren't, I always work on the basis that if I have to defend myself or mates/relatives then I will fight, we personally don't all go out of our way to look for trouble.

The bloke who got stabbed in the chest was a Millwall fan, and a mate of Chris Bethell who works for the 'Wall, we were speaking to him when we were held in the Police Cordon outside on the way to Upton Park station after being held in ground for a short while amazingly and he said pre match that some were on their way to the away end behind the home Bobby Moore, some of them turned off another way towards the Millwall section and walked straight into Wet Spam's mob and he got stabbed! At least some media mentioned that he was only a father with kids and was Millwall, stabbed by The Academy's 'heroes', at least the media did not imply that he committed Hari Kari as a Millwall fan, with the ups and downs of a team like us, this type of thing would have been wholesale!

It was like verbal tribal warfare inside the ground and a Police State in and out before and after, you know the form, it was electric in the ground far more so from the home sections than we have had before there from my experience.

West Ham United should be fined massively for the pitch invasions; there was one after each of their goals. The Stewards and Police did sod all about, nothing to do with Millwall at all.

On the night, we said it was amazing this, because if anyone goes on the pitch at the New Den, they are treated as if they are going to murder some of the opposition players, whereas today, they seemed to be able to do what they bloody well liked. We all said on the night that if that had happened at the New or Old Den we would have been shut down as in the past or fined the national debt!

See my comments at the end of this chapter about what happened re the punishment imposed for the Aggro,

One very fat, short wearing bare chested Hamster in fact ran on to the pitch from the stand to our left, misunderstanding the meaning of Chicken Run I think! Moreover, he was escorted and returned back to his seat by a steward! If that had been at our ground he would have been treated like an opponent of Stone Cold Steve Austin in a wrestling match, this fat git was probably asked if he was comfortable and would like a pie! Of course, he bloody would!

We said Kenny Jackett during these invasions that he should walk our team off and say that his team felt intimidated by the home fan mass invasions, knowing our luck if he had done this West Ham United would have been given the game as we refused to play them, or some bollocks!

In the game Millwall outplayed them for the first 90 minutes, they hit the post, but we had 4 or 5 good chances, in fact Dunne should have scored straight after Bomber's goal, we really got behind them as usual, it was a real Millwall night, the players came over to us after the game and threw their shirts in to our end after negotiating the thronged Stewards in front of us and we sang among other things -'We're Proud Of You Millwall!'

After this at the end of the game we were held in and around the ground for about half hour and then were allowed back to Upton Park station, from there I got a tube to Barking and then a Mainline train from there to Limehouse station right near me, I was indoors by Midnight.

It is always like tribal warfare Millwall v Wet Spam Untied, but the Police caused a hell of a lot of the problems, their halving Millwall's allocation from what Wet Spam had originally given us.

Therefore it caused Millwall to either turn up with no tickets, get tickets from West Ham mates in their section, got them online or simply turned up for the inevitable mass ruck! It had obviously not occurred to the Police that if they had ALL Millwall in one section they could pen us in and they would know where everyone was, too easy that!

It was like verbal warfare inside the ground and a Police State in and out before and after, you know the form!

Harry Redknapp ex hamster player and manager said in the red top gutter press The Sun on Thursday 27th August 2009 that we should never be allowed to play each other again, he said something like 'If it is a cup draw, then it should be redrawn and if in league it should be played behind closed doors' what a Botox desperately needed foreskin faced stupid prick!

At Wigan Athletic on 15th May 2011 when HOF organized a fly past of a small plane with a banner behind it that said Avram Grant Millwall Legend praising Agent Avram as he was known at Millwall and his sterling work when Wigan Athletic equalized after their clawing back from their 2 – 0 deficit and later beating the Spammers to relegate them. It must have pleased Harry Boy a treat; we would be playing each other twice in 2011/2012.

Strange but true on a coach trip to Chesterfield in August 2016 we drove past Lords when England where playing Pakistan in ODI as crowds flooded in and as we passed a crossing Avram Grant walked by spooky or what!

To emphasize who we wanted to play and implying that we had done it on purpose when we lost against Swansea City we sang in the last home game of our season 2010/11 a fortnight before the Hammers demise – 'Down For The West Ham, We're staying down for the West Ham!'

When we lost and our Play Off possibility had disappeared and the 'Appy 'Ammers looked like coming to join us which they did!

I have said to umpteen Hamsters I know that their opening Olympic Stadium game should be against us, that will sort the seats out for you! Let's be honest their first ever game at Upton Park was v us so why not the same there!

Back to Harry Boy wonder what masterplan he would have come up with had this happened, returning to the League Cup game I think that he was in panic mode because Wet Spam Untied, the alleged Academy, one of the darlings of the Premier League and the purported 1966 World Cup winners, would themselves get hammered big time by the FA for their Aggro and pitch invasions inside Upton Park/The Boleyn Ground or whatever it was f***ing called.

He basically said that West Ham fans are not like that! What planet does he live on or come from!!!!

Some of the worst in ground violence that I have ever personally seen was West Ham United v Manchester United, when Man U won the league at Wet Spam in 1967 by beating the hamsters there 6 – 1, I was only about 9 at the time and my Dad took me to it as all the top players at the time, Moore, Hurst, Best, Stiles, Charlton, Law etc. were playing in the game, the day from memory inside the ground was a bloody parade of dart and missile thrown blood strewn damaged victims, with a continual parade of ejected culprits all afternoon, it was just like the film 'ID' for those who have seen it.

For 'Arry Boy to say what he did he conveniently must have never heard of the early years Mile End mob, the ICF, Cass Pennant, Bill Gardener, Carlton Leach, read any of their or other ICF/Mile End authors books or seen any of the films like 'Rise Of The Footsoldier', 'Green Street', 'Green Street 2 : Stand Your Ground' ; the remade version of 'The Firm', which was specifically about clashes between Millwall and West Ham United Firms, not the Gary Oldman original, which had very flimsily hidden Firm names and not forgetting the West Ham United Top Boy Cass Pennant autobiographical film 'Cass!'

If they did what he suggests, what would he do assemble an acceptable list –

Say ban all Leeds United v Cardiff City games, in fact Leeds United, Stoke City, Portsmouth or Bristol City v anyone they play and Cardiff City v Swansea City or anyone else the 2 taffs play.

Burnley v Blackburn Rovers, Sheffield Wednesday v Sheffield United, Newcastle United v Sunderland, Spurs v Arsenal/Chelsea or West Ham United,

Does Southampton v Portsmouth ring any bells as you were Pompey's manager?

Carrying on compiling the banning list Manchester United v Leeds United/Manchester City or Liverpool, Birmingham City v Aston Villa or Wolves, Leicester City v Chelsea, Notts Forest v Derby County, West Bromwich Albion v Wolves etc. games!

His option I assume would be to suggest that we only have happy clappy family clubs games, like say Wycombe Wanderers v Charlton athletic, if that ever happened I would lapse in to a tedium induced coma !!!

Carlton Cole, seemed to also leap in to the defend the Premier League Spamsters fray by using the Race Card, as he claimed that we racially abused him with monkey noises etc., which some may very well have done, but Jason Price was also allegedly abused by the home fans.

What about their equalizing goal scorer Junior Stanislas, making gestures at us when he scored, isn't that inciting the crowd at what was a hot bed night anyway? Strangely this was never mentioned and he was not booked for it!

I think any abuse of Carlton Cole was because we saw him being mooted as the main cog in the England forward line and all thought my God are we in trouble internationally if he is one of our main goal scoring forwards! The FA was investigating these apparent racist outbursts.

To me it seems that Wet Spam Untied sat down post all the home fan Aggro and decided to try to blame us for something, you know 'They are Millwall so obviously it is all their fault!' Wrong!!!

The BBC and Charlie Nicholas on Sky according to the House of Fun went in to overdrive mode to try to find something that they could use to blame us for all the Aggro, why?

Prior to our trip to Hamsters Central during our game, at home the Tuesday before against Oldham Athletic, there was our customary plethora of anti-West Ham abuse and to highlight the Asian nature of Newham some sang – 'We're going to Bangladesh!' and 'We're going to Bollywood!'

On the Racist front I admit that we did sing the following at the game –

'Your Mum is from Bangladesh!'/'You're just a town full of Pakis' and 'You're all on Ramadan!'

We also sang 'Your Coat's from Pakistan' in response to 'Your Coat's from Matalan!' that the Chicken Run sung at our section. These were like the Oldham Athletic game chants to highlight the undoubted Muslim Asian ghetto nature of the surrounding area.

On the player front in response to West Ham United player Callum Davenport being stabbed several times In the legs, with his Mother also being attacked, and there was a mooted amputation of his leg.

To highlight this we sang in response to the whole ground singing 'Stand Up If You Hate Millwall' –

'Stand up if you've got 2 legs!' another new chant on the night went –

'Wow Callum, wow Callum, Wowo – he used to have good skills, now looks like Heather Mills!'

We know how to aid anyone's physical recovery!

On Monday 28th September 2009 West Ham United were charged on four counts of failing t to control their supporters whilst Millwall FC were charged on three counts following events at the Carling Cup fixture. The FA alleged that both clubs failed to ensure that their supporters conducted themselves in an orderly fashion.

Specific charges relating to West Ham United FC include:

Failure to ensure their supporters refrained from violent, threatening, obscene and provocative behaviour.

Failure to ensure their supporters refrained from racist behaviour.

Failure to ensure their supporters didn't throw missiles, harmful or dangerous objects onto the pitch.

Failure to ensure their supporters didn't enter the field of play.

Amazingly or not, Specific charges relating to Millwall FC include:

Failure to ensure their supporters refrained from violent, threatening, obscene and provocative behaviour.

Failure to ensure their supporters refrained from racist behaviour.

Failure to ensure their supporters didn't throw missiles, harmful or dangerous objects onto the pitch.

Are the FA f***ing mad? Or is it a Premier League do not have aggro aka they have loads of money ruse, I know what I think chaps!

In January 2010 the Independent group who had looked at all FA charges, found Millwall innocent of all the supposed charges Wet

Spam Untied were found guilty of all bar the racist behaviour and throwing missiles, but guilty of all others, a couple of days after the decision was made they imposed a fine of £115,000 plus costs of 5,000, amazing that it was not all Millwall's fault somehow obviously, we are usually blamed for absolutely everything, however whilst it is great that justice has been done a few things – will Millwall get their legal costs lay out back, for the massively expensive legal Defence team that they had to put together because of the FA's completely fatuous charges, will we bollocks I seriously doubt it, if we did try to get it back they would just fine us for something else, if we sued the FA for it being their fault that the Legal Defence team was needed, also a fine of £115,000 the main fine, is completely inappropriate in my Millwall mind because if we were at home and had actually done what they did inside and outside the ground the punishment would be

- A) We would have been fined a king's ransom
- B) We would have been banned from playing in the Carling Cup the next season
- C) The New Den would have been closed for a set period as we have had to endure several times in the past at the Old Den

As one of my Millwall cousin's Paul had implied after the fun that had happened at Upton Park/The Boleyn or whatever, one of the FA's main men Wet Spam Untied legend Sir Trevor Brooking must have sucked some serious cock to keep it all dragging on forever and to keep the punishment to be so relatively light, what do I know I have Millwall paranoia!!

At Wycombe Wanderers away in February 20th 2010 in praise of the great man's influence against us Sir Trevor got the following homage's 'One Trevor Brooking, There's Only One Trevor Brooking, With A Packet Of Sweets, And An Ice Cream Van, Brooking's Got Madeleine McCann!' and 'Brooking Is A Sex Case, La La La La!

On Saturday 17th September 2011, we clashed again at the New Den, with access anywhere near the away end, or our own main Club Shop totally blocked to us, I am sure Harry Boy Redknapp must have been appalled that this game went ahead! F*** him, there was Police aplenty and it did not kick off big time as he had applied that us naughty Millwall would do against his sainted Hammers.

West Ham United got 2000 tickets in the North Stand Upper Tier only.

Millwall had said to the Police must not make it home fan only or played behind closed doors as it will kick off big time away from the grounds where they would not be able to control or away fans would get tickets in the home bits, so they would have no control there either

The game was a 0 – 0 draw meaning Wet Spam Untied had still not beaten us at home since 1988, Premier League my arse!

The anti-Wet Spammers chants-

In homage to the Millwall Legend –

'Avram Grant, Avram Grant! And ' Avram Grant My Lord Wowo, Avram Grant, Avram Grant My Lord Wowo Avram Grant, Avram Grant My Lord Wowo Avram Grant, Oh Lord Avram Grant!

Carlton Cole got – 'You Knicked My Stereo! Moreover 'You're Just a S*** Emile Heskey!' a bigger insult than being a burglar in my book!

Robert Green got – 'Wanker Wanker!' with appropriate gestures and 'You Let Your Country Down!' After his World Cup f*** up v USA, in 2010

Kevin Nolan got – 'You're Just a S*** Joey Barton!' his ex-Toon Army colleague.

Not West Ham but a reference –

Joey Barton himself playing for QPR at The New Den 19th October 2013 got

'Barton, Barton You're A C***!'and 'You Scouse C***'

James Tomkins who was taken off looking alarmed at how we could be so nasty to his him and his fellow Hamsters got – 'Your Bottles Gone, Your Bottles Gone!'

Karren Brady now at West Ham United got – 'Karren Brady is a slapper, is a slapper!' and 'We can smell your C*** from here!' Two golden oldies from her Birmingham City bullshit spouted following major aggro at St Andrews.

What A Difference A Day Makes –

The next day, I went to Fulham v Manchester City with Swedish Millwall mates Michael and his eldest son Christoffer as they were over for the above game; it was like entering Narnia, especially after the day before v the enemy.

To highlight this I saw only six Police cavalry, there were No Riot Police, No Police on Motorbikes, No Rabid Police Alsatians, and No Truncheon wielding fully armoured Plod, No Meat Wagons, and No Hoolie Vans! No post-match segregation and nobody was kept in the ground for an eternity or kettled outside,

I am awake aren't I ?

I did see a helicopter hovering but this was just nearby not hovering above us like a gunship! We could not find a pub anywhere near the bloody ground,

To highlight the surreal nature of it all we sat in a Neutral zone behind goal that was essentially in Man City's away section but occupied by Fulham and Man City and tourists from everywhere flashing cameras..

I thought that I had entered a parallel universe, a neutral zone would be right up our street at Millwall, would it b***ocks, be interesting to see what we get if we go to Fulham, doubt it will be quite the same! I found out when I watched a match on Sky Sport from the Cottage, that the Neutral zone only applies to games that are not sold out, i.e. there was not one when their local rivals Chelski played there in April 2012, so with us, sold out or not It would revert to our usual massed Police State!

Wet Spam in Nam FA Cup 3rd Round
Saturday 7th January 2012

A month before our trip to Upton Park in February 2012, we played on their manor at Dagenham and Redbridge in the FA Cup, 6 of us went Paul, Nathan and Dave Simms who live in Chingford/Chigwell and Harlow and drove over there, myself, Simon and Patrick Barrett went there via tube, we went in Cafe opposite as Simon was starving, The ordered food was taking yonks so I left them there as it was clocking on and the others were already in ground.

When I got to ground there were queues as they were checking tickets more due to dodgy ones knocking about and a lot of people were turned away.

Simon said that when they arrived just before KO, about 15 West Ham tried to attack young Millwall in the park outside, older Wall saw this steamed into them, they buggered off and Old Bill closed ranks around it.

After game we were held in ground then allowed out through park where we had to go through small gap, so in dribs and drabs, we all got through and the 6 of us walked down to near station and we separated Paul/Dave/Nathan to go to car and me, Simon and Pat to Dagenham East.

When we three got there you could hear noise from downhill past the station, and the Old Bill went steaming past in umpteen meat wagons, what had happened was that Vermin were gathered down there and threw bottles etc. at Millwall, who then charged at them and they all run, they never wanted to attack a large group of Millwall as you will see later.

Dagenham East was shuttered and we were all milling about outside until they finally opened shutters and we were all ferried on to a Special that went directly to Tower Hill, where I went home via Tower Gateway DLR and Simon and Patrick went back to Whitechapel on tube to get bus home from there.

I got a text on the night that the other 3 were attacked by Vermin on the way back to their car and had had to go to Police station they were all thankfully okay but it had been dodgy for them.

I spoke to Dave on the Sunday morning and he told me what had happened, he said that Old Bill had cordoned people going back to cars and only let them through in dribs and drabs.

He said that they were walking towards their car on a main road, several hundred yards away when about 50 – 60 Vermin came charging downhill, saw Paul's Lion badge knew they were Millwall and Dave got attacked from behind with a kick, Dave fought back and Old Bill then came charging in having seen fracas, he said Plod were about 50 yards behind them, they nicked the bloke who attacked him and Vermin all run when Plod turned up.

Re Nam the East London name for Dagenham we all knew the possibilities of them turning up so were alert that it could kick off, but Nathan said to me that it was good that all 6 of us had not been there together when they turned up because we would have all fought the Vermin, would very well have lost due to being outnumbered about 10 to 1, but we would no doubt been arrested, simply for being Millwall!!!

I heard that there were around 250 Millwall plotted up in The Barking Dog a Wetherspoons pub at Barking, strangely no show by West Ham. So straggler attacks it was, true heroism, no show when Millwall are firmed up, but happy to attack dribs and drabs of easy looking targets mob handed and flashing blades in some cases, f***ing heroes to a man! The Vermin heroes had adopted an attack stragglers policy, like the tactic adopted by Wolves, too frightened to attack large groups.

Dave said it was like Custer's Last Stand, I said it was lucky you had not been stabbed like that Wall bloke was at Upton Park in same attack style mate, they must have seen Dave is a short man who is over retirement age and thought he was an easy target, wrong!

Dave/Paul and Nathan had to give statements at Plod shop as man was charged by Dave with assault.

Dave said he got a phone call later Saturday night asking if he would drop charge as the assailant had said he was sorry, he had no criminal record and was a married man with kids, who was being released on the Monday after game! I said he sounds like a nice bloke mate should ask him round for dinner!

Dave said no I am not withdrawing assault charge, I was attacked when walking along with my two sons so he deserves it, he came hurtling down with a Vermin mob so what was he doing there if he was innocent? Bloody right let the b****** suffer I said to Dave when he told me that he should definitely press charges, let's be honest what else was the Vermin there for?

I said in all truthfulness Dave the Old Bill are just trying to save themselves the f***ing paperwork.

If the Nam Filth had done their job and cleared streets when we were held in ground there would not have been any aggro. It was the same Police Intelligence Eek! That the Old Bill had adopted at Carling Cup game at Upton Park, hence the Wall bloke getting stabbed by a West Ham mob near a Council estate.

After Nam game we said that it would not surprise us if game at Vermin's in February would be home fan only.

I thought this likely as I looked on West Ham website Sunday after Nam and there was sod all on there about Millwall game re tickets, ticket news about games weeks later but not that one.

I said after aggro at Nam the Old Bill will say Upton Park is unpoliceable, it is if you leave pubs near ground open all day and F*** up the policing as usual!!!

Amazingly we were all wrong and we received an allocation, albeit of less than 1500.

Wet Spam Untied Championship away Saturday 4th February 2012

A game that we lost 2 – 1 thanks to a fantastically inept refereeing when he allowed the most blatant foul in all Christendom on Forde before their winner, moving away from the result to the chants –

Us to them

Regarding their proposed/possible move to the Olympic Stadium in Stratford –

'You're just the shit end of Westfield!'

The huge shopping area near the London Stadium

When the PA announced home fans in the Chicken Run should only go towards Barking Road, we sang – 'It's for your own Protection!'

Them to us

'You're going back to your caravan!'

Their Gypsy reference due to the row of caravans parked along Ilderton Road South Bermondsey end I thought but one of my mates Tony Russell was told we are Gypsys because we are based in South London in the Hamsters mind a Romany stronghold, eh!.

Our reply to them

'You're going back to your Taliban!

Our response allied to the predominantly Asian nature of Newham

Them to us

'You're going down with the Redknapp!'

Strange chant as he was an ex Hammer I thought, whether he was now Spurs manager and in court over tax evasion whilst at Pompey or not.

Our reply to them

'You're going down on your Mother!'

Naturally, from us – the Bobby Moore, Avram Grant and Trevor Brooking Sex offender chants got frequent airings.

We Want West Ham In The Cup Away At Olympic Stadium

I would just like to say that I and in fact all of us Wall have more chance of winning the lottery than Millwall drawing West Ham United in any cup especially if it was at their free council funded money pit The London Stadium aka the Olympic Stadium, the balls would magically disappear back in to the back quicker than Lewis Hamilton could do a lap in the stadium in his F1 car.

I would love to see what on earth the people pulling the balls out of the bag as It were did if Millwall were drawn away in FA Cup or League Cup, I put that not Milk Cup, EFL, Littlewoods, Carabao along with many other names so that you know that I meant the League Cup.

If at Den might be tolerated behind closed doors or if home or away moved to some unreachable venue because if that draw happened and it was to be at their Olympic Free Stadium it would never ever be allowed.

With the incompetent stewarding at their stadium apparently unable to handle Watford, so what on earth would they make of us!! Bearing in mind the violent history between each other alongside Wet Spam Untied Unhappy 'Ammers fighting amongst their own sections or Watford, in the first few games at their new Council owned paid f*** all for it stadium.

The reason I believe for shit stewarding, no police inside, stupid restrictions on access, lack of signposting or lighting outside for night matches, so an Orient supporting mate of mine who went to the first ever game there in Europa League Qualifier, this is all a ploy by the money grabbing Porn Baron bastards behind the 'Ammers who would love to see the stadium turned into a soulless money pit, filled with people who are not Football fans in reality let alone support West Ham, in my opinion as a Cockney born in East End, believe it is a lets destroy East End traditions and history, lets replace with right on Gastro Pub lodgers!

I am sorry to admit this but I Actually went to the London Stadium in February 2019, when a club I am in got 10 free tickets, I went incognito, refraining from wearing my customary Millwall shirts, scarf and bobble hat or taking my rattle! This was on a Friday night against Fulham, not exactly us, and there is a section they block off with barriers around away section outside, I thought well that would work a treat if we ever played there not!!!

CHAPTER 14
'Me And Me Mates'

Me, Me, Me on a Personal Note –
If you have read my other Millwall books you'll know all of the people mentioned in this chapter, to start is a plethora about me, and what then follows is a collection of personal stories.

There comes a time when age begins to creep up on you as Mandy Smith found out with Bill Wyman. Football is a perfect place to realise it, as you watch players that you consider ready for the knacker's yard who turn out to be younger than you are, this is as good an indicator of the ageing process as any, the same applies when you have seen a player play his entire career from debut to retirement as I have done with the likes of Kitchener, Stevens and Sheringham to name just three.

As you get older the clincher is when the managers are younger than you, then you really know it's time to retire to Eastbourne, take up Bowls and get in a couple of cases of Sanatogen, hopefully that's a few years off yet! Watching Millwall isn't exactly conducive to not giving you worry lines and grey hair, that's for sure, they can turn you to drink as well, not that I need much turning if truth be told.

I must have a 'joiner' mentality, as I have been tempted over the years to buy -

Millwall shares, at top dollar 20p obviously, I bought these for sentimental value only and because I like waving my money go bye bye. I certainly did not think that I would be making a killing in the

Square Mile that is for sure. I bought a Lions card, much maligned at a time, but from which I have had my money back with interest over the years in the form of discounts on season tickets and the like.

I was a member of the now sadly defunct Away travel club. I have also been a member of IMSA and am of the MSC, not forgetting my many many years as a season-ticket. I now obviously have a Teamcard of the home and away variety as well. It appears that any excuse to get my name or ugly mug on anything associated with Millwall and I must have it. The mug shot of me on Millwall's file unfortunately makes me look like the 'Mad Axeman' or one of Reggie and Ronnie's henchmen, based on which I would not let me in to a ground anywhere in the country or sell me any tickets in the first place!

Charlton fan pastime moment – I have a confession to make whenever I watched Countdown I always hoped that when the contestant asked Carol Vorderman for 3 vowels in a row and she picked out

'E, I, O'. On October 27th 2004 it came out twice!!! Which had me air pumping from my living room armchair – a bit of a worry isn't it?

Something strange happened to me outside the WACA Cricket ground in Perth, Western Australia a few years ago when I was on holiday visiting an old schoolmate Ian, who now lives there. This was in the mid-1990s and unfortunately, I was away over the period when we knocked Arsenal and Chelsea out of the FA Cup. Sadly, I missed the victorious games at Highbury and Stamford Bridge. I saw us lose at QPR though. I was in Australia ostensibly for a holiday but also to see the final Ashes Test in the1994/95 series. We had tickets for all five days of this game and on each day, the ground was awash with English club Football shirts. On one particular day upon leaving the ground, I was approached by a man with his little boy who came dashing over to me having spotted my Millwall shirt. Once he found out that I was the genuine article and had flown over from London, he shook me warmly by the hand and told his son excitedly that I was a real live Millwall supporter in the flesh, in a real live Millwall shirt. It took me aback a bit, after all, it is not normal for a Millwall shirt to elicit such an excited and positive response, it is certainly not the usual case is it?

Enough of me a few home stories about my Millwall mates –

My mates and I have been accompanied in the stands/terraces by numerous players at home and away matches over the years, for example Richard Sadlier, Alex Rae, Teddy Sheringham, Tony Warner, Tim Carter, Marc Bircham, Kasey Keller, Neil Harris, Byron Webster, Gary Alexander, Joe Dolan, Stuart Nethercott, Jay Simpson,

Darren Morgan and Tim Cahill to name but a few, we also sat next to Dennis Wise's dad at Watford on New Years Day 2005 and I met Mahlon Romeo's dad Jazzy B outside Northampton Town away a few seasons back.

A fellow East Ender and old Grammar schoolmate, Colin Briden a Lion for as long as me now lives in Bridport in Dorset, consequently up until fairly recently he had been an infrequent visitor to Millwall. Nonetheless, to demonstrate right place, right time perfectly he somehow managed to be at a game at the Old Den that was filmed by Channel 4 for the 1990 documentary 'No One Likes Us' and managed to appear at the very top of the programme whist walking back to meet me after buying a programme outside the ground, not that I begrudge it but that should have been my 15 minutes of fame! Just joshing Col! He was a season ticket holder for several recentish years, making the long trek down from the West country for home games, truly devotion to duty and not forgetting a big dent to his wallet!

Another mate Micky Fisher who I used to go to home and away matches with in the late 1980s – and 1990s, named one of his sons Terry Hurlock Fisher, good eh!

We went to a game against West Ham United at the Old Den 3rd December 1988 when Paul Ince scored a highly dodgy goal in front of the CBL. Following this 1-0 defeat we headed back to the East End for a commiseration Light Ale.

En route we stopped off at his flat, as we walked in, Micky said to his girlfriend Sandra –

'Those F***ing C...s Beat Us Again!'

He then said that his kids had started swearing adding – 'I Can't Think Where They Get It From!'

Without a hint of irony, I said neither can I Mick!

I used to go to lots of away matches with Micky in the late Eighties early Nineties.

As a city dweller from Millwall E14 when confronted with the cows, grass, sheep and the smell of muck spreading, i.e. the country, Micky would come over all townie. Every time we passed a farmhouse seemingly in the middle of the nowhere, he would comment – 'F... living there, four hours walk just to get a paper and a packet of fags every morning!'

The next anecdote is not about a Millwall mate but it's relevance will become apparent –

A Tottenham supporting mate of mine Tony, told me of a visit that he and his cousin Terry, an Arsenal supporter had made to Charlton for a night match a couple of years ago to watch Spurs.

He said that whilst sitting in the stands at Happy Valley Terry had an argument with some anoraks, who then chased him around the stand corridors. Apparently, he only just managed to escape unscathed. When I was told this story, I obviously fell about in hysterics – 'Charlton!'

Once I stopped rolling about on the floor with my legs in the air and laughing, Terry, who was there when I was being relayed the story, said that it was not funny and had been very iffy at the time. I said – 'I'm sure it was, here's a tip for the future – wear a Millwall shirt and see if they attack you then'.

This was unusual as the only time a Charlton fan generally gets irate is if you steal their trainspotting lists or denigrate their anorak, maybe Terry said something derogatory about Millets?

One of my long-time home mates Clive Whates is just a little bit excitable at games.

He once jumped so high at one match when sitting high up in the CBL that his head barely missed crashing into the stand roof, he also has a habit of clapping very loudly and is not the man you want to sit in front of if you've got delicate lugholes. In season 2001/2 on the day that Dion Dublin made his debut against Stockport County he claimed that he would not be at the game because had to take his kids to see 'The Tweenies'.

As you can imagine he took just a bit of ribbing after this, but still insists that it was his kids who wanted to go – we believe you.

He has a workmate whose name is Dick, who is another CBL regular, with his daughter Joanne, both mentioned much earlier in The 'Wall Dedications, prior to each match I usually like to get in a pre-match slash before taking up my seat. At one particular game I noticed that Dick was at the urinal and I was just about to say – 'Hello Dick!' When I realised how it might sound just a bit dodgy in a gents toilet and thought better of it!

Especially if we were playing Brighton!!!!

Clive and I have developed a couple of concepts whilst sitting at quiet games in the last couple of years, for example – When Neil Harris went through a lean spell in 2000/1 we tried to think of a phrase we could use as the opposite of a purple patch. We came up with the idea of a purple knob, as in –

'Harris is going through a purple knob at the moment!'

Which does not bear visualising and after what happened to him at the end of that season, it was just a bit too close to the proximity of his problem for comfort, if you get my drift, to continue – We also came up with the concept of replacing season tickets with arse indentation moulds, like Homer Simpson's settee. Therefore if anyone sat in the wrong seat their behind would not fit.

Rather like the Cinderella slipper principle, if your buttocks fit perfectly into the grooves it is your seat. No two Arses are the same you know. It would certainly stop glory hunters I would say, it would also highlight the phrase 'Bums on seats!'

A Coach One Regular mate Tony Russell, told me once about an incident he had had at Palarse when a Nigel securely behind Police lines was calling him a Prick, Tony felt obliged to point out to the suburbanite tosser, the following I am a C*** mate not a Prick! Strangely the Old Bill dragged Tony off for being grammatically correct to a Palarse need an escort at your own ground Ultra Palarse tosser, so much for education education education eh!!

If you've read my other Millwall books you'll know that one of my long-time home companions Simon Barrett invariably took his son Patrick to home and away games with him and used to take his daughter Lisa as well. Pat had been a regular at home now for many years; he has also been a season-ticket/Teamcard holder now for a good few years and has also been an away traveller for a good while as well, in fact, by 2003/4, he had been to nearly 40 away grounds in England and was then only 13. He also went with us to Ferencvaros in the next season in Hungary as you will see in a later chapter. As he was frequently in our company, he was like watching a reflection of how we behave, In 2016 he departed these shores to live in Australia, for reference, nothing to do with Millwall he and his girlfriend wanted to go and live there so they did, he subsequently came back to live in London after a couple of years down under and is back in his spiritual home with a Teamcard in place.

My mate Ian Glasby also a Gooner, who is Lee's brother, Lee is the one that I mentioned in the Dr Jekyll And Mr Millwall incident earlier, Ian is the one that I mentioned who also lives in Australia albeit in Perth whereas Pat was on the far other side of the continent, he was in England because their mother was seriously ill and I persuaded him to come to his first ever Millwall match during his stay, a night match against Rotherham United at the New Den, he said of Patrick 'He's like a little bloke, like a miniature version of you lot!'

Our own sort of Mini Me, he is bigger now and proper grown up like!

Patrick has been a good source of laughs over the years some examples –

His birthday is very near to Christmas and I used to buy him some Millwall related items to cover both events, many years ago when he was about eight. I handed his dad Simon an unmarked plastic bag containing a shirt, shorts, etc. Pat smelt a rat and said – 'What's in the bag?'

Simon in an attempt to cover up said – 'Barrie's bought you some pyjamas for your birthday',

I said to Simon -'Cheers! That doesn't make me sound like an old perv does it!'

He once sang 'Let 'Em Come' and 'No One Likes Us' when asked for a Christmas song at school!

Against Sheffield Wednesday at home on Saturday 22nd March 2003 the away fans sang -

'Wednesday Till I Die!' Pat said – 'That means they have only got 4 days to live then!'

He played against a West Ham United boy's team for his local boy's side wearing a Millwall shirt underneath his team's shirt and he made a point of lifting his shirt to flash it off to the junior Hammers when he scored.

Finally, on a trip to Leeds United in December 2004 on a club coach he was commenting about all the villages we were passing up north, he said 'Bal there's villages everywhere, there's one over there in a valley' I said 'Pat that 'village' is Sheffield!'

Simon's Grandson Rudie has now been going with us since he was less than 4, he is at the time of writing 13.

He has been a season ticket holder for a few seasons now and had his first away game on 14th November 2009 at Brentford, when I got the full 'Are We There Yet' gamut, this started as soon as we boarded the train at Waterloo, when I had to explain that we had not actually left Waterloo yet and on the way received numerous what's thats? So had to explain what a train platform was, why the train kept stopping, what lights were, what the seats were, how trains ran, what trains were. I said to Simon, you really should take him on a coach trip to Carlisle you would love it mate!

He has now been to several away grounds his farthest one being Sheffiield Wednesday on August 24th 2013.

I said to him in 2013/4, that I did not start going to Millwall at home until I was 8 and look what I am like God help you Rudie!

Before Simon and I used to travel away together, he had a few tales to tell -

Simon said he once sat in the seats at Plymouth surrounded by home fans wearing every club shirt under the sun except Argyll's, including people in Crystal Palace and West ham shirts, popular choices with us Lions as you can imagine, there's support your local team for you!

Bizarrely at Home Park at the time they also had a club shop in the away end for some strange reason.

As a youth, he went to Manchester United on January 14th 1989, for the 3 – 0 defeat game.

He travelled up to the game on an early train with Peter Ironside and a Man U fan friend Ali; they came out of Piccadilly station and headed into the shopping area, where he said that there were crowds like Oxford Street. Even so, they were ambushed by a 40 strong mob of home fans, his mate Ali was punched in the face, and as Simon went to his aid he was hit from behind and knocked out, he was then continually kicked like a rag doll, Peter was also attacked and received a broken arm.

The shoppers carried on around the incident as though nothing was happening.

Once the attack was over, battered, bruised and with Simon covered in blood, they headed to a local pub to try to clean themselves up and to get some help, where the landlord very helpfully set his Rottweiler dogs on them. They left the pub sharpish and took themselves off to the local Hospital, where they were treated. As time was creeping towards kick off, they were forced to leave Peter in casualty to get plastered and went to the game; Simon was standing on the away terrace when after a while Peter suddenly turned up with his arm in a sling clutching an X ray bag, devotion to duty of a high level. Simon said that his only regret for the day was that Rhino had missed a couple of early chances to put us ahead!

Simon used to travel away with Mick and his dad Eddie, who I mentioned in the Dedications earlier, both were away travel veterans like us, I also went to many an away match with them once I had met Simon.

Simon and Mick once travelled on a club coach to Norwich, after the game they were standing in a chip shop and saw the club coach sail past the window, prompting them to have to dash from the shop and chase their coach up the road.

They once drove to an away match and pulled up at a set of traffic lights, where a persistent window washer kept cleaning Mick's car windscreen, despite the fact that Mick, who is not a small bloke, kept telling him – 'I don't want my windows cleaned mate, I'm not paying you!'

Nevertheless, the chamois man carried on washing. Mick repeated the above and decided that his only option was to get out of the car, punch this man in the head, shove his limp body out of the road, get back into his car and drive off, which he did, it obviously being the only sensible way to resolve the situation.

Mick has had some interesting incidents of his own -

He took his wife to a game at the New Den against Rotherham United and whilst sitting on the CBL lower, a wayward blast by Willie Gueret in the pre match kick about hit her in the face, hard enough to break her glasses, which he found hilarious, but strangely, she didn't!

He went to Man City for the infamous game a few years back and tried to get a cab to the ground from Moss Side and the man in the cab office said – 'Are you from London?'

When he replied that he was, the reply was – 'Well f***ing walk then!' Charming.

He was slashed with a knife outside Cardiff station by home fans, before yet another infamous game a few years back, receiving a chest wound that needed stitches.

The Police helpfully told him that it was his own fault for being at the station in the first place!

He was in a pub in Stockport full of Millwall fans, several years ago following our 5-1 hiding at Stockport County when home fans invaded the pub and a knife fight broke out.

He was hit in the face with a brick outside of Burnley's ground on 22nd April 2000, a game that we lost 4-3, this was after the game when the home fans threw missiles at the Millwall train contingent.

He has a missing front tooth as a permanent reminder.

He is not called Lucky Mick for nothing! Well, at all actually.

Long time home and away companion Mad Ted has a deep sense of what is right and wrong and aside from his frequent steward search arguments he has also appeared, not infrequently, on away club videos, when he has wrestled with home stewards, who he deemed to be out of order, for man handling any pitch encroaching kids. He once lambasted a double-decker King's Ferry coach full of Charlton fans at a service station. His main complaint was a coach company directed tirade along the lines of –

'They park their bloody coaches at our ground but won't take us!'

Which they did not at the time, the situation was not helped by the fact that it was a Charlton coach and whilst our coach was like the Sahara desert, alcohol wise, the Anoraks appeared to be knocking back beer on their flash new coach like a works beano; Ted being Diabetic doesn't drink but still saw the inequality in it all and felt that he had to tell them so.

Dave Simms, another of my regular home and away companions, was standing on the away terrace at Fulham a few years back, when he took his eye of the ball and a wayward shot flew into the crowd hitting him slap bang in the unmentionables. Naturally, we thought it was hilarious, as you do.

However, Dave was left to consider balls of a different kind and had to try to stop his eyes watering for the remainder of the match. For the record Dave worked for Millwall's executive club for donkey's years and he had his car flipped over in the car park in the riot that occurred after the Derby County Play Off.

He was also the man fighting on a low stand roof at West Bromwich Albion at a League Cup 2nd round, 2nd leg tie on 25th October 1983, a 5-1 defeat. For anyone who was there and who remembers the incident, now you know who it was. With his two sons Nathan and Paul Simms mentioned throughout this book as you will see are two other Hard core Home and away Wall fans as their Dad Dave is.

Nathan son Harry was Mascot v Notts Forest at home Good Friday 30th March 2018.

Two Of Those Days!

Over the succeeding years I have been to Birmingham City's St Andrews many times and seen trouble on several occasions, however first trip to Brummieland and my first proper away match, my actual first one being with my cousin Roy to Watford, this Brummie game was as a thirteen-year-old in 8th April 1972 and it was one of the most eventful. I briefly mentioned this game in my first book 'Tuesday Night In Grimsby' I travelled to this vital old Division 2 promotion clash with 3 people, schoolmates Colin Briden and another old school chum Paul White, with our quartet completed by Paul's cousin from Swindon who for some bizarre reason travelled with us. We got to the station early and due to my sodding about for want of a better expression when wearing a trilby in my skinhead era, I put the train ticket in the hat band, won a game of cards that we were playing, threw my trilby in the air and, I managed to lose my train ticket at Euston station and I told my mates to travel up to Birmingham without me. I myself bought another ticket and caught a later train, which turned out to be a Hoolie special. As it arrived at New Street we began chanting 'F*** Off Birmingham, I Said F*** Off Birmingham' to Ringo Starr hit Back Off Boogaloo as we disembarked the train to announce our arrival, we then chased away the home fans who were waiting outside the station.

The Police then stopped and searched us all, confiscating numerous weapons, including knives, before letting us free to run amok around the Bullring Shopping area. I then found myself walking to the ground alone after the train contingent I was with had dispersed to pubs and cafes on the long march to the ground. Consequently I was attacked outside the ground by a six-foot black Brummie adult, receiving several blows for my trouble, merely for wearing Millwall silk scarves around my wrists, a custom at the time, and failing the 'Got the time mate?' Quiz.

I picked myself up and paid to get into the first stand that I came to, which turned out to be the home end behind the goal, I only had enough to pay my entrance fee, not enough to get a programme, I stood there on red alert all afternoon with Millwall's 'Boys', thankfully we were not attacked by the home fans who gave us a wide berth all afternoon.

After the game I left the ground and searched the streets for my lost mates. As I walked back towards the station, I saw that Millwall fans were following a black Brummie fan.

He looked terrified, and kept looking over his shoulder in expectation of an imminent attack, which obviously came, he was jumped, bundled into a doorway and mercilessly kicked and punched, callous or not after what had happened to me before the game I had little sympathy for his plight.

Luckily I found my mates in Brum and we headed back to London together, thank gawd as I now had no money left and did not fancy walking back to East London from Euston!

Finally, to close this chapter a game that I mentioned in 'I Was Born Under The Cold Blow Lane' that perfectly shows that I do not only suffer Football related travel disasters -

I pre brain injury used to sing in a band and we had a wedding booking for the night of one match at Crystal Palace.

As it was a fairly local trip, I thought that I would be okay to go to the match and do the gig as well, especially as one of my mates the aforementioned Dave had agreed to drive me to the venue in St Albans. Consequently after the game we got a train from Norwood Junction back to London Bridge station we then headed by tube to Victoria Park in Mile End where Dave had parked his van, we got on board with plenty of time to spare and he dropped his aforementioned son's Paul and Nathan off at their home in Chingford on the way to the M25. We then easily got on to the motorway however we unfortunately did not know which way we were heading around this orbital road so we were unsure if we were heading towards or away from the St Albans turn off. I had a new mobile that I had only received in the post that morning because of this I had only been able to charge it for about half an hour. I had turned it off at the game to save the battery so at least I was able to phone one of my band mates, who were already there and setting up, to let him know that I was on the way and I would be there shortly, or so I hoped!

Due to our disorientation, we pulled off the motorway a couple of times and set off in the opposite direction hoping to get our bearings. With time racing on I began to get several agitated 'Where the F... are you?' phone calls from band mates. I assured them that all was fine, well sort of! To add to the Motorway farce, by now darkness was falling and Dave's van had no internal lights so although I had a map and directions to the venue I could no longer see it. Never mind I thought I've still got the mobile so I'll get my band mates to guide me in, naturally in mid phone call the mobile battery died on me and as Dave did not have a mobile at the time all our means of communications had now been cut off.

It was at this point that I began to lose my calm demeanour and panic began to set in, largely because by now the agreed performance time was looming, in truth I thought that I would not make it at all. Luckily, we eventually reached the St Albans junction; we came off the motorway and then hared up a country lane. In our haste, we then sailed by the turn off that we should have taken and we had to do a U-turn in a narrow lane, much to the annoyance of the other motorists who hooted and waved their fists at us. We then took the right road and set off hell for leather for the venue.

We arrived after we should have started playing and as we approached, I saw that members of my band and the groom were waiting outside. To announce our arrival I dived out of the van apologetically hysterical and Dave got out and relieved himself up against the nearest tree in full view of everyone – Hello the Londoners are here! Fortunately, the Bridegroom saw the funny side and I managed to quickly get changed and give a panic powered 'the show must go' on performance.

CHAPTER 15
The Many 'Joys' of Away Travel aka 'Been There Done That!'

Away Grounds that I have visited to see Millwall as at the time of publishing this book –
1. Arsenal Highbury
2. Aston Villa
3. Barnet Underhill/The Hive
4. Barnsley
5. Birmingham City
6. Blackburn Rovers
7. Blackpool
8. Bolton Wanderers Burnden Park/Reebok Stadium aka Macron Stadium
9. Bournemouth
10. Bradford City
11. Brentford
12. Brighton & Hove Albion Goldstone/Withdean/AMEX American Express Community Stadium
13. Bristol City
14. Bristol Rovers Eastville/Twerton Park/Memorial Stadium
15. Burnley
16. Burton Albion
17. Bury
18. Cambridge United now in the Conference
19. Cardiff City Ninian Park/Cardiff City Stadium

20. Carlisle United
21. Charlton
22. Chelsea
23. Cheltenham Town
24. Chester City Deva Stadium
25. Chesterfield Saltergate/Proact Stadium
26. Colchester United Layer Road/Weston Homes Community Stadium
27. Coventry City Highfield Road/Ricoh Arena
28. Crewe Alexandra
29. Crystal Palace
30. Dagenham & Redbridge twice both in the FA Cup when they were Amateur and when professional
31. Derby County Baseball Ground/Pride Park
32. Doncaster Rovers Keepmoat Stadium
33. Everton
34. Exeter City
35. Fleetwood Town Highbury Stadium!
36. Fulham
37. Gillingham
38. Grimsby Town
39. Hartlepool United
40. Hereford United
41. Huddersfield Town McAlpine Stadium aka Galpharm Stadium
42. Hull City Boothferry Park/KC Stadium aka KCOM Stadium
43. Ipswich Town
44. Leeds United
45. Leicester City Filbert Street/The Walker Stadium
46. Leyton Orient
47. Lincoln City
48. Liverpool
49. Luton Town
50. Macclesfield Town

51. Manchester City Maine Road
52. Manchester United
53. Middlesbrough Ayresome Park/Riverside
54. MK Dons
55. Newcastle United
56. Northampton Town Sixfields Stadium
57. Norwich City
58. Notts County
59. Notts Forest
60. Oldham Athletic
61. Oxford United Manor Ground/Kassam Stadium
62. Plymouth Argyle
63. Portsmouth
64. Port Vale
65. Preston North End
66. Queens Park Rangers
67. Reading Elm Park/Madejski Stadium
68. Rochdale
69. Rotherham United Millmoor/AESSEAL New York Stadium
70. Rushden and Diamonds
71. Scunthorpe United
72. Sheffield United
73. Sheffield Wednesday
74. Shrewsbury Town New Meadow
75. Southampton The Dell/St Mary's
76. Southend United
77. Stockport County
78. Stoke City Victoria Ground/Britannia Stadium
79. Sunderland Roker Park/Stadium of Light
80. Swansea City Vetch Field/Liberty Stadium
81. Swindon Town
82. Tottenham Hotspur
83. Tranmere Rovers
84. Walsall Fellows Park/Bescot Stadium

85. Watford
86. West Bromwich Albion
87. West Ham United
88. Wigan Athletic Springfield Park/JJB Stadium
89. Wimbledon Plough Lane/National Hockey Stadium Milton Keynes/Cherry Red Records Stadium
90. Wolverhampton Wanderers
91. Wrexham
92. Wycombe Wanderers
93. Yeovil Town
94. York City.

Millwall Away Amateur/Conference or special

95. Ferencvaros Ulloi Ut Stadium Budapest Hungary in the UEFA Cup
96. Millennium Stadium Cardiff in the FA Cup Final
97. Wembley Stadium original in the Autowindscreen Final
98. Wembley Stadium new one for the League 1 Play Off Final in May 2009, 2010, 2016 and 2017 plus FA Cup Semi Final in May 2013
99. Telford Amateur in the FA Cup
100. Altrincham Amateur in the FA Cup
101. Staines Town Amateur in the FA Cup

For reference I have called the Stadium at the away grounds what it was called when I attended there, as you know grounds nowadays seem to change their name frequently, so I stayed with what it was called when I went there.

Grounds that I have seen live and visited at non Millwall games at -

Dorchester Town Blue Square Conference South
AIK in Stockholm Sweden both at the Rasunda (the 1958 World Cup Final Stadium) and the Friends Arena
Hammarby in Stockholm Sweden both at Soderstadion and Tele2 Arena
Djurgardens IF in Stockholm Sweden at Tele2 Arena live and a tour of Stockholm's Olympiastadion they used to play in, which was used for 1912 Olympics
Malmo Swedbank Stadion in Malmo Sweden
FC Copenhagen Parken Stadium in Copenhagen Denmark.

Worst away trips ever –

Some contenders
Reading on 6th August 2011.
Bloody shame that they did not have one of the Samaritans signs they have when you come off motorway towards Barnsley, which I mention later on the bridge over the M4 when someone committed suicide by jumping off this bridge in to traffic, gridlocking the M4 and slip road on to it from M25 when we tried to drive to Reading.

Kill yourself by all means like this but not during the football season and before the kick off, you showboating div!!! Sorry bang goes my sympathy gene!

We eventually arrived at the Madejski about 5 minutes late amazingly as we were walking about on the M4 itself at around 2.30pm!

Another real monster away trip in same season Brighton and Hove Albion Valentines night horror show Tuesday 14th February 2012 our first visit to AMEX. We had a driving plan, the 4 of us, Nathan driving, me, his Brother Paul and father Dave as passengers, our plan was to drive to Lewes park there and get the shuttle train the short distance back to Falmer and after the match from Falmer back to Lewes, which is right next to the AMEX Stadium exactly how Hull City's old ground Boothferry Park used to be like.

We were heading to Lewes station to get shuttle train but saw a Football Park and Ride sign so decided to go that way, we went around the roundabout on the A23, on to a slip road near Lewes roundabout on to an unlit side road, with a Hamburger stand but no lights and no road signs, it was Lewes Kingston Roundabout it transpired, but it might as well have been Kingston Jamaica the amount of herb and spliffs that we all needed for the homeward journey!

There was only a Burger Refreshment stall for identification near the Park and Ride that was all, we paid the man on Park and Ride with a luminous coat and a torch but no other lights only and an impossible to see blue and white bollard, we did not get a ticket so were none the wiser where the hell we actually were, we walked up to A23 verge where we then had to get a Range Rover to the ground, the driver was initially overloaded, did a run to ground he then reappeared shortly after and drove us the short distance to the AMEX the 4 of us and two more Millwall fans, he said on way back get 28 or 29 bus as there was no pick up, after game.

After the match we followed his directions going past Falmer station, through an underpass and ended up near the University but could not find any bus stop apart from a 25 bus one, so we asked umpteen stewards and Old Bill where it was and all of whom knew f**k all, so, we went back to the main reception at ground.

Spectacularly on the way there I managed to fall down a very muddy slope, tried to get up and fell over 2 more times, so three times in total, I also managed to lose my glasses, one good thing though was that my coat and jeans both have lovely clear complexions having got a mud bath!

We went in to AMEX main reception, spoke to a nice lady there who was bemused and asked another Steward about the place that we were trying to describe, vagueness across the board aplenty, following the discussions a Steward led us to get a Park and Ride bus to Mill Road.

Which was the one that he thought that it was, but no, it was not so we got a bus back to ground that was parked behind our one and went back in to main reception again.

We terrified the nice lady when we appeared again, as we were now officially totally lost, we asked how many Park and Rides there were? She said three, we said get us a cab and we will go around all of them until we find our one, fortunately financially a bloke walked in as we were discussing our options who ran the car park and knew exactly where we meant so he got us a cab, Our cab turned up shortly he briefed the driver where we wanted to go to the get back to Nathans car.

So we drove the shortish distance, along the A23 arrived at the right Park and Ride, and miraculously we found our car, but this had taken an age as it was after 11 pm when we got aboard so one and a half hours after leaving ground, no bollard, man with torch/luminous jacket, Football Park and Ride signs or the Burger stall, which added to the adventure..

For reference the AMEX is right near the station and the Millwall special directly to London Bridge was amazingly well signposted with Millwall badges on large multiple placards!

But Park and Ride or Buses were a complete mystery to all and sundry.

It was a new ground for us all and I know that it is named American Express Community Stadium or AMEX Stadium, but to use and Americanisation this was a real disorganised cluster F***!

Consequently for our future trips, the next one another night match, Dave and I, went on the club coach, for the next trip there a Saturday, Dave, Nathan, Paul and I drove around, past the stadium looking for a parking space, no joy so we drove back to AMEX asked if we could park where coaches/Park and Ride buses park, were told no but there was a pub/hotel that did frequent shuttle buses, and allowed you to park in their grounds so we drove there and low an behold it did exist, so we parked up, had a beer and something to eat before getting the shuttle the AMEX, they pick you up after the game and take you back to your car, you buy tickets to do this, but it is no more expensive and far more efficient than trying to find somewhere to park, so the next time we did exactly the same thing, sorted took a while to discover but sorted

Burton Albion away Saturday 24th February 2018

Usual route to MI via Victoria Station, which was closed off, so headed for Haymarket via Strand this was also closed so we did two circuits around Trafalgar Square and up Charing Cross Road, to Camden getting through London in a weird and wonderful way. On arrival in Derbyshire Sat Nav went pear-shaped near Burton and we ended up two double decker coaches in a Residential Cul De Sac, as it did in Derby County on a previous trip, a bloke sitting in front of me used his Sat Nav on Mobile and he and his 9 year old son shouted out directions to ground where we arrived nearly KO time, toilet very small and packed, so went inside shoved in end of stand, went out during game and failed to get a programme had a piss though, went back to centre block and found Dave, Paul, Nathan, Kay and Charlie, view horrendous sun in eyes as so low, in line with goal but could not see through net, and guessed what was happening, at end I went to go to loo it was rammed, I saw a Disabled toilet and remembered I had a Radar Key as disabled so sod queueing I used my key on that door easy!!!

Other away horror contenders mentioned in my previous books Burnley Turf Moor when tyres went pear-shaped and hub cap fell off in Essex on way back making it a bit dangerous to say the least, and Hartlepool United in FA Cup when whole of motorway seemed to be coned on way back to London making journey home to London a bit of a bind to say the least ...

But the winner is -

Aston Villa Saturday 9th December 2017 One If Not The Worst Away Journeys Ever

The journey was a nightmare from start to finish, three Kingsferry Double Decker coaches at New Den, leaving at 10am one left and we on coach 1 found that other coaches battery was flat, so we tried to edge up close to it to use Jump leads, we had a van in front of us, so were asked to push coach to near other coach as he could not move, some on board did this and nearly rammed the gates, when we had pulled alongside, the other driver incorrectly attached the leads, which started smoking! So, they were taken off and his battery was then charged.

Following this palaver, we left The New Den At about 10.45am, naturally we then drove to the M1 only to hit bad traffic at J11 due to a bad accident. We also followed Salt Spreaders on M1 and M6 which added to the fun as we were bombarded with salt and with all problems, we could not stop at Services due to time running out.

We then drove on to meet West Midlands finest on J7 of the M6 having passed Villa Park on our way there then there changing the required Junction to further up, our driver said to stroppy copper that being late and unable to stop at Services his Tachometer was on verge of going overtime and he would be fined, the copper took no notice at all and he and a fellow Plod car drove us all around Birmingham, sailing past Whitton Station a short walk to Villa Park, West Midlands finest then drove us in to a side street traffic jam, and in the end people behind us on second coach were let off and as we could see Villa Park over the horizon, so people on Coach 1 demanded to be able to get off, and managed to break the door in the process, with Coach 1 now not able to move we were able to dismount and sped the longish distance to Villa Park, when we were allowed in at 3.11pm naturally finding a seat was practically impossible and finding my friends who had taken another route via Kent and Waltham Abbey even more so.

Are We There Yet?

Hearing young voices on coaches or trains chirping up the chapter title is just one of the many joys of travelling away; this chapter is meant as a guide to highlight the many other pleasures (?) of the away travel experience as I mentioned earlier re Rudie

Before I start for real, I have a question –

Whatever happened to the Millwall Away travel club that I was obviously a member of, which sold combined discount travel packages? Bring it back I say!

I recall as a young boy that I had a revelation one day when it suddenly dawned on me that you could actually go to the away matches as well as the home games. No more did I have to wonder just what all these exotic names were, I could actually go to see them for myself if I was so inclined, places like – Grimsby, Carlisle, Doncaster, Rochdale, Rotherham, Barnsley, Scunthorpe, Hartlepool and the like.

Prior to this revelation, any empty Millwall Saturday was generally occupied with -

Being taken to Spurs by my dad, playing with my Subbuteo, 'Action-Man' or 'Johnny 7', watching Grandstand or Kent Walton's wrestling on World Of Sport with Dickie Davies and his badger like hairdo, the only other option was to indulge in the pleasures of the palm.

All of which were at least cheaper alternatives to yomping all over England as I have done in the many many succeeding years.

Nowadays I treat Saturday away trips like mini weekend holiday breaks, usually of a mystery trip variety, with all the adventures of a real holiday except that usually you don't lose your luggage and don't get the chance of a holiday romance, although I suppose you could have a passionate fling on the Club Coach in the Loo, then again perhaps not!

To be able to go away frequently you need to be organised – getting coach, match or train tickets in advance, organising time off work for nationwide midweek jaunts, etc. It is therefore advisable to have the following to assist in your away travel quest -

A) Self-employment.

B) Job flexibility and or an understanding boss.

C) Plenty of free time and spending cash.

D) An accommodating or no wife.

I am not married and I worked for myself for 15 years prior to going back into work before subsequently suffering a severe brain injury so no longer working; I therefore fulfilled most of the ideal conditions for an away traveller. Unfortunately, I also have pangs of guilt if I do not go to away matches, as it feels like infidelity, which is a bit of a worry.

From a Self Employed work perspective, all I simply had to do was to organise any work to fit in with my travel plans, take the phone off the hook and off I went.

Being in gainful employment means having to plan your life around Football to a degree, especially for any midweek away matches.

Setting Off For The Coach

When I go to Weekend away games, especially the long trips, it usually means getting up with the lark.

There is nothing like getting out of bed after a couple of hours kip with the alluring prospect of spending four or five hours on a trip to some godforsaken place up North on a club coach, I must love it really

I have certainly done it hundreds of times, best early rising was up at 4am on Sunday 5th May 2019 last game of the season early kick off so 6am coach to Wigan Athletic, as no trains running in north over weekend this was only option other than going up a day or so earlier staying in north and coming back after May Bank Holiday so 4.30am mini cab it was.

There have been added hardships for any crack of dawn trips –

In the old days when it was a Bank Holiday if I had not been able to cadge a lift to the coach departure point it has meant having to yomp across the river.

Either through Rotherhithe Tunnel, a carbon monoxide fuelled monotonously tiled treat, or if

I did not fancy bloody great lung fulls of noxious gas I would have to go via Tower Bridge.

This in the half-light of dawn when the East London line actually normally ran but either had not started running for the day or just could not be arsed. This route march at Christmas time for the usual 'local' Derby at some far-flung outpost was invariably carried out bleary eyed through lack of sleep and excess alcohol consumption. On the occasions when I have gone via the bridge route, it has at least been more scenic I suppose, but it was still a bloody trek from Stepney or Limehouse where I lived. I focussed on the incinerator chimney, as it saved me from having to think where I was going.

One good thing about Millwall supporters in my experience is that any Lions fans heading south in their cars to the ground who spot fellow Millwall shirted supporters on foot, will always offer you a lift, I suppose there are not that many of us so we need to stick together. To the multitude of people who have offered me lifts to home and away Den trips much obliged. Gawd bless ya!

To lower the tone one tip for the inexperienced traveller -

Before travelling it is essential to have a good clear out, as it were, so I would recommend an enema, erotic or otherwise and Ex Lax, accompanied by a slash of horse proportions, just in case the coach does not have a loo, it breakdowns or you are caught in traffic without a service station toilet stop in sight.

Even nowadays despite far better transport options available this still has be done to catch a coach at the New Den in case the Millwall Café with its toilet facilities was not open.

Ticket Checking Away Travel Newby's or Big Home Game Debutantes

By this I mean the people who come on to your stand away by intently gawping at the ticket to see where their designated seat is, this also happens at home when you have a big cup tie mostly, at home people who you have never seen before gawp up with a ticket in their hands, the amount of people who I have had to explain the Millwall away travel ethos of sit where you bloody well like everybody else will and stewards will not check, same principle at home when strangers emerge on CBL that is an designated seat block specific only stand, where people look for their seats well as CBL seats as far as I know are not number, you must be a boyscout if you can actually find your allegedly designated seat!

Food, Glorious Food

In the early 1980s, I would travel to away matches by car with yet another old schoolmate Steve Kimberley who I mentioned in the Dedications. For these trips we had a couple of rituals before we left the smoke, firstly we had to confirm that we had adopted our mum's advice about always wearing clean underpants on any journey, we did this verbally taking each other's work for it I might add.

The principle of clean pants was simple -

If we had an accident and consequently had to go to hospital, where any Tom, Dick or Harry would get to see the condition of the pants that we had on, we would not be open to ridicule.

Therefore, even If we went through the windscreen, thereby ruining our boyish good looks forever, we were at least pristine in the pants department – sound thinking.

Once we had confirmed that we adhered to the pants ethos our other ritual was to head to the nearest Pie and Mash shop for two and two and liquor. This would act as ballast before we set off; it was like a Cockney Last Supper, with our thinking being that if we did have an accident or did not return at least we would have some proper London nosh inside us.

Steve stopped going away in the late 1980s and since then I have gone by train, coach, car, donkey or whatever with numerous various different companions.

Over the succeeding years if I was going by coach, it seemed like a good idea to prepare an away travel kit, a bit like a packed lunch or a picnic. The checklist for this away travel kit would consist of -

1. Several drinks in screwed top bottles (non-alcoholic naturally).
2. Crisps, sandwiches or other snacks.
3. A pen to do the crosswords.
4. Umpteen tabloids
5. An Android Device/I Pad with games on that you can play to wile away the time on way up and also imterwobble to check scores and league tables on way back

In the previous years I have been on many away coach trips where 2 of my regular companions Simon and Dave have usually cleared out Tesco's and the local cake shop themselves to add to the rations that I had already bought, so we have had enough food between us for about a fortnight let alone a day trip. If I am on my own. I buy sandwiches at any service station that we stop at, ostensibly to waste time. Sandwiches that are sold at a price that would make even a West End eatery blanch.

Irrespective of this for some reason I usually feel a moral obligation to empty my wallet into the bulging coffers of these money pits. I should probably seek therapy, if I am in the land of the meat and potato pie – i.e. the North. I then have to buy a pie in the ground, It is not easy staying fat it takes work you know, being a season ticket Holder in the local chip shop also helps.

On the just plain odd food front at the infamous 4-1 defeat at Brighton in the Play – Off Semi Final, I stood on the open side terrace behind some blokes who kept chanting throughout the game –

'Cheese and biscuits, cheese and biscuits, soup, soup!' You explain it!

Here is another tip –

If you try to save money by preparing sandwiches yourself on the night before an early start, do not make them if you get home at 3am after a long night guzzling Carling Black Label in an East End nightclub as I once did. You know how it is; all of a sudden, I thought I was Marco Pierre White, Cordon Bleu Chef, sandwiches a speciality. Sadly, in the real world outside of an alcohol-induced illusion I was anything but.

Apart from lack of culinary talent, there are a couple of other post piss-up sandwich making problems –

Firstly, falling asleep in mid-sandwich preparation and waking up with the sandwiches stuck to the side of your cheek, which I thankfully managed to avoid in this instance.

Secondly, and something that I did do was to complete the sandwiches and then forget to wrap them in cling film or put them into the fridge to keep fresh, preferring instead to leave them on the kitchen table to take the air. Consequently, I eventually made it to bed satisfied with my culinary efforts, woke up after a couple of hours' fitful sleep scraped my tongue and with bloodshot eyes and my head banging like a drum solo by John Bonham, I headed into the kitchen.

I then tried to track down the 'Resolve' before mustering the strength to feast my eyes on my previous night's handiwork, which in the cold light of day left just a bit to be desired.

Laid out in front of me was – Butter smeared everywhere, bits of filling and crumbs aplenty, with the finished sandwiches now crusty, dried up curly specimens reminiscent of British Rail's finest.

The curl was so pronounced that I could have packed them in a Pringle's container.

Still as they say beggars can't be choosers, so I took them anyway thinking that if the worst comes to the worst I can graciously offer them around on the coach!

In closing a real oddity at Derby County's Pride Park Wednesday 20th February 2019, in the refreshment area they had a poster saying Millwall Fans Special – Pie and Mash and Liquer, my God I was shocked, and so were all the rest of the 377 away travellers as I saw no one eating this at all, I assume thinking I am not coming up North to have their non London version, I will have it when in London!!!

Passing The Time On A Coach

There is a monotonous regularity to any coach trip –
Firstly I read the papers before I leave the ground and crack into the crisps early doors.

Then I continue to eat as if it is going out of fashion in an effort to stave off the boredom of watching the thousands of motorway cones that are invariably stretched out ahead of us.

In Lottery Larry timescale as the trip progressed due to the nature of coach-induced tedium I then sometimes bought umpteen scratch cards and scratch away to my hearts content when this was the away coach norm, re-read the papers or try to watch the on board action videos.

Why are there never any Harry Munk films? Don't answer that.

You cannot really watch the videos properly anyway, because you invariably cannot see or hear them very well if at all sometimes. There is always the option of listening to the inane chatter all around or the radio I suppose however, this is regularly not tuned in properly and is like listening to short wave or doesn't work at all.

You cannot really play cards on a coach and having a Jodrell Bank to pass the time is frowned on, as the person in front would end up with hair gel like Cameron Diaz in 'There's Something About Mary'. I suppose if there are any lovers on board, male and female ideally, to pass the time they could join the 'Bog Seat High Club' – the sex in a coach toilet society,

They would probably have more chance of getting away with this than of having a sly fag (cigarette). This is because the driver of the 'No Smoking' coach is like a bloodhound, spotting a sly puff a mile away and then attacking the affected area immediately with his trusty air freshener.

Moving to the eccentrically bizarre, I went on a coach trip to Scunthorpe United in the season that we played them again in the Play Off Final at Wembley with brothers Paul and Nathan Simms, who sat together whilst I sat behind with sadly deceased Millwall Coach One eccentric Marmalade, for those who do not remember him he was the man who adorned himself in about 14 layers of clothing, for example umpteen coats, shirts, a scarf, an apron, flags, and a titfer, etc. in order to go to the on coach toilet he had to strip down to is inner garments to be able to fit in the bog. To do this, he disrobed in the coach aisle with the coach bombing along the motorway.

He did this whilst the coach inhabitants serenaded him with the Striptease tune 'The Stripper', as he discarded his multiple layers of clothing he piled them high on his now empty seat next to me. Once he felt that he had shed enough he went to his ablutions, whilst I sat next to his clothes mountain. He reappeared having completed his call of nature, and he came out of the trap and then proceed to reclothe himself whilst standing in the aisle again.

He appeared to follow a highly defined dressing regime, which took a fair time, enabling the coach to serenade him again with 'The Stripper' what fun coach trips are, errrr!!!

Things to Avoid

Number one based on the above do not sit next to Marmalade if he was still alive, which sadly he isn't.

I have learnt over my years of travelling that there are people and things it is best to avoid, on a coach trip I suggest that you avoid sitting next to anyone who gets coach sick for one!

This is always a treat; there are a multitude of other things –

Try To Avoid Toilet Visits – Avoid having a slash whilst standing up on a moving coach, or a train for that matter, as this is a real adventure. Because of the motion, especially of a coach, the usual result is that it multiplies a man's normal aiming problems by ten and inevitably ends in a damp floor, wet walls and the toilet goer giving themselves a golden shower. I would also suggest you try to avoid going to the loo after someone has used it and almost certainly flooded it.

With more optimism than logic I have noticed that some train toilets have baby changing facilities blimey that must be entertaining! You may as well have an open razor shave in there because as you are driven along; you are about as likely to succeed. Just trying to stand up or turn around in a coach/train cubicle is bad enough, without having to juggle a baby wriggling like an eel.

I would suggest that you avoid toilets in away grounds, as Millwall do have a nasty habit of putting various items in them. It is also advisable to make sure that your shoes do not have any holes, as you will often find yourself ankle deep in, erm... water. In fact, it is probably best to avoid toilets full stop!

Why not wear adult size pampers and avoid going to the loo at all?

A more radical option is to have a catheter and a bag fitted for the day.

Try To Avoid The Inevitable –

Always try to avoid games were ex-players are playing against you.

Few things are certain in life but one thing that is guaranteed to happen, especially away, or at home for that matter, is that an ex-player will inevitably score against you. Even the ones who could not hit the Millennium Dome/O2 Arena very close in with a beach ball before they left Millwall. I am sure that you are not safe with ex playing against you because however inept they were as a Lion at very least they will play a blinder against you in a 'Get rid of me would you, I'll show you!' Fashion

Equally ominous is this other certainty –

As you drift into range of any local radio stations their match review will say something like –

'City have not won at home all season, largely due to the goal drought of star striker ...

who has not scored in the last 10 games. New manager ... hopes to end a losing run of ... matches against the Lions ...'

As a seasoned away traveller, I know that this is the time to turn the car or coach around, as you can be sure with a high degree of certainty that today is the day that the home side choose to break their duck, the stuttering goal machine will clank back into life and the players will lift their game to impress their new boss.

Trust me it has happened too many times over the years to be a fluke, you mark my words.

Try To Avoid Predicting What The Away Trip Will Be Like –

There are three things to avoid saying on the way to an away match –

1) I have never seen Millwall lose there.

2) No, there is never any trouble there.

3) There is never any atmosphere there.

Life has a way of making you look a fool, so once spoken we will get beat, it will be like a Hoolie World War 3 and the home crowd will roar like The Kop on a European Cup glory night.

Try To Avoid Blowing Your Cover -

Try to avoid waving at fellow Lions at an away match when you are attempting to get into a pub incognito, as Steve Kimberley and I were trying to do in the 1980s at York City.

We were just on the verge of getting past the bouncers when Johnny Lynch, another long suffering home and away Lion and drinking companion at my East End local who I mentioned in my Dedications as well, waved at us and shouted my name from the Millwall train escort across the road.

I acknowledged him and almost blew our cover in the process, just as we were trying to get into the pub. Luckily, the bouncers were a bit thick and did not notice that we were in fact Millwall supporters, i.e. exactly the sort of people who they were trying to stop getting in.

Try To Avoid The Terrors Of The Terraces/Stands -

Try to avoid open uncovered terraces where the atmosphere, such as it is, disappears into the ether, you should also try to avoid family clubs and the dead from the arse up club atmospheres, all of which I find depressing.

Try to avoid games at grounds like the pre renovated Cambridge United or Colchester United where there are only about a dozen steps on the behind goal terraces, the type of grounds where no matter how high up you get you still cannot get a good perspective of the far end and you have therefore got no idea how far out an attack or free kick is at that the end, naturally hopefully Millwall won't be in the pits of the EFL and terraces open or not will not be an option.

Try to avoid being at full away grounds at a vital game when the home side score a late, late vital goal against you. Leaving you to withstand the home crowd going bonkers all around you, whilst you stand there staring blankly with that horrible sinking feeling in the pit of your stomach.

Try To Avoid Trying To Find The Ground By Stealth -

I don't mean a Stealth Bomber pre Sat Nav you had to avoid relying on the scan the skies for the floodlight pylon trick if lost at away matches it can be very risky at some more volatile away grounds anyway this is now largely pointless; because most of today's new stadia all seem to have lights on the stand roofs.

Try To Avoid Putting Your Tickets In A Safe Place -

Avoid putting match tickets in a safe place for any all-ticket game, like the sideboard indoors for example.

Their absence in your wallet will only be discovered after an arduous trek, when you are frantically scrabbling about in your pocket and wallet outside the entrance to the away ground itself.

To avoid this I have an essential away travel routine -The check and recheck policy of a compulsive disorder paranoid. The spectacles, testicles, wallet and watch dance of Harry Enfield's 'You don't want to do it like that!' Man. Drive yourself mad by continually checking that you have all the required match, train and coach tickets for the day before you leave home. If you adopt the holiday procedure of checking and double-checking, as you would do for air tickets and your passport, you cannot go wrong. You'll leave the house a gibbering wreck, but It is better to be safe than sorry. You can make it more complicated by buying a batch of tickets for different matches at the same time, you then have to convince yourself that you have the right tickets for the right game, it adds to the fun.

Try To Avoid Taking Any Notice Of Your Match Ticket -

You can then avoid sitting in the correct designated seat at an away game, unless it is a good seat of course. If you sit in the right seat you do not have the up to the kick-off thrill of someone throwing you out as you are in their seat.

Try To Avoid Mad Ted's Civil Liberties Speeches -

Long time home and away companion Ted – aka Mad Ted, Nutty, The Mad One and Puff Teddy or

P Diddy Teddy more recently has many times confronted a hapless steward for not having the authority to frisk him at away matches, so try to avoid being behind Ted whilst a steward tries to search him and he launches into his – 'You're violating My Human Rights!' speech.

Finally on a personal note – Try to avoid Northern away grounds that have run out of meat and potato pies!

'You Don't Want To Do That'

At many grounds, anonymity is definitely the key, Millwall for example.

I am all for showing my club allegiance and damn the consequences, but it is not such a good idea at many away grounds, when bang goes your anonymity and probably your windows as well.

At hostile away grounds, you do not want to do any of the following -

A) Put a car window sticker on your car.
B) Leave a London newspaper or Millwall programme in plain sight in your car.
C) Have personalised Millwall car number plates.
D) Leave a scarf, miniature scarf or Millwall flag, etc in the back window of your car.
E) Leave a little miniature club kit in the front windscreen of your car.
F) Wander the streets dressed in Millwall clobber like a tourist looking for the ground..

Regarding point A above a Karate Club sticker on your windscreen on the other hand is a good idea as added security. As an aside, Paul Simms, who along with Nathan and I are all Karate Veterans, were on the way home from an away match and once sat behind a car in Bethnal Green that had the ultimate deterrent on its rear window and boot – A Millwall 'No One Likes Us' sticker and Galatasaray stickers. The type of items that may make you think that the car owner likes a row!

Who invented Football related window stickers anyway?

My theory is that it was a windscreen window replacement company who did it as a marketing tool, maybe that's why Auto Windscreen have sponsored Football competitions and teams – guilt?

Perhaps every sticker should say 'Follow Me I'm off to Auto Windscreens' along with any Football alliance.

I am waiting for some honest car stickers something like -

'Follow me I'm a Bandwagon Jumping Glory Hunter Too' or 'I Have Not Been To Old Trafford In Person Either'.

The whole idea of humorous window stickers is a bit odd to me 'My Other Car's A Porsche' yes I know that's why you chose to put

569

it on a 30 year-old Hillman Imp. I know it's supposed to be a joke, I personally think 'My Other Car's In The Crusher/My Other Car's Been Repossessed' would be funnier.

I saw one car sticker, which I did find funny at Ipswich in 2002/3 – 'My Other Car's A Tractor!'

Regarding point B above Simon went to Bristol City with Mick and Eddie and unfortunately, Simon left The Hackney Gazette in the back of their car. So keen were the West Country folk to read it, that they smashed a window to get to it, leaving the return journey to London a smidge windy, courtesy of there new West Country style air-conditioning

At most grounds nowadays there seems to be a rash of illustrated ground regulation posters shooting up, with little idiot proof drawings of things that you cannot take into the ground, highlighted with a circle and a cross in red showing what is not allowed, items like –

Darts, bottles, flagpoles, aerosols, half-eaten meat pies, bad breath, etc.

The New Den had thermos flasks shown as a banned item why? Presumably, it was to stop you bringing things in it things like boiling hot stewed tea, Vodka or hydrochloric Acid in the thermos, strange. I am sure that if you were pedantic, your particular weapon of choice was not shown as a banned item and it was refused admittance, you would have a case at the Court of Human Rights, so why not try – A chainsaw, a rabid pit-bull, a phial of anthrax, a double-barrelled sawn-off shotgun, a bazooka or a flame-thrower? All of which I have yet to see on the 'not acceptable' list pictograms anywhere, so that must mean that they are okay I assume?

The other recentish nationwide phenomenon was the anti abusive/homophobic/racist chanting legislation with people advised to shop any culprit or to get a steward to ask them to desist. The ethos of not being too beastly to the away team and fans to anybody whose formative Football years were spent at the Old Den is a rather bizarre concept, no true Lion is going to report an abuser in their midst to a steward are they? They may tell them to shut up or words to that effect, or offer them an encouraging slap to drive home the point but not grass them up to a steward.

We do often go a bit too far, but to me that is what it is all about, it's all part of the fun, all part of the cathartic Football fan experience. Intimidate the opposition that is the way to go, this has always been the Millwall way and I hope it always will be. Anyway, abusive language and chanting is usually a bit too widespread from both Millwall and the home fans so the stewards and Police would be spoilt for choice in finding a culprit to eject and would have to eject everyone.

All of these recentish restrictions smack to me of political correctness gone too far, whatever happened to freedom of speech? Is it just another attempt to create the mythical state of Football family atmospheres? No Ta!

The Away Traditions And Memories

Some traditions and customs have cropped up over the years, in no particular order -

Feigning sleep when the coach driver's collection comes round for a kick off.

The keep the ball policy, pre cinder track ball-boy tossers, particularly popular at away grounds when we were losing, in a pathetic attempt by us to get the game abandoned due to lack of balls.

Millwall traditionally always used to take a high percentage of their home crowd away.

This was particularly noticeable in the early years of the 1980s when we seemed to have about a quarter plus of our average home crowd following us away, something that I cannot confirm as the programmes at the time did not have an away fan listing, but it certainly seemed that way.

There is the Lions tradition of being very loud and obnoxious, with Millwall's away following being voted most vocal away fans in nearly all of the club fanzines of teams that we visited in 2000/1 for example.

There was the fairly modern tradition of Millwall Fanzine sellers often plying their wares at away grounds.

As I mentioned in in my other books a great away Millwall tradition is to spot the celebrity down on their luck, I forgot to mention – Tommy Cooper, The Marx Brothers, The Three Stooges, The Chuckle Brothers, Mr Bean and Norman Wisdom masquerading as our side under the likes of Peter Anderson, Jimmy Nicholl, Willie Donachie and Steve Lomas. As a special closing variety twist under Ian Holloway we had the privilege of Worzel Gummidge appearing as our manager and with all our team picked from The Goons, The Goodies and Monty Python's Flying Circus!

There are the Jews Hill traditionalists who attempt to keep the great freeloading tradition alive by trying to cadge a lift home from away games on our team coach.

There is the old train tradition of spotting the grounds that you pass on the way and the subsequent policy of dashing to the windows, like an excited kid when he first sees snow.

This is repeated at train stations, thus enabling us to have a mutual gawping session with the locals and to gaze upon the massed ranks of the local constabulary, who are on any station platform where we could conceivably get off.

There was a tradition of Invading and emptying out Platform based shops without paying whenever we have had train problems and stopped at a train station for any length of time, with beer being particularly popular in the looting.

There was the tradition of being at games when our teetotal specials have arrived at our destination station, and then been emptied out onto coaches and buses to be ferried to the ground, which we had to do at Coventry City, Manchester City, Liverpool, Everton, and Bristol City, in the past. Whether this was to protect us from them or them from us, I do not know.

It was certainly a good idea at Manchester City, where we had a double header of League and FA Cup games in December 1989/January 1990. The best policy was not to go wandering off to make your own way back to the distant Piccadilly station, whilst taking in the breathtaking sights of DSS shops and urban decay that was Mosside at the time. Because you would almost certainly be met by a large group of locals very willing to give you a dose of the local hospitality. For these two particular games, it prompted a few stragglers to wander off on their own only to return briskly to the ground to try to catch a lift on the bus, with discretion being the better part of valour.

A Millwall tradition, prevalent at home as well, was to unveil the bloody great big Millwall flag of St George. This flag if viewed from a distance looked clean, but was in fact filthy up close and personal, it was no wonder that those underneath it handed it along so quickly, this has now disappeared, it has not been prevalent at games for several seasons.

There is a great long-standing Millwall tradition of singing over any away club PA announcements especially those that start 'This is a message for the Millwall fans...'

This prompts we away fans to petulantly sing all the way through it so that we have no chance of properly hearing it. The usual nature of the message from what you can make out is to tell us that we would be kept in the ground after the match and that the London-bound train at any night match would depart at 8:20pm, i.e. halfway through the game, with the next one being the milk train at 5am the next morning. An added complication being that, the Police would not let us out of the ground anyway and the station was a half hour walk away.

I have my own away tradition of keeping away match paraphernalia, like any match or travel tickets, programmes, Police welcome notices and even home club badged napkins, why I don't know, I usually throw them into a box in a cupboard never to be looked at again, which again is a bit of a worry.

573

In Football's answer to a parade, there is a tradition prevalent at a Bertie Big Bollocks away game and that is to drive up the motorway with a scarf/flag in the back window, with club shirts on or with a scarf billowing out from a side window blowing in the speed-induced wind. This allows like-minded individuals to hoot and wave in recognition, especially when passing club coaches. Alternatively, if you pass any away fans, you can then give them a damned good wankering, or royal waving as we used to call it at school, accompanied by a fist shake and growling display as applicable.

To finish this section a couple of modern traditions that the recent fashion for all-seater stadia has thrown up, for example: –

Even though we pay a king's ransom for a seat, it is often the case that we stand up for the whole game at away matches, particularly the 'trouble' ones, when it often pays to be on a war footing.

In these instances we usually stand for the first half, sit down at half time and then stand up again for the second half, strange isn't it?

At the less volatile games when we do sit down the game is punctuated by the Football crowd equivalent of an aerobics class, where we stand up, sit down, stand up, sit down, all afternoon in a manner Zebedee would be proud of. It is probably the only exercise that some people get.

The 'It's Millwall!' Traditions

Visiting clubs where every pub in the county is shut and the habit of stitching us away fans up to cover Police costs and for us to effectively pay a premium for the privilege of being manhandled and buggered about by hundreds of riot Police, with Bristol Rovers, Hull City, Leicester City, Doncaster Rovers, West Ham United, Leeds United, Manchester City and Crystal Palace away in the recent or recentish past immediately springing to mind, however you will find numerous other examples, well practically every Millwall away match to be honest.

Another ploy is moving our away games about with gay abandon, so –

Games are moved to Saturday or Sunday noon kick-offs, Friday night or to midweek nights, at towns where there is no London-bound train after dark.

For example Bank Holiday games are usually moved to the following day, especially if the game is at a seaside club, to stop us doing what Leeds United fans did in the 1980s I think at Bournemouth I assume, in their case massively invade the place and then go bonkers, it could also be to stop us having a paddle or a winkle stall feast, bizarrely this aside Southend United away in 2007/8 was allowed on Saturday 25th August which was the August Bank Holiday weekend, I am amazed that the Old Bill didn't think that we would knick Southend Pier or the Kursaal to take back to London with us, very odd!!!

They also seem to schedule games to coincide with the following -

Train strikes, Major road works, rail engineering works or tube problems, terrorist attacks on New York and Royal deaths! Naturally, my Millwall conspiracy theory mindset makes me wonder if this is all just a coincidence or is it a sinister ploy? These are just some examples, naturally it does not stop us travelling, we still go to games by one means or another, as they say where there is a will there is a way and an inheritance tax free castle if you are Prince Charles!

In the recentish past with ITV digital and the Police conspiring together I had the privilege of going to an away match on every day or night of the week, completing the set at West Bromwich Albion with a Thursday night trip in 2001, for this much thanks.

The scheduling backfired though on one occasion, I wanted to go to Bradford City in 2001/2, as this was a new ground for me at the time. The original game was scheduled for an ITV digital match on a Thursday night, which I could have made, only for the bastards to pull out and for the game to be switched back to its original Saturday slot, which due to other commitments I could not make.

Thus robbing me at the time of a new ground.

This brings me on to the ground gathering tradition, whilst I have been to 100 plus different grounds, watching Millwall this includes going to various grounds for different clubs when they have moved, i.e I have been to 3 different Bristol Rovers grounds Eastville, Twerton Park and the Memorial Stadium for example it also includes Amateur Clubs, Wembley Stadium, The Millennium Stadium and Budapest, I am not an anorak, honest! However I do like to gain new grounds, but only if Millwall are playing. I personally would not go to a game simply to notch another ground. It is part of the fun to find out how the home fans respond to the perceived threat of a visit by Millwall. I do not like missing any away match if I can help it, but I like many other frequent away travellers seem to put in a special effort to get to any new club or new ground. Why I do not know? There is no prize for it.

Not a tradition but always an old favourite of mine was standing outside of the ground, especially one with a nice acoustically enhancing shed end, whilst waiting to go in and listening to Millwall songs reverberate from inside the ground.

Coach Dwellers

For those who do not regularly travel on Kings Ferry, say Coach One, whilst the curtain things by the windows are and old style Millwall blue, the coach seats are covered in claret and blue – eek!!!!

For the record, for anyone who did not know, pre Kingsferry which are pukka the standard Millwall coach was normally –

1) Of a less than pristine vintage,
2) Was supposedly alcohol free,
3) Had a definite modern era No Smoking policy.

4) Had limited or no facilities.

In addition, everyone on board would be treated like terrorists on arrival at the away ground; we usually all receive the full body search, blood, urine and breathalyser tests treatment, sadly only slightly exaggerated. Traditionally it is also obligatory that every coach be filled with the following –

- A) A goodly percentage of smokers who are all dying for a fag and gagging to fill their lungs with tobacco smoke. This prompts chain smoking or a world record 'Shove as many fags in your gob as you can' attempt as soon as we stop at the services or it did before the English No Smoking Revolution.
- B) There will occasionally be those on board who appear to be drinking Coke/Lemonade, which is really laced with alcohol, as you will find out as their behaviour deteriorates.
- C) Every car driver on board will consistently know a better route than the coach driver.
   Mind you from my experience, it does seem that some coach drivers would rather navigate by the stars than use one of those new-fangled maps or Sat Navs.
- D) There will be a cache of very moody pre release DVDs or videos. many of which have not yet been released or were still on at the pictures at the time.

There is another type of coach dweller, the 'Don't tell the Missus if you see her' traveller, the sort of man who says to his wife – 'I have got to work tonight dear' or 'I am just nipping out to get some fags love, don't wait up!' Just prior to setting off up North for a midweek night match.

A policy that came unstuck in the recentish past due to the amount of Live TV games that Millwall appeared in, as it made anonymity harder to achieve. For example if the wife of the secretive one happened to be watching the live match on telly and hubby's mug suddenly appeared on the screen.

It was rolling pin on the bonce, sleep in the spare room, no nookie for a fortnight time as soon as he arrived home!

Strange Roads – Bizarre Shorts

In the old days, we used to pick up the club coaches near to the church on New Cross Road/Old Kent Road, close by 'The Albany'. For midweek matches it meant that we East Enders had to get off the coach here, in the middle of the night and then try to get a cab home from the nearby Shaka Zulu mini cab office. The African drivers who worked there did not know where Rotherhithe Tunnel was let alone Stepney or anywhere else in the East End. It was always exactly what you needed after an arduous coach trip. This was how I met long term home and away mate Simon, when he shared a northbound mini cab with Dave Murray and me who I mentioned in the Dedications following a Tuesday night jaunt to Grimsby Town, an away match trip that made me name my first book Tuesday Night In Grimsby.

Some of the stranger incidents from my travels –

At one away match on a club coach we were surrounded by a Volkswagen Beetle Rally, so for a few miles we were looking down on scores of lurid coloured strange shaped little cars, it was all very surreal and a bit like something that you would see in 'Austin Powers' or 'The Prisoner'.

On a couple of occasions I have seen a sky full of hot air balloons on trips to Bristol and in the course of travelling the land.

I have seen all of the major snooker venues -

The Guildhall Preston, The Crucible Sheffield, The Hexagon Reading and The Wembley Conference Centre for our Auto Windscreen Final. Just thought I would mention it.

On a night trip up north on 3rd November 1998 we formed a convoy on the M1 with some Celta Vigo coaches on their way back from Aston Villa after a UEFA Cup tie, not a sight that you usually see.

When Princess Diana died a junior Lions coach en route to an away match at Northampton, if memory serves, stopped off at Althorp to lay flowers and pay their respects.

To highlight the fact that it is not only an inner-city problem at one recent away match up North, we drove past dumped and rotting cars plonked slap bang in the middle of the countryside fields.

To continue – on a rustic theme I have seen hundreds of dead animals over the years, that must have been killed by speeding cars and who were strewn along the sides of the motorways.

On the live animal front, I have passed many thousands of sheep, horses and cows in my time and we have passed acres of oil seed rape over the years.

For a townie like me, sitting behind horseboxes, complete with a horse's arse poking out, and sheep transports on the motorways is always an oddity.

At Crewe away on Tuesday 30th November 2004 me and Laurie an Essex mate, who I mention in Dedications at the front, went into a pub before the game where it was £1.50 a pint and they were giving away free chip butties! A shock to the system for a perennially stitched up Londoner like myself.

Once inside Gresty Road Crewe had a tractor parked behind one goal, prompting us to enquire vocally 'Why's your tractor in the ground?' A good question I thought.

On a few away trips, we encountered Theo.

The one that sticks in mind was early in his reign at a Friday night match at Wigan's Springfield Park. After the match, our homebound coach broke down outside the ground.

He stood nervously amongst us as we waited to see if the driver could rectify the problem.

You could sense that he hoped that our coach would start, as he probably had visions that we would all clamour on to the roof of his flash car like 48 asylum-seekers coming through the Channel Tunnel and try to hold on all the way back to London. Luckily, for him the coach driver sorted out the problem and we came back in the conventional manner.

In the old days, the club used to print a map and or instructions on how to drive to away matches. From memory, these used to be fantastically detailed about how to get out of London and then a bit vague for the rest of the trip. These types of travel details have recently reappeared; however, in the modern era they are not really necessary because driving to games nowadays has taken on a high-tech slant, we ourselves often use internet maps, which you can programme to go from outside of your front door to a chip shop at your chosen destination. On some of the maps that we have had, it has also given the weather forecast for the trip and I imagine, if you asked nicely, it would tell you how friendly the natives were, the likely match score and how good the pies were, etc. It is all witchcraft I tell you! Why can't service stations install internet access so that you could get this sort of map on the way? I would have thought it was good idea, the only drawback being that the services map shop owner would probably take a hammer to it.

A classic example of delusions of grandeur -

During our previous stay in the then called Division 2, Millwall used England's Green Flag coach; sadly, the illusion was shattered when Bowry and Newman came down off the coach and not Owen and Beckham.

I went to a night match at Bury in March 2001 and noticed in their programme that they had an advertisement for 'Support-A-Plates', a customised car number plate. This boon in the anonymity stakes also had the Bury website info on was a bargain at £29.99 and was advertised with the line 'Why not have the Bury FC badge on your car number plates?' How about the old bang goes your windows reason.

For anyone interested at Donington there was a photo/sketch machine called 'Portrait Studio' that did a sketch from a mug shot or whatever else you choose to stick in front of the lens, it then gave you a choice of a drawing in 4 different types of pencil styles or in pen and ink. It was able to do this apparently because it had studied the styles of umpteen world-renowned portrait artists to ascertain the perfect portrait style or so the blurb on the machine said. It also produced caricatures if you wanted. All of which you can select from the menu – I say again witchcraft!

Various teams including Wolves, West Brom and Stoke to name but 3 had 2 Muppets, one male one female. I had an entertainment idea – Why not put on a half time Muppet sex show and beam it live on to the big screens? No? Oh, well just a thought.

For a game in the 1970s, I turned up at Paddington with another old schoolmate Richard Hulls and a couple of his mates to go to Oxford United, only to find that the game had been snowed off.

This was in the era when silk club named scarves worn around the wrists were all the rage, dressed like this we decided to head off with other Lions to St Pancras to join up with Spurs for their trip to Leicester City. Thankfully on arrival with the Spurs fans looking at us suspiciously we came to our senses and didn't go, as we all collectively thought 'What the bloody hell are we doing here?' And we headed back home instead.

Just to show how my mind works -

I went to a gig at the Old Vic on a Sunday night with a non-Football mate Ian Smith and Chelsea fan Barry Church and some of their mates, two of whom had come down from Birmingham especially for this John Hiatt gig. One of the Brummies was staying in London and the other one was going back to Birmingham after the gig, I thought to myself -'Fancy trekking all the way from Birmingham and back for a gig, I wouldn't do that' However, I would not bat an eyelid about doing a midweek round trip of 400 miles plus to watch Millwall. On a similar tack, I have often had to get up on a Saturday or Sunday morning in a pre sunrise gloom to head to the New Den to get a coach for a long trip in winter. Before setting off I have looked out of the window on to the marina where I live, and seen blokes sitting in the dark, cold and rain fishing and thinking – 'They must be mad!' I would then set out on a fifteen-hour round coach trip. You tell me who the mad one is?

I recall going to Everton on a club coach with Simon for a midweek game, our 4-2 Coca Cola Cup win on 4th October 1995. On the way up we pulled into a service station and stopped next to a coach load of Wycombe Wanderers fans on their way to Manchester City. As I stood beside our coach one of their fans headed towards me, I prepared myself to lamp him, assuming his intentions were hostile, as you would do. He came up to me shook me warmly by the hand and wished Millwall all the best for the night, unusual to say the least and like the similar Australian incident that I mentioned it was certainly not what I am used to. Just a bit too civilised if you ask me.

At Southampton's old ground The Dell several years ago the massed away contingent were being held in the Guantanemo Bay style cages behind the goal and the police foolishly let some Junior Lions on to the pitch to get them away from the crush only for them then to run amok behind the goal. We breed them young at the Millwall.

Near Stoke City there is an area called Dresden! I thought would be disasterous for them if Neil 'Bomber' Harris lived up to the World War 2 Bomber Marshal of the RAF that his nickname comes from and he decided to do as that man did to the German Dresden and bombed the shit out of the place, that would mess up their Potteries!

Near Nottingham Forest on the Motorway I saw signs for 'Gotham', something to do with Batman and Robin I presumed! I would think that they would not want the luridly coloured be tighted oppo of Batman but they would prefer a Lincoln Green tighted Robin Hood to help the Caped Crusader in their case I presume!

At Coventry City's Ricoh Arena in December 2005 we sat in the Jewson Stand behind the goal with our tickets proclaiming that we were sitting in Vomitory 37.

Our 1 – 0 defeat did make me feel a bit sick as it happens, very strange!

At Ipswich Town in March 2006 I noticed in the gents that the hand drying blower had a warning of 'Warning Electricity!' How else would it bloody well work? The good country folk of Suffolk have probably never seen that there new fangled electricity before!

At Leyton Orient in August 2006 I was surprised to see that the home programme had 'EIO' on the front, I thought that was nice putting our goal celebration on the front! It was only after a while that I twigged that it was 'E10' the Leyton postcode, shame.

Later in August 2006 at Cheltenham Town, apart from our rural and semi pro style surroundings bring us down to earth, making us realise how low we had fallen, there was the bizarre sight of there being a bowling green right outside the away entrance, with a game of elderly white clad OAPs in full flow as we exited the ground. There was also the rather odd announcements from the PA announcer that the police would walk Millwall fans back to the station in an escort the quickest way as time was tight, only for there to be no sign of them as we left the ground, their arrangements having been scuppered by late leaving Lions, additionally the PA asked the home fans to remain in the ground for 5 minutes at the end of the match to let us out, not a bad idea I suppose but odd nonetheless.

I still find it a bit bizarre to encounter 'local' Lions fans at away matches speaking in their own regional accents who presumably only come out for the local games, in a similar vein I also find it strange to have Scots, Brummie and Geordie Lions travelling up with us from London.

Finally, for anyone of a train spotting mentality any away match that you drive to is also an excellent opportunity to spot Eddie Stobart Lorries and if you are particularly sad, you can take the name and number as well. I was once in a car with a mate on a motorway, not football related but the same principle applies. An Eddie Stobart lorry sailed past us and I said to my mate Keith, who was driving -

'Look another Eddie Stobart Lorry, how many f***ing Lorries does he have?' To which Keith replied – 'He's only got one but he isn't half busy!'

Good answer, what sort of anorak collects lorry numbers anyway? Continuing the bizarre –

The Lancashire Bizarre Health And Safety Alert!!! There's Been A Burnley –

For anyone who has read my other Millwall books about visiting the mystic land of Burnley FC, here are some points that I would mention from my trip to Turf Moor on 8th February 2014.

I went on my own on Coach one, when we arrived at the proof that it's grim Oop Norf spot that is Burnley, we arrived early so were forced to go to the Burnley Cricket Club for a beer as the turnstiles were not opening until 1.45pm, which was a good 45 minutes after we arrived at the ground, It did not take too much forcing I will be honest!

So I walked around there where I had a couple of pints that for reference seemed to be at around 1990s London prices, me like!!

After the cheap sherbets I walked to the ground at 2pm, went and bought my essential I am up North Meat and Potato Pie, then had a slash where I found that the toilets in the Away David Fishwick stand do not have that modern convenience wash basins, so the only way you can wash your hands if you had done a number one job was to piss on them!

I know that the away section is like a football ground museum piece but I thought washing your hands after ablutions might have reached the North, obviously I am wrong!

Continuing the fun that is Turf Moor, the steward at the top of the stairway entrance demanded that he saw my ticket and that I sat in the right seat,

I did say you know that you are playing Millwall today don't you, and sitting in the right seat is not exactly a priority with us lot mate!

I did not elaborate but for reference I think although I have been to hundreds of away games with Millwall, the only places that I have sat in the right seat were on my trip to the old Wembley for the Autowindscreen Final, my five trips at the point of writing to the new Wembley four Play Off Finals and one FA Cup Semi Final,

Old Trafford for the FA Cup Semi Final and the FA Cup Final at the Millennium stadium, not a high percentage, but I wished the jobsworth good luck and launched my journey to my ticketed seat up the stone age monolith that is the away end at Burnley.

If you had not been there he seats are all wood with surrounding metal frames, and the steps are twice the height of the steps at normal football grounds, for reference you will know what I mean if you ever stood on the Rookery End at Watford pre all seater stadiums, imagine that with seats plonked on it and you have a Burnley.

If you were a mountain climber be a piece of piss but if you were born in the modern world it was a real adventure climbing to my seat, which was near the top of the stand, good on the thighs and all that, but seats splinter your arse once you plonk it down as you need to from the exhaustion of climbing to your seat.

So here are a few tips for any trips you make to Burnley –

Close your eyes so that you do not have to view the architectural splendour that is the town/city of Burnley, where Millwall mate Johnny Lynch once said to me on a coach trip to there, they seem to be building slums to replace the slums already here! Back to my close your eyes suggestion only open your eyes when you arrive at the ground, I would just like to point out that this particular suggestion should not be adopted if you are driving!

You will probably have to visit the loo, so have a bottle of water and a bar of soap or bottle of handwash with you! What I would recommend was that if someone has just visited the bogs in this stand do not send them to order food for you! Just a recommendation I thought I should pass on.

Take mountaineering gear to ascend the steps in the stand.

Take the stewards 'You must sit in the correct seat' ethos, with a pinch of salt, because you may well find that your seat is behind the metal posts holding up the roof of the stand, so f*** sitting there for a game of soldiers! I sat in the right row but moved to another seat further away from the pillars nearer to behind the goal, steward might have found it naughty if he had discovered what I had done but so bloody what! Take a pair of tweezers with you to get the splinters out of you arse from the wooden seat and have some Savlon on you to repair the damage caused by them, you might also take some WD40 to oil the metal part of the seat, perhaps that is a bit ott, okay then take breathing equipment if you find that your seat is at the top of the stand, because you will need it!

The Yorkshire Bizarre –

Although the above Health and Safety alerts at Burnley were sort of meant to be serious If you want proof that we are in a health and safety nanny state, at Sheffield United, as our coach arrived outside Brammall Lane in 2010/11, a female steward came on board and welcomed us to the delights of Sheffield, then said 'has anybody got a flag that they want to take inside? Because if you have it must be fire proof with a fire safety certificate otherwise you won't be able to take inside Brammall Lane to celebrate with when you score as it is against our health and safety rules!' yea gods, I did say to Paul Simms one of my mates who I had travelled with who was about to have a post coach fag – 'Watch it mate we may also need a fire safety certificate for our clothes in case anyone spontaneously combusts after another reffing disaster!'

Darren Deadman's reffing display could cause that easily, I myself had to put a bucket of water on my nut for 90 minutes in case it exploded!

I have a strange concept that you only need driving directions to get to the away ground, you do not need a return route as all London roads will be sign posted, wrong!

I adopted this stupid policy when we drove to Huddersfield Town for the Play Off Semi Final First Leg in May 2010, we found Huddersfield easily with our directions but could not find an easy way back to London, so we toured Yorkshire beauty spots like Halifax, Leeds and Bradford for yonks trying to find an M1 South sign.

In the process of this tour we noted the Huddersfield penchant for having Hot Tub shops, why the bloody hell would you want what is essentially an outdoor bath in Huddersfield?

It is not a sun drenched hot spot is it?

For reference this is next door to a funeral parlour, I think it was called Hot Tub World, when I went there again for Ian Holloway's first game 11th January, if Lomas had still been in charge I would have booked myself in Hot Tub World post game, drowned myself and organised my burial at sea in the Funeral Parlour before I went in Hot Tub World and did the suicidal deed. Luckily when Lomas went my feeling about having to endure another Lomas inspired horror show and having to drown myself so that I did not have to watch anymore went away, a bliss! Little did I know what things would be like under Hollowhead, suicide before the match at Huddersfield Town been preferable than enduring that C***s footballing nous!

On a trip through Yorkshire to Middlesbrough on 15th October 2011, which I went to on my jack on a club coach, I noticed whilst gawping out of the coach window that we went past The World Of James Herriot, I thought must go there, I will undoubtedly be taught the correct technique for shoving my arm up a cow's arse! Moving on...

In conclusion of the Yorkshire beauty spots returning to the previous season – Barnsley, when we went there for the final game of the season on 7th May 2011 we had a lovely tour around a roundabout directed by a police motorcyclist, who eventually led us to pull in behind another Kings Ferry coach, in their case a double decker, this was done as it is essential that we get a police escort in to what bizarrely for football grounds is a very well signposted one.

Still this didn't stop the Old Bill motorcyclist going in the opposite direction of the signs that said Barnsley FC,.

That aside when we parked up behind the leading Kings Ferry coach, we pulled up on a road above the Motorway next to a lampost that had a a poster that said – 'In Despair call The Samaritans 24 hours 08457 109090'

Bloody hell I assume it was to stop the public diving headlong on to the motorway below, mind you it could have been there for any team in freefall relegation mode, to protect their fans mental health, if everyone parks up here for a police escort, bizarre I thought!

The Western Bizarre –

Bloody shame that they did not have one of the above mentioned Samaritans signs on the bridge over the M4 when someone commited suicide by jumping off bridge in to traffic, gridlocking the M4 and slip road on to it from M25 when we tried to drive to Bizarre day Number One Reading on Saturday 6th August for the first game of the 2011/12 season.

Kill yourself by all means like this but not during the football season and before the kick off, you showboating div!!! Sorry there goes my sympathy gene!

We eventually arrived at the Madejski about 5 minutes late amazingly as we were walking about on the M4 itself at around 2.30pm!

Number two Southampton FA Cup 4th Round Replay Tuesday 7th February 2012, three of us myself, Paul and David Simms decided to drive to Sarfampton, we arranged to meet in Lowell Street where I live in Limehouse at 3.30pm, This is because Paul Simms at the time worked nearby to me in Canary Wharf.

Dave had driven down from Harlow to meet us two in the car we were going to drive in and drove down to meet us in this car, all okay.

Paul was going to drive so Dave parked up and we boarded the car put our seatbelts on and Paul put the key in the ignition started the engine and nothing, he made several attempts still no luck, we tried to push start the car still no luck, so we got the jump leads out and flagged other drivers down.

The first one came over in a Mercedes Benz, parked near us to enable us to attempt the jump start, Dave tried to open the bonnet, no joy to add to the fun he managed to break something at the front of the bonnet.

As no joy we tried car number two, this was a brand spanking new car the bonnet was opened and we found that all the engine was sealed and there was nowhere to attach the jump leads, so third attempt, Dave went in to the flats near where we were found a driver in there who gave us longer jump leads drove out to us, parked his car in front of us we attached the new jump leads, and Paul tried the engine, third time lucky we started, this was now about 4pm.

Anyway we drove through the East End over Tower Bridge to the Elephant and Castle on to A3 – M3, we stopped at a Petrol Station to get some petrol keeping the engine running for fear that it might not start again if we stopped it. At the Petrol stop Dave topped up the distilled water and tightened the Battery connections, and all seemed tickety boo, we continued to Southampton and drove all over the shop as the customary Football signs seemed to appear then vanish, we asked several people and were given umpteen different directions! Amazingly we found St Mary's and parked up near the away end.

Due to all the palaver we arrived not long before the kick off, settled down on a freezing cold night watched a great game, that we won 3 – 2 having been 1 – 0 up, then 2 -1 down 13 minutes before end, only to equalise with less than 10 minutes to go and score a brilliant goal in injury time!!!!

We went back to the car without knowing if it would start or not, it did yahoo!

I had done my usual trick of only doing an AA map of the outward directions not the return trip, so we drove all over the shop and luckily found the M3, only to encounter a diversion on Junctions 5/6 I think, again found the diversion a mystery tour and found ourselves in country lanes, we eventually found our way

589

back at the M4, amazingly near Reading, and drove home to London from there.

Finally Gone West third Western bizarre Cardiff City away 31st March 2012 which I went to on a club coach on my jack, we left the New Den at 7am and made our way through London to the M4, pretty much as soon as we got on to the motorway the trouble began.

We went over a weighbridge and were ordered in to the first services Heston as we had exceeded the allowable 7.5 tons weight limit apparently, this was because our coach had not taken any notice of the diversion signs as the other two coaches had, we did not really know what the problem was but we thought best not antagonize them, thank Christ I had lost three stone in previous few months or I may have to be winched to away games if they bring in a weight restriction, I.e. Put scales by door so you have to weigh in as well as being strip searched and anally probed every away coach trip that encounters a weight restriction!

The male and female who pulled us in weren't actually Old Bill but private f***ing Traffic Enforcement officers, who in my opinion were just Jobsworths Bertie big bollocking themselves with their company that they were not afraid of anyone as they had pulled over a Millwall coach!

In fact the female one of the duo actually said something like 'You are Millwall you should be used to it!' what does that mean if we were Premier League top knobs we would be escorted in with our servants

to feed us grapes and be chauffer driven there? Talk about perception of what Millwall fans are like!

When she also implied we would be held there for quite a while, it being three or so hours pre kick off at 12.30pm and were still well over a hundred Miles from Welsh Wales consequently I thought that we would miss the game and I text Millwall friends and family who could not make trip, to tell them of the situation and that I hoped the games on radio if we have to listen from here!!!

Our decision re not slagging the Jobsworths was because we did not want to give them an excuse to turn us around back to New Den, after doing their alleged duty they let us go after ballsing us about for about 10 mins, so we drove on to what we thought would be a Welsh Wales Heddlu Police State, amazingly when we did arrive at Services near Cardiff with our being the last coach to arrive of our three on the day the Old Bill pretty much drove us straight out, presumably because they had held the other two coaches long enough in their plans as they had not been held on M4 as we had, also it was not like the customary Police State we usually get in Cardiff or Swansea.

To show that the Cardiff City Stadium is nothing like Ninian Park used to be like, which was similar in hostility to the Old Den the new all singing and dancing arena, looks like umpteen others, as it is an Identikit pretty much soulless non-atmospheric arena in my opinion.

One original bizarre thing, on entry to the ground Stewards were handing out plastic cups that you had

to pour any liquid stuff in to before they took even plastic bottles from you,

One thing that I was worried about was that I had a pasty in the ground and thought should I look at

Google to try to get a Cardiff Mini Cab company? This idea was in case I myself was now over the accepted weight limit?

I did not do it and to be honest I did not have to as it turned out because our coach actually went the way home that it should have done on the way west, i.e. followed the diversion signs, so I could have been the size of the King Of Tonga if I had fancied!

Real welcome in the hillsides at the next game there post-Christmas 2012 on Saturday 29th December 2012, outside the ground there is an Away Parking only area which is right outside Visitors section, inside the ground there was one TV that had Millwall's 2011/12 season video on, pre match on concourse, a Play station Stand that you could play at, most of the Refreshment staff had

Millwall home shirts on and there were posters all around the concourse saying 'Thank You for travelling 300 miles today' with a Millwall lions background and pictures of Millwall players and Kenny Jackett, unfortunately one of the players shown was Chris Wood who had decided to join Leicester City rather than us, in honour of this Paul decided that on Poster nearest to us he would black his face out with a pen so he did!

Not Western But Two More Bizarre Trips

I went to Notts Forest on my own on Saturday 4th November 2012 and it was an entertaining day, the wheelchair lift attachment on Coach 1 became stuck when wheelchair regular away traveller Kenny wanted to go to the services, it was fine getting him off the coach, but the coach lift device jammed and we were stuck at the Services until it was fixed, which fortunately it was.

We then drove in too Nottingham when we went passed Trent Bridge County Cricket ground, which I thought was odd as although I have been to The City Ground about a half a dozen times I had never seen it before I found out why, the reason was because the coach driver drove in towards the ground and we were at the Notts Forest end, a policeman got on board and directed the driver to the away end, marvellous as he must have driven there numerous times before, I said I think that what passes for a Sat Nav on a Millwall coach is someone on board saying ' It is that way you c***!'

Inside the ground there were a couple of strange incidents, in front of me there was a bloke standing with his son who had smuggled in a tin of Stella Artois in his jeans, I said how the f*** did you get that in, he said if you have your child with you they don't search you so a guzzling he could go !!!!

As we rattled goals in at 3-1 a bloke behind said I hope that we don't get a fourth as I have had a bet on Millwall winning 3-1, I said mate if we do get a fourth I will give you my wallet, we did and I offered to make up his lost winnings, but thankfully he turned my offer down as he was delirious!

Finally on strange journey trip I went to Sheffield Wednesday on Friday 23rd August 2013 with Swedish Millwall fan Michael Karlstrom and his wife Catarina, they flew in to Stanstead from Stockholm and I met them for Michael to drive up to Sheffield stay overnight in a hotel go to Sheffield FC the oldest Football club in the world and to Sheffield dog racing, the night before our match there with Sheffield Wednesday on Saturday 24th August.

We left Stanstead in a hire car about 12.30pm or so and encountered the customary traffic jams on M11 caused by roadwork's, we then went on to M25 to get on to M1, here we encountered one of the most annoying things I have ever encountered, there were traffic jams all the way from Watford where we had joined M1 to Sheffield, this was caused by the Motorway system showing Queues ahead and slower speeds that you had to travel, I said to Michael this must be due to Roadwork's but it transpired that it must have been a brilliant transport plan as we passed a sign up in Yorkshire that said something like Speed Easing Ends! What a fantastic idea, all it caused was over a hundred miles of traffic congestion and meant that it took over 4 hours to complete our journey! I know it was the weekend of a Bank Holiday but what a nightmare piece of planning, one if not the worst pointless driving journeys that I have ever encountered.

Most Annoying Clubs Fans At Away Games Award

My award for most Noisy annoying bastards goes to Hull City at the KCOM Arena on Tuesday 26th Feb 2019, because in addition to 2017/18 visit they now bang a bleeding drum in addition to banging on metal fence at the back of their section, this was not there the season before, they were right close to us and annoying does not start to describe them!

Town and Stadium Signposts

A couple of questions –

Is it only my dodgy peepers or can you never find the place where you are travelling to on the Motorway signs, until you pretty much get there? Apart from the above mentioned Cardiff City arena where there were actually illuminated signs on the M4 that told you what JCT, in this case number 33 that you had to turn off at, bizarre!

Also why do Stadium signs only ever appear, if they exist at all that is, as you actually have the ground in sight?

Bizarre Away Sponsors

Modern all-seater stadia have led to some bizarre depictions, sponsors, cock-ups and missed opportunities – for example, there still isn't a Gary Glitter junior Enclosure yet I see? Sorry bad taste!

A few years ago, we went to Macclesfield for a night game and we marvelled at 'The Samaritans' adverts all around their ground. As Macclesfield went on to get relegated that season I imagine that the local branch must have done a roaring trade. Given the anguish that most people's teams put their fans through I'm surprised that a side hasn't gone the whole hog and opened a 'Samaritans' stand, complete with your own personal councillor sitting next to you, who could then guide you through the horrors of yet another woeful, hapless display.

Whilst many clubs have names or club badges picked out in their seats there are also various depictions of ex stars heads at clubs around the country, for example –

At Preston they have the heads of Sir Tom Finney, Bill Shankly and ex goalkeeping hero Alan Kelly, who I had never heard of.

At Portsmouth on the KJC stand behind the goal there is someone depicted who I did not know from Adam, why not have the head of the Looney with the bell, trumpet, blue hair and big top hat?

Some faces on the stand ideas that have not yet been tried -

As Wigan Athletics' JJB was really a shrine to the sport of rugby league, how about -

'It's An Up And Under' With a picture of Eddie Waring's head depicted on the main stand?

Another marketing opportunity not yet taken up is to hire out the oceans of empty seats at Wigan, how about. – 'This Space for Hire' or 'Empty Stand'?

At Carrow road Norwich, they could have had a depiction of Iwan Roberts head, utilising his gap-toothed grin as an exit. How about a pictogram of Peter Beardsley facing the away fans at Anfield or St James's Park that would keep the pigeons off the pitch and put the willies up the away fans, if you will pardon the Brighton ground expression! Given the megalomaniac nature of some club's chairmen, I find it strange that none of them has yet constructed a new stand to the exact dimensions of their own head, thus doubling its capacity at a stroke!

Finally, the most humorous incident of real stand artistry was on Crystal Palace's Holmsdale End. Which was constructed with insufficient blocks to spell out 'Crystal Palace', shame, never mind they could have just spelt out 'We Are F...ed' in homage to the right royal shafting that Uncle Ron Noades inflicted on the heart leading the head, businessman (sic) Mark Goldberg and his financial wizardry, an opportunity missed there.

Kit Man Cock Up

What is the kit mans job? I could be wrong but I think that it is to bring the kit! Well I have seen teams at both The Dens play in Millwall's away kit, the most famous being when Derby County won the Division 2 Championship at the Old Den under Dave Mackay in 1968/9 I may have a selective memory but I cannot ever remember Millwall playing away in the home teams kit, that was not until we played at Sheffield Wednesday's Hillsborough on 22nd August 2013, when we played the first half in Wednesday's black and yellow away kit but the second in our Orange away kit, bizarre, I wonder where he had taken that, I cannot be arsed to check so either he drove back to London and got it, left it at hotel and went to get it, or he had really brought it and lost it at Hillsborough?

Actual answer – I found out that the away kit was flown up by Helicopter from London hence proper away kit in second half Sheffield Wednesday kit man said that was what happened and kit not only job!

Returning To The Smoke

Having sat numb arsed on a lengthy coach or car journey, counted the traffic cones and watched the miles agonisingly counting down. It is not until I arrive within striking distance of the capital or I see things like the Nissan 'Welcome to London' sign as you come off the M1, that I know that I can relax, it is not too far to go now.

After such a long trek it's often a case that even the thought of seeing the Holloway Road or Shoreditch seems like something to look forward to, especially when returning from the horrors of the likes of Oldham, Burnley, Rotherham and of course Brummie land.

It's at these times that the proposition of crossing the Thames, driving up the Embankment or through Greenwich cheers me up no end and makes me realise just what I have been away from as I view the Thames and London at night in all its splendour -

Big Ben
HMS Belfast
The Illuminated Bridges
The Houses of Parliament

The London Eye
St Paul's Cathedral
The Up lit buildings
Park Plaza Hotel
The Globe Theatre
The Gherkin
The Millennium Dome
The Shard
The O2
The London Eye
Canary Wharf
The Savoy
The Tate Modern
The Tower of London
Tower Bridge
The Maritime buildings, etc, etc.

All of which help to erase any thoughts of the places that I have just visited from my mind.

Put it this way it is not quite like driving into Burnley!

It is definitely a case of thank God I am back in the smoke – I am happy now.

CHAPTER 16
Mad Lions And Englishmen Stand Out In The Morning Sun

The Brighton Play Offs at the Old Den and the Autowindscreen Final and 2003/4 FA Cup Semi and Cup Final queues were bad but this was the best or worst depending on how you look at it.

This was largely because like Brighton the queue was for both the home and away games and was open to season ticket holders and members alike, Birmingham City, Play-Off Semi-Final legs 2001/2002.

All that could have made it worse was having a bloody great clock in front of the queue to prove that time does in fact standstill, doesn't fly when you're not enjoying yourself and every second really does take a minute and every minute does take an hour.

As usual I had volunteered to get our clans tickets and I set off from my flat at 7.15am, arriving at the ground at about 8 am, an hour before opening time.

There were rumours that some people had got there at 4am, which makes no sense at all to me, at the very best they would have at least a four and a half to five hour wait, let's face it they were not going to open a ticket window in the middle of the night were they.

The car park and streets had been cleared of cars and there were barriers laid out to form a winding queue that went up and down in front of the West Stand, as I approached I noticed that even by this early stage it was building up ominously and there were already some 300 to 400 people in the queue in front of me. Being a veteran of this sort of thing, I treat it as an away trip, so I take newspapers, food, drinks and a pen to do the crosswords and psyche myself up for a bloody long wait.

Whilst I thought I was prepared, it was nothing to some others, for example, several people had brought portable seats to sit on. Now that is organized!

These were mostly women, veterans of the January sales no doubt

When I left my flat it had been a bit nippy, so my trusty old leather coat seemed like the best bet, with all those around me in the queue in short-sleeved shirts looking out of place.

Naturally as the sun woke up and started beating down, my coat seemed less sensible and I stood in the winding queue sweating like a stuck pig on a spit.

The media later said that the fair-skinned ones of which I am one my being blonde as a child, in the queue, who had queued in the baking sun for hours, had suffered sunburn, mind you whilst I packed all the items that I deemed necessary, I had not thought that sunscreen would really be required, fortuitously the queue at the ground coincided with a doctor's convention at the ground, which was sound planning as they could counsel the agitated and treat the heat stroke as it turned out.

As I queue I tend to recite a mantra in my head adding up the tickets I require, so that I do not forget what I have to get, I also continually count and recount the money and the season ticket vouchers, it drives me mad but I am sure everyone does it.

I myself had to get both home and away tickets; I was not concerned about the home tickets, as they should be guaranteed, I was concerned about the away allocation however.

The original plan was that anybody from season-ticket holders to members could buy tickets for the away match, at one ticket each; fortunately, they changed their mind by the time that the tickets went on sale and our away ticket allocation was thankfully only sold to season-ticket holders, which is how I think it should be.

What this policy change meant was that getting an away ticket was now far more likely, even so in the interest of paranoia, despite the fact that the queue was not split in to home and away and I had no real concept of what game(s) people were getting tickets for, I pessimistically assumed that those ahead of me were all season ticket holders and all wanted away tickets. Consequently, I found myself doing a mental calculation about the limited number of away tickets available, this consisted of– Number of people in front of me multiplied by the estimated number of tickets they wanted, minus the total number of original tickets available (2800) equals the number of tickets left for the away match by the time that I got to the window.

Warren one of the Essex contingent was several hundred people behind me and he must have been working on the same equation, because when he spotted me nearer to the front he came over and asked if I could get their away tickets for them just in case. I agreed and he gave me his vouchers and money and said that he would queue up to get their home tickets.

We are all regular Home and Awayers so in my opinion we should all be guaranteed tickets over and above any away Johnny-come-lately.

I had to get tickets in various stands for the home game, 11 in all and I now had to get 14 for the away game plus 7 coach tickets, which was the easy part, one bloke in front of me bought 64 home tickets!

Who decided that we should sell six tickets per season ticket for the home game?

I believe we had 7000 season-ticket holders, so with the ludicrous home ticket policy, if every season ticket holder, took up their full allocation we would need a ground twice the size of the current Den to fit everyone in, isn't CSE math's marvellous? A recipe for disaster and that is not just with the benefit of hindsight. I had eight season tickets with which I bought all the home tickets, which meant that in theory, if I understood how it worked, I could have bought 48 tickets. Our block in the CBL is practically a season-ticket holder only area as it is, so where would all the interlopers have sat? In addition, how on earth would you manage the reserved seating stands? Anyway, what was to stop me buying my full allocation of tickets and then selling them on for a profit to Brummies or other club fans? This was not the first game this crazy policy had been used; it was certainly an accident waiting to happen, rant over.

On the plus side amazingly Millwall opened up the food and drink stalls and the toilets, however in order to get anything you had to leave the queue whilst somebody kept your place for you.

Why they didn't have mobile food wagons going up and down the vast queue I do not know, they would have made a bomb.

During the morning, Theo Paphitis arrived to a chorus of abuse for the way that the ticket selling appeared to be totally unorganised.

Confusion had reigned on the day regarding what you could and could not get with what membership or season ticket, with PA announcements seemingly made on the fly.

As Theo went through the doors I was talking to a bloke in front of me, who said – 'I bet he goes upstairs and bangs one out at the thought of all the money that he's going to make out of this!'

Graphic but possibly true.

Queues are a great place for observing human nature, there is generally always a good camaraderie with many strangers conversing like old friends, it is rather like the spirit of the Blitz, as we are all mentally in the same boat. A queue is also a rumour mill as well with the usual talk that tickets were being sold on the internet and by telephone, whilst we queued up like mugs in the baking sun.

On a lighter note it was comical to see some kids in school uniforms queuing up; it is good to see that following Millwall takes preference to schoolwork!

Something else that added to the farcical nature of it all was that everyone in the queue had Millwall ring tones on their mobiles, everybody either had – 'No One Likes Us' or 'Let 'Em Come'.

As usual, this prompted the ridiculous sight of umpteen people scrabbling to find their phone, whenever a mobile rang, unsure if it was for them. I had previously noticed this phenomenon at away matches throughout the season. I personally had mine on vibrate and I kept it in my jeans front pocket, I thought that I might as well enjoy myself while I am at it.

As the ticket window opening time got closer the queue was snaking back and forth several times across the car park, out through the gates and up Bolina Road as far as the railway arches.

At 8.30am, they opened the first window and there were three open by 9.15am, I only saw at most five windows open in all the time that I was there, which was just not enough, after all this was our biggest day since the Wembley Final and the Wigan Play–Offs.

In a perverse way the closer, that you get to the front of the queue the more frustrating it becomes, because the wait for some reason seems longer. One reason is that it appears that the people at the window ahead of you are there for an age, they seem to be the kind of people who wait until they get to the window before they take out their vouchers or sort their money out, not me I had the vouchers taken out of the season ticket books as soon as I got to the ground and I had the financial side of things tied up by then as well, that was until I had to revise it for the extra tickets the Essex Boys wanted.

After four and a half hours at 12.30pm, I got to the head of the queue, by which time my legs had seized up, so that when my turn came I stumbled forward like a zombie.

When I eventually got to the window I noticed that the people behind them had a haunted shell-shocked look on their faces, even at this early stage. Their spirits would not have been lifted by the seemingly endlessly snaking queue outside that is for sure.

Grateful it was all over I headed away from the ground as the day of the long and sun-baked queue continued and went blood doning.

At about 5pm Dave Murray rang me to say that he had got there at 4pm and he asked me how I had done, very well, as it turned out. He said that the queue was still well outside of the gates when he arrived and people were getting more and more agitated and sun burnt, he eventually rang me at 10.30pm after six-and-a-half hours wait and said that when he left they were still queuing up.

He also said that Mark McGhee and Theo had come out to quell the angry mob and that he had heard that touts had been selling tickets in the toilets, at three times face value, the way it was organized it was practically set up for this to happen.

Even though some people during the day seemed to be working in shifts, handing the baton to another person when they had done their bit, it seemed that everyone had queued up for at least several hours, with my four and a half hour one-man stint appearing to be getting off lightly.

It was said on the TV and in the press that many people had queued for nine hours, which I can well believe and there were numerous complaints about it being much worse than the Auto windscreen queue, which it was. Queues eh! Don't you just love them?

I do because obviously, being English queuing is all part of my genetic make-up

Oh, I nearly forgot my standing for umpteen hours in the sun in a thick coat to get tickets several times, i.e. for 2004 FA Cup Final v Manchester United, 2008/9 v Scunthorpe United and 2009/10 Swindon Town Play Off Finals.

Away Season Ticket Time

In 2016/7 in an I am bored with queuing for tickets scenario brought on largely by the Gillingham clash where we did not get tickets due to the crap allocation and the way Millwall sold the tickets, i.e. no restriction on number of Teamcards any one person could turn up with in queue, selling them online and on telephone at same time, this led to me writing to Millwall to say that there should be a preference system for hard core away travelers, with a pecking order so that we week in week out away Millwall took precedent over every now and then merchants, so before Millwall's announcement I mention later I went the Away Season Ticket route where you pay £20 allied to your Season Ticket that you already have for home and they take your tickets out of the allocation first, take your money from Debit/Credit card details you put on Away Season Ticket application and put your ticket aside for collection or postal delivery where you get the receipt for your payment, this means come what may I get a ticket and without the joys of queuing and having the possibility of missing out as a lot of Hard Core away Wall did, at the start of 2016/7 Millwall announced that they had taken on board my preference for real away travellers system, good news and it was not only said by me that this should happen as it was common talk in the personal queues at The Den.

CHAPTER 17
'UEFA Cup We Had A Laugh!'

In some sort of alternative universe Millwall were in the UEFA Cup!

Merely by virtue of being English, we were a seeded team and went straight in to the first round proper with the big boys. I honestly thought that we would be drawn against an obscure team from a former Soviet satellite republic; however in the end we drew Hungarian champions Ferencvaros.

They had come in to the competition via the Champions League and it transpired that they were a persistent trouble club themselves, which if nothing else proves that the draw wasn't rigged I suppose.

As a bit of background for those who do not know the merest hint of Millwall fans setting foot on continental Europe for a pre-season tour of Germany in 2001/2 had prompted a resounding 'Nein!' And a cancellation of the tour pronto before Deutschland's 'Boys', lederhosened up and felt hatted in their version of a Football casual could pit their hooligan wits against England's most notorious fans.

Unsurprisingly the prospect that everybody, be they Millwall or other club's fans, talked about was the vague possibility of the UEFA Cup draw bringing up the dream pairing of Galatasaray and Millwall and for us a jolly jaunt to Leeds fan murdering Istanbul.

Can you imagine what the response would have been?
1. The nation and media would be in uproar.
2. The press and TV would be having kittens.

3. There would be questions raised in the House of Commons.
4. They would have to wake up, or in some cases dig up, the House of Lords to put through an Emergency Bill to ban us.
5. The full might of Britain and Turkey's Diplomatic Corps would be involved in hours of frantic talks behind the scenes in an effort to avoid a major International incident.
6. They would issue banning orders to everyone in London, Essex and Kent just to be on the safe side.
7. They would shut all the kebab shops and declare martial law in Wood Green, again just in case.

As the Turkish side failed to reach the UEFA Cup this was not to be, however as I said above the eventual team, we drew were themselves equally notorious Football Hooligans it was to transpire.

I thought it only fitting to give you my memories of Millwall's historic games in the UEFA Cup, the away part of which has previously appeared in a different form in Sweden on Millwall Enough Said website.

Millwall v Ferencvaros UEFA Cup 1st Leg Thursday 16th September 2004 The New Den

For this first and quite probably last European adventure, we were drawn at home first.

Naturally, we were far more interested in the jaunt to Budapest.

In the home leg despite having the better of the game and leading 1 – 0 we conceded an away goal making the away leg fraught from both a Footballing and Hooligan perspective.

Unsurprisingly we sang a plethora of stereotypical chants on the match night -

'We hate goulash and we hate goulash, we are the goulash haters!'/'You can stick your f…ing goulash up your arse!'/'We hate pikeys (gypos)!'/'You dirty foreign bastards!'

When we went 1 – 0 up we sang – 'Pikeys pikeys what's the

score?' Not forgetting the less abusive –'We're the famous Millwall and we're going to Hungary, Hungary, Hungary!'/'Grandad's going on a European tour!' And 'Get your passports out, get your passports out!'

Ferencvaros' 245 fans sang uninteligible chants in their very strange language whilst nazi saluting and bobbing up and down in the North stand upper tier for most of the night.

In response we 'EIO'd' and arm pumped, it looked like the Eurovision Dance contest.

In response to their strange actions we naturally took the piss out of our Eastern European visitors,

Milllwall mate Clive who could not get to the 2nd Leg pointedly said 'You're laughing now wait and see how funny it is with 15,000 of the buggers doing it!' A very wise assessment as it turned out.

'What I Did On Me Holidays' – Ferencvaros v Millwall UEFA Cup 2nd Leg Thursday 30th September 2004. Ulloi Ut Stadium Budapest, Hungary

5 of us decided to travel to Budapest, myself and my mates Paul, Nathan and Simon with his son Pat.

Simon got the forms from Millwall to apply for the match tickets via the club ballot, an unfair method of allocation I thought, why not merely offer tickets to those who travel away regularly, not just those who show up for big games? Whatever the rights and wrongs of the ballot system I gathered everyone's Teamcards and relevant passport info and put in our match ticket applications I included details of our travel and hotel arrangements on the applications my thinking being that it proved that we were serious about how we were travelling and staying in Budapest.

Despite the small allocation of Millwall tickets we decided that we were going come what may and we trawled the internet for a good flight/hotel deal before we had heard the result of the ticket ballot.

After a few days surfing we booked a package via an online travel company with flights on Malev Hungarian airlines and a double and triple room in the three star Stadion Hotel in the less than beautiful downtown area of Pest.

Because we had already booked our flights and accomodation we obviously decided to forego the option of applying for the couple of hundred available club plane places, we decided to make our own travel arrangements for two reasons.

Firstly we would be stuck if we did not all get flight or tickets, for example what if 12 year old Pat got a match ticket/flight ticket and his dad Simon didn't?

Secondly we thought that it was best to spend a few days in Budapest and booked to fly out early on Wednesday 29th September from Heathrow and we were due to return on the late afternoon of Friday 1st October, thus giving us ample time to sightsee and try to get match tickets in Hungary if required this was because the club plane version was a travel out and return on the same day trip, consequently we wouldn't get to see any of Budapest. For reference I had several friends who had travelled to Budapest on Holiday in the past who all assured me that it was a beautiful city, more of which later.

I personally deposited the applications safely at Millwall and quite quickly the flight document and hotel vouchers arrived, all that we needed for our trip now was the minor detail of the match tickets.

As the days passed without hearing anything all our paranoia was setting in nicely. I personally filled in all our forms and as I mentioned earlier I put everything conceivable on them, for example every number on the Teamcard, passports info, flight and hotel details, etc, nonetheless although I was sure I hadn't made a mess of the forms I would still not be happy until all we 5 had the Match tickets in our grubby mitts.

Then it was announced that the draw had been made and we had heard nothing, the club said that you would not be contacted unless you were successful, so you would not find out if you had tickets until the postman shoved them through your letterbox, the club had more faith in our postal system than I do, this scenario I had tried to sidetrack by saying I will come and pick up my ticket do not post as post in Limehouse is erratic to say the least, Millwall said yes to this and when I heard that tickets were being sent out I called Millwall and found out despite my instructions and their agreement they had been sent in post, I said what if they do not turn up, Millwall said no duplicate tickets are available sir, I said well lets hope they bloody well turn up then!

Gradually news was filtering through that people had received their tickets, for example my cousin Gavin, who had applied for match and Club flight tickets had been successful, consequently I was getting even more jumpy.

Paul Simms found an MSC link where it said that they had the list of lucky applicants and you could Email to see if you had come through the draw.

As I had everyone's info I Emailed Jim Webb at MSC to check if we had been successful and after several days wait I thankfully got a reply to say that we had all come through, thank god, it turned out that the lists they held were random and unalphabetical consequently searching them for names from the deluge of Email must have been a nightmare. I sat back happy that I had not made a balls of the applications and waited like a kid at Christmas for the postman to arrive.

Texts began arriving from my mates that they had there's and when I heard the rattle of the letterbox and soft plop of an envelope landing on the carpet I ran downstairs like an exited eight year old.

Silly old bugger you may well say but I had a feeling that Millwall in Europe would be a once in a lifetime affair and I was glad that we were not going to miss it.

We continually hit Ferencvaros' website which was available in Hungarian, German and thankfully English, it contained warnings not to travel without tickets and had pictures of the 'stadium' which looked like we were heading back to the old 4th division, more of which later.

In the days leading up to departure I got my and Simon's Hungarian Fiorents and noticed that most of the notes seemed to have pictures of people who looked like Vlad The Impaler on them, sorry wrong country I know, but it gave us a feel for the Eastern European adventure that we were about to embark upon.

Our flight was due to depart at 7am on Wednesday 29th so Simon and Pat stayed at my East End flat, as we had to be at Heathrow two hours before our flight, Nathan and Paul were going to pick us up at around 3am. Pat was hyper during the preceeeding evening he was exclaiming that this would be the best holiday he'd ever had, seeing Millwall and with his dad and mates.

We had a couple of hours fitful sleep and went to meet Nathan at the designated meet, he arrived and we set off to the airport. With no traffic on the road we consequently arrived at around 4am and then drove all around the airport looking for the long stay car park, we eventually found it and caught our bus back to the terminal, we went to sign in and found the lower level of the airport was full of travelling Celtic fans on their way AC Milan, we got our boarding passes and headed upstairs to get some food and wait for our flight to be called, we found the upper floor contained numerous Hearts fans en route to portuguese side SC Braga. Our flight was called and we headed to the gate where there were several Police who gave everyone's passports a cursory glance, we then boarded our small plane, it was chockful of Millwall fans, mostly able bodied men, Pat was by far the youngest on board.

Pat was still hyper and wanted to sit in the window seat, as Simon doesn't like heights or going over water he gladly let him sit there. We took off and were shortly served a breakfast that consisted of ham, scrambled eggs and what looked like seaweed, this delightful concoction and accompanying smell led to Simon who I was sitting next to being sick into his sickbag, a very good start then.

The flight was short and only a few hours so we arrived at Budapest's Ferihegy airport at 10.45am local time. We headed through customs and I turned on my mobile which sparked into life with Welcome to Hungary messages from the local phone network.

We went out of the airport to the cab rank and boarded two cabs to our hotel.

I was in one cab with Simon and Pat and as the nature of the East European country that we were now in became apparent, Pat suddenly became quiet before exclaiming 'Dad, It's a shithole!'

Quite what he thought it would be like I don't know. We drove through Pest and arrived at our hotel, which was a stones throw from the Ferenc Puskas aka Nep Stadium (Stadion) the national Football stadium. Thankfully our 3 star hotel was really quite posh, it had a free swimming pool and sauna and more importantly a fully stocked bar.

We dropped off our luggage in our adjoining rooms, Simon and Pat in one bedroom room and Paul, Nathan and I in the other. We made ourselves briefly at home before setting off to explore Budapest, the weather was surprisingly sunny and warm. Close to our hotel the area was pretty rundown, a bit like skid row, although luckily it transpired that we were only around a mile from Ferencvaros' stadium.

We continued walking towards the main part of town and stopped off at a Flea market very near to our hotel that was so rough that no self respecting flea would go within ten miles of it!

We left the Flea market and eventually reached the city centre itself where we found that the street near the train station contained tram lines in its centre and had a McDonalds, Pizza Hut and KFC, that's Americanisation, democracy and joining the EU for you!

As you might have gathered from the list of restaurants above, which we used for our daily meals we didn't quite go for the authentic Hungarian experience, to be honest we never even had a whiff of goulash, although I did have a spicy Hungarian topping on my pizza.

Simon admitted that he had actually had goulash, although not in Hungary sadly but in the East End hospital canteen where he works! He beat us lot on that one in the culinary stakes.

The Hungarian language is massively different to English and because along with Finnish it is a language that has no connnection with any other language whatsoever, everything looked very alien.

We had been given a map by the hotel that was all in Hungarian and French neither of which languages I know at all! So about as useful as a chocolate teapot, despite this with me as group map reader we continued our blind leading the blind walk. There was not a single shop sign that we saw that made any sense at all to us, adding to the alien feel. I've never been anywhere so foreign myself.

On our walk we noticed that despite the impressive architecture every building appeared to be covered in fly posters and grafitti, despite Budapest's Americanisation that I mentioned it still looked pretty rundown and the locals all looked Gypsyesque all of whom having bought their clothes at Millets.

It was certainly not the picturesque city that we were expecting and that my friends who had been there had mentioned. It appeared to me that under communist rule everyone was too frightened to do anything but now they were free they went mad and plastered everything.

We continued our yomp and eventually reached the bridges over the Danube, we crossed over into Buda and found that it was infinitely nicer than Pest with great architecture however despite the cathedrals, medieval architecture and hillside statues many edifices still had grafitti and posters on them

Walking along the banks of the Danube looking towards Pest was surreal as it gave us a sense of Déjà vu it looked and felt just like walking along the Thames Embankment, a strange feeling. We climbed up a steep incline that led to a park that overlooked the city and river and although sweating and panting it was worth it as the view was very impressive.

We then decided to stop off for a beer in a roadside bar where we were joined by a couple of Millwall fans a white male and a mixed race girl with dreadlocks, who I had seen at numerous away grounds over the years. We had a chat and it transpired that they did not have match tickets having failed in the ballot, thereby putting its unfairness into perspective, they said that they were going to the ground and would try to get some Tickets there even if it was in the home section, we wished them luck.

We walked further along the river and continued our ramble back to the hotel via a different bridge and found ourselves in a much nicer part of town that looked like the West End with shops like Prada, etc.

On our lengthy march various Millwall mates rang from London or Budapest to see what was happening, we told them it was actually a bit of a dive in places and we hadn't seen that many Millwall about.

Dave Murray and Bob – two Millwall regulars had arrived in Budapest on Tuesday and Dave rang to see if we had arrived, I said that we had and were yomping about and he said that they were currently on a boat trip up the Danube.

We decided to have something to eat and stopped at a McDonalds for another authentic Hungarian meal NOT! Inside there were several other ticketless Millwall, as a few of us had Millwall shirts on they came over and we had another 'we're alright Jack' chat, they too were going to try to get tickets at the ground we also wished them well and set off again.

We eventually arrived back at our hotel foot weary and collapsed in our rooms for a well deserved rest.

Pat by now wasn't well he had a headache and was sick so his dad Simon had to stay with him in the hotel and had the pleasure of watch Hungarian TV all night this consisted of Hungarian game-shows, German shows and soap operas and BBC World Service, what fun he had!

We found out from a very helpful hotel employee, a Ferencvaros fan, that the ground was only a ten minute bus/tram ride from where we were staying.

Simon suggested that it would be a good idea to find where the ground was to save any traumas the next day, so with Simon snuggled up in front of the telly looking after Pat, Nath, Paul and I set off at around 8pm.

Despite our Tram stop travelling instructions we almost immediately got lost, thankfully after wandering the streets we eventually found the tramline that we needed. This was located in the middle of a very busy multi carriageway road and we had to take our life in our hands by dodging through the speeding traffic, eventually we reached the tram stop and boarded a tram without a ticket and only a rudimentary idea of where we were going, consequently we rode up and down the tram network, baffled, due to the Hungarian language signs everywhere and our distinct lack of Hungarian. Consequently we continually got on and off the trams displaying an Englishman's reserve by not asking anyone where the ground was, preferring to politely get lost instead.

We decided to get off at a stop that said Ferencvaros, sadly this was miles from where the ground actually was and we found ourselves in an industrial site.

We got back on to a tram and continued our Budapest shuttle, eventually getting on and off of around a dozen trams without actually paying a Fiorent.

Eventually through the tram windows we saw some floodlights that looked like a football ground so we got off, we then found ourselves in the middle of an amateur football club's training session, fortuitously we were not far from the Ulloi Ut stadium (sic.) near the Nepliget Coach station that we had sailed past frequently.

The reason that we kept missing the ground was because it looked more like some sort of industrial complex than a football ground, especially at night. We had a wander around the outside and found that the visitors section was very near to the main road where the trams ran on a corner section beneath a flyover. It all looked a bit grim in truth, we then had a wander around the Underground metro station and decided that it had aggro written all over it and we would definitely not be getting an underground train to the ground. It looked exactly as had been predicted in the Millwall literature that we had seen prior to travelling to Hungary. After our scouting mission and again going up down the tram network we eventually arrived back at our hotel at around 10.30pm having wasted a couple of hours valuable drinking time we decided to have a couple of beers in the hotel whilst waiting for the cab that we had booked to arrive, as there didn't appear to be any such thing as Hungarian beer we had a couple of lightning quick Austrian beers. Luckily just as the hotel bar was about to shut the cab arrived and we headed to the posher part of town that we had been in during the afternoon.

We asked our cabbie for an area with bars and we alighted at a West End style street side bar-restaurant that was playing trendy jazz. We found that the prices were around the same price as we would pay in London.

Prices have apparently shot up since Hungary's EU membership.

After a couple of beers here, we then set off in pursuit of further watering holes and we passed several small groups of Millwall doing exactly the same, in all our time in Budapest we never saw any large groups of Millwall fans despite hoping that we would.

After a short backstreet wander we found an 'authentic' Hungarian bar Not ! Called The Captain Cook near the Danube, we sat down and were served draught pints with a head so large that it would make a northerners eyes light up. So alarming was the amount of froth that Nathan took pictures of the mega headed pints on his Mobile and sent picture messages back to his mates in dear old blighty.

615

We left this bar after a few beers, wandered around couldn't find anywhere better so went back to The Captain Cook, where they claimed that we hadn't paid the bill, the dodgy buggers, untrue as we paid as we went, it was just a scam, however beggars can't be choosers and we coughed up the unpaid amount, around a fiver and carried on drinking. I did say if you want to stitch Millwall fans up, we can comeback here tomorrow with a couple of 100 Wall fans and burn your fucking bar down, they ignored this advice.

We then went back to our hotel eventually arriving back at around 2am having now been awake for almost 48 hours.

On the next Morning following our previous nights exploits Nathan and Paul were dead to the world.

Naturally Simon was bright eyed and bushy tailed and couldn't wait to do something, at 9ish Simon knocked on my, Paul and Nathan's door and he, Pat and I went down to have breakfast in the hotel, where there were quite a few Millwall dotted around the large dining area, we had a breakfast of frankfurters, scrambled eggs, tea and cornflakes before heading back to our rooms where we then left Pat with Paul and Nathan in our room and Simon and I headed out to try to find the ground in daylight.

We had a wander around the area behind the hotel and found a huge space aged arena that was metallic silver and looked like a UFO, it was huge. There were also several shops, a bus terminal and a nearby metro station. We decided to walk to the ground. I knew after our epic trek of the previous night that the stadium was very near Nepliget Hungary bus station which was around half an hours walk from our hotel, luckily it was a beautiful warm late summer day, as it was for our entire visit.

We walked up to the Ulloi Ut stadium and in daylight we found that Ferencvaros, the apparent Manchester United of Hungary, had a ground with all the charm of Wimbledon's Plough Lane. When we arrived mid morning we found that the outside of the away end was being encircled by high metal fences. Simon and I went into Ferencvaros' small club shop near the away section, there were dozens of Millwall milling about trying to get tickets, we had a chat with several people and found that although Londoners were being turned away in the queue the Hungarians who were queueing for their tickets were more than happy to get them for you.

Good that they would get the ticketless fans tickets, but for Millwall fans it seemed like a recipe for disaster. Simon bought several items in the shop and we set off back to the hotel, en route we decided to have a look at the stadiums that we had passed on the way up, these were only a short walk from Ferencvaros.

One of them was an athletics stadium and the another was a football ground, we chose to explore the latter.

From the outside this football ground looked like Wigan's Springfield Park, it was open to the elements and rust filled, the ticket windows looked like a mediaeval castle's arrow slits and welcomingly had broken glass all around their inner edge.

We walked up to an open doorway and found a man sitting at a desk with team photos behind him and on the surrounding walls, Although the man's level of English was as good as our level of Hungarian we found that it was the ground of MTK, who it turned out were another top Hungarian side.

We asked this man if there was a club shop, he stared at us blankly, we said 'Souvenirs?' And Simon waved his bag of goodies at him and he said 'Yes!' And pointed upstairs, Simon and I climbed the stairs and found ourselves in a corridor full of offices with secretaries typing, etc.

We wandered aimlessly before coming upon an office with a man sitting at a desk with trophies behind him, we again said 'Club shop, souvenirs?' He nodded got up and came to a safe near the door, he opened it and gave us MTK pennants and small replica kits like those that people hang in their cars.

He wouldn't take any money from us so we thanked him and set off downstairs nodding thankingly at the desk clerk as we left, it was all very bizarre.

We went back to the hotel roused the others and went out for something to eat and a bit of a wander.

Essex boys Mark & Laurie were coming in on an afternoon flight on the day of the match, they rang me when they touched down and I said that they should meet us at our hotel for a pre match snifter, we didn't want to get totally on it, because Simon's Man U mate Ali had relayed tales of his European jaunts with them where people had been turned away if they smelt of drink, as a precaution I brushed my teeth and chewed gum to disguise my guzzling.

We had a few pleasant beers whilst Laurie kept mumbling that he couldn't believe that we were in a Budapest hotel waiting to watch Millwall in Europe. Mark and Laurie said that at Luton airport where they departed from they were checking passports religiously and pulling people out for questioning, which they were, they had not done this on Wednesday when we left Heathrow.

Everyone else in my group had been having a pre match siesta but they eventually came down and joined us in the hotel lobby bar for a beer before we set off to the ground a couple of hours before kick off. We left the hotel and headed to a nearby tram stop, as we waited without a tram in sight a very helpful Hungarian asked us if we were Millwall, which we obviously admitted that we were, he told us that there had been a Tram accident and that we should get the Metro to the game, which we didn't fancy after our previous nights jaunt, so as we knew exactly where we were going we walked.

There were around half a dozen other Millwall walking with us and a short distance from the ground we all went into a McDonalds for yet another American feast.

We then continued to the game along largely empty streets, as we approached they appeared to be selling numerous bizarre foodstuffs including Pretzels, we later heard rumours of some of the stalls outside selling knives! What a bloody good idea!

Strangely the home club did not produce a match programme.

We arrive outside the away area at around 8.15pm 45 minutes before the kick off and it was chaos.

They had completed the fencing off of the away area that Simon and I had seen them doing earlier. These security barriers now radiated out from the away end and spread out into the main road near the metro entrance from across the road we saw one Millwall fan in an England shirt getting a kicking despite giving as good as he got. There was a vast amount of police and stewards ringing the inside of this fence. We couldn't find our way in to our section so we wandered among home fans and were quite frankly lucky not to also get a kicking. The away sections of the ground were on a corner located underneath a motorway flyover, in truth the whole stadium inside and out was like a cross between the three Bristol Rovers grounds, Eastville, Twerton Park and the Memorial Stadium that I had been to, please see these 2 pictures of our away section

We eventually found the away entrance where we then had to fight our way into the ground through heavy-handed stewards and riot police, in total we were searched 4 times before being allowed into the ground. Inside the ground we met up with my cousin Gavin and mates Bob & Dave, etc.

The full majesty of the stadium came into focus once inside, it really was a tip, even the grim Hungarian Club's website photos that we had seen before travelling did not do it justice, it was the equivalent of a very bad amateur ground, it would certainly not get a safety certificate in England.

Inside the stadium we were penned into the far right corner, very apt in a nazi ground! Below is a photograph that features the 3 bespectacled ones myself Nathan and Paul behind the metal fencing that surrounded our section, Simon and Pat sat away from us, due to Pat's young age I think.

There was one main section with an overspill to our right besides a 'no mans land' area, and a 'grandstand'. We were surrounded by stewards and Riot Police all night and were being filmed and gawped at by the OTT security for the whole match, naturally nothing unusual for all of us Millwall Away travel regulars.

We did our customary away trick of finding the best position and we found ourselves as you will see from the photograph near to the front of the stand and as you will also see surrounding the pitch there was a high perimeter fence topped off with wire mesh it was not an easy viewing experience, it was rather like peering through fishnet stockings all night, although sadly without the Naked Female leg Flesh poking through it, good though that would have meant naked lady and we would not have been able to see anything at all of the game, to continue in reality we stood on our seats all night in an attempt to try to at least see some of the match, I know we only paid £9 for the tickets but this was ridiculous.

To our left behind the massed security ranks there was an empty area behind the goal with green bushes and a statue, for some bizarre reason, something else that we do not see in England was the home fans behind the opposite goal lighting flares and there was also the home fans equivalent of Grandad leading the home Ultras singing by shouting through a megaphone.

It was a hostile atmosphere, nothing to a veteran of the Old Den though, anyway I prefer volatile atmospheres myself. During the game the home fans continued their racist abuse and nazi salutes as they had done at our home game, but this time on the grand scale, Millwall's black players, especially Mark McCammon, had to endure monkey noises, etc.

As per our games in England we were filmed and photographed all night whilst the racist home fans were ignored, still that's our reputation for you.

To add to their hostility the home fans did throat slitting gestures and threw missiles towards what passed for Ferencvaros' 'executive boxes' to the right of the away section, prompting Theo Paphitis, etc to duck for cover.

On the small matter of the game itself we were very unlucky and although we found ourselves 3 – 1 down we battered them in second half unfortunately all to no avail.

Some Millwall chants to give you a feel for the night, in addition to the previous chants from the New Den Leg we also sang – To the massed home Stewards and the Fradi Fans – 'You're fat and your Mum's a brass!'/'You fat bastard, you fat bastard you ate all the goulash!'/'Pie and Mash, Pie and Mash, Pie and Mash!'/'Going Home To Your Caravans!' And 'You're just a third world country!'

We also sang 'Gary, Gary!' in response to the home fans sarcastic pidgen English chants when they beat us of 'Bye, bye Millwall!'

Our chant was in reference to the Christmas 'Only Fools And Horses' Foreign asylum seekers version.

We also sang –

'Engerland!'/'Rule Britannia' and 'God Save The Queen!' And '3 – 1 and a long way home!'

There were some Millwall banners around the ground, the best in my opinion being 'Pie 'N' Mash Brigade' and 'The Wise Men Cometh'.

After the match as we were escorted right around the inside of the ground to the airport coaches by military style riot police whilst surrounded by Stewards, who all looked like WWE wrestlers and were apparently in fact the home team's hooligans, who many Millwall on the Route March commented that they had seen fighting with our visiting fans during the day. These stewards ringed the outer perimeter and many were sarcastically rubbing their eyes in mock crying that we had lost, the cheeky buggers!

As we were been escorted I went to a loo inside the ground that smelt like it hadn't been hosed since the Russian tanks were rolling through Hungary, I almost fainted, the state of the urinals sum up the tip that was the Ulloi Ut stadium. Because of my call of nature I found myself at the back of the escort with very sinister black Ninja clad and jack booted riot police a mere couple of steps behind me.

After the forced march all around the ground we found ourselves at the other end of the Stadium near the official Millwall coaches. Unfortunately the 7 of us wanted to go back towards the tram stops near the bus station, so after being held for a short while behind police lines we were allowed out on to the main road and found ourselves further away from our hotel. We crossed the wide road towards the tramlines and made our way back towards the nearest stop to the ground itself.

As we stood at the open air tram stop, we had numerous home fans milling about near us and more alarmingly there were hundreds of Fradi hooligans just across the road drinking whilst being surrounded by army/police, We all admitted that we had never felt so exposed at an away match in our lives, we had a quick chat and decided that standing here was not a good idea so decided to walk. back to our hotel, this as a Grey Gunmetal army like Water cannon passed us whilst driving along the road towards the massed home Hooligans.

After our yomp we got back to our hotel safely at around midnight and after dropping Simon and Pat off myself, Paul, Nathan, Mark and Laurie got a couple of cabs, for a Beer or as many as possible to be honest! We told the Cabbies to take us to a late bar and we ended up in an apparent authentic Hungarian Bar, in truth though it was much more specifically an authentic British pub, right near the Danube, The John Bull pub, apparently the scene for previous violent clashes with the locals, all was calm tonight though, it was populated by several dozen Millwall and was so English looking that it was very surreal. We naturally drank like fish and left the bar at 2.30am, myself, Nathan and Paul headed back to our hotel and said that the other 2 could doss down in our room if they liked but they declined. Consequently Mark and Laurie tried unsuccessfully to find a place to carry on drinking, so having failed they headed to the Ferenghy Airport to doss down for the night along with numerous fellow Lions.

On our last morning some of us had our Hotel Breakfast and then left our hotel deciding to get a cab to Buda to do our tourist bit, i.e. traipsing around a cathedral, on the way we got Financially stiffed by our 2 cabbies, that aside we agreed a price and a time with one of the cab drivers for him to come back and pick us up to take us to the airport several hours later.

The Taxis left and we set off on our tourist jaunt around Buda's picturesque old buildings and then went to a restaurant where we scrabbled through our pockets for change in order to get something to eat, it was all pretty desperate. Although we were on tenterhooks that the Cabby wouldn't turn up we wandered around and found one really humourous item at a souvenir stall Osama Bin Laden Russian dolls! As he was the Terrorist enemy not bizarrely we decided against buying any!!!

Luckily our driver arrived and we set off to the airport on the flyover above Ferencvaros ground. Humourously we drove by a man selling porno at the roadside, looking very similar to the flower sellers on our roadsides despite the smut that he was selling; this was on the motorway to the airport, as a selling point picturesquely he was covered head to foot in wank mags, what a splendid idea!!

We arrived at Ferenghy airport at 4pm for our 6.15pm flight back to Heathrow.

Unfortunately having paid the cab fare we had now spent practically all of our Hungarian money so we scrabbled in our pockets like beggars trying to find enough for a drink and a bag of crisps, we were so poor that we seriously considered breaking into an airport charity machine!

The airport was naturally full of Millwall heading back home including the Rasta girl and white bloke who we had met at the bar in Buda, Simon spoke to them and found that they had managed to buy over the odds tickets for the home section at the ground, however when they tried to get into the match on the night the stewards tore the tickets up and threw the pieces in their face, this was not an isolated incident from what we heard, apparently others either got in to the overspill section to our right or were thrown out on to the street.

We ourselves did not see any violence other than the chaos outside the stadium on the night although we heard plenty of rumours. It appeared that during the day anyone who looked English, i.e. who didn't look like a dosser, was attacked on the Metro individually.

Following the previously mentioned home fan Metro attacks on individuals Millwall firmed up and apparently ran the home hooligans all around the Metro network.

There was also apparently violent pub clashes during the day of the match prompted by home fans gesturing through pub windows at Millwall fans, these pubs were apparently wrecked with the home fans given a hiding. We heard that the subsequent stabbings of several Millwall fans were in response to Lion hooligan victories during the day. On our plane home people swapped stories and we heard from various people that the Police had said that no one else's fans had given the home hooligans such robust opposition and actually praised them for it! Apparently others sides fans including notorious hooligans like Feyenoord had merely taken a beating and left the country.

On arrival back in London the tabloids were full of pictures of the 'Battle of Budapest'.

Whoever was to blame for the on street violence the Hungarian club were quite rightly fined more than £26,000 by UEFA for the problems in and around the Ulloi Ut stadium on the night

I later heard that Ferencvaros wanted to play at Ferenc Puskas Stadion aka Nep Stadion but 'the powers that be' wanted to limit travelling Millwall, aka our perceived Hooligan hordes! Hence the Football Stadium tip that we were forced to play in. The Nep stadion was huge and directly across the road from our hotel, we could see into it from our balcony window, it would have been very handy.

As the succeeding days past and Budapest was just a memory I was brought back to earth when a mega expensive mobile bill dropped on the mat!!!

*As I mentioned earlier a version of this chapter appeared in 'Millwall Enough Said' Millwall Sweden's website fanzine.

CHAPTER 18
'Mad Ted's Big Adventure' – Carlisle United Away Saturday 7th October 2006 2pm; League 1 Won 2-1

The final Chapter –
This was my fifth away trip of the season but my first ever visit to Carlisle United, the longest journey that a Londoner can make, some 310 miles.

For the record Carlisle United would be my 84th League club and 97th League ground, due to clubs moving to new homes. One result of our relegation was that it allowed me to add not only Carlisle United but also Cheltenham Town to my new clubs list and Swansea City's Liberty Stadium to my new ground total. In this season, I had to miss Yeovil Town and Doncaster Rovers away because I was in Hospital from November 2006 until March 2007.

To make matters more interesting today the League had moved the kick off forward to 2pm so that fans could watch England v Macedonia on TV. This did not apply to any travelling fans obviously, as we would be on the move at the time; however what it meant was that I would have an hour less in bed on what would already be a very early start, whichever way we travelled, for this early hour kick off many thanks – Not!

We had originally planned to travel by train, however due to some of our usual travelling companions undecided about whether to go to the game or not, we failed to book the train in time to get a decent discount and by the time, we sorted out who was going the prices had risen prohibitively.

Our other option was driving up in a mini bus, however this was also stymied when two of our prospective drivers dropped out, which meant that we only had one driver, Paul Simms, who understandably did not want to take on a 600+ trip on his own.

Eventually four of us decided to make the long trip north by club coach, myself, Paul, Laurie and Mad Ted, who was the only one of us to have been there before, my 3 companions will be familiar to those of you who have read my other Millwall books and this one as well.

The club coach was due to leave the Den at 5.30am, but due to fluctuating numbers, the club's official coach was forced to merge with the Junior Lions coach and consequently we had to leave at 5am because we had the mascot on board, who had to be at the ground by 12.30pm.

On Saturday morning my alarm went off at 3.55am and I headed drowsily to Rotherhithe Tunnel where Paul was picking me up at 4.30am, he soon arrived with the others already aboard and we made the short trip south of the river. We parked up at the Den and boarded a Kings Ferry double Decker coach, plumping for seats on the upper deck near the front.

The coach eventually left at 5.15am and within minutes, we were to hit a massive traffic jam near the Elephant and Castle. This was largely because hundreds of Africans were emerging from a Nigerian nightclub, where they were straying into the road and fighting in the side streets as they made their way home, it was a very bizarre sight at this early hour I can tell you.

We eventually cleared the area and headed to the M1 via the West End.

The early part of the journey was a bit surreal as a full moon shone down on us for several hours before the sun could be bothered to rouse itself. En route, we stopped off to pick up a Milton Keynes based Lion before pulling in to Leicester Forest services at

8am for 45 minutes; this was to be our only rest stop on the way up as it was to turn out. By the time, we were at the services the sun was now beating down and it was a bright if chilly day. Having stocked up on massively overpriced Service Station food we set off north again,

As we progressed through the northernmost parts of North West England the scenery was spectacular, with rolling hills and lush green valleys, Carlisle in Cumbria for those who do not know is near the picturesque Lake District. Apart from commenting on the beautiful scenery, everyone also commented that they had never seen so many sheep; enough of the fluffy creatures to put a Welshman in to carnal raptures seemingly inhabited each hillside and remote farm that we passed!

To explain it there were more sheep than you could shake a shepherd at!

Something that was rather alarming was that as we neared Carlisle the motorway signs simply said Carlisle with 'Scotland' as the only other available destination, which is another country! Chilly Jockoland as Jimmy Greaves used to all it was only a dozen or so miles further north.

We eventually completed our journey, which had been lengthy and scenic but rather uneventful on largely empty motorways, and arrived after 7 hours outside Carlisle's Brunton Park at 12.15am, where we parked in a car park behind the away section that resembled a sand quarry.

As we still had almost 2 hours before kick-off the four of us headed towards the city centre to find a pub or a Chip shop. En route we passed the obligatory T shirted northerners all seemingly oblivious to the cold wind that blew around us. After about 10 minutes' walk we noticed several police vans parked outside a pub on the other side of the road, we crossed over to investigate and found the police busy body-searching several young home fans, for the record Carlisle themselves have a noted hooligan firm the BCF, Border City Firm. There was a chip shop near to this pub but we decided to give it a miss and asked the police for an away fan friendly pub, they pointed us to a pub called The Griffin just a short walk from this other pub and near the oldie worldie train station.

We reached the pub, walked past the bouncers on the door and entered a bar that was awash with Millwall's boys. Inside it was full of Burberry, Stone Island bedecked souls, and it became obvious that today we would have a large firm at the game; there were numerous faces there, many from Millwall's golden hooligan age of years gone by. We went to buy a drink and pleasingly found that Lager was 2/3rds of London prices. We then drank our drinks as we watched Nottingham Forest being humiliated by the might of Scunthorpe United on the pub's large TV screens.

In the pub I met up with Millwall Sweden's Mattias he told me that he had made the trip on a National Express coach that had taken 12 and a half hours, blimey I thought our trip was lengthy!

For reference from a Scandinavian point of view not much of a distance to the Swedish based away traveller from what Millwall Sweden's Henrik Lundgren told me, that aside it was a hell of a trot in English terms, as the time it took Mattias listed above shows.

As we stood drinking a Millwall, away regular came into the pub and announced that the publican would not let some Millwall kids in, so at his behest we staged a minor protest outside the pub, with dozens of us marching through the doors to confront the owner and the bouncers.

They eventually grudgingly relented and let them in, discretion being the better part of valour as we say.

Once back inside we loudly sang a collection of Millwall songs with anti-West Ham and 'Bobby Moore is no more' being particularly popular, strange as the scum would not hear us as we over 300 miles from Upton Park! Unless the pub was bugged and they were, listening in on very sophisticated devices or had inordinately acute hearing!

With the kick off approaching, we could see police, including London's finest, gathering outside the pub, they then came inside and announced that we should all drink up as they were going to escort us to the ground.

We did as they asked and began to gather outside when a pale blue three wheeler car with 3 locals on board was pulled over right in front of us by the police, we found this highly amusing as it was the type of car that Del Boy used in 'Only Fools and Horses', Lottery Larry would have been in raptures!

Having been released they sheepishly drove past our massed ranks as we sang – 'There's only one Derek Trotter!'

With a couple of hundred Millwall now outside the pub, the police marched us mob handed behind slow moving police vans through the City Centre in the opposite direction to where we knew the ground was and away from the home boys pub that we had passed earlier. We sang our Millwall repertoire as we walked along the main street with shoppers and locals gawping at us.

The police then led us down a side street where some foolish Carlisle fans made themselves known from a pub's Beer Garden, this led to a Millwall charge towards the pub, which the local police quickly nipped in the bud.

We then continued our circuitous walk to the ground like a singing invading army through residential streets and sometime later emerged on the road that we knew that the ground was on.

As we neared Brunton Park we passed Carlisle RFC where some Carlisle boys were gathered, unfortunately for them there were only around a dozen of them and they quickly went into reverse as dozens of Millwall surged towards them, the police again quickly regained control and we set off for the ground.

We arrived outside the stadium just as the team intro music; Robbie Williams 'Let Me Entertain You' was being played on the club PA. Outside the home parts of the ground, we exchanged the usual North v South pleasantries with some locals through the fences. Mad Ted did this to such a degree that he first had a police dog set on him before being pinned up against a wall and then wrestled to the ground by three police officers. This provoked a violent reaction from much of the Millwall being escorted that rose to his defence, which prompted the police to draw their batons and wade in, strangely, it then calmed down and they released Ted who was able to go into the ground with us.

We got through the away turnstiles just after the game had kicked off and made our way onto the open Petteril End terrace behind the goal.

The whole day so far had had a nostalgic edge to it, it was just like a match in the late 1970s, early 1980s, this feeling was compounded by Carlisle's ground which was really a return to a bygone age, what I like to call a real football stadium –

It had the open terrace that we were on, a covered terrace at the opposite end that had a roof like a Toblerone, this was the home for some idiot who banged a big bass drum continually throughout the game and also the stand from where the police dragged out several missile throwers as Millwall attacked this end in the first half after the linesman had grassed them up to the ref. There was a grandstand to our right, which had three disparate shaped sections, with terracing at the front and primitive executive boxes between the two parts.

The ground was completed by one largish new stand the Cumberland Building Society Stand to our left, which housed the more mouthy home fans.

The home fans did not seem to have much of a repertoire of songs apart from 'Carlisle' and 'United', and 'We hate Cockneys'. The only other chant I can recall was 'Who are ya?' to which we replied with the sarcastic – 'You're just a small town in Scotland' and 'You Scotch C…s!'

In the game, which was played out in a very strong wind, the referee Mr. G Law, ably supported by his officials managed to give Carlisle every possible decision, despite this we took the lead thanks to an Alan Dunne deflected volley on 27 minutes at the opposite end of the ground, which sent us in to raptures.

This was short lived as we then gave away a soft equaliser on

35 minutes, scored by very recent Leeds loanee Jermaine Beckford, who made a two-fingered gesture to we away fans behind his shorts, charming!

Poul Hubertz then pounced on an under-hit header back to the keeper on 38 minutes, sliding it beneath the advancing goalie to make it 2 – 1 to us, hoorah!

Once again, this lead was threatened as Millwall gave away a penalty for handball in front of we gathered away fans, we did our best to put him off, which must have worked as fortunately the taker Chris Lumsdon hit the post and we went in at half time in the lead.

Paul headed off to the Refreshment stall and I went to the toilet, before re-joining him.

Next to the toilet the home fans were trying to break through a wooden fence to get in to our end, unwise and ultimately unsuccessful. I re-joined Paul at the Refreshment counter where he gave me the devastating news that despite being massively Northern they did not sell pies! What!

Consequently, despite being in shock I had to settle for a Burger, Paul plumped for a Cheeseburger, which he had to have without cheese as they had run out of cheese, they had also run out of Hot Dogs, bloody marvellously organised from a food flogging front, I don't think.

The second half continued in much the same fashion as the first with Millwall holding their own and the referee continuing to give Carlisle every decision, but fortunately missing an apparently blatant handball by Tony Craig, which I didn't see, this is not an Arsene Wenger moment as we were up the other end, honest!

Never mind, we had three blatant penalties turned down at Crewe Alexandra in a game in the same season so it all levels out. Millwall went into a defensive shell for the final third of the game with the scoreboard behind us tortuously counting down the minutes, it then flashed up a crowd of 8,413 with an away turnout of 513, something that I had never seen at a ground before.

Not a bad turn out for such a lengthy trip, mind you it would be a new ground for many of us as we had not played there for years and you could add to this the hooligan element. For the record during the game, the home crowd had been sporadically vocal and we got behind the team manfully, despite not having the assistance of a roof to enhance us.

As injury time dragged on seemingly forever Millwall during the latter part of the game sang –

'How the F*** Are We Going to Get Home?'

Eventually after something like 7 minutes of injury time being played at the end of the match, and the scoreboard's clock seemingly frozen in time, the ref blew the whistle, we celebrated our second away win in a week, and Carlisle United's first home defeat of the season, as the team came over to applaud us.

We then set off happily into the car park where I headed to the coach, Mad Ted however decided instead to abuse and then throw a rock at some home fans, drawing the attention of the police again who remarkably released him for the second time, it was certainly his lucky day.

Whether there were any clashes between Millwall and Carlisle's boys after the game on the way back to the train station I have no idea, it certainly had the feel and potential to kick off.

Having boarded the coach, we set off back to London cheerily looking forward to our lengthy trek.

Whilst the journey had been comfortable enough, the DVD only worked on the monitor downstairs, all we had upstairs was the sound and no pictures, which was very off putting.

There was an electric clock in front of us upstairs that was partially broken and set to the wrong time, which was also annoying; however, for us Englishmen the most irritating thing was that the drivers could not get England's game on the radio.

Although we did have a couple of people on the coach with hand held TVs relaying the gory details of yet another poor England performance to one and all, still mustn't grumble Millwall won!

By the way, as you may have gathered from the exploits that I have mentioned, the reason for the title was that this had been Mad Ted in his element, he was bonkers all day and hyperactive on the coach, it was amazing that he had not been nicked – he was very lucky, very mad but very lucky.

The coach once again stopped at Leicester Forest Services and we then headed back south to negotiate the dreadful London traffic and arrive back at the Den at 11.35pm, Paul then dropped me off and I was at home by midnight, following a proper Football away day – a successful 14 hours plus in the saddle, bloody marvellous.

* A version of this chapter appeared in 'Millwall Enough Said' Millwall Sweden's fanzine in October 2006.

The 'Wall = Passion NOT Patience

This is the 3rd book that I have had published in English about my lifetime supporting Millwall F.C.

The 1st book was entitled 'Tuesday Night In Grimsby (Diary of a Masochist)' and the 2nd one was entitled 'I Was Born Under The Cold Blow Lane'.

These 2 books were later reproduced as one combined book in Germany, where it was translated into German by the publisher and renamed 'Millwall For Life: Lebenslang Millwall.'

This book continues my lifetime devotion to my team, whom I have supported home and away for 5 decades, to verify this my Millwall Date of Birth was 29th August 1966 so 2016 was my 50th Anniversary supporting Millwall!

It highlights what being perceived as England's Hooligan Public Enemy Number One is really like.

It features anecdotes of both home and away games that I and my numerous Millwall friends and family have attended, it features a plethora of diverse chants that we have heard or been involved in over the years, it features a story of Millwall's two legs against Ferencvaros in the UEFA Cup, it highlights the joys (sic) of away travel and the animosity between Millwall and West Ham United.

You will hopefully find it an entertaining book; I have tried to show humorously what it is really like to follow a team with a reputation like ours and highlight what you have to endure from all angles when the perception is that adverse against you.

I hope that you enjoy it.

Please note all the photographs used come from various and numerous different Internet sources, including Millwall FC who agreed I could use them.

© Barrie Stradling 2019